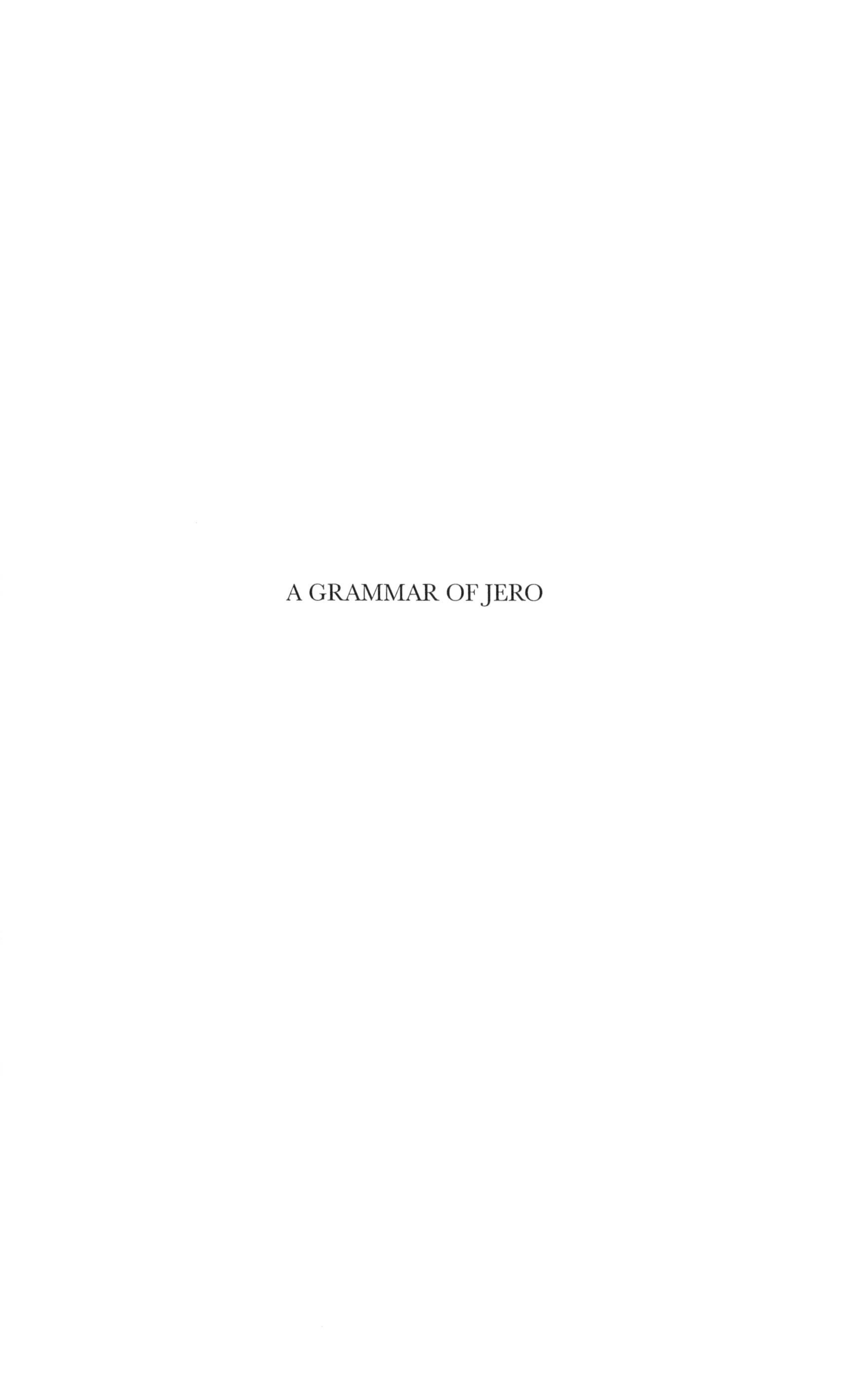

A GRAMMAR OF JERO

BRILL'S TIBETAN STUDIES LIBRARY

EDITED BY

HENK BLEZER
ALEX MCKAY
CHARLES RAMBLE

LANGUAGES OF THE GREATER HIMALAYAN REGION

EDITED BY

GEORGE L. VAN DRIEM

VOLUME 5/3

A GRAMMAR OF JERO

With a Historical Comparative Study of the Kiranti Languages

BY

JEAN ROBERT OPGENORT

BRILL
LEIDEN · BOSTON
2005

This book was published with financial support from the International Institute for Asian Studies (IIAS), Leiden, the Netherlands.

On the cover: A typical house in the village of Mohanṭār, where the author collected his first data on Jero in March 1998.

This book is printed on acid-free paper.

Library of Congress Cataloging-in-Publication Data

A C.I.P. record for this book is available from the Library of Congress.

ISSN 1568-6183
ISBN 90 04 14505 2

PRINTED IN THE NETHERLANDS

In Loving Memory of My Dear Guru

चन्द्र बहादुर राई
(आषाढ १९८९ – १७ माघ २०६१)

Candra Bahādur Rāī

(June/July 1932 – 30 January 2005)

पाप, जम्मा ७२ बर्स ७ मैना ब्लेनुम रै ।
नौठाङ फेरि न्वाम्निमा, योर स्वाचा ।
बुब्ज्वाम, सार्जङ, हलैंडनोम ताऽवा,
जाँ रोबियर ।

CONTENTS

LIST OF DIAGRAMS AND MAPS

ABBREVIATIONS

1	first person
2	second person
3	third person
A	agent
a	Āmboṭe dialect of Jero
ABL	ablative marker
ACG	marker of the general active verbal adjective
ACP	marker of the particular active verbal adjective
AD	*anno domini*
adj	adjective
adv	adverb
AFF	suffix of the affirmative
ATT	marker of the attributive verbal adjective
BA	Bahing
BN	Bantawa
CH	Chamling
cmp	compound
CND	marker of the conditional gerund
CNN	marker of the connective gerund
COM	comitative marker
conj	conjunctive
CTT	contemporaneous time suffix
d / ^{d}	dual
DETR	detransitivising marker
down / ^{down}	at a lower elevation than the point of reference
DM	Dumi
DU	dual number marker
emph / EMPH	emphatic
e / ^{e}	exclusive
f.	feminine
FCT	marker of the factual verbal adjective
H	Hodgson (1857, 1858)
HA	Hayu
HMG	His Majesty's Government of Nepal
hrz / ^{hrz}	horizontally
i / ^{i}	inclusive
IMP	imperative marker
ind	indefinite and interrogative word
INF	infinitival marker
intens	intensifier
ir	irregular

IRR	irrealis marker
KH	Khaling
KU	Kulung
LI	Limbu
lit.	literally
LIT	Literary Jero (published in *Libju-Bhumju* magazine)
LSN	Linguistic Survey of Nepal (unpublished material)
LTH	Literary Thulung by Agam Sing Rai, cited by Allen (1975)
LN	nominaliser of loan verbs
LOC	locative marker
m.	masculine
m	Mohanṭāre dialect of Jero
MAN	marker of the gerund of manner
MID	inflectional middle marker
n	noun (in lexicon); non- (in glosses)
NEC	marker of necessity
NEG	negative marker
Nep.	Nepali
nom	nominal
NSG	marker of the negative state gerund
num	numeral
Ø	zero (phonologically empty)
OPT	optative marker
P	patient
p / ^{p}	plural
part	particle
PAS	marker of the passive verbal adjective
PAT	patient postposition
pers	personal pronoun
PFG	marker of the perfect gerund
PK	Proto-Kiranti
PL	plural number marker
poss	possessive pronoun
postp	postposition
PPT	past prior time marker
PRG	marker of the present gerund
PUR	verbal adjective of purpose
quant	quantifier
RES	reifying marker
s / ^{s}	singular
S	subject
SIM	similaritive marker
SML	marker of the simultaneous gerund
SRC	source marker
SU	Sunwar
SUP	supine marker
TH	Thulung
THM	theme marker

up / ^{up} at a higher elevation than the point of reference

v verb, verbal

v-1a verb of the first conjugation, (a) class

VDC Village Development Committee

vi intransitive verb

vm middle verb

VOL volitional marker

vr reflexive verb

vs. versus

VS *Vikram Saṃvat* era

vt transitive verb

w Wamdyal dialect of Wambule

WA Wambule

YA Yamphu

Σ verb root

[ ] phonetic transcription (phone); etymological note

/ / phonological transcription (phoneme)

< > morphological transcription (morpheme)

A × B major or minor interlingual variation, or major intralingual variation, viz. A and B are members of the same word family (in Tibeto-Burman reconstruction)

~ alternates (allomorphs, allophones); minor intralingual variation (in Tibeto-Burman reconstruction)

≈ likely morphosemantically related forms

+ components of a *portemanteau* morpheme

* reconstructed, unattested or ungrammatical form, or rejected analysis

<jɔkt- (*~ jo-)> verb of which the root <jɔkt-> is attested, but of which the root <jo-> has not been found, but is expected for structural reasons

▪ used to list different etyma (in Kiranti reconstruction)

? doubtful form or analysis

- word-internal morpheme boundary; boundary between the components of a compound

= boundary between a full word and a phrasal affix

≡ boundary between a full word and a phrasal affix, and word-internal morpheme boundary (in citation forms)

/C/ consonant

/V/ vowel

< derives from

> yields (in diachronic analysis)

→ yields (in synchronic analysis); direction of a transitive relationship

↔ reciprocal transitive relationship

|X — after X

... phonetic pause

.... unquoted part

EDITORIAL FOREWORD

This description of the Jero language appears in sequel to the author's Wambule grammar. Jero is related to Wambule and spoken in an adjacent area, but remains different enough to merit a grammar of its own. This volume is testimony to the author's enduring commitment and continued service to the language communities where he stayed and made so many dear friends. The book also contains a historical comparative study of the Kiranti languages, the branch of the Tibeto-Burman language family to which both Jero and Wambule belong. This systematic reconstruction is the most recent and complete study of Proto-Kiranti to date and supersedes all earlier lexical and phonological comparisons of Kiranti languages.

George van Driem
ཐིམ་ཕུག། Thimphu, 5 December 2004

INTRODUCTION

This book is the main spin-off of my descriptive research on the Wambule language. The present book offers the first-ever published detailed analysis of the phonology, morphology and syntax of Jero, the previously undescribed and endangered Kiranti language most closely related to Wambule. The research for this grammar of Jero was sponsored by the Netherlands Organisation for Scientific Research (NWO) and the Niels Stensen Stichting. The publication of this volume was made possible with financial support from the International Institute of Asian Studies (IIAS) at Leiden.

The Jero and Wambule data presented here were collected during six trips which I undertook to Nepal from November 1996 to December 2004. The data on the Wambule language were primarily collected in the village of Hilepānī in Okhalḍhuṅgā district, where I lived with the late Candra Bahādur Rāī and his family. I am also very much indebted to Bālkājī Rāī and Nava Vāmbule, who helped me with some phonetic and phonological issues regarding plain /l-/ and preglossalised /ʔl-/ in their 'Ɔmdɛl' (Wamdyal) dialect of Wambule. The data on the southern Jero dialect were gathered during a two week trip to the village of Mohanṭār in March 1998, where I lived with Jaya Kumār Rāī, a young farmer in his early twenties, and his parents. The data on the northern Jero dialect of Āmboṭ village were collected in Kathmandu in January 2003 (VS 2059), where I had the chance of working together with Rām Kumār Rāī and Gam Bahādur Rāī. Rām Kumār Rāī, born in VS 2040, is a student of biology at Amrit Science Campus. Gam Bahādur Rāī, born in VS 2017, is the founder and managing director of Edelweiss Treks & Expeditions.

The Jero data presented in this book were mostly collected by direct elicitation, that is by presenting the informant with words and sentences in Nepali for translation into Jero. The testing material was oriented to the Kiranti languages and included checks for major structural features that have hitherto been observed in Kiranti languages.

A preliminary and tentative analysis provided by the method of direct elicitation is no adequate alternative to an in-depth grammatical description, which makes available a large body of detailed and diverse typological knowledge on a single language. The present grammatical survey of Jero should therefore not be compared with the comprehensive grammatical descriptions of Dumi, Limbu, Wambule or Yamphu, which are based on a extensive acquaintance of the languages in question.

Nevertheless, to ensure that the material elicited represented authentic spoken data, I worked with at least two informants for each dialect. Where possible, I listened to native conversation and to personal use of the elicited forms. Data were double-checked when the informant showed hesitation or doubt. I also analysed three unpublished lists of about 102 words each, which were collected within the framework of the Linguistic Survey of Nepal (LSN), and culled Jero literary forms (LIT) from the trilingual *Libju-Bhumju* magazine. This magazine on Wambule language and culture regularly features poems and short stories written in other Kiranti languages, such as Jero, Bantawa, Thulung and Bahing.

Most of the lexical material on the Āmboṭe dialect of Jero was tape-recorded several weeks after the initial elicitation. I also recorded a short interview with Rām Kumār Rāī, posing 50 questions in Nepali for translation into Jero. Rām replied in Jero and subsequently translated his response into Nepali. The material on tape was intended for the initial acoustic analysis of spoken Jero.

The presentation of this short grammar of Jero owes a great deal to my exhaustive grammar of Wambule, allowing easy comparison between the two closely related languages. The present work attempts to reconcile various types of data in a clear and uniform way. In order to achieve this purpose, a number of conventions have been introduced.

Phonologically based orthography. Jero and Wambule are written in a phonologically based orthography that uses the symbols from the International Phonetic Alphabet. Orthographic forms are generally italicised. However, phonetic, phonological and morphological data are placed between the brackets recognised for the different levels of linguistic analysis and are not italicised. Orthography and phonological transcription use the same symbols, but differ from one another in that the orthography distinguishes several allophones. The orthography is presented in Section 2.5 (p. 78).

Transliterated orthography. Nepali is the Indo-Aryan tongue that functions as the chief language of literature and administration in Nepal and as the *lingua franca* of the diverse tribes. Nepali is written in indological transliteration from the *Devanāgarī* script. The system of transliteration is based on spelling, not on pronunciation or phonology. The Roman transliteration of the *Devanāgarī* script uses the following symbols:

अ *a* आ *ā*
इ *i* ई *ī*
उ *u* ऊ *ū*
ऋ *ṛ*
ए *e* ऐ *ai*
ओ *o* औ *au*
ं *ṃ* ः *ḥ*

क *k*	ख *kh*	ग *g*	घ *gh*	ङ *ṅ*
च *c*	छ *ch*	ज *j*	झ *jh*	ञ *ñ*
ट *ṭ*	ठ *ṭh*	ड *ḍ*	ढ *ḍh*	ण *ṇ*
त *t*	थ *th*	द *d*	ध *dh*	न *n*
प *p*	फ *ph*	ब *b*	भ *bh*	म *m*
य *y*	र *r*		ल *l*	व *v*
श *ś*		ष *ṣ*		स *s*
		ह *h*		

In contrast to the consonants, which are represented by one symbol each, all but one (i.e. अ *a*) of the vowels in the *Devanāgarī* script have two symbols each. The vowel characters, which are given above, are used in initial positions and after other vowels. By contrast, the vowel ligatures ा *ā*, ि *i*, ी *ī*, ु *u*, ू *ū*, ृ *ṛ*, े *e*, ै *ai*, ो *o* and ौ *au* are used after consonants. The combinations that can be made with the consonant क् k are the following: क *ka* (no vowel ligature), का *kā*, कि *ki*, की *kī*, कु *ku*, कू *kū*, कृ *kṛ*, के *ke*, कै *kai*, को *ko* and कौ *kau*. Besides the ordinary consonant characters, which are given above, there is a large set of conjunct consonants, which are two or more consonant characters joined together and operating as one graphemic unit, e.g. ङ्ख *ṅkh* and ष्ट *ṣṭ*. An overview of these conjunct consonants can be found in Clark (1989) and Matthews (1990).

The inherent अ *a* is only transliterated where it is pronounced, even though it is not generally deleted with a *virām* (्) in the *Devanāgarī* script. The *śirbindu* (ं) written above a vowel is commonly transcribed as *ṃ*, and may be used to represent the nasal consonants /m, n, ŋ/. The nasal consonant represented by a *śirbindu* is homorganic with the following obstruent, or /m/ before /s, h/. The *candrabindu* (ँ) is generally used to indicate a nasalised vowel, and transliterated by placing a tilde (˜) above the vowel. However, in relation to vowel symbols that are written above the horizontal line that unites the orthographic word in *Devanāgarī*, a *śirbindu* is also commonly used to indicate nasality.

The orthographic distinctions between इ *i* and ई *ī* and between उ *u* and ऊ *ū* are rendered in the transliteration, although they do not correspond to any phonological length distinctions in modern spoken Nepali. The orthographic distinction between अ *a* and आ *ā* involves a phonemic distinction in quality between the vowels /ʌ/ and /a/. The orthographic distinctions between श *ś*, ष *ṣ* and स *s* and between व *v* and ब *b* are also preserved in the transliteration, even though they do not necessarily represent phonemic distinctions. There is only one alveolar fricative /s/ in modern spoken Nepali. Orthographic व *v* usually represents the same phoneme as orthographic ब *b*, i.e. /b/, and less frequently the phoneme /w/.

A distinctive mark of Jero written in *Devanāgarī* script is its use of the digraph ल्अ *ʔl*, which consists of a 'half' ल *l* plus the vowel character अ *a*, e.g. ल्आ *ʔlā* 'hand'. This digraph represents a glottalised lateral /ʔl/, which, however, has not been identified in the spoken Jero material on which this grammar is based. Literary forms are basically intended here as supplementary information.

Spelling for Nepali. There is no official and universally accepted standard of spelling for Nepali. As a standard, I have chosen to take Bālkṛṣṇa Pokhrel *et al.* (VS 2040). If a certain spelling does not appear there, I have looked at Chandra Lal Singh (1971) or rendered the spelling given by other Nepali authors. For geographical names, I have adopted the spelling used on the district maps 'Okhalḍhuṅgā' (number 13), 'Udaypur' (number 14) and 'Sindhulī' (number 20), published by His Majesty's Government of Nepal. If the Nepali spelling does not appear there, I have adopted the transliterated spelling used on the most detailed maps of all, i.e. those entitled '2786 14A

Svalpā Bhañjyāṅ', '2786 14B Māne Bhañjyāṅ', '2786 14C Baserī Bajār', '2786 14D Limpāṭār' and '2786 15A Chyāsimṭār', which are issued by the Survey Department of His Majesty's Government of Nepal and which have a seemingly acceptable transliterated spelling, with the modification that the graphemes *ch*, *chh* and *w* on these maps have been uniformly replaced by *c*, *ch* and *v*. Names such as Kathmandu and Nepal are given in their more or less acceptable English form. Labels to designate the different Nepali verb forms are taken from T.W. Clark's (1989) *Introduction to Nepali.*

Data from other languages. Information about the languages related to Jero have been collected from the following publications: Āṭhpahariyā by Karen Ebert (1997a), Bahing by Brian Houghton Hodgson (1857, 1858), Bantawa by Werner Winter (2003), Chamling by Karen Ebert (1997b), Dumi by George van Driem (1993), Hayu by Boyd Michailovsky (1981), Khaling by Sueyoshi Toba and Ingrid Toba (1975), Kulung by Gerard Tolsma (1999), Thulung by Nicholas Allen (1975), Yamphu by Roland Rutgers (1998), Limbu by Vairāgī Kāĩlā *et al.* (VS 2059), Sunwar by Dora Bieri and Marlene Schulze (1971) and Wambule by myself (Opgenort 2004b). Reconstructed Proto-Tibeto-Burman forms are generally taken from Matisoff (2003), but also from Benedict (1972) if marked specifically. I have adopted the morphophonological and phonological spellings used by the different authors, but uniformly placed bound morphemes between conventional European structuralist morpheme brackets, e.g. Kulung <-si>, and written lexemes in italicised orthography, e.g. Kulung k^{h}*ousi* 'cotton'. Reconstructed forms are preceded by an asterisk. The glosses, translations and labels are those given by the different authors. English translations are provided for quotes from sources in foreign languages.

CHAPTER ONE

THE JERO LANGUAGE AND ITS RELATIVES

The Jero are a Kiranti ethnic group of Nepal who speak a Tibeto-Burman language of the same name. The ethnolinguistic term 'Kiranti' applies to the Tibeto-Burman peoples native to the hill tracts of eastern Nepal, specifically the Limbu and Rai. The Limbu (Nep. *Limbū*) are the easternmost ethnic group of Kiranti people. The Rai (Nep. *Rāī*) consist of various groups speaking closely related languages.

1.1 *The Kiranti languages*

The Kiranti languages were first investigated by the English administrator, ethnologist and naturalist Brian Houghton Hodgson (1857, 1858). Hodgson, the former British Resident in Nepal, did not only write extensive contributions on Hayu ('Háyu, or Váyu') and Bahing ('Báhinggyá'), but also compiled word lists of Bantawa (the 'Rúngchhénbúng', 'Chhingtángya' and 'Wáling' lists), Chamling ('Rodong, or Chámling'), Dumi ('Dúmi'), Dungmali ('Dungmáli'), Khaling ('Kháling'), Kulung ('Kulúng'ya'), Lohorung ('Lóhórung'), Mewahang ('Báláli'), Nachiring ('Náchheréng'), Sampang ('Sángpáng'), Wambule ('Chouras'ya'), Yakkha (the 'Yákha' and 'Lámbichhong' lists) and Thulung ('Thulung'gya'). On the basis of Hodgson's material, Sten Konow presented his short notes on different Rai languages some 50 years later (Grierson 1909).

In more recent times, an increasing number of Rai languages have become the object of detailed linguistic research. Up till now, grammatical sketches and more comprehensive grammatical analyses have been written on Thulung (Allen 1975), Khaling (Toba 1979), Hayu (Michailovsky 1981, 1988a), Limbu (van Driem 1987), Dumi (van Driem 1993), Āṭhpahariyā (Ebert 1997a), Chamling (Ebert 1997b),Yamphu (Rutgers 1998), Kulung (Tolsma 1999) and Wambule (Opgenort 2002, 2004b). Comparative studies dealing with Kiranti languages are Shafer (1966), Glover (1971), Benedict (1972),

Winter (1986, 1987), Michailovsky (1988b, 1994, 2003) and Starostin (1994-2000).

On the basis of phonological developments, lexical isoglosses, what is known from grammar and the ethnic divisions recognised by the Kiranti people themselves, van Driem (2001: 615) presents the following Kiranti subgroups from east to west:

LIMBU

Eastern Limbu: Pāñcthare, Tamarkhole
Western Limbu: Phedāppe, Chathare

EASTERN KIRANTI

Greater Yakkha: Yakkha, Chɨlɨng, Āṭhpahariyā
Upper Aruṇ: Lohorung, Yamphu, Mewahang

CENTRAL KIRANTI

Khambu: Kulung, Nachiring, Sampang, Sām
Southern: Chamling, Puma, Bantawa, Chintang, Dungmali

WESTERN KIRANTI

Midwestern: Thulung
Chaurasiya: Ombule, Jero
Upper Dūdhkosī: Dumi, Khaling, Kohi
Northwestern: Bahing, Sunwar, Hayu

On the basis of Toba's recent work, the Kiranti language Tilung, 'of which very little is known except the name and the approximate location' (van Driem 2001: 715) can now be listed as a Central Kiranti language. Toba (2004: 146) observes that 'Tilung shares 14% cognates with Thulung, 60% with Chamling, and 26% with Bahing. This indicates a close relationship with Chamling, but not whether this relationship is the result of recent adjusting or whether it was there to begin with. It is noteworthy that Tilung is so close to Chamling but not so to Umbule, although geographically very close to a village of Umbule speakers.'

The total number of speakers of Kiranti languages is difficult to establish because of a serious lack of reliable statistical information. According to the 1995 census, Limbu is spoken by roughly 254,000

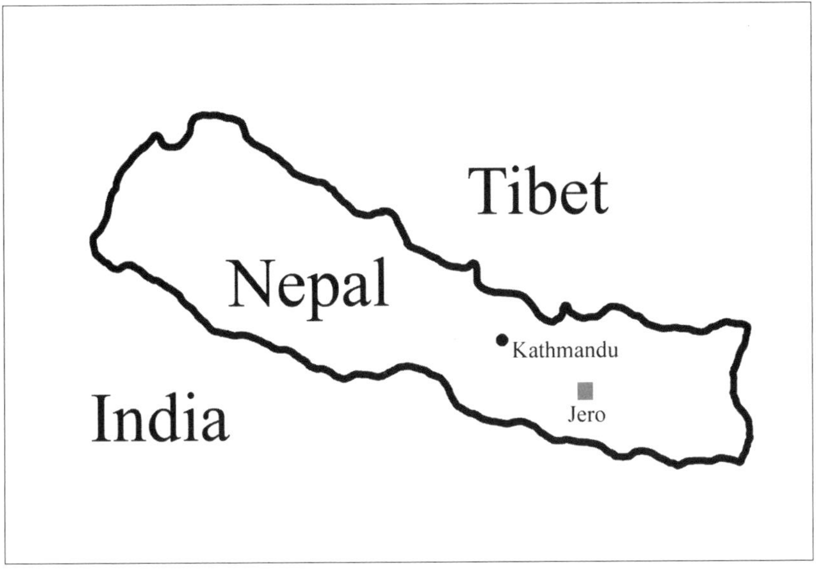

Map 1: Location of the Jero speaking area in eastern Nepal

people living in Nepal (HMG 1995). The 2001 population census though puts the number of ethnic Limbu at 359,379, of which 333,633 speak Limbu (HMG 2002). The number of ethnic Rai varies between around 439,000 (HMG 1995) and 635,151 (HMG 2002), of which 539,967 individuals speak a Rai language as their mother tongue.

1.2 *The Jero language and its dialects*

The Jero Rai language is known from the literature by several names. Hanßon (1991) mentions the names 'Jerung', 'Jero', 'Jerum', 'Zero', 'Zerum' or 'Jerunge'. The informants whom I consulted preferred the term 'Jero' to designate their language, adding that the term 'Jeruŋ' (Jerung) is a toponym that is used in the names of several villages within the Jero speaking area as well as the name of a village in the neighbouring Wambule-speaking area.

The Jero speaking area is situated in Okhalḍhuṅgā and Sindhulī districts. Hanßon (1991) claims that there are three to four dialects. My informants claimed that there are two major dialects:

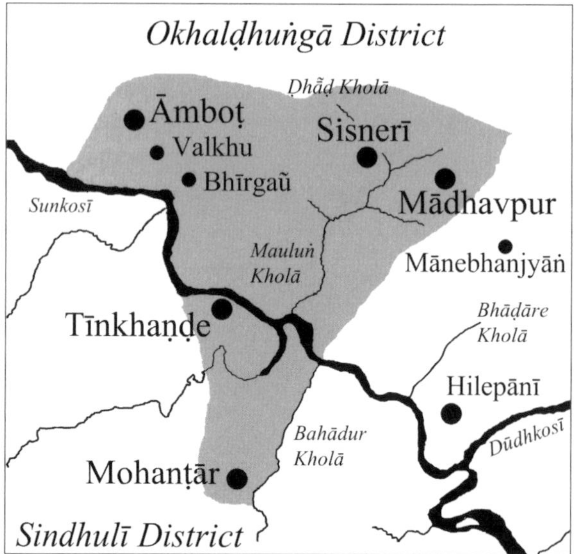

Map 2: The Jero speaking area

- The northern dialect is spoken around the Mauluṅ Kholā in Okhalḍhuṅgā district, i.e. in the area roughly to the west of the Bhāḍāre Kholā, to the south of the Ḍhā̃ḍ Kholā, to the north of the Sunkosī river, and as far west as the village of Āmboṭ. Villages are Gairājerūṅg, Ḍā̃ḍājeruṅ, Ciurībot, Tumak, Vināse, Kallerī, Sisnerī, Phoksiṅṭār and Mādhavpur.

- The southern dialect is spoken in Sindhulī district in several villages along the west bank of the Bahādur Kholā, to the south of the Sunkosī river as far south as the village of Mohanṭār. Villages are Tīnkhaṇḍe, Sokhuḍihīṭār, Pāṭiṭār, Geruḍā̃ḍā, Deukīḍā̃ḍā, Hathiṭār, Dalse and Mohanṭār.

Hanßon (1991) places the number of speakers of Jero at between 1,000 and 2,000. According to the 2001 population census though, only 271 people speak Jero (HMG 2002).

1.3 *The Jero language and its linguistic relatives*

The Kiranti languages Bahing, Sunwar, Thulung, Hayu and Khaling are close relatives of Jero, but the language most closely related is its eastern neighbour Wambule (Ombule, Umbule). The intimate relationship between Jero and Wambule has been acknowledged for some time. On the basis of short word lists collected within the framework of the Linguistic Survey of Nepal, Hanßon (1991) points out that the differences in phonology and lexicon between Jero and Wambule argue for a definition of the former as a language of its own, rather than as a dialect of Wambule. The Jero and Wambule peoples also insist on differentiating between two distinct ethnolinguistic groups, even though they also acknowledge the intimate relationship between their ethnicities and languages.[1]

The data presented below show that Jero and Wambule are indeed very closely related from a lexical, phonological and morphological viewpoint. The additional fact that the two speeches are to a very large extent mutually intelligible may perhaps argue for the view that Jero and Wambule can be treated as two separate sets of dialects of a single language. A suitable name for the language combining the Jero and Wambule dialect groups may well be 'Chaurasia'. This name is an anglicised version of the historical Nepali name *Caurāsiyā* or 'Eighty-Four' counties, which roughly designated the present-day Wambule and Jero speaking area in the old administrative system of His Majesty's Government of Nepal. The unit combining Jero and Wambule is to be understood as a entirely linguistic construct based on identifiable lexical, phonological and morphosyntactic similarities. The ethnolinguistic situation, however, is that no Jero considers himself to be Wambule and *vice versa*.

1.3.1 *Lexical and phonological comparison between 13 languages*

As mutual intelligibility is not only influenced by purely linguistic factors but also by sociological and individual factors, the criterion of

[1] Note also that the name 'Jero' is not only the name of an ethnic Kiranti group but also a designation for a particular Wambule clan. Many Jero clan names have apparent Wambule cognates, e.g. *Topile*$_a$ (WA *Topile*), *Dʌŋkhʌmcu*$_a$ (WA *Dwaŋkhumco*), *Laimcu*$_a$ (WA *Laimco*) and *Rɔke*$_a$ (WA *Rwake*).

mutual intelligibility alone cannot be safely used to establish the relation between different speeches. A description of quantifiable similarities and differences in lexicon, phonology and morphology is more useful to determine the relationship between two or more speeches.

Two major criteria which enable the identification and classification of subgroups in Kiranti involve shared lexical isoglosses and phonological developments. The Kiranti languages are classified here on the basis of 14 lexical and 31 phonological isoglosses discussed below. The Kiranti languages examined in this minor comparative study are Jero, Wambule, Bahing, Sunwar, Hayu, Thulung, Khaling, Dumi, Bantawa, Chamling, Kulung, Yamphu and Limbu. The full list of etyma is given in Appendix 4 (p. 337) below.

1.3.1.1 *Lexical isoglosses*

Kiranti subgroups can firstly be identified on the basis of isoglosses for different words which bundle together. The lexical isoglosses used in Section 1.3.1.3 (p. 40) to classify Kiranti subgroups refer to the following words for which I have found correspondences in 12 or more of the 13 languages examined:

1.	'axe'	2.	'become'
3.	'causativiser'	4.	'count'
5.	'do, make'	6.	'fear (n)'
7.	'give'	8.	'hear'
9.	'lie down, go to sleep'	10.	'one'
11.	'search, look for'	12.	'swallow'
13.	'wait (for)'	14.	'write'

1.3.1.2 *Phonological developments*

The second major criteria which enables the identification of subgroups in Kiranti involves phonological developments, in particular shared developments of initial obstruents. Some progress in the reconstruction of the Proto-Kiranti phonemic system has already been made, most importantly by Boyd Michailovsky. The present study incorporates data which only recently have become available.

As a point of departure, I will present the Proto-Tibeto-Burman syllable canon and the inventory of phonemes proposed by Matisoff (2003). Matisoff argues that the Proto-Tibeto-Burman syllable consists of the following structural elements: an onset comprising a root-initial consonant (C_i) which can be preceded by up to two consonantal prefixes (P_2, P_1), and optionally followed by a liquid or semi-vowel glide (G); and a vocalic nucleus consisting minimally of a simple vowel (V), followed optionally by a restricted set of possible final consonants (C_f) and/or a suffix (s):

$$(P_2) \quad (P_1) \quad C_i \quad (G) \quad V(:) \quad (C_f) \quad (s)$$

Matisoff (2003) generally follows Benedict (1972) in reconstructing the Proto-Tibeto-Burman consonant and vowel phonemes given in Diagram 1. Contrastive vowel length is posited according to the proto-syllable canon.

/*p/	/*t/	/*ts/	/*tś/	/*k/
/*b/	/*d/	/*dz/	/*dź/	/*g/
		/*s/	/*ś/	/*h/
		/*z/	/*ź/	
/*m/	/*n/		(/*ń/)	/*ŋ/
/*w/	/*l/	/*r/	/*y/	
/*i/	/*e/	/*a/	/*o/	/*u/

Diagram 1: Proto-Tibeto-Burman phonemes following Matisoff (2003)

A two-way contrast in manner of articulation between voiceless and voiced is reconstructed for Proto-Tibeto-Burman obstruents, even though many modern Tibeto-Burman languages including the Kiranti languages have more manners of articulation. Other manners of articulation in present-day Tibeto-Burman languages, such as aspiration, prenasalisation and preglottalisation, are analysed as prefix-induced types of secondary articulation.

The Proto-Tibeto-Burman obstruents are reconstructed with stops at three points of articulation (labial, dental, velar) and two series of affricates (dental, palatal). Nasals are reconstructed at four points of articulation. Other positions of articulation found in many modern Tibeto-Burman languages, such as postvelar, retroflex and labiodental, seem to represent secondary positions of articulation. For instance, retroflex consonants in some Tibeto-Burman languages seem to be derived from proto-clusters with medial liquids. However, in Kiranti, retroflex stops are largely confined to loan words from Nepali.

Prefixes are of great importance for the reconstruction of Proto-Tibeto-Burman (Wolfenden 1929, Benedict 1972, Matisoff 2003). Matisoff (2003: 99-143) argues that the 'glottogenetic' or 'laryngealising' prefixes <*s-> and <*ʔə-> are among the most important and semantically transparent of all Tibeto-Burman prefixes. Tibeto-Burman <*s-> before verb roots expresses a directive, causative or intensive meaning, whereas <*s-> before noun roots often represents a reduction of the syllable _*sya_ 'animal, flesh, body'. Tibeto-Burman <*ʔə->, which Benedict (1972) lists as <*a->, appears with kinship terms, as a nominal prefix marking a third person possessive, as a bulk-provider with nouns, as a verb prefix showing agreement with a third person subject, as a nominaliser of verbs and as a verbal suffix indicating stativity or intransitivity. The suffixes <*s-> and <*ʔə-> occur equally well before obstruents and sonorants and tend to induce aspiration or glottalisation to the root-initial.

The Tibeto-Burman proto-prefixes only left indirect traces in the modern Kiranti languages. Several transitive verbs in Kiranti seem to reflect a prior Tibeto-Burman <*s->, which could devoice, glottalise or aspirate an originally voiced initial consonant. For instance, the verb 'erect, arise, wake up' which can be reconstructed with initial /*p-/ or /*ph-/ in Kiranti, is the transitive counterpart of intransitive 'get up, stand up, arise', which can be reconstructed with initial /*b-/ at the Proto-Kiranti level.

The regular correspondences between Kiranti initial obstruents given in Diagram 2 are adapted from Michailovsky (1994). Michailovsky (1994: 768) notes that the reconstruction of a voiceless aspirated series is somewhat doubtful, as it does not correspond very reliably across the group, adding that 'the aspiration of individual lexical items may not have been fixed at the time of Common Kiranti, and it may be necessary to reconstruct prefixes in PK [Proto-Kiranti].'[2]

	WESTERN						EASTERN			
PK	HA	BA	SU	DM	KH	TH	KU	CH	BN	LI
*p-	p-	p-	p-	p-	p-	b-	b-	b-	b-	ph-
*ph-	ph-	ph-	ph-	ph-	ph-	ph-	ph-	ph-	ph-	ph-
*b-	b-	b-	b-	b-	b-	b-	p-	p-	p-	p-
*t-	t-	t-	t-	t-	t-	ɖ-	d-	d-	d-	th-
*th-	th-	th-	th-	th-	th-	th-	th-	th-	th-	th-
*d-	d-	d-	d-	d-	d-	d-	t-	t-	t-	t-
*c-	c-, ts-	ts-	ky-, c-/ts-	ts-	c-	c-	ch-	ch-	tsh-	s-
*ch-	ch-	s-	s-	ts-	ch-	ch-	ch-	ch-	tsh-	s-
*j-	dz-	dz-	gy-, j-/dz-	dz-	j-	j-	c-	c-	ts-	ts-
*k-	k-	k-	k-	k-	k-	k-	kh-	kh-	kh-	kh-
*kh-	kh-	kh-	kh-	kh-	kh-	kh-	kh-	kh-	kh-	kh-
*g-	g-	g-	g-	g-	g-	g-	k-	k-	k-	k-
*kw-	-	ʔb-	ʔw-	-	-	p-	-	-	-	-

Diagram 2: Kiranti initial obstruent correspondences following Michailovsky (1994)

In addition, Michailovsky does not reconstruct breathy voiced consonants because voiced aspiration appears to have developed sporadically from plain voiced initials under Indo-Aryan influence. There is a considerable variation between plain voiced and breathy voiced initials in Bahing and Thulung. Allen (1975: 12) notes that 'aspiration of voiced stops, whether or not before liquids, differs from that of voiceless ones in that in many words it is subject to free or dialectal variation.' He further adds that 'Word-initially there is considerable dialectal fluctuation between dental and retroflex.' (p. 15).

---

[2] Indeed, some etyma show a variation between voiceless unaspirated, preglottalised and voiceless aspirated obstruents at the Proto-Kiranti level. Even within a single modern language, there can be some variation in phonation types, such as between the Jero and Wambule words meaning 'calf of leg' (initial /p-/ and /ph-/), 'shut, close' (initial /t-/ and /th-/) and 'smoke (n)' (initial /k-/ and /kh-/).

Michailovsky argues that the Kiranti languages have undergone complex phonological changes for the voiceless series of Proto-Kiranti obstruents depending on the place of articulation. The Western Kiranti languages preserve the Proto-Kiranti initial obstruent series.

PROTO-SERIES:

*p-	*t-	*c-	*k-
*ph-	*th-	*ch-	*kh-
*b-	*d-	*j-	*g-

In Thulung and in the Eastern Kiranti languages Kulung, Chamling and Bantawa, initial /*p-/ and /*t-/ were preglottalised in a first sound change, which did not take place in the Western Kiranti languages and in Limbu, the latter of which must have split off from the other Eastern Kiranti languages by that time.

FIRST SOUND CHANGE: GLOTTALISATION

Kulung, Chamling, Bantawa, Thulung

*ʔb-	*ʔd-	*c-	*k-
*ph-	*th-	*ch-	*kh-
*b-	*d-	*j-	*g-

Later, a second sound change occurred in parallel in Limbu and in the neighbouring Eastern languages. In Kulung, Chamling and Bantawa, the non-glottalised voiceless initials /*c-/ and /*k-/ were aspirated and merged with /*ch-/ and /*kh-/, whereas the voiced series /*b-/, /*d-/, /*j-/ and /*g-/ were devoiced. In Limbu, all plain voiceless initials were aspirated and merged with /*ph-/, /*th-/, /*ch-/ and /*kh-/, whereas the voiced series /*b-/, /*d-/, /*j-/ and /*g-/ were devoiced.

SECOND SOUND CHANGE: DEVOICING AND ASPIRATION

Kulung, Chamling, Bantawa				*Limbu*			
*ʔb-	*ʔd-	*ch-	*kh-	ph-	th-	s-	kh-
*ph-	*th-	*ch-	*kh-	ph-	th-	s-	kh-
*p-	*t-	*c-	*k-	p-	t-	c-	k-

Some time later, a third sound change occurred in the languages with preglottalised /*ʔb-/ and /*ʔd-/, which became plain voiced /*b-/, /*d-/ or /*ɖ-/.

THIRD SOUND CHANGE: DEGLOTTALISATION

Kulung, Chamling, Bantawa				*Thulung*			
b-	d-	ch-	kh-	b-	ɖ-	c-	k-
ph-	th-	ch-	kh-	ph-	th-	ch-	kh-
p-	t-	c-	k-	b-	d-	j-	g-

The more recent reconstruction of Proto-Kiranti undertaken by Sergei Starostin (1994-2000) is based on data from Sunwar, Thulung, Khaling, Dumi, Kulung, Yamphu and Limbu.

PK	SU	TH	KH	DM	KU	YA	LI
*p-	p-	p-	p-	p-	p-	p-	p-
*ʔp-	p-	b-	p-	p-	b-	Ø	ph-
*ph-	ph-	ph-	ph-	ph-	ph-	ph-	p-/ph-
*b-	b-	b-	b-	b-	b-/p-	p-	p-/ph-
*bh-	b-	b-/bh-	bh-	b-/bh-	b-/p-	p-	p-/ph-
*t-	t-	t-	t-	t-	t-	t-	t-
*ʔt-	t-	d- (ḍ-)	t-	t-	d-	Ø	th-
*th-	th-	th-	th-	th-	th-	th-	th-
*d-	d-	d-	d-	d-	d-/t-	t-	t-/th-
*dh-	d-	d-/dh-	dh-	d-/dh-	d-/t-	t-	t-/th-
*c-	c-	c-	c-	c-	c-	c-	c-
*ʔc-	c-	c-	c-	c-	ch-	s-	s-
*ch-	s-/ś-	ch-	ch-	c-	ch-	s-	s-
*ʒ-	ʒ-	ʒ-	ʒ-	ʒ-	ǯ-	c-	c-
*ʒh-	ʒ-	ʒ-/ʒh-	ʒh-	ʒ-	ǯ-/c-	c-	c-
*k-	k-	k-	k-	k-	k-	k-	k-
*ʔk-	k-/kh-	k-	k-	k-	kh-	kh-	kh-
*kh-	kh-	kh-	kh-	kh-	kh-	kh-	kh-
*g-	g-	g-	g-	g- (/h-)	g-/k-/h-	h- (/k-)	Ø/h-
*gh-	g-	g-/gh-	gh-	g-/gh-	g-/k-	h- (/k-)	k-

Diagram 3: Kiranti initial obstruent correspondences following Starostin (1994-2000)

Diagram 3 is adapted from the system of correspondences which he presented in March 2000 at Leiden University. This table shows that the bilabial, alveolar, affricate and velar series make a phonemic distinction between voiceless, preglottalised voiceless, voiceless aspirated, plain voiced and breathy voiced consonants. In addition, there is also one glottal stop phoneme /*ʔ-/. The nasal phonemes are bilabial /*m-/, alveolar /*n-/, palatal /*ń-/ and velar /*ŋ-/. There is also an alveolar lateral /*l-/, an alveolar trill /*r-/, a palatal trill /*ŕ-/, a bilabial approximant /*w-/, a palatal approximant /*j-/, and three voiceless fricatives, i.e. alveolar /*s-/, uvular /*χ-/ and glottal /*h-/.

Starostin's idea of reconstructing preglottalised sounds at the Proto-Kiranti level is very informative, even though his reconstruction seems to suffer from a bias towards Khaling. For instance, the Protoform for 'father' is **pǟ́ ~ pǟ́p*, which is obviously modelled after Khaling *'päp*, with a high tone and the vowel /æ/. However, Michailovsky (1975, 1995) already pointed out that only the vowels /*i/, /*e/, /*a/, /*o/ and /*u/ need to be reconstructed for Bahing, Khaling and Dumi on the basis of internal reconstruction. In addition, Michailovsky strongly argues that that the Khaling tones have arisen from the influence of final consonants: 'The generalization that suggests itself is that verb roots in final stops have the high tone, and roots in final nasals (in fact, continuants) have the low tone, regardless of any stem augment.' (Michailovsky 1975: 209).

My own analysis of Proto-Kiranti initials is based on data from 13 Kiranti languages, viz. Jero, Wambule, Bahing, Sunwar, Hayu, Thulung, Khaling, Dumi, Bantawa, Chamling, Kulung, Yamphu and Limbu. I follow Michailovsky (1994) in not reconstructing a series of breathy voiced consonants and retroflex consonants, as the Kiranti languages of Nepal seem to have developed these series under the influence of Indo-Aryan languages, first occurring in loans from Nepali, but now occurring in native words as well. However, I follow Starostin (1994-2000) in reconstructing a preglottalised manner series. I propose a four-way contrast in manner of articulation for obstruents: voiceless, preglottalised[3], voiceless aspirated and voiced. The Kiranti

[3] The preglottalised obstruents /*ʔp-, *ʔt-, *ʔc-, *ʔk-/ and preglottalised /*ʔm-, ʔn-, ʔl-/ are perhaps best analysed as consonant clusters (such as /*kw-/ and /*ry-/) rather than as single consonant phonemes (such as /*p-/ and /*ph-/). In any case, there is some evidence for distinguishing preglottalised sounds from plain sounds as distinct units at the Proto-Kiranti level.

obstruents reconstructed include three positions of articulation (bilabial, alveolar, velar) and one series of affricates (alveolar).

PK	JE	WA	BA	SU	HA	KH	DM	TH	CH	BN	KU	YA	LI
*p	p	p	p	p	p	p	p	p	p	p	p	p	p
*ʔp	p	p	p	p	p	p	p	b	b	b	b	Ø	ph
*ph	ph	ph	ph	ph	ph	ph	ph	ph	ph	ph	ph	ph	ph
*b	b	b	b	b	b	b	b	b	p/b	p/b	p/b	p	p
*t	t	t	t	t	t	t	(?)	t	(?)	t	t	t	t
*ʔt	t	t	t	t	t	t	t	ḍ	d	d	d	Ø	th
*th	th	th	th	th	th	th	th	th	th	th	th	th	th
*d	d	d	d	d	d	d	d	d/ḍ	t/d	t/d	t/d	t	t
*c	c	c	c	c	c	c	c	c	c	c	c	c	c
*ʔc	c	c	c	c	c	c	c	c	ch	ch	ch	s	s
*ch	s	s	s	(?)	ch	ch	c	ch	ch	ch	ch	s	s
*j	j	j	j	j/gy	j	j	c	j	c	c	c/j	c	c
*k	k	k	k	k	k	k	k	k	k	k	k	k	k
*ʔk	k	k	k	k	k	k	k	k	kh	kh	kh	kh	kh
*kh	kh	kh	kh	kh	kh	kh	kh	kh	kh	kh	kh	kh	kh
*g	g	g	g	g	g	g	g	g	k	k/g	k/g	k	k
*kw	m	ɓ	ʔb	b/g	x/b	k	k	b/p	k	k(h)	k(h)	h	k(h)
*m	m	m	m	m	m	m	m	m	m	m	m	m	m
*ʔm	m	ɓ	m	m	m	m	m	m	m	m	m	m	m
*n	n	n	n	n	n	n	n	n	n	n	n	n	n
*ʔn	n	ɗ	n	n	n	n	n	n	n	n	n	n	n
*ŋ	ŋ/n	ŋ/n	ŋ/n	ŋ	n˜	ŋ/n	ŋ	ŋ/n	ŋ	ŋ	ŋ	n	n/ŋ
*l	l	l	l	l	l	l	l	l	l	l	l	l/r	l
*ʔl	l/ʔl	l/ʔl	l	l	l	l	l	l	l	l	l	l/r	l
*r	r	r	r	r	r	r	r	r	r	r/y	r	y	y
*ry	r/y	r/y	r/y	r/y	y	r	r	r/y	r	r/y	g	y	y
*y	y	y	y	y	y	y	y	y	y	y	y	y	y
*w	w	w	w	w	w	w	w	w	w	w	w	w	w
*s	s	s	s/ʃ	s/ʃ	s	s	s	s	s	s	s	s	s
*h	h	h	h	h	h	h	h	h	h	h	h	h	h
*Cl	Cl	Cl	Cl	Cr	Cl	Cl	C/l	Cl	C/l	C/l	C/l	C/l	C/l
*Cr	Cr	Cr	Cr	Cr	C	Cr	C	Cr	C	C	C	C	C

Diagram 4: Kiranti initial consonant correspondences

One might tentatively propose that aspirated and preglottalised initial consonants have arisen under influence of the glottogenetic Tibeto-Burman prefixes <*s-> and <*ʔə->. In addition to preglottalised obstruents, which have only left indirect traces in modern Kiranti, I also propose to reconstruct preglottalised nasals and liquids, which have left direct traces in Wambule and Jero, and which therefore seem to justify the reconstruction of preglottalised sounds in Kiranti.

The regular opposition between nasal and implosive consonants constitutes the most striking difference between Wambule and the other Kiranti languages. Wambule seems to occupy a special place among its closest linguistic relatives because the implosive stops /ɓ-/ and /ɗ-/ can be partly traced back to Proto-Wambule /*ʔm-/ and /*ʔn-/, probably reflecting Proto-Kiranti preglottalised nasals which can be further traced back to the Tibeto-Burman glottogenetic prefixes <*s-> or <*ʔə-> followed by a root-initial consonant /*m, *n/. Compare, for instance, Wambule *ɓisi* 'eye' and *ɗwabu* 'ear' with the Proto-Lolo-Burmese word *s-myak*^{H} 'eye' and *ʔ-na*^{2} 'ear', which are reconstructed with the glottogenetic prefixes <*s-> and <*ʔə-> at the Proto-Tibeto-Burman level. There is no direct evidence that Tibeto-Burman <*s-> led to the development of a voiceless aspirated manner series of obstruents in Kiranti and that <*ʔə-> gave rise to preglottalised sounds. However, in Kiranti words where aspiration is irregularly spread and in variation with the preglottalised consonants, the prefixes <*s-> and <*ʔə-> may have alternated before obstruents.

(i) *Proto-Kiranti /*p-/*

The voiceless unaspirated Proto-Kiranti obstruent /*p-/ is reflected in words which regularly have initial /p-/ in the modern Kiranti languages, e.g. 'bat', 'father', 'sweet potato' and 'wring, squeeze'.

BAT:

Proto-Tibeto-Burman **ba:k*.

- /*p-/: Jero *pɔkti*$_{\text{am}}$; Wambule *pwakti*; Bahing *pákati*; Sunwar *'pakatiyti*; Thulung *pakti*; Khaling *'paakti*; Kulung *papiwa*.

FATHER:

Proto-Tibeto-Burman **pu* 'male, father, grandfather', *p^w*a* 'man, father, husband, person', **wa* 'man, father, husband, person'.

- /*p-/: Jero *papa*$_{am}$; Wambule *papa*, *pap*, *po*; Bahing *-po* in *ápo*; Hayu *-pɷ* in *uxpɷ*; Thulung *pap*; Khaling *'päp*; Chamling *-pa* in *kok-pa* 'grandfather'; Dumi *papa*, *pu*; Bantawa *(-)pa*, *pa=pa*; Kulung *pa*; Yamphu *-pa*; Limbu *pa*.

(ii) *Proto-Kiranti /*ʔp-/*

Preglottalised Proto-Kiranti /*ʔp-/ is reflected in words which regularly have initial /p-/ in Jero, Wambule, Bahing, Sunwar, Khaling, Dumi and Hayu, /b-/ in Thulung, Chamling, Bantawa and Kulung, an initial vowel in Yamphu and /ph-/ in Limbu, e.g. 'axe', 'bamboo', 'bind, tie', 'causativiser', 'come (across a horizontal plane)', 'do, make', 'earth, soil', 'flower', 'head', 'owl' and 'pig, hog'. The aspiration in Jero, Wambule, Bahing, Sunwar and Hayu seems to be secondary development.

FLOWER:

Proto-Tibeto-Burman **ba:r* 'bloom flower', *b^w*at* 'flower', **b/s-wat* 'flower'.

- /*ʔp-/: Jero *phuri*$_{am}$; Wambule *phuri*; Bahing *phúng*; Sunwar *phuu*; Thulung *buŋma*; Khaling *pungme*; Dumi *puma*; Chamling *bungwa*; Bantawa *buŋ+ga*; Kulung *buŋ*; Yamphu *œʔwa*.

PIG, HOG:

Proto-Tibeto-Burman *p^w*ak*, **wak.*

- /*ʔp-/: Jero *pa*$_{am}$ 'pig', *cuppa*$_{am}$ 'piglet'; Wambule *pa* 'pig', *cuppa* 'piglet'; Bahing *po*; Sunwar *poo*; Thulung *boa*; Khaling *'po*; Dumi *poʔo* 'pig', *poksœ* 'piglet'; Chamling *bose*; Bantawa *bak*; Kulung *bo:* 'pig', *bokc*^{h}*a* 'piglet'; Yamphu *akma* 'pig', *akpasa* 'piglet'; Limbu *phak*.

(iii) *Proto-Kiranti /*ph-/*

The voiceless aspirated Proto-Kiranti obstruent /*ph-/ is reflected in words which regularly have initial /ph-/ in the modern Kiranti languages, e.g. 'break, burst', 'flour' and 'spread'.

FLOUR:

- /*ph-/: Jero *phuli*$_{am}$; Wambule *phuli*; Thulung *phul*; Kulung *p*^{h}*ul*; Limbu *phe:rum*.

SPREAD:

- /*ph-/: Khaling *'phen-nä*; Dumi *phiŋni* 'spread out, grow wider'; Bantawa *phes-(u)*; Yamphu *phe'ma* 'spread out'.

(iv) *Proto-Kiranti /*b-/*

The plain voiced Proto-Kiranti obstruent /*b-/ is reflected in words which regularly have initial /b-/ in the Western Kiranti languages Jero, Wambule, Bahing, Sunwar, Hayu, Khaling, Dumi and Thulung, /p-/ or sometimes /b-/ in the Central Kiranti languages Chamling, Bantawa and Kulung, and /p-/ in the Eastern Kiranti languages Yamphu and Limbu, e.g. 'banana', 'be, sit', 'cow', 'die', 'get up, stand up, arise', 'give', 'millet', 'run (away)', 'thumb', 'touch' and 'white'.

COW:

- /*b-/: Jero *biya*$_{a}$ 'bullock'; Wambule *biya*; Bahing *bing* 'bull'; Sunwar *bii*; Thulung *beno* (LTH *beoneo*); Khaling *bay*; Dumi *bhiʔi* (/b-/ expected); Chamling *pyupa*; Bantawa *pit-ma*; Kulung *pi*; Yamphu *bik*; Limbu *pit*.

GET UP, STAND UP, ARISE:

Proto-Tibeto-Burman **m-sow* 'arise, awake(n)'.

- /*b-/: Jero *bukcap*$_{a}$, *bukcam*$_{m}$; Wambule *bukcam*, *bu:cam*; Bahing *bwóko*; Sunwar *'book-tsa*; Hayu *bɶk-*; Thulung *bək-*; Bantawa *puk-(a)*; Kulung *po:ma*; Yamphu *pu'kma*; Limbu *po:kma*.
  - ≈ 'Transitive' initial /*ph-/: Khaling *'phu-nä*; Dumi *phikni*.

(v) *Proto-Kiranti /*p-/, /*ʔp-/, /*ph-/ or /*b-/*

Several words seem to exhibit an alternation between two or more morphosemantically related Proto-Kiranti roots with /*p-/, /*ʔp-/, /*ph-/ or /*b-/, e.g. 'ashes', 'ask for, beg', 'bring (across a horizontal plane)', 'calf of leg', 'dress', 'erect, arise, wake up', 'ginger', 'hang up, suspend', 'sew' and 'suck'.

BRING (ACROSS A HORIZONTAL PLANE):

- /*ʔp-/: Bahing *pito*; Sunwar *'pit-tsa*; Hayu *pit-*; Khaling *'pan-nä*; Dumi *pitnɨ*; Chamling *baid-*; Bantawa *bitt-(u)*; Kulung *baima*.
  /*ph-/: Jero *phiccap*$_a$, *phiccam*$_m$; Wambule *phiccam*; Thulung *phit-*; Limbu *phɛpma*.

ERECT, ARISE, WAKE UP:

Proto-Tibeto-Burman **m-sow* 'arise, awake(n)'.

- /*p-/: Bahing *pok-* (Michailovsky 1975); Sunwar *pook-tsa* 'pick up'; Hayu *pɷk-*; Kulung *po:ma*; Yamphu *pu'kma*.
  /*ph-/: Jero *phukcam*$_m$; Wambule *phukcam*; Thulung *phək-* 'raise, waken'; Khaling *'phu-nä* 'raise'; Dumi *bhoknɨ* 'put' (/ph-/ expected); Limbu *pho:ŋma*.

In addition, the words 'knee' and 'tear (n)' can be for the moment reconstructed with initial /*p-/ or /*ʔp-/, whereas 'be able' and 'wind (n)' have /*ph-/ or perhaps /*ʔp-/.

(vi) *Proto-Kiranti /*t-/*

Quite interestingly, the voiceless unaspirated Proto-Kiranti obstruent /*t-/ is currently only reflected in word 'knee' in a few languages which have initial /t-/. This suggests an early merger of Proto-Kiranti /*t-/ and /*ʔt-/. However, there are several items listed below that can be reconstructed with /*t-/ or /*ʔt-/.

KNEE:

Proto-Tibeto-Burman **put-s*.

- /*t-/: Khaling *tamcu*; Kulung *tumc^hi*; Yamphu *tumruk*; Limbu *thumboʔ*, *thuŋboʔ* (initial unexplained; /t-/ expected).

(vii) *Proto-Kiranti /*ʔt-/*

Preglottalised Proto-Kiranti /*ʔt-/ is reflected in words which regularly have regularly initial /t-/ in Jero, Wambule, Bahing, Sunwar, Hayu, Khaling and Dumi, /ḍ-/ in Thulung, /d-/ in Chamling, Bantawa and Kulung, an initial vowel in Yamphu and /th-/ in Limbu, e.g. 'beat, play (instrument)', 'beat, strike', 'drink', 'one' and 'swallow'.

BEAT, STRIKE:

Proto-Tibeto-Burman **dip* × **tip*, **dup* × **tup*.

- /*ʔt-/: Jero *tupcap*$_{a}$, *tupcam*$_{a}$; Wambule *tupcam*; Bahing *teuppo*; Sunwar *'tup-tsa*; Hayu *top-*; Thulung *Dep-*; Khaling *'thu-nä* 'beat (heart)' (initial unexplained; /t-/ expected); Dumi *da:pnɨ* (initial unexplained; /t-/ expected); Chamling *dip-*; Bantawa *dup-(u)* 'work metal' (*dhup-(u)* 'hit'); Kulung *dəima*; Yamphu *upma* 'batter'; Limbu *thamma* 'beat (cloth in washing), smash, thrash, knock down'.

DRINK:

Proto-Tibeto-Burman **ʔam* 'eat, drink'.

- /*ʔt-/: Jero *tu:cap*$_{a}$, *tu:cam*$_{m}$; Wambule *tu:cam*; Bahing *túg-no*; Sunwar *tuu-tsa*; Hayu *tũ'ta* 'drunk'; Thulung *Du(ŋ)-*; Khaling *tu-nä*; Dumi *tiŋnɨ*; Chamling *dungma*; Bantawa *duŋ-ma*; Kulung *du:ma*; Yamphu *uŋma*; Limbu *thuŋma*.

(viii) *Proto-Kiranti /*th-/*

The voiceless aspirated Proto-Kiranti obstruent /*th-/ is reflected in words which regularly have initial /th-/ in the modern Kiranti languages, e.g. 'come up', 'cough (n)', 'hear', 'sell, exchange', 'sew', 'spittle, saliva', 'stretch' and 'year'.

HEAR:

Proto-Tibeto-Burman **r/g-na* 'ear, hear, listen', **s-ta-s* 'hear'.

- /*th-/: Jero *thɔcap*$_{a}$, *thɔ-*$_{m}$; Wambule *thwacam*; Hayu *tha(t)-*; Thulung *theos-*; Khaling *thö-nä* 'see, get'.

YEAR:

Proto-Tibeto-Burman **s-ni(:)ŋ* × **s-nik*.

- /*th-/: Jero *-thoce*$_{am}$, *-thot*$_{a}$, *tho-*$_{a}$; Wambule *-thoce*, *-thoḍ*; Bahing *thó*; Sunwar *-thotse*; Thulung *thə*; Khaling *tho*.
  ≈ /*d-/: Bantawa *doŋ*; Kulung *-doŋ*; Limbu *tɔŋ*.

(ix) *Proto-Kiranti /*d-/*

The plain voiced Proto-Kiranti obstruent /*d-/ is reflected in words which regularly have initial /d-/ in Jero, Wambule, Bahing, Sunwar, Hayu, Khaling and Dumi, /d-/ or sometimes /ḍ-/ in Thulung, /t-/ or sometimes /d-/ in Chamling, Bantawa and Kulung, and /t-/ in Yamphu and Limbu, e.g. 'become', 'big, large, great', 'blow (by mouth)', 'chase away', 'cover', 'dig', 'fall down, fall off', 'head', 'like, be fond of', 'meet, visit', 'shake, move, agitate', 'suffice', 'taste (eat an example)', 'tomorrow', 'village' and 'year'.

TASTE (EAT AN EXAMPLE):

- /d-/: Jero *dɔmcap*$_{m}$ 'be tasted', Wambule *dwapcam*; Bahing *damso*; Sunwar *tham-tsa* 'taste' (initial unexplained; /d-/ expected); Thulung *deop-*; Khaling *'däm-nä*; Dumi *da:p-nɨ*; Bantawa *dutt-(u)* (*dhutt-(u)*; /d-/ as expected); Kulung *damma*.

VILLAGE:

Proto-Tibeto-Burman **dyal* × **tyal*.

- /d-/: Jero *dɛl*$_{am}$; Wambule *dyal*; Bahing *dyal*; Thulung *del*, *Del*; Khaling *del*; Dumi *de:l*; Bantawa *ten*; Kulung *tel*; Limbu *tɛn* 'place'.

(x) *Proto-Kiranti /*t-/, /*ʔt-/, /*th-/ or /*d-/*

Several words seem to exhibit an alternation between two or more morphosemantically related Proto-Kiranti roots with either /*t-/, /*ʔt-/, /*th-/ or /*d-/, e.g. ‘follow, go after’, ‘fall down, fall off’, ‘finish, complete’, ‘heart’, ‘make drink’, ‘push’, ‘shut, close’ and ‘spit’.

FALL DOWN, FALL OFF:

- /*t-/: Thulung *ta(n)-* ‘fall down as when walking’.
  /*ʔt-/ or /d-/: Chamling *dha-* (/d-/ expected); Bantawa *dha-(a)* (/d-/ expected); Kulung *dima*.
  /*th-/: Khaling *thi-nä*; Dumi *thi:ni*; Limbu *tha:ma* ‘come down, fall down’.

SPIT:

Proto-Tibeto-Burman **m/s-tu:k* ‘spit, spew’, **ts(y)il* × **til* ‘spit, spittle, saliva’.

- /*t-/ or /*ʔt-/: Bahing *téwo*; Sunwar *’took-si-tsa*.
  /*th-/: Jero *thukcap*$_{a}$; Wambule *thukcam*; Thulung *thaŋki*, *thəŋki*; Khaling *khi ’thu-nä*; Kulung *t*^{h}*uwa*; Limbu *tho:ŋ-ma*.

In addition, the words ‘kick’, ‘lick’ and ‘moon’ can for the moment be reconstructed with initial /*t-/ or /*ʔt-/, whereas ‘cloth, wear’ and ‘hurt, ache’ may have initial /*t-/ or /*d-/. The words ‘back, behind, after’ and ‘what’ can take either initial /*ʔt-/ or /*d-/.

(xi) *Proto-Kiranti /*c-/*

The voiceless unaspirated Proto-Kiranti obstruent /*c-/ is reflected in words which regularly have initial /c-/ in the modern languages, e.g. ‘be able’, ‘game’, ‘grandchild’, ‘heart’, ‘kiss’, ‘tasty’ and ‘tear, rend’.

BE ABLE:

- /*c-/: Jero *capcam*$_{m}$; Wambule *capcam*; Bahing *chápo*; Sunwar *tsap-tsa*; Thulung *caps-*; Khaling *’cäm-nä*; Dumi *tsa:pni*; Chamling *camma*; Bantawa *cap-(a)*; Limbu *cup-tama* ‘be convenient, favourable, opportune’.

LEARN, STUDY:

Proto-Tibeto-Burman **s-lwap* ‘practice, learn’.

- /*c-/: Jero *cei-*$_{m}$; Wambule *ceicam*; Bahing *cháyin̠so*; Sunwar *’sheen-si-tsa* (initial unexplained; /c-/ expected); Thulung *cen-* ‘teach’; Khaling *’ceysi-nä*; Dumi *tsen’sini*; Chamling *cuima*; Bantawa *cint-(a)ncin-*; Yamphu *cimma*.

(xii) *Proto-Kiranti /*ʔc-/*

Preglottalised Proto-Kiranti /*ʔc-/ is reflected in words which regularly have initial /c-/ in Jero, Wambule, Bahing, Sunwar, Hayu, Khaling, Dumi and Thulung, /ch-/ in Chamling, Bantawa and Kulung, and /s-/ in Yamphu and Limbu, e.g. ‘bird’, ‘finger, toe’, ‘hate (n)’, ‘pinch, nip; sting (by insect)’, ‘shut, close’ and ‘write’.

BIRD:

Proto-Tibeto-Burman **bya* ‘bee, bird’, **wa* ‘bird, feather’, **s-ŋak* ‘bird’.

- /*ʔc-/: Jero *cikmu*$_{m}$, *cipmu*$_{a}$; Wambule *cwagbo*; Bahing *chikba*; Sunwar *’tsiikbi*; Thulung *cəkpu*; Bantawa *choŋ-ga*, *choŋ-wa*. Kulung *c*^{h}*owa*; Yamphu *soŋ(w)a*.

SHUT, CLOSE:

Proto-Tibeto-Burman **dzyiːp* ‘shut, close, close together’.

- /*ʔc-/: Bahing *tsok-* (Michailovsky 1994); Sunwar *’tsooksho* ‘shut, lock’; Thulung *cəks-* ‘shut up’; Khaling *’cenä*; Bantawa *chekt-(u)*; Kulung *c*^{h}*ima*; Yamphu *sækma*; Limbu *sakma*, *supma*.

(xiii) *Proto-Kiranti /*ch-/*

The voiceless aspirated Proto-Kiranti obstruent /*ch-/ is reflected in words which regularly have initial /c-/ in Dumi, /ch-/ in the Western Kiranti languages Khaling and Thulung and the Central Kiranti languages Chamling, Bantawa and Kulung, and /s-/ in the Western Kiranti languages Jero, Wambule and Bahing and the Eastern Kiranti languages Yamphu and Limbu, e.g. 'dance (n)', 'dry, dry up', 'day after tomorrow', 'song', 'suck' and 'sweep'.

DANCE (N):

Proto-Tibeto-Burman **gan* 'run, dance, kick', **ga:r* × **s-ga* 'dance, sing, leap, stride'.

- /*ch-/: Thulung *cheoms-*; Khaling *chwaam-nä* (v); Dumi *tsəm*; Chamling *themma* (initial unexplained; /ch-/ expected); Yamphu *simmama* (v).

SONG:

Proto-Tibeto-Burman **ga:r* × **s-ga* 'dance, sing, leap, stride'.

- /*ch-/: Jero *sa:laŋ*$_{\mathrm{m}}$, *sa:ʔlɛŋ*$_{\mathrm{a}}$; Wambule *sa:laŋ*; Bahing *swá-long*; Bantawa *cham*; Kulung *c*^{h}*am*; Yamphu *semluma* 'song', *semla* 'voice'; Limbu *sam*, *sam-lo*.

(xiv) *Proto-Kiranti /*j-/*

The plain voiced Proto-Kiranti obstruent /*j-/ is reflected in words which regularly have initial /j-/ in the Western Kiranti languages Jero, Wambule, Bahing, Hayu, Khaling, Dumi and Thulung, /j-/ or sometimes /gy-/ in Sunwar, /c-/ or sometimes /j-/ in the Central Kiranti languages Chamling, Bantawa and Kulung, and /c-/ in the Eastern Kiranti languages Yamphu and Limbu, e.g. 'break', 'buy', 'eat', 'know (by learning)', 'plough', 'sour', 'sweet' and 'wind (n)'.

EAT:

Proto-Tibeto-Burman **dzya* 'eat, food, feed', **dzya-s* 'eat, food, feed', **dzya-t* 'eat, food, feed'.

- /*j-/: Jero *jacap*$_{\mathrm{a}}$, *jacam*$_{\mathrm{m}}$; Wambule *jacam*; Bahing *jáwo*; Sunwar *'dza-tsa*; Hayu *dza-*; Thulung *jam* 'cooked rice, food'; Khaling *jö-nä*; Dumi *dzuni*; Chamling *ca-ma*; Bantawa *ca-(a)*, *ca-(u)*; Kulung *cama*; Yamphu *ca'ma*; Limbu *cama*.

SOUR:

Proto-Tibeto-Burman **su:r* × **swa:r* 'sour, be acid', **s-kyu:r* × **s-kywa:r* 'sour, be acid'.

- /*j-/: Jero *jurtɔp*$_{a}$, *jurto*$_{m}$; Wambule *jurco*; Bahing *jeujeum*; Sunwar *gyur-sho*; Thulung *jhiur-* 'be sour', *jiujiur* 'variety of bitter fruit'; Khaling *jujur*; Dumi *tsɨrpɨ* (initial unexplained; /j-/ expected); Kulung *jujurpa*.

(xv) *Proto-Kiranti /*c-/, /*ʔc-/, /*ch-/, /*j-/ or /*s-/*

Several words seem to exhibit an alternation between two or more morphosemantically related Proto-Kiranti roots with either /*c-/, /*ʔc-/, /*ch-/ or /*j-/ as well as /*s-/.

MORTAR:

Proto-Tibeto-Burman **t(s)um* × *(t)sum*, **tśrum*.

- /*ʔc-/: Sunwar *'tsumlo*; Chamling *chippu*, *chippukhung*; Bantawa *chum+puk*; Kulung *c*^{h}*umbo*.
  /*s-/: Jero *sumlo*$_{a}$; Wambule *sumlo*; Thulung *'siuŋkhra*; Khaling *samkhraa*; Dumi *siŋkho*; Yamphu *summak*; Limbu *sumdaŋ*.

URINE:

Proto-Tibeto-Burman **g-ts(y)i-t/n*, **ʐəy*.

- /*ʔc-/: Bahing *charníku*; Sunwar *'tsarnaku*; Hayu *tsɪ-*; Khaling *'cekmö*; Dumi *tsirkhɨm*; Chamling *chʌrs-* 'urinate'; Bantawa *cheys-(a)*; Kulung *c*^{h}*ema* 'urinate'; Yamphu *se'ma* 'urinate'; Limbu *seʔma:t* 'urinate'.
  /*s-/: Jero *sɔrki*$_{am}$; Wambule *swarki*; Thulung *sar(s)-* 'urinate'.

The words which show this alternation are 'cough (n)', 'cover', 'fly (n)', 'mortar', 'new', 'urine', 'winnow' and 'wring, squeeze'. In addition, the words 'catch', 'cheek', 'hang up, suspend', 'millet', 'question', 'twist' and 'wash (up, oneself), bathe' can for the moment be reconstructed with initial /*c-/ or /*ʔc-/. By contrast, 'dress', 'finish, complete', 'hide, conceal', 'small, little' and 'spit' may take initial /*c-/ or /*j-/ whereas 'lungs' is reconstructed with /*j-/ or /*s-/.

(xvi) *Proto-Kiranti /*k-/*

The voiceless unaspirated Proto-Kiranti obstruent /*k-/ is reflected in words which regularly have initial /k-/ in the modern languages, e.g. 'bark, skin', 'chase away', 'lizard', 'maternal uncle' and 'stick, attach'.

BARK, SKIN:

Proto-Tibeto-Burman **kok* × *kwa(:)k.*

- /*k-/: Jero *kɔkte*$_{am}$; Wambule *kwakte*; Bahing *kokte* 'skin'; Sunwar *krusul* 'bark', *'kusul* 'skin'; Hayu *kuktsho*; Thulung *kokte*; Khaling *'kaa.*

  ≈ /*k-/: Dumi *-kə* in *səkkə*; Kulung *-ko-* in *sokowar*; Yamphu *-k* in *sauk.*

STICK, ATTACH:

Proto-Tibeto-Burman **g(y)it/k* × **k(y)it/k* 'tie, bind'.

- /*k-/: Jero *kɛpcap*$_{a}$, *kɛpcam*$_{m}$; Wambule *kyapcam*; Bahing *kyapcho* 'glue'; Sunwar *keptsok* 'greasy'; Hayu *kik-*; Thulung *kep-;* Khaling *kay-nä* 'stick into', *'kem-nä* 'stick'; Dumi *kepni*; Bantawa *khep* in *cük+khep=cük+khep* 'sticky' (initial unexplained; /k-/ expected); Kulung *kemma*; Yamphu *ki'pma* 'stick onto'; Limbu *kapma.*

(xvii) *Proto-Kiranti /*ʔk-/*

Preglottalised Proto-Kiranti /*ʔk-/ is reflected in words which regularly have initial /k-/ in Jero, Wambule, Bahing, Sunwar, Hayu, Khaling, Dumi and Thulung, but /kh-/ in Chamling, Bantawa, Kulung, Yamphu and Limbu, e.g. 'bite, peck', 'buy', 'chew, masticate', 'cloud', 'cover', 'look' and 'stretch'.

CARRY:

Proto-Tibeto-Burman **ba* 'carry on back', **tam* 'carry on shoulder'.

- /*ʔk-/: Jero *kurcap*$_a$, *kurcam*$_m$; Wambule *kurcam*; Bahing *kúro*; Sunwar *kur-b mur* 'porter'; Thulung *kur-*; Khaling *kar-nä*; Dumi *kɨrnɨ*; Chamling *khur-*; Bantawa *khuy-(u)*; Kulung *khurma*; Yamphu *khi'ma*; Limbu *ku:ma* (initial unexplained; /kh-/ expected).

LOOK:

Proto-Tibeto-Burman **hyen* 'hear, listen, look, see'.

- /*ʔk-/: Jero *kicap*$_a$, *kicam*$_m$; Wambule *kwacam*; Bahing *kwó-gno* 'see'; Sunwar *koo-tsa* 'see, look at'; Khaling *'ko-nä* 'know how to do something'; Chamling *khanga-*, *khõ-*; Bantawa *kha-(u)*, *khaŋ-(u)*; Kulung *kho:ma* 'see'; Yamphu *khaŋma*.

(xviii) *Proto-Kiranti /*kh-/*

The voiceless aspirated Proto-Kiranti obstruent /*kh-/ is reflected in words which regularly have initial /kh-/ in the modern Kiranti languages, e.g. 'arm, hand', 'axe', 'black', 'call (v)', 'fry', 'elbow', 'follow, go after', 'go', 'pus', 'shave', 'theft, thief' and 'touch'.

THEFT, THIEF:

Proto-Tibeto-Burman **r-kəw* × **r-kun* × **r-kut* 'steal, thief'.

- /*kh-/: Jero *khus*$_{am}$ 'theft'; Wambule *khus* 'theft', *khujiwa* 'male thief'; Bahing *kunchaniwa* 'theft', *kuncha* 'thief' (initial unexplained; /kh-/ expected); Sunwar *khuy 'pa-tsa* 'steal'; Thulung *khu-* 'steal', *khuciubo* 'thief'; Khaling *'khepä* 'thief'; Dumi *khi:nɨ* 'steal'; Chamling *khuma* 'steal'; Bantawa *khü+ka+ba*; Kulung *k*^{h}*uma* 'be a thief'; Yamphu *khusubaŋ* 'thief'; Limbu *khu:pma* 'steal'.

AXE:

Proto-Tibeto-Burman **r-p^wa*.

- /*kh-/: Jero *khu*$_{am}$; Wambule *khu*; Bahing *khá*; Sunwar *khraa* (initial unexplained; /kh-/ expected); Hayu *khoʔ-joŋ*; Thulung *kho*.

(xix) *Proto-Kiranti /*g-/*

The plain voiced Proto-Kiranti obstruent /*g-/ is reflected in words which regularly have initial /g-/ in the Western Kiranti languages Jero, Wambule, Bahing, Sunwar, Hayu, Khaling, Dumi and Thulung, /k-/ or sometimes /g-/ in the Central Kiranti languages Chamling, Bantawa and Kulung, and /k-/ in the Eastern Kiranti languages Yamphu and Limbu, e.g. 'arm, hand', 'be (identity)', 'bend', 'come up', 'crow', 'fingernail', 'give', 'hide, conceal', 'pick up', 'tiger, leopard' and 'tooth'.

BEND:

Proto-Tibeto-Burman **gu(:)k* × **m-ku(:)k* 'crooked, bent, knee, angle'.

- /*g-/: Wambule *gupcam*; Bahing *guk-* (Michailovsky 1994); Sunwar *'guk-* (Michailovsky 1994); Hayu *guk-*; Thulung *gum-*; Khaling *'ghu-nä*; Dumi *kɨm'sinɨ*; Bantawa *kuŋt-(u)*; Kulung *kumma*; Yamphu *kuŋliŋ* 'curly, twisted'; Limbu /-kɔk/ in *pɛgɔk* 'manner of being twisted'.

CROW:

Proto-Tibeto-Burman **ka-n*.

- /*g-/: Jero *gagmu*$_{m}$, *ga:gab*$_{a}$; Wambule *gagbo*; Bahing *ga-gágpa*; Sunwar *khada* (initial unexplained; /g-/ expected); Thulung *gāpu*, *goāpu* (LTH *gagakpu*); Khaling *'gaakphö*; Dumi *gogo*; Bantawa *ka-gak*, *gagak*; Kulung *gagappa*; Limbu *ka:k-wa*, *a:k-wa*.

  ≈ Yamphu: *araʔwa*.

(xx) *Proto-Kiranti /*k-/, /*ʔk-/, /*kh-/ or /*g-/*

Several words exhibit an alternation between two or more morpho-semantically related Proto-Kiranti roots with /*k-/, /*ʔk-/, /*kh-/ or /*g-/, e.g. 'big, large, great', 'bitter', 'cook, boil', 'cooked liquid vegetable or meat dish', 'earth, soil', 'house', 'smoke (n)' and 'spittle, saliva'. In addition, the words 'door', 'one', 'song' and 'pinch, nip; sting (by insect)' can for the moment be reconstructed with initial /*k-/ or /*ʔk-/, whereas 'fear (n)' has either /*k-/ or /*g-/. The words 'flour' and 'hear' can be reconstructed with either initial /*ʔk-/ or /kh-/.

BITTER:

Proto-Tibeto-Burman **b-ka-n* 'bitter, liver'.

- /*k-/ or /*ʔk-/: Bahing *kaba*; Sunwar *'ka-sho.*
  /*kh-/: Jero *khatto*$_{m}$; Wambule *khaco*; Thulung *khes-* 'taste bitter'; Khaling *khäpä*; Dumi *kha:kpi*; Bantawa *khük*; Kulung *khikpa*; Yamphu *khiʔiye*; Limbu *khi:k*.

HOUSE:

Proto-Tibeto-Burman **k-yim* × **k-yum.*

- /k-/ or /ʔk-/: Jero *kulu*$_{a}$, *kul*$_{am}$; Wambule *kuḍu*; Hayu *kem*; Khaling *kam*; Dumi *ki:m*.
  /kh-/: Bahing *khyim*; Sunwar *khiin*; Chamling *khim*; Bantawa *khim*; Kulung *k*^{h}*im*; Yamphu *khim*; Limbu *khim*, *him*.

(xxi) *Proto-Kiranti /kw-/*

There appears to be some Kiranti evidence for distinguishing /*k-/ from /*kw-/ as distinct units at the Proto-Kiranti level. Initial /*kw-/ seems to have undergone reanalysis in various Kiranti groups because of the fact the semi-vowel /*w/ is capable of phonetic interaction with the syllable's initial consonant and its nuclear vowel. In the Western Kiranti languages Wambule, Bahing and Sunwar, for instance, the semi-vowel /*w/ was so bound to the velar stop /*k/ that these languages regularly treated the sequence like a unitary labiovelar phoneme /k^{w}-/, which later developed into a bilabial implosive /*ʔw-/ or

/*ʔb-/ (Opgenort 2004a). The regular reflex of Proto-Kiranti /*kw-/ is Jero /m-/, suggesting a development from Proto-Chaurasia /*ʔm-/. Proto-Chaurasia /*ʔm-/ is also derived from the Proto-Kiranti preglottalised bilabial nasal /*ʔm-/, which is discussed further below.

WOUND:

Proto-Tibeto-Burman **r-ma-t* 'wound, injured'.

- /*kw-/: Jero *mari*$_{\text{am}}$; Wambule *ɓari*; Bahing *ʔbar* (Michailovsky 1994); Sunwar *gaar*; Hayu *buʔma* (Michailovsky 1994); Thulung *par* 'sore, skin lesion of any kind'; Khaling *'kwaar*; Dumi *kar*; Bantawa *khen*; Kulung *k^{h}er*; Yamphu *huwa*; Limbu *ka:n*.

WATER:

Proto-Tibeto-Burman **m-ti-s* 'wet, soak', **ti(y)* 'water'.

- /*kw-/: Jero *ka:ku*$_{\text{am}}$, *ka:k*$_{\text{am}}$; Wambule *ka:ku*, *kak*; Bahing *pwáku*; Sunwar *baakku*; Thulung *ku*; Khaling *ku*; Dumi *kɨ*; Kulung *kawa*.
  - ≈ /*kw-/: Chamling *wa*; Bantawa *caʔ+wa*; Yamphu *wa-* in *wajokma* 'water'; Limbu *wa*.

The words 'cool (v)', 'potato, yam', 'water' and 'wound' reflect a Wambule implosive which corresponds to initial Proto-Kiranti /*kw-/ because several Kiranti languages have velar segments as regular correspondences of the Wambule implosive /ɓ-/. In the word 'water', by contrast, either the semi-vowel or the initial consonant /*k-/ was lost.

CHICKEN:

Proto-Tibeto-Burman **ʔa:r*, **ha:r* 'fowl, chicken, quail'.

- ?/*kw-/: Jero *mɔkɔm*$_{\text{am}}$ 'chicken', *ma-* in *maphlɛm*$_{\text{am}}$ 'wing'; Wambule *ɓo* 'chicken', *ɓa-* in *ɓaphlyam* 'wing'; Bahing *ʔbá* (Michailovsky 1994); Sunwar *bwa* (Michailovsky 1994); Hayu *xo'co*; Thulung *po*, *pa-* in *pasiurium* 'feather', *ba-* in *baphlem* 'wing'; Khaling *phö*; Dumi *pawœm*; Chamling *wasa*; Bantawa *wa*; Kulung *wa:*; Yamphu *wa*; Limbu *waʔ*.

In the words 'cheek', 'chicken', 'come out, go out', 'eat, bite', 'language, word, speech', 'net', 'shadow, spirit', 'shoulder' and 'spider', by contrast, the Wambule implosive stop /ɓ-/ regularly corresponds to /m-/ in Jero but to plosive stops in other Kiranti languages. These words may also be reconstructed with /*kw-/, yielding /p- ~ ph- ~ b- ~ bh- ~ g- ~ w-/ in the modern languages.

SHOULDER:

- $^{?}$/*kw-/: Jero *masεm*$_{\text{m}}$; Wambule *ɓasyam*; Bahing *balam*; Sunwar *balaa*; Thulung *'balam* 'shoulder blade'; Khaling *'bhaataa* (/bh-/ expected); Dumi *bokto*; Bantawa *bak+taŋ*; Kulung *bouto* ($^{?}$<**bokto*); Yamphu *akkŕaŋ* (<**paktaŋ*); Limbu *phɔkthaŋ*.

(xxii) *Proto-Kiranti /*m-/*

The Proto-Kiranti bilabial nasal /*m-/ is reflected in words which have initial /m-/ in the modern Kiranti languages, e.g. 'catch', 'die' (= 'forget'); 'fire' (and the derived compound forms 'ashes' and 'smoke (n)'); 'forget', 'mankind, person', 'mother', 'search, look for', 'wash (up, oneself), bathe', 'wash, rinse' and 'what'.

FIRE:

Proto-Tibeto-Burman **mey*.

- /*m-/: Jero *mi*$_{\text{am}}$; Wambule *mi*; Bahing *mí*; Sunwar *mii*; Thulung *mu*; Khaling *mi*; Dumi *mi*; Chamling *mi-* in *midhima* 'ashes'; Bantawa *mi*; Kulung *mi*; Yamphu *mi*; Limbu *mi*.

MANKIND, PERSON:

Proto-Tibeto-Burman **r-mi(y)-n* 'man, person'.

- /*m-/: Jero *mucu*$_{\text{am}}$; Wambule *muyo*; Bahing *múryeu*; Sunwar *mur*; Thulung *miuciu*; Khaling *min*; Dumi *mi:n*; Chamling *mina*; Bantawa *mü+na* 'man'; Kulung *misi*; Yamphu *-mi* in *yaʔmi*; Limbu *mɔna*.

(xxiii) *Proto-Kiranti /*ʔm-/*

The Proto-Kiranti preglottalised bilabial nasal /*ʔm-/ is reflected in words which regularly have initial /m-/ in the modern Kiranti languages except Wambule, which has /ɓ-/ instead, e.g. 'buffalo', 'eye', 'remember, think', 'tail', 'tear (n)' and 'woman'. The words 'banana', 'be, sit', 'bear (n)', 'beat, play (instrument)', 'black', 'blow (by mouth)', 'causativiser', 'cloud', 'do, make', 'finish, complete', 'hail', 'silence, quietness', can for the moment be reconstructed with either /*m-/ or /*ʔm-/.

EYE:

Proto-Tibeto-Burman **s-mik* × **s-myak*.

- /*ʔm-/: Jero *misi*$_{\mathrm{am}}$; Wambule *ɓisi*; Bahing *michi*; Sunwar *miiktsi*; Thulung *miksi*; Khaling *mas*; Dumi *miksi*; Chamling *micu*; Bantawa *mük*; Kulung *muksi*; Yamphu *mik*; Limbu *mik*.

REMEMBER, THINK:

- /*ʔm-/: Jero *mimcap*$_{\mathrm{a}}$; Wambule *ɓimcam*; Bahing *mimto*; Sunwar *mim-tsa*; Thulung *mim-*; Khaling *mam-nä*; Dumi *minni*; Bantawa *mitt-(a)*; Kulung *mi:ma*; Yamphu *miʔma*; Limbu *niŋ-waʔ*.

(xxiv) *Proto-Kiranti /*n-/*

The Proto-Kiranti alveolar nasal /*n-/ is reflected in words which regularly have initial /n-/ in the modern Kiranti languages, e.g. 'back, behind, after', 'brain', 'day after tomorrow', 'elbow', 'pinch, nip; sting (by insect)', 'priest', 'push', 'rest, relax' and 'smell'.

REST, RELAX:

Proto-Tibeto-Burman **g-na-s* 'be, live, stay, rest, alight, perch'.

- /*n-/: Jero *naicam*$_{\mathrm{m}}$; Wambule *naicam*; Bahing *náso* 'take rest'; Sunwar *'nayk-tsa*; Thulung *ŋemsi-* (initial unexplained; /n-/ expected); Khaling *nöl mü-nä*; Bantawa *nant-(a)*; Kulung *nomcima*; Yamphu *nœ'ʔma* 'rest a burden'; Limbu *naʔsiŋma*.

SMELL:

Proto-Tibeto-Burman **m/s-nam.*

- /*n-/: Jero *ŋɔmcap*$_{a}$, *ŋɔmcam*$_{m}$ (initial unexplained; /n-/ expected); Wambule *ŋwamcam* (initial unexplained; /n-/ expected); Bahing *námo*; Sunwar *nam-tsa* 'smell, sense odour'; Hayu *nam-*; Thulung *nem-*; Khaling *nwaam-nä*; Dumi *nəmnɨ*; Chamling *namma*; Bantawa *nam*; Kulung *namma*; Yamphu *namma*; Limbu *namma*.

(xxv) *Proto-Kiranti /*ʔn-/*

The Proto-Kiranti preglottalised alveolar nasal /*ʔn-/ is reflected in words which regularly have initial /n-/ in the modern Kiranti languages except Wambule, which has /ɗ-/ instead, e.g. 'chew, masticate', 'ear', 'be good, be healthy', 'head strap', 'name', 'nose', 'spittle, saliva' (possibly a compound with 'brain') and 'sun'.

NOSE:

Proto-Tibeto-Burman **s-na* × **s-naːr.*

- /*ʔn-/: Jero *nusum*$_{am}$; Wambule *ɗusum*; Bahing *néu*; Sunwar *neen*; Hayu *-no* in *tsoʔno*; Thulung *neo*, or *na-* in *nakhli* 'nasal mucus'; Khaling *nö*; Dumi *nu*; Chamling *nabro*; Bantawa *na+bu*; Kulung *nap*; Yamphu *naʔu*; Limbu *nɛboʔ.*

SUN:

Proto-Tibeto-Burman **nəy* 'sun, day' (Matisoff 2003), **nam* 'sun' (Benedict 1972).

- /*ʔn-/: Jero *nɔm*$_{am}$; Wambule *ɗwam*; Bahing *nam*; Sunwar *naa*; Thulung *nepsuŋ*; Khaling *nwaam*; Dumi *naːm*; Chamling *nam*; Bantawa *nam*; Kulung *nam*; Yamphu *nam*; Limbu *nam*.

In addition, the words 'be (identity)', 'dirtiness on the body', 'like, be fond of', 'new', 'pus', 'rub', 'tiger, leopard' and 'year' can for the moment be reconstructed with either /*n-/ or /*ʔn-/.

(xxvi) *Proto-Kiranti /*ŋ-/*

The Proto-Kiranti preglottalised alveolar nasal /*ŋ-/ is reflected in words which have initial /ŋ-/ or /n-/ in the modern Kiranti languages, e.g. 'ask for, beg', 'banana', 'before, front', 'cheek' (a compound with 'face'), 'cook, boil', 'count', 'cover', 'dream', 'finish, complete', 'fish', 'fry', 'hear', 'hurt, ache', 'sit down' and 'weep, cry'.

FISH:

Proto-Tibeto-Burman **s-ŋya*.

- /*ŋ-/: Jero *mõ*$_{a}$, *mũ*$_{a}$, *mu*$_{m}$ (initial unexplained; /ŋ-/ expected); Wambule *ŋwaso*; Bahing *gná*; Thulung *ŋō*; Khaling *ngö*; Dumi *ŋɨ*; Chamling *ngasa*; Bantawa *ŋa*, *ŋa+sa*; Kulung *ŋa*; Yamphu *na*; Limbu *na*, *ŋa*.

SIT DOWN:

- /*ŋ-/: Jero *niːcap*$_{a}$, *niː-*$_{m}$; Wambule *niːcam*; Bahing *niso* 'sit'; Sunwar *nit-tsa* 'sit', *'nit-tsa* 'sit cross legged'; Khaling *ngäy-nä*; Dumi *ŋaːnsinɨ* 'sit down'.

(xxvii) *Proto-Kiranti /*l-/*

The Proto-Kiranti plain lateral /*l-/ is reflected in words which regularly have initial /l-/ in the modern Kiranti languages, e.g. 'become', 'before, front', 'bow', 'go', 'language, word, speech', 'lick', 'tongue' and 'wait (for)'. Note that Yamphu also has /l-/ and /r-/ as regular reflexes of the Proto-Kiranti lateral /*l-/. Rutgers (1998) notes that the liquid phonemes /r/ and /l/ occur contrastively in word-initial position but that 'In the speech of older people, an occasional word may be pronounced with either of the liquids as initial.' (p. 34). This variation seems to be the result of a historical development described by van Driem (1990) following which word-initial /*r-/ disappeared as a result of the merger of Proto-Tibeto-Burman /*r-/ and /*y-/ in initial position in Eastern Kiranti, leaving Proto-Tibeto-Burman /*l/ and /*r/ in complementary distribution so that they were re-analysed as two allophones of a single liquid phoneme /l/. Van Driem further adds that the original allophonic distribution of the Eastern Kiranti liquid phoneme /l/ is best reflected in Limbu and least preserved in Rai languages such as Yakkha, Mewahang and Yamphu, where /l/ and /r/ appear to have resurfaced as independent phonemes much earlier than in Limbu.

LICK:

Proto-Tibeto-Burman **m/s-lyak* 'lick, tongue, eat (of animals), feed (animals)'.

- /*l-/: Jero *lɔkcap*$_{a}$; Wambule *lɔkcam*$_{w}$, *lwakcam*; Khaling *'laa-nä*; Dumi *lyəknɨ*; Bantawa *lek-(u)*; Kulung *lo:ma*; Yamphu *rœˈkma*; Limbu *lakma*. Thulung *lep-* can perhaps also be added.

TONGUE:

Proto-Tibeto-Burman **s-lyam* 'tongue, flame'.

- /*l-/: Jero *lɛm*$_{am}$; Wambule *lɛm*$_{w}$, *lyam*; Bahing *lyam*; Sunwar *leen*; Thulung *lem*; Khaling *lem*; Dumi *le:m*; Chamling *lem*; Bantawa *lem*; Kulung *lem*; Yamphu *lem*; Limbu *lɛso:t*, *lɛso:ppa*.

(xxviii) *Proto-Kiranti /*ʔl-/*

The Proto-Kiranti preglottalised lateral /*ʔl-/ is found in the words 'arm, hand', 'leg, foot', 'lie, act of lying', 'liver', 'red', 'road, path', 'silence, quietness', 'stone', 'sell, exchange', which regularly have initial /l-/ in the modern Kiranti languages except Jero and Wambule, which have /*ʔl-/ instead in one or more of their dialects. The words 'catch', 'come out, go out', 'dance (n)', 'door', 'hail', 'know (by learning)', 'leave, quit, abandon', 'millet', 'run (away)', 'search, look for', 'shadow, spirit', 'song', 'suffice', 'swallow' and 'tooth' can be reconstructed with /*l-/ or /*ʔl-/.

ROAD, PATH:

Proto-Tibeto-Burman **lam*.

- /*ʔl-/: Jero *lam*$_{am}$; Wambule *ʔlam*$_{w}$, *lam*; Bahing *lam*; Sunwar *'laan*; Hayu *lom*; Thulung *lam*; Khaling *läm*; Dumi *lam*; Chamling *lam*; Bantawa *lam*; Kulung *lam*; Yamphu *ram*; Limbu *lam*.

STONE:

Proto-Tibeto-Burman **r-luŋ* × **k-luk.*

- /*ʔl-/: Jero *-luŋ* in *phuluŋ*$_{am}$; Wambule *ʔluŋ*$_{w}$, *luŋ*; Bahing *lung*; Sunwar *-lu* in *phullu*; Hayu *lɷ'phɷ*; Thulung *luŋ*; Khaling *lung*; Dumi *lu*; Chamling *longto*; Bantawa *luŋ*; Kulung *luŋ*; Yamphu *ruŋguʔwa*; Limbu *luŋ*.

(xxix) *Proto-Kiranti /*r-/*

Proto-Kiranti /*r-/ corresponds to /r-/, /y-/ or /g-/ in the modern Kiranti languages as the result of complex historical developments. According to van Driem (1990), word-initial Tibeto-Burman /*r-/ regularly went to /y-/ in the historical evolution of the Eastern Kiranti languages Limbu, Yakkha, Mewahang and Yamphu. The merger of /*r-/ and /*y-/ can perhaps be explained by assuming that /*r-/ used to be pronounced as palatal [ɽ] with audible friction. The reintroduction of the phoneme /r/ in Eastern Kiranti must be attributed to Indo-Aryan influence taking place around the time of the Gorkha conquest of the Kiranti area (AD 1776-1786). By contrast, the Western and Central Kiranti languages regularly preserved Proto-Kiranti /*r-/ as /r-/.

Proto-Kiranti /*r-/ is reflected in words which regularly have /r-/ in Western Kiranti and Kulung and /y-/ in Eastern Kiranti, e.g. 'cool (v)', 'obey', 'potato, yam', 'twist' and 'wring, squeeze'. The words 'bone', 'dirtiness on the body', 'good, nice, fine', 'language, word, speech', 'rain, shower', 'say', 'wait (for)' and 'write' can perhaps also be added to this group because these words also have /r-/ in Western Kiranti. However, I have not found reflexes of these words in Eastern Kiranti. The word 'stand' can perhaps also be added, but in this case the Western Kiranti languages Jero, Wambule and Thulung show initial /y-/, which is possibly the result of some confusion with the reflexes of another, distinct Proto-Kiranti unit, viz. /*ry-/.

TWIST:

- /*r-/: Sunwar *rop-tsa*; Thulung *rim-* 'twist'; Khaling *'ramnä* 'twist, wring'; Dumi *ri:pni*; Bantawa *ript-(u)*; Kulung *rəmma*; Limbu *lipma* (initial unexplained; /*y-/ expected).

STAND:

Proto-Tibeto-Burman **g-r(y)ap.*

- /*r-/ > /y-/: Jero *yɔmcap*$_{\mathrm{a}}$, *yɔmcam*$_{\mathrm{a}}$; Wambule *yamcam*; Thulung *yem-*, *yep-*; Bantawa *ʔep(a)* (Winter 2003), *yéba* (H); Lohorung *yébe* (H); Yamphu *ye'pma*; Mewahang *yépok* (H); Yakkha *yé-bá-chi-ni*; Limbu *yɛpma*;

  /*r-/ > /r-/: Bahing *rápo* (H); Sunwar *'rap-tsa*; Khaling *'rem-nä* 'erect'; Dumi *repnɨ*; Chamling *repa-*; Dungmali *rebe* (H); Kulung *t*^{h}*o remma* (Tolsma 1999), *thórépa* (H); Nachiring *répa* (H); Sampang *ripá* (H).

(xxx) *Proto-Kiranti /*ry-/*

There appears to be some Kiranti evidence for distinguishing /*r-/ from /*ry-/ as distinct units at the Proto-Kiranti level. Initial /*ry-/, much like initial /*kw-/ discussed above, seems to have undergone reanalysis in various Kiranti groups because the semi-vowels /*y/ and /*w/ are basically capable of phonetic interaction with the syllable's initial consonant and its nuclear vowel. The evidence for /*ry-/ is provided by words that have /g-/ (< fricative velar /*γ/) in modern Kulung but either /r-/ or /y-/ in Western and Central Kiranti and /y-/ in Eastern Kiranti, e.g. (*r*-initial) 'body', 'damage, destroy', 'laugh' and 'shade', and (*y*-initial) 'rub', 'salt' and 'be sharp'.

SALT:

Proto-Tibeto-Burman **gryum*, **g-ryum.*

- /*ry-/ > /y-/: Bantawa *yum*; Dungmali *yúm* (H); Lohorung *yúm* (H); Yamphu *yum*; Mewahang *yúm* (H); Yakkha *yúm* (H); Limbu *yum.*

  /*ry-/ > /r-/: Khaling *ram*; Dumi *rɨm*; Chamling *rúm* (H); Nachiring *ram* (H); Sampang *rúm* (H).

  /*ry-/ > /g-/: Kulung *rum* (Tolsma 1999), *gúm* (H).

Note that a merger of /*ry-/ and /*y-/ in Eastern Kiranti may actually have conditioned the subsequent merger of plain /*r-/ and /*y-/. In Western Kiranti, by contrast, /*ry-/ merged with /*y-/ or /*r-/, whereas /*r-/ generally remained unaffected.

LAUGH:

Proto-Tibeto-Burman **r(y)ay* × **r(y)a-t(s)*.

- /*ry-/ > /y-/: Hayu *jɪt-*; Lohorung *yichae* (H); Yamphu *yi'tcama*; Mewahang *yúcha'* (H); Limbu *e:pma* (<**ye:pma*).
  /*ry-/ > /r-/: Jero *rɛnda recap*$_a$, *rɛnda recam*$_m$; Wambule *ryanda ryacam*; Bahing *riso*; Sunwar *'rit-tsa* 'laugh, smile'; Thulung *ris-*; Khaling *ren-nä*; Dumi *ri:nɨ*; Chamling *ri-* ~ *rya-*; Bantawa *réta* (H); Dungmali *ríge* (H); Nachiring *rhésa* (H); Yakkha *rísa* (H).
  /*ry-/ > /g-/: Kulung *gema* (Tolsma 1999), *gésa* (H); Sampang *ghísá* (H).

(xxxi) *Proto-Kiranti /*y-/*

The Proto-Kiranti palatal semi-vowel /*y-/ is reflected in words which regularly have initial /y-/ in Western, Central and Eastern Kiranti languages, e.g. 'also', 'back, behind, after', 'come down', 'grind', 'hear', 'like, be fond of', 'mouse', 'net', 'small, little' and 'suck'.

COME DOWN:

- /*y-/: Jero *yacap*$_a$, *yacam*$_m$; Wambule *ywacam*; Bahing *yú-wo*; Sunwar *'yi-tsa* 'descend'; Hayu *ju(t)-*; Thulung *yok-*; Khaling *ye-nä*; Dumi *yi:nɨ*; Chamling *i-* (<**yi-*); Bantawa *yi-(a)*; Kulung *yuma*; Yamphu *yu'ma*; Limbu *yu:ma*.

SMALL, LITTLE:

Proto-Tibeto-Burman **z(y)əy* 'little, small, tiny'.

- /*y-/: Jero *yɔkko*$_m$; Wambule *ywakka*; Bahing *yáke*; Thulung *yakke*; Hayu *jaŋ-* 'be small'; Khaling *yaahki*.

(xxxii) *Proto-Kiranti /*w-/*

The Proto-Kiranti labiovelar semi-vowel /*w-/ is reflected in words which regularly have initial /w-/ in modern Kiranti, e.g. 'bear (n)', 'cloth, wear', 'husband', 'lie, act of lying', 'rain, shower',

CLOTH, WEAR:

Proto-Tibeto-Burman **gwa-n* × **kwan* 'wear, put on, clothe', **s-g-w(y)a-n/t* 'wear, clothe', **w(y)a-t* × **wit* 'wear, clothe'.

- /*w-/: Jero *wa*$_{am}$; Wambule *wa*; Bahing *wá'*; Sunwar *waa*; Khaling *gö* (initial unexplained; /w-/ expected); Dumi *gu* (initial unexplained; /w-/ expected); Hayu *-wa* in *cuʔwa*; Chamling *wa-kha*; Bantawa *war-a* 'is worn'; Kulung *waima* 'wear (cloths, jewellery)'; Yamphu *wæ'ʔma* 'wear ornaments or a watch'; Limbu *wa:pma* 'adorn, decorate'.

RAIN, SHOWER:

Proto-Tibeto-Burman **rwa-s*, **r-wa* ×**s-wa* ×**g-wa*.

- /*w-/: Jero *hwarsi*$_{a}$ (initial unexplained; /w-/ expected), *war-si*$_{m}$; Wambule *warsi*; Thulung *wō*; Khaling *wö*; Dumi *hu* (initial unexplained; /w-/ expected); Bantawa *wa-ta-(a)* (v); Kulung *wa*; Yamphu *wari*; Limbu *wage:k*.

By contrast, Jero and Wambule /wa-/ in the following words is derived from the vowel /*o-/.

SCREAM, CROW:

Proto-Tibeto-Burman *ʔa:w* 'shout'.

- /*o-/: Jero *wakcapa*$_{a}$, *wa:capa*$_{a}$; Wambule *wakcam*; Hayu *ok-* ; Thulung *ok-*, *hok-*; Khaling *'o-nä*; Dumi *u:kni*; Bantawa *ʔokt-(a)*; Kulung *o:ma*; Yamphu *wo'ma*; Limbu *u:ma*.

YELLOW:

Proto-Tibeto-Burman **b-wa* 'white, yellow'.

- /*o-/: Jero *waʔɔmjimo*$_{m}$; Wambule *waʔwamjwam*, *waʔwam-jim*; Bahing *womwome*; Sunwar *haw* (initial unexplained); Thulung *om-om*; Khaling *ööm*; Bantawa *ʔom+pi*; Kulung *omlo:pa* 'white'; Limbu *ɔm*.

(xxxiii) *Proto-Kiranti /*s-/*

The Proto-Kiranti sibilant /*s-/ is reflected in words which regularly have initial /s-/ in the modern Kiranti languages. However, Bahing and Sunwar occasionally have the palatal sibilants /sy-/ or /ʃ-/, which seems to be the result of a language-internal historical development. The words reconstructed with /*s-/ which have /s-/ in Bahing and/or Sunwar are 'dance (n)', 'dry, dry up', 'hair', 'kill', 'louse', 'wash, rinse' and 'yesterday'. The words 'bee', 'flesh, meat', 'husked and polished grain, especially rice' and 'wood, firewood' have palatal /sy-/ or /ʃ-/ in Bahing and/or Sunwar.

KILL:

Proto-Tibeto-Burman **g/b-sat.*

- /*s-/: Jero *sɛccap*$_{a}$, *sɛccam*$_{m}$; Wambule *syaccam*; Bahing *sáto*; Sunwar *'sayk-tsa*; Hayu *sɪt-*; Thulung *set-*; Khaling *'sen-nä*; Dumi *setnɨ*; Chamling *seima*; Bantawa *set-(u)*; Kulung *seima*; Yamphu *seʔma*; Limbu *sɛpma.*

WOOD, FIREWOOD:

Proto-Tibeto-Burman **siŋ* × **sik* 'tree, wood'.

- /*s-/: Jero *siŋ*$_{a}$; Wambule *siŋ*; Bahing *sing* 'tree'; Sunwar *shii*; Hayu *siŋ*; Thulung *səŋ* 'wood, tree'; Khaling *sang*; Dumi *sɨ*; Chamling *suŋ*; Bantawa *süŋ*; Kulung *siŋ*; Yamphu *siŋ*; Limbu *siŋ*.

(xxxiv) *Proto-Kiranti /*h-/*

Proto-Kiranti /*h-/ is reflected in words which regularly have initial /h-/ in the modern Kiranti languages, e.g. 'be able', 'be alive, survive', 'arm, hand', 'bark (v)', 'bark, peel', 'blood', 'blow (by mouth)', 'cut off, mow', 'dry, dry up', 'finger, toe', 'one's own child's father-in-law', 'one's own child's mother-in-law', 'open', 'pus', 'question', 'red', 'self', 'set (sun), sink', 'wait (for)', 'wash, rinse', 'what' and 'wind (n)'.

BLOOD:

Proto-Tibeto-Burman **s-hywəy.*

- /h-/: Jero *usu*$_{m}$, *yusu*$_{a}$ (<**husu*); Wambule *usu* (<**husu*); Bahing *hési*; Sunwar *hush*; Khaling *hi*; Dumi *hiː*; Hayu *ji* (<**hi*); Bantawa *hü*; Kulung *hi*; Yamphu *hari*; Limbu *-khiʔ* in *makkhiʔ* (<**mak-hiʔ*).

OPEN:

Proto-Tibeto-Burman **m-ka* 'open, opening, mouth, door'.

- /*h-/: Jero *hɔl-*$_{m}$; Wambule *hwalcam*; Bahing *hókko*; Thulung *hoak-*, *hol-* 'open'; Khaling *'haa-nä* 'open', *hwaal-nä* 'break open'; Hayu *ho-*; Dumi *haːknɨ*; Bantawa *hok-(u)*; Kulung *həlma*; Yamphu *hemma*; Limbu *hɔmma*.

(xxxv) *Consonant clusters*

Most Western Kiranti languages have /Cr-/ and /Cl-/ clusters which consist of an initial bilabial or velar plosive plus /*l/ or /*r/. Dumi, however, lacks these clusters and, in this respect, resembles Central and Eastern Kiranti languages such as Kulung and Limbu. In Limbu, /*khr-/ merged with /*khl-/ sometimes yielding /h/ in the modern language. Proto-Kiranti /*Cl-/ regularly went to Sunwar /*Cr-/. Proto-Kiranti /*gr-/ sometimes yielded Wambule and Jero /r-/.

ARROW:

Proto-Tibeto-Burman **g/b/m-la-y*.

- /*bl-/: Jero *blu*$_{am}$; Wambule *blo*; Bahing *blá*; Sunwar *-bra* in *libra*; Hayu *blo*, *bo*, *liwo*; Thulung *blə* 'metal arrow head'; Bantawa *bhe* (/b-/ expected); Kulung *bei* (loss of /*l-/); Yamphu *-la* in *thula*; Limbu *-la* in *toːŋ-la* 'arrow-stick'.

FAECES, STOOL:

Proto-Tibeto-Burman * *kləy* 'excrement'.

- /*khl-/: Jero *-ki* in *saŋki*$_{a}$ and *-khi* in *saŋkhi*$_{m}$ (loss of /l-/); Wambule *khli*; Sunwar *'khrii* 'faeces'; Thulung *khli*; Khaling *khli*; Dumi *khil*; Chamling *-khle* in *nakhle* 'snot' (lit. 'nose-shit'); Bantawa *khü*; Kulung *k*^{h}*il*; Yamphu *hi*; Limbu *hi*.

The words 'be alive, survive', 'arrow', 'boil, simmer', 'dog', 'faeces, stool', 'forget', 'lie down, go to sleep', 'leave, quit, abandon', 'moon', 'say' and 'tear (n)' reflect Proto-Kiranti /*Cl-/. By contrast, the words 'bite; gnaw', 'break, burst', 'call (v)', 'count', 'finger, toe', 'grind', 'hate (n)', 'horn', 'jump', 'meet, visit', 'run (away)', 'spread', 'sweep', 'tasty' and 'weep, cry' reflect Proto-Kiranti /*Cr-/.

BITE; GNAW:

Proto-Tibeto-Burman **hap* 'bite, snap at, mouthful', **g-wa-t* 'bite, chew'.

- /*kr-/: Jero *kraccap*$_a$, *kra[k]-*$_m$; Wambule *kraccam*; Bahing *kráto*; Khaling *'kän-nä*; Dumi *ka:tni*.
  /*khr-/: Sunwar *'khrayk-tsa* 'bite'; Thulung *khret-* 'bite, rend, nibble', *ghrək-* 'gnaw'; Bantawa *khett-(u)*; Yamphu *hæ'ʔma* 'bite, nibble'; Limbu *haʔma* 'bite'.

JUMP:

Proto-Tibeto-Burman **p(r)ok*.

- /*pr-/: Jero *prɛkcam*$_m$; Wambule *pryakcam*, *precam*; Bahing *próko*; Sunwar *preek-tsa*; Thulung *prok-*; Khaling *'pro-nä*; Chamling *phũima* (initial unexplained); Bantawa *phint-(a)* (initial unexplained); Yamphu /-pruk-/ in *am-brukma* 'jump up and down'; Limbu *pimma*.

1.3.1.3 *Relative closeness between pairs of Kiranti languages*

The Kiranti languages can be classified into subgroups on the basis of the 14 lexical isoglosses and 31 phonological isoglosses discussed above.[4] Diagram 5 and Diagram 6 give the isogloss reference and a lower case letter (a, b, c, d, e) referring to a particular word listed in Section 1.3.1.1 (p. 6) or to an initial consonant in Diagram 4 (p. 13).

Diagram 5 and Diagram 6 allow us to quantify the relative closeness between pairs of Kiranti languages by determining how often the letters in the columns are identical for each pair of languages. The absolute numbers are converted into percentages of the 14 lexical and 31 phonological agreements possible. The degree of closeness in Diagram 7 is calculated by dividing the sum of the lexical and phonological averages by two.

---

[4] The 31 phonological isoglosses used here for the classification of Kiranti subgroups refer to the 32 sound correspondences given in Diagram 4 (p. 13) with the exception of the correspondences of /*kw-/, which are too diverse to be useful here.

LEXICAL ISOGLOSSES													
PK	JE	WA	BA	SU	HA	KH	DM	TH	CH	BN	KU	YA	LI
1	a	a	a	a	a	b	b	a	(?)	b	b	b	c
2	a/b	a	a	a	a	b	c	(?)	b	b	c	b	b
3	a	a	a	a	a	b	b	a	b	b	b	b	b
4	a/b	a	a	a	a	a	a	b	a	a	b	b	b
5	a	a	a	a	a	b	b	a/b	b	b	b	c	d
6	a	a	a	a	(?)	a	a	a	b	b	b	b	b
7	a	a	a	a	b	c	c	a	c	c	c	c	c
8	a	a	b	b	a	a/b	b	a	c	c	c	d	d
9	a	a	a	a/b	b	a	b	a/b	b	a/b	b	b	b
10	a	a	a	a	a	b	b	a	c	c	c	c	b
11	a	a	b	a	a	b	b	a	b	b	b	c	d
12	a	a	a	a	a	b	b	a	(?)	b	b	b	b
13	a	b	a	a	a	c	c	b	c	c	c	c	c
14	a	a	a	a	b	a	b	a	b	b	b	b	b

Diagram 5: Lexical comparison between 13 Kiranti languages

PHONOLOGICAL ISOGLOSSES													
PK	JE	WA	BA	SU	HA	KH	DM	TH	CH	BN	KU	YA	LI
*p	a	a	a	a	a	a	a	a	a	a	a	a	a
*ʔp	a	a	a	a	a	a	a	b	b	b	b	c	d
*ph	a	a	a	a	a	a	a	a	a	a	a	a	a
*b	a	a	a	a	a	a	a	a	a/b	a/b	a/b	b	b
*t	a	a	a	a	a	a	(?)	a	(?)	a	a	a	a
*ʔt	a	a	a	a	a	a	a	b	c	c	c	d	e
*th	a	a	a	a	a	a	a	a	a	a	a	a	a
*d	a	a	a	a	a	a	a	a/b	a/c	a/c	a/c	c	c
*c	a	a	a	a	a	a	a	a	a	a	a	a	a
*ʔc	a	a	a	a	a	a	a	a	b	b	b	c	c
*ch	a	a	a	(?)	b	b	c	b	b	b	b	a	a
*j	a	a	a	a/b	a	a	c	a	c	c	a/c	c	c

Diagram 6: Phonological comparison between 13 Kiranti languages

PK	JE	WA	BA	SU	HA	KH	DM	TH	CH	BN	KU	YA	LI
*k	a	a	a	a	a	a	a	a	a	a	a	a	a
*ʔk	a	a	a	a	a	a	a	a	b	b	b	b	b
*kh	a	a	a	a	a	a	a	a	a	a	a	a	a
*g	a	a	a	a	a	a	a	a	b	a/b	a/b	b	b
*m	a	a	a	a	a	a	a	a	a	a	a	a	a
*ʔm	a	b	a	a	a	a	a	a	a	a	a	a	a
*n	a	a	a	a	a	a	a	a	a	a	a	a	a
*ʔn	a	b	a	a	a	a	a	a	a	a	a	a	a
*ŋ	a/b	a/b	a/b	a	c	a/b	a	a/b	a	a	a	b	a/b
*l	a	a	a	a	a	a	a	a	a	a	a	a	a
*ʔl	a	a	b	b	b	b	b	b	b	b	b	b	b
*r	a	a	a	a	a	a	a	a	a	a/b	a	b	b
*ry	a/b	a/b	a/b	a/b	b	a	a	a/b	a	a/b	c	b	b
*y	a	a	a	a	a	a	a	a	a	a	a	a	a
*w	a	a	a	a	a	a	a	a	a	a	a	a	a
*s	a	a	a/b	a/b	a	a	a	a	a	a	a	a	a
*h	a	a	a	a	a	a	a	a	a	a	a	a	a
*Cl	a	a	a	b	a	a	c/d	a	c/d	c/d	c/d	c/d	c/d
*Cr	a	a	a	a	b	a	b	a	b	b	b	b	b

Diagram 6 continued

	WEST							CENTRAL			EAST	
	WA	BA	SU	HA	KH	DM	TH	CH	BN	KU	YA	LI
JE	93	91	91	79	68	47	86	39	46	39	37	37
	WA	84	84	72	61	44	83	32	39	32	27	27
		BA	93	73	69	56	77	41	47	40	32	32
			SU	79	64	56	79	41	44	40	32	34
				HA	52	51	72	44	49	45	37	37
					KH	81	64	56	74	60	50	50
						DM	45	67	76	74	55	57
							TH	44	47	51	37	37
								CH	91	82	65	63
									BN	91	77	72
										KU	74	68
											YA	82

Diagram 7: Relative closeness in percentages between 13 Kiranti languages

According to the results provided by the method used here, the Kiranti languages most closely related are Wambule and Jero (93%), on one hand, and Bahing and Sunwar (93%), on the other. The Western Kiranti languages Jero, Wambule, Bahing and Sunwar show the greatest mutual affinity with an average of about 90% for the four languages. Thulung and Hayu are more distantly related to these four languages with averages of about 81% and 76% respectively. Even more distantly related to these four languages, with an average degree of closeness of about 58%, are Khaling and Dumi, which are each other's closest relatives (81%). The Western Kiranti languages can be classified as followed on the basis of the relative distance from Central Kiranti.

WESTERN KIRANTI (→ CENTRAL KIRANT)

Chaurasiya: Jero, Wambule
Northwestern: Bahing, Sunwar
Farwestern: Hayu
Midwestern: Thulung
Upper Dūdhkosī: Khaling, Dumi

As for Central and Eastern Kiranti languages, Bantawa and Chamling are each other's closest relatives (91%) whereas Kulung is more distantly related. The language most closely related to Limbu is Yamphu (82%). The Kiranti languages least related (27%) are Western Kiranti Wambule and Eastern Kiranti Yamphu and Limbu.

1.3.2 *Morphological comparison between Western Kiranti languages*

Jero and Wambule are not only very closely related from a lexical and phonological viewpoint, the languages also share a considerable part of their nominal and verbal morpheme inventory. The following is a morphological comparison between the Western Kiranti languages Jero, Wambule, Bahing, Sunwar, Hayu, Thulung, Khaling and Dumi.

Case marking morphemes. The case markers in Jero and Wambule constitute a closed class of bound morphemes which are used to distinguish different grammatical roles from one another. In both languages, case markers can be analysed as phrasal affixes, which are morphemes that are structurally dependent upon the preceding unbound forms (or full words), such as nominal and adverbial lexemes, with which they show limited morphophonological interaction. The Jero case markers are discussed in Section 3.3 (p. 87).

	JERO	WAMBULE
by	*≡ku*$_{\mathrm{a}}$, *≡k*$_{\mathrm{am}}$, *≡khu*$_{\mathrm{m}}$, *≡k*$_{\mathrm{am}}$	*≡kho*, *≡k*
from	*=ŋo*$_{\mathrm{m}}$, *≡ŋ*$_{\mathrm{m}}$	*≡ŋo*, *≡ŋ*
	=na=ku$_{\mathrm{a}}$, *=na=k*$_{\mathrm{a}}$	*=lo=ŋo*, *=lo=ŋ*
in	*=na*$_{\mathrm{a}}$, *=n*$_{\mathrm{am}}$, *=ma*$_{\mathrm{a}}$, *=no*$_{\mathrm{m}}$, *=n*$_{\mathrm{am}}$	*≡lo*, *≡l*, *≡no*, *≡n*
of	*=ŋaŋ*$_{\mathrm{m}}$, *=ŋ*$_{\mathrm{am}}$	*=ŋaŋ*, *=ŋ*
toward	*-la*$_{\mathrm{am}}$, *-l*$_{\mathrm{am}}$	*≡la*, *≡l*
with	*=na*$_{\mathrm{a}}$, *=n*$_{\mathrm{am}}$, *=no*$_{\mathrm{m}}$, *=n*$_{\mathrm{am}}$	*=no*, *=n*

	BAHING	SUNWAR
by	*-mi*	*-mi*
from	*-ng* in *ding* 'from'	*lee ngon* 'away from'
in	*-di*	*-mi*
of	*-ke*	*-ke*, *-nga*
toward	*lá*	*-ge*
with	*nung*	*-nu*

	HAYU	THULUNG
by	*-ha*	*-ka*
from	*-khen*	*-lam*
in	*-he*	*Da*
of	*-mɷ*	*-ku*
toward	—	*theo*
with	*-noŋ*	*-nuŋ*

	KHALING	DUMI
by	*-ä*	*-ʔa*
from	*-kaa*, *-laakaa*	*-ləkə*
in	*-bi*, *-yu*, *-goyu*	*-bi*
of	*-po*	*-po*
toward	*-thaa*	*lambɨ*
with	*-kolo*	*-kəy*

Personal pronouns. The personal pronouns in Wambule and Jero are only distinguished for person, but not for number and inclusivity/exclusivity. That is to say, personal pronouns without overt number markers have singular, dual or plural reference. Nominal number marking in Jero and Wambule can be analysed as the expression of an intended meaning. The pronouns are presented in Section 3.6 (p. 105).

	JERO	WAMBULE
I, we	*uŋgu*$_{am}$, *uŋ*$_{am}$	*uŋgu, uŋ*
you	*inne*$_{am}$, *in*$_{am}$	*unu, un*
he, they	*aŋgu*$_{am}$, *aŋ*$_{am}$	*aŋgu, aŋ*

	BAHING	SUNWAR
I	*gó*	*go-*
you^{s}	*ga*	*ge-/go-y*
he	*harem*	*eko* 'this', *meko* 'that'
we^{d}	*gósuku*^{de}	*go 'niikshi*
	gósi^{di}	
you^{d}	*gási*	*ge 'niikshi*
they^{d}	*harem dausi*	*meko 'niikshi*
we^{p}	*góku*^{pe}	*go puki*
	gói^{pi}	
you^{p}	*gáni*	*ge puki*
they^{p}	*harem dau*	*meko puki*

	HAYU	THULUNG
I	*gu, gu'u*	*go*
you^{s}	*gon*	*gana*
he	*komi*	*gu*
we^{de}	*gu, gu'u*	*guku* (= we^{pe}?)
we^{di}	*gu, gu'u*	*guci*
you^{d}	*gontshe*	*gaci*
they^{d}	*komi*	*guci*
we^{pe}	*gu, gu'u*	*gucuku* (= we^{de}?)
we^{pi}	*gu, gu'u*	*guy*
you^{p}	*gone*	*gani*
they^{p}	*komi*	*gumi*

	KHALING	DUMI
I	*ung*	*aŋ*
you^{s}	*in*	*an*
he	*am*	*ɨm*
we^{de}	*ocu*	*antsɨ*
we^{di}	*ici*	*intsi*
you^{d}	*eci*	*antsi*
they^{d}	*amsu*	*ɨmnɨ*
we^{pe}	*ok*	*aŋkɨ*
we^{pi}	*ik*	*iŋki*
you^{p}	*en*	*ani*
they^{p}	*amhäm*	*hammɨl*

Possessive pronouns. Possession in Jero and Wambule can be marked by means of a series of syntactically restricted morphemes which show no morphophonological interaction with the word they precede. The Kiranti languages generally make a formal distinction between three numbers, three persons, and forms including and excluding the person addressed. Note also that there is only one form expressing 'our^{di}' and 'your^{d}'. The Jero and Wambule words are formally very similar. The topic of possessive pronouns is discussed in Section 3.7 (p. 107).

	JERO	WAMBULE
my	*am*$_{am}$	*a*
your^{s}	*im*$_{am}$	*i*
his, her	*aŋ*$_{m}$, *aŋam*$_{a}$	*aŋ*
our^{de}	*ancum*$_{am}$	*ancuk*
our^{di}	*incim*$_{am}$	*inci*
your^{d}	*incim*$_{am}$	*inci*
their^{d}	*ancim*$_{am}$	*anci*
our^{pe}	*akkum*$_{am}$	*ak*
our^{pi}	*ikkim*$_{am}$	*ik*
your^{p}	*inim*$_{am}$	*in*
their^{p}	*anim*$_{am}$	*an*

BAHING

my	*á*
your^{s}	*í*
his, her	*á*
our^{de}	*wási*
our^{di}	*ísi*
your^{d}	*ísi*
their^{d}	*ási*
our^{pe}	*wakke*
our^{pi}	*íkke*
your^{p}	*íni*
their^{p}	*ani*

	HAYU	THULUNG
my	*aŋ*	*a*
your^{s}	*uŋ*	*i*
his, her	*a*	*u*
our^{de}	*aŋtshe*	*aci*
our^{di}	*uŋtshe*	*aci*
your^{d}	*uŋtshe*	*ici*
their^{d}	*atshe*	*uci*
our^{pe}	*ã·ki*	*aki*
our^{pi}	*ũ·ki*	*iki*
your^{p}	*uni*	*ini*
their^{p}	*ami*	*uni*

	KHALING	DUMI
my	*aapo, ungpo*	*oː-*
your^{s}	*inpo*	*a-*
his, her	*ampo*	*ɨ-*
our^{de}	*os-, ocupo*	*antsɨ-*
our^{di}	*icipo*	*intsi-*
your^{d}	*es-*	*intsi-*
their^{d}	*us-, uspo*	*ɨmnɨ-*
our^{pe}	*ok-, okpo*	*aŋkɨ-*
our^{pi}	*ik-, ikpo*	*iŋki-*
your^{p}	*enpo*	*ani-*
their^{p}	*amhämpo*	*ham-*

Simplex verbs. Jero and Wambule simplex verbs consist of a verb root plus one or more person and number agreement suffixes. Tense is not a grammatical category in the two languages. By contrast, Khaling has a preterite tense suffix <-t>, which precedes the person and number agreement markers. Similarly, Bahing, Hayu, Thulung and Dumi have suffixes indicating tense and showing agreement for person and number. Dumi also has several agreement prefixes. The following are affirmative paradigms of <bak-> 'be, sit' in Jero and Wambule, the non-preterite paradigms of <bok-> and <bɷk-> 'rise' in Bahing and Hayu (Michailovsky 1975, 1981), the non-preterite paradigm of <jar-> 'fall' in Thulung (Allen 1975) and the non-preterite paradigm of <duk-> 'stub, knock' in Dumi (van Driem 1993).

VI	JERO	WAMBULE	BAHING
1s	*ba-ŋ-ma*	*ba-ŋ-me*	*boŋ-ŋa*
1di	*ba-ŋ-ci-m*	*ba-ŋ-ci-m*	*bok-sa*
1de	*ba-ŋ-cu-m*	*ba-ŋ-cuk-m*	*bok-su*
1pi	*baː-ki-m*	*baː-ki-m*	*boŋ-ja*
1pe	*baː-ku-m*	*baː-ku-m*	*bok-ka*
2s	*ba-n-Ø-ne*	*baː-nu-me*	*boŋ-e*
2d	*ba-ŋ-ci-m*	*ba-ŋ-ci-m*	*bok-si*
2p	*baː-ni-m-me*	*baː-ni-m*	*boŋ-ni*
3s	*baː-Ø-m*	*baː-Ø-m*	*boŋ-Ø*
3d	*ba-ŋ-ci-m*	*ba-ŋ-ci-m*	*bok-se*
3p	*ba-m-me*	*ba-m-me*	*boŋ-me*

VI	HAYU	THULUNG	DUMI
1s	*bɷk+ŋo*	*jar-ŋu*	*duk-t-ə*
1di	*bɷk+tshik*	*jar-ci*	*duk-t-i-Ø*
1de	*bɷk+tshok*	*jar-cuku*	*duk-t-ɨ-Ø*
1pi	*bɷk+ke*	*jar-i*	*duk-k-i-t-i*
1pe	*bɷk+kok*	*jar-ku*	*duk-k-ɨ-t-a*
2s	*bɷk+Ø*	*jar-na*	*a-duk-t-a-Ø*
2d	*bɷk+tshik*	*jar-ci*	*a-duk-t-Ø-i*
2p	*bɷk+ne*	*jar-ni*	*a-duk-t-Ø-ini*
3s	*bɷk+Ø*	*jar-Ø*	*duk-t-a-Ø*
3d	*bɷk+tshik*	*jar-ci*	*duk-t-Ø-i*
3p	*bɷk+me*	*jar-mi*	*ham-duk-t-a*

Jero and Wambule do not mark temporal distinctions in the verb, but instead a fundamental distinction is made between affirmative verbs that end in the suffix <-me> and factual verbal adjectives that end in the suffix <-mei>. The negative prefix <a-> is mutually exclusive with the affirmative ending in the suffix <-me>. In addition, the same types of nouns and adjectives are derived from verbs by suffixation of, for instance, the infinitive marker <-si> or the supine marker <-phu> to verb roots to which no person and number agreement suffixes are added. Jero and Wambule use identical periphrastic constructions with auxiliary verbs which add a dimension of some kind (inception, ingression, termination, continuation) to the meaning expressed by the main verbal or deverbative constituent. Jero verbal morphology is dealt with from Chapter 4 (p. 125) onwards.

1.3.3 *The distance between Jero and Wambule*

The data presented above show that the lexical, phonological and morphological distance between Jero and Wambule is smaller than the distance between each of the two languages and the other Kiranti languages. Nevertheless, the Jero language remains different enough from Wambule to merit a grammatical description of its own. So far the degree to which Jero has been influenced by Wambule and *vice versa* has not been established. It may well have been the case that intermarriage between the Jero and Wambule has caused a strong linguistic assimilation between two already inherently closely related tongues.

CHAPTER TWO

PHONOLOGY AND MORPHOPHONOLOGY

This chapter deals with the Āmboṭe Jero sound system. The phonological analysis is based on a classical phonemic approach, in which the qualification of the minimal units of the sound system is given in terms of their distribution and identity. Sounds are considered phonemic if substitution of one sound for another causes a change in meaning. If substitution does not cause a change in meaning or if two sounds do not occur in the same environments, they can be considered allophonic realisations of the same phoneme. Neutralisation is the loss of contrast between two or more phonemes in a particular environment. I will also provide an overview of the major phonological factors that affect the formal realisation of morphemes.

2.1 *Vowels*

The Jero vowel inventory is given in Diagram 8. The language makes a qualitative contrast which involves four degrees of vowel height dimension and three degrees in the front-back dimension. Jero distinguishes the close front vowels /i/ and /iː/, a half-close front vowel /e/, a half-open front vowel /ɛ/, the open central vowels /a/ and /aː/, a half-open unrounded back vowel /ʌ/, a half-open rounded back vowel /ɔ/, a half-close back vowel /o/, and the close back vowels /u/ and /uː/. Vowel nasalisation is marginally distinctive in Jero.

	FRONT	CENTRAL	BACK
CLOSE	/iː/ /i/		/u/ /uː/
HALF-CLOSE	/e/		/o/
HALF-OPEN	/ɛ/		/ɔ/ /ʌ/
OPEN		/a/ /a/	

Diagram 8: Āmboṭe Jero vowel phonemes (excluding nasalised vowels)

The phonemic contrast between /i/ and /iː/, /a/ and /aː/ and /u/ and /uː/ is a quantitative distinction in vowel duration. By contrast, the distinction between /ɛ/ and /e/ and between /ɔ/ and /o/ can be characterised in terms of vowel duration and vowel quality in some phonological environments, whereas the distinction is merely qualitative in other phonological environments. The difference between the native phoneme /ɔ/ and the loan phoneme /ʌ/ is one of lip rounding.

2.1.1 *Distinctive length contrasts between vowels*

The initial acoustic analysis of spoken Jero suggests that stress and tone are not phonemically relevant. The syllable that is based on the root of verbs and deverbatives and on the initial syllable of nouns and other parts of speech is generally more prominent than the other syllables due to an increase of loudness. Loudness is not always concurrent with highest pitch. The stressed open syllable of polysyllabic words is characterised by a distinctive contrast between the phonemes /i/ and /iː/, /ɛ/ and /e/, /a/ and /aː/, /ɔ/ and /o/, /u/ and /uː/, and /ʌ/.

The phoneme /i/ is a short unrounded close front vocoid [i]. The phoneme /iː/ is a long unrounded close front vocoid [iː].

/sicap/	[sit͡sap̚]	'to die, be dead'
/siːcap/	[siːt͡sap̚]	'to thread'

The phoneme /ɛ/ is a short unrounded half-open front vocoid [ɛ], which is frequently realised with a non-contrastive glide [j] or as a more close vocoid [e] before /i/. In Mohanṭāre, the phoneme /ɛ/ is often realised as a lowered vocoid [ɛ̞] or [æ], which is quite similar to Dutch /ɛ/ in *met* 'with'. The phoneme /e/ is generally realised as a long unrounded half-close front vocoid [eː] in the initial open syllable of polysyllabic words and as a shorter allophone [eˑ ~ e] in other syllable types, such as closed or medial syllables.

/sɛri/	[sʲɛri]	'body louse'
/seri/	[seːri]	'husked grain'

The phoneme /a/ is a short half-rounded open central vocoid [a]. The phoneme /a:/ is a long half-rounded open central vocoid [a:].[5]

/cacuŋma/ [ʦaʦuŋma] 'granddaughter'
/ca:cap/ [ʦa:ʦap̚] 'to ascend, go up'

The phoneme /ɔ/ is a short rounded half-open back vocoid [ɔ], which is often realised with a non-contrastive glide [w]. The phoneme /o/ is usually realised as a long rounded half-close back vocoid [o:] in the initial open syllable of polysyllabic words and as a shorter allophone [o˙ ~ o] in other syllable types.

/lɔsu/ [lɔsu] 'leg, including foot'
/rosu/ [ro:su] 'horn'

The vowel /u/ is a short rounded close back vocoid [u]. The vowel /u:/ is a long rounded close back vocoid [u:].

/nucap/ [nuʦap̚] 'to be well, be healthy'
/tu:cap/ [tu:ʦap̚] 'to drink'

The vowel /ʌ/ is usually realised as a short half-open unrounded vocoid [ʌ] or a more central vocoid [ə]. This vowel generally occurs in loans from Nepali. In native forms, by contrast, [ʌ] can be analysed as an irregular allophone of [ɔ].[6]

/mʌsi/ [mʌsi] 'marrow' (<Nep. *masī*)
vs. /mɔkɔm/ [mɔkɔm] 'chicken'

/dʌro/ [dʌro] 'firm, fast' (<Nep. *daro*)
/sʌbʌi/ [sʌbʌi] 'all' (<Nep. *sabai*)

---

[5] Note that the difference between /a/ and /a:/ sometimes appears to be fairly unstable. The realisation of /a/ as a lengthened vocoid [a˙] was rather common in the speech of young Rām Kumār Rāī. The frequent lenghtening of Jero /a/ in his speech is perhaps related to the normal phonetic realisation of Nepali /a/ in the many loan words. Nepali /a/ is a relatively long vowel that is rarely realised as the phonetic norm of the short vowel /a/ in Jero.

[6] The unrounded realisation [ʌ] in native Jero words was occasionally produced in response to a lack of understanding of what my informants actually said.

In addition to the vowel phonemes presented above, Jero has the diphthongs /iu/, /ei/[7], /ɛu/, /ai/, /au/, /ʌi/, /ʌu/, /ɔi/, /ɔu/ and /ui/. Both vocalic elements have equal duration, but the first vocalic element is generally realised with a higher pitch than the second element.

/kiuma/	[kiuma]	'I look at him'
/seicap/	[seiʦap̚]	'to know (a person)'
/dɛuma/	[dɛuma]	'I will dig'
/ai/	[ai]	'this'
/khauma/	[k^{h}auma]	'k.o. ceremony'
/pʌini/	[pʌini]	'k.o. vessel' (<Nep. *painī*)
/nʌuthal/	[nʌut^{h}al]	'later, after'
/thɔime/	[t^{h}ɔime]	'he hears it'
/thɔume/	[t^{h}ɔume]	'I hear it'
/buisi/	[buisi]	'raw cotton'

The sequences /iu/, /ei/, /ɛu/, /ai/, /au/, /ɔi/, /ɔu/, and /ui/ are often found in finite verb forms, in which there is a morpheme boundary between the initial vocoids [i], [e ~ ɛ], [a], [ɔ] and [u] and the final vocoids [i] and [u]. The initial vocoids generally correspond to the morphophonemes <i>, <ɛ>, <a>, <ɔ> and <u> of the verb root. By contrast, the final vocoids can be identified as the morphophonemes <i> and <u> of the following person and number agreement suffixes. The presence of a morpheme boundary suggests that /iu/, /ei/, /ɛu/, /ai/, /au/, /ʌi/, /ʌu/, /ɔi/, /ɔu/ and /ui/ are best analysed as sequences of two juxtaposed vowels rather than complex nuclei functioning as single units within the sound system. However, this claim cannot be made unequivocally.

The qualitative and quantitative contrasts found in the initial stressed open syllable of polysyllabic words are also present in the open syllable of polysyllabic verbs that follows the syllable of the negative prefix <a->. Word stress regularly falls on the root following the negative prefix, but the negative prefix can also be stressed.

/nɔkim/	[ˈn^{w}ɔkim]	'we^{pi} are'
/nɔki/	[aˈn^{w}ɔki]	'we^{pi} are not'

[7] The vocoid [e] in /ei/ appears to be an allophone of /ɛ/ before /i/.

/blaːkim/	[ˈblaːkim]	‘we^{pi} will come’
/ablaːki/	[aˈblaːki]	‘we^{pi} will not come’

The distinctiveness of vocalic quality and quantity is also maintained in monosyllabic words that are morphophonologically derived from bisyllabic words with an initial open syllable. This is illustrated in the following verb and non-verb forms. See also Section 2.3.3 below (p. 73).

/lame/	[lame]	‘it will become’
→ /lam/	→ [lam]	
/baːme/	[baːme]	‘he will sit, he will be’
→ /baːm/	→ [baːm]	
/niːme/	[niːme]	‘he is afraid’
→ /niːm/	→ [niːm]	
/sime/	[sime]	‘he is dead’
→ /sim/	→ [sim]	
/lɔsu/	[lɔs]	‘leg, including foot’
→ /lɔs/	→ [lɔs]	
/rosu/	[roːsu]	‘horn’
→ /ros/	→ [roːs]	

There is also a phonological contrast between the native short and long vowels (i.e. all the vowels but /ʌ/) before the glottal stop /ʔ/ in syllable-initial and syllable-final positions. This is illustrated in the following series of words:

/kaʔu/	[kaʔu]	‘friend’
/kraːʔme/	[kraːʔ̚me]	‘they^{p} bite’
/nɛʔe/	[nɛʔe]	‘it is said’
/teʔu/	[teːʔu]	‘son, boy’
/kɔʔlo/	[k^{w}ɔʔ̚lo]	‘one’
/toʔla/	[toːʔ̚la]	‘above, up’

Note also that short vowels in the environments defined above can be lengthened when receiving prosodic stress. As a result, phonetic vowel length is not always relevant for the meaning of a word. In other words, long vowel duration in the stressed open syllable of polysyllabic words and related environments is not always concurrent with phonemic length. Nonetheless, vowel length is marked here in indigenous Jero words where a long vowel duration but no alternative short vowel duration has been recorded, where a long vowel duration is recurrent, and where present-day morphological patterns suggest that the attested phonetic vowel duration is in fact phonemic.[8]

2.1.2 *Neutralisations*

Distinctive vowel length seems to form a marginal part of the Jero sound system, especially in non-verbs. Since differences in vowel length are not considered to be distinctive other than in the environments specified above, I propose that the opposition between the short and long vowel phonemes is neutralised in the remaining phonological environments. From a phonetic point, the long vowels usually lack pertinent duration and become physically indistinguishable from the short vowels that have the same quality in terms of vowel height and front-back dimension. The phonological transcription uses the short vowel symbols /i, a, u/ for these length-neutralised sounds. By contrast, the distinction between the half-close and half-open vowels /ɛ/ and /e/ and /ɔ/ and /o/ is maintained in medial open syllables and in initial, medial and final closed syllables of polysyllabic words. As the vowels /e/ and /o/ in closed syllables are often realised with shorter durations than are normal in open initial syllables, I consider the distinction between /ɛ/ and /e/ and between /ɔ/ and /o/ to be essentially qualitative. Hence I prefer to transcribe /ɛ/ vs. /e/ and /ɔ/ vs. /o/ rather than /e/ vs. /eː/ and /o/ vs. /oː/.

---

[8] In my 2004 grammar of Wambule, by contrast, vowel length is only marked as phonologically distinctive in indigenous Wambule words in which my informants in general rejected short vowels. However, comparative evidence from Jero actually suggests that the Wambule words *kaku* 'water', *nathoce* 'next year' and *Raḏu* 'Rai', which were recorded with the short vowel [a] in the speech of some Wambule speakers, can perhaps also be analysed as having free variants with [aː] as this long vowel was also frequently found in the speech of others, viz. *kaːku*, *naːthoce* and *Raːḏu*. At any rate, vowel duration has a low functional load in Wambule and Jero.

MEDIAL OPEN SYLLABLES

/hedicap/	[heːditsap˺]	'to climb, mount'
/pacewa/	[patseːwʌ]	'silly stunt'
/riptɛwa/	[rip˺tɛwʌ]	'shade'
/jajale/	[dzadzale]	'the palm of the hand'
/tɛŋthoce/	[tɛŋtʰoːtsɛ]	'this year'
/gutulum/	[gutulum]	'tone ball'

CLOSED MONOSYLLABLES

/nim/	[nim]	'act of lying'
/cɛm/	[tsʲɛm]	'call, summon'
/cel/	[tseːl]	'question' (< /cela/?)
/haŋ/	[haŋ]	'why'
/nɔm/	[nɔm]	'sun'
/hur/	[hur]	'mouth'

INITIAL CLOSED SYLLABLES

/bipcap/	[bip˺tsap˺]	'to suck'
/nenne/	[nenne]	'youˢ say'
/dɛnne/	[dɛnne]	'youˢ dig'
/camda/	[tsamda]	'game'
/dɔkcap/	[dɔk˺tsap˺]	'to be sufficient'
/bosrɛmpu/	[bosrɛmpu]	'big spider'
/culle/	[tsulle]	'stinging nettle'

MEDIAL CLOSED SYLLABLES

/ninibbɔn/	[ninib˺bɔn]	'three days ago'
/masrɛmpu/	[masrɛmpu]	'pinion, feather'
/mayaŋga/	[majæŋga]	'egg'
/dubɔlki/	[dubɔlki]	'big earthenware vessel'
/nunusso/	[nunussʷo]	'three days from now'

FINAL CLOSED SYLLABLES

/anim/	[anim]	'theirᵖ'
/rapcimtep/	[rap˺tsimtep˺]	'ant'
/cimtɛp/	[tsimtɛp˺]	'a little'

/noʔmar/	[noːʔ̚mar]	'head strap'
/bɛthɔŋ/	[bɛtʰɔŋ]	'Gurkhali knife'
/kaŋkoʈ/	[kaŋkoʈ̚]	'locust'
/akkum/	[ak̚kum]	'our^{pe}'

The distinction between the half-close and half-open vowels /ɛ/ and /e/ and /ɔ/ and /o/ is not always clearly maintained, however. The distinction seems to be lost in open monosyllabic words and in the unstressed final open syllable of polysyllabic words. The final neutral vowels /e/ and /o/ vary between half-close /e/ and /o/ and half-open /ɛ/ and /ɔ/. Short and long realisations of the vowel phonemes are also considered to be allophonic. Long and very long realisations are common in open monosyllables, whereas shorter realisations are frequent in the final open syllable of polysyllabic words.

OPEN MONOSYLLABLES

/mi/	[miː]	'fire'
/ni/	[niː]	'name'
/ma/	[maː]	'liver'
/pa/	[paː]	'pig'
/su/	[suː]	'meat'
/blu/	[bluː]	'arrow'
/gle/	[gleː]	'lie down'
/ke/	[keː ~ kʲɛː]	'look at me'
/do/	[doː ~ dɔː]	'distribute'
/ho/	[hɔ]	'yes, it is' (<Nep. *ho*)

FINAL OPEN SYLLABLES

/misi/	[misi]	'eye'
/thoni/	[tʰoːni]	'one year ago'
/inne/	[inne]	'you'
/magge/	[mag̚ge]	'egg'
/yɔmala/	[yɔmala]	'below'
/biya/	[bijæ]	'bullock'
/jɔpro/	[ʥɔpro]	'lungs'
/mɔkko/	[mɔk̚ko]	'just now'
/jɔmcu/	[ʥɔmʨu]	'shaman'
/thalu/	[tʰalu]	'where'

Final /e/ and /o/ vary between [ɛ ~ e] and [ɔ ~ o] in the morphological process of attachment of abbreviated phrasal suffixes, such as the comitative and genitive case markers. See also Section 2.3.2 below (p. 71).

/inne=n/	[innen]	'with you'
/jɛnje=ŋ/	[ʥɛnʥɛŋ]	'pertaining to buttocks'
/jero=ŋ/	[ʥeːrɔŋ]	'pertaining to the Jero'

2.1.3 *Nasalised vowels*

Nasalised vowels have been attested in a relatively small group of words. The absence of free variation between vowel nasalisation and vowels that are followed the velar consonant /ŋ/ argues for the view that vowel nasalisation is best analysed as a separate phonological feature instead of a subphonemic realisation of the velar nasal consonant.

/sĩ/	[sĩː]	'blowing one's nose'
/cɛ̃kmu/	[cʲɛ̃k̚mu]	'chick'
/mũ/ ~ /mõ/	[mũː] ~ [mõː]	'fish'
/phuŋmũ/	[pʰuŋmũ]	'eel' (with /mũ/ 'fish')

2.2 *Consonants*

The system of Jero consonants is presented in Diagram 9. The system incorporates five series of obstruents (plosives and affricates) with the laryngeal settings voiceless, voiceless aspirated, plain voiced and breathy voiced, plus a glottal stop. The other consonants are voiced. There is a series of nasals at three points of articulation, one fricative, one trill, two laterals and three approximants.

The breathy voiced consonants /bh, dh, ḍh, jh, gh/, the voiceless aspirated affricate /ch/ and the retroflex consonants /ṭ, ṭh, ḍ, ḍh/ are mostly found in loans from Nepali. Even though the phoneme /ḍ/ also regularly occurs in native Jero words, the use of retroflex or postalveolar stops in place of apico-alveolar stops in indigenous forms seems to be generally determined by personal style or preference.

VOICELESS	/p/	/t/	/ṭ/	/c/	/k/
ASPIRATED	/ph/	/th/	/ṭh/	/ch/	/kh/
VOICED	/b/	/d/	/ḍ/	/j/	/g/
BREATHY	/bh/	/dh/	/ḍh/	/jh/	/gh/
GLOTTAL					/ʔ/
NASAL	/m/	/n/			/ŋ/
FRICATIVE		/s/			
TRILL		/r/			
LATERAL		/l/			ल्अ /ʔl/
APPROXIMANT	/w/	/y/			/h/

Diagram 9: Āmboṭe Jero consonant phonemes

All the consonants, with the exception of the glottal stop /ʔ/, occur in word-initial position. The glottal stop has phonemic status as a syllable-initial consonant in intervocalic and postvocalic positions and as a syllable-final consonant. Pre-consonantal syllable-final obstruents are subject to neutralisation of the contrast between the different phonation types. Affricate obstruents are not generally found in syllable-final position, except in loans from Nepali. The approximants /h/, /y/ and /w/ do not appear in syllable-final position. The phoneme /h/ does not generally occur in intervocalic position, except in negated verbs with the root-initial consonant /h/ and in loans from Nepali. The phonemes /y/ and /w/ appear as initials in word-initial and intervocalic positions.

2.2.1 *Obstruents*

The phonemic contrasts between the series of voiceless unaspirated, voiceless aspirated and plain voiced obstruents are illustrated for indigenous words with velar, alveolar, bilabial and glottal places of articulation. Voiceless, voiceless aspirated and voiced obstruents are contrastive in initial positions.

The phoneme /k/ is a voiceless unaspirated dorso-velar stop [k]. The phoneme /kh/ is a voiceless aspirated dorso-velar stop [k^h]. The phoneme /g/ is a voiced dorso-velar stop [g].

/kɔkcap/	[kʷɔk̚ʦap̚]	'to dig'; 'to bite, sting'
/khɔkcap/	[kʰʷɔk̚ʦap̚]	'to cook, boil'
/gɔkcap/	[gʷɔk̚ʦap̚]	'to give; to let'

The affricate series basically consists of two native phonemes. The phoneme /c/ is a voiceless unaspirated lamino-alveolarised affricate [ʦ]. The phoneme /j/ is a voiced lamino-alveolarised affricate [ʣ]. The phoneme /ch/ is a voiceless aspirated lamino-alveolarised affricate [ʦʰ], which is generally found in loans.

/curcap/	[ʦurʦap̚]	'to press, twist'
/jurcap/	[ʣurʦap̚]	'to be sour'
/chana/	[ʦʰaˑna]	'roof' (<Nep. *chānu*)

The phoneme /t/ is a voiceless unaspirated apico-alveolar stop [t]. The phoneme /th/ is a voiceless aspirated apico-alveolar stop [tʰ]. The phoneme /d/ is a voiced apico-alveolar stop [d].

/tumcap/	[tumʦap̚]	'to finish, complete'
/dumcap/	[dumʦap̚]	'to become'
/thukcap/	[tʰuk̚ʦap̚]	'to spit at someone'
/dukcap/	[duk̚ʦap̚]	'to shake, move, agitate'

In indigenous Jero words, the use of retroflex or apico-postalveolar stops in place of alveolar stops is generally determined by personal style or preference. However, the intervocalic retroflex flap [ɽ], which is analysed as an allophone of the phoneme /ɖ/, is a common sound in native Jero words. The phoneme /ʈ/ is a voiceless unaspirated apico-postalveolar stop [ʈ]. The phoneme /ʈh/ is a voiceless aspirated apico-postalveolar stop [ʈʰ]. The phoneme /ɖ/ is a voiced apico-postalveolar stop [ɖ] in word-initial position or a flap [ɽ] in intervocalic and postvocalic positions.

/kaŋkoʈ/	[kaŋkoʈ̚]	'locust'
/buɖum/	[buɽum]	'monkey'
/phuɖim/	[pʰuɽim]	'wind, storm, tempest'

The distinction between dental and retroflex stops is phonemic in Nepali, and this distinction is maintained in Jero.

/ʈaɖo/	[ʈa·ɽo]	'far' (<Nep. *ṭāḍho*)
/ʈhaũ/	[ʈ^{h}aũ]	'place' (<Nep. *ṭhāũ*)
/ɖori/	[ɖo·ri]	'rope' (<Nep. *ḍori*)

The phoneme /p/ is a voiceless unaspirated bilabial stop [p]. The phoneme /ph/ is a voiceless aspirated bilabial stop [p^{h}]. The phoneme /b/ is a voiced bilabial stop [b].

/pumci/	[pumʦi]	'knee'
/phuŋmũ/	[p^{h}uŋmũ]	'eel'
/phukcap/	[p^{h}uk̚ʦap̚]	'to erect, lift'
/bukcap/	[buk̚ʦap̚]	'to get up'

The voiceless unaspirated, voiceless aspirated and plain voiced obstruents found in word-initial positions are also found in syllable-initial positions.

/papa/	[papa]	'father'
/braphu/	[brap^{h}u]	'centipede'
/bubu/	[bubu]	'white'

Note that the glottal stop /ʔ/, which serves as a hiatus in word-initial position, has phonemic status in intervocalic position.

/kaʔu/	[kaʔu]	'friend'
vs. /ka:ku/	[ka:ku]	'water'

Final obstruents are commonly realised without any clear audible release. Voiceless stops are common in word-final positions.

/mat/	[mat̚]	'late, a little later'
/cimtɛp/	[ʦimtɛp̚]	'a little'

However, plain voiced stops are also found in word-final position, albeit marginally. The distinctiveness of voicing is apparently maintained in abbreviated monosyllabic morphs which are derived by means of a rule of final-vowel deletion from the corresponding bimorphemic basic forms that have intervocalic stops. See Section 2.3.3 (p. 73) on full and abbreviated morphs.

/naʔa/	[naʔa]	'only'
→ /naʔ/	→ [naʔ]	
/daku/	[daku]	'memory, remembrance'
→ /dak/	→ [dak]	
/parkoti/	[parko·ti]	'sweet potato'
→ /parkot/	→ [parkot]	
/ŋaba/	[ŋaba]	'fragrance'
→ /ŋab/	→ [ŋab]	

By contrast, final affricates and voiceless aspirated stops have not been found in native words. The abbreviated morphs of basic forms with intervocalic affricates take a word-final stop.

/ticu/	[tiʦu]	plural marker
→ /tit/	→ [tit]	

Syllable-final stops share the voicing of the following syllable-initial obstruent. Voiced [g˺, d˺, b˺] are used before voiced obstruents. Voiceless [ʔ˺, k˺, t˺, p˺] are found before voiceless and voiceless aspirated obstruents and before other consonants such as nasal and fricatives. The syllable-final stops /p, t, k/ might be analysed as archiphonemes that have two allophonic realisations relating to voicing. I have not found words with final [k˺] before initial /p/, final [t˺] before initial /k, p/, and final [p˺] before initial /k/. This peculiarity might be attributed to a second type of neutralisation between the distinctive points of articulation.

SYLLABLE-FINAL VELARS

/akkum/	[ak˺kum]	'our^{pe}'
/rakcap/	[rak˺ʦap˺]	'to influence'
/hujɔktɔp/	[huʥɔk˺tɔp˺]	'how'

/pɛkmar/	[p^{j}ɛk˺mar]	'egg of a louse'
/kaksi/	[kak˺si]	'earth, soil'
/kligji/	[klig˺ʥi]	'throat, neck'
/magge/	[mag˺ge]	'egg'

SYLLABLE-FINAL ALVEOLARS

/blatcap/	[blat˺ʦap˺]	'to come, arrive'
/mɛttɛp/	[mɛt˺tɛp˺]	'girl'
/satni/	[sat˺ni]	'yesterday'

SYLLABLE-FINAL BILABIALS

/bipcap/	[bip˺ʦap˺]	'to suck'
/riptɛwa/	[rip˺tɛwʌ]	'shade'
/lapthɔl/	[lap˺t^{h}ɔl]	'before'
/cuppa/	[ʦup˺pa]	'piglet'
/lapphu/	[lap˺p^{h}u]	'before'
/hupni/	[hup˺ni]	'pus'
/rɛpmu/	[r^{j}ɛp˺mu]	'chin'
/gupsu/	[gup˺su]	'tiger, leopard'
/labji/	[lab˺ʥi]	'husked grain'
/nibbɔn/	[nib˺bɔn]	'two days ago'

The synchronic phonemic status of the syllable-final glottal stop follows, amongst others, from its contrastivity with vowels that are not followed by a glottal stop. In other words, the presence of the glottal stop is not predictable in this environment.

SYLLABLE-FINAL GLOTTALS

/naʔa/	[naʔa]	'only'
vs. /nake/	[nake]	'animal'
/toʔla/	[to:ʔ˺la]	'above, up'
vs. /tolupe/	[to:lupe]	'the name of a Jero clan'
/tu:ʔme/	[tu:ʔ˺me]	'they^{P} drink' (root <tu:t->)
vs. /tupme/	[tup˺me]	'they^{P} hit' (root <tup->)

Verbal morphology suggests that the syllable-final glottal stop /ʔ/ might be historically analysed as a neutralising consonant for /t/.

SYLLABLE-FINAL GLOTTALS AND ROOT-FINAL <T>

/kraːʔme/	[kraːʔ̚me]	'they[P] bite' (root <krat->)
/phaːʔme/	[pʰaːʔ̚me]	'they[P] can' (root <phat->)
vs. /baːme/	[baːme]	'he is' (root <baː->)

Comparative evidence also suggests a possible link between Wambule implosives and Jero /mVʔ/ or /nVʔ/ syllables, which consist of initial /m/ or /n/, a nuclear vowel and a final glottal stop.

SYLLABLE-FINAL GLOTTALS AND WAMBULE IMPLOSIVES

/maʔla/	[maʔ̚la]	'spirit' (WA *ɓala*)
/mɛʔlum/	[mɛʔ̚lum]	'tail' (WA *ɓulum*)
/noʔmar/	[noːʔ̚mar]	'head strap' (WA *ɗobir*)

Voiceless aspirated consonants occur before other consonants with which they also form clusters in word-initial position, i.e. bilabial and velar stops followed by /r, l/.

SYLLABLE-INITIAL VOICELESS ASPIRATED OBSTRUENTS

/maphlɛm/	[mapʰlɛm]	'late, a little later'
/kakhrɔm/	[kakʰrɔm]	'vessel'

I propose to place the syllable boundary before the voiceless aspirated consonants. By consequence, there are no syllable-final voiceless aspirated consonants in indigenous Jero words.

2.2.2 *Nasals*

Jero has a series of voiced nasals at three points of articulation, viz. /m, n, ŋ/. The three nasals are distinctive in all phonological environments. The phoneme /m/ is a voiced bilabial /m/. The phoneme /n/ is a voiced alveolar nasal [n], which has an allophone [ɳ] before retroflex plosives. The phoneme /ŋ/ is a voiced velar nasal [ŋ]. The following series of words show nasals in initial, medial and final positions.

/mi/	[mi]	'fire'
/ni/	[ni]	'name'
/ŋa:bu/	[ŋa:bu]	'assistant priest'
/anɔmi/	[anɔmi]	'they are not'
/ganani/	[ganani]	'come^{p} up!'
/gaŋaci/	[gaŋaʦi]	'come^{d} up!'
/tɛmbar/	[tɛmbar]	'today'
/tɛncap/	[tɛnʦap˺]	'to make drink'
/tɛŋthoce/	[tɛŋt^{h}o:ʦɛ]	'this year'

2.2.3 *The fricative, trill and laterals*

Jero has one fricative /s/, one trill /r/ and two laterals /l/ and ल्अ /ʔl/, the latter of which is found in written literary Jero. The phoneme /r/ is a voiced apico-alveolar trill [r]. The fricative /s/ is a voiceless lamino-alveolarised sibilant [s]. The phoneme /s/ does not occur as a verb root final. The phoneme /l/ is a voiced apico-alveolar approximant [l]. The following series of words show the consonant phonemes /s/, /r/ and /l/ in initial, medial and final positions.

/sɔkane/	[sɔkane]	'cough'
/rɔke/	[r^{w}ɔke]	'the name of a Jero clan'
/lɔki/	[l^{w}ɔki]	'let us^{pi} go'
/phuli/	[p^{h}uli]	'flour'
/phuri/	[p^{h}uri]	'flower'
/rusu/	[rusu]	'bone'
/ul/	[ul]	'there'
/hur/	[hur]	'mouth'
/hus/	[hus]	'how'

There does not seem to be a direct link between the Āmboṭe cluster /ʔl/ and the digraph ल्अ *ʔl* in e.g. ल्आ *ʔlā* 'hand', which represents a preglottalised lateral /ʔl/ that is also found in the Wamdyal (and perhaps also Udaipure) dialect of Wambule. Note, however, that a preglottalised lateral sound is not found in the Hilepāne dialect on which my 2004 book *A Grammar of Wambule* is based.[9] The preglottalised lateral /ʔl/ occurs in word-initial positions, whereas the Āmboṭe cluster /ʔl/ appears in medial positions. A preglottalised lateral phoneme has not been established in the spoken Āmboṭe material on which this grammar is based.

/beʔli/	[beːʔ̚li]	'she-goat'
/sɔʔlɔm/	[sɔʔ̚lɔm]	'*Shorea robusta*'
/poʔle/	[poːʔ̚le]	'vagina'
/saːʔlɛŋ/	[saːʔ̚lɛŋ]	'song'
/siʔlim/	[siʔ̚lim]	'green leafy vegetable'

2.2.4 *Approximants*

Jero has three approximants /h, y, w/, of which the phonemes /h, w/ do not occur as verb root finals. The phonemes /y, w/ appear as prevocalic elements in syllable-initial positions and marginally as postconsonantal segments before the open central vowel /a/.

The approximant /h/ is a voiceless glottal [h].

/hipsu/	[hip̚su]	'tree, *Bassia butyracea*'
/hɔmcap/	[hʷɔm̚ʦap̚]	'to sink; to set (sun)'
/hupni/	[hup̚ni]	'pus'

---

[9] The preglottalised lateral /ʔl/ is found in the following Wamdyal words: *ʔla* 'hand, arm', *ʔlaccam* 'to upset, overturn', *ʔlaci* 'vagina', *ʔlaicam* 'to be turned upside down, turn round', *ʔlajabo* 'a kind of mythological living being', *ʔlakacim* 'red', *ʔlam* 'road, path', *ʔlantho* 'opposite, reversed', *ʔlaːcam* 'to give birth to', *ʔlɛkku* 'earthquake', *ʔleicam* 'to change clothes', *ʔliba* 'silence', *ʔLibju* 'an important Wambule forefather', *ʔlico* 'weighing, being heavy or light in weight', *ʔlikcam* 'to spring up, sprout', *ʔlim* 'manner of performing an action right away', *ʔlima* 'lie, act of lying', *ʔlimcam* 'to return, come back', *ʔliːphu* 'kind of vessel', *ʔliːcam* 'to sell', *ʔlɔcam* 'to have sex (rude term)' (vs. *lɔcam* 'to go'), *ʔlɔsu* 'leg', *ʔlucchu* 'marten', *ʔlukcam* 'to pour out', *jiji ʔlum* 'it is sweet', *ʔluŋ* 'stone' and *ʔlupcam* 'to cover'. By contrast, the plain lateral /l/ is found in the words *lakcam* 'to jump, leap over', *lɛccam* 'to take, take for sex (said by men)', *lɛm* 'tongue', *lɛpcam* 'to spread out a bedding', *lɛpsu* 'the back of the head', *lɛtam* 'bedding, bed', *le* 'manner of handing over', *likcam* 'to set fire to', *lɔcam* 'to go' (vs. *ʔlɔcam* 'to have sex (rude term)'), *lɔccam* 'to hew out', *lɔkcam* 'to boil', *lɔkcam* 'to lick', *lo* 'locative marker', *locam* 'to wait for', *lu* 'manner of inserting something', *lumbo* 'deep' and *lupcam* 'to cover' (also *ʔlupcam*).

The phoneme /y/ is realised as a voiced lamino-palatal approximant [j]. The sound [j] is analysed as subphonemic before the front vowels /i, iː, ɛ, e/. The pronunciation of /ya/ is between [jæ] and [æ].

/yaksi/	[jæk̚si]	'salt'
/yɔya/	[jɔjæ]	'down here (of place)'
/yunti/	[junti]	'lip'
/sɛri/	[sʲɛri]	'body louse'
/gyaŋgu/	[gjæŋgu]	'snail'

The phoneme /w/ is realised as a bilabial approximant [w] with a simultaneous articulation in the direction of the velar region. The sound [w] is not found in combination with front vowels and is analysed as subphonemic before the back vowels /u, uː, ɔ, o/.

/wa/	[wʌ]	'clothes'
/waːcap/	[wʌːʦap̚]	'scream'
/swam/	[swʌm]	'hair'
/hwarsi/	[hwʌrsi]	'rain'

The difference between the labialised midvowel /ɔ/ [ʷɔ] and the sequence /wa/ [wʌ] and that between the palatalised midvowel /ɛ/ [ʲɛ] and the sequence /ya/ [jæ] occasionally proved difficult to perceive. However, the labialisation and palatalisation of the phonemic sequences often seemed to be stronger than the ongliding of the midvowels. Unlike the Hilepāne dialect of Wambule, where /*ɔ/ and /*wa/ generally went to /wa/ while /*ɛ/ and /*ya/ went to /ya/, the original phonemic distinction between the vowels and the sequences has been retained in Jero and in the Wamdyal dialect of Wambule. Note that in literary sources both /ɔ/ and /wa/ are often transcribed as *vā*, and that both /ɛ/ and /ya/ are frequently rendered as *yā*. These orthographic conventions do not reflect the phonemic reality.

2.2.5 *Consonant clusters*

In addition to the post-consonantal sequences /ya/ and /wa/, Jero permits syllable-initial clusters which consist of two consonants of which the first element is /k, kh, g/ or /p, ph, b/ and the second is /l, r/.

/plɛtcap/	[plɛt̚ʦap̚]	'to dry something'
/prakcam/	[prak̚ʦam]	'to run' (Mohanṭāre)
/phrakcap/	[pʰrak̚ʦap̚]	'to break open'
/blatcap/	[blat̚ʦap̚]	'to come, arrive'
/bracap/	[braʦap̚]	'to spread'
/kligji/	[klig̚ʥi]	'throat, neck'
/krampu/	[krampu]	'*Garuga pinnata* tree'
/khlɛkcap/	[kʰlɛk̚ʦap̚]	'to paint'
/khricap/	[kʰriʦap̚]	'to count'
/glecap/	[gleːʦap̚]	'to lie down'
/gramji/	[gramʥi]	'hate, hatred'

2.3 *Morphophonology*

An overview is given here of the morphophonological regularities that are found throughout the Jero language. Phonologically conditioned alternation between morphemes is handled here by setting up a basic form which undergoes modification in a certain environment. This basic morph is considered to be an underlying representation that consists of actual phonemes, which are written between conventional European structuralist morpheme brackets, e.g. <blaː-mi-me> 'they^{P} come'. The phonemic form is considered to be derived from the basic form through morphophonological rules. The actual morph consists of autonomous phonemes or archiphonemes, which are written between slanted brackets, e.g. /bla-m-me/ 'they^{P} come'.

2.3.1 *Morphophonemic and phonemic vowel length*

The neutralisation of the phonemic contrasts between /i/ and /iː/, /a/ and /aː/, and /u/ and /uː/ in certain environments, rather than, for instance, limited distribution of the long vowel phonemes, is primarily suggested by systematic alternations between the different phonemic forms of a verb within a single paradigm. These alternations can be explained if we set up a monosyllabic basic form of the verb root which shows vowel length distinctions at the morphophonemic level.

Thus, take a look at the different forms of the transitive verb *gacam* vi <ga> 'to come up', which has a short morphophoneme <a>, and the intransitive verb *bakcam* vi-2 <bak- ~ ba:-> 'to be, sit', which has the long morphophoneme <a:> in the secondary root alternant. The distinction between the morphophonemes <a-> and <a:-> is retained in the first person inclusive forms, but lost in the second person singular and third person plural forms.

<ga->		'to come up'
/ganne/	[ganne]	'you^{s} will come up'
/gakim/	[gakim]	'we^{pi} will come up'
/gamme/	[gamme]	'they^{p} will come up'
<ba:->		'to be, sit'
/banne/	[banne]	'you^{s} are'
/ba:kim/	[ba:kim]	'we^{pi} are'
/bamme/	[bamme]	'they^{p} are'

The verbs *lucap* vi-1a-i <lu-> 'to feel, cause a mental and bodily sensation' and *hu:cap* vi-1b <hu:-> 'to shout, cry' illustrate the neutralisation of the contrast between /u/ and /u:/ in closed syllables.

<lu->		'to feel'
/lunne/	[lunne]	'you^{s} felt'
/lukim/	[lukim]	'we^{pi} felt'
/lumme/	[lumme]	'they^{p} felt'
<hu:->		'to shout, cry'
/hunne/	[hunne]	'you^{s} shouted'
/hu:kim/	[hu:kim]	'we^{pi} shouted'
/humme/	[humme]	'they^{p} shouted'

By contrast, the verbs *lɔcap* vi-1a-i <lɔ-> 'to go' and *docap* vi-1b <do-> 'to fall' show that the distinction between /ɔ/ and /o/ is preserved in this morphophonological environment. The long vowel /o/ lacks a long duration in the second person singular and third person plural forms, but is still physically distinguishable from the short vowel /ɔ/, which has a different quality.

<lɔ->		'to go'
/lɔnne/	[lɔnne]	'you^{s} will go'
/lɔkim/	[lɔkim]	'we^{pi} will go'
/lɔmme/	[lɔmme]	'they^{p} will go'
<do->		'to fall'
/donne/	[donne]	'you^{s} will fall'
/dokim/	[doːkim]	'we^{pi} will fall'
/domme/	[domme]	'they^{p} will fall'

2.3.2 *Bound morphemes*

A formal distinction can be made between two types of bound morphemes, i.e. morphemes which cannot stand on their own in an utterance. Lexical affixes are bound morphemes which are attached to other morphemes with which they form one phonological and grammatical word. Phrasal affixes, by contrast, are bound morphemes which attach to unbound morphemes and which form constituents within the phrase as a whole.

Lexical affixes. The boundary between roots and lexical affixes is analysed as phonologically and grammatically word-internal. Roots are the basic forms of a word which carry the lexical meaning. Lexical affixes are attached to other morphemes with which they form one phonological and grammatical word. Lexical affixes attach to each constituent of a phrase individually. Their scope of application is restricted to the word of which they form part. Examples of lexical affixes are the negative prefix, the person and number agreement suffixes, the verbal suffixes which follow the agreement suffixes and the non-finite deverbalising suffixes. A word-internal morpheme boundary is indicated by a hyphen (-) in transcription.[10]

Open monosyllabic roots, such as the verbs <baː-> 'be, sit' and <ga-> 'come up', show qualitative and quantitative vowel contrasts before lexical suffixes depending on whether the root syllable is open

[10] A hyphen is also used to indicate the boundary between the components of ordinary and reduplicative compounds in derivational morphology. The boundary between the components of compounds is phonologically word-external from the point of view of the component lexemes.

or closed. In the following examples, the contrasts at the morphophonological level are pertinent at the phonological level.

<ba:->
/ba:-ŋ-a-ci/ [ba:ŋat͡si] 'be^{d}, sit^{d}!'

<ga->
/ga-ŋ-a-ci/ [gaŋat͡si] 'come^{d} upwards!'

Phrasal affixes. The second type of morphosyntactically bound forms are phrasal affixes. Phrasal affixes are structurally dependent upon the preceding unbound forms or full words, such as nominal and adverbial lexemes, with which the affixes show limited morphophonological interaction. Phrasal suffixes differ from lexical suffixes in that they are constituents within the phrase as a whole. The syntactic positions in which these word-like bound morphemes occur are rather limited. Phrasal affixes generally occur in phrase-final position. The morpheme boundary between a full word and the following phrasal affix is indicated by means of the symbol (=) in transcription. Examples of phrasal affixes are the Jero case markers (e.g. source, locative, comitative, genitive), the discourse markers meaning 'also' and 'exactly', and the reifying morpheme, which creates nominal constituents from various word classes.

Open monosyllabic lexemes, such as the adverb *na* 'before', do not show any phonemic length distinction before phrasal suffixes, such as the marker <=se> 'exactly, precisely'. Open monosyllabic lexemes are generally realised with a long duration in this morphophonological environment.

/na=se/ [na:se ~ na:s^{j}ɛ] 'much before'

This phonetic peculiarity suggests that the morpheme boundary between unbound lexemes and phrasal suffixes is word-external from the point of view of the unbound lexemes.

Many lexical or phrasal affixes have abbreviated forms that show a contraction with the root, stem or lexeme to which they are attached. The phonological basis of the alternation can be advanced as an argument in favour of the view that not only lexical affixes but also phrasal affixes are morphologically bound and form a phonological unit with the morpheme to which they are attached. The formation of abbreviated morphs is discussed next.

2.3.3 *Full and abbreviated morphs*

Jero morphemes can have two alternants of which the full form ends in a consonant that is followed by a vowel, whereas the corresponding abbreviated form ends in the intervocalic consonant of the full form. Abbreviated forms are generally obtained from basic morphs through a morphophonological process of morpheme-final vowel deletion.

<kulu> →	/kulu/	'house'
	/kul/	*idem*

As in Wambule, there is no apparent difference in meaning between the two forms. The abbreviated forms are commonly used in connected allegro speech, whereas the full forms are used in more carefully enunciated speech, as citation forms or in combination with certain bound morphemes.

The use of abbreviated bound allomorphs is dependent on the phonological form of the preceding morpheme. Abbreviated forms of suffixes can be attached if the preceding morpheme ends in a vowel, whereas the full forms can always be used.

<dome> →	/dome/	'he will fall'
	/dom/	*idem*
<lɔme> →	/lɔme/	'he will go'
	/lɔm/	*idem*
<=ku> →	/=ku/	(source marker)
	/=k/	*idem*

2.3.4 *Final and post-final <t>*

Verbs which show paradigmatically conditioned root alternations between the root-final elements <pt ~ m> (vt-2c), <tt ~ n> (vt-2d), <kt ~ V:> (vt-2e), <yt ~ y> (vt-2f), <rt ~ r> (vt-2g) and <lt ~ l> (vt-2h) are characterised by the presence of two successive consonants in the pri-

primary root alternant, i.e. final <p, t, k, y, r, l> plus post-final <t>. In addition, class (vt-2b) of verbs ending in <V:t ~ V:> is characterised by the presence of a post-final consonant <t> following a long root vowel. I have not found direct evidence for a class of verbs ending in <mt ~ t>, but the verbs listed under <-mt> in Section 4.1.3 (p. 131) are good candidates.

Post-final <t> is generally deleted in word-final and syllable-final positions, viz. before suffixes with an initial consonant. The deletion is phonologically motivated since Jero does not generally permit any consonant clusters in final positions.

<tu:t-cu>	/tu:-cu/	'drinking'
<tupt-ca-me>	/tup-ca-p/	'to beat'
<phatt-ni-Ø-me>	/phat-ni-Ø-m/	'you^{s} could'
<jɔkt-ni-Ø-me>	/jɔk-ni-Ø-m/	'you^{s} knew it'
<tɛrt-ni-Ø-me>	/tɛr-ni-Ø-m/	'you^{s} received it'

Post-final <t> is retained if the segment can be integrated into the structure of the following syllable. This is illustrated in the following forms:

<tu:t-i-Ø-me>	/tu:t-i-Ø-m/	'he drank it'
<japt-i-Ø-me>	/japt-i-Ø-m/	'he bought it'
<phatt-i-Ø-me>	/phatt-i-Ø-m/	'he could'
<gɔkt-i-Ø-me>	/gɔkt-i-Ø-m/	'he gave it'
<tɛrt-i-Ø-me>	/tɛrt-i-Ø-m/	'he receive it'

Paradigmatic root-final <t> is generally assimilated to the following consonant. Recall that syllable-final /t/ in pre-consonantal position can be analysed as an archiphoneme which phonetically assimilates to the following consonant.

<phitt-phu>	/phip-pu/	'in order to bring'
<phitt-ti>	/phit-ti/	'bring'
<phatt-ni-Ø-me>	/phat-ni-Ø-m/	'you^{s} can'
<kratt-ka-Ø>	/krak-ka-Ø/	'bite^{s} him!'
<phɛtt-si>	/phɛs-si/	'serve out'

2.3.5 *Post-agreement suffixes with initial <m>*

The morpheme <-mei>$_{am}$ of the factual verbal adjective, which is discussed in Section 4.4 (p. 165), and the morpheme <-me>$_{am}$ of the affirmative, which is discussed in Section 4.5 (p. 169), belong to the group of post-agreement suffixes with initial <m>. These suffixes have a strong effect on the realisation of the preceding simplex person and number agreement suffixes <-mi>$_{am}$ (23/ns), <-ni>$_{am}$ (2) and <-ŋu>$_{am}$ (1s). The post-agreement suffixes with initial <m> are subject to the following morphophonological variation:

(a) The vowel <e> in the suffixes <-mei>$_{am}$ and <-me>$_{am}$ becomes /a/ in first person singular, first person dual exclusive and first person plural exclusive forms, which, as a rule, do not have simplex person and number agreement suffixes ending in <i>, e.g. <si-ŋu-me> (die-1s-AFF) → /si-ŋ-ma/$_{am}$ 'I died', <po-cuwa-me> (do-1deAS-AFF) → /po-cu-ma/$_{a}$ 'we^{de} did it' and <baː-kuwa-mei> (be/sit-1peAS-FCT) → /baː-ku-mai/$_{a}$ 'we^{pe} sat'. Morpheme-final /ai/ of factual verbal adjective freely alternates with /ʌi/. Word-final /a/ is usually dropped in first person dual and plural exclusive forms, but commonly retained in first person singular forms, e.g. <po-kuwa-me> (do-1peAS-AFF) → /po-ku-ma/$_{a}$ ~ /po- ku-m/ $_{a}$ 'we^{pe} did it'.

(b) The suffix-initial consonant <m> of the suffixes <-mei>$_{am}$ and <-me>$_{am}$ is /n/ after the abbreviated morph /-n/ of the second person suffix <-ni>$_{am}$ (2), e.g. <lɔ-ni-Ø-me> (go-2-23s-AFF) → /lɔ-n-Ø-ne/$_{am}$ 'you^{s} went' and <ja-ni-Ø-me> (eat-2-23s-AFF) → /ja-n-Ø-ne/$_{am}$ 'you^{s} ate it'. Note that the suffix consonant <m> is not changed after the basic morph /-ni/$_{am}$ of the second person suffix <-ni>$_{am}$ (2), e.g. <hipt-ni-Ø-me> (see-2-23s-AFF) → /hip-ni-Ø-m/ 'you^{s} saw it', in which the abbreviate morph /-m/ of the suffix <-me>$_{am}$ of the affirmative can be used instead.

(c) The suffix-initial consonant <m> of the post-agreement suffixes <-mei>$_{am}$ and <-me>$_{am}$ are not changed in other morphophonological environments. The affirmative suffix <-me>$_{am}$ is regularly realised as /-me/$_{am}$ after vowels and consonants, but it can also be realised as /-m/$_{am}$ after vowels through the process of word final vowel deletion, e.g. <do-Ø-me> (fall-23s-AFF) → /do-Ø-me/$_{a}$ ~ /do-Ø-m/$_{a}$ 'he fell'. The suffix <-me>$_{am}$ is not reduced to /-m/$_{am}$ after a consonant, however, e.g. <pa-mi-me> (do-23/ns-AFF) → /pa-m-me/$_{am}$ 'they^{P} did it'.

2.4 *Phonology of Nepali loans*

The informants whom I consulted mastered Nepali pronunciation perfectly. As far as I could tell, their pronunciation of loan forms generally seemed to be in accordance with Nepali phonology.

/ʌ/ /a/
/i/
/u/
/e/ /ʌi/
/o/ /ʌu/

/k/	/kh/	/g/	/gh/	/ŋ/
/c/	/ch/	/j/	/jh/	
/ṭ/	/ṭh/	/ḍ/	/ḍh/	
/t/	/th/	/d/	/dh/	/n/
/p/	/ph/	/b/	/bh/	/m/

/y/ /r/ /l/ /w/
/s/
/h/

The Nepali vowel system shows a qualitative contrast between six monophthongs and two diphthongs. There is no phonological contrast in quantity between the Nepali vowels. The contrast between the Jero phonemes /i/ and /iː/, /a/ and /aː/, and /u/ and /uː/, which is considered to be relevant in specific phonological environments, is not clearly maintained in loans from Nepali, where the distinction between short and long vowel durations is not phonologically relevant. As a general rule, however, /i/ and /u/ in loans from Nepali are pronounced as Jero /i/ and /u/, whereas /a/, /e/ and /o/ in loans are intermediate in phonetic duration between the short and long vowels in indigenous Jero words, even though the duration of these phonetically lengthened vowels varies depending on speaker and environment. For instance, stressed /a/, /e/ and /o/ are very similar to the long vowels /aː/, /e/ and /o/ in native Jero words, whereas Nepali /a/, /e/ and /o/ appear to be rather short before the high vowels /i/ and /u/ and the corresponding semi-vowels /y/ and /w/. In addition, the vowels /e/ and /o/ in Nepali are sometimes assimilated to the short vowels /ɛ/ and /ɔ/ in Jero. The Nepali vowel /ʌ/ is usually realised as the short vowel /ʌ/ in Jero, but a more rounded allophone [ɔ] was also heard, albeit rarely. The vowels /ʌ/, /a/, /e/, /i/, /o/ and /u/ in loans from Nepali are generally represented by *ʌ*, *a*, *e*, *i*, *o* and *u* in the orthography.[11]

Nasalisation has phonemic status in loan words. Nasalised vowels are also retained in my orthography, except in words in which a velar nasal /ŋ/ was heard. In the latter case, nasalised vowels in loans are not rendered as vowels plus a tilde (˜) but as sequences of vowels plus a velar nasal.

The system of Nepali consonants incorporates five series of plosive stops and affricates with the laryngeal settings voiceless, aspirated, plain voiced and breathy voiced, which are spread over five distinctive points of articulation, viz. velar, retroflex, dental and bilabial plosives and alveolar/palatal affricates. The other consonants are all voiced. There is a series of nasals at three points of articulation, one fricative, one trill, one lateral and three approximants.

/bĩɖ/	[bĩɽ]	'handle' (<Nep. *bĩḍ*)
/bidesi/	[bideˑsi]	'foreigner' (<Nep. *videśī*)
/jati/	[ʤaˑti]	'good' (<Nep. *jāti*)
/bihan/	[bi^{h}æn]	'morning' (<Nep. *bihān*)
/bɛla/	[bɛla]	'time' (<Nep. *belā*)
/cheparo/	[ʦ^{h}eˑparo]	'lizard' (<Nep. *chepāro*)
/bhãɖo/	[b^{h}ãˑɽo]	'pot' (<Nep. *bhā̃ḍo*)
/pakhra/	[paˑk^{h}ra]	'arm' (<Nep. *pākhurā*)
/car/	[ʦaˑr]	'four' (<Nep. *cār*)

[11] Since the length of the initial vowels in the native Jero word *maːla* 'language' and the loan word *mala* 'garland' (<Nep. *mālā*) can be quite similar, one could propose to assimilate Nepali /a/ to Jero *aː* in those environments in which there is a distinctive length contrast between the vowels in native Jero words. However, as in Wambule, I have decided to mark length distinctions in indigenous words only.

/bɔkra/	[bɔkra]	'skin, rind' (<Nep. *bokro*)
/boka/	[bo·ka]	'billy-goat' (<Nep. *bokā*)
/ɖhoka/	[ɖ^{h}o·ka]	'door' (<Nep. *ḍhokā*)
/buɖi/	[buɽi]	'old' (<Nep. *buḍhī*)
/bhus/	[b^{h}us]	'husk' (<Nep. *bhūs*)
/guleli/	[gule·li]	'pellet-bow' (<Nep. *gulelī*)
/bhʌtkʌi/	[b^{h}ʌtkʌi]	'destruction' (<Nep. *bhatkāi*)
/cʌlʌi/	[ʦʌlʌi]	'movement' (<Nep. *calāī*)
/gʌrib/	[gʌrib̚]	'poor' (<Nep. *garib*)

2.5 *The orthography and rule of transcription*

The orthography used for transcribing Jero distinguishes the vowel and consonant phonemes by using the same symbols as the phonological transcription. The orthography differs from the phonological transcription in the following two ways:

- the orthography represents the predictable allophones of the consonant archiphonemes in pre-consonantal syllable-final position by using *p* ~ *b* (/p/ before labials stops), *c* ~ *j* (/t/ before affricates), *ʈ* ~ *ɖ* (/t/ before post-alveolar stops), *t* ~ *d* (/t/ before alveolar stops) and *k* ~ *g* (/k/ before velar stops).

- the vowel archiphonemes are rendered as short vowel graphemes.

Loans from Nepali are transcribed according to the pronunciation given by my informants. In the examples, the English gloss of loan forms is generally rendered in italicised characters. However, abbreviated glosses such as CNT, EMPH, EXCL, NEW, LN, PAT and THM are never italicised. All loans are listed in the Jero-English lexicon, in which the non-native origin of the borrowings is indicated.

As a general rule of transcription for the examples, words are broken up into morphs which are transcribed in phonologically based orthography. The spelling reflects the phonological realisation after morphophonological rules have applied. Mohanṭāre forms are followed by ($_{m}$) and Āmboṭe forms by ($_{a}$).

CHAPTER THREE

NOMINALS AND ADVERBIALS

This chapter on nominal and adverbial morphology deals with former elements of noun classification and gender marking, number markers, case markers, postpositions, discourse markers and various nominal and adverbial word forms. Nominals are words that have some of the attributes of nouns, but not all. The group of nominals comprises personal pronouns, demonstrative pronouns, indefinite and interrogative words, adjectives, and numeral and non-numeral quantifiers. Reified verbs, verbal nouns and verbal adjectives are also nominals, but the morphosyntax of these deverbative forms is discussed in Sections 4.4 (p. 165) and 5.2 (p. 187). Adverbials are a heterogeneous group of words which serve to specify constituents other than nouns. Adverbials are commonly used as modifiers of verbs and adjectives.

3.1 *Improductive nominal suffixes*

Although many nouns cannot be divided up into smaller morphological units, some nouns incorporate bound elements with a more or less clear meaning. Noun classifying elements represent non-productive nominal suffixes, most of which are attached to bound roots with an unclear meaning. In addition, Jero shows traces of an improductive grammatical device to mark gender distinctions. The Jero gender distinctions are related to the sex distinction between male and female.

3.1.1 *The suffix 'person'*

MORPHEME	<-cu>$_{\text{am}}$
GLOSS	person

The suffix <-cu>$_{\text{am}}$ 'person' is cognate of Wambule <-co> 'person' in e.g. *waco* 'husband', Bahing <-cha> in e.g. *wancha* 'husband', Hayu <-tso> 'person, man' in e.g. *ka'tso* 'friend', Dumi <-tsu> in e.g. *tsatsu* 'grandson', Khaling <-co> in e.g. *'nokco*, and Kulung <-c^{h}o> in e.g. *nokc^{h}o* 'priest'. This suffix occurs in a number of kinship terms and in clan terminology.

cacu$_{\text{am}}$	'grandson'
Dʌŋkhʌmcu$_{\text{a}}$	'the name of a Jero clan'
jɔmcu$_{\text{am}}$	'shaman'
Laimcu$_{\text{a}}$	'name of a Jero clan'
mucu$_{\text{am}}$	'man, person'
Setalcu$_{\text{a}}$	'the name of a Jero clan'
wacu$_{\text{m}}$	'husband'
yɔkcu$_{\text{am}}$	'child, infant'

3.1.2 *The suffix 'grain'*

MORPHEME	<-ji>$_{\text{am}}$
GLOSS	grain

The suffix <-ji>$_{\text{am}}$ 'grain' is a reflex of Proto-Tibeto-Burman **dzya* 'eat' and Proto-Kiranti **ja* 'grain'. This suffix is cognate of Wambule <-ja> 'grain' in e.g. *carja* 'finger millet, *Eleusine coracana*', Bahing <-já> in e.g. *chárjá* 'millet (kodo)', Dumi *dza:* 'rice; cooked grain', Khaling *jä* 'grain', Kulung *ja* 'cooked rice, food (in general)', Yamphu <ca-> in e.g. *cari* 'seed', Āṭhpahariyā <ca-> in e.g. *cama* 'rice, food', and Limbu <-chaʔ> in e.g. *wɛtchaʔ* 'husked rice'.

carji$_{\text{am}}$	'finger millet, *Eleusine coracana*'
garji$_{\text{am}}$	'rice plant'
labji$_{\text{a}}$	'husked grain'

3.1.3 *The suffix 'water'*

MORPHEME	<-ku>$_{\text{am}}$
GLOSS	water

The suffix <-ku>$_{\text{am}}$ 'water' can be traced back to Proto-Tibeto-Burman **klu(:)ŋ* × **k(l)uk* 'river, valley' and Proto-Kiranti **ku* 'water'. The water suffix is cognate of Wambule <-ku> 'water' in e.g.

Glwaku 'the Dūdhkosī river', Bahing <-ku> in e.g. *pwáku* 'water', Sunwar <-ku> in e.g. *baakku* 'water', Dumi *ki* 'water; source, tap' and Khaling *ku* 'water'.

Glɔku$_{\text{m}}$ 'the Dūdhkosī river'
ka:ku$_{\text{am}}$ 'water'

3.1.4 *The suffix 'tree, wood'*

MORPHEME <-si>$_{\text{am}}$
GLOSS tree

The suffix <-si>$_{\text{am}}$ 'tree, wood' is related to Proto-Kiranti **siŋ* 'tree', Wambule <-si ~ -ci ~ -chi> 'tree, wood' in e.g. *kuksi* 'the tree *Ficus cunia*', Bahing *sing* 'tree', Sunwar *shii* 'wood, firewood', Dumi <-si> in e.g. *pi:sibhu* 'the tree *Castanopsis indica*', Khaling *sung* 'wood, fallen tree', Kulung *siŋ* 'firewood', Yamphu <-si> in e.g. *usrœ'ksi* 'the Chinese sumac tree *Rhus javanica*', Hayu, Āṭhpahariyā and Limbu *siŋ* 'wood', and Limbu <-siŋ> in *yaŋsiŋba* 'the tree *Schima wallichii*'.

kuksi$_{\text{am}}$ 'the tree *Ficus cunia*'
mεsi$_{\text{m}}$ 'the tree *Elaeagnus parvifolia*'

3.1.5 *The suffix 'fruit'*

MORPHEME <-si>$_{\text{am}}$
GLOSS fruit

The suffix <-si>$_{\text{am}}$ 'fruit' is cognate of Proto-Tibeto-Burman **sey* 'fruit', Proto-Kiranti **sit* 'fruit, bear fruit', Wambule <-si ~ -ci> 'fruit' in e.g. *twaksi* 'mango' and *balci* 'banana', Bahing *síchi* 'fruit', Sunwar <-si> in e.g. *'wobisi* 'cucumber', Dumi <-si> in e.g. *dzasi* 'fruit', Hayu <-si> in e.g. *pakamsɪ* 'mango', Thulung <-si> in *Doksi* 'mango', Khaling <-si> in e.g. *lengaasi* 'banana', Kulung *se* 'fruit' or <-si> in e.g. *liŋo:si* 'banana', Yamphu <-si> in e.g. *phana'si* 'jack-fruit', Āṭhpahariyā *sa* 'fruit', Limbu and Limbu *se?* 'seed, fruit'.

tɔksi$_{\text{am}}$ 'mango'

3.1.6 *The suffix 'small object'*

MORPHEME	<-si>$_{am}$
GLOSS	small object

The suffix <-si>$_{am}$ 'small object' is cognate of Proto-Tibeto-Burman **z(y)əy* 'small, minute', Proto-Kiranti **ci* 'small, little', Wambule <-si ~ -ci> 'small object' in e.g. *ɓisi* 'eye' and *pumci* 'knee', Sunwar <-tsi> in e.g. *miiktsi* 'eye' and *pooktsi* 'knee', Dumi <-si> in e.g. *khoʔsi* 'cotton', Khaling <-cu> in e.g. *tamcu* 'knee', Kulung <-si> and <-c^{h}i> in e.g. *muksi* 'eye, sepal of a flower' and *tumc*^{h}*i* 'knee' and Āṭhpahariyā <ci-> in e.g. *cipa* 'some, a little'.

hwarsi$_{a}$ ~ *warsi*$_{m}$	'rain, shower'
kaksi$_{am}$	'earth, soil, mud'
misi$_{am}$	'eye'
nɛksi$_{m}$	'elbow'
yaksi$_{am}$	'salt'

3.1.7 *The suffixes 'day'*

MORPHEME	<-so>$_{am}$
GLOSS	day

MORPHEME	<-ni>$_{am}$
GLOSS	day

The Jero suffix <-so>$_{am}$ 'day' is cognate of the Wambule suffix <-so> 'day' in e.g. *saiso* 'yesterday'. The Jero suffix <-ni>$_{am}$ 'day' is cognate of the Wambule suffix <-ḍi> 'day' in e.g. *saḍi* 'two days ago' and Khaling <-ne> in *aathaasne* 'day before yesterday' and *'samne* 'three days later'. The suffix <-ni>$_{am}$ is a reflex of Proto-Tibeto-Burman **nəy* 'sun, day'.

nunusso$_{a}$	'three days from now'
nusso$_{a}$ ~ *nuso*$_{m}$	'day after tomorrow'
sa:satni$_{a}$	'two days ago'
satni$_{a}$	'yesterday'

saʔni$_{m}$	'two days ago'
saiso$_{m}$	'yesterday'

3.1.8 *The suffix 'bird'*

MORPHEME	<-mu>$_{am}$
GLOSS	bird

The suffix <-mu>$_{am}$ 'bird' is cognate of Proto-Tibeto-Burman **bya* 'bee, bird' or **wa* 'bird, feather', Wambule <-bo> 'bird' in e.g. *cwag-bo* 'bird' and *gagbo* 'crow', Bahing <-ba> in *chikba* 'bird', Sunwar <-bi> in *'tsiikbi* 'bird', Dumi *phu* 'chicken' or *pawœm* 'chicken' and the formative <-pu> in e.g. *silpu* 'bird', Khaling <-pu> in *salpu* 'bird' or <-phö> in *'gaakphö* 'crow', Kulung <-wa> in e.g. *k*^{h}*elwa* 'kind of bird', the Chamling 'bird noun class marker' <-wa> in e.g. *khlawa* 'a species of bird', Yamphu <-a ~ -wa> in e.g. *soŋa* or *soŋwa* 'bird' and *araʔwa* 'crow, raven', Āṭhpahariyā <wa-> in e.g. *kakwa* or *kaʔwa* 'crow', and Limbu *pu* 'bird' and <-wa> in e.g. *ka:kwa* 'crow'.

cipmu$_{a}$ ~ *cikmu*$_{m}$	'bird'
cεũmu$_{a}$ ~ *cεʔmu*$_{m}$	'chick'
gagmu$_{m}$	'crow'

3.1.9 *The suffix 'flesh, meat'*

MORPHEME	<-su>$_{am}$
GLOSS	flesh

The suffix <-su>$_{am}$ 'flesh, meat' is related to the Wambule suffix <-so> 'flesh, meat' in e.g. *gyapso* 'barking deer' and *gumso* 'tooth'. This Jero suffix is found in many animal names and is morphosemantically related to nouns meaning 'flesh' or 'meat', such as Proto-Tibeto-Burman **sya-n*, Proto-Kiranti **sya*, Jero *su*, Wambule *so*, Bahing *syé*, Sunwar *she*, Dumi *su*, Khaling *sö*, Kulung *sa*, Yamphu *sa*, Āṭhpahariyā *sa* and Limbu *sa*.

gεpsu$_{m}$	'barking deer'
gumsu$_{am}$	'tooth'

gupsu$_{am}$	'tiger'
mesu$_{am}$	'buffalo'

3.1.10 *The masculine suffixes*

MORPHEME	<-pa>$_{am}$
GLOSS	masculine

MORPHEME	<-pu>$_{am}$
GLOSS	masculine

MORPHEME	<-ʔu>$_{am}$
GLOSS	masculine

The masculine suffixes <-pa>$_{am}$ ~ <-pu>$_{am}$ ~ <-ʔu>$_{am}$ are cognate of the Proto-Tibeto-Burman masculine suffix *<-pa> (Benedict 1972) and the noun *$p^{w}a$ 'man, father, husband, person', which have given, for instance, Proto-Kiranti **pa* 'father', the Wambule masculine marker <-pa ~ -po ~ -p ~ -wa> in e.g. *papa* ~ *pap* 'father' and *kawa* 'friend', Bahing <-pa ~ -po ~ -wa> in *ápa* 'my father', *ípo* 'thy father' and *táwa* 'boy', Hayu <-pɷ ~ -wo> in *uxpɷ* 'father' and *taˑwo* 'son', Dumi *papa* or *pu* 'father', Khaling *'päp* 'father', Yamphu <-pa ~ -p-> 'male person' and Āṭhpahariyā <-ba ~ -pa>.

papa$_{am}$	'father'
hilpu$_{a}$	'one's own child's father-in-law'
hupu$_{am}$	'grandfather'
kaʔu$_{am}$	'friend'
teʔu$_{am}$	'son, boy'

3.1.11 *The feminine suffixes*

MORPHEME	<-ma>$_{am}$
GLOSS	feminine

MORPHEME	<-mu>$_{am}$
GLOSS	feminine

MORPHEME	<-me>$_{am}$
GLOSS	feminine

The feminine suffixes <-ma>$_{am}$ ~ <-mu>$_{am}$ ~ <-me>$_{am}$ can be traced back to Proto-Tibeto-Burman **ma-n* 'mother, feminine suffix', which has given, for instance, Proto-Kiranti **ma* 'mother', Wambule feminine <-ma ~ -mo ~ -me ~ -m ~ -be> in e.g. *mama* ~ *mam* 'mother' and *cacwame* 'granddaughter', Bahing <-ma ~ -mi ~ -mo> in e.g. *áma* or *ámó* 'my mother', *ímo* 'thy mother' and *támi* 'girl', Hayu <-mi ~ -mu> in e.g. *ta'mi* 'daughter' and *umu* 'mother', Dumi *mama* or *mu* 'mother', Khaling *'mäm* 'mother', Yamphu <-ma ~ -m-> 'female person' and Āṭhpahariyā <-ma> in e.g. *tuma* 'grandmother'.

cacuŋma$_{a}$ ~ *cacume*$_{m}$	'granddaughter'
mama$_{am}$	'mother'
hilmu$_{a}$	'one's own child's mother-in-law'
humu$_{am}$	'grandmother'
saŋmu$_{am}$	'dog'
salme$_{m}$	'young woman'
sɛrme$_{am}$	'mother-in-law'

3.2 *Number markers*

MORPHEME	*nimpha*$_{am}$ ~ *nim*$_{m}$
GLOSS	DU

MORPHEME	*ticu*$_{am}$ ~ *tit*$_{am}$
GLOSS	PL

The Jero number markers are morphologically unbound forms which are syntactically restricted in the sense that they cannot be used on their own as a sentence. The number markers always appear after the head, which is generally a noun or nominal, and they precede grammatical role marking elements such as case markers and postpositions. The lexeme to which the number markers are attached is usually the abbreviated morph of morphemes which permit an alternation between full and abbreviated forms. A formal distinction is made between the dual number marker *nimpha*$_{am}$ ~ *nim*$_{m}$ and the plural number marker *ticu*$_{am}$ ~ *tit*$_{am}$.

The basic meaning expressed by the nominal number markers relates to the pluriformity of referents. The dual marker marks exactly two referents and is semantically equivalent to English *a couple of* or *a pair of.* The plural marker stresses three or more referents. The nominal number markers are absent in the case of singular referents.

1_a	*In*	*nimpha=ku*	*ai*	*kam*	*haŋ*	*tan-ci-m?*
	you	DU=SRC	this	*work*	why	stop-d-AFF

Why did you stop [doing] this work?

2_a	*Uŋ*	*ticu*	*lɔ-ca-me?*
	I/we	PL	go-PUR-RES

[Somewhere] we^{p} should go [to]?

Unlike English, in which number marking involves a binary opposition between a zero morpheme for singular referents and the morpheme <-s> for more than one referent, nominal number marking in Jero is best analysed as the expression of an intended meaning. For instance, the personal pronoun *uŋgu*$_{am}$ ~ *uŋ*$_{am}$ 'I, we' without number markers can have either singular, dual or plural reference. The number markers serve to specify the exact number of referents.

uŋgu$_{am}$	'I, we'
uŋ nimpha$_{am}$	'we^{d}'
uŋ ticu$_{am}$	'we^{p}'

The pluriformity of referents can also be indicated by cross reference with verbs. However, it should be noted that although finite verbs may indicate the number of referents, cross reference cannot always be used as a criterion to establish the number of referents. In the case of non-human entities, for instance, Jero verbal morphology generally marks singular number for arguments with plural reference, e.g. (90).

An additional part of the meaning expressed by the number markers involves the concept of manifoldness. Manifoldness indicates various types or varieties of the referent denoted. For instance, the plural form *hepa ticu*$_{\text{am}}$ (cooked.grain PL) refers to three or more varieties of cooked grain, such as rice, maize and barley.

3.3 *Case markers*

Case markers constitute a closed class of bound morphemes which are used to distinguish different grammatical roles from one another. The use of grammatical role markers with nouns and nominals is also best analysed in terms of the expression of an intended meaning. The intention on the part of the speaker may be to clearly distinguish the core arguments of the verb in those situations in which verbal morphology offers no clues as to 'who does what to whom'.

Case markers can not only be identified as phrasal suffixes in relation to nominal lexemes, but they can also be associated with adverbs and verbs, at least from a historical point of view. For instance, the locative marker can be identified in the locative adverbs *alu*$_{\text{am}}$ 'here' and *thalu*$_{\text{am}}$ 'where, somewhere'. Case markers are analysed as lexical suffixes in adverbs and gerunds.

The arguments of a verb that do not take grammatical role marking morphemes are analysed as unmarked forms. Grammatical roles which commonly appear in the unmarked form are the subject of intransitive and middle verbs, the patient of transitive verbs and the goal. However, grammatical subjects are occasionally marked with the source marker, patients can be marked with the patient postposition, and agents also appear in the unmarked form.

The nominal role marking system in Jero gives evidence for what some linguists would call 'intra-clausal ergativity', which is a term used to describe a formal parallel between subjects and patients. In (3), the subject *didi-bʌini* 'sisters' of the intransitive verb *bakcap*$_{\text{a}}$ ~ *bakcam*$_{\text{m}}$ vi-2 <bak- ~ ba:-> 'to be, sit' appears in the unmarked form, and the patient *kaksi* of the transitive verb *phuicap*$_{\text{a}}$ ~ *phuit-*$_{\text{m}}$ vt-2f <phuyt- ~ phuy-> 'to dig, root' in (6) also appears in this form.

3$_{\text{a}}$	*Im*	*didi-bʌini*	*ba-m-me?*
	your^{s}	*elder.sister-younger.sister*	be/sit-23/ns-AFF

Do you^{s} have sisters?

The nominal constituents *im pacha* 'your^{s} clan' and *am pacha* 'my clan' in example (4) also appear in the unmarked form. These nominals function as the subject of the unexpressed copula of identification *nɔcap*$_{a}$ ~ *nɔcam*$_{m}$ vi-1a-i <nɔ-> 'to be'.

4_{a}	a.	*Im*	*pacha*	*hai*	*dɔt?*
		your^{s}	*clan*	what	thing
	b.	*Am*	*pacha*	*Topile*	*Jero.*
		my	*clan*	Topile	Jero

a. What is your^{s} clan?

b. I am a Topile Jero.

This example illustrates that nominal predicates need not always be accompanied by copula verbs in Jero. The presence of an overt linking device between nominals is exemplified in (89) and (101) below.

3.3.1 *The source marker*

MORPHEME	<=ku>$_{a}$ ~ <=khu>$_{m}$
GLOSS	SRC

The source marker <=ku>$_{a}$ ~ <=khu>$_{m}$ marks the source of an action. This marker has the regular allomorphs *=ku*$_{a}$ ~ *=khu*$_{m}$ ~ *=k*$_{am}$. The source marker is often used in relation to instrumental and agent arguments.

5_{m}	*Lʌura=khu*	*tup-ca-m.*
	stick=SRC	beat-PUR-RES

[Something] to hit with a stick.

6_{m}	*Mɔkɔm=khu*	*kaksi*	*phuit-i-Ø-m.*
	chicken=SRC	earth	root-3npA-23s-AFF

The chicken rooted in the soil.

7_{a}	*Uŋgu=ku*	*ai*	*kam*	*pa-u-mai*	*ba:-Ø-m.*
	I/we=SRC	this	*work*	do-1s-FCT	be/sit-23s-AFF

I have done this work.

8_a *Uŋ* *ticu=ku* *saŋmu* *lai* *tum-ki-Ø-m.*
I/we PL=SRC dog PAT beat-1piAS-23s-AFF
We^{pi} punched the dog.

In Āmboṭe Jero, the source suffix is also used with the locative case suffix to mark the ablative sense of a starting point, conveying the sense of ‘from’, e.g. (19) and in the following example:

9_a *Inne* *husulu* *im* *gaũ=na=ku* *al*
you when your^s *village*=LOC=SRC here
ya-n-Ø-ne?
come.down-2-23s-AFF
When did you^s come (down) here from your^s village?

The source marker has the status of lexical suffix in perfect gerunds, the morphology of which is dealt with in Section 6.1 (p. 195).

3.3.2 *The locative marker*

MORPHEME <=na>$_a$ ~ <=no>$_m$
GLOSS LOC

The locative case marker <=na>$_a$ ~ <=no>$_m$ indicates the place or time of the event. This suffix has the regular allomorphs =*na*$_a$ ~ =*no*$_m$ ~ =*n*$_{am}$ ~ =*ma*$_a$. The Āmboṭe suffix <=na>$_a$ is apparently realised as =*ma*$_a$ after words ending in /m/, but the realisation =*ma*$_a$ can also be a loan from the Nepali postposition *mā*. The locative marker <=na>$_a$ ~ <=no>$_m$ has only been found in relation to unbound lexemes.

10_m *Uŋ* *kul=no* *ba-ŋ-ma.*
I/we house=LOC be/sit-1s-AFF
I will be home.

11_a *Ulu=s* *jhola=n* *ba:-Ø-m.*
there=exactly *bag*=LOC be/sit-23s-AFF
It is exactly there in the bag.

12_a *Im* *kul=na* *hukɔl* *ba-m-me?*
your^{s} house=LOC how.much be/sit-23/ns-AFF
How many [deities] are there in your^{s} house?

There is also another locative morpheme in Jero, viz. the marker <-lu>$_{am}$. This lexical suffix has the regular allomorphs *-lu*$_{am}$ ~ *-l*$_{am}$ and forms part of words with adverbial functions, such as the adverb *alu* 'here' and the present gerund *pacalu* 'while doing'. These adverbial forms are discussed in Sections 3.8.2 (p. 109) and 6.2 (p. 199).

3.3.3 *The comitative marker*

MORPHEME	<=na>$_{a}$ ~ <=no>$_{m}$
GLOSS	COM

The comitative marker <=na>$_{a}$ ~ <=no>$_{m}$ is homophonous with the locative case marker. The comitative marker has the regular allomorphs *=na*$_{a}$ ~ *=no*$_{m}$ ~ *=n*$_{am}$. The comitative marker serves as a coordinator of arguments and as the comitative case marker.

Two or more nominal phrases can be coordinated without any overt marker of linking, e.g. *uŋgu inne*$_{a}$ 'I and you', with the comitative marker on the first coordinated argument, e.g. (13) and (14), or with the comitative case marker attached to both coordinated arguments, e.g. (15). A single comitative marker conveys the meaning 'and', whereas the comitative marker on two coordinated arguments expresses the meaning 'both ... and'. Note that the finite verbs in (13) and (14) agree with the sum of the person and number of all coordinated arguments.

13_a *Uŋgu=na* *inne* *bla-ŋ-ci-m.*
I/we=COM you come-dS-d-AFF
I and you [= we^{di}] will go.

14_a *Uŋgu=na* *aŋgu* *bla-ŋ-cu-m.*
I/we=COM he/they come-dS-1deAS-AFF
I and he [= we^{de}] will go.

15_a	*Uŋgu=na*	*inne=na.*
	I/we=COM	you=COM

Both you and I.

The second function of the comitative marker is to mark the grammatical role of the comitative, conveying the meaning 'with, in the company of'. The comitative argument is the entity which assists in the action. The sense of 'in the company of' is also marked by means of a genitive complement plus the postposition *kwa*$_a$, which is discussed in Section 3.4.6 below (p. 97).

16_a	*Uŋgu=n*	*lɔ-cu?*
	I/we=COM	go-ACP

Will [you, he, they] go with me/us?

A comitative argument can often be distinguished from a coordinated one by the verbal agreement, since the finite verb does not agree with the argument in the comitative role, as in the following example.

17_a	a.	*Inne*	*im*	*kul=na*	*khamma*	*ba-n-Ø-ne*
		you	your^s	house=LOC	alone	be/sit-2-23s-AFF
		ki?				
		or				
	b.	*Uŋ*	*kaʔu=n*	*ba-ŋ-ma.*		
		I/we	friend=COM	be/sit-1s-AFF		

a. Do you^s live on your^s own?
b. I live with a friend.

3.3.4 *The ablative marker*

MORPHEME	<=ŋo>$_m$
GLOSS	ABL

The Mohanṭāre ablative case marker <=ŋo>$_m$ is used to mark the starting point of an action. This marker has the regular allomorphs =*ŋo*$_m$ ~ =*ŋ*$_m$. The ablative case marker functions as a phrasal suffix in relation to adverbs of place, e.g. *thalu=ŋ*$_m$ (where=ABL) 'from where' in (18). In Āmboṭe, by contrast, a starting point seems to be generally marked by means of the source marker or a sequence that consists of the locative and source case suffixes, e.g. (19).

18_{m} *Inne* *thalu=ŋ* *bla-n-Ø-nei?*
you where=ABL come-2-23s-FCT

From where did you^{s} come?

19_{a} *Ai* *dui* *jʌna* *bidesi* *thalu=na=k*
this *two* *person* *foreigner* where=LOC=SRC
bla-ŋ-ci-m?
come-dS-d-AFF

From where did these two foreigners come?

The ablative suffix seems to be related to the final velar nasal consonant plus vowel of the verbal morpheme <-dɔŋo>$_{a}$ ~ <-dɔŋ>$_{am}$ of the conditional gerund. This gerund is discussed in Section 6.3 (p. 201).

3.3.5 *The genitive marker*

MORPHEME	<=ŋaŋ>$_{a}$ ~ <=ŋ>$_{am}$
GLOSS	GEN

The genitive case marker <=ŋaŋ>$_{a}$ ~ <=ŋ>$_{am}$ indicates possession and related semantic functions such as membership within a set or a part-whole relation. The Āmboṭe marker has the allomorphs =*ŋaŋ*$_{a}$ ~ =*ŋ*$_{a}$.

20_{a} *Papa=ŋ* *kul.*
father=GEN house

Father's house.

21_{a} *Tin* *jʌna* *didi=ŋ* *biha*
three *person* *elder.sister*=GEN *marriage*
dum-Ø-me.
become-23s-AFF

Three elder sisters are married.

3.3.6 *The similaritive marker*

MORPHEME	<=se>$_{am}$
GLOSS	SIM

The suffix <=se>$_{am}$ marks similarity and expresses the meaning of sameness, likeness or equality. This suffix has the regular allomorphs =*se*$_{am}$ ~ =*sε*$_{m}$ ~ =*s*$_{am}$. In Āmboṭe, the similaritive suffix forms part of a case sequence with the locative marker.

22$_a$ *Hwarsi* *ya-Ø-m=na=se=p*
rain come.down-23s-AFF=LOC=SIM=RES

ba:-Ø-m.
be/sit-23s-AFF

It looks like it will rain.

In Mohanṭāre, by contrast, the similaritive suffix can be directly attached to a preceding noun, e.g. (98) below. The similaritive case suffix is lexicalised as the marker -*se*$_{am}$ ~ -*sε*$_{m}$ ~ -*sa*$_{a}$ ~ -*s*$_{am}$ in demonstrative adverbs of direction and manner, which are discussed in Sections 3.8.2 (p. 109) and 3.8.3 (p. 111) below.

3.4 *Postpositions*

Postpositions constitute a class of syntactically bound morphemes in phrase-final position which are also used to distinguish grammatical roles from one another. Postpositions are syntactically restricted forms that are not subject to allomorphy which is dependent on the phonological form of the preceding word.

3.4.1 *The directive postposition*

MORPHEME	<lam>$_a$
GLOSS	via

The directive postposition <lam>$_a$ indicates the direction of the verbal event, conveying the sense of 'towards', 'via' or 'though'.

23_{a} *Kul cheu lam.*
house *side* via

Towards the side of the house.

24_{a} *Inne Kirãt bat lam rɛk-si phat-ni-Ø-m?*
you *Kiranti* *thing* via write-INF can-2-23s-AFF

Can you[s] write in [a] Kiranti language?

25_{a} *A-nɔ-Ø, thɔ-m-me lam a*
NEG-be-23s hear-23/ns-AFF via ?or

ne-m-me lam bhʌne.
say-23/ns-AFF via *as.for*

No, [the people learn sacred texts] through what they[p] hear and tell.

The postposition <lam>$_{a}$ seems to be related to the noun *lam* 'road, path, route, way' and to the lexical suffix <-la>$_{am}$. The latter suffix, which has the regular allomorphs *-la*$_{am}$ ~ *-l*$_{am}$, can be found in postpositions of location such as *yɔmala*$_{m}$ ~ *yɔmal*$_{am}$ 'below, towards the lower side', which are discussed in Section 3.4.4 (p. 95), and in adverbs of direction such as *asal*$_{a}$ 'here', which are dealt with in Section 3.8.2. (p. 109).

3.4.2 *The postpositions 'in front of, before'*

MORPHEME	*lapphu*$_{am}$ ~ *lapthɔl*$_{a}$
GLOSS	front/before

The postpositions and adverbs *lapphu*$_{am}$ and *lapthɔl*$_{a}$ express the spatial sense of 'in front', but more often the temporal sense of 'before, previously, formerly, firstly'. The form *lapthɔl*$_{a}$ seems to incorporate the abbreviated allomorph *-l*$_{am}$ of the locative marker <-lu>$_{am}$.

26_{a} *Kul lapthɔl.*
house front/before

In front of the house.

27_{a}	*Uŋgu*	*tin*	*bʌrsa*	*lapphu*	*al*
	I/we	*three*	*year*	front/before	here

ya-ŋ-ma.
come.down-1s-AFF

I came (down) here three years ago.

3.4.3 *The postposition 'behind, after'*

MORPHEME	*nʌuthal*$_{a}$ ~ *nʌuṭhal*$_{m}$
GLOSS	behind/after

The postposition and adverb *nʌuthal*$_{a}$ ~ *nʌuṭhal*$_{m}$ 'behind, after' expresses the spatial sense of 'behind, after, at the end' and the temporal sense of 'after, later'. The form *nʌuthal*$_{a}$ ~ *nʌuṭhal*$_{m}$ seems to incorporate the abbreviated allomorph *-l*$_{am}$ of the locative marker <-lu>$_{am}$. There is also another adverb, viz. *nʌuṭhaŋ*$_{am}$ 'behind, after; later', which seems to incorporate the abbreviated morph of the ablative marker <=ŋo>$_{m}$.

28_{a}	*Kul*	*nʌuthal.*
	house	behind/after

Behind the house.

29_{a}	*Pʌḍ-ʌi*	*la-sa-k*	*nʌuṭhaŋ*
	read/study-LN	become-MAN-PFG	behind/after

hai *pa-n-Ø-ne?*
what do-2-23s-AFF

What will you^{s} do after you^{s} have finished your studies?

3.4.4 *Postpositions of location*

Jero has a small series of postpositions and adverbs which indicate the side towards which the location given by the context is situated. The forms I recorded refer to a location further away from the speaker and hearer, and additionally specify that this location is situated at a horizontal, higher or lower level relative to the point of orientation.

nɔmala$_{\text{m}}$ ~ *nɔmal*$_{\text{a}}$	'beside, towards the horizontal side'
tɔmala$_{\text{m}}$ ~ *tɔmal*$_{\text{am}}$	'above, towards the upper side'
yɔmala$_{\text{m}}$ ~ *yɔmal*$_{\text{am}}$	'below, towards the lower side'

The postpositions of location incorporate the lexicalised forms *-la*$_{\text{am}}$ ~ *-l*$_{\text{am}}$ of the directive marker. I have not recorded any forms **amala* ~ **amal*$_{\text{a}}$ 'hither' and **umala* ~ **umal*$_{\text{a}}$ 'thither', referring to locations near the speaker or hearer. See also Section 3.8 (p. 108).

30$_{\text{a}}$ *Phutur tɔmal.*
head above

a. Above the head.
b. The head is above.

3.4.5 *The postposition 'beside'*

MORPHEME	*pum*$_{\text{a}}$
GLOSS	beside

The postposition *pum*$_{\text{a}}$ 'beside' marks a location next to something or somewhere. As in Wambule, this morpheme seems to be a grammaticalised instance of the noun *pum* 'base, foundation, bottom'. See also Section 3.4.11 (p. 99).

31$_{\text{a}}$ *Pum=na mɛʔlum.*
bottom=LOC tail

At the bottom [is] the tail.

32$_{\text{a}}$ *Ui pum=ma.*
there beside=LOC

[It is] next to there.

3.4.6 *The postpositions 'in the company of' and 'together'*

MORPHEME	*kwa*$_a$
GLOSS	in.the.company.of

MORPHEME	*kwaya*$_a$
GLOSS	together

The postposition *kwa*$_a$ and the formally related and possibly derived adverb and postposition *kwaya*$_a$ convey the sociative meaning of 'in the company of'. The postpositions are attached to a genitive form.

33$_a$ a. *Munu=ŋ* *kwa* *ba-n-Ø-ne?*
who=GEN in.the.company.of be/sit-2-23s-AFF

b. *Am* *didi=ŋ* *kwa*
my *elder.sister*=GEN in.the.company.of

ba-ŋ-ma.
be/sit-1s-AFF

a. With whom do you[s] live?
b. I live with my elder sister.

34$_a$ *Munu=ŋ* *kwaya?*
who=GEN together

With whom [are your sisters married]?

3.4.7 *The postposition 'without'*

MORPHEME	*sɔŋku*$_a$
GLOSS	without

The postposition *sɔŋku*$_a$ marks a non-comitative, non-accompanying and non-instrumental argument of the verb. This postposition seems to be a combination of an unknown element *sɔŋ-* plus the source marker *-ku*$_a$ or the marker *kwa*$_a$ 'in the company of'. No examples.

3.4.8 *The postposition 'on top of'*

MORPHEME	*toʔla*$_a$
GLOSS	top

The postposition *toʔla*$_a$ 'above, on top of' marks a place on top of something or to a higher point of something.

35$_a$ *Kul* *toʔla.*
house top
On top of the house.

3.4.9 *The postposition 'aside from'*

MORPHEME	*bahek*$_a$
GLOSS	aside from

The postposition *bahek*$_a$ 'aside from, except for, not considering' is a loan from Nepali *bāhek*, which marks an excluded argument.

36$_a$ *Uŋgu* *bahek.*
I/we *aside.from*
Except me.

3.4.10 *The postposition 'than'*

MORPHEME	*bhʌnda*$_{am}$
GLOSS	than

The postposition *bhʌnda*$_{am}$ 'than' is a loan from the Nepali word *bhandā*, which literally translates as 'while saying' or 'in the saying'. Examples (37) and (38) show that this loan postposition is used in the expression of a comparison between two or more entities, in which the word or phrase preceding *bhʌnda* is conceptualised as the point of reference for the comparison.

37a *Ai* *mucu* *bhʌnda*
this person *than*

uŋ *cimtɛp* *ba-ŋ-ma.*
I/we small be/sit-1s-AFF

I am smaller than this person.

38m *Ai* *mucu* *sʌpp-ʌi* *bhʌnda*
this person *all.*EMPH-EMPH *than*

yɔkko *ba:-Ø-m.*
small be/sit-23s-AFF

This person is smallest of all.

3.4.11 *The postposition 'next to'*

MORPHEME	*cheu*am
GLOSS	side

Reference to a location next to something else can not only be made by means of the indigenous postposition *puma* 'beside', which is introduced in Section 3.4.5 above (p. 96), but also by means of the postposition *cheuam* 'side, next to' to which locative and directive markers are added. Jero *cheuam* is a loan from Nepali *cheu*, which as a noun means 'side, edge, end' and as a postposition conveys the sense of 'next to, near'.

39a *Kul* *cheu=na.*
house *side*=LOC

Next to the house.

40a *Kul* *cheu* *lam.*
house *side* via

Towards the side of the house.

3.4.12 *The patient postposition*

MORPHEME	*lai*$_{\text{am}}$
GLOSS	PAT

The postposition *lai*$_{\text{am}}$ is a loan from Nepali *lāī*. In the case of living beings, and less often with inanimate entities, this postposition marks the grammatical patient of a verbal event. The grammatical patient is a recipient participant in (41) and (42) but a patient participant in (43).

41$_{\text{m}}$	*Kwal*	*muṭhi*	*seri*	*gɔk-kha-Ø*
	one	*handful*	husked.grain	give-IMP-SAS

	nɔi	*phɔi-ce*	*lai!*
	that.hrz	ask.for-ACG	PAT

Give^{s} one handful of husked grain to that beggar!

42$_{\text{a}}$	*Aŋ*	*tit*	*lai*	*hep*	*phɛs-si*
	he/they	PL	PAT	cooked.grain	serve.out-INF

pʌrchʌ?
is.necessary

Do you [generally] have to serve out cooked grain to them [i.e. the spirits of the dead ancestors]?

43$_{\text{a}}$	*Uŋgu*	*lai*	*Nepal=na*	*tɛr-su*	*pa-n-Ø-ne?*
	I/we	PAT	*Nepal*=LOC	receive-MAN	do-2-23s-AFF

Will you^{s} meet me in Nepal?

3.4.13 *The postposition 'as far as'*

MORPHEME	*sʌmba*$_{\text{m}}$ ~ *sʌmma*$_{\text{a}}$
GLOSS	as far as

The postposition *sʌmba*$_{\text{m}}$ ~ *sʌmma*$_{\text{a}}$ 'as far as, up to, until' is a loan from Nepali *samma*. This postposition marks a place until which something moves or a moment until which the action is carried out.

44_{m}

Al	*sʌmba.*
here	*as.far.as*

Until here.

45_{m}

a.

Inne	*lai*	*tʌya*	*dui*	*bʌrsa*	*lagchʌ*	*hɔla.*
you	PAT	still	*two*	*year*	*will.happen*	*may.be*

b.

Tʌya	*lagchʌ*	*hɔla,*	*dui*	*bʌrsa*	*sʌmmʌ.*
still	*will.happen*	*may.be*	*two*	*year*	*as.far.as*

a. You will probably still need two years.
b. I will probably still need as much as two years.

3.5 *Discourse markers*

Discourse markers are morphemes which mark relationships between elements of different sentences. The Jero discourse markers are generally attached to the final constituent of a phrase, following nominal number markers and grammatical role marking case suffixes and postpositions.

3.5.1 *The marker 'also, too, even'*

MORPHEME	<=ya>$_{am}$
GLOSS	also

The phrasal suffix <=ya>$_{am}$ 'also, too, even' indicates inclusivity or additivity with another element of the discourse. This suffix has the regular allomorphs =*ya*$_{am}$ ~ =*i*$_{am}$.

46_{m}

Uŋgu=i	*lɔ-ŋ-ma.*
I/we=also	go-1S-AFF

I too will go.

In a negative context, the phrasal suffix =*ya*$_{am}$ ~ =*i*$_{am}$ 'also, too, even' is also used in relation to indefinite and interrogative words. Here the indefinite and interrogative words correspond to English *nobody*, *nothing*, *never*, *nowhere*, etc. The inclusive suffix serves to strengthen the negation, conveying the emphatic sense of 'even, at all'.

47_a *Hai (=ya)* *dum-Ø-mei* *a-ba-Ø.*
what (=also) become-23s-FCT NEG-be/sit-23s
Nothing (at all) is the matter.

3.5.2 *The marker 'exactly, precisely'*

MORPHEME	<=se>$_{am}$
GLOSS	exactly

The phrasal suffix <=se>$_{am}$ conveys the emphatic sense of 'exactly, precisely'. This suffix, which has the regular allomorphs =*se*$_{am}$ ~ =*s*$_{am}$, is usually translated into Nepali by means of the particle *nai.*

48_a *Jati=s* *ba:-Ø-m.*
good=exactly be/sit-23s-AFF
It is precisely good.

49_a *Inne* *inne=s* *tum-ni-Ø-m.*
you you=exactly beat.self-2-23s-AFF
You^{s} beat yourself.

50_a *Uŋ* *kul=na=se* *ba-ŋ-mai* *thiyo.*
I/we house=LOC=exactly be/sit-1s-FCT *was*
I was right at home.

51_a *Gaũ=na=s* *ba-m-me.*
village=LOC=exactly be/sit-23/ns-AFF
They^{p} live right in the village.

3.5.3 *The marker 'on the contrary'*

MORPHEME	*ke*$_a$
GLOSS	contrary

The particle *ke*$_a$ 'on the contrary' marks that the action expressed by the verb is contrary to what is expected in a given situation. This marker is translated into Nepali by means of the particle *po.*

52_{a} *Use=p* *pa-si* *ke* *mil-ʌi*
like.that=RES do-INF contrary *agree*-LN
la-Ø-m *rʌi.*
become-23s-AFF NEW

In contrast to what was expected, it turned out to work in that way.

The marker *rʌi* indicates that the speaker has just come to the knowledge of an event, implying an event which is contrary to expectation, sudden or even surprising.

53_{a} *Keṭi* *ke* *thɔ-m-me,* *tʌra* *aŋgu*
girl contrary hear-23/ns-AFF *but* he/they
pʌrdʌina, *aŋ* *tit* *lai.*
is.not.necessary he/they PL PAT

The girls listen, however, but they do not need [to learn sacred texts of the oral tradition].

3.5.4 *The marker 'only'*

MORPHEME	*naʔa*$_{am}$ ~ *naʔ*$_{a}$
GLOSS	only

A constituent that is modified by the particle *naʔa*$_{am}$ ~ *naʔ*$_{a}$ 'only' marks one alternative to the exclusion of others.

54_{a} *Uŋgu* *naʔa* *ka:ku* *tu:-ʔ-ma.*
I/we only water drink-1s-AFF

Only I will drink water.

55_{m} *Nɔi* *naʔa* *a-nɔ-Ø,* *sʌpp-ʌi*
that.hrz only NEG-be-23s *all*.EMPH-EMPH
phik-kha-Ø!
bring.hrz-IMP-sAS

Bring[s] everything, not only that [which is at the same altitude as the speaker]!

3.5.5 *The theme marker*

MORPHEME	*da*$_a$ ~ *ḍa*$_m$
GLOSS	THM

The theme marker *da*$_a$ ~ *ḍa*$_m$ is a loan from the Nepali particle *ta*. This marker is used to provide a background or point of departure for the following piece of information. The theme particle often indicates a slight adversative or contrasting nuance.

56$_a$

Uŋgu=k	*da*	*inne*	*lai*	*tɛr-phu*
I/we=SRC	THM	you	PAT	receive-SUP

bla-ŋ-mai	*ba:-Ø-me.*
come-1s-FCT	be/sit-23s-AFF

I have come to meet you.

3.5.6 *The contrastive topic marker*

MORPHEME	*cai*
GLOSS	CNT

The phrase-final particle *cai* is a loan from the Nepali contrastive topic particle *cāhī̃*. The contrastive morpheme is used to individualise or single out the entity or event referred to by the modified constituent from several other possibilities.

57$_a$

Uŋgu	*lɔ-ku-dɔŋ*	*inne*	*cai*	*alu*
I/we	go-1peAS-CND	you	CNT	here

bak-si	*pʌrcha*
be/sit-INF	*is.necessary*

As for you, you will have to stay here if we^{pe} go.

3.6 *Personal pronouns*

Personal pronouns are unbound nominal morphemes which are used to refer to the speaker, the addressee and another person or human-like entity (deities, spirits of the dead ancestors), whose referents are presumed to be clear from the context.

uŋgu$_{am}$ ~ *uŋ*$_{am}$	'I, we'
inne$_{am}$ ~ *in*$_{am}$	'you'
aŋgu$_{am}$ ~ *aŋ*$_{am}$	'he, she, they'

The personal pronouns are only distinguished for person, but not for number. Duality or plurality can be marked explicitly by adding nominal number markers to the abbreviated morphs of the pronouns.

uŋ nimpha$_{am}$	'we^{d}'
uŋ ticu$_{am}$	'we^{p}'
in nimpha$_{am}$	'you^{d}'
in ticu$_{am}$	'you^{p}'
aŋ nimpha$_{am}$	'they^{d}'
aŋ ticu$_{am}$	'they^{p}'

The following examples illustrate that the first person pronoun *uŋ* is used to refer to inclusive and exclusive arguments. The pronoun *uŋ* refers to a first plural exclusive subject in (58) but to first a plural inclusive subject in (59).

58$_{a}$	*Uŋ*	*ba:-ku-mai*	*na*	*bla:-Ø-m.*
	I/we	be/sit-1peAS-FCT	previously	come-23s-AFF

He has already come to the place where we^{pe} are sitting.

59$_{a}$	*Uŋ*	*lɔ-ki!*
	I/we	go-1piAS

Let us^{pi} go!

Here are some other examples. In (60) the plural marker is added to the second person pronoun, whereas the number of the subject is unmarked and unknown in (61).

60_a	*In*	*ticu*	*al*	*pi-n-a-ni!*
	you	PL	here	come.hrz-pS-IMP-23p

You[P] come here (across a horizontal plane)!

61_a	*Uŋgu*	*Jero*	*ho.*
	I/we	Jero	*is*

a. I am Jero.
b. We are Jero.

62_a	a.	*Purkha*	*tit*	*thal*	*ba-m-me?*
		ancestor	PL	where	be/sit-23/ns-AFF

Dulo=n *ba-m-me?*
hole=LOC be/sit-23/ns-AFF

b. *Aŋ* *a-ba:-mi.*
he/they NEG-be/sit-23/ns

Culo=n *ba-m-me.*
fireplace=LOC be/sit-23/ns-AFF

a. Where do the [spirits of the dead] ancestors live? Do they[P] live in holes?
b. They[P] do not live [in holes]. They[P] live in the [white ashes inside the] fireplace.

Example (62) illustrates that pronouns need not be overtly expressed if the referents are known from the context or from verbal morphology. The use of pronouns in Jero resembles the situation in Nepali, where pronouns need not be overtly expressed if the referents are known from the context or from verbal morphology, but where the use of personal pronouns does not automatically trigger emphasising or contrastive functions.

3.7 *Possessive pronouns*

Possession can be marked by means of a series of syntactically restricted morphemes which show no morphophonological interaction with the word they precede.

am$_{am}$	'my'
incim$_{am}$	'our^{di}; your^{d}'
ancum$_{am}$	'our^{de}'
ikkim$_{am}$	'our^{pi}'
akkum$_{am}$	'our^{pe}'
im$_{am}$	'your^{s}'
inim$_{am}$	'your^{p}'
aŋam$_{a}$ ~ *aŋ*$_{m}$	'his, her'
ancim$_{am}$	'their^{d}'
anim$_{am}$	'their^{p}'

Jero makes a formal distinction between three numbers, three persons, and forms including and excluding the person addressed. A first person dual inclusive possessor and a second person dual possessor are marked by means of the same pronoun. Possession can also be marked by means of personal pronouns to which the genitive case marker is attached.

63$_{a}$	*Im*	*gumsu*	*hai*	*dum-Ø-me?*
	your^{s}	tooth	what	become-23s-AFF

a. What has become of your^{s} tooth?
b. What is the matter with your^{s} tooth?

64$_{a}$	*Aŋ*	*ticu=ŋ*	*hepa*	*thalu*	*baː-Ø-m?*
	he/they	PL=GEN	cooked.grain	where	be/sit-23s-AFF

Where is their^{p} [portion of] cooked grain?

3.8 *Demonstratives*

The group of demonstratives comprises nominal and adverbial words. The demonstrative system is based on five bound morphemes which indicate a location relative to the point of orientation given by the context.

<a->$_{am}$	'near (near the speaker)'
<u->$_{am}$	'distal (near the hearer)'
<nɔ->$_{am}$	'yonder (at the same elevation)'
<tɔ->$_{am}$	'yonder (up)'
<yɔ->$_{am}$	'yonder (down)'

The morpheme <a->$_{am}$ marks a position relatively near the point of reference or near the speaker. The morpheme <u->$_{am}$ marks a position relatively further away from the point of reference or near the hearer. The bound morphemes <nɔ->$_{am}$, <tɔ->$_{am}$ and <yɔ->$_{am}$ mark locations which are relatively far away from the point of reference or from the speaker and hearer, and also specify that these locations are situated at the same elevation as the point of reference, or either higher or lower than that.

The morphemes <a->$_{am}$ 'near' and <u->$_{am}$ 'distal' do not only refer to the strict spatial location of the event but also mark temporal settings. In addition, these morphemes can also be used anaphorically and derive their interpretation from a previously expressed element in the context. The demonstrative morphemes <nɔ->$_{am}$, <tɔ->$_{am}$ and <yɔ->$_{am}$ can be identified in the series of demonstrative postpositions and adverbs of location discussed in Section 3.4.4 above (p. 95).

3.8.1 *Demonstrative pronouns*

The Jero demonstrative pronouns are fixed combinations of the five demonstrative morphemes presented above plus a kind of nominalising element <-ya>. This nominalising element has the regular allomorphs *-ya*$_{a}$ ~ *-i*$_{am}$.

aya$_{a}$ ~ *ai*$_{am}$	'this (near the speaker)'
uya$_{a}$ ~ *ui*$_{a}$	'that (near the hearer)'
nɔya$_{a}$ ~ *nɔi*$_{am}$	'that (at the same elevation)'

tɔi$_{am}$	'that (up)'
yɔya$_{a}$ ~ *yɔi*$_{am}$	'that (down)'

Independently used demonstrative pronouns function as the head of an argument or as a predicator. Demonstrative pronouns which are used as the head of an argument take all the markers required by syntax. Noun modifying demonstratives precede the nominal head, e.g. (65). The morphosemantics of the periphrastic verb form *pasi pleuma* is discussed in Section 7.4 (p. 210).

65$_{m}$	*Uŋgu*	*ai*	*kam*	*pa-si*	*ple-u-ma.*
	I/we	this	*work*	do-INF	stop-1s-AFF

I will stop doing this work.

66$_{a}$	*Tɔi*	*cipmu.*
	that.up	bird

That bird [which is relatively far away and higher than the point of reference].

Suffixation of the nominalising marker <-cu>$_{am}$ to abbreviated demonstrative pronouns yields comparative forms which mark that the entity referred to by the demonstrative is relatively further away than another distant entity which is located at the same elevation as the point of reference, or either higher or lower than that.

67$_{a}$	*Tɔicu*	*cipmu.*
	that.further.up	bird

That bird [further and higher than another bird flying further and higher than the point of reference].

3.8.2 *Demonstrative adverbs of place and direction*

The adverbs of place consist of the five bound morphemes presented above plus the locative marker <-lu>$_{am}$ or the vertical bound markers <-na>$_{a}$ ~ <-no>$_{m}$ 'at the same elevation', <-ta>$_{a}$ ~ <-to>$_{m}$ 'at a higher elevation' and <-ya>$_{a}$ ~ <-yo>$_{m}$ 'at a lower elevation'.

alu$_{am}$ ~ *al*$_{am}$	'here (near the speaker)'
ulu$_{am}$ ~ *ul*$_{a}$	'there (near the hearer)'
nɔna$_{a}$ ~ *nɔno*$_{m}$ ~ *nɔn*$_{a}$	'there (at the same elevation)'
tɔta$_{a}$ ~ *tɔto*$_{m}$ ~ *tɔt*$_{a}$	'up there'
yɔya$_{a}$ ~ *yɔyo*$_{m}$ ~ *yɔi*$_{am}$	'down there'

The following examples illustrate the use of adverbs of place.

68$_{a}$ a. *Inne* *thal* *ba-n-Ø-ne?*
you where be/sit-2-23s-AFF

b. *Uŋ* *alu=s* *ba-ŋ-ma.* *Uŋ* *al*
you here=exactly be/sit-1s-AFF I here

Kaṭhmanḍu *Cabʌhil=na* *ba-ŋ-ma.*
Kathmandu *Cābahil*=LOC be/sit-1s-AFF

a. Where do you[s] live?

b. I live exactly here. I live in Cābahil in Kathmandu.

69$_{m}$ *Am* *kul* *yɔi* *baː-Ø-m.*
my house down.there be/sit-23s-AFF

My house is down there.

70$_{a}$ *Kul* *al* *jap-cu?*
house here buy-ACP

Will you buy a house here?

The adverbs of direction consist of the five bound demonstrative morphemes to which the lexicalised instances *-sa*$_{a}$ ~ *-sɛ*$_{m}$ and *-l*$_{am}$ of the similaritive and directive markers are added.

asal$_{a}$	'here (towards the speaker)'
usal$_{a}$	'there (towards the hearer)'
nɔsal$_{a}$ ~ *nɔsɛl*$_{m}$	'there (at the same elevation)'
tɔsal$_{a}$ ~ *tɔsɛl*$_{m}$	'up there'
yɔsɛl$_{m}$	'down there'

3.8.3 *Demonstratives of manner*

The demonstratives of manner basically consist of the five demonstrative morphemes to which the similaritive marker <-se>$_{am}$ is added. The following Mohanṭāre forms have been recorded as adverbs:

ase$_{m}$ ~ *as*$_{m}$	'in this way, like this, thus, so'
use$_{m}$ ~ *us*$_{am}$	'in that way, like that, thus, so'
nɔse$_{m}$	'in that way (hrz)'

The basic adverbial forms can be extended by means of suffixation of the reifying morpheme <=me>$_{am}$, which creates nominal constituents.

ase=p$_{a}$ ~ *ase=m*$_{m}$	'(something) like this, thus, so'
use=p$_{a}$ ~ *use=m*$_{m}$	'(something) like that, thus, so'
nɔse=p$_{a}$ ~ *nɔse=m*$_{m}$	'(something) like that (hrz)'
tɔse=p$_{a}$	'(something) like that (up)'
yɔse=p$_{a}$	'(something) like that (down)'

In Mohanṭāre Jero, reified demonstrative forms are used as noun modifiers. In Āmboṭe Jero, by contrast, reified forms can be used as noun modifiers and as verb modifiers.

71$_{m}$

Use=m	*kul.*
in.that.way=RES	house

A house like that (near the hearer).

72$_{a}$

Ase=p	*pa-ha-Ø!*
in.this.way=RES	do-IMP-SAS

Do [it] in this way!

73$_{a}$

Haŋ	*ase=p*	*ḍhilo*	*pa-n-Ø-nei?*
why	in.this.way=RES	*delay*	do-2-23S-FCT

Why are you[s] this late?

3.8.4 *Adverbs of altitude*

The following series of deictic adverbs point to the vertical level of or the vertical motion towards a place indicated by the context.

pɛttu$_{a}$ ~ *pɛtthu*$_{m}$	'horizontally'
gattu$_{a}$ ~ *gatthu*$_{m}$	'up, upwards'
hɛttu$_{a}$ ~ *hɛtthu*$_{m}$	'down, downwards'

3.9 *Indefinite and interrogative words*

Indefinite and interrogative words are unbound forms which include nominals and adverbials. Indefinite and interrogative nominals can be used independently or in noun modifying position.

hai$_{am}$	'what, something'
haŋ$_{a}$ ~ *haiŋa*$_{m}$ ~ *haiŋaŋ*$_{m}$ ~ *haiŋo*$_{m}$ ~ *hayaŋ*$_{m}$ ~ *hayɔŋ*$_{m}$	'why'
hujɔktɔp$_{a}$	'how, what sort of'
hukɔl$_{am}$	'how many, how much'
hus$_{am}$	'how, as'
husulu$_{a}$ ~ *husul*$_{a}$ ~ *husɛl*$_{m}$	'when, ever'
munu$_{am}$ ~ *mun*$_{a}$ ~ *mundo*$_{m}$	'who, somebody'
thalu$_{am}$ ~ *thal*$_{am}$	'where, somewhere'
thamalu$_{a}$ ~ *thamal*$_{am}$	'whereto, whither'

The adverbs *husulu*$_{a}$ ~ *husul*$_{a}$ ~ *husɛl*$_{m}$ 'when, ever' and *thalu*$_{am}$ ~ *thal*$_{am}$ end in the locative marker <-lu>$_{am}$. The adverb *thalu*$_{am}$ can be extended by means of the ablative case suffix to form *thalu=ŋ*$_{m}$ 'from where, from somewhere' in Mohanṭāre Jero, or by means of the locative and source case sequence to form *thalu=na=ku*$_{a}$ ~ *thalu=na=k*$_{a}$ 'from where, from somewhere' in Āmboṭe Jero.

74$_{a}$	*Im*	*bicar=na*	*husul*	*biha*	*po-cu?*
	your^{s}	*opinion*=LOC	when	*marriage*	do-ACP

When do you^{s} think you^{s} will get married?

75_{m}	*Im*	*kul*	*thal*	*ho?*
	your^{s}	house	where	*is*

Where is your^{s} house?

The adverb *thamalu*$_{a}$ ~ *thamal*$_{am}$ 'whither' that I recorded also ends in the locative marker, but comparative evidence from Wambule suggests that the locative ending is actually incorrect. That is to say, the Wambule cognate form ends in the directive marker <-la>$_{am}$ instead.

The nominal form *hujɔktɔp*$_{a}$ consists of the morph *hu-*, which seems to be related to the adverb *hus* 'how, as', plus the attributive verbal adjective *jɔktɔp*$_{a}$ 'characterised by knowing'. This deverbative is derived from the verb *jɔkcam*$_{m}$ vt-(2e) <jɔkt- (~ *jo-)> 'to know (by learning)'.

76_{m}	*Hai*	*pa-ca-m?*
	what	do-PUR-RES

What [thing] to do?

77_{a}	*Hai*	*ja-n-Ø-ne?*
	what	eat-2-23s-AFF

What did you^{s} eat?

78_{m}	*Haiŋo*	*bla-n-Ø-ne?*
	why	come-2-23s-AFF

Why are you^{s} coming?

79_{m}	*Hukɔl*	*ja-n-Ø-ne?*
	how.much	eat-2-23s-AFF

How much did you^{s} eat?

80_{a}	*Hukɔl*	*mucu*	*bla-m-me?*
	how.much	person	come-23/ns-AFF
	Kɔʔl	*mucu*	*bla:-Ø-m.*
	one	person	come-23s-AFF

How many people will come? One person will come.

The sense of 'when' can also be expressed by means of the phrase *hai bɛl?*$_{a}$, in which the word *hai*$_{am}$ 'what' occurs in adnominal modifying position of the loan noun *bɛl*$_{a}$ 'time' (<Nep. *belā*).

81$_{a}$	*Hai*	*bɛl*	*jo-cu?*
	what	*time*	eat-ACP

When will [we, you, he, they] eat?

Adnominal *hai* 'what' in the following sentence conveys the sense of 'what kind of'.

82$_{a}$	a.	*Inne*	*hai*	*kam*	*pa-n-Ø-ne?*
		you	what	*work*	do-2-23s-AFF
	b.	*Uŋ*	*pʌḍ-ʌi*		*la-ŋ-ma.*
		you	*read/study*-LN		become-1s-AFF
	c.	*Hai*	*dɔt*	*bisʌya?*	
		what	thing	*subject*	

a. What kind of work do you^{s} do?
b. I study.
c. What subject?

The nominals *hai*$_{am}$ 'what, something' and *mun*$_{a}$ 'who, somebody' are often used with the noun *dɔt*$_{a}$ 'thing, matter' in what is allegedly a more polite or formal interrogative form.

83$_{a}$	*Mun*	*dɔt*	*pi-Ø-me?*
	who	thing	come.hrz-23s-AFF

Who will come?

84$_{a}$	a.	*Im*	*ni*	*hai*	*dɔt?*
		your^{s}	name	what	thing
	b.	*Ram*	*Kumar*	*Rai.*	
		Rām	*Kumār*	*Rāī*	

a. What is your name?
b. Rām Kumār Rāī.

Jero has many related words for 'why', viz. *haŋ*$_{a}$ ~ *haiŋa*$_{m}$ ~ *haiŋaŋ*$_{m}$ ~ *haiŋo*$_{m}$ ~ *hayaŋ*$_{m}$ ~ *hayɔŋ*$_{m}$. The word for 'because' is *haŋ-bhʌne*$_{a}$, which is a calque of Nepali *kina bhane*.

85$_{a}$

Haŋ	*jo-cu?*
why	eat-ACP

Why will [I, we, you, he, they] eat [this]?

86$_{a}$

Haŋ-bhʌne	*alu*	*ʌru*	*jat=na=p*
because	here	*other*	*ethnic.group*=LOC=RES

ba:-Ø-m.
be/sit-23s-AFF

[We do not to perform rituals in honour of the deities and ancestors in Kathmandu] Because there are people of other ethnic groups living here.

3.10 *Adjectives*

The majority of indigenous words that denote qualities and attributes are deverbatives. However, not all adjectival meanings are expressed by adjectives that are derived from verbs. Most of the true adjectives are common loans from Nepali. Here are some examples:

ʌndha$_{m}$ 'blind in both eyes' (<Nep. *andho*)
bʌndʌ$_{m}$ 'shut, confined, closed, stopped' (<Nep. *banda*)
basi$_{m}$ 'stale, kept for a long time' (<Nep. *bāsī*)
birami$_{am}$ 'ill, sick' (<Nep. *birāmī*)
gʌira$_{m}$ 'deep, profound' (<Nep. *gahirā*)
gʌrib$_{am}$ 'poor' (<Nep. *garib*)
khusi$_{m}$ 'pleased, glad, happy' (<Nep. *khusī*, *khuśī*)
nʌrʌm$_{m}$ 'soft, mild, tender' (<Nep. *naram*)
sʌjilo$_{m}$ 'easy' (<Nep. *sajilo*)
saro$_{m}$ 'hard, difficult' (<Nep. *sāhro*, *sāro*)
ubhinḍo$_{m}$ 'standing on one's head' (<Nep. *ubhiṇḍo*)
ulṭo$_{m}$ 'opposite, reversed, turned inside out' (<Nep. *ulṭo*).

Jero also possesses a class of underived native adjectives. The group of indigenous adjectives is small, however. The Jero adjectives can be used dependently as a noun modifier, and independently as a nominal head or predicate.

cimtɛp$_{a}$	'small, little, inferior'
daŋma$_{a}$	'self'
khamma$_{a}$ ~ *kha:ma*$_{m}$	'alone'
nɛntha$_{a}$	'new'
yɔkko$_{m}$	'small, little, inferior'

The antonym of the adjectives *cimtɛp*$_{a}$ 'small, little, inferior' and *yɔkko*$_{m}$ 'small, little, inferior' is the attributive verbal adjective *khɔl-tɔp*$_{a}$ ~ *khɔlto*$_{m}$ 'big, large, great'.

In the following example, the adjective *khamma*$_{a}$ functions as a nominal head that is preceded by the possessive pronouns *im*$_{am}$ 'your^{s}' and *am*$_{am}$ 'my'. In example (17) above, the nominal predicate *kham-ma*$_{a}$ is accompanied by the copula verb *bakcap*$_{a}$ ~ *bakcam*$_{m}$ vi-2 <bak- ~ ba:-> 'to be, sit'.

87$_{a}$ a. *Im* *khamma?*
your^{s} alone

b. *Am* *khamma.*
my alone

a. [Did you^{s} come] alone?
b. [I came] alone.

The following words of colour can also be used in adnominal modifying position without additional modification and can thus be analysed as adjectives. However, these adjectives seem to be poly-morphemic.

bupcip$_{a}$ ~ *bubjɛŋmo*$_{a}$	'white'
khucɛp$_{a}$ ~ *khucɛm*$_{m}$ ~ *khucɛŋmo*$_{a}$	'black'
lakcip$_{a}$	'red'
waʔɔmjimo$_{m}$ ~ *waʔɔmjɔkto*$_{m}$	'yellow'

The word *waʔɔmjimo*$_{m}$ takes the bound element <-jimo>$_{m}$, of which the Wambule cognate form <-jimo> expresses the notion of 'knowl-edge obtained through the senses'. The word *waʔɔmjɔkto*$_{m}$ consists of the colour form *waʔɔm*$_{m}$ plus the attributive verbal adjective *jɔkto*$_{m}$. This adjective is derived from the transitive verb *jɔkcam*$_{m}$ vt(-2e) <jɔkt- (~ *jo-)> 'to know (by learning)'. The final *-p*$_{a}$ in *bupcip*$_{a}$, *khucɛp*$_{a}$ and *lakcip*$_{a}$ might be analysed as a lexicalised abbreviated morph of the reifying morpheme <=me>$_{am}$, which creates nominal constituents. See Section 3.14 below (p. 123).

3.11 *Numerals and numeral classifiers*

With the general exception of the word for 'one', the Jero numerals are loans from Nepali. The following are the numerals 'one' to 'five':

kɔʔlo$_{a}$ ~ *kɔʔl*$_{a}$ ~ *kwal*$_{m}$	'one'
dui$_{am}$	'two' (<Nep. *duī*)
tin$_{am}$	'three' (<Nep. *tīn*)
car$_{am}$	'four' (<Nep. *cār*)
pãc$_{am}$	'five' (<Nep. *pā̃c*)

As in Nepali, Jero requires under certain circumstances the use of numeral classifiers with all the numerals except the native numeral for 'one'. The two loan classifiers are selected by the noun on the basis of semantic correlation.

jʌna$_{am}$ ~ *jʌn*$_{m}$	human classifier
gɔʈa$_{a}$ ~ *gɔʈ*$_{a}$	non-human classifier

Human referents generally select the human classifier, which is a loan from Nepali *janā* 'person'. Non-human referents require the non-human classifier, which is a loan from *vaṭā* 'piece, article'. The non-human classifier may also be used in relation to human referents. See also example (19).

88$_{a}$

Inne	*dui*	*jʌna*	*aŋgu*	*tin*	*jʌna*
you	*two*	*person*	he/they	*three*	*person*

lai	*hepa*	*gɔk-ka-ci!*
PAT	cooked.grain	give-IMP-23d

You two give them three [some] cooked grain!

89_{m} *Nɔi* *dui* *jʌn* *munu* *nɔ-ŋ-ci-m?*
that.hrz *two* *person* who be-dS-d-AFF

Who are those two people [at the same altitude as the speaker]?

90_{a} *Kul=na=p* *dui* *gɔʈ* *mi* *baː-Ø-m?*
house=LOC=RES *two* *piece* fire be/sit-23s-AFF

Are there two fires inside the house?

91_{a} a. *Im* *gaũ=na* *hukɔl* *jʌna* *mucu*
your^{s} *village*=LOC how.much *person* person

ba-m-me?
be/sit-23/ns-AFF

b. *Ɛti* *khera* *chʌ* *jʌna* *ba-m-me:*
so.much *time* *six* *person* be/sit-23/ns-AFF

papa-mama, *didi* *car* *jʌna,*
father-mother *elder.sister* *four* *person*

kɔʔl *bʌini.*
one *younger.sister*

a. How many people [of your family] live in your^{s} village?
b. At this time, there are six people: [my] parents, four elder sisters and one younger sister.

92_{a} a. *Hukɔl* *jʌna* *didi-bʌini?*
how.much *person* *elder.sister-younger.sister*

Hukɔl *jʌna* *bʌini?*
how.much *person* *younger.sister*

b. *Chʌ* *jʌna* *didi,* *kɔʔl* *jʌna*
six *person* *elder.sister* one *person*

bʌini.
younger.sister

a. How many sisters [do you have]? How many younger sister?
b. Six elder sisters and one younger sister.

Note that the noun *mi* 'fire' in (90) has plural reference, but is marked as a singular argument in the finite verb. See also Section 3.2 above (p. 85). In examples (91) and (92), the classifier *jʌna*$_{am}$ is used in connection with the interrogative *hukɔl*$_{am}$ 'how much, how many'. The native Jero numeral for 'one' does not require the use of numeral classifiers, e.g. *jʌna*$_{am}$ is present in (92) but absent in (91) and (93).

93$_a$ *Us* *nɔ-Ø-mʌi* *inne* *kɔʔl* *naʔ* *teʔu*
in.that.way be-23s-FCT you one only son

ba-n-Ø-ne?
be/sit-2-23s-AFF

So you[s] only have one son?

Classifiers are not used when telling time. In Nepali, classifiers are also not used when counting and enumerating and with nouns denoting dates, periods of time, measures, weights and receptacles and in the expression of age.

94$_a$ *Ai* *kɔʔl* *dui* *bʌrsa* *nʌuthaŋ* *maŋ*
this one *two* *year* behind/after now

sik-ʌi *la-ŋ-ma.*
learn-LN become-1s-AFF

I will learn it one or two years later, and I am learning it now [too].

3.12 *Quantifiers and intensifiers*

Quantifiers are qualifying nominals that express a contrast in quantity between entities.

cicir$_a$	'a little, few, some'
cimmaŋ$_m$	'a little, few, some'
cimtɛp$_a$	'a little, few, some'
ɛti$_a$	'so much, this much' (<Nep. *yati*)
khɔlse$_a$	'an amount of'
sʌb$_a$ ~ *sʌp*$_m$	'all, whole' (<Nep. *sab*)
thupro$_a$	'a heap of, a pile of' (<Nep. *thupro*)

The use of the quantifier *sʌb*$_{a}$ ~ *sʌp*$_{m}$ 'all, whole' in relation to superlatives is exemplified in (38) above. The quantifier *cicir*$_{a}$ 'a little, few, some' is used in the following example.

95$_{a}$	a.	*Sɔmdu*	*inne*	*jɔk-ni-Ø-me?*
		sacred.text	you	know-2-23s-AFF
	b.	*Cicir*	*jɔk-Ø-ma.*	
		a.few	know-1s-AFF	

a. Do you^{s} know sacred chanted texts?
b. I know a little.

Intensifiers are qualifying adverbials that have a heightening or lowering effect on the meaning of another element in the sentence, such as a verb, an adverb, or an adnominal modifier such as an adjective or quantifier.

asi$_{am}$	'few, scarce, less'
bʌḍi$_{a}$ ~ *bʌḍe*$_{m}$	'more, larger' (<Nep. *baḍhī*)

The native intensifier *asi*$_{am}$ marks a lowering effect with quantifiers, e.g. *asi khɔlse*$_{a}$ 'some, few, a small amount', and with adjectives or deverbatives, e.g. *asi khɔlto*$_{m}$ 'little big'. The loan intensifier *bʌḍi*$_{a}$ ~ *bʌḍe*$_{m}$ marks a heightening effect, e.g. *bʌḍe roto*$_{m}$ 'very high, very tall'. The quantifying phrase *as khɔlse*$_{a}$ was translated as 'much, many'. The element *as*$_{a}$ in this phrase may perhaps be analysed as the abbreviated morph of the demonstrative adverb *ase*$_{m}$ ~ *as*$_{m}$ 'in this way'. The element *-se* in the quantifier *khɔlse*$_{a}$ 'an amount of' can perhaps be analysed as the marker 'exactly, precisely'.

The following loan words can function as a quantifier and as an intensifier.

dherʌi	'very many; very, too' (<Nep. *dherai*)
jʌmma	'in all, in full' (<Nep. *jammā*)
saro	'very, much' (<Nep. *sāhro*)

3.13 *Nouns and adverbs of time*

Nouns that refer to notions of time are generally loans from Nepali, such as *bʌrsa*$_{m}$ 'year' (<Nep. *barṣa*), *coṭi*$_{m}$ 'time, turn' (<Nep. *coṭi*) and *din*$_{am}$ 'day' (<Nep. *din*). Indigenous words that refer to notions of time are mostly adverbial forms. The following adverbs express general temporal notions, covering the range from 'much previously' in the past until 'later' in the future:

na ke$_{a}$ ~ *na-na*$_{m}$ ~ *na=se*$_{am}$	'much previously'
na$_{am}$	'previously, formerly, already'
lapphu$_{am}$ ~ *lapthɔl*$_{a}$	'before, previously, formerly'
maŋ$_{am}$	'now, at this time, at the time'
mɔko$_{a}$ ~ *mɔkko*$_{a}$ ~ *mɔkke*$_{m}$	'just now, presently'
tɛŋu$_{a}$ ~ *tɛŋ*$_{am}$	'now, from now on'
nʌuṭhaŋ$_{m}$	'afterwards, after, later'
mat$_{a}$ ~ *matto*$_{a}$ ~ *mattol*$_{a}$ ~ *mattɔlo*$_{m}$	'later, a moment later'

The complex forms *na=se* [na:se] en *na ke* [na:ke] consist of the adverb *na*$_{am}$ [na:] 'previously, formerly, already' to which the phrasal suffix <=se>$_{am}$ 'exactly, precisely' or the phrase-final particle *ke*$_{a}$ 'on the contrary' are added. The adverb *na-na*$_{m}$ is a reduplicated form. Reduplication is a common way of expressing emphasis.

96$_{a}$	*Na=se*	*pa-u-mai*	*thiyo.*
	previously=exactly	do-1s-FCT	*was*

I did it just before.

97$_{a}$	*Mɔko*	*bat*	*po-ci-mei*	*satni=p=na=s*
	just.now	*thing*	do-d-FCT	yesterday=RES=LOC=SIM
	lu-ŋ-ma.			
	feel-1s-AFF			

For me it seems like the conversation we[di] were having just now is like the one we had yesterday.

The series of temporal adverbs from 'today' until three days in the past and four days in the future is given in two series. The first series gives the Āmboṭe forms and the second series the Mohanṭāre forms. These adverbs incorporate the two ancient suffixes <-so> 'day' and <-ni> 'day' introduced in Section 3.1.7 above (p. 82). Rām Kumār Rāī claimed that the form *sa:satni*$_{a}$ 'two days ago' in the first series is child language, whereas *nibbɔn*$_{a}$ is the ordinary word. The Mohanṭāre adverbs for 'three days ago', 'two days ago' and 'yesterday' are cognate of Wambule *tha:thaccum* 'three days ago', *thaccum* 'two days ago' or *saḍi* ~ *saḍ* 'two days ago' and *saiso* 'yesterday'.

ĀMBOṬE

ninibbɔn$_{a}$	'three days ago'
nibbɔn$_{a}$ ~ *sa:satni*$_{a}$	'two days ago'
satni$_{a}$	'yesterday'
tɛmbar$_{am}$	'today'
phɔpma$_{am}$	'tomorrow'
nusso$_{a}$	'day after tomorrow'
nunusso$_{a}$ ~ *sukmul*$_{a}$	'three days from now'
pyakmul$_{a}$	'four days from now'

MOHANṬĀRE

tha:thaccum$_{m}$	'three days ago'
thaccum$_{m}$ ~ *saʔni*$_{m}$	'two days ago'
saiso$_{m}$	'yesterday'
tɛmbar$_{am}$	'today'
phɔpma$_{am}$	'tomorrow'
nuso$_{m}$	'day after tomorrow'
sukul$_{m}$	'three days from now'

The series of temporal adverbs from 'two years ago' until 'next year' is given here. These four adverbs have a basic suffixal element <-thoce>$_{am}$ or prefixal element <tho->$_{a}$, both meaning 'year'.

thɔmbar-thoni$_{a}$	'two years ago'
thoni$_{a}$ ~ *numthoce*$_{m}$	'one year ago'
tɛŋthoce$_{a}$	'this year'
na:thot$_{a}$	'next year'

3.14 *Nominalisation and reification*

MORPHEME	<=me>$_{\text{am}}$
GLOSS	RES

Nominalisation is the derivational process of forming nominals from different types of word classes and the result of such a process. Nominalisers are morphemes which trigger this process. Derived nominals function as any underived noun or nominal, which can be used as an argument, as a predicator or as an adnominal modifier. Different types of nouns and adjectives are derived from non-finite verbs by suffixation of, for instance, the infinitive marker <-si>$_{\text{am}}$, the supine marker <-phu>$_{\text{am}}$ and the attributive verbal adjectival marker <-tɔ>$_{\text{a}}$ ~ <-to>$_{\text{m}}$ to verb roots without person and number agreement suffixes. Non-finite deverbatives are discussed in Chapter 5 (p. 183).

Another common way of forming nominals is by suffixation of the reifying morpheme to the final constituent of a phrase. The term 'reify' can be defined as 'transforming into a thing' or 'giving the character of a thing'. Reification is the morphological process of reifying and the result of this process. Nominalisation by means of reification applies to several word classes. The factual reification of verbs is discussed in Section 4.4 (p. 165). The reification of other word classes is discussed here.

Nouns, adjectives and adverbs can be turned into nominal constituents by suffixation of the reifying suffix <=me>$_{\text{am}}$ (RES). This Jero suffix is cognate of the Wambule reifying suffix <=me>. The Jero suffix has the regular allomorphs *=me*$_{\text{am}}$ ~ *=p*$_{\text{a}}$ ~ *=m*$_{\text{am}}$. In (97) above, for instance, the adverb *satni* 'yesterday' is turned into the nominal *satni=p* (yesterday=RES) 'the one from yesterday'. Likewise, in example (98), the similaritive adverb *saiso=se* (yesterday=SIM) 'like yesterday' is turned into the nominal *saiso=se=m* 'the one like yesterday' by suffixation of the reifying suffix.

98$_{\text{m}}$	*Lapphu*	*Dʌlse*	*lɔ-ŋ-mai*	*saiso=se=m*
	before	*Dalse*	go-1s-FCT	yesterday=SIM=RES
	mɔ-ŋ-ma.			
	sense-1s-AFF			

It seems like yesterday that I went to Dalse.

The following examples show the suffixation of the reifying marker to locative complements. In the first example, the adverb *alu* 'here' is turned into the nominal constituent *alu=p* 'the ones from here'.

99_{a}

Uŋgu	*hepa*	*ja-u-m*	*bhʌne,*	*sʌb-ʌi*
I/we	cooked.grain	eat-1s-AFF	*as.for*	*all*-EMPH

alu=p	*mucu=ya*	*hepa*	*ja-si*	*pʌrchʌ.*
here=RES	person=also	cooked.grain	eat-INF	*is.necessary*

If I eat cooked grain, all the people here also have to eat cooked grain.

100_{a}

India=na=p	*jeṭha-bhena*	*Sampaŋ,*
India=LOC=RES	*eldest.male-sister's.husband*	Sampang

Ilam=na=p	*Subba,*	*rʌ*	*gaũ=na=p*	*Jero.*
Ilām=LOC=RES	*Limbu*	*and*	*village*=LOC=RES	Jero

The husband of my eldest sister in India is Sampang, the one from Ilām is Limbu, and the one in [my] village is Jero.

3.15 *Emphatic forms*

MORPHEME	<-ʌi>$_{am}$
GLOSS	EMPH

Loans from Nepali, such as nouns, adjectives, quantifiers, intensifiers and other adverbs, have emphatic forms which are formed by suffixation of the emphatic morpheme <-ʌi>$_{am}$ or by reduplication of the final consonant. The emphatic marker <-ʌi>$_{am}$ is a loan from the Nepali suffix *-ai*. The suffixation of the emphatic morpheme is generally accompanied by deletion of the word-final vowel, e.g. *thupro*$_{a}$ → *thupr-ʌi*$_{a}$ 'a heap of, a pile of, a lot of'. Here are some examples:

sʌb$_{a}$ ~ *sʌp*$_{m}$	'all'
sʌb-ʌi$_{a}$ ~ *sʌp-ʌi*$_{m}$	'really all'

Note that the word *sʌppʌi*$_{m}$ is emphasised twice by reduplication of final /p/ and by suffixation of the emphatic marker <-ʌi>$_{am}$.

CHAPTER FOUR

FINITE VERB FORMS

Verbs can be identified as a distinct grammatical group on the basis of criteria that relate to their function and distribution and to grammatical categories that are typically associated with them, e.g. negation and transitivity. From the point of view of the constituents of sentence structure, verbs function as a predicator, expressing the relationship between the different arguments of a clause. Deverbatives, i.e. words that are derived from verbs, may function as an adnominal modifier and as an argument.

This chapter addresses the Jero verb lexeme and the morphosyntax of the negative, the simplex verb, the factual verbal adjective, the affirmative, the imperative and the optative. The factual verbal adjective is syntactically closely related to the non-finite verbal adjectives discussed in Chapter 5 below. This chapter on finite verbal morphology does not address the morphosyntax of the ablative and the irrealis, which can also be used as the predicator of a main clause. The latter finite forms generally occur in subordinate clauses in complex sentences, which are discussed in Chapter 6 below.

4.1 *The Jero verb*

The Jero verb is analysed here from three viewpoints. Firstly, three main verb types can be distinguished on the basis of the inflectional category of transitivity. Secondly, verbs can be classified in various conjugations and verb classes on the basis of paradigmatically conditioned root alternation and shared allomorphy that affects the verb roots and the morphemes that are bound to them. Thirdly, the verb root is analysed in terms of a morphophonological syllable, serving the description of the phonology and morphophonology of the verb and revealing some synchronic differences between Jero and Wambule.

4.1.1 *Transitivity*

Jero verbs can be classified into three main types on the basis of formal and semantic criteria that involve the inflectional category of transitivity. The notion of transitivity has bearing on the core arguments (subject, agent, patient) that are cross-referenced in the finite verb, and involves a conceptualisation of the way in which the arguments initiate the verbal action or are affected by it. A distinction can be made between intransitive, middle and transitive verbs.

Intransitive verbs show person and number agreement with one argument, which functions as the intransitive subject. For instance, the affirmative verb *bla-n-Ø-ne*$_{a}$ 'you^{s} come' contains two agreement markers, viz. the allomorph *-n* of the morpheme <-ni> (2) and the phonologically empty morpheme <-Ø> (23s). The two agreement morphemes are used to mark a second person singular subject in the verb. The verb *khrɔm-Ø-me*$_{m}$ 'he cries', by contrast, contains one agreement morpheme, viz. <-Ø> (23s), which is used to mark a third person singular subject in intransitive verbs.

bla-n-Ø-ne$_{a}$	(come-2-23s-AFF)	'you^{s} come'
khrɔm-Ø-me$_{m}$	(cry-23s-AFF)	'he cries'

The intransitive subject can be conceived of as the argument which by either its own free will or through lack of volition initiates the action expressed by the verb.

Middle verbs also show person and number agreement with one argument, which functions as the middle subject. For instance, the affirmative verb *ca-n-Ø-ne*$_{a}$ 'you^{s} ascend' also contains the morphemes <-ni> (2) and <-Ø> (23s), which mark a second person singular subject in the middle verb. The verb *tum-si-Ø-me*$_{m}$ 'he cried' contains the agreement morpheme <-Ø> (23s), which is suffixed to the middle marker <-si> (MID) to mark a third person singular subject in middle verb forms.

ca-n-Ø-ne$_{a}$	(ascend-2-23s-AFF)	'you^{s} ascend'
tum-si-Ø-me$_{m}$	(hit.self-MID-23s-AFF)	'he hits (for) himself'

Self-benefactive, reflexive and passive readings can be ascribed to the meaning of middle verbs in Jero. The middle subject differs from the intransitive subject by the fact that the cross-referenced actant may or may not have initiated the action, but is most certainly affected by it. In other words, the middle subject can be identified as the entity which undergoes the effect of the action expressed by the verb.

Transitive verbs show agreement with two arguments, which function as the agent and the patient. The agent initiates the action. The patient is affected by the action. For instance, in the affirmative verb form *pa-n-ne*$_{a}$ 'you^{s} do it' the morphemes <-ni> (2) and <-Ø> (23s) mark a second person singular agent, whereas the patient is formally left unmarked in the verb. By contrast, the negative verb *a-tɛr-ʔu-m*$_{m}$ 'I do not receive them^{p}' contains the allomorph *-ʔu* of the agreement morpheme <-ŋu> (1s), which refers to the first person singular agent, and the allomorph *-m* of the agreement morpheme <-mi> (23/ns), which refers to the third person plural patient here. The morpheme <-mi> (23/ns) generally marks that minimally one of the actants involved in the verbal scenario is a second or third person and that minimally one actant, but not necessarily the same actant, is non-singular.

pa-n-ne$_{a}$	(do-2-23s-AFF)	'you^{s} do it'
a-tɛr-ʔu-m$_{m}$	(NEG-receive-1s-23/ns)	'I do not receive them^{p}'

4.1.2 *Conjugations and verb classes*

Jero intransitive, middle and transitive verbs may have one or more different roots and can be classified in various conjugations on the basis of paradigmatically conditioned root alternation. Identical configurations are found in other Kiranti languages, especially in Wambule, where a conjugation represents a fixed pattern of paradigmatically conditioned root alternation. Paradigmatically conditioned root alternation can be formulated in terms of the morphophonological quality of the root-final segments (root rimes), and involves either the root vowel, the root-final consonant or both.

Verbs of the first intransitive conjugation, middle verbs and verbs of the first transitive conjugation are characterised by a single invariable root throughout the entire finite paradigm. Verbs of the second intransitive conjugation have different roots in finite and non-finite forms, whereas verbs of the second transitive conjugation are characterised by a fixed pattern of paradigmatically conditioned alternation between a primary and a secondary root. Note that a distinction is made here between the different roots of a single verb morpheme and the different forms of a single root. Different roots are distributed according to a fixed pattern of paradigmatically conditioned root alternation. By contrast, different root forms are forms of a single root which are morphophonemically conditioned by the presence or absence of suffixes which form their environment.

For instance, the verb *makcam*$_{m}$ vt-2e 'to catch, capture' has two paradigmatically conditioned root alternations, viz. <makt-> and <ma:->. The paradigmatic root <makt-> is realised as the root form /makt-/ before the suffix <-i>$_{am}$ (3npA) in the third person singular agent affirmative form *maktim* 'he caught it'. The paradigmatic root <makt-> is realised as the root form /mak-/ before the suffix <-ni>$_{am}$ (2) in the second person singular agent affirmative form *maknim* 'you^{s} caught it'. In other words, the basic root form /makt-/ is preserved before suffixes with an initial vowel, e.g. <makt-> + <-i> → /makt-i/, whereas the root form /mak-/ is obtained from the paradigmatically conditioned root alternation <makt-> by the general rule of deletion of post-final <t> before suffixes with an initial consonant, e.g. <makt-> + <-ni> → /mak-ni/ (see also Section 2.3.4, p. 73).The paradigmatically conditioned root alternation <ma:-> is realised as the basic root /ma:-/ before the second person suffix <-ni>$_{am}$ (2) in the second person plural agent affirmative form *ma:nimme* 'you^{p} caught it'. The fact that the paradigmatically conditioned root alternants <makt-> and <ma:-> both occur before the second person morpheme <-ni>$_{am}$ (2) shows that the different forms of a verb cannot be accounted for in terms of the modification of a single verbal base under the presence or absence of suffixes which form their environment.

Verbs that share a given conjugation can be further classified into various classes on the basis of shared allomorphy that affects the verb roots and the morphemes that are bound to them. Verb classes are defined in terms of the root-final elements. Eighteen classes have been identified thus far: five classes of verbs which belong to the first intransitive conjugation, one class of verbs which belong to the second intransitive conjugation, three classes of verbs which belong to the middle conjugation, one class of verbs which belong to the first transitive conjugation and eight classes of verbs which belong to the second transitive conjugation.

INTRANSITIVE VERBS

(vi-1a-i) Verbs ending in <V>, e.g. *dicap*$_{m}$ ~ *dicam*$_{m}$ vi-1a-i <di-> ‘to go (and come back)’, *lacap*$_{a}$ ~ *lacam*$_{m}$ vi-1a-i <la-> ‘to be, become’ and *lɔcap*$_{a}$ ~ *lɔcam*$_{m}$ vi-1a-i <lɔ-> ‘to go’.

(vi-1a-ii) Verbs ending in <V>, e.g. *gacap*$_{a}$ ~ *ga-*$_{m}$ vi-1a-ii <ga-> ‘to come up’, *picap*$_{a}$ ~ *picam*$_{m}$ vi-1a-ii <pi-> ‘to come (across a horizontal plane)’ and *yacap*$_{a}$ ~ *yacam*$_{m}$ vi-1a-ii <ya-> ‘to come down’.

(vi-1b) Verbs ending in <V:>, e.g. *docap*$_{a}$ vi-1b <do-> ‘to fall, fall down’, *glecap*$_{a}$ ~ *glecam*$_{m}$ vi-1b <gle-> ‘to lie down’ and *hu:cap*$_{a}$ ~ *hu:-*$_{m}$ vi-1b <hu:-> ‘to shout, cry; to bark’.

(vi-1c) Verbs ending in <m>, e.g. *dumcap*$_{a}$ ~ *dumcam*$_{m}$ vi-1c <dum-> ‘to be, become’, *khrɔmcap*$_{a}$ ~ *khrɔmcam*$_{m}$ vi-1c <khrɔm-> ‘to cry, weep’ and *yɔmcap*$_{a}$ ~ *yɔmcam*$_{m}$ vi-1c <yɔm-> ‘to stand, stand up’.

(vi-1d) Verbs ending in <l>, e.g. *walcap*$_{a}$ ~ *walcam*$_{m}$ vi-1d <wal-> ‘to walk’.

(vi-2) Verbs ending in <Vk ~ V:>, e.g. *bakcap*$_{a}$ ~ *bakcam*$_{m}$ vi-2 <bak- ~ ba:-> ‘to be, sit’, *blakcap*$_{a}$ ~ *blak-*$_{m}$ vi-2 <blak- ~ bla:-> ‘to come, arrive’ and *wakcap*$_{a}$ vi-2 <wak- ~ wa:-> ‘to scream, shriek’.

MIDDLE VERBS

(vm-1a) Verbs ending in <V:>, e.g. *ca:cap*$_{a}$ ~ *ca:-* vm-1a <ca:-> ‘to ascend, go up’, *necap*$_{a}$ ~ *necam*$_{m}$ vm-1a <ne-> ‘to say, quote, relate’ and *ni:cap*$_{a}$ ~ *ni:-*$_{m}$ vm-1a <ni:-> ‘to sit down, be seated’.

(vm-1b) Verbs ending in <m>, e.g. *himcap*$_{a}$ vm-1b <him-> ‘to see oneself; to be or get seen’ and *tumcap*$_{a}$ ~ *tumcam*$_{m}$ vm-1b <tum-> ‘to hit oneself’.

(vm-1c) Verbs ending in <r>, e.g. *mɛrcap*$_{a}$ ~ *mɛrcam*$_{m}$ vm-1c <mɛr-> ‘to wash oneself’, *mɔrcap*$_{a}$ vm-1c <mɔr-> ‘to come out, go out’ and *tɛrcap*$_{a}$ vm-1c <tɛr-> ‘to be received; to be met’.

TRANSITIVE VERBS

(vt-1) Verbs ending in <V>, e.g. *dɛcap*$_{a}$ vt-1 <dɛ-> 'to dig', *kicap*$_{a}$ ~ *kicam*$_{m}$ vt-1 <ki-> 'to look at, watch', *plɛcam*$_{m}$ vt-1 <plɛ-> 'to stop, quit' and *thɔcap*$_{a}$ vt-1 <thɔ-> 'to ask for'.

(vt-2a) Verbs ending in <V_1 ~ V_2>, e.g. *jacap*$_{a}$ ~ *jacam*$_{m}$ vt-2a <ja- ~ jo-> 'to eat' and *pacap*$_{a}$ ~ *pacam*$_{m}$ vt-2a <pa- ~ po-> 'to do'.

(vt-2b) Verbs ending in <Vːt ~ Vː>, e.g. *tuːcap*$_{a}$ ~ *tuːcam*$_{m}$ vt-2b <tuːt- ~ tuː-> 'to drink'.

(vt-2c) Verbs ending in <pt ~ m>, e.g. *hipcap*$_{a}$ ~ *hipcam*$_{m}$ vt-2c <hipt- ~ him-> 'to see', *japcap*$_{a}$ ~ *japcam*$_{m}$ vt-2c <japt- ~ jam-> 'to buy' and *tupcap*$_{a}$ ~ *tupcam*$_{m}$ vt-2c <tupt- ~ tum-> 'to beat, strike'.

(vt-2d) Verbs ending in <tt ~ n>, e.g. *paccap*$_{a}$ ~ *paccam*$_{m}$ vt-2d <patt- ~ pan-> 'to cause someone to do something', *plɛccap*$_{a}$ ~ *plɛccam*$_{m}$ vt-2d <plɛtt- ~ plɛn-> 'to dry' and *phaccap*$_{a}$ vt-2d <phatt- ~ phan-> 'can, be able'.

(vt-2e) Verbs ending in <kt ~ Vː>, e.g. *dakcam*$_{m}$ vt-2e <dakt- ~ daː-> 'to like', *gɔkcap*$_{a}$ ~ *gɔkcam*$_{m}$ vt-2e <gɔkt- ~ go-> 'to give; to let' and *rɛkcap*$_{a}$ ~ *rɛk-*$_{m}$ vt-2e <rɛkt- ~ re-> 'to write, draw'.

(vt-2f) Verbs ending in <yt ~ y>, e.g. *phuicap*$_{a}$ ~ *phuit-*$_{m}$ vt-2f <phuyt- ~ phuy-> 'to dig, root (in soil)'.

(vt-2g) Verbs ending in <rt ~ r>, e.g. *kurcap*$_{a}$ ~ *kurcam*$_{m}$ vt-2g <kurt- ~ kur-> 'to carry' and *tɛrcap*$_{a}$ ~ *tɛrcam*$_{m}$ vt-2g <tɛrt- ~ tɛr-> 'to get, receive; to meet'.

(vt-2h) Verbs ending in <lt ~ l>, e.g. *khɛlcap*$_{a}$ ~ *khɛlcam*$_{m}$ vt-2h <khɛlt- ~ khɛl-> 'to touch' and *mɛlcap*$_{a}$ ~ *mɛlcam*$_{m}$ vt-2h <mɛlt- ~ mɛl-> 'to fall asleep, sleep'.

Paradigmatically conditioned root alternants of a single verb are given in their morphophonemic form and separated by (~). The conjugation of a particular verb is indicated after the citation form. An intransitive verb is indicated as 'vi-', a middle verb as 'vm-' and a transitive verb as 'vt-'. The subcategories are indicated by a system of numbers (1, 2) for the type of conjugation and which is followed by letters (a, b, c, d, e, f, g, h) and roman numbers (i, ii) for the verb classes.

4.1.3 *The verb root syllable*

The Jero verb root can be described in terms of a morphophonological syllable <(C_i)V(C_f)> with a post-final segment <t> in some transitive verbs. C_i is a optional syllable-initial consonant or consonant cluster. V is the obligatory syllable nucleus. C_f is the optional syllable-final consonant. There are no syllable-final consonant clusters in Jero. The post-final segment <t> in transitive verbs seems to be a reflex of the Proto-Tibeto-Burman 'directive' or 'applied' suffix *<-t> (Wolfenden 1929, Benedict 1972). In modern Jero verb forms, this former suffix appears to have a causative or transitivising sense. The segment <t> is paradigmatically conditioned and realised as the initial consonant of the suffix syllable or deleted according to the morphophonological regularities presented in Section 2.3.4 (p. 73).

Initial consonants. C_i is an optional syllable-initial consonant or consonant cluster that consists of bilabial or velar stops followed by <r> or <l>. The single consonants <p, ph, b, t, th, d, c, j, k, kh, g, m, n, ŋ, r, l, s, h, w, y> and the consonants clusters <pl, pr, phr, bl, br, kl, kr, khl, khr, gl> have been found to occur in C_i position in verb roots. The cluster <gr> is absent in verb roots, but found in non-verbs such as *gramji*$_a$ 'hate'. The absence of <phl> in verbs and non-verbs seems to be accidental. Wambule permits the syllable-initial consonant clusters <gr> and <phl> in verb roots.[12] Note the lack of the single initial consonant <ch>, which is neither found in native Wambule words. Note also that <w> is only found before <a, a:>, whereas <y> occurs before <a, ɔ, o, u, u:> in verb roots. I have no ready explanation for the absence of <a:> after initial <y>.

Final consonants. C_f is the optional syllable-final consonant <p, t, k, m, n, l, r, y>. The lack of final <ŋ> in verb roots may be accidental, as

[12] For instance, Wambule has <gr> in *grwapcam* 'to throw, cast' and <phl> in *phlocam* 'to break open by oneself'.

final <ŋ> is found in non-verbs such as <haŋ> 'why' and as a syllable-final consonant in Wambule verbs.[13] As in Wambule, final <c, s> have not been found in Jero verb roots. The absence of final fricatives and affricates in verb roots seems to be structural in the Chaurasia area.

Vowels. Although ten vowel phonemes are distinguished in modern Jero, only five need to be reconstructed diachronically for verb roots. Length seems to be secondary in Jero, resulting from the loss of root-final consonants, especially /k/. This phonological development is primarily suggested by present-day paradigmatically conditioned root alternation of verbs belonging to class (vi-2) and (vt-2e), e.g. *bakcap*$_{a}$ ~ *bakcam*$_{m}$ vi-2 <bak- ~ ba:-> 'to be, sit' and *gɔkcap*$_{a}$ ~ *gɔkcam*$_{m}$ vt-2e <gɔkt- ~ go-> 'to give; to let', but also by related pairs of verbs such as *rakcap*$_{a}$ ~ *rakcam*$_{m}$ vt(-2e) <rakt- (~ *ra:-)> 'to influence' vs. *ra:cap*$_{a}$ vm-1a <ra:-> 'to influence, arouse' and *wakcap*$_{a}$ vi-2 <wak- ~ wa:-> 'to scream, shriek' vs. *wa:cap*$_{a}$ v(i) 'to scream, shriek'.

VI	**-i-*	**-e-*	**-a-*	**-o-*	**-u-*
-k		ɛk[1]	ak ~ a:[2a] ak[2b]	ɔk[3]	uk[4]
-m			am[5]	ɔm[6]	um[7]
-l			al[8]		
-r				ɔr[9]	ur[10]
-V	i[11]		a[12]	ɔ[13]	u[14]
-V:	i:[15]	e[16]	a:[17]	o[18]	u:[19]

Diagram 10: Jero intransitive verb root rimes

The 19 different attested intransitive verb root rimes are given in Diagram 10. With respect to the intransitive verbs ending in <-k>, the rimes on the upper line (a-forms) refer to the paradigmatically condi-

[13] Quite interestingly, final <k> in Jero verb roots frequently corresponds to final <ŋ> in Wambule, e.g. Jero <nak->$_{a}$ vs. Wambule <daŋ-> 'chew', Jero <yak->$_{m}$ vs. Wambule <yaŋ-> 'cut down', and Jero <tɔk->$_{m}$ vs. Wambule <twaŋ-> 'swallow'. In Wambule, paradigmatic root-final <ŋ> is realised as the velar nasal /ŋ/ or the velar stop /k/ before suffix-initial /c, s/. So we find the root forms /ɗak-/, /yak-/ and /twak-/ before the suffix <-ca> of the verbal adjective of purpose.

tioned roots found in some verb morphemes, whereas the rimes on the lower line (b-forms) are morphophonologically conditioned forms of verb that are considered to be subject to the same pattern of paradigmatically conditioned root alternation as the a-forms in the upper line. The intransitive rimes occur in the following verb forms:

<-k> (1) *prɛkcam*$_{m}$ v(i) 'to jump'; (2a) *bakcap*$_{a}$ ~ *bakcam*$_{m}$ vi-2 'to be, sit', *blakcap*$_{a}$ ~ *blak-*$_{m}$ vi-2 'to come, arrive somewhere', *wakcap*$^{2}{}_{a}$ vi-2 'to scream, shriek'; (2b) *brakcap*$_{a}$ v(i) 'to break, burst', *prakcam*$_{m}$ v(i) 'to run'; (3) *dɔkcam*$_{m}$ *v(i)* 'to fall'; and (4) *bukcap*$_{a}$ ~ *bukcam*$_{m}$ v(i) 'to get up, stand up'.

<-m> (5) *yamcap*$_{a}$ v(i) 'to be rotten'; (6) *khrɔmcap*$_{a}$ ~ *khrɔmcam*$_{m}$ vi-1c 'to weep', *yɔmcap*$_{a}$ ~ *yɔmcam*$_{m}$ vi-1c 'to stand'; and (7) *dumcap*$_{a}$ ~ *dumcam*$_{m}$ vi-1c 'to be, become'.

<-l> (8) *walcap*$_{a}$ ~ *walcam*$_{m}$ vi-1d 'to walk, go'.

<-r> (9) *sɔrcap*$_{a}$ ~ *sɔr-*$_{m}$ v(i) 'to dry, dry up'; and (10) *burcap*$_{a}$ v(i) 'to shout, rebuke', *jurcap*$_{a}$ ~ *jur-*$_{m}$ v(i) 'to be sour'.

<-V> (11) *dicap*$_{a}$ ~ *dicam*$_{m}$ vi-1a-i 'to go (and come back)', *picap*$_{a}$ ~ *picam*$_{m}$ vi-1a-ii 'to come (across a horizontal plane)', *sicap*$_{a}$ ~ *sicam*$_{m}$ vi-1a-i 'to die'; (12) *gacap*$_{a}$ ~ *ga-*$_{m}$ vi-1a-ii 'to come up', *lacap*$_{a}$ ~ *lacam*$_{m}$ vi-1a-i 'to be, become', *yacap*$^{1}{}_{a}$ ~ *yacam*$_{m}$ vi-1a-ii 'to come down', *yacap*$^{2}{}_{a}$ v(i) 'to be sharp'; (13) *lɔcap*$_{a}$ ~ *lɔcam*$_{m}$ vi-1a-i 'to go (away)', *nɔcap*$_{a}$ ~ *nɔcam*$_{m}$ vi-1a-i 'to be'; and (14) *lucap*$_{a}$ ~ *lucam*$_{m}$ vi-1a-i 'to feel, cause a mental or bodily sensation', *nucap*$_{a}$ ~ *nucam*$_{m}$ vi-1a-i 'to be well'.

<-V:> (15) *hi:cap*$_{a}$ v(i) 'to be long', *ni:cap*$^{2}{}_{a}$ vi-1b 'to be afraid'; (16) *blecap*$_{a}$ ~ *ble-*$_{m}$ v(i) 'to be alive', *glecap*$_{a}$ ~ *glecam*$_{m}$ vi-1b 'to lie down', *hecap*$^{1}{}_{a}$ ~ *he-*$_{m}$ v(i) 'to be left over'; (17) *da:-* $_{a}$ vi-1b 'to like', *wa:cap*$_{a}$ v(i) 'to scream, shriek'; (18) *brocap*$_{a}$ v(i) 'to be tasty', *docap*$_{a}$ vi-1b 'to fall', *hocame*$_{a}$ ~ *ho-*$_{m}$ vi-1b 'to burn'; and (19) *hu:cap*$_{a}$ ~ *hu:-*$_{m}$ vi-1b 'to shout, cry'.

As in Wambule, Jero does not have intransitive verb ends in <p, t>. The absence of the vowel *-i-* before the root-final consonants *-k*, *-m*, *-l*, and *-r* in intransitive verbs seems to be an accidental gap, as the vowel *-i-* is found before these root-final consonants in middle and transitive verbs.

VM	*-*i*-	*-*e*-	*-*a*-	*-*o*-	*-*u*-
-*m*	im[20]		am[21]	ɔm[22]	um[23]
-*r*		ɛr[24]		ɔr[25]	
-*V:*	i:[26]	e[27]	a:[28]	o[29]	
-*Vy*			ai[30]		

Diagram 11: Jero middle verb root rimes

The 11 different attested middle verb rimes found are given in Diagram 11. There are no middle verb ends in <p, t>, as in Wambule. The middle rimes occur in the following verb forms:

<-m> (20) *himcap*$_a$ vm-1b 'to see oneself'; (21) *damcap*$_a$ v(m) 'to be or get lost'; (22) *bɔm-*$_m$ v(m) 'to be covered', *dɔmcap*$_m$ v(m) 'to be tasted', *kɔmcap*$_a$ ~ *kɔmcam*$_m$ v(m) 'to cover oneself'; and (23) *tumcap*^1_a ~ *tumcam*$_m$ vm-1b 'to beat oneself'.

<-r> (24) *mɛrcap*$_a$ ~ *mɛrcam*$_m$ vm-1c 'to wash oneself', *tɛrcap*$_a$ ~ *tɛrcam*$_m$ vm-1c 'to be received'; and (25) *mɔrcap*$_a$ vm-1c 'to come out, go out'.

<-V:> (26) *ni:cap*^1_a ~ *ni:-*$_m$ vm-1a 'to sit down'; (27) *necap*$_a$ ~ *necam*$_m$ vm-1a 'to say'; (28) *ca:cap*$_a$ ~ *ca:-*$_m$ vm-1a 'to ascend, go up', *ra:cap*$_a$ vm-1a 'to influence, arouse', *tha:cap*$_a$ ~ *tha:cam*$_m$ vm-1a 'to warm oneself'; and (29) *jocam*$_m$ v(m) 'to seem, look like', *pocap*$_a$ vm-1a (reciprocal auxiliary).

<-Vy> (30) *naicam*$_m$ v(m) 'to rest', *paicap*$_a$ v(m) 'to dress oneself'.

VT	*-i-	*-e-	*-a-	*-o-	*-u-
-pt	ipt ~ im[31a] ip[31b]	εp[32]	apt ~ am[33]	ɔp[34]	upt ~ um[35a] up[35b]
-tt	itt[36a] it[36b]	εtt ~ εn[37a] εt[37b]	att ~ an[38a] at[38b]	ɔt[39] / ot[40]	ut[41]
-kt	ik[42]	εkt ~ e[43a] εk[43b]	akt ~ aː[44a] ak[44b]	ɔkt ~ o[45a] ɔk[45b]	uk[46]
-mt	im[47]	εm[48]	am[49]	ɔm[50]	um[51]
-nt		εn[52]			
-lt		εlt ~ εl[53]	al[54]	ɔl[55]	
-rt	ir[56]	εrt ~ εr[57a] εr[57b]	ar[58]	ɔr[59]	urt ~ ur[60a] ur[60b]
-V	i[61]	ε[62]	a ~ o[63a] a[63b]	ɔ[64]	
-Vːt	iː[65]	e[66]		o[67]	uːt ~ uː[68]
-Vyt	uyt ~ uy[69]	ei[70]		ɔi[71]	

Diagram 12: Jero transitive verb root rimes

The 41 different attested transitive verb rimes found are given in Diagram 12. The rimes ending in post-final <t> on the upper line (a-forms) refer to the paradigmatically conditioned roots found in some verb morphemes, whereas the rimes on the lower line (b-forms) are morphophonologically conditioned forms of verb which may possibly be considered to be subject to the same or a similar pattern of paradigmatically conditioned root alternation. The b-forms appear to be generally derived from the a-forms though the deletion of post-final <t> following the morphophonological regularities specified in Section 2.3.4 (p. 73). However, it cannot be excluded that Jero also has the transitive verb root syllable <(C_i)V(C_f)> without a post-final segment <t> after the syllable-final consonants <m, n, l, r, y> or after a long vowel in the nucleus. As in Wambule, post-final <t> seems to be obligatory after root-final <p, t, k>. The transitive rimes occur in the following verb forms:

<-pt> (31a) *hipcap*$_a$ ~ *hipcam*$_m$ vt-2c 'to see', *hipcam*$_m$ vt-2c 'to obtain'; (31b) *bipcap*$_a$ ~ *bipcam*$_m$ v(t) 'to suck', *khripcam*$_m$ v(t) 'to count'; (32) *kɛpcap*$_a$ ~ *kɛpcam*$_m$ v(t) 'to stick', *nɛpcap*$_a$ ~ *nɛpcam*$_m$ v(t) 'to push'; (33) *capcam*$_m$ vt(-2c) 'can, be able', *japcap*$_a$ ~ *japcam*$_m$ vt-2c 'to buy'; (34) *cɔpcap*$_a$ ~ *cɔpcam*$_m$ v(t) 'to put down', *hɔpcap*$^1{}_a$ ~ *hɔpcam*$_m$ v(t) 'to winnow', *hɔpcap*$^2{}_a$ v(t) 'to toss', *tɔpcap*$_a$ ~ *tɔpcam*$_m$ v(t) 'to strike'; (35a) *tupcap*$_a$ ~ *tupcam*$_a$ vt-2c 'to beat'; and (35b) *yupcap*$_a$ v(t) 'to suck'.

<-tt> (36a) *phiccap*$_a$ ~ *phiccam*$_m$ vt(-2d) 'to bring (across a horizontal plane)'; (36b) *ciccap*$_a$ v(t) 'to tear', *kliccap*$_a$ ~ *kliccam*$_m$ v(t) 'to hide', *ticcam*$_m$ v(t) 'to comb'; (37a) *nɛccap*$_a$ ~ *nɛt-*$_m$ vt(-2d) 'to hurt', *plɛccap*$_a$ ~ *plɛccam*$_m$ vt-2d 'to dry something', *sɛccap*$_a$ ~ *sɛccam*$_m$ vt-2d 'to kill'; (37b) *cɛccap*$^1{}_a$ v(t) 'to hang', *cɛccap*$^2{}_a$ v(t) 'to burn something', *hɛccap*$_a$ v(t) 'to bring down', *jɛccap*$_a$ v(t) 'to draw, pull', *lɛccap*$_a$, *lɛccam*$_m$ v(t) 'to take', *mɛccap*$_a$ ~ *mɛccam*$_m$ v(t) 'to feed', *phɛccap*$_a$ ~ *phɛccam*$_m$ v(t) 'to deal out (a meal)', *tɛccap*$_a$ v(t) 'to cut'; (38a) *kraccap*$_a$ ~ *kra[k]-*$_m$ vt-2d 'to bite with molars', *paccap*$_a$ ~ *paccam*$_m$ vt-2d 'to cause someone to do something', *phaccap*$_a$ vt-2d 'can, be able', *taccap*$_a$ vt-2d 'to stop, quit'; (38b) *blaccap*$_a$ ~ *bla[k]-*$_m$ v(t) 'to come, arrive somewhere', *daccam*$_m$ v(t) 'place, set up', *khaccap*$_a$ ~ *khaccam*$_m$ v(t) 'to bring up', *naccam*$_m$ v(t) 'to sting'; (39) *khɔccap*$_a$ v(t) 'to follow', *pɔccam*$_m$ v(t) 'to bind'; (40) *yoccam*$_m$ v(t) 'to throw overhand' (the vocalism *o* instead of *ɔ* is perhaps the result of the phonological environment, viz. *yVt*); and (41) *huccap*$_a$, *hu[k]-*$_m$ v(t) 'to blow up', *yuccap*$_a$ v(t) 'to throw overhand'.

<-kt> (42) *cikcam*$_a$ v(t) 'to find out', *phikcap*$_a$ v(t) 'to insert', *rikcam*$_m$ v(t) 'to cut off'; (43a) *jɛkcam*$_m$ vt(-2e) 'to begin, start', *rɛkcap*$_a$, *rɛk-*$_m$ vt-2e 'to write, draw'; (43b) *brɛkcap*$_a$, *brɛk-*$_m$ v(t) 'to sweep, brush', *cɛkcap*$^1{}_a$, *cɛkcam*$_m$ v(t) 'to break, fracture', *cɛkcam*$^2{}_m$ v(t) 'to find out', *khlɛkcap*$_a$, *khlɛk-*$_m$ v(t) 'to paint', *pɛk-*$_m$ v(t) 'to pluck, pull out', *sɛkcap*$_a$ v(t) 'to pluck',

thεkcap$_a$ v(t) 'to shut, lock', *ṭhεkcam*$_m$ v(t) 'to shut, lock'; (44a) *dakcap*$_a$ ~ *dakcam*$_m$ vt-2e 'to like', *makcam*^1_m vt-2e 'to catch, capture', *rakcap*$_a$ ~ *rakcam*$_m$ vt(-2e) 'to influence'; (44b) *makcam*^2_m v(t) 'to chew, masticate', *nakcap*$_a$ v(t) 'to chew, masticate', *phrakcap*$_a$ v(t) 'to break open', *takcap*$_a$ v(t) 'to place, set up', *yak-*$_m$ v(t) 'to cut down, fell'; (45a) *dɔkcap*$_a$ ~ *dɔkcam*$_m$ vt(-2e) 'to be sufficient', *gɔkcap*$_a$ ~ *gɔkcam*$_m$ vt-2e 'to give; to let', *jɔkcam*$_m$ vt(-2e) 'to know (by learning)'; (45b) *kɔkcap*^1_a v(t) 'to dig', *kɔkcap*^2_a v(t) 'to bite (said of a snake)', *khɔkcap*$_a$ ~ *khɔkcam*$_m$ v(t) 'to cook, boil', *lɔkcap*^1_a ~ *lɔkt-*$_m$ v(t) 'to boil, simmer', *lɔkcap*^2_a v(t) 'to lick'; and (46) *dukcam*$_m$ v(t) 'to shake, move', *phukcam*$_m$ v(t) 'to erect, lift', *suk-*$_m$ v(t) 'to prick, pierce', *thukcap*$_a$ v(t) 'to spit at someone'.

<-mt> (47) *dimcap*$_a$ v(t) 'to tread, trample', *mimcap*$_a$ v(t) 'to remember, think'; (48) *rεmcam*$_m$ v(t) 'to meet, visit'; (49) *damcap*$_a$ v(t) 'to lose', *hamcam*$_m$ v(t) 'to sink; to set', *khamcap*$_a$ v(t) 'to call, summon', *thamcap*$_a$ v(t) 'to sell'; (50) *hɔmcap*$_a$ v(t) 'to sink; to set', *khlɔmcap*$_a$ ~ *khlɔm-*$_m$ v(t) 'to put to sleep', *ŋɔmcap*$_a$ ~ *ŋɔmcam*$_m$ v(t) 'to smell, sniff'; and (51) *cumcap*$_a$ ~ *cumcam*$_m$ v(t) 'to catch', *hum-*$_m$ v(t) 'to boil in water', *sumcam*$_m$ v(t) 'to cover', *tumcap*^2_a v(t) 'to finish'.

<-nt> (52) *tεncap*$_a$ v(t) 'to make drink'.

<-lt> (53) *khεlcap*$_a$ ~ *khεlcam*$_a$ vt-2h 'to touch', *mεlcap*$_a$ ~ *mεlcam*$_m$ vt-2h 'to sleep'; (54) *calcap*$_a$ ~ *calcam*$_m$ v(t) 'to plait, twist', *dalcap*$_a$ ~ *dalcam*$_m$ v(t) 'to drive out', *malcam*$_m$ v(t) 'to search, seek'; and (55) *rɔlcam*$_m$ v(t) 'to shake down, knock down', *sɔlcap*$_a$ ~ *sɔl-*$_m$ v(t) 'to take out'.

<-rt> (56) *mircap*$_a$ ~ *mircam*$_m$ v(t) 'to scratch'; (57a) *tεrcap*$_a$ ~ *tεrcam*$_m$ vt-2g 'to get, receive'; (57b) *nεrcap*$_a$ v(t) 'to count', *phεrcap*$_a$ ~ *phεr-*$_m$ v(t) 'to sew'; (58) *kharcap*$_a$ ~ *kharcam*$_m$ v(t) 'to fry, pop'; (59) *khɔrcap*$_a$ ~ *khɔr-*$_m$ v(t) 'to plough', *mɔrcap*$_a$ v(t) 'to drive out, take out'; (60a) *kurcap*$_a$ ~ *kurcam*$_m$ vt-2g 'to carry'; and (60b) *curcap*$_a$ ~ *curcam*$_m$ v(t) 'to press (sugar cane or oil)', *murcap*$_a$ v(t) 'wash, rinse'.

<-V> (61) *gicap*$_a$ ~ *gicam*$_m$ v(t) 'to pick', *kicap*$_a$ ~ *kicam*$_m$ vt-1 'to look at', *khricap*$_a$ ~ *khricam*$_m$ v(t) 'to grind'; (62) *dɛcap*$_a$ vt-1 'to dig', *plɛcam*$_m$ vt-1 'to leave, quit'; (63a) *jacap*$_a$ ~ *jacam*$_m$ vt-2a 'to eat', *pacap*$_a$ ~ *pacam*$_m$ vt-2a 'to do, make'; (63b) *bracap*$_a$ ~ *bracam*$_m$ v(t) 'to spread, scatter', *macap*$_a$ ~ *macam*$_m$ v(t) 'to eat by biting', *placap*$_a$ v(t) 'to take'; and (64) *sɔcam*$_m$ v(t) 'to say, talk', *thɔcap*^1_a, *thɔ-*$_m$ v(t) 'to hear, smell', *thɔcap*^2_a vt-1 'to ask for'.

<-V:t> (65) *ki:t-*$_m$ v(t) 'to pull, stretch', *si:cap*$_a$ v(t) 'to thread (bind flowers)'; (66) *klecam*$_m$ v(t) 'to spread out', *khlecap*$_a$ v(t) 'to rub'; (67) *locam*$_m$ v(t) 'to wait, await', *yocam*$_m$ v(t) 'to swing'; and (68) *tu:cap*$_a$ ~ *tu:cam*$_m$ vt-2b 'to drink', *yu:cap*$_a$ v(t) 'to keep, support'.

<-Vyt> (69) *phuicap*$_a$ ~ *phuit-*$_m$ vt-2f 'to dig, root'; (70) *peicam*$_m$ v(t) 'to shell, peel', *seicap*$_a$ ~ *sei-*$_m$ v(t) 'to know a person', *teicam*$_a$ v(t) 'to make drink'; and (71) *phɔicam*$_m$ v(t) 'to ask for'.

The most striking formal difference between Jero and Wambule transitive verb morphology is the absence in Jero of transitive verbs that exhibit the presence of a post-final segment /s/ in certain finite forms. That is to say, Wambule transitive verbs that end in the long vowel phonemes <a:, e, i:, o, u:> and in the consonants <m, ŋ, y, r, l> (but not in <pt, kt, mt, yt, rt, lt>, which have post-final <t>) require the presence of a morphophonologically conditioned segment /s/ before the third person non-plural agent agreement morpheme <-u> (3npA), e.g. *tirsume* 'he received it' (root <tir->) and *tu:sume* 'he drank it' (root <tu:->). Post-final /s/ does not appear in other morphological environments, such as after verb roots ending in short vowels, e.g. *poume* 'he did it'. So far, post-final /s/, which can perhaps be traced back to the Proto-Tibeto-Burman 'causative' suffix *<-s> (Benedict 1972), has not been attested in Jero. The Jero verb forms *tɛrtime* 'he received it' (root <tɛrt->) and *tu:time* 'he drank it' (root <tu:t->), in which the verb root is followed by the cognate third person non-plural agent agreement morpheme <-i>$_{am}$ (3npA) suggest that Jero transitive verbs that end in a long vowel or in a final consonant generally take the paradigmatically conditioned post-final segment <t>.

Note that Jero and also Wambule have the root rimes *-akt* and *-ɔkt* (Wambule *-wakt*). In Dumi, however, no verb has a root in *-ak*. In Dumi and Bahing, **-a-* is backed by syllable-final *-k*, a phenomenon described as 'typical of this language area' by Michailovsky (1995: 4).

There appears to be a historical relationship between the root-final consonants /n/ and /y/ in *tɛncap*$_a$ v(t) 'to make drink' and *teicam*$_a$ v(t) 'to make drink'. It appears that root-final /y/ in some verbs is derived from root-final /*n/. Also compare the reflexes of the Proto-Kiranti etymon /*cen-/ 'learn, study' in some languages: Jero *cei-*$_m$, Wambule *ceicam*, Bahing *cháyinso*, Khaling *'ceysi-nä* and Dumi *tsen'sini*.

4.2 *The negative*

MORPHEME	<a->$_{am}$
GLOSS	NEG

The contradiction of the meaning of a verb is expressed by prefixation of the negative marker <a->$_{am}$ to corresponding positive forms. The negative marker is the only prefix found in Jero.

101$_a$	*Uŋgu*	*Jero*	*a-nɔ-ŋu.*
	I/we	Jero	NEG-be-1s

I am not a Jero.

102$_a$	*Aŋam*	*sɔndɔm*	*a-nu-Ø.*
	his/her	voice	NEG-be.well-23s

Her voice is not well [healthy or pleasant to hear].

103$_a$	*Kɔʔl*	*pacha=se*	*biha*	*a-dum-Ø.*
	one	*clan*=exactly	*marriage*	NEG-become-23s

One is not allowed to marry within one's own clan. [Reportedly, Jero people that belong to the same clan may only get married if they are separated by at least seven generations.]

The negative prefix can be attached to different types of finite verb forms, such as simplicia, imperatives and optatives, as well as several types of verbal adjectives.

4.3 *The simplex verb*

Simplex verbs, or simplicia, are finite forms which consist of a verb root and one or more suffixes which provide limited information on the person and number of the subject, agent and patient involved in the verbal action.

First person dual and plural inclusive simplex verbs and their negatives commonly serve as exhortatives, which are performative propositions for action to be taken by both the speaker and the hearer. Exhortatively used simplicia are generally translated into Nepali by means of first person forms of the aorist injunctive tense, e.g. *garaũ!* 'let us do!'.

104_{a}	*Uŋ*	*lɔ-ki!*
	I/we	go-1piAS

Let us^{pi} go away!

105_{m}	*Mi*	*tha-ŋ-ci!*
	fire	warm.self-dS-d

Let us^{di} warm ourselves near the fire!

Negated simplicia also serve as the negative counterpart of affirmative verb forms. Negated second person forms can be used to express prohibition, negative advice, denial of permission. Negated first person dual and plural inclusive forms also serve as negative exhortatives.

106_{a}	*Hep*	*a-jo-cu*	*a-nɔ-Ø-dɔŋ*
	cooked.grain	NEG-eat-ACP	NEG-be-23s-CND
	a-lɔ-kuwa.		
	NEG-go-1peAS		

If we^{pe} do not get diner, we^{pe} will not go.

107_{a}	*Uŋ*	*a-lɔ-ki.*
	I/we	NEG-go-1piAS

a. We^{pi} will/did not go away.
b. Let us^{pi} not go away!

Simplicia and their negatives also serve as deliberatives, which are questions by means of which the speaker tries to elicit the hearer's advice or assent.

108_{a}	*Uŋ*	*he-du-ŋu?*
	I/we	climb-go/come-1s

Shall I mount?

109_{m}	*Uŋ*	*pi-ŋu?*
	I/we	come.hrz-1s

Am I to come (across a horizontal plane)?

Simplex verbs contain a single person and number agreement suffix or a fixed string of suffixes with a maximum of three elements. The Jero simplex agreement suffixes given in Diagram 13 are spread over three functional positions. The morphemes in first functional position occur as the initial elements after the verb root, whereas those in the third position constitute the final elements of a string.

Intransitive and middle verbs generally use the same set of simplex agreement suffixes, which mark the person and number of the grammatical subject. Dual forms require the presence of the dual subject morpheme <-ŋ>$_{am}$. From the point of view of the verbal suffixes, the only formal difference between intransitive and middle conjugations involves the presence of the middle marker <-si>$_{am}$ before the second and third person singular morpheme <-Ø>$_{am}$ in middle forms. There are 9 different finite forms of intransitive and middle verbs. The distribution of the Jero simplex person and number agreement morphemes in intransitive and middle verbs is presented in Diagram 14.

In transitive verbs, by contrast, the agreement suffixes mark the person and number of the agent or the patient, a transitive relationship between the agent and the patient, or a combination of both. The distribution of the simplex person and number agreement morphemes in transitive verbs is presented in Diagram 15 and Diagram 16 below.

Simplex agreement morphemes		
1	<-aŋti>$_{m}$	(3s→1s)
	<-i>$_{am}$	(3npA)
	<-iŋ>$_{m}$	(2→1s)
	<-ki>$_{am}$	(1piAS)
	<-ku>$_{m}$	(1peAS)
	<-kuwa>$_{a}$	(1peAS)
	<-nati>$_{m}$	(3s→2s)
	<-ni>$_{am}$	(1s→2)
	<-ŋ>$_{am}$	(dS)
	<-ŋu>$_{am}$	(1s)
	<-si>$_{am}$	(MID)
2	<-ci>$_{am}$	(d)
	<-cu>$_{m}$	(1deAS)
	<-cuwa>$_{a}$	(1deAS)
	<-ni>$_{am}$	(2)
3	<-mi>$_{am}$	(23/ns)
	<-Ø>$_{am}$	(23s)
	<-ʔ>$_{m}$	(3dA)

Diagram 13: Simplex agreement morphemes (basic morphs)

vi & vm	MOHANṬĀRE	ĀMBOṬE
1s	<Σ-ŋu>	
2s	<Σ-ni-Ø>	
3s (vi)	<Σ-Ø>	
3s (vm)	<Σ-si-Ø>	
1di/2d/3d	<Σ-ŋ-ci>	
1de	<Σ-ŋ-cu>	<Σ-ŋ-cuwa>
1pi	<Σ-ki>	
1pe	<Σ-ku>	<Σ-kuwa>
2p	<Σ-ni-mi>	
3p	<Σ-mi>	

Diagram 14: Simplex intransitive and middle morphology

The following is a morphosemantic analysis of the Jero simplex person and number agreement system. The symbol (Σ) is used in this grammar to represent the verb root. Root Σ_1 is considered to be the primary root of verbs that subject to paradigmatically conditioned root alternation. Root Σ_2 is the secondary root. The root numbers are superfluous if verbs use a single invariable root.[14]

The Jero verbal agreement system uses synthetic and periphrastic forms to mark transitive relationships between agents and patients. The use of the periphrastic constructions seems to be the result of the loss of verbal morphology in modern Jero. There are two types of periphrastic constructions. The first type consists of a main verbal ending in <-su>$_{am}$ plus inflected forms of the auxiliary *pacap*$_a$ ~ *pacam*$_m$ vt-2a <pa- ~ po-> 'to do, make'. This type is used in Mohanṭāre 1s→2ns$_m$, 1pe→2p$_m$, 2s→1nse$_m$, 3s→1ns$_m$ and 3p→1ns$_m$ forms and in Āmboṭe 1s→2ns$_a$, 1de→2$_a$, 1pe→2$_a$, 2s→1$_a$, 2d→1$_a$, 2p→1$_a$, 3s→1$_a$, 3d→1$_a$ and 3p→1$_a$ forms. The second type consists of a main verbal ending in <-si>$_{am}$ plus inflected forms of the middle auxiliary *ra:cap*$_a$ vm-1a <ra:-> 'to influence, arouse, provoke'. This type is used in Āmboṭe 3→2s$_a$, 3→2d$_a$ and 3→2p$_a$ forms and has synthetic alternatives.

4.3.1 *The second and third person singular suffix*

MORPHEME	<-Ø>$_{am}$
GLOSS	23s

The suffix <-Ø>$_{am}$ marks second and third person singularity. This phonologically empty suffix is present in forms in which the person and number of the second or third person singular actant is not indicated by some other morpheme.

SUBJECT		
2s$_{am}$	<Σ-ni-Ø>	(Σ-2-23s)
3s$_{am}$ *vi*	<Σ-Ø>	(Σ-23s)
3s$_{am}$ *vm*	<Σ-si-Ø>	(Σ-MID-23s)

[14] Note that the information on Mohanṭāre transitive verb morphology has some qualitative and quantitative shortcomings, whereas Āmboṭe transitive verb morphology is characterised by paradigmatic simplifications.

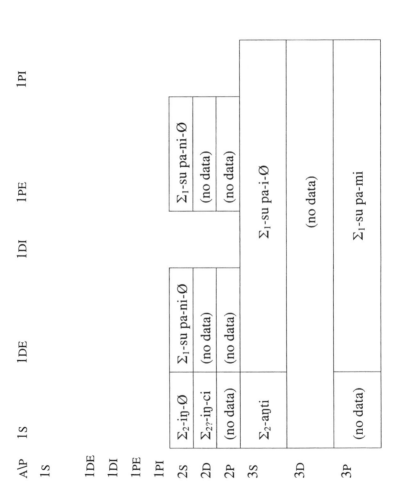

A\P	1S	1DE	1DI	1PE	1PI
1S					
1DE					
1DI					
1PE					
1PI					
2S	Σ_2-iŋ-Ø	Σ_1-su pa-ni-Ø		Σ_1-su pa-ni-Ø	
2D	$\Sigma_{2?}$-iŋ-ci	(no data)		(no data)	
2P	(no data)	(no data)		(no data)	
3S	Σ_2-aŋti	Σ_1-su pa-i-Ø			
3D	(no data)				
3P	(no data)	Σ_1-su pa-mi			

Diagram 15: Mohanṭāre Jero transitive conjugation (first person patients)

<table>
<tr><th>A\P</th><th>2S</th><th>2D</th><th>2P</th><th>3S</th><th>3D</th><th>3P</th></tr>
<tr><td rowspan="2">1S</td><td rowspan="2">Σ_2-ni-Ø</td><td>$\Sigma_{2?}$-ni-ci</td><td>$\Sigma_{2?}$-ni-ni</td><td rowspan="2">Σ_1-ŋu</td><td>Σ_1-ŋu-ci-mi</td><td>Σ_1-ŋu-mi</td></tr>
<tr><td colspan="2">Σ_1-su pa-ŋu</td><td colspan="2"></td></tr>
<tr><td>1DE</td><td colspan="3">(no data)</td><td>Σ_2-cu</td><td colspan="2">(no data)</td></tr>
<tr><td>1DI</td><td></td><td></td><td></td><td colspan="3">Σ_2-ci</td></tr>
<tr><td>1PE</td><td colspan="2">(no data)</td><td>Σ_1-su po-ku</td><td>Σ_2-ku</td><td colspan="2">(no data)</td></tr>
<tr><td>1PI</td><td></td><td></td><td></td><td colspan="3">Σ_2-ki</td></tr>
<tr><td>2S</td><td></td><td></td><td></td><td colspan="3">Σ_1-ni-Ø</td></tr>
<tr><td>2D</td><td></td><td></td><td></td><td>Σ_2-ci</td><td colspan="2">(no data)</td></tr>
<tr><td>2P</td><td></td><td></td><td></td><td>Σ_2-ni-mi</td><td colspan="2">(no data)</td></tr>
<tr><td>3S</td><td>Σ_2-nati</td><td>Σ_2-ci-mi</td><td>Σ_2-ni-mi</td><td colspan="3">Σ_1-i-Ø</td></tr>
<tr><td>3D</td><td>$\Sigma_{2?}$-ci-mi</td><td>(no data)</td><td>(no data)</td><td>Σ_1-i-ci-ʔ</td><td colspan="2">(no data)</td></tr>
<tr><td>3P</td><td>(no data)</td><td>(no data)</td><td>(no data)</td><td colspan="3">Σ_1-mi</td></tr>
</table>

Diagram 15 continued: Mohanṭāre Jero transitive conjugation (second and third person patients)

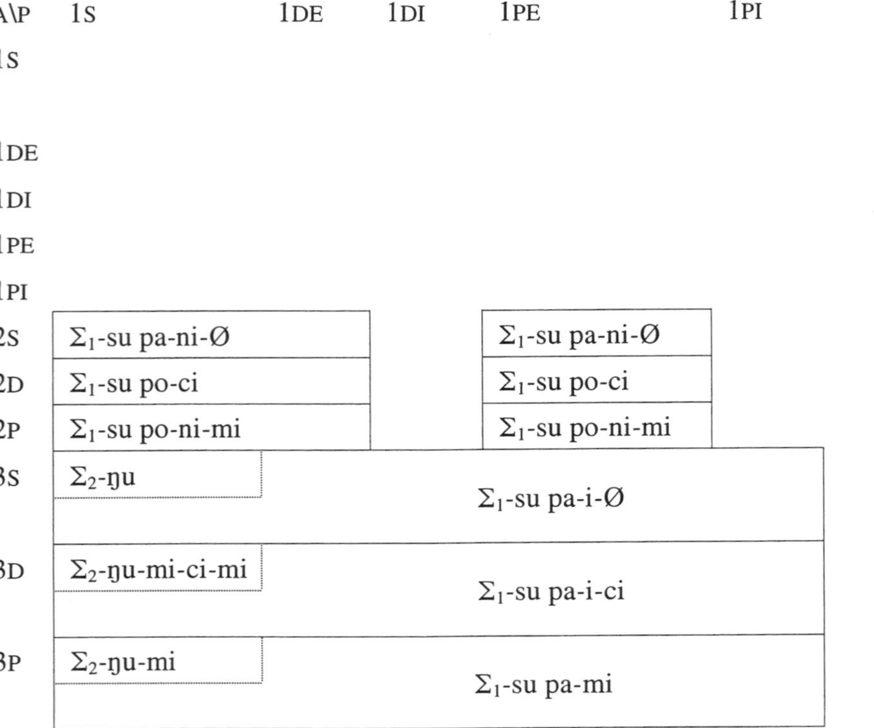

A\P	1S	1DE	1DI	1PE	1PI
1S					
1DE					
1DI					
1PE					
1PI					
2S	Σ_1-su pa-ni-Ø			Σ_1-su pa-ni-Ø	
2D	Σ_1-su po-ci			Σ_1-su po-ci	
2P	Σ_1-su po-ni-mi			Σ_1-su po-ni-mi	
3S	Σ_2-ŋu Σ_1-su pa-i-Ø				
3D	Σ_2-ŋu-mi-ci-mi Σ_1-su pa-i-ci				
3P	Σ_2-ŋu-mi Σ_1-su pa-mi				

Diagram 16: Āmboṭe Jero transitive conjugation (first person patients)

<table>
<tr><th>A\P</th><th colspan="2">2S</th><th colspan="2">2D</th><th colspan="2">2P</th><th>3S</th><th>3D</th><th>3P</th></tr>
<tr><td>1S</td><td colspan="2">Σ_2-ni-Ø</td><td colspan="4">Σ_1-su pa-ŋu</td><td>Σ_1-ŋu</td><td>Σ_1-ŋu-mi-ci-mi</td><td>Σ_1-ŋu-mi</td></tr>
<tr><td>1DE</td><td colspan="6">Σ_1-su po-cuwa</td><td colspan="3">Σ_2-cuwa</td></tr>
<tr><td>1DI</td><td colspan="6"></td><td colspan="3">Σ_2-ci</td></tr>
<tr><td>1PE</td><td colspan="6">Σ_1-su po-kuwa</td><td colspan="3">Σ_2-kuwa</td></tr>
<tr><td>1PI</td><td colspan="6"></td><td colspan="3">Σ_2-ki</td></tr>
<tr><td>2S</td><td colspan="6"></td><td colspan="3">Σ_1-ni-Ø</td></tr>
<tr><td>2D</td><td colspan="6"></td><td colspan="3">Σ_2-ci</td></tr>
<tr><td>2P</td><td colspan="6"></td><td colspan="3">Σ_2-ni-mi</td></tr>
<tr><td>3S</td><td rowspan="3">Σ_1-si
ra:-ni-Ø</td><td>Σ_2-ni-Ø</td><td rowspan="3">Σ_1-si
ra-ŋ-ci</td><td rowspan="2">Σ_2-ci-mi</td><td rowspan="3">Σ_1-si
ra:-ni-mi</td><td rowspan="3">Σ_2-ni-mi</td><td colspan="3">Σ_1-i-Ø</td></tr>
<tr><td>3D</td><td>Σ_2-ci-mi</td><td colspan="3">Σ_1-i-ci</td></tr>
<tr><td>3P</td><td>Σ_2-ni-mi</td><td>Σ_2-ni-mi</td><td colspan="3">Σ_1-mi</td></tr>
</table>

Diagram 16 continued: Āmboṭe Jero transitive conjugation (second and third person patients)

AGENT		
2s→1$_{a}$	<Σ-su pa-ni-Ø>	(Σ-MAN do-2-23s)
2s→1s$_{m}$	<Σ-iŋ-Ø>	(Σ-2→1s-23s)
2s→1nse$_{m}$	<Σ-su pa-ni-Ø>	(Σ-MAN do-2-23s)
2s→3$_{am}$	<Σ-ni-Ø>	(Σ-2-23s)
3s→1$_{a}$	<Σ-su pa-i-Ø>	(Σ-MAN do-3npA-23s)
3s→1ns$_{m}$	<Σ-su pa-i-Ø>	(Σ-MAN do-3npA-23s)
3s→3$_{am}$	<Σ-i-Ø>	(Σ-3npA-23s)

PATIENT		
1s→2s$_{am}$	<Σ-ni-Ø>	(Σ-1s→2-23s)
3→2s$_{a}$	<Σ-si raː-ni-Ø>	(Σ-INF provoke-2-23s)
3s→2s$_{a}$	<Σ-ni-Ø>	(Σ-2-23s)

4.3.2 *The 3s→1s suffix*

MORPHEME	<-aŋti>$_{m}$
GLOSS	3s→1s

The Mohanṭāre suffix <-aŋti>$_{m}$ marks a transitive relationship between a third person singular agent and a first person singular patient.

AGENT→PATIENT		
3s→1s	<Σ-aŋti>$_{m}$	(Σ-3s→1s)

The suffix is realised as the basic morph after root final consonants, e.g. <him-aŋti-m> (see-3s→1s-AFF) → *him-aŋti-m*$_{m}$ 'he saw me'. The suffix can also be realised without initial /a/ after root final vowels, e.g. <do-aŋti-m> (be.enough-3s→1s-AFF) → *do-ŋti-m*$_{m}$ 'it is enough for me'. The Mohanṭāre suffix <-aŋti>$_{m}$ is cognate of the Wambule suffix <-ŋati> (3s→1s). In Āmboṭe synthetic 3s→1s forms, the first person singular suffix <-ŋu>$_{am}$ (1s) is added to the secondary root alternant of verbs which are subject to paradigmatic root alternation, e.g. <go-ŋu- me> (give-1s-AFF) → *go-ŋ-ma*$_{a}$ 'he gave to me'.

4.3.3 *The dual suffix*

MORPHEME	<-ci>$_{am}$
GLOSS	d

The suffix <-ci>$_{am}$ marks duality of a subject, agent and patient.

SUBJECT		
1di/2d/3d$_{am}$	<Σ-ŋ-ci>	(Σ-dS-d)
AGENT		
1di/2d→3(s)$_{am}$	<Σ-ci>	(Σ-d)
2d→1s$_{m}$	<Σ-iŋ-ci>	(Σ-2→1s-d)
2d→1$_{a}$	<Σ-su po-ci>	(Σ-MAN do-d)
3d→1$_{a}$	<Σ-su pa-i-ci>	(Σ-MAN do-3npA-d)
3d→2s$_{am}$	<Σ-ci-mi>	(Σ-d-23/ns)
3d→3$_{a}$	<Σ-i-ci>	(Σ-3npA-d)
3d→3s$_{m}$	<Σ-i-ci-ʔ>	(Σ-3npA-d-3dA)
PATIENT		
1s→2d$_{m}$	<Σ-ni-ci>	(Σ-1s→2-d)
1s→3d$_{m}$	<Σ-ŋu-ci-mi>	(Σ-1s-d-23/ns)
3s→2d$_{m}$	<Σ-ci-mi>	(Σ-d-23/ns)
3→2d$_{a}$	<Σ-si ra-ŋ-ci>	(Σ-INF provoke-dS-d)
3np→2d$_{a}$	<Σ-ci-mi>	(Σ-d-23/ns)
AGENT↔PATIENT		
1s↔3d$_{a}$	<Σ-ŋu-mi-ci-mi>	(Σ-1s-23/ns-d-23/ns)

4.3.4 *The first person dual exclusive agent and subject suffix*

MORPHEME	<-cuwa>$_{a}$ ~ <-cu>$_{m}$
GLOSS	1deAS

The suffix <-cuwa>$_{a}$ and <-cu>$_{m}$ marks first person exclusive duality of an agent and subject argument. The patient is generally unmarked in first person dual exclusive agent forms. Āmboṭe transitive verbs with second person patients are periphrastic constructions which consist of a main verbal ending in <-su> and inflected forms of the verb *pacap* vt-2a <pa- ~ po-> ‘to do, make’. The Āmboṭe suffix <-cuwa>$_{a}$ is realised as the abbreviated morph *-cu*$_{am}$ before post-agreement suffixes. The final element <wa> of this morpheme is also found in the first person plural exclusive morpheme <-kuwa>$_{a}$. Whether a separate morphological status of the first person exclusive element <wa> should be preferred is unclear. The exclusive element <wa> seems to be cognate of the Wambule first person non-singular exclusive agent and subject morpheme <-ku> ($^{?}$< *-kwa*).

SUBJECT		
1de$_{a}$	<Σ-ŋ-cuwa>	(Σ-dS-1deAS)
1de$_{m}$	<Σ-ŋ-cu>	(Σ-dS-1deAS)

AGENT		
1de→2$_{a}$	<Σ-su po-cuwa>	(Σ-MAN do-1deAS)
1de→3$_{a}$	<Σ-cuwa>	(Σ-1deAS)
1de→3s$_{m}$	<Σ-cu>	(Σ-1deAS)

4.3.5 *The third person non-plural agent suffix*

MORPHEME	<-i>$_{am}$
GLOSS	3npA

The suffix <-i>$_{am}$ marks a third person non-plural agent:

AGENT		
3s→1$_{a}$	<Σ-su pa-i-Ø>	(Σ-MAN do-3npA-23s)
3s→1ns$_{m}$	<Σ-su pa-i-Ø>	(Σ-MAN do-3npA-23s)
3s→3$_{am}$	<Σ-i-Ø>	(Σ-3npA-23s)
3d→1$_{a}$	<Σ-su pa-i-ci>	(Σ-MAN do-3npA-d)
3d→3$_{a}$	<Σ-i-ci>	(Σ-3npA-d)
3d→3s$_{m}$	<Σ-i-ci-ʔ>	(Σ-3npA-d-3dA)

This morpheme is subject to the following morphophonologically conditioned alternation:

(a) The suffix <-i>$_{am}$ is realised as the basic morph *-i*$_{am}$ in third person singular agent forms, e.g. <ja-i-Ø-me> (eat-3npA-23s-AFF)

→ *ja-i-Ø-me*$_{am}$ 'he ate it' and <plɛtt-i-Ø-me> (dry-3npA-23s-AFF) → *plɛtt-i-Ø-m*$_{m}$ 'he dried it', and after root-final vowels in third person dual agent forms, e.g. <pa-i-ci-me> (do-3npA-d-AFF) → *pa-i-ci-m*$_{a}$ 'they^{d} did it' and <ja-i-ci-ʔ-me> (eat-3npA-d-3dA-AFF) → *ja-i-ci-ʔ-m*$_{m}$ 'they^{d} ate it'.

(b) The suffix <-i>$_{am}$ is realised as the phonologically empty morph *-Ø*$_{am}$ after root-final consonants in third person dual agent forms. The deletion of post-final <t> of the verb root seems to be somehow related to the phonologically empty realisation of the third person non-plural agent suffix, which surfaces as the basic morph *-i*$_{am}$ under (a). In Mohanṭāre, root-final <t> is also deleted and the preceding vowel becomes long before <-i>$_{am}$, e.g. <plɛtt-i-ci-ʔ-me> (dry-3npA-d-3dA-AFF) → *ple-Ø-ci-ʔ-m*$_{m}$ 'they^{d} dried it'. However, the other root-final consonants are not subject to additional morphophonologically conditioned modification in this dialect, e.g. <makt-i-ci-ʔ-me> (catch-3npA-d-3dA-AFF) → *mak-Ø-ci-ʔ-m*$_{m}$ 'they^{d} caught it' and <kurt-i-ci-ʔ-me> (carry-3npA-d-3dA-AFF) → *kur-Ø-ci-ʔ-m*$_{m}$ 'they^{d} carried it'. In Āmboṭe Jero, by contrast, there is no morphophonologically conditioned modification in addition to deletion of post-final <t>. Final <t> and the other root-final consonants are retained, e.g. <patt-i-ci-me> (cause.to.do-3npA-d-AFF) → *pat-Ø-ci-m*$_{a}$ 'they^{d} made him [do something]', <gɔkt-i-ci-me> (give-3npA-d-AFF) → *gɔk-Ø-ci-m*$_{a}$ 'they^{d} gave [something] to him' and <tɛrt-i-ci-me> (receive-3npA-d-AFF) → *tɛr-Ø-ci-m*$_{a}$ 'they^{d} received it'.

4.3.6 *The 2→1s suffix*

MORPHEME	<-iŋ>$_{m}$
GLOSS	2→1s

The Mohanṭāre suffix <-iŋ>$_{m}$ marks a transitive relationship between a second person agent and a first person singular patient. Singularity and duality of the agent are marked by means of the suffixes <-Ø>$_{am}$ (23s) and <-ci>$_{am}$ (d).

AGENT→PATIENT		
2s→1s$_m$	<Σ-iŋ-Ø>	(Σ-2→1s-23s)
2d→1s$_m$	<Σ-iŋ-ci>	(Σ-2→1s-d)

The suffix <-iŋ>$_m$ (2→1s) is cognate of Wambule <-ŋi> (2→1s). Comparative evidence suggests that plurality of the second person agent is marked by means of the suffixes <-ni>$_{am}$ (2) and <-mi>$_{am}$ (23/ns), i.e. 2p→1s *<Σ-iŋ-ni-mi>$_m$ (Σ-2→1s-2-23/ns).

Āmboṭe Jero generally uses periphrastic forms to mark transitive relationships between second person agents and first person patients. These agreement constructions consist of a main verbal ending in <-su> and singular, dual and plural agent forms of the verb *pacap* vt-2a <pa- ~ po-> 'to do, make', e.g. <gɔkt-su pa-ni-Ø-me> (give-MAN do-2-23s-AFF) → *gɔk-su pa-n-Ø-ne*$_a$ 'you^{s} gave to me/us^{e}'. In Mohanṭāre Jero, however, the use of periphrastic constructions is restricted to relationships between second person agents and first person non-singular patients, e.g. <tɛr-su pa-ni-Ø-me> (receive-MAN do-2-23s-AFF) → *tɛr-su pa-n-Ø-ne*$_m$ 'you^{s} met us^{e}'. The synthetic forms 2s→1s$_m$ <Σ- iŋ-Ø> and 2d→1s$_m$ <Σ-iŋ-ci> are used here to mark transitive relationships between second person agents and first person singular patients, e.g. <tɛr-iŋ-Ø-me>$_m$ (receive-2→1s-23s-AFF) → *tɛr-iŋ-Ø-ma*$_m$ 'you^{s} met me'.

4.3.7 *The first person inclusive agent and subject suffix*

MORPHEME	<-ki>$_{am}$
GLOSS	1piAS

The suffix <-ki>$_{am}$ marks a first person plural inclusive agent and subject argument. In transitive verbs, the patient is unmarked.

SUBJECT		
1pi$_{am}$	<Σ-ki>	<Σ-1piAS>

AGENT		
1pi→3$_{am}$	<Σ-ki>$_m$	<Σ-1piAS>

4.3.8 *The first person exclusive agent and subject suffix*

MORPHEME	<-kuwa>$_{a}$ ~ <-ku>$_{m}$
GLOSS	1peAS

The suffixes <-kuwa>$_{a}$ and <-ku>$_{m}$ mark a first person plural exclusive agent and subject.

SUBJECT		
1pe$_{a}$	<Σ-kuwa>	(Σ-1peAS)
1pe$_{m}$	<Σ-ku>	(Σ-1peAS)

AGENT		
1pe→2$_{a}$	<Σ-su po-kuwa>	(Σ-MAN do-1peAS)
1pe→2p$_{m}$	<Σ-su po-ku>	(Σ-MAN do-1peAS)
1pe→3$_{a}$	<Σ-kuwa>	(Σ-1peAS)
1pe→3s$_{m}$	<Σ-ku>	(Σ-1peAS)

In transitive verbs, the patient is formally unmarked. As in Āmboṭe, Mohanṭāre apparently also uses periphrastic forms to mark transitive relationships between first person plural exclusive agents and second person patients. This is primarily suggested by the second person plural patient form 1pe→2p$_{m}$ <Σ-su po-ku> (Σ-MAN do-1peAS). The Āmboṭe suffix <-kuwa>$_{a}$ is realised as the abbreviated morph *-ku*$_{am}$ before post-agreement suffixes.

110$_{a}$ *Kaṭhmanḍu=na* *ba:-ku-m.*
Kathmandu=LOC be/sit-1peAS
We[pe] will live in Kathmandu.

The final element <wa> of the first person plural exclusive morpheme is also found in the Āmboṭe first person dual exclusive suffix <-cuwa>$_{a}$.

4.3.9 *The second and third person and non-singular actant suffix*

MORPHEME	<-mi>$_{am}$
GLOSS	23/ns

The suffix <-mi>$_{am}$ marks that minimally one of the actants involved in the verbal scenario is a second or third person and that minimally one actant, but not necessarily the same actant, is non-singular. In the case of intransitive and middle verbs, the subject marked in the finite verb is both second or third person and non-singular.

SUBJECT		
2p$_{am}$	<Σ-ni-mi>	(Σ-2-23/ns)
3p$_{am}$	<Σ-mi>	(Σ-23/ns)
AGENT		
2p→1$_{a}$	<Σ-su po-ni-mi>	(Σ-MAN do-2-23/ns)
3d→2s$_{am}$	<Σ-ci-mi>	(Σ-d-23/ns)
3p→1$_{a}$	<Σ-su pa-mi>	(Σ-MAN do-23/ns)
3p→1ns$_{m}$	<Σ-su pa-mi>	(Σ-MAN do-23/ns)
3p→2np$_{a}$	<Σ-ni-mi>	(Σ-2-23/ns)
3p→3$_{am}$	<Σ-mi>	(Σ-23/ns)
PATIENT		
1s→3d$_{m}$	<Σ-ŋu-ci-mi>	(Σ-1s-d-23/ns)
1s→3p$_{m}$	<Σ-ŋu-mi>	(Σ-1s-23/ns)
3→2p$_{a}$	<Σ-si ra:-ni-mi>	(Σ-INF provoke-2-23/ns)
3s→2d$_{m}$	<Σ-ci-mi>	(Σ-d-23/ns)
3np→2d$_{a}$	<Σ-ci-mi>	(Σ-d-23/ns)
AGENT↔PATIENT		
1s↔3d$_{a}$	<Σ-ŋu-mi-ci-mi>	(Σ-1s-23/ns-d-23/ns)
1s↔3p$_{a}$	<Σ-ŋu-mi>	(Σ-1s-23/ns)
2p↔3$_{a}$	<Σ-ni-mi>	(Σ-2-23/ns)
2p↔3s$_{m}$	<Σ-ni-mi>	(Σ-2-23/ns)

In the form 3p→2np$_{a}$ <Σ-ni-mi>, the suffix <-mi>$_{am}$ (23/ns) refers to the third person plural agent, but not to the second person non-plural (i.e. singular and dual) patient, whereas the suffix <-ni>$_{am}$ (2)

marks a second person patient. In other words, the two simplex agreement morphemes refer to different actants. By contrast, in the form 2p↔3_{a} <Σ-ni-mi>, the two agreement suffixes refer to the same actant, which is a second person plural argument. Here, the third person argument is formally left unmarked in the finite verb.

Note that the suffix <-mi>$_{\text{am}}$ (23/ns) occurs twice in the Āmboṭe form 1s↔3d <Σ-ŋu-mi-ci-mi>$_{\text{a}}$ (Σ-1s-23/ns-d-23/ns), whereas the suffix occurs only once in the Mohanṭāre form 1s→3d <Σ-ŋu-ci-mi>$_{\text{m}}$ (Σ-1s- d-23/ns).

The suffix <-mi>$_{\text{am}}$ (23/ns) is subject to the following morphophonologically conditioned variation:

(a) The suffix <-mi>$_{\text{am}}$ (23/ns) is generally realised as *-m*$_{\text{am}}$ after agreement suffixes which end in a vowel morphophoneme, e.g. <kran-ŋu-mi-ci-mi-me> (bite-1s-23/ns-d-23/ns-AFF) → *kraŋ-ŋu-m-ci-m-me*$_{\text{a}}$ 'they^{d} bit me', and <ma:-ni-mi-me> (catch-2-23/ns-AFF) → *ma:-ni-m-me*$_{\text{m}}$ 'you^{p} caught it'.

(b) After verb roots which end in a vowel phoneme, word-final <-mi>$_{\text{am}}$ (23/ns) is also realised as *-m*$_{\text{am}}$ in Mohanṭāre Jero, e.g. <a-ja-mi> (NEG-eat-23/ns) → *a-ja-m*$_{\text{m}}$ 'they^{p} did not eat it', whereas the suffix is realised as *-mi*$_{\text{am}}$ in Āmboṭe Jero, e.g. <a-lɔ-mi> (NEG-go-23/ns) → *a-lɔ-mi*$_{\text{a}}$ 'they^{p} did not go' and <a-thɔ-mi> (NEG-ask.for-23/ns) → *a-thɔ-mi*$_{\text{a}}$ 'they^{p} did not ask for it'. Before post-agreement suffixes with initial <m>, such as the suffix <-me> of the affirmative, the suffix <-mi>$_{\text{am}}$ (23/ns) is realised as *-m*$_{\text{am}}$ in both dialects, e.g. <ja-mi-me> (eat-23/ns-AFF) → *ja-m-me*$_{\text{am}}$ 'they^{p} ate it', <thɔ-mi-me> (ask.for-23/ns-AFF) → *thɔ-m-me*$_{\text{a}}$ 'they^{p} asked for it' and <dɛ-mi-me> (dig-23/ns-AFF) → *dɛ-m-me*$_{\text{a}}$ 'they^{p} dug'.

(c) The suffix <-mi>$_{\text{am}}$ (23/ns) is realised as *-im*$_{\text{am}}$ after verb roots ending in a consonant phoneme, e.g. <wal-mi-me> (walk-23/ns-AFF) → *wal-im-me*$_{\text{m}}$ 'they^{p} walked', <a-khrɔm-mi> (NEG-cry-23/ns) → *a-khrɔm-im*$_{\text{m}}$ 'they^{p} did not cry' and <mɔr-mi-me> (get.out-23/ns-AFF) → *mɔr-im-me*$_{\text{a}}$ 'they^{p} got out'. Note that the root-final nasal <m> is deleted before <-mi>$_{\text{am}}$ (23/ns) in Āmboṭe, e.g. <dum-mi-me> (become-23/ns-AFF) →

du-im-me$_{a}$ 'they^{p} became' and <tum-mi-me> (beat.self-23/ns-AFF) → *tu-im-me*$_{a}$ 'they^{p} beat themselves'.

(d) In Mohanṭāre Jero, post-final <t> of transitive verbs is generally deleted before the suffix <-mi>$_{am}$ (23/ns), which is subsequently realised as *-ʔim*$_{m}$. The root-final consonants are modified as follows:

- Root-final <p> is deleted, e.g. <japt-mi-me> (buy-23/ns-AFF) → *ja-ʔim-me*$_{m}$ 'they^{p} bought it'.

- Root-final <t> and <k> are deleted and the preceding vowel of the verb root is lengthened, e.g. <plɛtt-mi-me> (dry-23/ns-AFF) → *ple-ʔim-me*$_{m}$ 'they^{p} dried it' and <a-makt-mi> (NEG-catch-23/ns)→ *a-maː-ʔim*$_{m}$ 'they^{p} did not catch it'.

- The other root-final consonants remain unchanged, however, e.g. <kurt-mi-me> (carry-23/ns-AFF) → *kur-ʔim-me*$_{m}$ 'they^{p} carried it' and <khɛlt-mi-me> (touch-23/ns-AFF) → *khɛl-ʔim-me*$_{m}$ 'they^{p} touched it'.

(e) In Āmboṭe, post-final <t> of transitive verbs is also generally deleted before the suffix <-mi> (23/ns). The morpheme <-mi> (23/ns) is realised as *-ʔmi*$_{a}$ in word-final position or *-Ø*$_{a}$ or *-ʔ*$_{a}$ before post-agreement suffixes with initial <m>, which have a haplological effect on the realisation of the agreement suffix <-mi> (23/ns). The root-final consonants are modified as follows:

- Root-final <p> and <k> are retained after the deletion of post-final <t>, e.g. <tupt-mi-me> (beat-23/ns-AFF) → *tup-Ø-me*$_{a}$ 'they^{p} beat him' (<**tup-ʔ-me*) and <rɛkt-mi-me> (write-23/ns-AFF) → *rɛk-Ø-me*$_{a}$ 'they^{p} wrote it' (<**rɛk-ʔ-me*).

- Root-final <Vt> becomes a long vowel, e.g. <phatt-mi-me> (can-23/ns-AFF) → *phaː-ʔ-me*$_{a}$ (<**phaː-ʔmi-me*) 'they^{p} could [do] it' and <a-phatt-mi> (NEG-can-23/ns) → *a-phaː-ʔmi*$_{a}$ 'they^{p} could not [do] it'.

- Post-final <t> of root-final <Vːt, rt> is deleted and the preceding root segments remain unchanged, e.g. <tuːt-mi-me> (drink-23/ns-AFF) → *tuː-ʔ-me*$_{a}$ 'they^{p} drank it' and <tɛrt-mi-me> (receive-23/ns-AFF) → *tɛr-ʔ-me*$_{a}$ 'they^{p} received him'.

4.3.10 *The 3s→2s morpheme*

MORPHEME	<-nati>$_{m}$
GLOSS	3s→2s

The Mohanṭāre suffix <-nati>$_{m}$ marks a transitive relationship between a third person singular agent and a second person singular patient.

AGENT→PATIENT		
3s→2s	<Σ-nati>$_{m}$	(Σ-3s→2s)

The suffix is has only been recorded as the basic morph *-nati*$_{m}$, e.g. <him-nati-me> (see-3s→2s-AFF) → *him-nati-m*$_{m}$ 'he saw you^{s}' and <tɛr-nati-me> (receive-3s→2s-AFF) → *tɛr-nati-m*$_{m}$ 'he met you^{s}'. This Mohanṭāre suffix is cognate of the Wambule suffix <-nati> (3s→2s). In Āmboṭe synthetic 3s→2s forms, the second person suffix <-ni>$_{am}$ (2) and the second and third person singular morpheme <-Ø>$_{am}$ (23s) are added to the secondary root alternant of verbs which are subject to paradigmatic root alternation, e.g. <go-ni-Ø-me> (give-2-23s-AFF) → *go-n-Ø-ne*$_{a}$ 'he gave to you^{s}'.

4.3.11 *The second person suffix*

MORPHEME	<-ni>$_{am}$
GLOSS	2

The suffix <-ni>$_{am}$ marks a second person actant in intransitive, middle and transitive verbs. Singularity or plurality of the second person actant is generally specified by means of the suffixes <-Ø>$_{am}$ (23s) and <-mi>$_{am}$ (23/ns). The recorded Mohanṭāre 1s→2p form <Σ-ni-ni>$_{m}$ might actually be incorrect.

SUBJECT		
$2s_{am}$	<Σ-ni-Ø>	(Σ-2-23s)
$2p_{am}$	<Σ-ni-mi>	(Σ-2-23/ns)

AGENT		
$2s \rightarrow 1_{a}$	<Σ-su pa-ni-Ø>	(Σ-MAN do-2-23s)
$2s \rightarrow 1nse_{m}$	<Σ-su pa-ni-Ø>	(Σ-MAN do-2-23s)
$2s \rightarrow 3_{am}$	<Σ-ni-Ø>	(Σ-2-23s)
$2p \rightarrow 1_{a}$	<Σ-su po-ni-mi>	(Σ-MAN do-2-23/ns)

PATIENT		
$1s \rightarrow 2p_{m}$	<Σ-ni-ni>	(Σ-1s→2-2)
$3 \rightarrow 2p_{a}$	<Σ-si ra:-ni-mi>	(Σ-INF provoke-2-23/ns)
$3 \rightarrow 2s_{a}$	<Σ-si ra:-ni-Ø>	(Σ-INF provoke-2-23s)
$3s \rightarrow 2s_{a}$	<Σ-ni-Ø>	(Σ-2-23s)
$3p \rightarrow 2np_{a}$	<Σ-ni-mi>	(Σ-2-23/ns)

Āmboṭe verb forms that mark transitive relationships between a second person plural agent and third person patients and verb forms that mark transitive relationships between third person agents and a second person plural patient are morphologically identical. The second person morpheme is directly added to the verb root, which is the secondary root of verbs which are subject to paradigmatically conditioned root alternation.

AGENT↔PATIENT		
$2p \leftrightarrow 3_{a}$	<Σ-ni-mi>	(Σ-2-23/ns)
$2p \leftrightarrow 3s_{m}$	<Σ-ni-mi>	(Σ-2-23/ns)

The second person suffix <-ni>$_{am}$ (2) is subject to the following morphophonologically conditioned variation:

(a) After verbs roots ending in a vowel and before the agreement suffix <-Ø>$_{am}$ (23s) and post-agreement suffixes with initial <m>, the suffix <-ni> is realised as *-n*$_{am}$, e.g. <ba:-ni-Ø-me> (be/sit-2-23d-AFF) → *ba-n-Ø-ne*$_{am}$ 'you^{s} were, you^{s} sat' and <ja-ni-Ø-me> (eat-2-23s-AFF) → *ja-n-Ø-ne*$_{m}$ 'you^{s} ate it'. In corresponding negative forms, word-final <-ni> can be realised as *-ni*$_{am}$ and *-n*$_{am}$, e.g. <a-ja-ni-Ø> (NEG-eat-2-23s) → *a-ja-ni-*

Ø$_{m}$ 'you^{s} did not eat it', <a-ne-ni-Ø> (NEG-say-2-23s) → *a-ne-ni-Ø* ~ *a-ne-n-Ø*$_{m}$ 'you^{s} did not say' and <a-thɔ-ni-Ø> (NEG-ask.for-2-23s) → *a-thɔ-ni-Ø*$_{a}$ 'you^{s} did not ask for it'.

(b) The suffix <-ni> is realised as the basic morph *-ni*$_{am}$ in the remaining environments, e.g. <tum-ni-Ø-me> (beat.self-2-23s-AFF) → *tum-ni-Ø-m*$_{m}$ 'you^{s} beat yourself', <dum-ni-mi-me> (become-2-23/ns-AFF) → *dum-ni-m-me*$_{m}$ 'you^{s} became' and <ya-ni-mi-me> (come.up-2-23/ns-AFF) → *ya-ni-m-me*$_{m}$ 'you^{s} came up'. Note that post-final <t> is generally deleted, e.g. <makt-ni-Ø-me> (catch-2-23s-AFF) → *mak-ni-Ø-m*$_{m}$ 'you^{s} caught it' and <tatt-ni-Ø-me> (stop-2-23s-AFF) → *tat-ni-Ø-m*$_{a}$ 'you^{s} stopped doing it'.

4.3.12 *The 1s→2 suffix*

MORPHEME	<-ni>$_{am}$
GLOSS	1s→2

The suffix <-ni>$_{am}$ marks a transitive relationship between a first person singular agent and a second person patient. The number of the patient is marked by means of the suffixes <-Ø>$_{am}$ (23s), <-ci>$_{am}$ (d), and perhaps also <-ni>$_{am}$ (2).

AGENT→PATIENT		
1s→2s$_{am}$	<Σ-ni-Ø>	(Σ-1s→2-23s)
1s→2d$_{m}$	<Σ-ni-ci>	(Σ-1s→2-d)
1s→2p$_{m}$	<Σ-ni-ni>	(Σ-1s→2-2)

4.3.13 *The dual subject suffix*

MORPHEME	<-ŋ>$_{am}$
GLOSS	dS

Dual intransitive and middle forms require the dual subject morpheme <-ŋ>$_{am}$. In Āmboṭe, his suffix is also used in the periphrastic 3→2d form, which consists of a main verbal ending in <-si>$_{am}$ plus second person dual forms of the middle verb *ra:cap*$_{a}$ vm-1a <ra:-> 'to influence, arouse'.

SUBJECT		
1di/2d/3d$_{am}$	<Σ-ŋ-ci>	(Σ-dS-d)
1de$_{a}$	<Σ-ŋ-cuwa>	(Σ-dS-1deAS)
1de$_{m}$	<Σ-ŋ-cu>	(Σ-dS-1deAS)
PATIENT		
3→2d$_{a}$	<Σ-si ra:-ŋ-ci>	(Σ-INF provoke-dS-d)

The dual subject suffix is subject to the following morphophonologically conditioned alternation:

(a) The allomorph *-ŋ*$_{am}$ is generally used after verb roots ending in a vowel, e.g. <ne-ŋ-ci-me> (say-dS-d-AFF) → *ne-ŋ-ci-m*$_{am}$ 'we^{di}/you^{d}/they^{d} said' and <si-ŋ-cu-me> (say-dS-1deAS-AFF) → *si-ŋ-cu-ma*$_{a}$ 'we^{de} will die'.

(b) In Mohanṭāre, the dual subject suffix is realised as *-uŋ*$_{m}$ in first person dual exclusive forms and as *-iŋ*$_{m}$ in other dual forms after verb roots ending in a consonant, e.g. <tum-ŋ-cu-me> (beat.self-dS-1deAS-AFF) → *tum-uŋ-cu-m*$_{m}$ 'we^{de} hit ourselves' and <tum-ŋ-ci-me> (beat.self-dS-d-AFF) → *tum-iŋ-ci-m*$_{m}$ we^{di}/you^{d}/they^{d} hit ourselves/yourselves/themselves'. The epenthetic vowels /i/ and /u/ which precede the velar nasal of the agreement suffix show harmony with the vowel of the following simplex person and number agreement suffix.

(c) In Āmboṭe Jero, by contrast, the dual subject agreement suffix is realised as *-ŋaŋ*$_{a}$ after middle verb roots ending in a consonant, e.g. <mɔr-ŋ-cu-me> (wash.self-dS-1deAS-AFF) → *mɔr-ŋaŋ-cu-m* 'we^{de} washed ourselves'. The dual subject agreement suffix is also realised as *-ŋaŋ*$_{a}$ after intransitive verb roots ending in the bilabial nasal <m>, which is modified into a velar nasal, e.g. <dum-ŋ-cu-me> (become-dS-1deAS-AFF) → *duŋ-ŋaŋ-cu-m* 'we^{de} became', <dum-ŋ-ci-me> (become-dS-d-AFF) → *duŋ-ŋaŋ-ci-m* 'we^{di} became'. By contrast, the dual subject agreement suffix is realised the morph *-ŋu*$_{a}$ after middle verb roots ending in <m>, e.g. <tum-ŋ-ci-me> → *tuŋum-ci-m* (hit. self+dS-d-AFF) 'we^{di} hit ourselves' and <tum-ŋ-cu-me> → *tuŋum-cu-m* (hit.self+dS-1deAS-AFF) 'we^{de} hit ourselves'.

4.3.14 *The first person singular suffix*

MORPHEME	<-ŋu>$_{am}$
GLOSS	1s

The suffix <-ŋu>$_{am}$ marks a first person singular argument, which is a subject or agent argument in Mohanṭāre, and also a patient in Āmboṭe Jero. The first person singular morpheme is directly added to the verb root. Transitive verbs that are subject to paradigmatically conditioned root alternation show that the first person singular morpheme is attached to the primary verb root if reference is made to an agent argument, whereas the secondary root alternant is used if reference is made to a patient argument.

SUBJECT		
1s$_{am}$	<Σ-ŋu>	(Σ-1s)
AGENT		
1s→2ns$_{am}$	<Σ-su pa-ŋu>	(Σ-MAN do-1s)
1s→3s$_{m}$	<Σ-ŋu>	(Σ-1s)
1s→3d$_{m}$	<Σ-ŋu-ci-mi>	(Σ-1s-d-23/ns)
1s→3p$_{m}$	<Σ-ŋu-mi>	(Σ-1s-23/ns)
AGENT↔PATIENT		
1s↔3s$_{a}$	<Σ-ŋu>	(Σ-1s)
1s↔3d$_{a}$	<Σ-ŋu-mi-ci-mi>	(Σ-1s-23/ns-d-23/ns)
1s↔3p$_{a}$	<Σ-ŋu-mi>	(Σ-1s-23/ns)

Verb forms that mark transitive relationships between a first person singular agent and third person patients and those that mark transitive relationships between third person agents and a first person singular patient are morphologically identical.

The suffix <-ŋu>$_{am}$ (1s) is subject to the following morphophonological alternation:

(a) In intransitive and middle forms ending in a vowel, the suffix is realised as *-ŋu*$_{am}$ in negative forms and as *-ŋ*$_{am}$ before post-agreement suffixes with initial <m>, e.g. <a-ne-ŋu> (NEG-say-1s) → *a-ne-ŋu*$_{m}$ 'I did not say', <a-nɔ-ŋu> (NEG-be-1s) → *a-nɔ-ŋu*$_{a}$ 'I was not', <lɔ-ŋu-me> (go-1s-AFF) → *lɔ-ŋ-ma*$_{am}$ 'I went' and <baː-ŋu-me> (be/sit-1s-AFF) → *ba-ŋ-ma*$_{am}$ 'I sat'. Final <-ŋu>$_{am}$ can also be realised as the abbreviated morph *-ŋ*$_{am}$ in Mohanṭāre, e.g. <a-ne-ŋu> (NEG-say-1s) → *a-ne-ŋ*$_{m}$ 'I did not say' and <a-di-ŋu> (NEG-go/come-1s) → *a-di-ŋ*$_{m}$ 'I did not go (and come back)'.

(b) In intransitive and middle forms ending in /l, r/, the first person singular agent and subject suffix is realised as *-uŋ*$_{m}$ in Mohanṭāre, e.g. <wal-uŋ-me> (walk-1s-AFF) → *wal-uŋ-ma*$_{m}$ 'I walked', and as the basic morph *-ŋu*$_{am}$ in Āmboṭe, e.g. <mɔr-ŋu-me> (wash.self-1s-AFF) → *mɔr-ŋu-m*$_{a}$ 'I washed myself'.

(c) In intransitive and middle forms ending in <m>, the suffix is realised as *-ŋ*$_{am}$ before post-agreement suffixes with initial <m> in Mohanṭāre. The verb root loses its final <m>, e.g. <tum-ŋu-me> (beat.self-1s-AFF) → *tu-ŋ-ma*$_{m}$ 'I will hit myself'. Root-final <m> becomes <ŋ> in Āmboṭe, where <-ŋu>$_{am}$ is realised as the basic morph, e.g. <tum-ŋu-me> (beat.self-1s-AFF) → *tuŋ-ŋu-ma*$_{a}$ 'I will beat myself'.

(d) In transitive forms ending in a short vowel, the first person singular suffix is realised as *-u*$_{am}$ before post-agreement suffixes with initial <m>, e.g. <dɛ-ŋu-me> (dig-1s-AFF) → *dɛ-u-m*$_{a}$ 'I will dig', <ki-ŋu-me> (look.at-1s-AFF) → *ki-u-m*$_{a}$ 'I will look at it', <thɔ-ŋu-me> (ask.for-1s-AFF) → *thɔ-u-m*$_{a}$ 'I will ask for it'. The vowel of transitive forms ending in <a> can also be realised as /ʌ/ before the vowel /u/ of the first person singular agreement suffix, e.g. <ja-ŋu-me> (eat-1s-AFF) → *jʌ-u-ma*$_{am}$ 'I ate it'.

(e) In negated transitive forms ending in post-final <t>, the post-final segment and the final stops are generally deleted and the first person singular suffix is realised as *-ʔu*$_{am}$, e.g. <a-japt-ŋu> (NEG-buy-1s) → *a-ja-ʔu*$_{m}$ 'I did not buy it', <a-patt-ŋu> (NEG-cause.to.do-1s) → *a-pa-ʔu*$_{a}$ 'I did not cause him to do [something]', <a-makt-ŋu> (NEG-catch-1s) → *a-ma-ʔu*$_{m}$ 'I did not catch him' and <a-tɛrt-ŋu> (NEG-receive-1s) → *a-tɛr-ʔu*$_{m}$ 'I did not receive it'.

(f) Before post-agreement suffixes with an initial <m>, by contrast, the first person singular suffix is generally realised as *-ʔ* in transitive forms ending in post-final <t>. In Mohanṭāre, the post-final segment and the final stops are deleted, whereas the other final consonants remain unchanged, e.g. <hipt-ŋu-ma> (see-1s-AFF) → *hi-ʔ-ma*$_{m}$ 'I saw him', <plɛtt-ŋu-ma> (dry-1s-AFF) → *plɛ-ʔ-ma*$_{m}$ 'I dried it', <makt-ŋu-ma> (catch-1s-AFF) → *ma-ʔ-ma*$_{m}$ 'I caught him', <khɛlt-ŋu-ma> (touch-1s-AFF) → *khɛl-ʔ-ma*$_{m}$ 'I touched him' and <tɛrt-ŋu-ma> (receive-1s-AFF) → *tɛr-ʔ-ma*$_{m}$ 'I received him'. In Āmboṭe, by contrast, post-final <t> is also deleted, but here the first person singular suffix is phonologically empty after root-final stops and root-final <p> and <t> become /p/, e.g. <hipt-ŋu-ma> (see-1s-AFF) → *hip-Ø-ma*$_{a}$ 'I saw him' (<**hip-ʔ-ma*), <patt-ŋu-ma> (cause.to.do-1s-AFF) → *pap-Ø-ma*$_{a}$ 'I made him do [something]' (<**pat-ʔ-ma*) and <rɛkt-ŋu-ma> (write-1s-AFF) → *rɛk-Ø-ma*$_{a}$ 'I wrote it' (<**rɛk-ʔ-ma*). The first person singular suffix is the regular allomorph *-ʔ* after other root-final segments, e.g. <tɛrt-ŋu-ma> (receive-1s-AFF) → *tɛr-ʔ-ma*$_{a}$ 'I received it' and <tuːt-ŋu-ma> (drink-1s-AFF) → *tuː-ʔ-ma*$_{a}$ 'I drank it'.

As in the case of the suffix <-mi>$_{am}$ (23/ns), the presence of glottal stops in agreement morphemes can be linked up with the presence of post-final <t> of transitive verb stems. Post-agreement suffixes with initial <m> have the same haplological effect on the realisation of the suffix <-ŋu>$_{am}$ (1s) as on that of the suffix <-mi>$_{am}$ (23/ns).

4.3.15 *The middle suffix*

MORPHEME	<-si>$_{am}$
GLOSS	MID

The suffix <-si>$_{am}$ marks a middle scenario in third person singular forms, in which the middle suffix precedes the phonologically empty second and third person singular agreement morpheme.

SUBJECT		
3s$_{am}$	<Σ-si-Ø>	(Σ-MID-23s)

The middle morpheme does not occur in the other forms of the middle paradigm. This restricted distribution is also found in Wambule.

4.3.16 *The third person dual agent suffix*

MORPHEME	<-ʔ>$_{m}$
GLOSS	3dA

The Mohanṭāre suffix <-ʔ>$_{m}$ marks a third person dual agent. This suffix does not appear in third person singular and plural agent forms.

AGENT		
3d→3s	<Σ-i-ci-ʔ>	(Σ-3npA-d-3dA)

The third person dual agent agreement morpheme <-ʔ>$_{m}$ distinguishes 1di/2d→3 forms, which generally take the secondary verb root, from 3d→3s forms, which generally take the primary verb root.

1di/2d→3(s)	<Σ-ci-me>$_{m}$	(Σ-d-AFF)
<jo->	*jo-ci-m*$_{m}$	'we^{di}/you^{d} ate it'
<kur->	*kur-ci-m*$_{m}$	'we^{di}/you^{d} carried it'
3d→3s	<Σ-i-ci-ʔ-me>$_{m}$	(Σ-3npA-d-3dA-AFF)
<ja->	*ja-i-ci-ʔ-m*$_{m}$	'they^{d} ate it'
<kurt->	*kur-Ø-ci-ʔ-m*$_{m}$	'they^{d} carried it'

The vowel-final root of the verb *jacam*$_{m}$ vt-2a <ja- ~ jo-> 'to eat' shows that the presence of the glottal stop morpheme <-ʔ>$_{m}$ is not somehow morphophonologically linked up with the presence of post-final <t> of transitive verb roots. However, the presence of <-ʔ>$_{m}$ may be related to the zero realisation of the morpheme <-i>$_{m}$ (3npA) after root-final consonants in third person dual agent forms. That is to say, the only phonological difference between *kurcim* 'we^{di}/you^{d} carried it' and *kurciʔm* 'they^{d} carried it' is the glottal stop.

From a comparative point of view, the suffix <-ʔ>$_{m}$ might also be analysed as a consonantal copy of the third person non-plural agent suffix <-i>$_{am}$. Note that the Jero suffix <-i>$_{am}$ is cognate of the Wambule suffix <-u> (3npA), which is realised as the consonant *-k* [ʔ] in complex verb forms with bound verb roots, e.g. Wambule <hipt-lwa-u-ci-me> (see-go-3npA-d-AFF) → *hip-lwa-k-ci-m* 'they^{d} went away and looked at him'. The Mohanṭāre suffix <-ʔ>$_{m}$ might therefore well represent a consonantal allomorph of a morpheme which has a vowel in the basic morph. Alternatively, one could state that Mohanṭāre Jero has a special third person dual agent suffix <-cik>$_{m}$. This analysis is not adopted here for structural reasons, mainly because the dual morpheme <-ci>$_{am}$ (d) can be followed by other agreement morphemes, notably <-mi>$_{am}$ (23/ns), and because the dual morpheme is generally contrastive with the morpheme <-Ø>$_{m}$ (23s).

4.4 *The factual verbal adjective*

MORPHEME	<-mei>$_{am}$
GLOSS	FCT

Suffixation of the morpheme <-mei>$_{am}$ to a simplex verb form yields a factual verbal adjective with imperfective aspectualising capacities. Negatives are formed by prefixation of the negative marker <a->$_{am}$ to the corresponding positive forms of the deverbative nominal. Factual verbal adjectives are generally translated into Nepali by means of first perfect participles, e.g. <ba:-ŋu-mei> (be/sit-1s-FCT) → *ba-ŋ-mai*$_{am}$, Nep. *baseko* '[I] was, [I] sat, [I] stayed'.

Factual verbal adjectives express statements of fact concerning the event expressed by the modified verb. For instance, the phrase *I said it* is turned into *that which I said* or *the fact that I said it*. Factual verbal adjectives can be used as an adnominal modifier like an ordinary adjective, as a nominal argument which takes case markers and postpositions like nouns, and as the main predicator of a clause.

Factual verbal adjectives and the clauses that dependent on them have nominalising capacities and can therefore be used as an adnominal modifier. The grammatical role markers required by syntax are added to the nominal head of the clause.

111_a *Uŋgu=ku* *satni* *tɛr-ʔ-mai* *mucu.*
I/we=SRC yesterday receive-1s-FCT person

The person whom I met yesterday.

112_m *Ai* *saiso* *ungu=khu* *po-u-mʌi* *kam.*
this yesterday I/we=SRC do-1s-FCT *work*

This [is] the work which I did yesterday.

113_a *Inne=ku* *thoni* *rɛk-ni-Ø-mei* *kitap*
you=SRC one.year.ago write-2-23s-FCT *book*

Nepal=na *tɛr-si-Ø-m?*
Nepal=LOC receive.self-MID-23s-AFF

Is the book you wrote last year available in Nepal?

114_m *Inne* *saiso* *lɔ-n-Ø-nei* *kul.*
you yesterday go-2-23s-FCT house

The house to which you[s] went yesterday.

115_a *Uŋ* *ba:-ku-mai* *ṭhaũ=na* *bla:-Ø-m.*
I/we be/sit-1peAS-FCT *place*=LOC come-23s-AFF

He arrived at the place where we[pe] are/were sitting.

116_a *Karj-ʌi* *pa-m-mei* *bɛla=n* *thɔ-si*
work-EMPH do-23/ns-FCT *time*=LOC hear-INF

bak-si *pʌrchʌ,* *hus* *bu-l* *jo-si-Ø-m.*
be/sit-INF *is.necessary* how time-LOC seem-MID-23s-AFF

When [the priests] do their work, you have to be listening, and then [the know-how] is revealed.

Factual verbal adjectives and the clauses that dependent on them can also be used as a nominal head to which the grammatical role markers required by Jero syntax are attached. The following example is a common alternative for (115). See also (58) and (97) above.

117$_{a}$	*Uŋ*	*ba:-ku-mai=na*	*bla:-Ø-m.*
	I/we	be/sit-1peAS-FCT=LOC	come-23s-AFF

He arrived [at the place] where we^{pe} are/were sitting.

Factual verbal adjectives that are used as the main predicator of a clause are aspectually marked in the sense that the factual events described by them are presented without making reference to the inceptive and terminative boundedness of the event within the time interval selected by the speaker. In other terms, the factual verbal adjective presents the action expressed by the modified verb as an event of which the temporal boundaries are unconnected to present circumstances or the moment of speech. A factual verbal adjective relates to the background of another event, rather than to a dynamic action. In the following sentences, the factual verbal adjectives refer to past matters of fact which remain unconnected with present circumstances, i.e. 'you went then' and 'you were late then'. The use of an affirmative verb in example (118) would yield the sense of 'you^{s} started going home yesterday'.

118$_{m}$	*Inne*	*saiso*	*kul*	*lɔ-n-Ø-nei.*
	you	yesterday	house	go-2-23s-FCT

You^{s} went home yesterday.

119$_{a}$	*Uŋ*	*koṭha=n*	*ba-ŋ-mʌi*	*ɛti*	*bɛla.*
	I/we	*room*=LOC	be/sit-1s-FCT	*so.much*	*time*

I stayed in a room then.

A factual verbal adjective relates to the background of the dynamic event of arriving in the following example. In past time settings, factual verbal adjectives often co-occur with the loan particle *thiyo* 'was' (<Nep. *thiyo*) in constructions which indicate relevance at some point of reference in the past of a previous past action. The general implica-

tion is that some other past action succeeded the event described by the factual verbal adjective.

120_{a} *Aŋ* *ticu=k* *hep* *ja-ca* *pa-m-mei*
he/they PL=SRC cooked.grain eat-PUR do-23/ns-FCT
thiyo, *hus* *bu-l* *sʌmdhi*
was how time-LOC *one's.own.child's.father.in.law*
bla:-Ø-m.
come-23s-AFF

They^{P} were about to eat cooked grain when the father-in-law of their own child arrived.

121_{a} a. *Haŋ* *khamma* *ya-n-ne?*
why alone come.down-2-23s-AFF
b. *Kaʔu* *a-ba:-Ø-mei* *thiyo ...*
friend NEG-be/sit-23s-FCT *was*

a. Why did you come alone [to Kathmandu]?
b. I had no friend ... [so I came alone]

Factual verbal adjectives can also be accompanied by third person singular subject forms of the auxiliary *bakcap*$_{a}$ ~ *bakcam*$_{m}$ vi-2 <bak- ~ ba:-> 'to be, sit' in perfect constructions. Perfect constructions mark a past matter of fact with continuing relevance at some posterior point of reference in the past or in the present. In (7) above, the agent is marked with the source marker.

122_{a} *Uŋgu=k* *ai* *kitap* *pʌḍ-ʌi*
I/we=SRC this *book* *read/study*-LN
la-ŋ-mai *ba:-Ø-m.*
become-1s-FCT be/sit-23s-AFF

I have read this book.

123_{m} *Uŋ* *ai* *kam* *pa-u-mʌi* *ba:-Ø-m.*
I/we this *work* do-1s-FCT be/sit-23s-AFF

I have worked.

124$_{a}$ a. *Hukɔl* *bʌrsa* *dum-ni-Ø-mei* *ba:-Ø-me?*
how.much *year* become-2-23s-FCT be/sit-23s-AFF

b. *Uŋgu* *tin* *bʌrsa* *dum-Ø-me*
I/we *three* *year* become-23s-AFF

ba-ŋ-mʌi.
be/sit-1s-FCT

a. How many years has it been [now]?
b. It has been three years for me.

4.5 *The affirmative*

MORPHEME	<-me>$_{\mathrm{am}}$
GLOSS	AFF

Finite verbs in positive statements and questions require the suffix <-me>$_{\mathrm{am}}$ of the affirmative, which appears to be mutually exclusive with the negative prefix. The morpheme <-me>$_{\mathrm{am}}$ of the affirmative is subject to the morphophonological variation described in the previous section. The affirmative suffix is analysed as a grammaticalised or lexicalised instance of the reifying suffix <=me>$_{\mathrm{am}}$. This phrasal suffix is introduced in Section 3.14 above (p. 123). In contrast to the reifying suffix <=me>$_{\mathrm{am}}$, the – at least historically – related affirmative suffix <-me>$_{\mathrm{am}}$ has no clear nominalising capacities in modern Jero. Affirmative verbs are usually translated into Nepali by means of an aorist perfect tense for past time situations and by a simple indefinite tense for present or future time situations, e.g. <ba:-Ø-me> (be/sit-23s-AFF) → *ba:-Ø-m* 'it is' or 'it was' (Nep. *cha*, *bhayo*).

The factual verbal adjective renders factual statements and is imperfectively marked in the sense that it presents the action expressed by the modified verb as an event of which the temporal boundaries are unconnected to present circumstances or the moment of speech. By contrast, the affirmative verb marks dynamic actions which are closely linked up to the moment of speech or some other moment chosen as the point of reference. In (120) above, the affirmative marks past dynamic actions, whereas the factual verbal adjective forms the background of the dynamic action. The affirmatives in the following two examples refer to foregrounded events that are connected to or apply at the moment of speech.

125_a	*Mɔl*	*nɛt-i-Ø-m.*
	stomach	hurt-3npA-23s-AFF

My stomach hurts.

126_m	*Kul*	*yɔkko*	*ba:-Ø-m.*
	house	small	be/sit-23s-AFF

The house is small.

The following affirmative verb forms occur in question sentences.

127_a	*Inne*	*tɛr-ca-p*	*t̨haũ*	*thal*	*ba:-Ø-m?*
	you	receive-PUR-RES	*place*	where	be-23s-AFF

Where is the place where [I, we, he, they] shall meet you[s]?

128_a	*Hai*	*dum-Ø-me?*
	what	become-23s-AFF

What is the matter?

129_a	*Inne*	*hukɔl*	*bʌrsa*	*dum-Ø-me*	*al*
	you	how.much	*year*	become-23s-AFF	here
	ba-n-Ø-ne?				
	be/sit-2-23s-AFF				

For how many years have you[s] been here?

130_a	a.	*Im*	*papa-mama*	*kul=na*	*ba-m-me*	*ki?*
		your[s]	father-mother	house=LOC	be/sit-23/ns-AFF	*or*
	b.	*Kul=na=s*	*ba-m-me.*			
		house=LOC=exactly	be/sit-2-23s-AFF			

a. Do your parents live at home?
b. They live exactly at home.

The coordinating conjunctive particle ki_a 'or' in (130) occurs at the end of polar questions to give the implication of doubt between a positive or negative answer. See also (17) above.

The affirmative in (131) marks an event that is already taking place but has a past inception.

131_{a}	*Uŋ*	*khoku*	*si-ŋ-ma.*
	I/we	cold	die-1s-AFF

I am cold.

The affirmative in (132) expresses the liking of a particular kind of *khamsi* at the moment of speech. The affirmative verb in (133), by contrast, refers to a general action.

132_{a}	*Ai*	*khamsi*	*hujɔktɔp*	*lu-Ø-m?*
	this	cooked.liquid.dish	how	feel-23s-AFF

How do you^{s} like this *khamsi*?

133_{a}	*Khamsi*	*hujɔktɔp*	*lu-Ø-m?*
	cooked.liquid.dish	how	feel-23s-AFF

How do you^{s} like *khamsi* [in general]?

The affirmatives in the following three examples express probable or future actions. The particle ni_{am} is a loan from the Nepali assertive marker *ni*.

134_{m}	*Phɔpma*	*uŋ*	*ai*	*kam*	*pa-u-ma*	*hɔla.*
	tomorrow	I/we	this	*work*	do-1s-AFF	*may.be*

Perhaps I will do this work tomorrow.

135_{m}	*Phɔpma*	*uŋ*	*bla-ŋ-ma*	*ni.*
	tomorrow	I/we	arrive-1s-AFF	I.tell.you

I will come tomorrow, I tell you.

136_{m}	*Inne*	*hai*	*pa-n-Ø-ne?*
	you	what	do-2-23s-AFF

What will you^{s} do?

4.6 *The imperative*

The inflectional category of the imperative is used to express requests, entreaties, commands, orders and permission. Examples of imperative verbs are given in (41), (55), (60) and (72) above.

Imperatives are second person subject and agent forms which contain a set of person and number agreement suffixes that is paradigmatically distinct but formally and semantically related to the simplex person and number agreement morphemes. The imperative person and number agreement suffixes are given in Diagram 17. The imperative suffixes are spread over four functional positions which have to be established in order to account for all suffixal strings. The morphemes in the first functional position occur as the initial elements after the verb root, whereas those in the fourth functional position constitute the final elements of a suffixal string.

Imperative agreement morphemes		
1	<-n>$_{am}$	(pS)
	<-ŋ>$_{am}$	(dS)
	<-s>$_{am}$	(DETR)
2	<-ka>$_{am}$	(IMP)
3	<-ŋ>$_{am}$	(1sP)
	<-m>$_{am}$	(s→3ns)
4	<-ci>$_{am}$	(23d)
	<-ni>$_{am}$	(23p)
	<-Ø>$_{am}$	(sAS)

Diagram 17: Imperative agreement morphemes (basic morphs)

The distribution of the imperative person and number agreement morphemes used in intransitive, middle and transitive verbs is given in Diagram 18 and Diagram 19. Note that imperative verbs that mark a transitive relationship between a second person agent and a first person non-singular exclusive patient are periphrastic constructions which consist of a main verbal ending in <-su>$_{am}$ and third person patient imperative forms of the auxiliary *pacap*$_{a}$ ~ *pacam*$_{m}$ vt-2a <pa- ~ po-> 'to do, make'.

vi & vm	MOHANṬĀRE & ĀMBOṬE
2s (*vi-1a-i*) 2s (*vi-1a-ii*)	<Σ_1-s-ka-Ø> <Σ_1-ka-Ø>
2d	<Σ_2-ŋ-ka-ci>
2p	<Σ_2-n-ka-ni>

Diagram 18: Imperative intransitive and middle morphology

vt	MOHANṬĀRE & ĀMBOṬE
2s→1s	<Σ_1-ka-ŋ-Ø>
2d→1s	<Σ_1-ka-ŋ-ci>
2p→1s	<Σ_1-ka-ŋ-ni>
2s→1e	<Σ_1-su pa-ka-Ø>
2d→1e	<Σ_1-su pa-ka-ci>
2p→1e	<Σ_1-su pa-ka-ni>
2s→3s	<Σ_1-ka-Ø>
2s→3d	<Σ_1-ka-m-ci>
2s→3p	<Σ_1-ka-m-ni>
2d→3	<Σ_1-ka-ci>
2p→3	<Σ_1-ka-ni>

Diagram 19: Imperative transitive morphology

The following is a morphosemantic analysis of the Jero imperative person and number agreement morphemes.

4.6.1 *The singular agent and subject suffix*

MORPHEME	<-Ø>$_{am}$
GLOSS	sAS

The phonologically empty imperative suffix <-Ø>$_{am}$ marks a second person singular agent and subject in imperative verbs in which the number of the agent or subject is not overtly expressed by some other suffix. The imperative suffix <-Ø>$_{am}$ (sAS) is formally identical to the Jero simplex agreement suffix <-Ø>$_{am}$ (23s).

SUBJECT		
$2s_{am}$	<Σ(-s)-ka-Ø>	(Σ(-DETR)-IMP-SAS)
AGENT		
$2s \rightarrow 1s_{am}$	<Σ-ka-ŋ-Ø>	(Σ-IMP-1sP-SAS)
$2s \rightarrow 1e_{am}$	<Σ-su pa-ka-Ø>	(Σ-MAN do-IMP-SAS)
$2s \rightarrow 3s_{am}$	<Σ-ka-Ø>	(Σ-IMP-SAS)

4.6.2 *The second and third person dual suffix*

MORPHEME	<-ci>$_{am}$
GLOSS	23d

The imperative suffix <-ci>$_{am}$ marks duality of a second and third person argument. This imperative suffix is formally identical to the dual suffix <-ci>$_{am}$ (d) in simplex verbs.

SUBJECT		
$2d_{am}$	<Σ-ŋ-ka-ci>	(Σ-dS-IMP-23d)
AGENT		
$2d \rightarrow 1s_{am}$	<Σ-ka-ŋ-ci>	(Σ-IMP-1sP-23d)
$2d \rightarrow 1e_{am}$	<Σ-su pa-ka-ci>	(Σ-MAN do-IMP-23d)
$2d \rightarrow 3_{am}$	<Σ-ka-ci>	(Σ-IMP-23d)
PATIENT		
$2s \rightarrow 3d_{am}$	<Σ-ka-m-ci>	(Σ-IMP-s→3ns-23d)

4.6.3 *The imperative suffix*

MORPHEME	<-ka>$_{am}$
GLOSS	IMP

The suffix <-ka>$_{am}$ occurs in all imperative forms and is analysed as the primary marker of the imperative inflection. The imperative suffix <-ka>$_{am}$ is directly attached to the verb root, except in intransitive and middle forms, in which the suffix is preceded by the subject-marking morphemes <-s> (DETR), <-ŋ> (dS) and <-n> (pS). The imperative suffix has the following realisations:

<-ka> (IMP) →	-*ka*$_{am}$	| Σ_{vi} <V> —
	-*ha*$_{am}$	| Σ_{vt} <V> —
	-*a*$_{am}$	| Σ<rt, lt> — | Σ<-s> (DETR) — | Σ<-ŋ> (dS) — | Σ<-n> (pS) —
	-*pha*$_{am}$ ~ -*pa*$_{a}$	| Σ<pt> —
	-*kha*$_{am}$ ~ -*ka*$_{a}$	| Σ<tt, kt> —

Imperatives which illustrate the given allomorphy are: <ga-ka-Ø> (come.up-IMP-SAS) → *ga-ka-Ø*$_{a}$ 'come^{s} up!', <pa-ka-Ø> (do-IMP-SAS) → *pa-ha-Ø*$_{am}$ 'do^{s} it!', <kurt-ka-Ø> (carry-IMP-SAS)→ *kura*$_{m}$ 'carry^{s} it!', <bak-s-ka-Ø> (be/sit-DETR-IMP-SAS) → *bak-s-a-Ø*$_{am}$ 'be^{s}! sit^{s}!', <baː-ŋ-ka-ci> (be/sit-dS-IMP-23d) → *baː-ŋ-a-ci*$_{am}$ 'be^{d}! sit^{d}!' and <baː-n-ka-ni> (be/sit-pS-IMP-23p) → *baː-n-a-ni*$_{am}$ 'be^{p}! sit^{p}!'.

A formal distinction between -*pha*$_{am}$ and -*pa*$_{a}$, on one hand, and between -*kha*$_{am}$ and -*ka*$_{a}$, on the other, is made in the Āmboṭe dialect, where the imperative suffix is realised with an aspirated voiceless stop in first person singular patient forms and with a plain voiceless stop in third person patient forms, e.g. <kratt-ka-ŋ-Ø> (bite-IMP-1sP-SAS) → *krak-kha-ŋ-Ø*$_{a}$ 'bite^{s} me!' vs. <kratt-ka-Ø> (bite-IMP-SAS) → *krak-ka-Ø*$_{a}$ 'bite^{s} him!', <gɔkt-ka-ŋ-Ø> (give-IMP-1sP-SAS) → *gɔk-kha-ŋ-Ø*$_{a}$ 'give^{s} to me' vs. <gɔkt-ka-Ø> (bring-IMP-SAS) → *gɔk-ka-Ø*$_{a}$ 'give^{s} to him' and <tupt-ka-Ø> (beat-IMP-SAS) → *tup-pa-Ø*$_{a}$ 'hit^{s} him!'.

In the Mohanṭāre dialect of Jero, by contrast, the imperative suffix is always realised as aspirated -*pha*$_{am}$ and -*kha*$_{am}$ after root finals <pt>, <yt> and <kt>, e.g. <tupt-ka-ŋ-Ø> (beat-IMP-1sP-SAS) → *tup-pha-ŋ-Ø*$_{m}$ 'hit^{s} me!', <tupt-ka-Ø> (beat-IMP-SAS) → *tup-pha-Ø*$_{m}$ 'hit^{s} him!', <blatt-ka-Ø> (bring-IMP-SAS) → *blak-kha-Ø*$_{m}$ 'bring^{s} it!' and <makt-ka-Ø> (catch-IMP-SAS) → *mak-kha-Ø*$_{m}$ 'catch^{s} it!'.

4.6.4 *The s→3ns suffix*

MORPHEME	<-m>$_{am}$
GLOSS	s→3ns

The imperative agreement suffix <-m>$_{am}$ marks a transitive relationship between a second person singular agent and a third person non-singular patient.

AGENT→PATIENT		
2s→3d$_{am}$	<Σ-ka-m-ci>	(Σ-IMP-s→3ns-23d)
2s→3p$_{am}$	<Σ-ka-m-ni>	(Σ-IMP-s→3ns-23p)

The imperative suffix <-m>$_{am}$ (s→3ns) bears formal and semantic similarities with the simplex suffix <-mi>$_{am}$ (23/ns).

4.6.5 *The plural subject suffix*

MORPHEME	<-n>$_{am}$
GLOSS	pS

The imperative suffix <-n>$_{am}$ marks a plural subject in intransitive and middle imperative verbs.

SUBJECT		
2p$_{am}$	<Σ-n-ka-ni>	(Σ-pS-IMP-23p)

The plural subject attaches to the verb root and precedes the imperative morpheme <-ka>, which is realised as the morph *-a*$_{am}$ in this environment, e.g. <si-n-ka-ni> (die-pS-IMP-23p) → *si-n-a-ni*$_{a}$ 'die^{p}!'. The plural subject morpheme can be analysed as an abbreviated copy of the second and third person plural imperative morpheme <-ni>$_{am}$ (23p) or represent a kind of special plural counterpart of the dual subject imperative suffix <-ŋ>$_{am}$ (dS).

4.6.6 *The second and third person plural suffix*

MORPHEME	<-ni>$_{am}$
GLOSS	23p

The suffix <-ni>$_{am}$ marks a second or third person plural subject, agent and patient in the imperative.

SUBJECT		
2p$_{am}$	<Σ-n-ka-ni>	(Σ-pS-IMP-23p)
AGENT		
2p→1s$_{am}$	<Σ-ka-ŋ-ni>	(Σ-IMP-1sP-23p)
2p→1e$_{am}$	<Σ-su pa-ka-ni>	(Σ-MAN do-IMP-23p)
2p→3$_{am}$	<Σ-ka-ni>	(Σ-IMP-23p)
PATIENT		
2s→3p$_{am}$	<Σ-ka-m-ni>	(Σ-IMP-s→3ns-23p)

The second and third person plural imperative suffix is formally identical to the second person simplex suffix <-ni>$_{am}$ (2). In Āmboṭe, suffix-initial <n> is deleted after <-m> (s→3ns), e.g. <kratt-ka-m-ni> (bite-IMP-s→3ns-23p) → *krak-ka-m-i*$_{a}$ 'bite^{s} them^{p}!' and <gɔkt-ka-m-ni> (give-IMP-s→3ns-23p) → *gɔk-ka-m-i*$_{a}$ 'give^{s} to them^{p}!'.

4.6.7 *The first person singular patient suffix*

MORPHEME	<-ŋ>$_{am}$
GLOSS	1sP

A first person singular patient is marked by means of the imperative morpheme <-ŋ>$_{am}$. This suffix attaches to the imperative morpheme <-ka> and precedes the three agreement suffixes that mark the number of the second person agent.

PATIENT		
2s→1s$_{am}$	<Σ-ka-ŋ-Ø>	(Σ-IMP-1sP-sAS)
2d→1s$_{am}$	<Σ-ka-ŋ-ci>	(Σ-IMP-1sP-23d)
2p→1s$_{am}$	<Σ-ka-ŋ-ni>	(Σ-IMP-1sP-23p)

4.6.8 *The dual subject suffix*

MORPHEME	<-ŋ>$_{am}$
GLOSS	dS

The suffix <-ŋ>$_{am}$ (dS) marks a dual intransitive and middle subject. The imperative morpheme <-ka> is realised as *-a* after the dual subject marker, e.g. <si-ŋ-ka-ci> (die-dS-IMP-23d) → *si-ŋ-a-ci*$_{a}$ 'die^{d}!'. Note the metathesis in Mohanṭāre <khrɔm-ŋ-ka-ci> → *khrɔm-aŋ-ci*$_{m}$ (cry-dS+IMP-23d) 'cry^{d}!'.

SUBJECT		
2d$_{am}$	<Σ-ŋ-ka-ci>	(Σ-dS-IMP-23d)

4.6.9 *The detransitivising suffix*

MORPHEME	<-S>$_{am}$
GLOSS	DETR

The suffix <-s>$_{am}$ is a marker of non-transitive scenarios. This suffix is found in second person singular imperatives of middle verbs and most intransitive verbs. The imperative morpheme <-ka> is realised as *-a* after the detransitivising suffix, e.g. <si-s-ka-Ø> (die-DETR-IMP-sAS) → *si-s-a-Ø*$_{a}$ 'die^{s}!', <gle-s-ka-Ø> (lie.down-DETR-IMP-sAS) → *gle-s-a-Ø*$_{m}$ 'lie^{s} down!' and <la-s-ka-Ø> (become-DETR-IMP-sAS) → *la-s-a-Ø*$_{m}$ 'become^{s}!'.

SUBJECT		
2s$_{am}$	<Σ-s-ka-Ø>	(Σ-DETR-IMP-sAS)

Verbs that do not take the detransitivising suffix in the imperative are verbs of motion which belong to class (vi-1a-ii): *gacap*$_{a}$ ~ *ga-*$_{m}$ vi-1a-ii <ga-> 'to come up', *picap*$_{a}$ ~ *picam*$_{m}$ vi-1a-ii <pi-> 'to come (across a horizontal plane)' and *yacap*$_{a}$ ~ *yacam*$_{m}$ vi-1a-ii <ya-> 'to come down'. Thus, we find <ga-ka-Ø> (come.up-IMP-sAS) → *ga-ka-Ø*$_{m}$ 'come^{s} up!', <pi-ka-Ø> (come.hrz-IMP-sAS) → *pi-ka-Ø*$_{m}$ 'come^{s} (across a horizontal plane)!' and <ya-ka-Ø> (come.down-IMP- sAS) → *ya-ka-Ø*$_{m}$ 'come^{s} down!'.

Note that the Wambule cognate verbs *gacam* 'to come up', *picam* 'to come (across a horizontal plane)' and *ywacam* 'to come down' also lack the Chaurasia detransitivising suffix <-s>.

4.7 *Prohibition and absence of necessity*

MORPHEME	<-sano>$_{a}$
GLOSS	NEC

Prohibition, negative advice, denial of permission and absence of necessity can be expressed by several formal means, such as negative imperatives, negated second person simplex verbs and negative verbs ending in the suffix <-sano>$_{a}$.

Negative imperatives are formed by prefixation of the negative marker <a-> (NEG) to positive imperative forms, e.g. <a-di-s-ka-Ø> (NEG-go/come-DETR-IMP-sAS) → *a-di-s-a-Ø*$_{m}$ 'do^{s} not go (and come back)!' and <a-japt-kha-Ø> (NEG-buy-IMP-23s) → *a-jap-pha-Ø*$_{m}$ 'do^{s} not buy it!'.

Prohibition can also be expressed by negated second person simplex verbs, e.g. <a-japt-ni-Ø> (NEG- buy-2-23s) → *a-jap-ni-Ø*$_{m}$ 'you^{s} will not buy it!' and <a-ma:-ni-mi> (NEG-catch-2-23/ns) → *a-ma:-ni-m*$_{m}$ 'you^{p} will not catch it!'.

Suffixation of the marker <-sano>$_{a}$ to a negated simplex verb yields a verb form that indicates that is not needed, essential or required to perform the action express by the verb, e.g. <a-si-ni-Ø-sano> (NEG-die-2-23s-NEC) → *a-si-ni-Ø-sano*$_{a}$ 'you^{s} need not die!' and <a-sɛtt-ni-Ø-sano> (NEG-die-2-23s-NEC) → *a-sɛt-ni-Ø-sano*$_{a}$ 'you^{s} need not kill him!'. The verb forms ending in <-sano>$_{a}$ are translated into Nepali by means of infinitives followed by *pardaina* 'it is not necessary', which is the third person singular negative simple indefinite tense form of the verb *parnu* 'to be necessary, be situated'. The suffix <-sano>$_{a}$ appears to be morphosemantically related to the suffix <-ano>$_{a}$ ~ <-no>$_{m}$ of the optative, which is discussed next. See also Section 5.1.1 below (p. 183).

4.8 *The optative*

MORPHEME	<-ano>$_{a}$ ~ <-no>$_{m}$
GLOSS	OPT

Optatives are finite verb forms that are used to express the speaker's wishes and hopes, conveying the sense of 'may he do something!'. Optative forms are also used as a kind of third person imperative by means of which a command is given to a second person to allow a third person to perform the action denoted by the verb, conveying the sense of 'let him do something!'. Jero optatives are formed by suffixation of the morpheme <-ano>$_{a}$ ~ <-no>$_{m}$ to imperatives or simplicia. The Āmboṭe suffix <-ano>$_{a}$ is realised as the full morph *-ano*$_{a}$ after consonants and as the abbreviated morph *-no*$_{am}$ after vowels.

The optatives in the following two examples are based on imperative forms. For instance, the imperative optative <bak-s-ka-Ø-ano> (be/sit-DETR-IMP-SAS-OPT) → *bak-s-a-Ø-no*$_{am}$ 'let^{s} him sit!' in (138) can be contrasted with the simplex optative <baː-Ø-ano> (be/sit-23s-OPT) → *baː-Ø-no*$_{a}$ 'let^{s} him sit!'.

137$_{m}$	*Ai*	*mucu*	*hep*	*ja-ha-Ø-no!*
	this	person	cooked.grain	eat-IMP-SAS-OPT

Let^{s} this person eat cooked grain!

138$_{a}$	*Ikkim*	*kaʔu*	*bhuĩ=na*	*bak-s-a-Ø-no!*
	our^{pi}	friend	*ground*=LOC	be/sit-DETR-IMP-SAS-OPT

Let^{s} our^{pi} friend sit on the ground!

The optative in (139), by contrast, is based on a simplex base, viz. the third person singular simplex form <dum-Ø> (become-23s) → *dum-Ø* of the intransitive verb *dumcap*$_{a}$ vi-1c <dum-> 'to be, become'. The corresponding imperative is <dum-s-ka-Ø> (become-DETR-IMP-SAS) → *dum-s-a-Ø*.

139$_{a}$	*Im*	*kam*	*ran-tɔ-p*	*dum-Ø-ano!*
	Your^{s}	*work*	good-ATT-RES	become-23s-OPT

May your^{s} work become good!

The optative in example (140) also appears to have an imperative base. However, the optative *paisano* can also be analysed as having a simplex base if one supposes that the middle marker <-si>$_{\text{am}}$ is realised as the abbreviated morph -s_{a} before suffixes with an initial vowel. However, this claim cannot be made unequivocally.

140$_{\text{a}}$	a.	*Ai*	*mucu*	*wa*	*pai-s-a-Ø-no!*
		this	person	clothes	dress.self-DETR-IMP-SAS-OPT
	b.	*Ai*	*mucu*	*wa*	*pai-s-Ø-ano!*
		this	person	clothes	dress.self-MID-23s-OPT

Let^{s} this person get dressed!

CHAPTER FIVE

NON-FINITE DEVERBATIVES

Bare verb roots serve as a basis for suffixation of several morphemes that turn modified verb roots into deverbative constituents termed ‘verbal nouns’ and ‘verbal adjectives’. From the point of view of external morphosyntax, these deverbatives behave like ordinary nouns and adjectives.

5.1 *Verbal nouns*

Verbal nouns are derived nominals that refer to the entire verbal action, rather than to the arguments of the verb. In contrast to verbal adjectives, verbal nouns do not take the negative prefix. A distinction can be made between the infinitive, the supine and the nominaliser of loan verbs.

5.1.1 *The infinitive*

MORPHEME	<-si>$_{\text{am}}$
GLOSS	INF

The infinitive is a noun that is derived from a verb root by suffixation of the morpheme <-si>$_{\text{am}}$. In the next example, the infinitive serves as the main predicator of a clause.

141$_{\text{m}}$	*Khasi*	*jur-si.*
	work	be.sour-INF

[Religious] work is [emotionally] painful.

The infinitival predicator *pa-si* ‘do, make’ in the following example is accompanied by the loan particle *pʌrchʌ*$_{\text{am}}$ ‘it is necessary’. This word and the particle *pʌryo*$_{\text{m}}$ ‘it was necessary’ are borrowed from the Nepali third person singular simple indefinite tense form *parcha* and the aorist perfect tense form *paryo*, which are inflected forms of the verb *parnu* 'to be necessary, be situated'. These two loan particles are used with an infinitive in constructions that express that it is essential to achieve the action expressed by the infinitive. The simple indefinite tense form *parcha* is used for a general instance, i.e. 'it is generally necessary', whereas the aorist perfect tense form *paryo* refers to a particular instance, i.e. 'it was then necessary' or 'it is now necessary'.

142$_m$	*Pa-si*	*pʌrchʌ.*
	do-INF	*is.necessary*

It is [generally] necessary to do [these things].

143$_a$	*Hepa*	*khɔk-si*	*pʌrchʌ.*
	cooked.grain	boil-INF	*is.necessary*

It is [generally] necessary to boil grains.

144$_a$	*Hus*	*bu-lu*	*phipuwa*	*gɔk-si*	*pʌrchʌ?*
	how	time-LOC	ginger	give-INF	*is.necessary*

Do you [generally] have to give [them] ginger on that occasion?

Infinitives also co-occur with native auxiliary verbs, which add a dimension of some kind to the meaning expressed by the main verbal or deverbative constituent, such as inceptive and ingressive aspectualisation. The topic of auxiliaries is discussed in Chapter 7.

In the following examples, the infinitive functions as the subject of the verb *milʌi lacap*$_a$ vi-1a-i <la-> 'to agree, blend, go together'.

145$_a$	*Mama*	*tɛr-si*	*mil-ʌi*	*a-la-Ø*	
	mother	receive-INF	*agree*-LN	NEG-become-23s	
	ɛti	*bɛla,*	*haŋ-bhʌne*	*mama=ku*	*maŋ*
	so.much	*time*	*because*	mother=SRC	now
	hep	*ja-i-Ø-m*	*ba:-Ø-m.*		
	cooked.grain	eat-3npA-23s-AFF	be/sit-23s-AFF		

It is not convenient to meet mother at the moment because she is having dinner.

146$_a$ *Kul-deuta* *man-ʌi* *pa-si* *mil-ʌi*
house-*god* *observe*-INF do-INF *agree*-LN

a-la-Ø.
NEG-become-23s

[It is not acceptable to marry outside of one's own ethnic group because] It is not acceptable to perform rituals in honour of the indoor deities.

5.1.2 *The supine*

MORPHEME	<-phu>$_{am}$
GLOSS	SUP

The supine is a verbal noun that expresses the purpose of an action. The supine is formed by suffixation of the morpheme <-phu>$_{am}$ to the verb root. In Āmboṭe, this morpheme has the regular allomorph *-pu*$_a$ after root-final <pt> and <tt>, e.g. <hipt-phu> (see-SUP) → *hip-pu*$_a$ 'in order to see' and <phitt-phu> (bring.hrz-SUP) → *phip-pu*$_a$.

147$_a$ *In* *nimpha* *phɔpma=ya* *pheri* *ka:ku*
you DU tomorrow=also *again* water

phip-pu *lɔ-ŋ-ci-m.*
bring.hrz-SUP go-dS-d-AFF

Also tomorrow you two will go again in order to fetch water (across a horizontal plane).

148$_a$ *Uŋgu* *Jero* *ma:la* *sik-ʌi* *la-phu*
I/we Jero language *learn*-LN become-SUP

Nepal *ga-ŋ-mai* *ba:-Ø-m.*
Nepal come.up-1s-FCT be/sit-23s-AFF

I have come up [from the Netherlands] to Nepal in order to learn the Jero language.

149_m *Uŋ* *ḍa* *khet=no* *sag* *pɛk-phu*
I/we THM *field*=LOC *greens* pluck-SUP

di-ŋ-ma.
go/come-1s-AFF

I will go to the field in order to pluck greens (and come back).

5.1.3 *The nominaliser of loan verbs*

MORPHEME	<-ʌi>$_{am}$
GLOSS	LN

Nepali verbs which are used in a Jero syntagm are rendered as nominals which are derived by suffixation of the morpheme <-ʌi>$_{am}$ to the root of a verb or some part of that root. The nominaliser of loan verbs is a loan from the Nepali nominalising suffix *-āi*. The morpheme <-ʌi>$_{am}$ is formally identical to the emphatic morpheme <-ʌi>$_{am}$, which is a loan from the Nepali suffix *-ai*. Jero nominals that are derived from loan verbs are used with the intransitive auxiliaries *dumcap*$_a$ ~ *dumcam*$_m$ vi-1c <dum-> 'to be, become' or *lacam*$_a$ vi-1a-i <la-> 'to be, become' if the loan verb is intransitive. See also (52) and (148) above.

150_m *Dʌs* *rupiyã* *naʔa* *lag-ʌi* *dum-Ø-me.*
ten *rupee* only *happen*-LN become-23s-AFF

It only costs ten rupees.

151_a *Uml-ʌi* *la-Ø-mei* *magge.*
boil-LN become-23s-FCT egg

A boiled egg.

152_a *Inne* *thal* *pʌḍ-ʌi* *la-n-Ø-ne?*
You where *read/study*-LN become-2-23s-AFF

Where are you[s] studying?

By contrast, the native transitive auxiliary *pacap*$_{\mathrm{a}}$ ~ *pacam*$_{\mathrm{m}}$ vt-2a <pa- ~ po-> 'to do, make' is used if the loan verb is transitive.

153$_{\mathrm{a}}$	*Uŋgu*	*ciṭhi*	*pʌṭh-ʌi*	*pa-u-m.*
	I/we	*letter*	*send*-LN	do-1s-AFF

I will send a letter.

154$_{\mathrm{a}}$	*Aŋgu=ku*	*ḍhoka*	*khol-ʌi*	*pa-i-Ø-me.*
	he/they=SRC	*door*	*open*-LN	do-3npA-23s-AFF

He opened the door.

5.2 *Verbal adjectives*

Verbal adjectives differ from verbal nouns in that verbal adjectives can be modified by the negative prefix. Like ordinary adjectives, verbal adjectives commonly function as an adnominal modifier, as an argument of a verb or as a predicator in a clause. Unlike verbal nouns, non-finite verbal adjectives do not refer to entire verbal events, but to the arguments of the modified verb. The referent of the argument referred to by a non-finite verbal adjective in adnominal modifying position can be generally identified as the referent of the head nominal. A formal distinction can be made between two active verbal adjectives, the attributive verbal adjective, the verbal adjective of purpose and the passive verbal adjective. The morphosyntax of the factual verbal adjective, which is a finite form, is discussed in Section 4.4 above (p. 165).

5.2.1 *The particular active verbal adjective*

MORPHEME	<-cu>$_{\mathrm{am}}$
GLOSS	ACP

The particular active verbal adjective is formed by suffixation of the morpheme <-cu>$_{\mathrm{am}}$ to the verb root, which is usually the primary root form. However, the marker of the active verbal adjective is suffixed to the secondary root of transitive verbs ending in <Σa- ~ Σo->, such as *jacap*$_{\mathrm{a}}$ ~ *jacam*$_{\mathrm{m}}$ vt-2a <ja- ~ jo-> 'to eat'. The particular active verbal adjective refers to the performer of an action that applies at a particular moment. The performer can be identified as the subject of intransitive and middle verbs or as the agent of transitive verbs. The active verbal adjective is generally translated into Nepali by means of an infinitival participle, e.g. <tu:t-cu> (drink-ACP) → *tu:-cu*$_a$ 'the one drinking', Nep. *piune*.

155_a	*Su*	*tham-cu.*
	meat	sell-ACP

Someone who sells meat [at a particular moment].

156_a	*Ciya*	*tu:-cu*	*mucu.*
	tea	drink-ACP	person

A person who drinks tea [at a particular moment].

Particular active verbal adjectives that are used as a deverbative predicator often occur in short question sentences with future reference.

157_a	*Hai*	*jo-cu?*
	what	eat-ACP

What shall [I, we, you, he, they] eat?

158_a	*Munu=k*	*jo-cu?*
	who=SRC	eat-ACP

Who will eat?

159_a	*Mun*	*dɔt*	*lɔ-cu?*
	who	thing	go-ACP

Who will go?

160_a	*Nʌuthal*	*biha*	*po-cu?*
	behind/after	*marriage*	do-ACP

Will you get married later?

5.2.2 *The general active verbal adjective*

MORPHEME	<-ce>$_{\mathrm{am}}$
GLOSS	ACG

The general active verbal adjective is formed by suffixation of the morpheme <-ce>$_{\mathrm{am}}$ to the verb root. This type of active verbal adjective also refers to the performer of the action described by the modified verb, but slightly differs from the particular active verbal adjective in that the action expressed by the modified verb does not just apply at a particular moment, but has a more general basis. See also example (41).

161$_{\mathrm{a}}$	*Ciya*	*tuː-ce*	*mucu.*
	tea	drink-ACG	person

A person who [generally] drinks tea.

162$_{\mathrm{m}}$	*Mundo*	*blak-ce?*
	who	come-ACG

Who comes [regularly, habitually]?

5.2.3 *The attributive verbal adjective*

MORPHEME	<-tɔ>$_{\mathrm{a}}$ ~ <-to>$_{\mathrm{m}}$
GLOSS	ATT

The attributive verbal adjective is formed by suffixation of the morpheme <-tɔ>$_{\mathrm{a}}$ ~ <-to>$_{\mathrm{m}}$ to the verb root. This morpheme has an allomorph with initial /tt/ after roots ending in a short vowel morphophoneme, but without the effect of any emphatic force that is normally associated with consonant doubling. In Āmboṭe, the allomorph *-ttɔ*$_{\mathrm{a}}$ can also be used after long vowel morphophonemes, causing phonetic vowel shortening. In this dialect, the attributive verbal adjective is generally extended by means of the suffix *-p*$_{\mathrm{a}}$, which is analysed as a lexicalised instance of the phrasal reifying suffix <=me>$_{\mathrm{am}}$.

Like the two active verbal adjectives discussed here above, the attributive verbal adjective refers to the performer of the action described by the modified verb. The attributive form differs from the active forms that the verbal action is presented as an attribute, i.e. a trait or characteristic that distinguishes the performer, e.g. *cor po-ttɔ-p* (thief do-ATT-RES) 'a thief'.

163_{a}	*Hus*	*khɔl-tɔ-p!*
	how	big-ATT-RES

How big!

164_{a}	*Ciya*	*tu-ttɔ-p*	*mucu.*
	tea	drink-ATT-RES	person

A kind of person who drinks tea.

165_{a}	*Uŋgu*	*ma:la*	*sik-ʌi*	*la-ttɔ-p*	*mucu.*
	I/we	language	*learn*-LN	become-ATT-RES	person.

I am a kind of person who learns languages.

166_{m}	*Hai*	*jɔ-tto?*
	what	eat-ATT

He is a kind of person who eats what?

The following intransitive verbs frequently appear in the attributive form:

bro-to$_{m}$	*bro-ttɔ-p*$_{a}$	'tasty; agreeable'
jur-to$_{m}$	*jur-tɔ-p*$_{a}$	'sour'
khɔl-to$_{m}$	*khɔl-tɔ-p*$_{a}$	'big, large, great'
ran-to$_{m}$	*ran-tɔ-p*$_{a}$	'good'

5.2.4 *The verbal adjective of purpose*

MORPHEME	<-ca>$_{am}$
GLOSS	PUR

The verbal adjective of purpose is formed by suffixation of <-ca>$_{am}$ to the verb root. The verbal adjective of purpose refers to the intended application, function or purpose of an argument of the action described by the modified verb, expression the sense of ‘object used for performing an activity’ or ‘place for performing an activity’.

Unmodified verbal adjectives of purpose are commonly used as the main predicator of a clause or sentence. The verbal adjective of purpose is deontically marked in the sense that the speaker uses this type of deverbative to express what he want or intends or what somebody should do.

167_{a}	*Inne*	*tεr-ca*	*phɔpma*	*thalu?*
	you	receive-PUR	tomorrow	where

Where shall [I, we, he, they] meet you tomorrow?

168_{a}	*Hai*	*pa-ca?*
	what	do-PUR

What shall be done?

The verbal adjective of purpose is usually turned into a nominalised form by means of suffixation of <-me>$_{am}$. A reified verbal adjective of purpose is the usual citation form of a verb and corresponds to the Nepali infinitival verb form. However, a verbal adjective of purpose is most accurately translated into Nepali by means of a two-word phrase that consists of an infinitive in *-nu* plus the infinitival participle of the auxiliary *parnu* ‘to be necessary, be situated’. Thus, the word *sεc-ca-p*$_{a}$ ~ *sεc-ca-m*$_{m}$ (kill-PUR-RES) ‘to kill, put to death’ translates as *mārnuparne*. Reified verbal adjectives of purpose which are used as an adnominal modifier correspond to English *to* plus infinitive constructions, e.g. *lɔcam ṭhaũ* ‘the place to go to’, Nep. *jāne ṭhāũ*.

169_{m}	*Inne*	*phɔpma*	*lɔ-ca-m*	*ṭhaũ.*
	you	tomorrow	go-PUR-RES	*place*

The place where you shall go to tomorrow.

170_{a}	*Uŋ*	*lɔ-ca-p*	*lam.*
	I/we	go-PUR-RES	road

The road for me to go.

Reified verbal adjectives of purpose can also be used as the main predicator of a clause or sentence.

171_{m} *Hai* *pa-ca-m?*
what do-PUR-RES

What [thing] shall be done?

172_{a} *Lʌura=ku* *tup-ca-p.*
stick=SRC beat-PUR-RES

[Something] to hit with a stick.

173_{a} *Uŋ* *lɔ-ca-me?*
I/we go-PUR-RES

Do we have to go?

The use of unmodified verbal adjective of purpose with inceptive auxiliaries is discussed in Section 7.1 (p. 207). The suffix <-lu>$_{am}$ of the present gerund is suffixed to verbal adjectives of purpose in non-finite present gerunds, which are discussed in Section 6.2 (p. 199).

5.2.5 *The passive verbal adjective*

MORPHEME	<-mamcu>$_{a}$
GLOSS	PAS

The passive verbal adjective is formed by suffixation of <-mamcu>$_{a}$ to the verb root. This adjective refers to the subject or patient of the action described by the modified verb. The performer is said to have first person reference. In forms without case markers, the passive verbal adjectival suffix is extended by means of the reifying morph *-m*$_{a}$.

174_{a} *Uŋ* *nimpha* *wal-mamcu-m.*
I/we DU walk-PAS-RES

We walked.

175_a *Sa:ʔlɛŋ pa-mamcu-m.*
song do-PAS-RES

The song was performed (by us).

176_a *Ka:k a-tu:-mamcu=k ka:k-dak*
water NEG-drink-PAS=SRC water-notice

pa-i-Ø-m.
do-3npA-23s-AFF

I am thirsty because I have not drunk water.

CHAPTER SIX

GERUNDS

Gerunds or verbal adverbs are deverbative forms which qualify the action expressed by the main verb. The basic function of gerunds is as the predicator of a subordinate clause which marks the syntactic function of an adverbial with respect to the main clause of the complex sentence. Like verbal nouns and verbal adjectives, gerunds are used in several periphrastic constructions with auxiliaries. Gerunds differ from verbal nouns in that gerunds are subject to prefixal morphology. Gerunds differ from verbal adjectives, which are also subject to prefixal verbal morphology, in that gerunds cannot be used in adnominal modifying position. This chapter deals with the morphology of perfect gerunds, present gerunds, the conditional gerund and the irrealis, the simultaneous gerund, the connective gerund, gerunds of manner and the negative state gerund.

6.1 *Perfect gerunds*

MORPHEME	<-ku>$_{a}$ ~ <-khu>$_{m}$
GLOSS	PFG

MORPHEME	<-ma>$_{am}$
GLOSS	PPT

Perfect gerunds are formed by means of suffixation of a grammaticalised instance of the source marker <-ku>$_{a}$ ~ <-khu>$_{m}$ to a finite verb or a gerund of manner. Negatives are formed by prefixation of the negative marker to the corresponding positive forms. Sentences that contain a perfect gerund express a sequence of events in which the perfect gerund locates the event expressed by it as relatively prior to some other event chosen as the point of reference. The events expressed in the subordinate and the main clause reflect the chronological order of events. Perfect gerunds are perfect in the sense that they describe a prior event with ongoing relevance for the following or main event which serves as an orientation point. Clauses that contain a perfect gerund are often the equivalent of English adverbial subordinates introduced by the preposition *after*. Sometimes, perfect gerunds mark situations which occur in association with the main action and which are presented as a manner or circumstance under which the action in the main clause takes place.

The non-past perfect gerund is formed by suffixation of the marker <-ku>$_{a}$ ~ <-khu>$_{m}$ to a simplex verb. The non-past perfect gerund marks a non-past prior event of which the result continues up to the following event located in non-past time. The main verbs in the following examples are affirmatives and imperatives.

177$_{a}$	*Hepa*	*ja-u-k*	*lɔ-ŋ-ma.*
	cooked.grain	eat-1s-PFG	go-1s-AFF

I will eat cooked grain and go.

178$_{m}$	*Pi-n-Ø-khu*	*alu*	*bak-s-a-Ø!*
	come.hrz-2-23s-PFG	here	be/sit-DETR-IMP-SAS

Come^{s} (across a horizontal plane) and sit^{s} here!

179$_{m}$	*Am*	*ma:la*	*thɔ-n-Ø-khu*	*lɔ-s-a-Ø!*
	my	word	hear-2-23s-PFG	go-DETR-IMP-SAS

Listen^{s} to what I say and go!

The past perfect or pluperfect gerund is formed by suffixation of <-ku>$_{a}$ ~ <-khu>$_{m}$ to a simplex verb to which the past prior time suffix <-ma>$_{am}$ is added. The pluperfect marks a past prior event whose result continues up to the following event. The following event is usually located in past time, but may have an ongoing relevance into the present.

180$_{a}$	*Hepa*	*ja-u-ma-ku*	*kul*	*lɔ-ŋ-ma.*
	cooked.grain	eat-1s-PPT-PFG	house	go-1s-AFF

I ate cooked grain and went home.

181$_{a}$ *Ungu* *al* *bla-ŋ-ma-ku*
I/we here come-1s-PPT-PFG

kaʔu *lɔ-Ø-m.*
friend go-23s-AFF

I arrived here and [my] friend went away.

182$_{m}$ *Ka:ku* *tu:-si* *a-hi-ʔ-ma-khu*
water drink-INF NEG-obtain-1s-PTT-PFG

ka:k-dakhu *si-ŋ-mʌi* *ba:-Ø-me.*
water-notice die-1s-FCT be/sit-23s-AFF

I am thirsty because I have not been able to drink water.

The non-finite perfect gerund is formed by suffixation of <-ku>$_{a}$ ~ <-khu>$_{m}$ to a gerund of manner ending in <-sa>$_{am}$. The non-finite perfect gerund marks an event independently from the time expressed in the main clause.

183$_{a}$ *Pʌisa* *gɔk-sa-ku* *pi-ka-Ø!*
money give-MAN-PFG come.hrz-IMP-SAS

Come^{s} [across a horizontal plane] after you have given the money.

184$_{a}$ *Hep* *ja-sa-ku* *kulu* *lɔ-ŋ-mai.*
cooked.grain eat-MAN-PFG house go-1s-FCT

I ate cooked grain and went home.

185$_{m}$ *Hep* *ja-sa-khu* *lɔ-s-a-Ø!*
cooked.grain eat-MAN-PFG go-DETR-IMP-SAS

Go^{s} after you have eaten cooked grain.

186$_{m}$ *Al* *pi-sa-k* *bak-s-a-Ø!*
here come.hrz-MAN-PFG be/sit-DETR-IMP-SAS

Come^{s} here (across a horizontal plane) and sit^{s}!

187$_a$

Sikar	*pa-sa-k*	*bla:-ku-m.*
hunting	do-MAN-PFG	come-1peAS-AFF

We[pe] will come after the hunt.

188$_a$

Biha	*pa-sa-k*	*Kaṭhmanḍu=n*	*bak-cu*
marriage	do-MAN-PFG	*Kathmandu*=LOC	be/sit-ACP

ki	*gaũ=na*	*bak-cu?*
or	*village*=LOC	be/sit-ACP

Will you live in Kathmandu, or [return and] live in the village once you are married?

In the following example, the action expressed by the perfect gerund is presented as a manner or circumstance under which the action in the main clause takes place.

189$_a$

Aŋgu=ku	*hepa*	*mis-ʌi*	*pa-sa-k*
he/they=SRC	cooked.grain	*mix*-LN	do-MAN-PFG

ja-i-Ø-m.
eat-3npA-23s-AFF

He ate cooked grain mixed [with something].

The non-finite perfect gerund of the verb *necap*$_a$ ~ *necam*$_m$ vm-1a <ne-> 'to say, quote, relate' is generally used to report speech or render a person's thoughts.

190$_a$

'Hai	*bɛl*	*jo-cu?'*	*ne-sa-ku*
what	*time*	eat-ACP	say-MAN-PFG

aŋ	*ticu=k*	*inne*	*lai*	*tublo*	*pa-m-me.*
he/they	PL=SRC	you	PAT	question	do-23/ns-AFF

They[p] asked you when they/you would eat.

191$_a$

'Tɛŋu	*lɔ-ki!'*	*ne-sa-ku*	*ʌrko*	*mucu*
from.now	go-1piAS	say-MAN-PFG	*other*	person

uŋgu	*lai*	*nɛŋ-ŋu-m.*
I/we	PAT	say-1s-AFF

Another person told me that we[pi] should go.

Note that an affirmative verb to which the source marker is suffixed indicates the reason for the main event. The morphosemantics of *japsi aca?u* is discussed in Section 7.5 below (p. 210).

192_{m}	*Pʌisa*	*a-baː-Ø-me=khu*	*sɔblɛm*
	money	NEG-be/sit-23S-AFF=SRC	bread
	jap-si	*a-ca-ʔu.*	
	buy-INF	NEG-can-1s	

I could not [was not in a position to] buy bread because I had no money.

193_{m}	*Tɛmbar*	*hwarsi*	*ya-Ø-me=k*
	today	rain	come.down-23S-AFF=SRC
	uŋgu	*a-lɔ-ŋu.*	
	I/we	NEG-go-1s	

I will not go because it will rain today.

6.2 *Present gerunds*

MORPHEME	<-lu>$_{\text{am}}$
GLOSS	PRG

MORPHEME	<-bu>$_{\text{am}}$
GLOSS	CTT

Present gerunds mark the point in time at which the situation referred to by the main clause takes place. The present gerund locates the event expressed by the subordinate clause as occurring at the same time as the event expressed in the main clause. Present gerundive clauses are the equivalent of English adverbial subordinates introduced by *when* or *while*.

Finite present gerunds are formed by suffixation of a grammaticalised instance <-lu>$_{\text{am}}$ of the locative marker to a simplex verb to which the contemporaneous time suffix <-bu>$_{\text{am}}$ is added.

194$_{a}$	*Uŋgu*	*alu*	*bla-ŋ-bu-l,*
	I/we	here	come-1s-CTT-PRG
	kaʔu	*blaː-Ø-m.*	
	friend	come-23s-AFF	

When I arrived here, my friend came.

195$_{m}$	*Uŋ*	*saiso*	*kul*	*pi-ŋ-bu-lu,*
	I/we	yesterday	house	come.hrz-1s-CTT-PRG
	lam=no	*mucu*	*a-tɛr-ʔu-m.*	
	way=LOC	person	NEG-receive-1s-23/ns	

When I came home yesterday (across a horizontal plane), I did not meet any people on the road.

196$_{m}$	*Inne*	*Bharʌt*	*lɔ-n-Ø-bu-l,*
	you	*India*	go-2-23s-CTT-PRG
	thupro	*kaʔu*	*tɛr-ni-Ø-m?*
	a.lot.of	friend	receive-2-23s-AFF

Did you[s] encounter a lot of friends when you went to India?

Unlike the past prior time suffix <-ma>$_{am}$, which is restricted to past contexts, the contemporaneous time suffix marks past and non-past events. Non-finite present gerunds are formed by suffixation of <-lu>$_{am}$ to a verbal adjective of purpose.

197$_{a}$	*Thapu*	*naʔa*	*a-nɔ-Ø,*	*aŋam*	
	maternal.uncle	only	NEG-be-23s	his/her	
	buḍi=ya	*pasmi*	*pa-ca-lu,*		
	old.woman=also	*food.ceremony*	do-PUR-PRG		
	uŋgu	*lai*	*hepa*	*gɔk-su*	*pa-i-ci-m.*
	I/we	PAT	cooked.grain	give-MAN	do-3npA-d-AFF

Not only [my] maternal uncle, his wife too, they[d] gave me cooked grain while performing the *pāsnī* ceremony [of giving a child its first solid food].

198$_{a}$	*Satni*	*inne*	*lai*	*tɛr-ca-l*
	yesterday	you	PAT	receive-PUR-PRG

im	*mama*	*a-hi-ʔu.*
your^{s}	mother	NEG-see-1s

I did not see your^{s} mother when I met you yesterday.

6.3 *The conditional gerund and the irrealis*

MORPHEME	<-dɔŋo>$_{a}$ ~ <-dɔŋ>$_{am}$
GLOSS	CND

MORPHEME	<-so>$_{am}$
GLOSS	IRR

The conditional gerund is formed by suffixation of the morpheme <-dɔŋo>$_{a}$ ~ <-dɔŋ>$_{am}$ to simplicia.[15] The conditional gerund is commonly used as the main verb of a subordinate clause which expresses supposition or implicit condition.

Real conditional sentences indicate that if one event takes place, some other event will follow. The predicator of the main clause can be of several verbal and deverbative types which are used to depict events that are portrayed as actualised, occurring, set to occur or potential. Previous examples of real conditional sentences are (57), (99) and (106) above. Note that the subordinate conditional clause in (99) ends in the clause-final particle *bhʌne*$_{a}$ 'if; as for'. This particle is a loan from Nepali *bhane* 'if saying', which is the second perfect participle of the verb *bhannu* 'to say'. The Jero form *ja-u-m bhʌne* (eat-1s-AFF if) 'if I eat' is a calque of Nepali *khāẽ bhane*. The native equivalent of this periphrastic construction is the synthetic form *ja-u-dɔŋ* (eat-1s-CND). The following example contains positive and negative conditionals.

[15] Unlike the present gerundive endings /-bu-lu/$_{am}$ and /-bu-l/$_{am}$, which are split up into two productive morphemes, the conditional gerundive endings <-dɔŋɔ>$_{a}$ ~ <-dɔŋ>$_{am}$ have not been further analysed and are treated here as indivisible morphemes. Even though a lexicalised reflex of the ablative case marker <=ŋo>$_{m}$ can be recognised, the element <-dɔ>$_{am}$ cannot be identified as a separate morpheme.

199$_a$ *Su a-ba:-Ø-dɔŋ, gɔk-ca-p; a-nɔ-Ø-dɔŋo,*
meat NEG-be/sit-23s-CND give-PUR-RES NEG-be-23s-CND

su ba:-Ø-dɔŋ, gɔk-si pʌrdʌina.
meat be/sit-23s-CND give-INF *is.not.necessary*

If there is not meat, you have to give [ginger]; if not, if there is meat, you do not need to give [ginger].

Unreal conditional sentences express counterfactual or unknown conditions for past events. These sentences take an irrealis verb form in the main clause. Irrealis verbs are formed by suffixation of the morpheme <-so>$_{am}$ to simplicia.

200$_a$ *Aŋgu lɔ-Ø-dɔŋ, uŋgu=ya lɔ-ŋ-so.*
he/they go-23s-CND I/we=also go-1s-IRR

If he had gone, I too would have gone.

201$_a$ *Inne tɔt lɔ-n-Ø-dɔŋ da,*
you up.there go-2-23s-CND THM

hip-su po-ku-so.
see-MAN do-1peAS-IRR

If you^{s} had gone up there, we^{pe} would have seen you.

202$_m$ *Inne=khu uŋgu a-nɛʔ-iŋ-Ø-mʌi*
you=SRC I/we NEG-say-2→1s-23s-FCT

nɔ-Ø-dɔŋ, a-lɔ-ŋ-so.
be-23s-CND NEG-go-1s-IRR

If you^{s} had not said it to me, I would not have gone away.

6.4 *The simultaneous gerund*

MORPHEME	<-sʌi>$_{am}$
GLOSS	SML

The simultaneous gerund points to a situation that occurs simultaneously with the event denoted in the main clause, conveying the sense of 'whilst doing'. The simultaneous gerund is formed from a verb root by suffixation of the marker <-sʌi>$_{am}$.

203_{a}	*Uŋgu*	*lam*	*brɛk-sʌi*	*lɔ-ŋ-ma.*
	I/we	road	sweep-SML	go-1s-AFF

I went off sweeping the road.

204_{m}	*Nɔi*	*jhola*	*kur-sʌi*	*kur-sʌi*	*lɔ-Ø-m.*
	that.hrz	*bag*	carry-SML	carry-SML	go-23s-AFF

He went off carrying that bag (which is at the same elevation as the speaker).

6.5 *The connective gerund*

MORPHEME	<-ti>$_{am}$
GLOSS	CNN

Suffixation of the morpheme <-ti>$_{am}$ to the verb root yields a connective gerund. The connective gerund is used to describe a verbal event in which the actions expressed by the connective (e.g. 'give him') and by the main verb (e.g. 'bring') are conceptualised as a mentally linked whole expressing a single idea (e.g. 'bring for him').

205_{m}	*Aŋgu*	*lai*	*hepa*	*phit-ti*
	he/they	PAT	cooked.grain	bring.hrz-CNN
	gɔk-kha-Ø!			
	give-IMP-SAS			

Bring[s] him cooked grain (across a horizontal plane)!

6.6 *Gerunds of manner*

MORPHEME	<-sa>$_{am}$
GLOSS	MAN

MORPHEME	<-su>$_{am}$
GLOSS	MAN

Gerunds of manner are used in several periphrastic constructions in which the gerund of manner specifies the manner or circumstance under which the action specified by the accompanying main verb takes place.

The gerund of manner in <-sa>$_{am}$ is used with a lexicalised instance of the source marker in non-finite perfect gerunds, the morphosyntax of which is discussed in Section 6.1 above (p. 195). The gerund of manner ending in <-sa>$_{am}$ is also used with the auxiliary *bakcap*$_{a}$ ~ *bakcam*$_{m}$ vi-2 <bak- ~ ba:-> 'to be, sit' in periphrastic constructions that mark continuous aspectualisation. These constructions are discussed in Section 7.3 below (p. 209).

In Jero person and number agreement morphology, the gerund of manner ending in <-su>$_{am}$ is used with the auxiliary *pacap*$_{a}$ ~ *pacam*$_{m}$ vt-2a <pa- ~ po-> 'to do' to mark Mohanṭāre 1s→2ns$_{m}$, 1pe→2p$_{m}$, 2s→1nse$_{m}$, 3s→1ns$_{m}$ and 3p→1ns$_{m}$ simplex forms, Āmboṭe 1s→2ns$_{a}$, 1de→2$_{a}$, 1pe→2$_{a}$, 2s→1$_{a}$, 2d→1$_{a}$, 2p→1$_{a}$, 3s→1$_{a}$, 3d→1$_{a}$ and 3p→1$_{a}$ simplex forms, and Mohanṭāre and Āmboṭe 2s→1e, 2d→1e and 2p→1e imperative forms. The periphrastic agreement constructions are discussed above in Sections 4.3 (p. 140) and 4.6 (p. 172). See also examples (227) and (228) below.

6.7 *The negative state gerund*

MORPHEME	<-thum>$_{a}$
GLOSS	NSG

Suffixation of the morpheme <-thum>$_{a}$ to the verb root yields a negative state gerund. This gerund is used to express that the situation referred to in the main clause happened without the occurrence of the situation referred to in the gerundive clause. The negative state gerund can occur with or without the negative prefix. The final <m> of the marker of the negative state gerund seems to represent a lexicalised and abbreviated instance of the reifying marker <=me>$_{am}$.

206_a	*Hep*	*a-ja-thum*	*lɔ-ku-m.*
	cooked.grain	NEG-eat-NSG	go-1peAS-AFF

We[pe] went without having eaten cooked grain.

207_a	*Ka:k*	*(a-) tu:-thum*	*lɔ-ŋ-ma.*
	water	(NEG-) drink-NSG	go-1s-AFF

I went without having drunk water.

CHAPTER SEVEN

VERBAL CONSTRUCTIONS AND COMPLEX VERBS

Verbal constructions are periphrastic forms that consist of a main verbal noun, adjective or adverb plus an unbound auxiliary verb which adds a dimension of some kind to the meaning expressed by the main constituent. The resultant combination functions like two independent stems. The verbal categories such as negation and transitivity are marked in the auxiliary. By contrast, a complex verb consists of a main verb root and a bound verb root. The two roots function like a single stem to which inflectional and derivational affixes can be added.

7.1 *Inceptive auxiliaries*

MORPHEME	*pacap*$_{a}$ vt-2a <pa- ~ po->
GLOSS	do

MORPHEME	*necam*$_{m}$ vm-1a <ne->
GLOSS	say

MORPHEME	*rakcam*$_{m}$ vt-2e <rakt- (~ *ra:-)>
GLOSS	provoke

The Āmboṭe auxiliary *pacap*$_{a}$ vt-2a <pa- ~ po-> 'to do, make' and the Mohanṭāre auxiliaries *necam*$_{m}$ vm-1a <ne-> 'to say' and *rakcam*$_{m}$ vt-2e <rakt- (~ *ra:-)> 'to influence, arouse, tease, provoke' are used with a verbal adjective of purpose in periphrastic constructions that specify that the action is about to be performed. See also example (120).

208$_{a}$	*Uŋ*	*lɔ-ca*	*pa-u-m.*
	I/we	go-PUR	do-1s-AFF

I was about to go.

209_a *Uŋ* *lɔ-ca* *pa-u-mai* *ba:-Ø-m.*
I/we go-PUR do-1s-FCT be/sit-23s-AFF

I am about to go.

210_m *Uŋ* *lɔ-ca* *ne-ŋ-mʌi* *thiyo,*
I/we go-PUR say-1s-FCT *was*

tʌrʌ *inne* *bla-n-Ø-ne.*
but you arrive-2-23s-AFF

I was about to go, but [then] you[s] came.

211_m *Warsi* *ya-ca* *ya-ca*
rain come.down-PUR come.down-PUR

rakt-i-Ø-m.
influence-3npA-23s-AFF

Rain was about to fall.

212_m *Nɔm* *ham-ca* *ham-ca*
sun sink-PUR sink-PUR

rakt-i-Ø-mʌi *thiyo.*
provoke-3npA-23s-FCT *was*

The sun was about to go under [when something else happened].

7.2 *Ingressive auxiliaries*

MORPHEME	*thalʌi pacap*$_a$ vt-2a <pa- ~ po->
GLOSS	start do
MORPHEME	*jɛkcam*$_m$ vt(-2e) <jɛkt- (~ *je-)>
GLOSS	start

The periphrastic construction *thalʌi pacap*$_a$ vt-2a <pa- ~ po-> 'to start doing' and the native auxiliary *jɛkcam*$_m$ vt(-2e) <jɛkt- (~ *je-)> 'to start' focus on the beginning of the action denoted by the infinitive.

213$_{m}$ *Uŋgu* *ai* *ciṭhi* *rɛk-si* *jɛ-ʔ-ma.*
I/we this *letter* write-INF start-1s-AFF

I will start writing this letter.

214$_{a}$ *Uŋ* *kul* *lɔ-si* *thal-ʌi* *pa-u-m.*
I/we house go-INF *start*-LN do-1s-AFF

I started going home.

215$_{a}$ *Inne* *haŋ* *kam* *pa-si* *thal-ʌi* *a-pa-ni-Ø?*
you why *work* do-INF *start*-LN NEG-do-2-23s

Why won't you[s] start working?

7.3 *The continuous auxiliary*

MORPHEME	*bakcap*$_{a}$ ~ *bakcam*$_{m}$ vi-2 <bak- ~ ba:->
GLOSS	be/sit

The auxiliary *bakcap*$_{a}$ ~ *bakcam*$_{m}$ vi-2 <bak- ~ ba:-> 'to be, sit' is used with a gerund of manner in <-sa>$_{am}$ to specify that the event expressed by the gerund is a continuous or ongoing activity. The gerund is commonly extended by means of the abbreviated morph =s_{am} of the suffix <=se>$_{am}$ 'exactly'.

216$_{a}$ *Ja-sa=s* *ba:-Ø-m.*
eat-MAN=exactly be/sit-23s-AFF

He is eating [now].

The perfect form *ba-ŋ-mʌi ba:-Ø-m* in the following sentence marks a past matter of fact which lasted throughout a particular period of time, and with continuing relevance at the moment of speech.

217$_{m}$ *Uŋ* *kam* *pa-sa=s* *ba-ŋ-mʌi*
I/we *work* do-MAN=exactly be/sit-1s-FCT

ba:-Ø-m.
be/sit-23s-AFF

a. I have been working.

b. I have kept on working.

7.4 *Terminative auxiliaries*

MORPHEME	*taccap*$_a$ vt-2d <tatt- ~tan->
GLOSS	stop

MORPHEME	*plɛcam*$_m$ vt-1 <plɛ->
GLOSS	stop

The auxiliaries *taccap*$_a$ vt-2d <tatt- ~tan-> 'to stop, quit' and *plɛcam*$_m$ vt-1 <plɛ-> 'to stop, quit' place a focus on the end of the action denoted by the infinitive. See also example (65).

218$_a$	*Uŋgu=ku*	*ai*	*kam*	*pa-si*	*tap-Ø-ma.*
	I/we=SRC	this	*work*	do-INF	stop-1s-AFF

I will stop doing this work.

7.5 *Auxiliaries of capacity*

MORPHEME	*phaccap*$_a$ vt-2d <phatt- ~ phan->
GLOSS	can

MORPHEME	*capcam*$_m$ vt(-2c) <capt- (~ *cam-)>
GLOSS	can

The auxiliaries of capacity *phaccap*$_a$ vt-2d <phatt- ~ phan-> 'can, be able' and *capcam*$_m$ vt(-2c) <capt- (~ *cam-)> 'can, be able' are used to express that the agent has the physical or mental capacity or is in a position to carry out or bring about the event denoted by the infinitive. Note that the auxiliary verb in (219) shows agreement with a third person patient argument, which can be identified as the infinitive verb form *ki-si* but not as the noun phrase *uŋgu lai* 'to me'. See also examples (24) and (192).

219$_a$	*In*	*ticu=ku*	*uŋgu*	*lai*	*ki-si*	*phan-ni-m-me.*
	you	PL=SRC	I/we	PAT	look.at-INF	can-2-23/ns-AFF

You^p can look at me.

220$_a$ *Uŋ* *kud-ʌi* *la-si* *a-pha-ʔu.*
I/we *leap*-LN become-INF NEG-can-1s

I cannot leap.

7.6 *Auxiliaries 'to like'*

MORPHEME	*daː-*$_a$ vi-1b <daː->
GLOSS	like

MORPHEME	*dakcam*$_m$ vt-2e <dakt- ~ daː->
GLOSS	like

The auxiliaries *daː-*$_a$ vi-1b <daː-> 'to like' and *dakcam*$_m$ vt-2e <dakt- ~ daː-> 'to like' are used to express that the performer likes to carry out the action denoted by the accompanying infinitive.

221$_m$ *Pa-si* *da-ʔ-ma.*
do-INF like-1s-AFF

I like to do [something].

222$_a$ *Uŋ* *kul* *lɔ-si* *daː-Ø-m.*
I/we house go-INF like-23s-AFF

I like to go home.

223$_a$ *Uŋgu* *inne* *lai* *ki-si* *daː-Ø-m.*
I/we you PAT look.at-INF like-23s-AFF

I like to watch you.

The infinitives *lɔ-si* in (222) and *ki-si* in (223) can be replaced by the verb forms *lɔ-p* and *ki-p* if the activities referred to by the infinitive still have to be performed.

224$_a$ *Uŋgu* *kul* *lɔ-p* *daː-Ø-m.*
I/we house go-$^?$RES like-23s-AFF

I would like to go home.

225$_a$ *Uŋgu inne lai ki-p da:-Ø-m.*
I/we you PAT look.at-$^?$RES like-23s-AFF
I would like to look at you.

7.7 The auxiliaries 'to know'

MORPHEME *jɔkcam*$_m$ vt(-2e) <jɔkt- (*~ jo-)>
GLOSS know

The auxiliary *jɔkcam*$_m$ vt(-2e) <jɔkt- (*~ jo-)> 'to know (by learning)' is used to express that the performer possesses the knowledge to carry out the action denoted by the accompanying infinitive.

226$_m$ *Inne nɔi rεk-si jɔk-ni-Ø-m?*
You that.hrz write-INF know-2-23s-AFF
You^s do know [how] to write that [word]?

7.8 The auxiliary 'to give'

MORPHEME *gɔkcap*$_a$ ~ *gɔkcam*$_m$ vt-2e <gɔkt- ~ go->
GLOSS give

The auxiliary *gɔkcap*$_a$ ~ *gɔkcam*$_m$ vt-2e <gɔkt- ~ go-> 'to give' is used in two types of periphrastic constructions. The auxiliary is used with an infinitive in permissive constructions, which express the giving of permission or consent to someone to do something, conveying the meaning 'to let somebody do something'. The agent of the auxiliary refers to the entity who gives permission. The patient refers to the entity to whom permission is given.

227$_a$ *Lɔ-si gɔk-su pa-i-Ø-m?*
go-INF give-MAN do-3npA-23s-AFF
Will he let me/us go?

The auxiliary *gɔkcap*$_a$ ~ *gɔkcam*$_m$ vt-2e <gɔkt- ~ go-> 'to give' is used with a connective gerund in periphrastic constructions that stress that the action is performed on behalf of someone or something else, e.g. (205) above and in the following example.

228_{a}

Aŋ	*ticu=ku*	*am*	*kaʔu=na*	*uŋgu*	*lai*
he/they	PL=SRC	my	friend=COM	I/we	PAT

hepa	*phɛt-ti*	*gɔk-su*	*pa-m-me,*
cooked.grain	deal.out-CNN	give-MAN	do-23/ns-AFF

ulu=k	*uŋgu*	*dui*	*jʌna=ku*	*aŋ*	*ticu*
there=SRC	I/we	*two*	*person*=SRC	he/they	PL

lai	*khamsi*	*phɛt-ti*	*go-cu-m.*
PAT	cooked.liquid.dish	deal.out-CNN	give-1deAS-AFF

They^{p} served cooked grain to me and my friend, and we^{e} two served them^{p} *khamsi*.

229_{m}

Inne	*ḍhoka*	*khol-ʌi*	*pa-ti*	*gɔk-kha-ŋ-Ø!*
you	*door*	*open*-LN	do-CNN	give-IMP-1sP-sAS

Open^{s} the door for me!

7.9 *The provocative auxiliary*

MORPHEME	*ra:cap*$_{a}$ vm-1a <ra:->
GLOSS	provoke

Second person simplex forms of the middle auxiliary *ra:cap*$_{a}$ vm-1a <ra:-> 'to influence, arouse, provoke' are used with an infinitive in grammaticalised periphrastic constructions which express that the argument marked as the subject of the intransitive verb, by request or way of conduct, arouses or brings about the action described by the infinitive, conveying the figurative sense of 'to ask for something'.

230_{a}

Ui	*naʔa*	*a-nɔ-sa-ku,*	*sʌb-ʌi*
that	only	NEG-be-MAN-PFG	*all*-EMPH

inne	*lai*	*gɔk-si*	*ra:-s-a-Ø!*
you	PAT	give-INF	provoke-DETR-IMP-sAS

Ask^{s} him to give you everything, not only that!

In simplex agreement morphology, these periphrastic constructions are allegedly used to mark transitive relationships between third person agents and second person patients.

7.10 *The reciprocal auxiliary*

MORPHEME	*pocap*$_a$ vm-1a <po->
GLOSS	reciprocal

Preverbs are unbound invariable verb forms which are derived from the paradigmatic verb roots by means of morphological processes that involve some kind of modification of the verb root. Preverbs carry the main semantics of the verbal event in constructions in which they co-occur with the reciprocal auxiliary *pocap*$_a$ vm-1a <po->.

231$_a$	*Uŋ*	*nimpha*	*tum*	*po-ŋ-ci!*
	we	DU	hit	reciprocal-dS-d

Let us[di] hit each other!

7.11 *The causative auxiliary*

MORPHEME	*paccap*$_a$ ~ *paccam*$_m$ vt-2d <patt- ~ pan->
GLOSS	cause to do

The productive causative devise in Jero is a periphrastic construction that consists of a preverb plus inflected forms of the auxiliary *paccap*$_a$ ~ *paccam*$_m$ vt-2d <patt- ~ pan-> 'to cause to do', e.g. *rɛnda re paccam*$_m$ 'to cause someone to laugh', *khrɔm paccap*$_a$ 'to make weep, cause to cry' and *wal paccam*$_m$ 'to make walk, make go, make move, conduct, steer'.

In the following example, by contrast, the auxiliary *pacap*$_a$ ~ *pacam*$_m$ vt-2a <pa- ~ po-> 'to do' is used in relation with a preverb ending in /s/, which can perhaps be identified as the marker 'exactly'. The use of the verb meaning 'to do something' instead of 'to cause someone to do (something)' seems to be related to the marking of an unexpressed patient participant, i.e. *sɔmdu* 'sacred texts of the oral tradition', rather than a recipient participant such as 'to us' in the finite verb.

232$_a$	*Naksu*	*ticu*	*sik-ʌi*	*pas*	*pa-m-me.*
	family.priest	PL	*learn*-LN	do	do-23/ns-AFF

Family priests and the like teach [sacred texts of the oral tradition].

7.12 *Bound verb roots*

MORPHEME <-di- ~ -du->$_a$
GLOSS go/come

MORPHEME <-kha->$_m$
GLOSS come.up

The bound verb roots <-di- ~ -du->$_a$ 'go (and come back)' and <-kha->$_m$ 'come up' are suffixed to the paradigmatically conditioned roots of the main verb. The resultant stem combination functions like a single complex root to which verbal affixes can be attached. Examples of complex verbs are: *blandicap*$_a$ vi-1a-i <blan-di- ~ blan-du-> 'to arrive somewhere (by going)', *blaŋkha-*$_m$ <blan-kha-> 'to go up and arrive somewhere' and *hedicap*$_a$ <he-di- ~ he-du-> 'to climb, mount; to enter'. The verb root <-du-> of the root <-di- ~ -du->$_a$ 'go (and come back)' co-occurs with the person and number agreement morphemes <-ŋu>$_{am}$ (1s), <-cuwa> (1deAS) and <-kuwa> (1peAS). The verb root <-di-> is used before the other agreement morphemes, which generally have the suffix vowel <i>. See example (108).

APPENDIX ONE

JERO-ENGLISH LEXICON

The alphabetical order follows the order of the Latin alphabet with some adaptations. Unaspirated obstruents precede aspirated and murmured obstruents. Alveolar plosives precede retroflex plosives. Short vowels precede long vowels. Nasalised vowels are not distinguished in the alphabetical order from normal vowels. Diphthongs are treated like vowel sequences.

ʌ
a
a:
b
bh
c
ch
d
dh
ɖ
ɖh
ɛ
e
g
gh
h
i
i:
j
jh
k
kh
l
m
n
ŋ
ɔ
o
p
ph
r
s
t
th
ʈ
ʈh
u
u:
w
y
ʔ

The Nepali translations are those given by the informants in the field. In the case of full or partial loans from Nepali, the Nepali translation is preceded by the symbol (<). The spelling of Nepali represents the norm given in the *Nepālī Bṛhat Śabdakoś*. The scientific names of Nepali plants and trees are taken from Panday (1982), Shrestha (1979) and the Bulletins of the Department of Medicinal Plants issued by His Majesty's Government of Nepal (HMG 1982,

1984). If the name of a plant does not appear in one of these publications, I have consulted Turner (1931), who identifies a number of plants by their obsolete botanical names.

The forms culled from the three unpublished lists of about 102 words each, which were collected within the framework of the Linguistic Survey of Nepal (LSN) and kindly given to me by Werner Winter, are preceded by the following Roman numerals:

I The 'Badancha'[16] list represents the Jero variety spoken in Ratnāvatī VDC in Sindhulī district (southern Jero).

II The 'Madhavpur' list represents the Jero variety spoken in Mādhavpur VDC, to the east of the Mauluṅ Kholā or 'Melungkhola' (Hanßon 1991: 43) in Okhalḍhuṅgā district (northeastern Jero).

III The 'Balkhu-Sisneri' list represents the Jero variety spoken in Valkhu and Sisnerī VDC, to the west of the Mauluṅ Kholā in Okhalḍhuṅgā district (northwestern Jero).

The lexical entry of literary forms (LIT) is given in transliterated orthography which is preceded by numbers referring to the following sources:

1	Rāī, Aṅgadhan (VS 2051)	Tīkhaṇḍe dialect
2	Rāī, Aṅgadhan (VS 2052)	*idem*
3	Rāī, Aṃga Dhan (VS 2053)	*idem*
4	Rāī, Aṃgadhan (VS 2054)	*idem*
5	Rāī, Aṅgadhan (VS 2056)	*idem*
6	Rāī, Ramilā (VS 2051)	Mādhavpur dialect
7	Setālco, Nain Bahādur (VS 2057)	Sisnerī dialect

Literary forms 1 to 5 represent southern Jero, 6 represents northeastern Jero, and 7 represents northwestern Jero.

---

[16] Hanßon (1991: 43) hypothesises that 'the name Badanchha or Badamchha .... may be a thar name of dialectal importance or only a pacha (clan) within this group.' This name may be related to the Wambule clan name *Boḍwam*.

The root-final element *[k]* in forms such as *kra[k]-* is a morphophonologically conditioned ending rather than a paradigmatically conditioned root final segment.

— Ø —

-Ø$^{1}_{am}$ *suffix* second and third person singular simplex agreement morpheme.
-Ø$^{2}_{am}$ *suffix* singular agent and subject imperative agreement morpheme.
-Ø$^{3}_{am}$ see *-i*^{1}.
-Ø$^{4}_{a}$ see *-mi*^{1}.
-Ø$^{5}_{a}$ see *-ŋu*^{1}.

— ʌ —

ʌ̃$_{a}$ [<Nep. *ã*] *adv* yes, even, exactly.
-ʌi$^{1}_{am}$ [<Nep. *-āi*] *suffix* nominaliser of loan verbs. LIT 1 4 *-ai* in *paḍai* 'reading; learning' / 4 *pharkailaṅmā* 'I returned'; 6 *-ai* in *bujhai* 'understanding'; 7 *-ai* in *jammailāsāku* 'having come together'.
-ʌi$^{2}_{am}$ [<Nep. *-ai*] *suffix* emphatic marker. LIT 1 *-ai* in *jhaṇḍai* 'almost, nearly, closely'.
ʌjiŋgʌr$_{a}$ [<Nep. *ajiṅgar*] *n* big snake, python.
ʌndha$_{m}$ [<Nep. *andho*] *adj* blind in both eyes.
ʌnuhar$_{a}$ [<Nep. *anuhār*, *anuvār*] *n* face.
ʌnusar$_{a}$ [<Nep. *anusār*] *postp* according to.
ʌŋgalo$_{m}$ [<Nep. *ãgālo*] *n* bent arm, embrace, armful.
ʌrko$_{a}$ [<Nep. *arko*] *adj* other.
ʌru$_{a}$ [<Nep. *arū*] *adj* other (of more than two), more.
ʌul$_{a}$ [<Nep. *aul*] *n* fever.

— a —

a-$^{1}_{am}$ *prefix* negative marker. LIT 4 *ā-* in *āhipthu* 'in order to not see'; 6 *ā-* in *āphāccāl* 'while not being able'. Nep. *na-*.

a-$^{2}_{\text{am}}$ *bound morph* demonstrative which indicates a position relatively near the point of reference or near the speaker.

-a$^{3}_{\text{am}}$ see *-ka*.

a$^{4}_{\text{a}}$ *conj* or, or else. Nep. *athavā*.

ai$_{\text{am}}$ see *aya*.

akkum$_{\text{am}}$ *poss* our^{pe}. Nep. *hāmro*.

alu$_{\text{am}}$, **al**$_{\text{am}}$ *dem adv* here (near the speaker). Nep. *yahā̃*. **alu=na=ku**$_{\text{a}}$, **alu=na=k**$_{\text{a}}$, **al=na=ku**$_{\text{a}}$, **al=na=k**$_{\text{a}}$ *dem adv* from here. Nep. *yahā̃-dekhi*. **al sʌmba**$_{\text{m}}$ *dem adv* until here. Nep. *yahā̃samma*.

am$_{\text{am}}$ *poss* my. LIT 2 *ām*, 1 5 *āmme* 'that of mine'; 6 *āmme* 'that of mine'. Nep. *mero*.

ancim$_{\text{am}}$ *poss* their^{d}. Nep. *unī duījanāko*.

ancum$_{\text{am}}$ *poss* our^{de}. Nep. *hāmī duījanāko*.

anim$_{\text{am}}$ *poss* their^{p}. Nep. *unīharūko*.

-ano$_{\text{a}}$, **-no**$_{\text{am}}$ *suffix* optative marker.

anucap$_{\text{a}}$, **anucam**$_{\text{m}}$ *vi-1a-i* to be ill, be sick, be unhealthy, be not all right. LIT 4 *ānuce* 'not being well'. Nep. *niko nahunu*. See *nucap*.

aŋ$^{1}_{\text{m}}$, **aŋam**$_{\text{a}}$ *poss* his, her. Nep. *usko*.

aŋ$^{2}_{\text{am}}$ see *aŋgu*.

aŋam$_{\text{a}}$ see *aŋ*^{1}.

aŋgu$_{\text{am}}$, **aŋ**$_{\text{am}}$ *pers* he, she, they. Nep. *u, unī*. **aŋ nimpha**$_{\text{am}}$ *pers* they^{d}. **aŋ ticu**$_{\text{am}}$ *pers* they^{p}.

-aŋti$_{\text{m}}$, **-ŋti**$_{\text{m}}$ *suffix* simplex agreement morpheme which marks a transitive relationship between a third person singular agent and a first person singular patient. LIT 7 *-ṅti* in *puṅtimāyā* 'he did to me'.

aro$_{\text{a}}$ [<Nep. *āro*] *n* saw.

asal$_{\text{a}}$ *dem adv* towards here (of direction, towards the hearer).

ase$_{\text{m}}$, **as**$_{\text{m}}$ *dem adv* in this way, like this, thus, so. Nep. *yaso*. **ase=p**$_{\text{a}}$, **ase=m**$_{\text{m}}$ *dem adj & adv* (something) like this, thus, so. Nep. *yaso, yasto*. **ase=p=na=se=p**$_{\text{a}}$ *dem adj & adv* (something) like this. Nep. *yasto*.

asi$_{\text{am}}$ *intens* few, scarce, less. Nep. *thorai, kamtī, alikati*. **asi khɔlse**$_{\text{a}}$ *quant* some, few, a small amount. **asi khɔlto**$_{\text{m}}$ *v adj* little big. Nep. *alikati ṭhūlo*.

as khɔlse$_{\text{a}}$ *quant* much, many.

aya$_{\text{a}}$, **ai**$_{\text{am}}$ *dem pron* this (near the speaker). LSN I *a̭i*; II *a̭i*; III *a̭i*. LIT 2 5 *āī*. Nep. *yo*.

— b —

bʌɖʌi$_{a}$ [<Nep. *baḍhāi*] *n* increase, enlargement. **bʌɖʌi pacap**$_{a}$ *vt-2a* to increase, enlarge. Nep. *baḍhāunu.*

bʌɖe$_{m}$, **bʌɖi**$_{a}$ [<Nep. *baḍhī*] *intens* more, larger. **bʌɖe roto**$_{m}$ *v adj* very high, very tall. Nep. *dherai aglo.*

bʌini$_{a}$ [<Nep. *bahinī*] *n* younger sister.

bʌkʌino$_{m}$ [<Nep. *bakainu*] *n* the plant *Azedarachta indica*, the berries of which are used for necklaces (Turner 1931, Singh 1971).

bʌliyo$_{a}$ [<Nep. *baliyo*] *adj* strong.

bʌnʌi$_{m}$ [<Nep. *banāi*] *n* something made, something done, construction. **bʌnʌi pacam**$_{m}$ *vt-2a* to make, build, construct, produce. Nep. *banāunu.*

bʌndʌ$_{m}$ [<Nep. *banda*] *adj* shut, confined, closed, stopped. **bʌndʌ pacam**$_{m}$ *vt-2a* to shut, lock, close, cover, shut off. Nep. *banda garnu.*

bʌr$_{m}$ [<Nep. *bar*] *n* the Banyan tree *Ficus bengalensis.*

bʌrsa$_{m}$ [<Nep. *barṣa*] *n* year.

bʌulʌi$_{am}$ [<Nep. *bauhlāi*] *n* craziness, insanity. **bʌulʌi lacap**$_{a}$, **bʌulʌi lacam**$_{m}$ *vi-1a-i* to go crazy, go insane. Nep. *bauhlāunu.*

ba$_{a}$ *adv* manner of setting up or putting down. Nep. *ṭhaḍyāune vā basāune kisimsita.* **ba yɔmcap**$_{a}$, **ba yɔmcam**$_{a}$ *vi-1c* to stand up. Nep. *khaḍā hunu.*

badʌl$_{a}$ [<Nep. *bādal*] *n* cloud, mist (in sky), fog. See *kɔksɛl.*

baɖ$_{a}$ [<Nep. *bāṇ*] *n* arrow.

bãɖʌi$_{a}$ [<Nep. *bā̃ḍāi*] *n* division, share, allotment, distribution. **bãɖʌi pacap**$_{a}$ *vt-2a* to divide, share, allot, distribute. Nep. *bā̃ḍnu.*

bahek$_{a}$ [<Nep. *bāhek*] *postp* aside from, except, not considering, e.g. *uŋgu bahek*$_{a}$ 'except me'.

bakcap$_{a}$, **bakcam**$_{m}$ *vi-2* <bak- ~ ba:-> A to be, copula of location and qualification, sit, remain. B continuous auxiliary, used with a gerund of manner ending in <-sa>$_{am}$. LIT 1 2 5 *bā-* in 1 2 *bām* 'he is' / 5 *bākṭvāk* 'being'; 6 *bā-* in *bānne* 'you^{s} are'; 7 *bā-* in *pausāsbāṅmā* 'I am doing'. Nep. *basnu, hunu, rahanu.*

baluwa$_{a}$ [<Nep. *baluwā*] *n* sand.

banta$_{a}$ [<Nep. *bāntā*] *n* vomiting.

baŋra$_{am}$ [<Nep. *baṅgāro*] *n* back tooth, molar.

bar$_{m}$ [<Nep. *bār*] *n* fence.

basi$_{m}$ [<Nep. *bāsī*] *adj* stale, kept for a long time.

bat$_a$ [<Nep. *bāt*] *n* thing, matter. **bat pacap**$_a$ *vt-2a* to talk. Nep. *bāt garnu.*

baṭa$_m$ [<Nep. *bāṭā*] *n* a big-mouthed copper or brass vessel.

bɛla$_a$, **bɛl**$_a$ [<Nep. *belā*] *n* time. LIT 1 2 *byālā* in 1 *uibyālāsse* 'at exactly that time'; 7 *belā* in *belāmā* 'at the time'.

bɛŋge$_a$ *n* a kind of red ant.

bɛthɔŋ$_{am}$ *n* Gurkhali knife. LIT 2 *byaṭhvāṅ*. Nep. *khukurī.*

beli$_m$, **beʔli**$_a$ *n* she-goat. LIT 7 *belī*. Nep. *bākhrī*. See *beʔli.*

berne$_a$ [<Nep. *bernu*] *n* rectum.

besura$_{am}$ [<Nep. *besāro*] *n* a particular kind of falcon.

beʔli$_a$ see *beli.*

bicar$_a$ [<Nep. *vicār*] *n* A opinion. B thought, consideration, idea. **im bicar=na**$_a$ [Jero *im* 'your^s', Nep. *vicār* 'opinion', Jero locative *=na*] in your opinion. Nep. *timro bicārmā.*

bicchi$_a$ [<Nep. *bicchī*] *n* scorpion.

bichʌi$_a$ [<Nep. *bichyāi*] *n* spread (e.g. of a bedding). **bichʌi pacap**$_a$ *vt-2a* to spread out. Nep. *bichyāunu*. See *ochʌi pacap.*

bidesi$_a$ [<Nep. *videśī*] *n & adj* foreigner.

bĩḍ$_a$ [<Nep. *bĩḍ*] *n* handle.

bigrʌi$_a$ [<Nep. *bigrāi*] *n* ruin, becoming damaged. **bigrʌi lacap**$_a$ *vi-1a-i* to spoil, be ruined, become damaged. Nep. *bigranu*. **bigrʌi pacap**$_a$ *vt-2a* to spoil, ruin, damage. Nep. *bigārnu.*

biha$_a$ [<Nep. *bihā*, *bihe*] *n* marriage.

bihan$_{am}$ [<Nep. *bihān*] *n* morning, daybreak, period from 05.00 to 12.00 hours.

binti$_m$ [<Nep. *bintī*] *n* A request, supplication, prayer. B application, petition. **binti pacam**$_m$ *vt-2a* to request, supplicate, pray. Nep. *bintī garnu.*

bipcap$_a$, **bipcam**$_m$ *v(t)* to suck, draw the liquid out of something with one's mouth, extract with one's mouth. Nep. *cusnu*, *śoṣan garnu.*

biralo$_{am}$ [<Nep. *birālo*] *n* cat.

birami$_{am}$ [<Nep. *birāmī*] *adj* ill, sick.

bisʌya$_a$ [<Nep. *viṣaya*] *n* subject, topic.

biu$_a$ [<Nep. *bīu*] *n* seed. See *cicila*, *cinci.*

biya$_a$ *n* bullock, steer. LIT 7 *biyā*. Nep. *goru*. See *goru*$_m$.

blaccap$_a$, **bla[k]-**$_m$ *v(t)* A to come, arrive somewhere. B to bring, fetch. LSN II *bla-(*s-)*; III *bla-ś-*. Nep. *āunu*, *āgaman hunu*, *lyāunu.*

blakcap$_{a}$, **blak-**$_{m}$ *vi-2* <blak- ~ bla:-> to come, arrive somewhere (from no fixed direction). LIT 5 *blām* 'he came'. Nep. *āunu, āgaman hunu.*

blandicap$_{a}$ *vi-1a-i* <blan-di- ~ blan-du-> to arrive somewhere (by going). Nep. *āipugnu.*

blaŋkha-$_{m}$ *vi* to go up and arrive somewhere.

blattɔp$_{a}$ *v adj* characterised by arriving. Nep. *āune.*

blecap$_{a}$, **ble-**$_{m}$ *v(i)* to be alive, be living, be in life, survive, escape from death, be saved. LIT 4 *blecām.* Nep. *bā̃cnu, jīvit rahanu, jiū̃do hunu.*

blu$_{am}$ *n* arrow. Nep. *dhanu.*

blu-lekhe$_{m}$ [Jero *blu* 'arrow' + *lekhe* 'bamboo bow'] *n cmp* arrow and bow.

bɔkra$_{m}$ [<Nep. *bokro*] *n* skin, rind, peel. See *kɔkte.*

bɔm-$_{m}$ *v(m)* to be covered. Nep. *chopinu, ḍhākinu.* **kum bɔm-**$_{m}$ *v* to bend down, hang down, stoop, bow. Nep. *nuhunu.*

bɔmbar$_{am}$ *n* a particular kind of big lime. Nep. *nibuvā.*

bɔmti$_{m}$ *n cmp* thumb, big toe. Nep. *buḍhīaū̃lī.* See *buḍi-bɔmti, buḍi-brɛmci.*

bɔna$_{a}$ *n* oar. Nep. *ḍhuṅgā khiyāune ḍā̃ḍā.*

bobo$_{a}$ *n* cob (of maize), ear (of grain). Nep. *makai, junelo ādi bhuṭdā viksita bhaeko svarup.*

boka$_{a}$ [<Nep. *bokā*] *n* billy-goat.

bosrɛmpu$_{a}$ *n* a species of big spider.

bracap$_{a}$, **bracam**$_{m}$ *v(t)* to spread, scatter, sow. Nep. *charnu, charpasṭa pārnu.*

brakcap$_{a}$ *v(i)* to break, burst. Nep. *cū̃ḍinu.*

braktɔp$_{a}$ *v adj* characterised by breaking. Nep. *cū̃ḍine.*

braphu$_{a}$ *n* centipede. Nep. *khajuro.*

brɛkcap$_{a}$, **brɛk-**$_{m}$ *v(t)* to sweep, brush. Nep. *baḍhārnu.*

brɛmci$_{am}$ *n* finger, toe. Nep. *aū̃lo.*

Briŋmu$_{a}$, **Briŋku**$_{m}$ *n* the Sunkosī river. Nep. *Sunkosī.*

brocap$_{a}$ *v(i)* A to be tasty. B to be agreeable, be beautiful. Nep. *mīṭho hunu, svādilo hunu, ramāilo hunu, rāmro hunu.*

broto$_{m}$, **brottɔp**$_{a}$ *v adj* A tasty. B agreeable, beautiful. Nep. *mīṭho, svādilo, ramāilo, rāmro.*

-bu$^{1}_{am}$ *suffix* contemporaneous time suffix, used in combination with the locative marker *-lu*$_{am}$ ~ *-l*$_{am}$ in present gerunds. LIT 1 4 *-bu* in 1 *mällī diṅbul* 'when I went around looking here and there' / 4 *mwarduṅbul* 'when I emerged'. Nep. *kher.*

bu-$^{2}_{a}$ *bound morph* time. See *hus.*

bubjɛŋmo$_{a}$ *adj* white. Nep. *seto, śvet, dūdh ādiko raṅ.*

bubu$_{a}$ *n* white. Nep. *seto, śvet, dūdh ādiko raṅ.* See *bupcip.*

bubuyaya$_{a}$ *n* very white, pure white. Nep. *ekdamai seto.*

buḍa$_{a}$ [<Nep. *būḍhā.* Masculine form] I *n* old man, elder, husband. II *adj* old, aged.

buḍi$_{a}$ [<Nep. *būḍhī.* Feminine form] I *n* old woman, elder, wife. II *adj* old, aged.

buḍi-bɔmti$_{m}$ [<Nep. *būḍhī* 'old' + Jero *bɔmti* 'thumb, big toe'] *n cmp* thumb, big toe.

buḍi-brɛmci$_{a}$ [<Nep. *būḍhī* 'old' + Jero *brɛmci* 'finger'] *n cmp* thumb, big toe.

buḍim$_{m}$, **buḍum**$_{a}$ *n* monkey, especially the white langur, a big monkey with a long tail. Nep. *bā̃dar, vānar, kapi.* See *buḍum.*

buḍi-mauli$_{a}$ [<Nep. *būḍhī* 'old' + *māvalī* 'belonging to the mother's family'; term of reference] *n cmp* maternal uncle-in-law. See *hupu.*

buḍum$_{a}$ see *buḍim.*

buisi$_{am}$ *n* raw cotton, cotton plant, cotton wool. Nep. *kapās.*

bukcap$_{a}$, **bukcam**$_{m}$ *v(i)* A to get up, stand up, arise, wake up, awake. B to be standing, be erect, be upright, stand. Nep. *uṭhnu, biũjhnu, ũbho lāgnu, khaḍā hunu, ubhinu.*

bupcip$_{a}$ *adj* white. Nep. *seto, śvet, dūdh ādiko raṅ.*

burcap$_{a}$ *v(i)* A to shout, rebuke, swear. B to swear, abuse. Nep. *karāunu, hapkāunu, gālī garnu.*

— bh —

bhʌnda$_{am}$ [<Nep. *bhandā*] *postp* than.

bhʌne$_{a}$ [<Nep. *bhane*] *part* A if (conditional). B as for.

bhʌtkʌi$_{am}$ [<Nep. *bhatkāi*] *n* destruction, obliteration. **bhʌtkʌi pacap**$_{a}$, **bhʌtkʌi pacam**$_{m}$ *vt-2a* to destroy, obliterate, demolish, break down, tear down. Nep. *bhatkāunu.*

bhā̃ḍo$_{am}$ [<Nep. *bhā̃ḍo*] *n* pot.

bhai$_{a}$ [<Nep. *bhāi*] *n* younger brother.

bhale$_{am}$ [[<Nep. *bhāle*] *n* rooster, cock. **bhale=ŋ**$_{a}$ *genitive* that of the cock.

Bharʌt$_{a}$ [<Nep. *Bhārat*] *n* India. Cf. *India*$_{a}$.
Bhau-Cacu$_{a}$ *n* the name of a particular Jero clan.
bhitra$_{am}$ [<Nep. *bhitra*] *adv* inside, e.g. *kul bhitra* 'inside the house'.
bhitta$_{am}$ [<Nep. *bhittā*] *n* inner wall.
bhorla$_{am}$ [<Nep. *bhorla*] *n* the tree *Bauhinia vahilii*. **bhorla=ŋ kokolo**$_{m}$ *n* the nut-like kernel of the tree *Bauhinia vahilii*, which is contained in a sheath-shaped shell.
bhũḍi$_{a}$ [<Nep. *bhũḍī*] *n* belly. See *mɔl*.
bhuĩ$_{am}$ [<Nep. *bhuĩ*] *n* ground, earth, floor. See *kaksi*.
bhus$_{m}$ [<Nep. *bhūs*] *n* husk, chaff.
bhusna$_{a}$ [$^{?}$<Nep. *bhusunu* 'a particular kind of very small black fly'] *n* mosquito.
bhut$_{a}$ [<Nep. *bhūt*] *n* ghost, evil spirit, devil. See *mʌsan*, *sama*.
bhutla$_{a}$ [<Nep. *bhutlo*] *n* feather (small). See *masrɛmpu*.
bhyaguta$_{am}$ [<Nep. *bhyāguto*] *n* frog. See *paha*.

— c —

cʌkku$_{a}$ [<Nep. *cakku*] *n* penknife.
cʌlʌi$_{m}$ [<Nep. *calāi*] *n* movement. LIT 3 *calai*. **cʌlʌi pacam**$_{m}$ *vt-2a* to cause to move, move. LIT 3 *calaidumcā* 'to move (vi)'. Nep. *calāunu*.
cʌrʌi$_{am}$ [<Nep. *carāi*] *n* grazing. **cʌrʌi lacap**$_{a}$, **cʌrʌi lacam**$_{m}$ *vi-1a-i* to graze. Nep. *carnu*.
-ca$_{am}$ *suffix* marker of the verbal adjective of purpose. LIT 1 2 4 *-cā* in 1 *pācām* 'to do' / 2 *lvācām* 'to go' / 4 *blecām* 'to be alive'; 6 *cā-* in *āphāccāl* 'while not being able'.
Cabʌhil$_{a}$ [<Nep. *Cābahil*] *n* the name of a *ṭol* 'division' of Kathmandu.
cacu$_{am}$ *n* grandson. Nep. *nāti*.
cacume$_{m}$, **cacuŋma**$_{a}$ *n* granddaughter. Nep. *nātinī*.
cai$_{a}$ [<Nep. *cāhĩ*] *part* contrastive topic marker, which is used to individualise or single out the entity or event referred to by the modified constituent from several other possibilities.
caksi$_{a}$ *n* beer made from *carji* 'finger millet, *Eleusine coracana*'. Nep. *jirmā*.
calcap$_{a}$, **calcam**$_{m}$ *v(t)* to plait, twist, make a rope, roll up (e.g. a cigarette). Nep. *bāṭnu*, *ḍorī banāunu*.

camda$_{a}$, **cam**$_{a}$, **camdo**$_{m}$ *n* game. LIT 2 3 *cāmdo* in 2 *cāmdopāimyai* 'he played'; 7 *cāmdo*. Nep. *khel*. **camda pacap**$_{a}$, **cam pacap**$_{a}$, **camdo pacam**$_{m}$ *vt-2a* to play a game. LIT 3 *cāmdo pācām*. Nep. *khelnu*.

capcam$_{m}$ *vt(-2c)* <capt- (~ *cam-)> A can, be able. B [in Mohanṭāre] auxiliary of capacity, used with an infinitive. LIT 2 *cāpt-* in *cāptīm* 'he could [do it]'. Nep. *saknu*. See *phaccap*.

car$_{am}$ [<Nep. *cār*] *num* four.

carji$_{am}$ *n* finger millet, *Eleusine coracana*, also identified as *Paspalum scrobiculatum* (Shrestha 1979). Nep. *kodo, kuanna*.

caːcap$_{a}$, **caː-**$_{m}$ *vm-1a* <caː-> to ascend, go up. LSN II *ca-ś-*. LIT 3 *cā-cām*. Nep. *uklanu*. See *hedicap*.

cɛccap$^{1}_{a}$ *v(t)* to hang, hang up, suspend. Nep. *jhunḍyāunu*. See *jhunḍʌi*.

cɛccap$^{2}_{a}$ *v(t)* to burn something. Nep. *ḍaḍāunu*.

cɛkcap$^{1}_{a}$, **cɛkcam**$_{m}$ *v(t)* to break, fracture. Nep. *bhā̃cnu*.

cɛkcam$^{2}_{m}$, **cikcam**$_{a}$ *v(t)* to find out, get knowledge, become aware of, have knowledge. LSN I *čiʔ-*. Nep. *thāhā pāunu*.

cɛ̃kmu$_{a}$, **cɛũmu**$_{a}$, **cɛʔmu**$_{m}$ *n* chick. Nep. *kukhurāko bacco, callo*.

cɛm$_{am}$ *n* call, summon. Nep. *bolāhaṭ*. **cɛm paccap**$_{a}$, **cɛm paccam**$_{m}$ *vt-2d* to call somebody. Nep. *bolāunu*.

cɛũmu$_{a}$, **cɛʔmu**$_{m}$ see *cɛ̃kmu*.

-ce$_{am}$ *suffix* marker of the general active verbal adjective. LIT 4 5 *-ce* in 4 *rānce* 'good' / 5 *pitigvākce* 'the one coming suddenly'.

cei-$_{m}$ *v(m)* to learn, study. Nep. *siknu*. See *sikʌi*.

cel$_{m}$ *n* request, question, interrogation. Nep. *praśna*. **cel pacam**$_{m}$ *vt-2a* to ask, inquire, make a request. Nep. *sodhnu*. See *tublo*.

cepʌi$_{a}$ [<Nep. *cepāi*] *n* pressure, depression. **cepʌi pacap**$_{a}$ [<Nep. *cepnu*] *vt-2a* to press, squeeze, depress.

-ci$^{1}_{am}$ *suffix* dual simplex agreement morpheme.

-ci$^{2}_{m}$ *suffix* second and third person dual imperative agreement morpheme.

ciccap$_{a}$ *v(t)* to tear, tear apart, rend, lacerate, rip (e.g. clothes). Nep. *cyātnu, cirnu, chednu*.

cicila$_{a}$ *n* grain, seed. Nep. *dānā*. See *biu, cinci*.

cicimo$_{m}$, **cicum**$_{m}$ *n* mouse. Nep. *mūso*. See *musa*.

cicir$_{a}$ *quant* a little, few, some. Nep. *ali ali, alikati, alikatā*.

cicum$_{m}$ see *cicimo*.

cij$_{m}$ [<Nep. *cīj*] *n* thing, object.

cikcam$_{a}$ see *cɛkcam*^{2}.

cikmu$_{m}$, **cipmu**$_{a}$ *n* bird. LSN I *čikŋu*; II *ciʔmu*; III *ciʔmu*.

cimmaŋ$_{m}$ *quant* a little, few, some. Nep. *ali, alikati, thorai.*

cimtɛp$_{a}$ I *adj* small, little, inferior. II *quant* a little, few, some. LSN II *cimṭɛp*; III *cimtep*. Nep. *sāno, ali, alikati, thorai.* See *yɔkko.*

cinci$_{am}$ *n* seed, grain. Nep. *dānā*. See *biu, cicila.*

cini$_{am}$ [<Nep. *cinī*] *n* sugar.

cipmu$_{a}$ see *cikmu.*

cirʌi$_{m}$ [<Nep. *cirāi*] *n* cut, incision. **cirʌi pacam**$_{m}$ *vt-2a* to split, rip up, cut, lacerate. Nep. *cirnu.*

cisʌi$_{a}$ [<Nep. *cisyāi*] *n* cold. **cisʌi pacap**$_{a}$ *vt-2a* to cool. Nep. *cisyāunu.*

ciso$_{a}$ [<Nep. *ciso*] *adj* wet, cold.

ciṭhi$_{m}$ [<Nep. *ciṭhī*] *n* letter (correspondence).

ciya$_{m}$ [<Nep. *ciyā*] *n* tea.

cɔk- *v* to carve (wood). Nep. *kāṭh khopera vā kũdera kunai vastu banāunu.*

cɔpcap$_{a}$, **cɔpcam**$_{m}$ *v(t)* to put down, place, keep. LIT 7 *cvāp-* in *cvāpsāku* 'having put down'. Nep. *rākhnu.*

cor$_{a}$ [<Nep. *cor*] *n* thief. **cor pottɔp**$_{a}$ [<Nep. *cor* 'thief' + Jero *pottɔp* 'characterised by doing'] *n* thief. See *khus.*

cor-brɛmci$_{am}$ [<Nep. *cor* 'thief' + Jero *brɛmci* 'finger'] *n cmp* index finger. Nep. *cor-aũlo.*

coṭi$_{m}$ [<Nep. *coṭi*] *n* time, turn.

-cu$^{1}_{am}$ *suffix* person marker.

-cu$^{2}_{am}$ see *-cuwa.*

-cu$^{3}_{am}$ *suffix* marker of the particular active verbal adjective. Possibly historically related to *-cu*^{1}.

-cu$^{4}_{am}$ *suffix* marker which creates comparative demonstrative pronouns from absolute forms, e.g. *nɔicu*$_{m}$ 'that which is relatively further away than *nɔi*$_{am}$, viz. another thing that is relatively far away and at the same elevation as the point of reference'. Possibly historically related to *-cu*^{1}.

culo$_{a}$ [<Nep. *culho*] *n* fireplace (for cooking). LIT 7 *culā.*

culle$_{a}$, **cutle**$_{m}$ *n* stinging nettle. Nep. *sisnu.*

cumcap$_{a}$, **cumcam**$_{m}$ *v(t)* to catch, hold, capture, seize by embracing, pounce upon. LSN I *cumʔ*; II *cuŋ-, cum-*; III *um-s-*. Nep. *samātnu, pakranu.*

cumma$_{a}$ [<Nep. *cummā*] *n* kiss. See *cuʔ.*

cup$_{a}$ [<Nep. *cup*] *adj* silent, quiet. **cup pacap**$_{a}$ *vt-2a* to be silent, be quiet.

cuppa$_{am}$ *n* piglet. Nep. *sũgurko bacco.*

curcap$_{a}$, **curcam**$_{m}$ *v(t)* A to press (sugar cane or oil). B to twist, wring, distort. Nep. *ukhu vā tel pelnu, baṭārnu.*

cutle$_{m}$ see *culle.*

-cuwa$_{a}$, **-cu**$_{am}$ *suffix* first person dual exclusive agent and subject simplex agreement morpheme.

cuʔ$_{m}$ *n* kiss. Nep. *cummā.* **cuʔ pacam**$_{m}$ *vt-2a* to kiss. Nep. *cummā khānu.* See *cumma.*

cyapu$_{a}$ [<Nep. *cyāpu*] *n* the lower jaw.

— **ch** —

chʌ$_{a}$ [<Nep. *cha*] *num* six.

chala$_{m}$ [<Nep. *chālā*] *n* skin (of a human being).

chamʌi$_{am}$ [<Nep. *chāmāi*] *n* touch, feeling, groping. **chamʌi pacap**$_{a}$, **chamʌi pacam**$_{m}$ *vt-2a* to touch, feel, grope. Nep. *chāmnu.*

chana$_{a}$ [<Nep. *chānu*] *n* roof, thatch.

chati$_{a}$ [<Nep. *chātī*] *n* chest, breast.

chekʌi$_{a}$ [<Nep. *chekāī*] *n* obstruction, hinder. **chekʌi pacap**$_{a}$ *vt-2a* to obstruct, hinder. Nep. *cheknu.*

cheparo$_{a}$ [<Nep. *cheparo*] *n* lizard.

cheu$_{am}$ [<Nep. *cheu*] I *n* side, edge, end. II *postp* next to, near, e.g. *kul cheu=na* 'next to the house'.

chopʌi$_{a}$ [<Nep. *chopāi*] *n* cover, shelter. **chopʌi lacap**$_{a}$ *vi-1a-i* to be covered, be hidden. Nep. *chopinu.* **chopʌi pacap**$_{a}$ *vt-2a* to cover, hide. Nep. *chopnu.*

— **d** —

Dʌlse$_{m}$ [<Nep. *Dalse*] *n* Dalse, the name of a Jero village.

Dʌŋkhʌmcu$_{a}$ [?= *Dɔŋkhɔmcu*] *n* the name of a Jero clan.

dʌro$_{a}$ [<Nep. *daro*] *adj* firm, fast, stable, sure.

dʌs$_{m}$ [<Nep. *das*] *num* ten.

da$_{a}$, **ɖa**$_{m}$ [<Nep. *ta*] *part* theme marker, which provides a background or point of departure for the following piece of information. LIT 1 *dā.*

daccam$_{m}$ *v(t)* place, set up, appoint. Nep. *thāpnu.*

daine$_a$ [<Nep. *dāhine*] *adv* right (as opposed to left). See *debre*.
daju$_a$ [<Nep. *dāju*] *n* elder brother.
daju-bhai$_a$ [<Nep. *dāju* 'elder brother' + *bhāi* 'younger brother'] *n cmp* brothers.
dak$_a$ see *daku*.
dakcap$_a$, **dakcam**$_m$ *vt-2e* <dakt- ~ da:-> A to like, be fond of, love, prefer. B [in Mohanṭāre] the auxiliary 'to like', used with an infinitive. Nep. *man parnu, hr̥dayale svīkār garnu*. **daksi ra:cap**$_a$ *vm-1a* to be pleased.
daku$_a$, **dak**$_a$, **dakhu**$_m$ *n* A memory, remembrance. B notice. LIT 1 *ḍākhu*, 4 *kākdākhu*. Nep. *samjhanā, smaraṇ*.
dal$_a$ [<Nep. *dāl*] *n* lentils.
dalaciŋma$_m$ *n* firefly, lightening bug. Nep. *jūnkīrī*. See *dalcip*.
dalcap$_a$, **dalcam**$_m$ *v(t)* to drive out, chase away, pursue. Nep. *dhapāunu, khednu, lakheṭnu*.
dalcip$_a$ *n* firefly, lightening bug. Nep. *jūnkīrī*. See *dalaciŋma*.
damcap$_a$ I *v(t)* to lose. II *v(m)* to be or get lost. Nep. *harāunu, harāinu*.
daŋma$_a$ *adj* self, by oneself, of one's own accord.
dari$_a$ [<Nep. *dāhrī*] *n* beard.
da:-$_a$ vi-1b <da:-> the auxiliary 'to like', used with an infinitive. Nep. *man parnu*.
dɛcap$_a$ *vt-1* <dɛ-> to dig, tear up soil with an implement, e.g. *uŋ dɛuma* 'I dig'. Nep. *khannu*. See *kɔkcap*.
dɛl$_{am}$ *n* village. LSN I *dæ̀l*; II *dɛl*; III *d̪ɛl*. LIT 1 4 *dyāl*; 7 *ḍyāl* in *ḍyālnase* 'exactly in the village'. Nep. *gāũ*. See *gaũ*.
dɛre$_a$ *n* afternoon, period from 12.00 till 18.00 hours. Nep. *diũso*.
debre$_a$ *adv* left (as opposed to right). See *daine*.
deuta$_a$ [<Nep. *deutā*] *n* god, divinity.
-di-$_a$, **-du-**$_a$ *bound morph* go (and come back). LIT 4 *-du-* in *mwarduṅbul* 'when I emerged'. See *dicap*.
dicap$_a$, **dicam**$_m$ *vi-1a-i* <di-> to go (and come back), do a job that involves a going, go working. LIT 1 *di-* in *māllī diṅbul* 'when I went around looking here and there'. Nep. *jānu, jāne kām garnu, kāmko lāgi jānu*. See *-di-*.
didi$_a$ [<Nep. *didī*] *n* elder sister.
didi-bʌini$_a$ [<Nep. *didī* 'elder sister' + *bahinī* 'younger sister'] *n cmp* sisters.
dikkur$_m$ *n* severe storm. Nep. *ā̃dhībeharī*. **dikkur pacam**$_m$ *vt-2a* to storm severely.

dimcap$_{a}$ *v(t)* to tread, trample, take support on one's feet. Nep. *kulcanu.*

din$_{am}$ [<Nep. *din*] *n* day.

dɔkcap$_{a}$, **dɔkcam**$_{m}$ *vt(-2e)* <(*dɔkt- ~) do-> to be sufficient, be enough. Nep. *kunai vastu paripūrṇa pugnu.*

dɔkcam$_{m}$ *v(i)* to fall, fall down (through the air), fall by sprinkling, drop off, descend, come or go down. Nep. *khasnu, jharnu.* See *docam.*

dɔmcap$_{m}$ *v(m)* to be tasted. Nep. *cākhinu.*

-dɔŋo$_{a}$, **-dɔŋ**$_{am}$ *suffix* marker of the conditional gerund, which is used as the main verb of a subordinate conditional clause, expressing supposition or implicit condition. See *bhʌne.*

dɔt$_{a}$ *n* thing, matter; used with *hai*$_{am}$ 'what' and *munu*$_{am}$ 'who' to form more polite or formal interrogative pronouns.

dɔyo$_{m}$, **do**$_{a}$ *n* allotment, distribution. LIT 6 *ḍoyā.* Nep. *bā̃ḍāi.* **dɔyo pacam**$_{m}$ *vt-2a* to distribute something. Nep. *bā̃ḍnu.* **do paccap**$_{a}$ *vt-2d* to distribute something to someone. Nep. *bā̃ḍi dinu.*

docap$_{a}$ *vi-1b* <do-> to fall, fall down (through the air), fall by sprinkling, drop off, descend, come or go down, e.g. *uŋ doŋma* 'I fell'. Nep. *khasnu, jharnu.* See *dɔkcam.*

-du-$_{a}$ see *-di-*$_{a}$.

dubɔlki$_{a}$ *n* a big earthenware vessel which is used to store alcoholic drinks. Nep. *māṭoko ṭhūlo ghaĩṭo.* See *li:phu.*

dudh$_{am}$ [<Nep. *dūdh*] *n* milk. **dudh teicam**$_{a}$ *v* to suckle, make someone drink milk.

Dudhkosi$_{a}$ [<Nep. *Dūdhkosī*] *n* the Dūdhkosī river. See *Glɔku.*

dui$_{am}$ [<Nep. *duī*] *num* two.

dukcam$_{m}$ *v(t)* to shake, move, agitate, wave. Nep. *hallāunu.* See *hʌlʌi.*

dukhʌ$_{a}$ [<Nep. *duḥkha*] *n* pain, grief. LIT 5 *duḥkha.*

dulo$_{a}$ [<Nep. *dulo*] *n* hole, open hole. See *dhɔŋga.*

dumcap$_{a}$, **dumcam**$_{m}$ *vi-1c* <dum-> to be, become. LIT 4 5 *dum-* in *dumme* 'it became', 2 *ḍum-* in *ḍumsī* 'become'; 7 *du-* in *duṅmā* 'I will become'. Nep. *hunu, bhainu, hoinu.*

dumsi$_{m}$ [<Nep. *dumsī*] *n* porcupine.

— dh —

dhʌnu$_a$ [<Nep. *dhanu*] *n* bamboo bow (for shooting arrows), with a bent handle. See *gurtha*.
dhago$_{am}$ [<Nep. *dhāgo*] *n* thread.
dhami$_a$ [<Nep. *dhāmī*] *n* wizard, sorcerer.
dherʌi$_m$ [<Nep. *dherai*] I *quant emph* very many, very much. II *intens emph* very, too.
dhɔndro$_m$, **dhɔndhro**$_a$ [<Nep. *dhotro*] *n* hole in which animals live. **dhɔŋga**$_m$ *n* hole, open hole. Nep. *pvāl, dulo*. See *dulo*.
dhursiŋ$_m$ *n* a kind of bush, *Colebrookia oppositifolia* (Shrestha 1979). Nep. *dhusre*.

— ɖ —

ɖa$_m$ see *da*.
ɖãɖa$_a$ [<Nep. *ḍā̃ḍā*] *n* hill, ridge.
ɖeri$_m$, **ɖori**$_a$ [<Nep. *ḍori*] *n* rope. **ɖori calcap**$_a$ *v* to make a rope. Nep. *ḍorī banāunu*.
ɖubʌi$_a$ [<Nep. *ḍubāi*] *n* act of sinking. **ɖubʌi lacap**$_a$ *vi-1a-i* to sink, drown, be submerged. Nep. *ḍubnu*. See *hamcam*.
ɖuɖuna$_a$ *n* shin. Nep. *pā̃sulo*. See *kɔŋko*.
ɖulʌi$_{am}$ [<Nep. *ḍulāi*] *n* walk. **ɖulʌi pacap**$_a$, **ɖulʌi pacam**$_m$ *vt-2a* to take for a walk. Nep. *ḍulāunu*.
ɖuŋga$_a$ [<Nep. *ḍuṅgā*] *n* small boat.

— ɖh —

ɖhiki$_a$ [<Nep. *ḍhikī*] *n* saw-shaped rice thresher.
ɖhilo$_{am}$ [<Nep. *ḍhīlo*] *n* delay, slackness.
ɖhoka$_{am}$ [<Nep. *ḍhokā*] *n* door.
ɖhukur$_m$ [<Nep. *ḍhukur*] *n* a species of turtledove, smaller than a pigeon.

— ε —

εs$_{a}$ [<Nep. *yas*] *dem pron* this. **εs pala**$_{a}$ *adv* this time.
εti$_{a}$ [<Nep. *yati*] *quant* so much, this much. **εti bεla**$_{a}$ *adv* this (much) time, now.

— e —

ebo$_{m}$ *v adj* new. Nep. *nayā̃*. See *nεntha*.

— g —

gʌira$_{m}$ [<Nep. *gahirā*] I *n* deep place, valley, abyss. II *adj* deep, profound.
gʌrib$_{am}$ [<Nep. *garib*] *adj* poor. LIT 5 *garib* in *garibṅāṅ* 'of poverty'. **gʌrib dumcap**$_{a}$, **gʌrib dumcam**$_{m}$ *vi-1c* to be in poverty. Nep. *garib hunu*.
gʌrjʌi$_{a}$ [<Nep. *garjāi*] *n* thunder, lightning. **gʌrjʌi lacap**$_{a}$ *vi-1a-i* to thunder. Nep. *garjanu*. See *gurum*.
Gʌurathoke$_{a}$ [?<Nep. *Gaurā* 'a name of the goddess Pārvatī' + *ṭhoke* 'pertaining to a blow'] *n* the name of a particular Jero clan.
gacap$_{a}$, **ga-**$_{m}$ *vi-1a-ii* <ga-> to come up. LIT 4 *ga-* in *gamuncvam* '(having) come'. Nep. *talabāṭa māthi āunu*.
gagmu$_{m}$, **gaːgab**$_{a}$ *n* crow. Nep. *kāg*. See *kag*.
gagri$_{a}$ [<Nep. *gāgrī*] *n* a small or medium sized copper water jar.
gai$_{am}$ [<Nep. *gāī*] *n* cow.
gajʌr$_{a}$ [<Nep. *gājar*] *n* carrot.
gala$_{a}$ [<Nep. *gālā*] *n* cheek. See *mambu*.
ganʌ$_{a}$ [<Nep. *gānu*] *n* anything knotty or swollen.
gaŋayɔma$_{m}$ *n* mosquito. Nep. *lāmkhuṭṭe*. See *bhusnap*.
garji$_{am}$ *n* rice plant, paddy, unhusked rice. LSN II *garolziŋ boṭ*; III *gardziŋ pɔrul*. Nep. *dhān*.
garji-seri$_{m}$ *n cmp* husked and polished rice. Nep. *cāmal*.
garo$_{a}$ [<Nep. *gāro*] *n* wall (of a building).
gattu$_{a}$, **gatthu**$_{m}$ *adv* up, upwards, above. Nep. *ũbho*, *māthitira*, *māstira*.
gā̃ṭho$_{a}$ *n* knot.

gaũ$_{a}$ *n* village. See *dɛl.*

gaːgab$_{a}$ see *gagmu.*

gɛpsu$_{m}$ *n* the barking deer *Muntiacus muntjak.* Nep. *mr̥ga, hariṇ.* See *mirgʌ.*

gɛtis$_{a}$ *n* pellet-bow. Nep. *gulelī.*

gerʌi$_{am}$ [<Nep. *gerāi*] *n* surrounding. **gerʌi pacap**$_{a}$, **gerʌi pacam**$_{m}$ *vt-2a* to surround. Nep. *gernu.*

gicap$_{a}$, **gicam**$_{m}$ *v(t)* to pick, pick up (from the ground). Nep. *ṭipnu, bhuĩbāṭa kehī ṭipnu.*

giddhʌ$_{a}$ [<Nep. *giddha*] *n* vulture.

gidi$_{a}$ [<Nep. *gidi*] *n* brain.

glecap$_{a}$, **glecam**$_{m}$ *vi-1b* <gle-> A to lie down, go to sleep, fall asleep. B to couch, rest, repose. LSN I *glom-s-, gloŋ-, gl*^{w}*am-*; II *glɛ-s*; III *glom-.* Nep. *sutnu, nidāunu, leṭnu.*

Glɔku$_{m}$ *n* the Dūdhkosī river. Nep. *Dūdhkosī.* See *Dudhkosi.*

gɔkcap$_{a}$, **gɔkcam**$_{m}$ *vt-2e* <gɔkt- ~ go-> A to give, endow. B to let. C auxiliary which is used with a connective gerund in periphrastic constructions that stress that the action is performed on behalf of someone or something else. D auxiliary which is used with an infinitive in permissive constructions, which express the giving of permission or consent to someone to do something, conveying the meaning 'to let somebody do something'. LSN I *g*^{w}*ɔ-n-*; II *g*^{w}*a-k-*; III *gok-.* LIT 5 *gvāk-* 'the one giving' in *pitigvākce* 'the one coming suddenly'. Nep. *dinu, pradān garnu.*

gɔṭa$_{a}$, **gɔṭ**$_{a}$ [<Nep. *vaṭā*] *class* non-human classifier, literally 'piece, article'. See *jʌna.*

golo$_{a}$ [<Nep. *golo*] *adj* round.

goru$_{m}$ [<Nep. *goru*] *n* bullock, steer, ox. See *biya.*

gramji$_{a}$, **gramsu**$_{m}$ *n* hate, hatred. Nep. *ghin, ghr̥ṇā.* **gramji lucap**$_{a}$ *vi-1a-i* to feel hate. **gramsu pacam**$_{m}$ *vt-2a* to hate (somebody). Nep. *ghin garnu.*

gũḍ$_{a}$ [<Nep. *gũḍ*] *n* nest.

guleli$_{a}$ [<Nep. *gulelī*] *n* bow for shooting mud pellets.

gumsu$_{am}$ *n* tooth. LSN I *gumsø*; II *gumśu*; III *gumsʏ.* Nep. *dā̃t.*

gundri$_{am}$ [<Nep. *gundri*] *n* woven straw mat.

gupsu$_{am}$ *n* tiger, leopard, panther. LSN II *gupśu*; III *gupsu.* Nep. *bāgh.*

gupsu-humu$_{a}$ [Jero *gupsu* 'tiger' + *humu* 'grandmother'] *n cmp* great-grandmother, especially paternal. Nep. *hajūr bākā āmā.*

gupsu-hupu$_{am}$ [Jero *gupsu* 'tiger' + *hupu* 'grandfather'] *n cmp* great-grandfather, especially paternal. Nep. *barājyū.*

gupha$_{a}$ [<Nep. *guphā*] *n* cave.

gurtha$_{a}$ *n* bow (for shooting arrows) with a bent handle. Nep. *dhanu.* See *dhʌnu.*

gurum$_{a}$ *n* thunder, lightning. Nep. *garjan.* **gurum pacam**$_{a}$ *vt-2a* to thunder. Nep. *garjanu.* See *gʌrjʌi.*

gutulum$_{a}$ *n* tone ball used to grind spices with. Nep. *masalā pīdhne ḍhuṅgā.*

gwarji$_{am}$ *n* nail, claw, talon. LSN II *gordzi*; III g^{w}*ardžɩ.* Nep. *naṅ.*

gyaŋgu$_{a}$ *n* snail. Nep. *ciplekīro.*

— **gh** —

ghʌcca$_{m}$ [<Nep. *ghaccā*] *n* push, thrust. **ghʌcca gɔkcam**$_{m}$ *vt-2e* to push, push away, shove, press forward. Nep. *ghaceṭnu.* See *nɛp-cap.*

ghʌĩʈi$_{am}$ [<Nep. *ghaĩṭī*] *n* a kind of small jar.

ghʌlɛk$_{a}$ [<Nep. *ghalek*] *n* a cloth worn over the shoulder by women.

ghãs$_{a}$ [<Nep. *ghā̃s*] *n* grass. LIT 2 5 *ghā̃s.*

ghoɖa$_{am}$ [<Nep. *ghoḍā*] *n* horse.

ghopʈʌi$_{a}$ [<Nep. *ghopṭyāi*] *n* upset, turn over. **ghopʈʌi lacam**$_{a}$ *vi-1a-i* to upset, overthrow. Nep. *ghopṭyāinu.*

ghuccuk$_{a}$ [<Nep. *ghuccuk*] *n* the back of the neck.

ghumʌi$_{a}$ [<Nep. *ghumāi*] *n* winding, turn, revolution. **ghumʌi lacap**$_{a}$ *vi-1a-i* to wander, go about. Nep. *ghumnu.* **ghumʌi pacap**$_{a}$ *vt-2a* to turn around, revolve. Nep. *ghumāunu.*

— **h** —

hʌlʌi$_{am}$ [<Nep. *halāi*] *n* shake, move, shift. **hʌlʌi pacap**$_{a}$, **hʌlʌi pacam**$_{m}$ *vt-2a* to shake, move, shift. Nep. *hallāunu.* See *dukcam.*

hʌriyo$_{a}$ [<Nep. *hariyo*] *n & adj* green.

-ha$_{am}$ see *-ka.*

hãga$_{a}$, **haŋga**$_{m}$ [<Nep. *hā̃gā*] *n* branch (of a tree).

hai$_{am}$ *ind* what, something, what kind of. LSN I *hai̭*; III *hai̭.* LIT 2 *hāi*, 4 *hāī.* Nep. *ke, je.* **hai bɛl?**$_{a}$ *n* which time, when. Nep. *ke belā?.* **hai**

dɔt$_a$ *n* what kind of thing. LSN II *ha̯ido*. **hai pacap**$_a$, **hai pacam?**$_m$ *vt-2a* what should [one] do?. Nep. *ke garne?*

haiŋa$_m$, **haiŋaŋ**$_m$, **haiŋo**$_m$, **hayaŋ**$_m$, **hayɔŋ**$_m$ [Jero *hai* 'what'] *ind* why, for what reason. LSN I *ha̯iŋo*. Nep. *kina*. See *haŋ*.

ham phalʌi pacap$_a$ [<Nep. *hām phālnu*] *vt-2a* to jump down. See *phalʌi*.

hamcam$_m$, **hɔmcap**$_a$ *v(t)* A to sink. B to set (said of the moon or sun). Nep. *ḍubnu, astāunu*. See *ḍubʌi*.

haŋ$_a$ *ind* why, for what reason. LSN II *haŋ*; III *haŋ*. LIT 6 *hāṅ*. Nep. *kina*. See *haiŋa*, *hayaŋ*, *hayɔŋ*.

haŋ-bhʌne$_a$ [<Jero *haŋ* 'why' + Nep. *bhane*] *conj cmp* because; a calque of Nepali *kina bhane*.

haŋga$_m$ see *hãga*.

harʌi$_m$ [<Nep. *harāi*] *n* loss. **harʌi dumcam**$_m$ *vi-1c* to get lost. Nep. *harāinu*.

hãs$_a$ [<Nep. *hā̃s*, *hāṃs*] *n* duck.

hawa$_a$ [<Nep. *hāvā*] *n* air, wind.

hayaŋ$_m$, **hayɔŋ**$_m$ see *haiŋa*.

hɛccap$_a$ *v(t)* to bring down. Nep. *māthibāṭa tala lyāunu*.

hɛttu$_a$, **hɛtthu**$_m$ *adv* down, downwards, below, beneath. LIT 4 *hyaṭhṭhū*. Nep. *tala*, *ũdho*, *talatira*.

hecap^1$_a$, **he-**$_m$ *v(i)* to be left over (said of food). Nep. *ubranu*, *bā̃kī rahanu*. See *hettɔp*.

hecap^2$_a$ *v* to wear around one's neck. Nep. *kā̃dh lāunu*.

hedicap$_a$ *vi* <he-di- ~ he-du-> A to climb, mount. B to enter. LIT 4 *heḍicām*. Nep. *caḍhnu*, *pasnu*.

hepa$_{am}$, **hep**$_a$ *n* cooked grain, especially rice. LSN I *hɛpa*; II *hɛpɔ*; III *hepa*. Nep. *bhāt*. **hepa ticu**$_{am}$ *n pl* three or more varieties of cooked grain.

hettɔp$_a$ *v adj* characterised by being left over. See *hecap*^{1}.

hilmu$_a$ [term of address] *n* one's own child's mother-in-law. Nep. *samdhinī*.

hilo$_a$ [<Nep. *hilo*] *n* mud, slime.

hilpu$_a$ [term of address] *n* one's own child's father-in-law. Nep. *samdhī*. See *sʌmdhi*.

himal$_a$ [<Nep. *himāl*] *n* mountain, especially in the Himalayas.

himcap$_a$ *vm-1b* <him-> A to see oneself. B to be or get seen, be visible, appear. Nep. *dekhinu*. See *himtɔp*.

himpu$_a$ *n* a big earthenware vessel which is used to store alcoholic drinks. Nep. *māṭoko ṭhūlo ghaĩṭo*. See *li:phu*.

himtɔp$_a$ *v adj* visible. Nep. *dekhine*. See *himcap*.

hipcap$_a$, **hipcam**$_m$ *vt-2c* <hipt- ~ him-> to see. LSN II *hi-p-*. LIT 4 *hip-* in *āhipthu* 'in order to not see'. Nep. *dekhnu*.

hipcam$_m$ *vt-2c* <hipt- ~ him-> to obtain, get. LIT 4 *āhipthu* 'to not obtain, not get'. Nep. *pāunu*.

hipsu$_a$, **hispu**$_m$ *n* the tree *Bassia butyracea* (Turner 1931). Nep. *chiuri*.

hitto$_m$, **hiṭṭɔp**$_a$ v *adj* long. LSN I *hiṭṭo*; II *hitto*; III *hitto*, *hushitop*. See *hi:cap*.

hi:cap$_a$ *v(i)* to be long. Nep. *lāmo hunu*.

hɔl-$_m$ *v* to open. LSN III *hwal-*. Nep. *kholnu*, *khulnu*. See *kholʌi*.

hɔla$_m$ [<Nep. *holā*] *part* marker of probability. LIT 1 2 *hvālā*.

hɔmcap$_a$ see *hamcam*.

hɔpcap^1$_a$, **hɔpcam**$_m$ *v(t)* to winnow, to move around winnowing basket. Nep. *niphannu*.

hɔpcap^2$_a$ *v(t)* to toss, throw, cast, hit (a target with a stone), strike, give a blow to, shoot (e.g. a bullet, an arrow, etc.). Nep. *hānnu*.

ho$_a$ [<Nep. *ho* 'is'] *part* A marker which is used to indicate a specific fact or occurrence in present time. B yes, used to indicate assent, agreement or affirmation.

hocame$_a$, **ho-**$_m$ *vi-1b* <ho-> to burn (e.g. wood). Nep. *balnu*, *salkanu*, *dankanu*.

huccap$_a$, **hu[k]-**$_m$ *v(t)* to blow up, inflate, blow (a fire). Nep. *phuknu*.

hujɔktɔp$_a$ *ind v adj* how, what sort of. Nep. *kasto*.

hukɔl$_{am}$ *ind* how much, how many. LSN I *hukol*; II *huko*; III *hutrob*. LIT 4 5 *hukvāl*. Nep. *kati*, *jati*.

hum-$_m$ *v(t)* to boil in water (e.g. an egg or lentils), cook by boiling, boil. LSN III *hum-*. Nep. *usinnu*, *umālnu*.

humu$_{am}$ *n* grandmother, especially paternal. Nep. *hajurāmā*.

hundʌri$_a$ [<Nep. *huṇḍarī*] *n* storm. See *huri*.

hupmi$_m$, **hupni**$_a$ *n* pus. Nep. *pīp*.

hupu$_{am}$ *n* A grandfather, especially paternal. B [in Āmboṭe; term of address] uncle-in-law. Nep. *hajurbā*, *āmāko māmālāī sambodhan gardā prayog garine śabda*. See *buḍi-mauli*.

hur$_{am}$ *n* mouth, snout, muzzle. LSN I *hu:r*; II *hur*; III *ɦur*. Nep. *mukh*, *tutuno*.

huri$_a$ [<Nep. *hurī*] *n* storm. See *hundʌri*.

hus$_{am}$ *ind* how, in what manner. Nep. *kaso, jaso.* **hus bulu**$_{a}$, **hus bul**$_{a}$ *ind & conj* when, ever, then. Nep. *kahile, jahile.* **hus pasaku**$_{m}$ *ind v adv* how, in what manner. LSN II *huśpaśok*; III *huśpasa*. Nep. *kasarī, kaso garī.*

husɛl$_{m}$, **husulu**$_{a}$, **husul**$_{a}$ *ind* when, ever. LIT 1 2 5 *husyāl*. Nep. *kahile, jahile.* See *hus, hai.*

huːcap$_{a}$, **huː-**$_{m}$ *vi-1b* <huː-> A to shout, cry. B to bark. Nep. *karāunu, bhuknu, gālī garnu.*

hwarsi$_{a}$, **warsi**$_{m}$ *n* rain, shower. LSN I *warsi-*; II *hor-s-*, *warśi*. Nep. *jharī, vr̥ṣṭi, barsāt.* LIT 5 *vārsī.* **warsi yacam**$_{m}$ *vi-1a-ii* to rain, shower. Nep. *pānī parnu.*

— i —

-i$^{1}_{am}$, **-Ø**$_{am}$ *suffix* third person non-plural agent simplex agreement morpheme. LIT 2 4 *-i* in 2 *cāmdopāimyai* 'he played' / 4 *pāim* 'he did'.

-i$^{2}_{a}$ see *-ni*^{2}.

=i$^{3}_{am}$ see *=ya*^{1}.

-i$^{4}_{am}$ see *-ya*^{2}.

-i$^{5}_{am}$ see *-ya*^{3}.

ikkim$_{am}$ *poss* our^{pi}. Nep. *hāmro.*

Ilam$_{a}$ [<Nep. *Ilām*] *n* the name of a district in eastern Nepal.

-im$^{1}_{am}$ see *-mi*^{1}.

im$^{2}_{am}$ *poss* your^{s}. Nep. *tero, timro, tapāīko.*

in$_{am}$ see *inne.*

incim$_{am}$ *poss* A our^{di}. B your^{d}. Nep. *hāmro, hāmī duījanāko, timīharūko, timī duījanāko, tapāīharūko, tapāī duījanāko.*

India$_{a}$ [<Eng.] *n* India. Nep. *Bhārat.* Cf. *Bharʌt*$_{a}$.

indreni$_{a}$ [<Nep. *indrenī*] *n* rainbow.

inim$_{am}$ *poss* your^{p}. Nep. *timīharūko, tapāīharūko.*

inne$_{am}$, **in**$_{am}$ *pers* you. LSN I *innɛ*; II *innɛ*; III *inne*. LIT 6 *inne* in *innelāī* 'to you'. Nep. *tã, timī, tapāī.* **in nimpha**$_{am}$ *pers* you^{d}. **in nimpha=ŋ**$_{am}$ *genitive pers* your^{d}. See *incim.* **in ticu**$_{am}$ *pers* you^{p}.

-iŋ$^{1}_{m}$ *suffix* simplex agreement morpheme which marks a transitive relationship between a second person agent and a first person singular patient.

-iŋ$^{2}_{m}$ see *-ŋ*^{3}.

— j —

jʌlewa$_{a}$ [<Nep. *jalevā*] *n* a species of black river bird with a long neck.

jʌmma$_{a}$ [<Nep. *jammā*] *quant & intens* in all, in full.

jʌna$_{am}$, **jʌn**$_{m}$ [<Nep. *janā*] *class* human classifier, literally 'person'. See *gwaṭa*.

jʌnmʌi$_{am}$ [<Nep. *janmāi*] *n* birth. **jʌnmʌi pacap**$_{a}$, **jʌnmʌi pacam**$_{m}$ *vt-2a* to beget, give birth to. Nep. *janmāunu*.

jʌra$_{a}$ [<Nep. *jaro*] *n* root.

jʌro$_{a}$ [<Nep. *jaro*] *n* fever.

jʌu$_{am}$ [<Nep. *jau*] *n* barley.

jacap$_{a}$, **jacam**$_{m}$ *vt-2a* <ja- ~ jo-> to eat (e.g. egg, rice, maize, biscuit, etc.). LSN I *dza-*, *dzɔ*; II *dza*, *dzo*; III *dza*. LIT 3 *jācām*. Nep. *khānu*. **jacam thok**$_{m}$ *n* food, foodstuffs. Nep. *khāne kurā*. **jacap cis**$_{a}$ *n* food, foodstuffs. Nep. *khāne cīj*.

jajale$_{m}$ *n* the palm of the hand. Nep. *hatkelā*.

jal$_{a}$, **jalu**$_{m}$ [<Nep. *jāl*] *n* netting, web.

jala$_{a}$ [<Nep. *jālā*] *n* net, snare, trap.

jalu$_{m}$ see *jal*.

japcap$_{a}$, **japcam**$_{m}$ *vt-2c* <japt- ~ jam-> to buy. LSN I *dzap-*; II *dzap-*; III *dza-ʔ/(p)-s-*.

jat$_{a}$ [<Nep. *jāt*] *n* ethnic group.

jati$_{a}$ [<Nep. *jāti*] *adj* good, right, wholesome.

jɛccap$_{a}$ *v(t)* to draw, pull. Nep. *tānnu*. See *kiːt-*.

jɛkcam$_{m}$ *vt(-2e)* <jɛkt- (~ *je-)> A to begin, start. B ingressive auxiliary, used with an infinitive. Nep. *thālnu*. See *thalʌi*.

jɛnje$_{am}$ *n* buttocks, bottom. Nep. *cāk*, *nitamba*, *pīdh*.

Jero$_{am}$ *n & adj* Jero. Nep. *Jero*, *Jeruṅ*. **Jero=ŋ maːla**$_{a}$ *n* the language of the Jero. Nep. *Jeroko bhāṣā*. **Jero maːla**$_{m}$ *n* Jero language. Nep. *Jero bhāṣā*.

jeṭha$_{am}$ [<Nep. *jeṭhā*] *n* first-born male.

jeṭha-bhena$_{a}$ [<Nep. *jeṭhā* 'first-born male' + *bhenā* 'elder sister's husband] *n cmp* husband of one's eldest sister.

-ji$_{am}$ *suffix* marker of grain.

jiji$_{m}$ *nom* sweet, delicious. Nep. *guliyo*. **jiji lucam**$_{m}$ *vi* to be sweet. Nep. *guliyo hunu*. See *lucam*.

jilli$_{a}$, **jitli**$_{m}$ *n* the tree *Bauhinia variegata* (Turner 1931). Nep. *koirālo*.

-jimo$_{m}$ *bound morph* knowledge obtained through the senses.

jitli$_{m}$ *n* see *jilli.*

jiu$_{a}$ [<Nep. *jīu*] *n* body, physic.

jɔkcam$_{m}$ *vt(-2e)* <jɔkt- (*~ jo-)> A to know (by learning). B [in Mohanṭāre] the auxiliary 'to know', which is used with an infinitive. LSN II *dzok-*; III *dzok-*. Nep. *jānnu.*

jɔktɔp$_{a}$, **jɔkto**$_{m}$ *v adj* characterised by knowing. Nep. *jānne.*

jɔmbal$_{am}$ *n* banana, banana tree. Nep. *kerā.*

jɔmcu$_{am}$ *n* shaman, religious authority with healing and clairvoyant capacities. Nep. *dhāmī, jhā̃krī, bijuvā.*

jɔpre$_{m}$, **jɔpro**$_{a}$ *n* lungs. Nep. *phokso.* See *phɔkso.*

jɔʔmu$_{am}$ *n* fat, grease or meat of a living creature. LSN I *dzogmu*; III *dzɔʔmu.* Nep. *boso.*

jocam$_{m}$ *v(m)* to seem, look like, appear, be, be like. Nep. *dekhinu, hunu, jasto hunu.*

jocu$_{a}$ *v adj* eating. See *jacap.*

josu$_{a}$, **jos**$_{am}$ *n* swimming. Nep. *pauḍī.* **jos pacap**$_{a}$, **jos pacam**$_{m}$ *vt-2a* swim. Nep. *pauḍī khelnu.*

jottɔp$_{a}$ *v adj* characterised by eating. See *jacap.*

julɛmo$_{m}$ *n* butterfly. Nep. *putalī.*

juŋga$_{a}$ [<Nep. *jũgā*] *n* moustache.

jurcap$_{a}$, **jur-**$_{m}$ *v(i)* to be sour. Nep. *amilo hunu.*

jurtɔp$_{a}$, **jurto**$_{m}$ *v adj* sour. Nep. *amilo.*

jyambale$_{a}$ *n* needle. LSN II *dzyambɔli*; III *dzɛmbaʔɛ.* Nep. *siyo.* See *waccɛm.*

jyaŋli$_{a}$ [<Nep. *jyāṅlī*] *n* sow, adult female hog.

— jh —

jhola$_{am}$ [<Nep. *jhola*] *n* bag.

jhumka$_{m}$ *n* earring (?).

jhunḍʌi$_{m}$ [<Nep. *jhunḍāi*] *n* hanging, suspension. **jhunḍʌi pacam**$_{m}$ *vt-2a* to hang, hang up, suspend. Nep. *jhunḍyāunu.*

— k —

≡k$^{1}_{am}$ see ≡*ku*^{2}.

-k$^{2}_{am}$ see -*ku*^{3}.

kʌchuwa$_a$ [<Nep. *kachuvā*] *n* turtle, tortoise.

kʌlʌm$_a$ [<Nep. *kalam*] *n* pen. LIT 2 *kalam.*

kʌlejo$_a$ [<Nep. *kalejo*] *n* liver. See *ma*^{5}, *ni.*

kʌmti$_a$ [<Nep. *kamtī*] *intens* less, insufficient.

kʌrʌŋ$_a$ [<Nep. *karaṅ*] *n* rib.

kʌreso$_a$ [<Nep. *kareso*] *n* ground immediately round a house, dust-pit or rubbish-shoot behind a house.

kʌtha$_m$ [<Nep. *kathā*] *n* story, fable, myth. **kʌtha sɔcam**$_m$ *v* to tell a story. Nep. *kathā hālnu.*

kʌʈerʌ$_a$ [<Nep. *kaṭero*] *n* shed, stall.

-ka$_{am}$, **-kha**$_{am}$, **-ha**$_{am}$, **-a**$_{am}$, **-pha**$_{am}$, **-pa**$_m$ *suffix* imperative agreement morpheme.

kag$_a$ [<Nep. *kāg*] *n* crow. See *gagmu.*

kakhrɔm$_a$ *n* vessel, especially one made from a large dried gourd. Nep. *ciṇḍo.*

kaksi$_{am}$ *n* earth, soil, mud, clay, ground. Nep. *māṭo*, *maṭṭī*, *jamin.* See *bhuī.*

kakhi$_{am}$ [<Nep. *kākhī*] *n* armpit.

kam$_{am}$ [<Nep. *kām*] *n* work. LIT 5 *kām*; 7 *kām.* **kam pacam**$_m$ *vt-2a* to work, perform labour. Nep. *kām garnu.*

kanaguju$_a$ [<Nep. *kānegujī*] *n* earwax.

kancha$_m$ [<Nep. *kānchā*] *n & adj* youngest-born male.

kanchi$_{am}$ [<Nep. *kānchi*] *n & adj* youngest-born female.

kanchi-brɛmci$_{am}$ [Nep. *kānchi* 'youngest-born female' + Jero *brɛmci* 'finger'] *n cmp* little finger or toe.

kaŋgale$_m$, **kɔŋgale**$_a$ *n* marten. Nep. *malsā̃pro.*

kaŋgyu$_m$ [<Nep. *kā̃iyo*] *n* comb.

kaŋkaŋ$_m$, **kaŋkoʈ**$_a$ *n* locust, grasshopper. Nep. *phaṭyāṅgro.*

karjʌi$_a$ [<Nep. *kārya*] *n emph* deed, work, occupation.

kaʈh$_a$ [<Nep. *kāṭh* 'wood, timber'] *n* a bed made of wood.

Kaʈhmanɖu$_a$ [<Nep. *Kāṭhmāṇḍū*] *n* Kathmandu.

kaʔu$_{am}$ *n* friend. LSN I *kaʔu*; II *kaʔu*; III *kaʔu.* LIT 4 *kāu*; 7 *kāvā* in *kāvāticu* 'friends and the like'. Nep. *sāthī.* See *sathi.*

kaːku$_{am}$, **kaːk**$_{am}$ *n* water. LSN I *kaku*; II *kaku*; III *kaku.* LIT 1 4 *kāk*; 7 *kāku.* Nep. *pānī*, *nadī.* **kaːk-daku**$_a$, **kaːk-dakhu**$_m$ *n* thirst. LIT 1 *kākḍākhu*, 4 *kākdākhu*; 7 *kāku dākhu* in *kāku dākhuku* 'as a result of thirst'. **kaːk-daku sicap**$_a$, **kaːk-dakhu sicam**$_m$ *vi-1a-i* to feel thirsty. Nep. *tirkhā lāgnu.* **kaːk-daku pacap**$_a$ *vt-2a* to feel thirsty. Nep. *tirkhā lāgnu.*

kɛpcap$_{a}$, **kɛpcam**$_{m}$ *v(t)* to stick, attach, glue. Nep. *ṭā̃snu*. See *ṭāsʌi*.

ke$_{a}$ *part* marker which indicates that the action expressed by the verb is contrary to what is expected in a given situation. Nep. *po*.

keṭa [<Nep. *keṭā*] *n* boy.

keṭi [<Nep. *keṭī*] *n* girl.

-ki$^{1}_{am}$ *suffix* first person plural inclusive agent and subject simplex agreement morpheme.

ki$^{2}_{a}$ [<Nep. *ki*] *conj* or.

kicap$_{a}$, **kicam**$_{m}$ *vt-1* <ki-> to look at, watch, look after. LSN I *ki*^{h}-, *k̭i*; II *ki*, *key-*; III *k̭i-*. Nep. *hernu*, *ā̃kha lagāunu*, *hervicār garnu*.

kilkile$_{a}$ [<Nep. *kilkile*] *n* uvula.

kimsul$_{am}$ *n* door, gate, main entrance which gives way to the courtyard. Nep. *dahilo*, *dailo*, *mūlḍhokā*.

Kirā̃t$_{a}$ [<Nep. *Kirā̃t*] *n & adj* Kiranti.

kitap$_{a}$ [<Nep. *kitāb*, *kitāp*] *n* book. LIT 2 *kitāb*.

ki:t-$_{m}$ *v(t)* to pull, stretch. Nep. *tānnu*.

klecam$_{m}$ *v(t)* to spread out (e.g. a mat or a *gundri*). Nep. *ochyāunu*, *bichyāunu*.

kliccap$_{a}$, **kliccam**$_{m}$ *v(t)* to hide, conceal. Nep. *lukāunu*, *chipāunu*, *cheknu*.

kligji$_{a}$ *n* throat, neck. Nep. *ghā̃ṭī*.

klɔ[k]-$_{m}$ *v* to unfasten, untie, let loose, take off (shoes, clothing), undo, unknot, take out, take off, pull out, remove (tooth). Nep. *phukālnu*.

kɔkcap$^{1}_{a}$ *v(t)* to dig. Nep. *khannu*. See *dɛcap*.

kɔkcap$^{2}_{a}$ *v(t)* to bite (said of a snake), sting. Nep. *ḍasnu*.

kɔksɛl$_{a}$, **kuksɛl**$_{m}$ *n* cloud, mist (in sky), fog. Nep. *bādal*. See *badʌl*.

kɔkte$_{am}$ *n* bark. Nep. *bokra*. See *bɔkra*.

kɔmcap$_{a}$, **kɔmcam**$_{m}$ I *n* blanket. II *v(m)* to cover oneself (with a blanket), wrap around oneself. Nep. *oḍhāunu*, *oḍhnu*.

kɔŋgale$_{a}$ see *kaŋgale*.

kɔŋko$_{a}$ *n* shin, lower part of the leg. Nep. *pā̃sulo*, *khuṭṭāko chepārī*. See. *kɔŋku*.

kɔŋku$_{m}$ *n* shin, lower part of the leg. Nep. *pā̃sulo*, *khuṭṭāko chepārī*. See *kɔŋko*.

kɔro$_{a}$, **kɔr**$_{a}$ *n* maternal uncle. Nep. *māmā*.

kɔr-gupsu-humu$_{a}$ [Jero. *kɔr* 'maternal uncle' + *gupsu* 'tiger' + *humu* 'grandmother'] *n cmp* maternal great-grandmother, mother of maternal grandfather.

kɔr-gupsu-hupu$_{a}$ [Jero. *kɔr* ‘maternal uncle’ + *gupsu* ‘tiger’ + *hupu* ‘grandfather’] *n cmp* maternal great-grandfather, father of maternal grandfather.

kɔr-humu$_{a}$ [Jero. *kɔr* ‘maternal uncle’ + *humu* ‘grandmother’] *n cmp* maternal grandmother. Nep. *hajurāmā*.

kɔr-hupu$_{a}$ [Jero. *kɔr* ‘maternal uncle’ + *hupu* ‘grandfather’] *n cmp* maternal grandfather. Nep. *hajurbā*.

kɔʔlo$_{a}$, **kɔʔl**$_{a}$, **kwal**$_{m}$ *num* one. LSN I *k*^{w}*ɔʈlo*; II *kɔ*; III *kwal*. LIT 6 *kvāl*; 7 *kvālo* in *kvālose*. Nep. *ek*, *euṭā*, *ekvaṭā*. **kɔʔl sʌi**$_{a}$ *num* one hundred. Nep. *ek say*. **kwal coʈiku**$_{m}$ *adv* A one time. B suddenly.

kope$_{a}$ *n* owl. Nep. *lāṭokosero*.

koʈha$_{a}$ [<Nep. *koṭhā*] *n* room.

kraccap$_{a}$, **kra[k]-**$_{m}$ *vt-2d* <kratt- ~ kran-> A to bite with molars or snout. B pick (a bone), gnaw. LSN II *kra-k-*. Nep. *ṭoknu*, *dārnu*, *hā̃s-le jasto khānu*.

krampa$_{m}$, **krampu**$_{a}$ *n* the tree *Garuga pinnata* (Turner 1931). Nep. *dabdabe rūkh*.

krɛktum$_{m}$, **krɛktup**$_{a}$ *n* termite, white or brown ant-like insect. Nep. *dhamirā*.

krɛmku$_{a}$, **krɛmkhu**$_{m}$ *n* hunger. LIT 1 *kryāmkhu*. Nep. *bhok*. **krɛmkhu pacam**$_{m}$ *vt-2a* to feel or be hungry. Nep. *bhok lāgnu*.

krɔtni$_{m}$ *n* shame, reserve. Nep. *lāj*. See *laji*.

-ku$^{1}_{am}$ see *-kuwa*^{1}.

≡ku$^{2}_{a}$, **≡khu**$_{m}$, **≡k**$_{am}$ *suffix* A source marker. B also used as a lexical suffix in perfect gerunds, which locate the event expressed by the modified verb as relatively prior to some other event chosen as the point of reference. LIT 6 *-ku* in *nesāku* ‘having said’; 7 *-ku* in *jam-mailāsāku* ‘having come together’, 7 *-k* in *dumsāk* ‘having been’, 7 *=ku* in *māmāku* ‘by mother’; 1 *-khū* in *plyāsakhū* ‘having left’, 1 4 *=khu* in *bainikhu* ‘by the younger sister’ / *rogkhu* ‘as a result of the disease’, 2 *=khū* in *ʔlākhū* ‘with hands’, 2 4 5 *-k* in *kursāk* ‘having carried’ / 4 *plyāsāk* ‘having left’. Nep. *le*.

-ku$^{3}_{am}$, **-k**$_{am}$ *suffix* marker of water.

kuco$_{am}$ [<Nep. *kūco*] *n* brush, especially one made of a bundle of grass.

kudʌi$_{a}$, **kuɖʌi**$_{m}$ [<Nep. *kudāi*] *n* running, galloping. **kudʌi lacap**$_{a}$ *vi-la-i* to leap, spring, hop. **kudʌi pacap**$_{a}$, **kuɖʌi pacam**$_{m}$ *vt-2a* make run, keep on the go, make gallop. Nep. *kudāunu*.

kuhina$_{m}$, **kuina**$_{m}$ [<Nep. *kuhinu*] *n* elbow. See *nɛksi*.

kuksi$_{am}$ *n* the tree *Ficus cunia* (Panday 1982, Shrestha 1979). Nep. *khanāyo, khaniũ.*

kuksɛl$_{m}$ see *kɔksɛl.*

kul$_{am}$ see *kulu*$_{a}$.

kul-deuta$_{a}$ [<Jero *kul* 'house' + Nep. *deutā* 'god'] *n cmp* deity who resides indoors in a Jero household. There are as many indoor deities as there are ancestors of a particular household. The *kul-deuta* have to be fed cooked grain from one's own field up to six times per annum, in particular on the occasion of the Hindu festivals *daśaĩ, tihār, caite daśaĩ* and *sāune sagrā̃tī*, which are national happenings throughout the entire Kingdom of Nepal, and *nvāgī*, which is a religious duty in honour of the ancestors, deities and spirits, which is intended to give them a portion of the new harvest. Rām Kumār Rāī does not obey the spirits of his ancestors in his house in Kathmandu, since there are people of other castes living there.

kuli$_{m}$ *n* face. Nep. *mukh.*

kulu$_{a}$, **kul**$_{am}$ *n* house. LSN I *kul*; II *kul*; III *kul*. LIT 1 *kul*. Nep. *ghar, ā-vās.*

kuma=na=p rusu$_{a}$ see *kuŋma-rusu.*

kuna$_{a}$ [<Nep. *kunu*] *n* corner, angle.

kunci$_{a}$, **khumci**$_{a}$ *n* smoke, visible vapour given off by a burning substance. Nep. *dhūvā̃.*

kuŋma-rusu$_{m}$ *n* vertebral column. Nep. *merudaṇḍa.* See *rusu.* **kuma=na=p rusu**$_{a}$ *n* vertebral column.

kurcap$_{a}$, **kurcam**$_{m}$ *vt-2g* <kurt- ~ kur-> to carry. LIT 3 *kurcām*, 2 5 *kur-* in *kursāk* 'having carried'; 7 *kur-* in *kursāku* 'having carried'. Nep. *boknu.*

kurkure$_{a}$ [<Nep. *kurkure*] *adj* soft, especially pertaining to cartilage or gristle, i.e. the tough elastic tissue that is found in the nose, throat and ear and in other parts of the body.

kurkucca$_{a}$ [<Nep. *kurkucco*] *n* heel.

kurti$_{a}$ *n* ground immediately round a house, dust-pit or rubbish-shoot behind a house. Nep. *kareso, karẽso, karā̃so.*

kurtima$_{a}$ *n* puppy. Nep. *kukurko bacco.*

kuryam$_{a}$, **kuryaŋma**$_{a}$, **kuryaŋmo**$_{m}$ *n* hen, mother-hen, chicken which lays eggs. Nep. *kukhurāko pothī, māupothī.*

kuṭmiro$_{m}$ [<Nep. *kuṭimiro*] *n* the tree *Litsea polyantha.*

-kuwa$^{1}_{a}$, **-ku**$_{am}$ suffix first person plural exclusive agent and subject simplex agreement morpheme. LIT 7 *-ku* in *pokumā* 'we^{pe} will do'.
kuwa$^{2}_{m}$ [<Nep. *kuvā*] *n* well, water-hole.
kwa$_{a}$ *postp* in the company of. Nep. *sãga*. Possibly related to *kwaya*$_{a}$.
kwal$_{m}$ see *kɔʔlo*.
kwaya$_{a}$ *postp & adv* together, in company with others. LIT 5 *kvāyās*; 7 *kvāyase* (with the marker 'exactly'?). Nep. *sãgai*. Possibly related to *kwa*$_{a}$.

— kh —

khʌi$_{m}$ [<Nep. *khai*] *part* I don't know. LIT 1 *khai*.
khʌppʌr$_{a}$ [<Nep. *khappar*] *n* skull.
-kha$^{1}_{am}$ see *-ka*.
-kha-$^{2}_{m}$ *bound morph* come up. See *blaŋkha-*.
khaccap$_{a}$, **khaccam**$_{m}$ *v(t)* to bring up. Nep. *talabāṭa māthi lyāunu*.
khalṭa$_{m}$ [<Nep. *khālṭo*] *n* hollow, hole, pit, depression.
khamcap$_{a}$ *v(t)* to call, summon, send for someone. Nep. *bolāunu*, *ḍāknu*.
khamma$_{a}$, **khaːma**$_{m}$ *adj* alone, without anything or anyone else, only. Nep. *eklo*, *mātra*.
khamsi$_{am}$ *n* cooked liquid vegetable or meat dish. Nep. *tihun*.
kharcap$_{a}$, **kharcam**$_{m}$ *v(t)* to fry, pop, sear (e.g. meat). Nep. *bhuṭnu*, *arālnu*.
khasi$_{a}$ [*sɔmdu* speech] *n* work. Nep. *kām*.
khatto$_{m}$ *v adj* bitter. Nep. *tīto*.
khauma$_{a}$ *n* the name of a religious ceremony which is performed as a funeral ceremony after the death of a relative. See *nul*.
khaːci$_{am}$ *n* middle, centre. Nep. *bīc*, *mājh*, *madhya bhāg*.
khaːma$_{m}$ see *khamma*.
khɛlcap$_{a}$, **khɛlcam**$_{a}$ *vt-2h* <khɛlt- ~ khɛl-> to touch. LIT 4 *khyālt-* in *khyāltim* 'it touched him'. Nep. *chunu*.
khel$_{a}$ [<Nep. *khel*] *n* game. See *camda*, *camdo*.
khelʌi$_{a}$ [<Nep. *khelāi*] *n* playing. **khelʌi pacap**$_{a}$ *vt-2a* to play. Nep. *khelnu*. See *camda*.
khera$_{a}$ [<Nep. *kheri*] *n* time.
khet$_{m}$ [<Nep. *khet*] *n* irrigated field used to grow grain crops, farm. LIT 7 *khet* in *khetbārin(a)* 'in the garden fields'.

khicul$_{a}$ *n* cooked *carji*. Nep. *ḍhīḍo*.

khirki$_{a}$ *n* a field to grow vegetables. Nep. *tarkārī ropne ṭhāũ*.

khlɛkcap$_{a}$, **khlɛk-**$_{m}$ *v(t)* to paint, smear on, plaster (with mud and dung). Nep. *lipnu, lippot ganu, potarnu*. See *lipʌi*.

khlecap$_{a}$ *v(t)* to rub. Nep. *dalnu*.

khlɔmcap$_{a}$, **khlɔm-**$_{m}$ *v(t)* to put to sleep, put to bed. Nep. *sutāunu*.

khɔccap$_{a}$ *v(t)* to follow, go after, go later. Nep. *pachi lāgnu, pachāunu*.

khɔkcap$_{a}$, **khɔkcam**$_{m}$ *v(t)* to cook, boil (e.g. rice, lentils). LSN I *k^hokti-*, **k^hwaʔ-*. Nep. *(bhāt) pakāunu*.

khɔltɔp$_{a}$, **khɔlto**$_{m}$ *v adj* big, large, great. LSN II *k^holṱo*; III *k^hɔlṱop*. Nep. *ṭhūlo, viśāl, jeṭho, mahān, ucca*. **khɔltɔp mucu**$_{a}$ *n* boss, chief.

khɔlse$_{a}$ *quant* an amount of, used with the intensifier *asi*$_{am}$ 'few, scarce, less' and in the quantifying phrase *as khɔlse*$_{a}$ 'much, many'.

khɔpme$_{m}$ *n* sow, female pig. Nep. *pothī sũgur, sũgurnī*.

khɔrcap$_{a}$, **khɔr-**$_{m}$ *v(t)* to plough. Nep. *jotnu, halo calāunu*. See *wakcap*^{1}.

khɔsrʌi$_{a}$ [<Nep. *khosrāi*] *n* scratching. **khɔsrʌi pacap**$_{a}$ *vt-2a* to scratch up. Nep. *khosranu*.

khoku$_{a}$, **khokhu**$_{m}$ *n* cold (of temperature), coldness, chill. Nep. *jāḍo, cisoko anubhav*. **khokhu pacam**$_{m}$ *vt-2a* to be cold (of temperature). Nep. *jāḍo hunu*. **khokhu sicam**$_{m}$ *vi-1a-i* to feel cold. Nep. *jāḍo lāgnu*.

kholʌi$_{am}$ [<Nep. *kholāi*] *n* opening. **kholʌi pacap**$_{a}$, **kholʌi pacam**$_{m}$ *vt-2a* to do open, make open. Nep. *kholnu*.

khopʌi$_{a}$ [<Nep. *khopāi*] *n* hole. **khopʌi pacap**$_{a}$ *vt-2a* to make a hole in. Nep. *khopnu*.

kholma$_{a}$ [<Nep. *kholmo*] *n* granary (for storing maize).

khor$_{a}$ [<Nep. *khor*] *n* enclosure, fold.

khricap$_{a}$, **khricam**$_{m}$ *v(t)* to grind, screw up, jack up. Nep. *pīdhnu, pinnu, pisnu*.

khripcam$_{m}$ *v(t)* to count. Nep. *gannu*.

khrɔm$_{a}$ *v* weep, cry. Nep. *runu*. **khrɔm paccap**$_{a}$ *vt-2d* to make weep, cause to cry. Nep. *runa lagāunu*.

khrɔmcap$_{a}$, **khrɔmcam**$_{m}$ *vi-1c* <khrɔm-> to weep, cry. LIT 1 *khrvām-* in *khrvāmmeī* 'he cried', 3 *khrvāmcām*. Nep. *roinu*.

≡khu$^{1}_{m}$ see *≡ku*^{2}.

khu$^{2}_{am}$ *n* axe, hatchet. LIT 2 *khu* in *khukursāk* 'having carried an axe'. Nep. *bancāro*.

khucɛm$_{m}$, **khucɛŋmo**$_{a}$, **khucɛp**$_{a}$ *adj* black. Nep. *kālo*.

khudo$_{a}$, **khuḍo**$_{m}$ [<Nep. *khudo*] *n* syrup, sugar cane, honey.

khumci$_{a}$ see *kunci*$_{a}$.

khursani$_{am}$, **khursan**$_{a}$ [<Nep. *khursānī*] *n* pepper, chilli pepper.

khus$_{am}$ *n* theft. Nep. *corī garāi, corī*. **khus pacam**$_{m}$ *vt-2a* to steal, loot, plunder, rob. Nep. *cornu*. **khus pɔce mucu**$_{m}$ *n* thief, burglar (literally 'theft doing person'). Nep. *cor, taskar*. **khus pottɔp**$_{a}$ *n* thief, burglar (literally 'theft doing'). Nep. *cor, taskar*. See *cor*.

khusi$_{m}$ [<Nep. *khusī, khuśī*] *adj* pleased, glad, happy. LIT 7 *khuśī*. **khusi bakcam**$_{m}$ *vi-2* to be pleased, be glad, be happy. Nep. *khusī hunu*.

khusiŋ$_{m}$ *n* handle (of an axe). LIT 6 *khusīṅā*. Nep. *bī̃ḍ*.

khuskʌi$_{m}$ [<Nep. *khuskāi*] *n* dislocation. **khuskʌi lacam**$_{m}$ *vi-1a-i* to be loosened, be dislocated (said of joints). Nep. *khuskanu*.

— l —

-l$^{1}_{am}$ see *-la*^{1}.

-l$^{2}_{am}$ see *-lu*.

lʌgatar$_{a}$ [<Nep. *lagātar*] *adv* incessantly.

lʌura$_{am}$ [<Nep. *laurā*] *n* stick, walking stick.

-la$^{1}_{am}$, **-l**$_{am}$ *suffix* directive marker, which is used as a lexicalised suffix in adverbs of direction, e.g. *asal* 'here'. Nep. *tira*. See *lam*^{1}.

la$^{2}_{am}$ [Wamdyal *ʔla*] *n* entire arm, including the hand. LSN I *laso*; II *la*; III *la*. LIT 2 *ʔlā* in *ʔlākhū* 'with one's hands' / *ʔlānwa* 'in one's hands'. Nep. *hāt, bāhulī, hasta*. **la tɔpcam**$_{m}$ *v* to clap one's hands. Nep. *tālī bajāunu*.

labji$_{a}$ [*sɔmdu* speech] *n* husked and polished grain, especially rice. Nep. *cāmal*. See *seri*.

lacap$_{a}$, **lacam**$_{m}$ *vi-1a-i* <la-> to be, become. LIT 4 *la-* in *pharkailaṅmā* 'I returned'; 6 *la-* in *lāgai lāse* 'exactly when happening'; 7 *lā-* in *jammailāsāku* 'having come together'. Nep. *hunu*.

laci$_{m}$ *n* vagina, the female sexual organ. Nep. *strīko jananendriya, bhag, yoni*.

lagʌi$_{m}$ [<Nep. *lagāi*] *n* happening, proceeding. LIT 6 *lāgai*. **lagʌi dumcam**$_{m}$ *vi-1c* to happen, proceed. Nep. *lagnu*.

lagchʌ$_{a}$ [<Nep. *lāgcha*] *part* it will happen.

lai$_{am}$ [<Nep. *lāī*] *postp* grammatical patient maker. LIT 5 *lāī* in *duḥkhī-lāī* 'pain'; 6 *lāī* in *innelāī* 'to you'.

Laimcu$_{a}$ *n* the name of a particular Jero clan.

laji$_{a}$ [<Nep. *lāj*] *n* shame, reserve. See *krɔtni*.

laka$_{a}$ [Wamdyal *ʔlaka-*] *n* red. Nep. *rāto, lāl.*

laka-laka$_{a}$ [Wamdyal *ʔlaka-*] *n cmp* very red. Nep. *ekdam rāto.*

lakcip$_{a}$ [Wamdyal *ʔlakacim*] *adj* red. Nep. *rāto, lāl.*

lam$^{1}_{a}$ *postp* directive marker, e.g. *kul lam*$_{a}$ 'towards the house'. Nep. *tira*. See *-la*^{1}.

lam$^{2}_{am}$ [Wamdyal *ʔlam*] *n* road, path, route, way. LSN I *lam*; II *lam*; III *lam*. Nep. *bāṭo, mārga.*

lapphu$_{am}$ *postp & adv* before, previously, formerly, in front of, before. Nep. *pahile, agāḍi*. See *lapthɔl.*

lapthɔl$_{a}$ *postp & adv* before, previously, formerly, in front of, before, e.g. *kul lapthɔl*$_{a}$ 'in front of the house'. Nep. *pahile, agāḍi.* See *lapphu.*

lɛccap$_{a}$, **lɛccam**$_{m}$ *v(t)* to take away, take with, escort, lead. LSN I *læk-*. Nep. *laijānu, lānu.*

lɛm$_{am}$ *n* tongue. LSN I *lɛm*; II *lɛm*; III *lɛm*. Nep. *jibro.*

lɛpsu$_{a}$ *n* the back of the head. Nep. *ṭāukoko pachāḍiko bhāg.*

lɛtam$_{am}$ *n* bedding, bed, mattress. Nep. *bichaunā, ochyān.*

lekhe$_{m}$ *n* a bamboo bow (for shooting arrows), with a straight handle. Nep. *dhanu*. See *blu.*

lipʌi$_{a}$ *n* paint, smear. **lipʌi pacap**$_{a}$ *vt-2a* to paint, smear on, plaster with mud and dung. Nep. *lipnu, lippot garnu*. Cf. *khlɛkcap.*

liːphu$_{m}$ [Wamdyal *ʔliːphu*] *n* a big earthenware vessel used to store alcoholic drinks. Nep. *māṭoko ṭhūlo ghaĩṭo*. See *dubɔlki, himpu.*

lɔcap$_{a}$, **lɔcam**$_{m}$ *vi-1a-i* <lɔ-> to go (away), make a journey. LIT 2 3 *lvācām*, 4 *lvā-* in *lvāṅmā* 'I will go'; 7 *lvā-* in *lvā̃ṅmā* 'I will go'. Nep. *jānu, prasthān garnu.*

lɔkcap$^{1}_{a}$, **lɔkt-**$_{m}$ *v(t)* to boil, simmer, bubble up. LSN III *l*^{h}*ok-(t)*. Nep. *umlanu, umlinu*. See *umlʌi.*

lɔkcap$^{2}_{a}$ *v(t)* to lick. Nep. *cāṭnu.*

lɔsu$_{am}$, **lɔs**$_{a}$ [Wamdyal *ʔlɔsu*] *n* leg, including foot. LSN I *laso*; II *lośu*; III *lośu*. Nep. *khuṭṭo, ghoḍā.*

locam$_{m}$ *v(t)* to wait, await, guard, keep watch. Nep. *parkhanu, pratīkṣā garinu, ruṅnu, kurnu*. See *rim.*

lokhʌrke$_{am}$ [<Nep. *lokharke*] *n* squirrel.

-lu$_{am}$, **-l**$_{am}$ *suffix* locative marker, which is used as a lexical suffix in adverbs, e.g. *alu*$_{am}$ 'here', and grammaticalised as the marker of the present gerund, e.g. *pacalu*$_{a}$ 'while doing'. LIT 1 4 *-l* in *māllī diṅbul* 'when I went around looking here and there' / 4 *mwarduṅbul* 'when I emerged'; 6 *-l* in *āphāccāl* 'while not being able'. Nep. *mā*. See *=na*^{1}. Apparently related to LIT 7 *=l* in *Libju-Bhumjul* 'at Libju-Bhumju'.

lucap$_{a}$, **lucam**$_{m}$ [Wamdyal *ʔlu-*] *vi-1a-i* <lu-> to cause a mental or bodily sensation. LIT 5 *lu-* in *luṅsai* 'as I felt it'. Nep. *anubhūt garnu*. See *jiji lucam, nim*^{1}.

luttɔp$_{a}$ [Wamdyal *ʔlu-*] *v adj* feeling, causing a mental or bodily sensation, tasty. Nep. *anubhūt garne.*

— m —

-m$^{1}_{am}$ *suffix* imperative agreement morpheme which marks a transitive relationship between a singular agent and a third person non-singular patient.

≡m$^{2}_{am}$ see *≡me*^{1}.

-m$^{2}_{am}$ see *-me*^{2}.

-m$^{3}_{am}$ see *-mi*^{1}.

Mʌha-Rɔke$_{a}$ [<Nep. *mahā* 'great'] *n cmp* the name of a subdivision of the Jero *Rɔke* clan.

-mʌi$_{am}$ see *-mei.*

mʌiju$_{a}$ [<Nep. *māiju*] *n* mother's brother's wife.

mʌjur$_{a}$ [<Nep. *majur*] *n* peacock.

mʌkʌi$_{am}$ [<Nep. *makai*] *n* maize, corn.

Mʌlɔŋ-Khola$_{a}$ [<Nep. *Maluṅ Kholā, Mauluṅ Kholā, Māluṅ Kholā*] *n cmp* the name of a stream in Okhalḍhuṅgā district in the vicinity of which the northern dialect of Jero is spoken.

mʌsala$_{a}$ [<Nep. *masālā*] *n* spices.

mʌsan$_{a}$ [<Nep. *masān*] *n* ghost. See *bhut, sama.*

mʌsi$_{a}$ [<Nep. *masī*] *n* marrow.

-ma$^{1}_{am}$ *suffix* past prior time marker in past perfect gerunds, e.g. *blaŋmaku*$_{a}$ 'after I had come'.

-ma$^{2}_{am}$ see *-me*^{2}.

-ma$^{3}_{am}$ *suffix* feminine gender marker. LIT 1 *-mā* in *māmā*; 7 *-mā* in *māmāku* 'by mother'. See *-me*^{3}, *-mu*^{1}.

=ma$^{4}_{a}$ see =*na*^{1}.

ma$^{5}_{a}$ *n* liver. Nep. *kalejo*. See *kʌlejo*, *ni*.

macap$_{a}$, **macam**$_{m}$ *v(t)* to eat by biting and tearing the food with one's teeth (e.g. meat, oranges, sugar cane, etc.). LSN II *ma-*. Nep. *ṭokera vā dārera khānu*.

magge$_{a}$ *n* egg. Nep. *phul*. See *mayaŋga*.

-mai$_{am}$ see *-mei*.

maili-brɛmci$_{m}$ [<Nep. *māhilī* 'second-born female' + Jero *brɛmci* 'finger'] *n cmp* middle finger.

majari$_{m}$ *n* spider. Nep. *mākuro*. See *makura*.

makura$_{a}$ [<Nep. *mākuro*] *n* spider. See *majari*.

mala$_{a}$ [<Nep. *mālā*] *n* garland.

makcam$^{1}_{m}$ *vt-2e* <makt- ~ ma:-> to catch, capture, snatch, seize, hold, take in hand. LSN II *mak-*. Nep. *samātnu*, *samāunu*, *hātmā linu*.

makcam$^{2}_{m}$, **nakcap**$_{a}$ *v(t)* to chew, masticate. Nep. *capāunu*.

malcam$_{m}$ *v(t)* to search, seek, look for. LIT 1 *māl-* in *māllī diṅbul* 'when I went around looking here and there'. Nep. *khojnu*, *khojī garnu*.

mama$_{am}$ *n* mother. LIT 1 *māmā*; 7 *māmā* in *māmāku* 'by mother'. Nep. *āmā*.

mambu$_{am}$ *n* cheek. Nep. *gālā*, *kapol*. See *gala*. **mambu=na=p rusu**$_{a}$ *n* the bone of the cheek. Nep. *gālāko hāḍ*.

mambu-rusu$_{m}$ *n cmp* cheek bone. Nep. *gālāko hāḍ*.

-mamcu$_{a}$ *suffix* marker of the passive verbal adjective. LIT 4 *-muncvam* in *gamuncvam* '(having) come'; 7 *-mancu* in *nemāncu* '(having) said'.

manʌi$_{m}$ [<Nep. *mānāi*] *n* observing, practice. **manʌi pacam**$_{m}$ *vt-2a* to observe, follow, practice. Nep. *mānnu*.

manto$_{m}$, **manthu**$_{a}$ *n* silence, quietness, quiet. Nep. *cup*.

maŋ$_{am}$ *adv* now, at this time, at the time, at that time, at the time when or of which one is writing or speaking. Nep. *ahile*.

ma[p]-$_{m}$ *v* to forget, not have the memory. Nep. *birsanu*, *samjhanā nahunu*.

maph$_{m}$ [<Nep. *māph*] *n* forgiveness, pardon. **maph gɔkcam**$_{m}$ *vt-2e* to forgive. Nep. *māph dinu*.

maphlɛm$_{am}$ *n* wing. Nep. *pakheṭā*.

mari$_{am}$ *n* A bruise, injury, open wound. B ulcer, blister, boil. Nep. *coṭ*, *ghāu*, *khaṭiro*.

masrɛmpu$_{a}$ *n* pinion, feather (big). Nep. *pvā̃kh*. See *bhutla*.

masεm$_{m}$ *n* shoulder. LIT 2 *māṃsyām*. Nep. *kā̃dh, kum.*

mattɔlo$_{m}$, **matto**$_{a}$, **mat**$_{a}$, **mattol**$_{a}$ *adv* late, a little later. Nep. *bhare, ek chin pachi.*

-**maya**$_{am}$ see *-mei.*

maya$_{a}$ [<Nep. *māyā*] *n* infatuation, love. **maya pacap**$_{a}$ *vt-2a* to be in love. Nep. *māyā garnu.*

mayaŋga$_{am}$ *n* egg. LSN II *maʔyaŋgɔ*. Nep. *phul*. See *magge.*

maʔla$_{a}$ *n* spirit, presence in mind, consciousness. Nep. *sāto, cetanā.*

maːla$_{am}$ *n* language, something said, word, speech, thing. LIT 7 *mālā*. Nep. *kurā*. **maːla sɔcam**$_{m}$ *v* to converse, speak, talk. Nep. *kurā garnu.*

maːmʌi$_{m}$ [term of address] *n* mother-in-law. Nep. *sāsū.*

maːmu$_{am}$ *n* any paternal aunt, any sister of ego's father, the wife of a *pusʌi*. Nep. *phupū.*

mεccap$_{a}$, **mεccam**$_{m}$ *v(t)* to feed, arrange and give food. Nep. *khuvāunu.*

mεlcap$_{a}$, **mεlcam**$_{m}$ *vt-2h* <mεlt- ~ mεl-> to sleep, be asleep, fall asleep (by some outer source). Nep. *bidāunu, bidramā parnu, sutnu.*

mεrcap$_{a}$, **mεrcam**$_{m}$ *vm-1c* <mεr-> to wash oneself, to wash up (e.g. hands), bathe oneself. LSN I *mur-, mεr-*; II *mur, myar-*; III *mur, mer*. Nep. *nuhāunu, snān garnu*. See *murcap.*

mεsi$_{m}$ *n* the tree *Elaeagnus parvifolia* (Panday 1982, Shrestha 1979), which has red and sweet edible fruits. Nep. *guhelī.*

mεtεme$_{m}$ *n* girl. LSN III *mεttεʔm*. Nep. *keṭī*. See *mεttεp.*

mεttεp$_{a}$ *n* girl. LSN II *mεṯṯεp*. Nep. *keṭī*. See *mεtεme.*

mεwa$_{am}$, **mewa**$_{a}$ [<Nep. *mevā*] *n* the papaya fruit *Carica papaya* (HMG 1984).

mεʔlum$_{a}$, **muʔlum**$_{m}$ *n* tail. LSN III *mεʔlum*. Nep. *pucchar*. See *pucchʌr.*

≡me$^{1}_{am}$, **≡p**$_{a}$, **≡m**$_{am}$ *suffix* reifying marker, used to create nominals from other parts of speech, e.g. *kul=na=p*$_{a}$ 'the one from home', *alu=p mucu*$_{a}$ 'the person from here'. LIT 1 2 4 *-m* in *pācām* 'to do' / 2 *lvācām* 'to go' / 4 *blecām* 'to be alive', 1 *=m* in *bhīrnvam* 'the one from the steep place', 2 *=m* in *hāi nwam* 'the one in what?'; 6 *-m* in *pācām.*

-me$^{2}_{am}$, **-ma**$_{am}$, **-m**$_{am}$, **-ne**$_{am}$ *suffix* marker of the affirmative. LIT 4 5 *me-* in 4 *nemme* 'they^{P} say' / 5 *bānimme* 'you^{P} are', 1 4 5 *-mā* in 1 *sīmā* 'I will die' / 4 *lvāṅmā* 'I will go' / 5 *nvāṅmā* 'I am', 1 2 4 5

-m in 1 *bām* 'it is' / 2 *cāptīm* 'he could [do it]' / 4 *siṅm* 'I will die' / 5 *blām* 'he arrived', 4 *-ne* in *lvānne* 'you^{s} will go'; 6 *-ne* in *bānne* 'you^{s} are'; 7 *-mā* in *lvā̃ṅmā* 'I will go'.

-me$^{3}_{am}$ *suffix* feminine gender marker. See *-ma*^{3}, *-mu*^{1}.

-mei$_{am}$, **-maya**$_{a}$, **-mai**$_{am}$, **-nei**$_{am}$, **-mʌi**$_{am}$ *suffix* marker of the factual verbal adjective. LIT 1 *-meī* in *khrvāmmeī* 'he cried', 1 *-māī* in *piṅmāī* 'I came (across a horizontal plane)'; 7 *-māyā* in *lāṅmāyā* 'I became'.

me pacap$_{a}$, **me pacam**$_{m}$ *vt-2a* to let cool off, make cold. Nep. *selāunu*.

mesu$_{am}$ *n* buffalo. Nep. *bhaĩsī*.

mewa$_{a}$ see *mɛwa*.

-mi$^{1}_{am}$, **-im**$_{am}$, **-m**$_{am}$, **-ʔ**$_{a}$, **-ʔim**$_{m}$, **-ʔmi**$_{a}$, **-Ø**$_{a}$ *suffix* simplex agreement morpheme which marks that minimally one of the actants involved in the verbal scenario is a second or third person and that minimally one actant, but not necessarily the same actant, is non-singular. LIT 4 5 *-m* in 4 *nemme* 'they^{p} say' / 5 *bānimme* 'you^{p} are'.

mi$^{2}_{am}$ *n* fire. LSN I *mi*; II *mi*; III *mi*. Nep. *āgo*. **mi lagʌi lacap**$_{a}$ *vi-1a-i*, **mi lagʌi dumcam**$_{m}$ *vi-1c* to catch fire, ignite, burn (e.g. of lamps). Nep. *āgo lāgnu*. **mi thaːcap**$_{a}$, **mi thaːcam**$_{m}$ *vm-1a* to warm oneself near a fire. Nep. *āgo tāpnu*.

milʌi$_{am}$ [<Nep. *milāi*] *n* agreement, blending. LIT 7 *milai*. **milʌi lacap**$_{a}$ *vi-1a-i*, **milʌi dumcam**$_{m}$ *vi-1c* to agree, blend, make go together. LIT 7 *milai ālāi* $^{?}$'even if it does not match'. Nep. *milnu*.

mimcap$_{a}$ *v(t)* to remember, think. LIT 1 *mim-* in *mimṅumyai* $^{?}$'they^{p} remember me'. Nep. *samjhanu*, *socnu*. See *sʌmjhʌi*.

mimti$_{m}$ *n* A memory, remembrance. B imagination. Nep. *samjhanā*, *kalpanā*. **mimti pacam**$_{m}$ *vt-2a* to remember, think. Nep. *kalpanā garnu*.

mircap$_{a}$, **mircam**$_{m}$ *v(t)* to scratch (e.g. by a cat). Nep. *koparnu*, *kotarnu*.

mirgʌ$_{a}$ [<Nep. *mr̥ga*] *n* the barking deer *Muntiacus muntjak* (Mishra and Mierow 1974). See *gɛpsu*.

misʌi$_{m}$ [<Nep. *misāi*] *n* mix, blending. **misʌi pacam**$_{m}$ *vt-2a* to mix, mix up, blend. Nep. *misāunu*.

misi$_{am}$ *n* eye. LSN I *mis*; II *miśi*; III *misi*. Nep. *ā̃khā*.

mɔ-$_{m}$ *v* to sense, feel, perceive. Nep. *anubhūt garnu*.

mɔkke$_{m}$, **mɔkko**$_{a}$, **mɔko**$_{a}$ *adv* just now, presently. Nep. *bharkhar*.

mɔkɔm$_{am}$ *n* chicken, fowl. LSN I *mokam*; II *mok'om*; III *mokɔm*. Nep. *kukhuro*.

mɔko$_{a}$ see *mɔkke*.
mɔl$_{am}$ *n* stomach, belly. Nep. *bhũḍī*. See *bhũḍi*.
mɔrcap$_{a}$ I *v(t)* to drive out, take out, cause to come out, pluck out, publish. II *vm-1c* <mɔr-> to come out, go out, get out. LIT 4 *mwar-* in *mwarduṅbul* 'when I emerged'. Nep. *nikālnu, niklanu*.
mõ$_{a}$, **mũ**$_{a}$, **mu**$_{m}$ *n* fish. LSN I *mu*; III *mu*. Nep. *mācha*.
moi$_{a}$ [<Nep. *mvāī*] *n* kiss.
moli$_{m}$, **moʔli**$_{a}$ *n* leaf. LSN I *motʔli*; II *moʔli*; III *moʔli*. Nep. *pāt*.
mũ$_{a}$ see *mõ*.
-mu$^{1}_{am}$ *suffix* feminine gender marker. See *-ma*^{3}, *-me*^{3}.
-mu$^{2}_{am}$ *suffix* marker of a bird.
mu$^{3}_{m}$ see *mõ*.
mucu$_{am}$ *n* mankind, human race, man, person. LSN I *mucu*; II *mucu*; III *mucu*. LIT 7 *mucu*. Nep. *mānāv, mānche*.
muḍki$_{m}$ [<Nep. *muḍkī*] *n* a punch, clenched fist.
mundo$_{m}$ *ind* who, somebody. LSN II *mundo*. Nep. *ko, jo*. See *munu*.
mundri$_{m}$ [<Nep. *mundrī*] *n* small ring, earring, nose ring.
munu$_{am}$, **mun**$_{a}$ *ind* who, somebody. LSN I *munu*; III *munu*$^{(?)}$. LIT 5 *mu-nu*. Nep. *ko, jo*. **mun dɔt**$_{a}$ *ind* who. See *mundo*.
murʌli$_{m}$ [<Nep. *muralī*] *n* flute, pipe.
murcap$_{a}$ *v(t)* wash, rinse. LSN I *mur-, mɛr-*; II *mur, myar-*; III *mur, mer*. Nep. *dhunu, pakhālnu*. See *mɛrcap*.
musa$_{a}$ [<Nep. *mūso*] *n* mouse. See *cicimo*.
muṭhi$_{am}$ [<Nep. *muṭhī*] I *n* fist. II *quant* a handful.
muʔlum$_{m}$ see *mɛʔlum*.

— **n** —

-n$^{1}_{am}$ *suffix* plural subject imperative agreement morpheme.
=n$^{2}_{am}$ see *=na*^{1}.
=n$^{3}_{am}$ see *=na*^{2}.
-n$^{4}_{a}$ see *-na*^{3}.
-n$^{5}_{am}$ see *-ni*^{3}.
nʌdi$_{a}$ [<Nep. *nadi*] *adv* river.
nʌjik$_{m}$ [<Nep. *najik*] *adv* near, close.
nʌmʌskar$_{m}$ [<Nep. *namaskār*] *n* obeisance, salutation, greeting.
nʌrʌm$_{m}$ [<Nep. *naram*] *adj* soft, mild, tender.

nʌuthal$_{a}$, **nʌuṯhal**$_{m}$ [with the locative marker *-l*] I *adv* back. II *postp* behind, e.g. *kul nʌuthal*$_{a}$ 'behind the house'.

nʌuṯhaŋ$_{am}$ *adv* afterwards, after, later. Nep. *pachi, pachāḍi, samay bitāera.* **nʌuṯha=m**$_{m}$ [with the reifying suffix *=m*] *nom* last.

=na$^{1}_{a}$, **=no**$_{m}$, **=n**$_{am}$, **=ma**$_{a}$ *suffix* locative marker, which is used as a phrasal suffix with unbound forms, e.g. *kul=na*$_{a}$ 'at home', *jhola=n*$_{a}$ 'in the bag', *pum=ma*$_{a}$ 'at the bottom'. LIT 1 2 4 5 *=nva* in 1 *kulnva* 'at home' / 2 *dhūlonva* 'in the dust' / 4 *jīvannva* 'in a life' / 5 *jindagīnva* 'in a life', 2 *=nwa* in *kalam nwa* 'in a pen', 5 *=nvā* in *ṭāḍhānvām* 'the one from far', 2 *=n* in 2 *byālān* 'at the time'; 6 *=n* in *andhyāron* 'in the dark'; 7 *=na* in *ḍyālnase* 'exactly in the village' / *pāhārna* 'in the hills'. Nep. *mā*. See *-lu*.

=na$^{2}_{a}$, **=no**$_{m}$, **=n**$_{am}$ *suffix* A comitative marker 'with, in the company of'. B also used as a coordinator of arguments, conveying the sense of 'and' or 'both ... and'. Nep. *sita, ra*.

-na$^{3}_{a}$, **-n**$_{a}$ *bound morph* marker which indicates a location at the same elevation as the point of reference. See *-no*^{4}.

na$^{4}_{am}$ *adv* previously, formerly, already. Nep. *agi, aghi.* **na ke**$_{a}$ *adv* much before, much previously, much formerly. Nep. *aghi nai.* **na-na**$_{m}$ *adv cmp* much previously, much formerly. Nep. *agi agi.* **na=se**$_{am}$ *adv* much before, much previously, much formerly. Nep. *aghi nai.*

naccam$_{m}$ *v(t)* A to sting (e.g. by a bee). B to pinch, nip, squeeze. Nep. *cimoṭnu, cimaṭnu.*

nãghʌi$_{a}$ [<Nep. *nā̃ghāi*] *n* jump (over something), transgression. **nã-ghʌi pacap**$_{a}$ *vt-2a* to jump over someone or something, transgress. Nep. *nā̃ghnu.*

naicam$_{m}$ *v(m)* to rest, take a breather, relax. Nep. *bisāunu, viśrām garnu, sustāunu.*

=na=k$_{a}$ see *=na=ku*.

nakcap$_{a}$ see *makcam*^{2}.

nake$_{a}$ *n* animal. Nep. *paśu.*

naksu$_{a}$ *n* family priest, spiritual leader of a particular family. Nep. *kulguru, purohit, puret, pūjārī, pūjāhārī, kulpūjārī.*

=na=ku$_{a}$, **=na=k**$_{a}$ [a sequence of the locative and source markers] *suffix* from, e.g. *kul=na=ku* 'from the house'

nalmu$_{a}$ *n* a species of tree.

nani$_{am}$ [<Nep. *nānī*] *n* child. **nani=ŋ kul**$_{a}$ *n* womb. Nep. *garbhāśay.*

nari$_{a}$ [<Nep. *nārī*] *n* A pulse. B wrist.

=na=se$_{a}$, **=na=s**$_{a}$ [a sequence of the locative and similaritive markers] *suffix* like, comparable to, similar to. =**na**=**se**=**p** [reified form] *nom suffix* like, e.g. *uŋ=na=se=p* ‘[something] like me’.

nasi$_{m}$, **nassi**$_{a}$, **ŋasi**$_{m}$ *n* type of home-brewed beer made from fermented rice, maize or barley. Nep. *jā̃ḍ*.

-**nati**$_{m}$ *suffix* simplex agreement morpheme which marks a transitive relationship between a third person singular agent and a second person singular patient.

naʔa$_{am}$, **naʔ**$_{a}$ *part* only. LIT 1 *ṅāā*. Nep. *mātra*.

naːthot$_{a}$ *adv* next year. Nep. *āune sāl*.

nɛccap$_{a}$, **nɛt-**$_{m}$ *vt(-2d)* <nɛtt- ~ (*nɛn-)> to hurt. Nep. *dukhnu*.

nɛksi$_{m}$ *n* elbow. Nep. *kuhunu*. See *kuhina*.

nɛm$_{m}$ *n* brain. Nep. *giḍī*.

nɛmki$_{am}$ [<Jero *nɛm* ‘brain’ + *khi* ‘shit’] *n* spittle, saliva. Nep. *thuk*.

nɛntha$_{a}$ *adj* new. Nep. *nayā̃*. See *ebo*.

nɛ[ŋ]-$_{a}$, **nɛ[ʔ]-**$_{m}$ *v* to say to someone. Nep. *bhanu*. See *nɛʔe*, *necap*.

nɛpcap$_{a}$, **nɛpcam**$_{m}$ *v(t)* to push, push away, shove, press forward. Nep. *dhakelnu*, *ghaceṭnu*. See *ghʌcca*.

nɛrcap$_{a}$ *v(t)* to count. Nep. *gannu*.

nɛttɔp$_{a}$ *v* characterised by hurting. Nep. *dukhne*.

nɛ[ʔ]-$_{m}$ see *nɛ[ŋ]-*.

nɛʔe$_{a}$ *part* marker of hearsay. Nep. *are*, *re*.

-**ne**$_{am}$ see *-me*[2].

-**nei**$_{am}$ see *-mei*.

necap$_{a}$, **necam**$_{m}$ *vm-1a* <ne-> A to say, quote, relate, inform, tell. B [in Mohānṭāre] inceptive auxiliary, used with a verbal adjective of purpose. LSN I *nɛ-s-*; II *ne-s-*. LIT 4 *ne-* in *nemme* ‘they[p] say’; 6 *ne-* in *nesāku* ‘having said’; 7 *ne-* in *nemāncu* ‘(having) said’. Nep. *bhannu*, *batāunu*.

Nepal$_{a}$ [<Nep. *Nepāl*] *n* Nepal. LIT 1 *Nepāl*.

nesaku$_{a}$ [Jero *ne-sa-ku* (say-MAN-PFG) ‘having said’] *v adj* perfect gerund which indexes indirect speech. LIT 6 *nesāku*. Nep. *bhanera*.

-**ni**$^{1}_{am}$ *suffix* simplex agreement morpheme which marks a transitive relationship between a first person singular agent and a second person patient.

-**ni**$^{2}_{am}$, -**i**$_{a}$ *suffix* second and third person plural imperative agreement morpheme.

-ni$^{3}_{am}$, **-n**$_{am}$ *suffix* second person simplex agreement morpheme. LIT 4 *-n* in *lvānne* 'you^{s} will go', 5 *-ni* in *bānimme* 'you^{p} are'; 6 *-n* in *bānne* 'you^{s} are'.

-ni$^{4}_{am}$ *suffix* marker of day.

ni$^{5}_{am}$ [<Nep. *ni*] *part* assertive particle, conveying the sense of 'I tell you' or 'you know'. LIT 5 *ni*.

ni$^{6}_{m}$ *n* liver. Nep. *kalejo*. See *kʌlejo*, *ma*^{5}.

ni$^{7}_{am}$ *n* name. LSN I *ni*; II *ni*; III *ni*. Nep. *nām*.

nidhar$_{a}$ [<Nep. *nidhār*] *n* forehead, brow.

nim$^{1}_{m}$ *n* fear. Nep. *ḍar*, *bhaya*, *trās*. **nim lucam**$_{m}$ *v* to fear, be afraid. Nep. *ḍarnu*.

nim$^{2}_{a}$ *n* lie, act of lying. Nep. *ḍhā̃ṭ*. **nim pacap**$_{a}$ *vt-2a* to lie. Nep. *ḍhā̃ṭ-nu*. **nim pottɔp**$_{a}$ *v adj* liar. Nep. *ḍhā̃ṭne*. See *nima*.

nim$^{3}_{m}$ see *nimpha*.

nima$_{m}$ *n* lie, act of lying. Nep. *ḍhā̃ṭ*. **nima han-**$_{m}$ *v* to lie, tell a lie to somebody. Nep. *arulāī ḍhā̃ṭnu*.

nimpha$_{am}$, **nim**$^{3}_{m}$ *number* nominal dual marker. LSN I **nimp^{h}a* 'both'.

ninibbɔn$_{a}$ *adv* three days ago, the day before the day before yesterday. Nep. *tīn din aghi*.

nibbɔn$_{a}$ *adv* two days ago, the day before yesterday. Nep. *asti*. See *saːsatni*.

niwa$_{am}$ *n* knowledge, wisdom. Nep. *jñān*, *cet*, *cetanā*, *buddhi*. **niwa ri-**$_{m}$ *v* to be or become dizzy or giddy. Nep. *riṅāunu*, *rīgaṭā lāgnu*.

niːcap$^{1}_{a}$, **niː-**$_{m}$ *vm-1a* <niː-> to sit down, be seated. Nep. *basnu*.

niːcap$^{2}_{a}$ *vi-1b* <niː-> to be afraid. Nep. *ḍarāinu*.

nɔ-$_{am}$ *bound morph* demonstrative which indicates a position which is relatively far away from the point of reference or from the speaker and hearer and at the same elevation.

nɔbu$_{am}$ *n* ear. LSN I *nobu*; II *nobu*. Nep. *kān*.

nɔcap$_{a}$, **nɔcam**$_{m}$ *vi-1a-i* <nɔ-> to be (copula of identification and categorisation). LIT 5 *nvā-* in *nvāṅmā* 'I am'. Nep. *hunu*.

nɔdɔŋ$_{a}$ [= *nɔ-Ø-dɔŋ* (be-23s-CND)] *vi-1a-i* if it is. LIT 6 *naḍaṅ*. Nep. *bhae*.

nɔi$_{am}$ see *nɔya*.

nɔicu$_{m}$ *dem pron* that which is relatively further away than another thing that is relatively far away and at the same elevation as the point of reference. Nep. *tyo terso*.

nɔm$_{am}$ *n* sun, sunlight. LSN I *nwam*; II *nom*; III *nwam*. Nep. *sūrya, ghām*. **nɔm mɔrcap**$_{a}$ *v* the sun to rise. **nɔm pacam**$_{m}$ *vt-2a* to be sunny, feel the sun. Nep. *ghām parnu*.

nɔmala$_{m}$, **nɔmal**$_{a}$ I *adv* beside, further, beyond, towards the horizontal side. II *postp* towards the same elevation, e.g. *phutur nɔmal* 'towards the same elevation as the head'. Nep. *ṭāḍhā, para*.

nɔna$_{a}$, **nɔn**$_{a}$, **nɔno**$_{m}$ *dem adv* there (of place, at the same elevation). Nep. *tyahā̃ terso*.

nɔsal$_{a}$, **nɔsɛl**$_{m}$ *dem adv* there (of direction, at the same elevation). Nep. *tyatā-tersotira*.

nɔse$_{m}$ *dem adv* in that way, like that, thus, so (at the same elevation as the point of reference). Nep. *tyaso terso*. **nɔse=p**$_{a}$, **nɔse=m**$_{m}$ *dem adj & adv* (something) like that (at the same elevation as the point of reference), thus, so. Nep. *tyasto terso*. **nɔse=p=na=se=p**$_{a}$ *dem adj & adv* (something) like that (at the same elevation as the point of reference).

nɔya$_{a}$, **nɔi**$_{am}$ *dem pron* that (at the same elevation). LSN III *ŋoi̯*. Nep. *tyo terso*.

-no$^{1}_{am}$ see *-ano*.

=no$^{2}_{m}$ see *=na*^{1}.

=no$^{3}_{m}$ see *=na*^{2}.

-no$^{4}_{m}$ *bound morph* marker which indicates a location at the same elevation as the point of reference. See *-na*^{3}.

nobir$_{m}$, **noʔmar**$_{a}$ *n* head strap for carrying a *ḍoko*. LIT 2 *novīr*. Nep. *nāmlo*.

nucap$_{a}$, **nucam**$_{m}$ *vi-1a-i* <nu-> to be well, be healthy, be good. LIT 4 *nu-* in *ānuce* 'not being well'. Nep. *niko hunu*.

nul$_{a}$ *n* the name of a religious ceremony which is performed as a funeral ceremony after the death of a relative. Also known as *khauma*.

num-$_{m}$ *bound morph* former, previous.

numthoce$_{m}$ *adv* one year ago, last year. Nep. *pohar, pohor*. See *-thoce*.

nunu$_{m}$ *n* child, baby. LIT 5 *nunu*. Nep. *baccā*. **nunu=ŋ kul**$_{m}$ *n* womb, literally 'baby's house'. Nep. *garbhāśay*.

nunusso$_{a}$ *adv* three days from now, the day after the day after tomorrow. Nep. *niparsi, nikoparsi, nikorsi*. See *sukmul*.

nuso$_{m}$, **nusso**$_{a}$ *adv* day after tomorrow, two days from now. Nep. *parsi*.

nusum$_{am}$ *n* nose. LSN I *nusum*; II *nuśum*; III *nusum*. Nep. *nāk*.

nusum-khli$_{m}$ *n cmp* snot, nasal mucus. Nep. *sĩgān*, *sĩghān*. See *sĩgan*.

— ŋ —

-ŋ$^{1}_{am}$ *suffix* dual subject imperative agreement morpheme.

-ŋ$^{2}_{am}$ *suffix* first person singular patient imperative agreement morpheme.

-ŋ$^{3}_{am}$, **-ŋaŋ**$_{a}$, **-ŋu**$_{a}$, **-uŋ**$_{m}$, **-iŋ**$_{m}$ *suffix* dual subject simplex agreement morpheme.

=ŋ$^{4}_{am}$ see *=ŋaŋ*^{2}.

-ŋ$^{5}_{am}$ see *-ŋu*^{1}.

≡ŋ$^{6}_{m}$ see *=ŋo*.

ŋaba$_{m}$, **ŋab**$_{am}$ *n* A fragrance, aroma. B smell, scent. Nep. *bāsnā*, *gandha*. **ŋab dɔmcap**$_{a}$ *v(m)* to smell. Nep. *sũghnu*, *vāsanā linu*. **ŋaba ŋɔmcam**$_{m}$ *v(t)* to smell, sniff. Nep. *sũghnu*, *vāsanā linu*.

ŋabu$_{m}$ *n* dream. Nep. *sapanā*, *svāpna*. **ŋabu mɔ-**$_{m}$ *v* to dream (literally 'sense a dream'). Nep. *sapanā garnu*.

-ŋaŋ$^{1}_{a}$ see *-ŋ*^{3}.

=ŋaŋ$^{2}_{m}$, **=ŋ**$_{am}$ *suffix* genitive marker, e.g. *papa=ŋ kul*$_{a}$ 'father's house'. LIT 5 *=ṅāṅ* in *jyānṅāṅ* 'of life'; 5 *=ṅ* in *goruṅ* 'of a bull'. Nep. *ko*, *kā*, *kī*.

ŋasi$_{m}$ see *nasi*.

ŋaːbu$_{a}$ *n* assistant priest. Nep. *sahapūjārī*.

ŋɔmcap$_{a}$, **ŋɔmcam**$_{m}$ *v(t)* A to smell, sniff (e.g. an aroma or fragrance). B smell bad, stink, stench. Nep. *sũghnu*, *vāsanā linu*, *ganhāunu*, *durgandha āunu*, *durnām calnu*.

=ŋo$_{m}$, **≡ŋ**$_{m}$ *suffix* ablative marker. LIT 1 2 *=ṅ* in *uluṅ* 'from there', 2 *husyālnvaṅai* 'from when'. Nep. *bāṭa*.

-ŋti$_{m}$ see *-aŋti*.

-ŋu$^{1}_{am}$, **-ŋ**$_{am}$, **-uŋ**$_{m}$, **-u**$_{am}$, **-ʔ**$_{am}$, **-ʔu**$_{am}$, **-Ø**$_{a}$ *suffix* first person singular simplex agreement morpheme. LIT 1 4 5 *-ṅ* in 1 *piṅmāī* 'I came (across a horizontal plane)' / *pharkailaṅmā* 'I returned' / 5 *nvāṅmā* 'I am', 1 *-˜* in *sĩma* 'I will die', 5 *-uṅ* in *vāluṅmā* 'I will walk'; 7 *-ṅ* in *duṅmā* 'I will become', 7 *-˜ṅ* in *lvā̃ṅmā* 'I will go', 7 *-u* in *paumāyā* 'he did'.

-ŋu$^{2}_{a}$ see *-ŋ*^{3}.

— ɔ —

ɔmbule$_{a}$ *n & adj* Wambule. Nep. *Umbule.*

— o —

ochʌi$_{a}$ [<Nep. *ochyāi*] *n* spreading (e.g. of a bedding). **ochʌi pacap**$_{a}$ *vt-2a* to spread out. Nep. *ochyāunu.* See *bichʌi.*

— p —

≡p$_{a}$ see ≡*me*[1].

pʌɖʌi$_{a}$ [<Nep. *paḍhāi*] *n* A reading. B learning, education. LIT 1 *paḍai,* 3 *paḍhai.* **pʌɖʌi lacap**$_{a}$ *vi-1a-i* to read, study. LIT 1 *paḍai pācām* 'to cause to study', 3 *paḍhaipācām.* Nep. *paḍhnu.*

pʌhẽlo$_{a}$ [<Nep. *pahẽlo*] *n & adj* yellow. See *waʔɔmjimo.*

pʌini$_{a}$ [<Nep. *painī*] *n* an earthenware vessel in which rice-spirit is distilled.

pʌiro$_{m}$ [<Nep. *pahiro*] *n* landslide.

pʌisa$_{am}$ [<Nep. *paisā*] *n* money. See *rɔkso.*

pʌital$_{a}$ [<Nep. *paitālo*] *n* sole (of a foot or shoe).

pʌlʌi$_{m}$ [<Nep. *palhāi*] *n* becoming green, sprouting. **pʌlʌi dumcam**$_{m}$ *vi-1c* to begin to sprout, become green after rain. Nep. *palhāunu.*

pʌrʌ$_{a}$ [<Nep. *para*] *n* aside, further, beyond. See *nɔmala.*

pʌrchʌ$_{am}$ [<Nep. *parcha*] *part* it is [generally] necessary. LIT 4 *parcha* in *sāmsīparcha* 'we must lose'; 7 *parcha* in *tyārsis parcha* 'we must meet'.

pʌrdʌinʌ$_{a}$ [<Nep. *pardaina*] *part* it is not [generally] necessary.

pʌrela$_{am}$ [<Nep. *parelā* 'eyelash'] *n* eyebrow, eyelash. See *rɔmpusɔm.*

pʌrewa$_{a}$ [<Nep. *parevā*] *n* pigeon, dove.

pʌryo$_{m}$ [<Nep. *paryo*] *part* it is [now] necessary, it was [then] necessary.

pʌʈhʌi$_{am}$ [<Nep. *paṭhāi*] *n* act of sending. **pʌʈhʌi pacap**$_{a}$, **pʌʈhʌi pacam**$_{m}$ *vt-2a* to send, dispatch something (to someone). Nep. *paṭhāunu.*

-pa$^{1}_{am}$ *suffix* masculine gender marker. LIT 1 *-pā* in *pāpā*. See *-pu*^{1}, *-ʔu*.

-pa$^{2}_{m}$ see *-ka*.

pa$^{3}_{am}$ *n* pig, hog, swine, boar. LSN I *pa*; II *pa*; III *pa*. Nep. *sũgur*.

pãc$_{am}$ [<Nep. *pā̃c*] *num* five.

pacap$_{a}$, **pacam**$_{m}$ *vt-2a* <pa- ~ po-> A to do, make. B [in Āmboṭe] inceptive auxiliary, which is used with a verbal adjective of purpose. LIT 2 4 *pā-* in 2 *pāsāk* 'having done' / 4 *pāim* 'he did it', 5 *pācām*; 6 *pācām*; 7 *po-* in *pokumā* 'we^{pe} will do'. Nep. *garnu*.

paccap$_{a}$, **paccam**$_{m}$ *vt-2d* <patt- ~ pan-> A to cause someone to do something, make someone do something. B causative auxiliary, which is used with a preverb. Nep. *garāunu, lagāunu*.

pacewa$_{a}$ *n* a kind of mischievous trick or silly stunt done for amusement. Nep. *ek kisim jiskāine*.

pacha$_{a}$ [<Nep. *pāchā*] *n* clan.

paḍa$_{a}$ [<Nep. *pāḍo*] *n* young buffalo bull.

paḍi$_{a}$ [<Nep. *pāḍī*] *n* young buffalo heifer.

paicap$_{a}$ *v(m)* to dress oneself, put on clothes. LIT 3 *pāīcām*. Nep. *lugā lagāunu*.

paha$_{a}$ [<Nep. *pāhā*] *n* a big frog.

pakhra$_{a}$ [<Nep. *pākhurā*] *n* upper arm (including the shoulder).

pala$_{a}$ [Nep. *pālo*] *adv* turn, rotation, time.

papa$_{am}$ *n* father. LIT 1 *pāpā*. Nep. *bābu, bubā*.

papa-mama$_{a}$ [Jero *papa* 'father' + *mama* 'mother'] *n cmp* parents.

parkoti$_{m}$, **parkot**$_{a}$ *n* sweet potato. Nep. *suṭhanī*.

pasmi$_{a}$ [<Nep. *pāsnī*] *n* the name of the life cycle ceremony of giving a child its first solid food, which is performed between the fifth to eighteenth month after birth.

paso$_{a}$ [<Nep. *pāso*] *n* trap.

pa-su$_{a}$ [Jero *pa* 'pig' + *su* 'flesh, meat'] *n cmp* pork. Nep. *sũgur māsu*.

pɛk-$_{m}$ *v(t)* to pluck, pull out (e.g. flower, spinach). Nep. *ṭipnu*.

pɛkmar$_{a}$ *n* egg of a louse.

pɛku$_{a}$ *n* a kind of small red monkey. Nep. *rāto bā̃dar ākārko ek prakārko bā̃dar*.

pɛttu$_{a}$, **pɛtthu**$_{m}$ *adv* horizontally. Nep. *terso, tersotira*. See *pɛttu*.

peicam$_{m}$ *v(t)* A to shell, peel, husk. B to set free, break off, cause to leave (e.g. grains of corn). Nep. *cũḍāunu, choḍāunu*.

picap$_{a}$, **picam**$_{m}$ *vi-1a-ii* <pi-> to come (across a horizontal plane). LSN I *pi-ŋ-, pi*; II *pi-k*^{h}*-*. LIT 1 5 *pi-* in 1 *piṅmāī* 'I came (across a horizontal plane)' / 5 *pitigvākce* 'the one coming suddenly', 3 *picām.* Nep. *samān bhaugolik avasthitibāṭa āunu.*

pimis$_{a}$ *n* tear. Nep. *ā̃su.* See *pitaŋke.*

pipʌl$_{m}$ [<Nep. *pipal*] *n* the tree *Ficus religiosa* (Panday 1982, Shrestha 1979).

pitaŋke$_{m}$ *n* tear. Nep. *ā̃su.* See *pimis.*

pitrʌ$_{a}$ [<Nep. *pitra, pitr̥*] *n* the spirit of the dead, ancestor.

placap$_{a}$ *v(t)* A to take. B to acquire. LIT 2 5 *plā-* in *plāsāk* 'having taken' / 5 *plāṭigvākṭvāk,* 3 *plācām.* Nep. *linu, prāpta garnu, grahaṇ garnu.*

plɛcam$_{m}$ *vt-1* <plɛ-> A to leave, quit, give up, stop, abandon, forsake. B [in Mohanṭāre] terminative auxiliary, which is used with an infinitive. LIT 1 4 *plyā-* in 1 *plyāsakhū* 'having left' / 4 *plyāsāk* 'having left'. Nep. *choḍnu, tyāgnu.* See *taccap.*

plɛccap$_{a}$, **plɛccam**$_{m}$ *vt-2d* <plɛtt- ~ plɛn-> to dry something, make dry. Nep. *sukāunu.*

pli$_{am}$ *n* penis. Nep. *lā̃ḍo, liṅga.*

pɔccam$_{m}$ *v(t)* to bind, tie, tie up, tie together. Nep. *bā̃dhnu.*

pɔkti$_{am}$ *n* a species of bat. Nep. *ek prakārko camero.*

pɔkhal$_{a}$ *n* white ashes. Nep. *seto kharānī.* See *pusmi, phucul.*

plɔŋkhi$_{m}$ *n* anus. Nep. *gudadvār.*

pɔpɔl$_{a}$, **phɔphɔl**$_{m}$ *n* the calf of the leg. Nep. *chepārī.*

pocap$_{a}$ *vm-1a* <po-> reciprocal auxiliary, the middle counterpart of *pacap*$_{a}$ ~ *pacam*$_{m}$ vt-2a <pa- ~ po-> 'to do, make'.

pottɔp$_{a}$ *v adj* characterised by doing something. See *pacap.*

pothi$_{a}$ [<Nep. *pothī*] *n* female animal, especially a bird.

poʔle$_{a}$ *n* vagina. Nep. *strīko jananendriya, bhag, yoni.*

prakcam$_{m}$ *v(i)* to run, run away, flee, escape. LSN I *prak-s-*; II *pra-s-*; III *prak-s-, praŋ-.* Nep. *bhāgnu, kudnu.*

prɛkcam$_{m}$ *v(i)* to jump. Nep. *uphranu, nāghnu, phaḍkanu.*

prithibi$_{a}$ [<Nep. *pr̥thvī*] *n* the world.

-pu$^{1}_{am}$ *suffix* masculine gender marker. See *-pa*^{1}, *-ʔu.*

-pu$^{2}_{a}$ see *-phu.*

pucchʌr$_{a}$ [<Nep. *pucchar*] *n* tail. See *mɛʔlum.*

pukulum$_{m}$ *n* chignon. Nep. *juro.*

pul$_{m}$ [<Nep. *pul*] *n* bridge.

pum$^{1}_{am}$ *n* bottom, base, foundation. Nep. *phed, surko bhāg, thālnī.*

pum$^{2}_{a}$ *postp* beside.

pumci$_{am}$ *n* knee. Nep. *ghũḍo.*

purkha [<Nep. *purkhā*] *n* ancestor.
pusmi$_{a}$ *n* black ashes. Nep. *kālo kharānī*. See *pɔkhal, phucul*.
putʌli$_{a}$ [<Nep. *putalī*] *n* butterfly.
pyāc$_{a}$ [<Nep. *pyāj*] *n* onion.
pyakmul$_{a}$ *adv* four days from now.

— **ph** —

phʌl-phul$_{am}$ [<Nep. *phalphūl*] *n cmp* fruit.
phʌrkʌi$_{m}$ [<Nep. *pharkāi*] *n* return, come-back. LIT 4 *pharkai*. **phʌrkʌi dumcam**$_{m}$ *vi-1c*, **phʌrkʌi lacam**$_{m}$ *vi-1a-i* to return, come back, go back. LIT 4 *pharkai lāṅmā* 'I will return'. Nep. *pharkanu*. **phʌrkʌi pacam**$_{m}$ *vt-2a* to return, bring back. Nep. *pharkāunu*.
-pha$_{am}$ see *-ka*.
phaccap$_{a}$ *vt-2d* <phatt- ~ phan-> A can, be able. B [in Āmboṭe and Mādhavpur] auxiliary of capacity, which is used with an infinitive. LIT 6 *phāc-* in *āphāccāl* 'while not being able'. Nep. *saknu*. See *capcam*.
phalʌi$_{a}$ [<Nep. *phālāi*] *n* throw. **phalʌi pacap**$_{a}$ *vt-2a* to throw out, throw away. Nep. *phālnu*. See *ham phalʌi pacap*.
pha:pu$_{am}$ *n* bamboo. Nep. *bā̃s*.
phɛccap$_{a}$, **phɛccam**$_{m}$ *v(t)* to deal out (a meal), take out of the pot. Nep. *paskanu*.
phɛmto$_{a}$ *n* cross-legging. LIT 7 *phyāmṭo* in *phyāmṭon(a)* 'in a cross-legged position'. Nep. *palētī, pailetī*. **phɛmto pacap**$_{a}$ *vt-2a* to sit cross-legged.
phɛrcap$_{a}$, **phɛr-**$_{m}$ *v(t)* to sew, perforate. Nep. *siunu, cepnu*.
pherʌi$_{m}$ [<Nep. *pherāi*] *n* change. **pherʌi pacam**$_{m}$ *vt-2a* to change, alter, reverse. Nep. *phernu*.
pheri$_{am}$ [<Nep. *pheri*] *adv* again.
phiccap$_{a}$, **phiccam**$_{m}$ *vt(-2d)* <phitt- (~ *phin-)> to bring (across a horizontal plane). Nep. *samān bhaugolik avasthitibāṭa lyāunu*.
phikcap$_{a}$ *v(t)* to insert, put in. Nep. *hālnu, pasālnu, ghusārnu*.
phila$_{m}$ [<Nep. *philo*] *n* upper leg, thigh. Nep. *tighro*.
phipuwa$_{a}$ *n* ginger, ginger-root. Ginger-root is used as a replacement of meat during worshipping ceremonies in honour of the ancestors. Nep. *aduvā*.

phɔicam$_{m}$ *v(t)* to ask for, beg, request, solicit. Nep. *māgnu*. **phɔice mucu**$_{m}$ *v adj* beggar. Nep. *māgne mānche*. See *thɔcap*^{2}.

phɔkso$_{a}$ [<Nep. *phokso*] *n* lungs. See *jɔpre*.

phɔpma$_{am}$ *adv* tomorrow. LSN I *ph*^{w}*apma*; II *p*^{h}*opmo*; III *phɔʔma*. Nep. *bholi*.

phɔphɔl$_{m}$ see *pɔpɔl*.

phrakcap$_{a}$ *v(t)* to break open, split, rip apart. Nep. *cirnu*.

-phu$_{am}$, **-pu**$_{a}$ *suffix* marker of the supine.

phucu$_{a}$ [$^{?}$<Nep. *phuco* 'small'] *n* a small snake.

phucul$_{m}$ *n* ash, wet ashes. Nep. *kharānī*, *bhasma*. See *pɔkhal*, *pusmi*.

phuḍim$_{m}$ *n* wind, storm, tempest, storm-wind. Nep. *batās*, *hurī*, *ā̃dhī*. **phuḍim pacam**$_{m}$ *vt-2a* to be windy, be stormy, blow.

phuicap$_{a}$, **phuit-**$_{m}$ *vt-2f* <phuyt- ~ phuy-> to dig, root (in soil), grub, scratch (said of chickens), tear up soil with an implement. Nep. *khosranu*, *khodalnu*, *khannu*.

phukʌi$_{a}$ [<Nep. *phuklāi*; used in connection with animate beings] *n* untying, unfastening. See *phuklʌi*. **phukʌi pacap**$_{a}$ *vt-2a* to untie, unfasten, unfold, loosen, take off.

phukcam$_{m}$ *v(t)* A to erect, lift, place upright. B to wake up someone, awake from sleep. Nep. *uṭhāunu*, *ṭhaḍyāunu*, *ṭhāḍo pārnu*, *nidrā-bāṭa jagāunu*, *biũjhāunu*, *uṭhībās lāunu*.

phuklʌi$_{am}$ [<Nep. *phuklāi*; used in connection with inanimate being] *n* untying, unfastening. See *phukʌi*. **phuklʌi pacap**$_{a}$, **phuklʌi pacam**$_{m}$ *vt-2a* to untie, unfasten, unfold, loosen, take off.

phuli$_{am}$ *n* flour. Nep. *pīṭho*.

phuluŋ$_{am}$ *n* stone. LSN I *p*^{h}*uluŋ*; II *p*^{h}*ulum*; III *p*^{h}*uluŋ*. Nep. *ḍhuṅgo*. **asi khɔlto phuluŋ**$_{m}$ *n* pebble (literally 'small stones'). Nep. *sāno ḍhuṅgo*.

phuŋmũ$_{a}$ [Jero *mũ* 'fish'] *n* eel. Nep. *bām*.

phuri$_{am}$ *n* flower. Nep. *phūl*.

phutir$_{m}$, **phutur**$_{a}$ *n* head. LSN I *p*^{h}*uṭir*; II *p*^{h}*utir*; III *p*^{h}*utir*. LIT 2 *phūtir*. Nep. *ṭāuko*, *śir*, *māth*.

— r —

rʌ$_{a}$ [<Nep. *ra*] *conj* and.

rʌi$_{am}$, **rʌicha**$_{a}$ [<Nep. *rahecha*] *part* marker which indicates that the speaker has just come to the knowledge of an event, implying an

event which is contrary to expectation, sudden or even surprising. LIT 4 *rai*, 4 *raichā*; 7 *raichā*.

rʌksi$_{a}$ [<Nep. *raksī*] *n* liquor, a particular kind of spirit made from fermented barley, Nepali *eau-de-vie*.

rakcap$_{a}$, **rakcam**$_{m}$ *vt(-2e)* <rakt- (~ *ra:-)> A to influence, arouse, provoke, tease, taunt, stir up. B [in Mohānṭāre] inceptive auxiliary, which is used with a verbal adjective of purpose. See *ra:cap*.

ram$_{m}$ *n* body, physic. LIT 5 *rām*. Nep. *jīu*, *śarīr*, *deha*.

rambhɛnda$_{a}$ [<Nep. *golbhẽḍā*, *golbhĩḍā*] *n* tomato.

rance$_{m}$ *v adj* good, nice, fine. LIT 4 *rānce*. Nep. *rāmro*, *asal*. **arance ŋab** *n* bad smell, bad scent. Nep. *narāmro gandha*.

rani$_{a}$ [<Nep. *rānī*] *n* queen.

rantɔp$_{a}$, **ranto**$_{m}$ *v adj* good, nice, fine. Nep. *rāmro*.

rapcimtep$_{a}$ *n* ant. Nep. *kamilā*.

rat$_{a}$ [<Nep. *rāt*] *n* night.

ra:cap$_{a}$ [in Āmboṭe] *vm-1a* <ra:-> A to influence, arouse, provoke, tease, taunt, stir up. B auxiliary which is used with an infinitive in periphrastic agreement constructions marking a transitive relationship between a third person agent and a second person patient. Nep. *calāunu*, *jiskyāunu*. See *rakcap*.

Ra:du$_{a}$, **Ra:ḍu**$_{m}$ *n & adj* Rai. LIT 7 *Rāḍu*. Nep. *Rāī*. **Ra:ḍu mucu**$_{m}$ *n* Rai person. Nep. *Rāī mānche*.

rɛkcap$_{a}$, **rɛk-**$_{m}$ *vt-2e* <rɛkt- ~ re-> to write, draw. LIT 3 *ryākcam*. Nep. *lekhnu*.

rɛmcam$_{m}$ *v(t)* to meet, visit, come across, find (a trace of someone), get, meet with, come together. Nep. *bheṭnu*, *barābarīmā āunu*.

rɛnda$_{am}$ *n* laugh. LIT 3 *ryāndā*. Nep. *hā̃so*. **rɛnda recap**$_{a}$, **rɛnda recam**$_{m}$ *v(i)* to laugh. LIT 3 *ryāndārecām*. Nep. *hā̃snu*. **rɛnda re paccam**$_{m}$ *vt-2d* to cause someone to laugh. Nep. *hā̃sna lagāunu*.

rɛnjab$_{a}$ *n* potato. Nep. *ālu*.

rɛpmu$_{am}$ *n* chin. Nep. *ciũḍo*.

recap$_{a}$, **recam**$_{m}$ see *rɛnda*.

rekha$_{a}$ [<Nep. *rekhā*] *n* line, mark.

rikcam$_{m}$ *v(t)* to cut off, mow. Nep. *kaciyāle dhān*, *khar ādi kāṭnu*.

riku$_{am}$ *n* dirtiness on the body. Nep. *mayal*, *mailo*, *śarīrmā jamne phohor*.

rim$_{a}$ *n* wait. Nep. *parkhāi*. **rim pacap**$_{a}$ *vt-2a* to wait for, guard, keep watch. Nep. *parkhanu*, *pratīksā garnu*. See *locam*.

rimsa$_{m}$ *n* shade (of a tree). Nep. *chahārī*. See *riptɛwa*.

riptɛwa$_{a}$ *n* shade (of a tree). Nep. *chahārī*. See *rimsa.*

ris$_{m}$ [<Nep. *rīs*] *n* anger, ire. **ris phukcam**$_{m}$ *v(t)* to make someone angry (the noun *ris* takes a possessed complement which refers to the person who is angry). Nep. *rīsāunu.*

Rɔke$_{a}$ *n* the name of a particular Jero clan.

rɔkso$_{a}$ [secretive language] *n* money. Nep. *paisā.*

rɔlcam$_{m}$, **rwalcap**$_{a}$ *v(t)* A to shake down, knock down. B to let fall, let drop, drop. C to cause to descend, bring down, lower, take down, shed. Nep. *jhārnu, khasālnu, orālnu, jharnu, khasnu.* See *rwalcap.*

rɔmpu-sɔm$_{m}$ *n cmp* eyelash. Nep. *parelā.* See *pʌrela.*

rokʌi$_{am}$ [<Nep. *rokāi*] *n* stop, hinder. **rokʌi pacap**$_{a}$, **rokʌi pacam**$_{m}$ *vt-2a* to stop, hinder, prevent, forbid, restrain. Nep. *roknu.*

rosu$_{am}$, **ros**$_{a}$ *n* horn. LSN II *rośu*; III *rośu*. Nep. *siṅ.*

roto$_{m}$ *v adj* high, tall. Nep. *aglo.*

rukh$_{am}$ [<Nep. *rūkh*] *n* tree.

rupiyã$_{m}$ [<Nep. *rupiyā̃*] *n* rupee.

rusu$_{am}$ *n* bone. Nep. *hāḍ.*

ruwa$_{a}$ [<Nep. *ruwā*] *n* cotton wool.

rwalcap$_{a}$ see *rɔlcam.*

rwate$_{a}$ *n* a species of red ant. Nep. *ek prakārko rāto kamilā.*

— s —

-s$^{1}_{am}$ *suffix* detransitivising morpheme.

≡s$^{2}_{am}$ see *≡se*^{1}.

=s$^{3}_{am}$ see *=se*^{2}.

sʌb$_{a}$, **sʌp**$_{m}$ [<Nep. *sab*] *quant* all, whole. **sʌbʌi**$_{a}$, **sʌpʌi**$_{m}$ [<Nep. *sabai*] *quant emph* really all, really the whole. **sʌppʌi**$_{m}$ [<Nep. *sabbai*] *quant emph emph* really all, really the whole (more emphatic that *sʌpʌi*).

-sʌi$^{1}_{am}$ *suffix* marker of the simultaneous gerund.

sʌi$^{2}_{am}$ [<Nep. *say*] *num* hundred.

sʌjilo$_{m}$ [<Nep. *sajilo*] *adj* easy.

sʌlkʌi$_{a}$ [<Nep. *salkāi*] *n* setting on fire. **sʌlkʌi lacap**$_{a}$ *vi-1a-i* to be set on fire, be lightened. Nep. *salkanu.*

sʌmba$_{m}$, **sʌmma**$_{a}$ [<Nep. *samma*] *postp* as far as, up to, until, for (i.e. duration of time). Cf. *sʌmma*$_{a}$.

sʌmdhi$_{a}$ [<Nep. *samdhī*] *n* one's own child's father-in-law. See *hilpu.*

sʌmjhʌi$_{am}$ [<Nep. *samjhāi*] *n* remembrance, reminder. **sʌmjhʌi lacap**$_{a}$ *vi-1a-i* to remember, understand. Nep. *samjhanu.* **samjhʌi pacap**$_{a}$, **sʌmjhʌi pacam**$_{m}$ *vt-2a* to remember, understand. Nep. *samjhanu.* See *mimcap.*

sʌmma$_{a}$ see *sʌmba*$_{m}$.

sʌp$_{m}$ see *sʌb.*

-sa$^{1}_{am}$ *suffix* marker of the gerund of manner. LIT 1 2 5 *-sā* in 1 *plyāsa-khū* 'having left' / 2 *kursāk* 'having carried' / 4 *plyāsāk* 'having left' / 5 *pāsāk* 'having done'; 6 *-sā* in *nesāku* 'having said', 6 *-sa* in *pāsaku* 'having done'; 7 *-sā* in *jammailāsāku* 'having come together'. See *-su*^{1}.

-sa$^{2}_{a}$ see *≡se*^{1}.

sā̃ḍe$_{m}$ [<Nep. *sā̃ḍhe*] *n* (wild) bull.

sag$_{m}$ [<Nep. *sāg*] *n* greens, green leafy vegetable, especially spinach. See *siʔlim.*

sā̃ghu$_{a}$ [<Nep. *sā̃ghu*] *n* bridge.

saili-brɛmci$_{m}$ [<Nep. *sā̃hilī* 'third-born female' + Jero *brɛmci* 'finger'] *n cmp* third finger.

saiso$_{m}$ *adv* yesterday. LSN I *sa̭iso.* See *satni.*

salco$_{m}$ *n* young man, youth, adolescent. Nep. *taruṇ, javān, yuvāk.*

sal$_{a}$ [<Nep. *sāl*] *n* year.

salme$_{m}$ *n* young woman, girl of marriageable age, young woman in the full bloom of youth. Nep. *taruṇī, yuvatī, paṭṭhī.* See *tʌruni.*

sama$_{m}$ *n* god, deity, divinity, supernatural being. Nep. *deutā, devatā.*

Sampaŋ$_{a}$ [<Nep. *Sāmpāṅ*] *n* A the name of a particular kind of Rai group; B a person belonging to that group.

samsa$_{a}$ *n* talk, conversation. Nep. *bāt, kuro.* See *ma:la.*

-sano$_{a}$ *suffix* marker which indicates that it is not needed, essential or required to perform the action expressed by the modified verb. Nep. *pardaina.*

saŋki$_{a}$, **saŋkhi**$_{m}$ *n* excrement, faeces, shit, dung, stool. Nep. *disā, guhu, viṣṭhā, phohor.* **saŋki pacap**$_{a}$ *vt-2a* to stool. Nep. *hagnu.* **saŋkhi prit-**$_{m}$ *v(t)* to suffer from diarrhoea.

saŋmu$_{am}$ *n* dog. LSN I *saŋŋu*; II *śaŋmu*; III *saŋmu.* Nep. *kukur, śvān, kuttā.*

sarʌi$_{m}$ [<Nep. *sārāi*] *n* shift, movement. **sarʌi dumcam**$_{m}$ *vi-1c* to shift, move. Nep. *sarnu.* **sarʌi pacam**$_{m}$ *vt-2a* to shift, move, transport (something). Nep. *sārnu.*

saro$_m$ [<Nep. *sāhro*, *sāro*] I *adj* hard, difficult. II *quant* great, much. III *intens* very, much.

sas$_a$ [<Nep. *sās*] *n* breath.

satni$_a$ *adv* yesterday. LSN II *śatni*; III *saʔni*. Nep. *hijo*. See *saiso*, *saʔni*.

sathi$_a$ [<Nep. *sāthī*] *n* friend, comrade. See *kaʔu*.

saʔni$_m$ *adv* two days ago, the day before yesterday. See *satni*, *thaccum*.

saːlimo$_a$ *n* a particular kind of bush, *Colebrookia oppositifolia* (Shrestha 1979). Nep. *dhusre*.

saːlaŋ$_m$, **saːʔlɛŋ**$_a$ *n* song. LIT 5 *sālāṅ*. Nep. *gānā*, *gīt*. See *saːʔlɛŋ*. **saːlaŋ pacam**$_m$ *vt-2a* sing a song. Nep. *gāunu*. **saːʔlɛŋ pottɔp**$_a$ *v adj* singer. Nep. *gāune*.

saːsatni$_a$ [child language] *adv* two days ago, the day before yesterday. Nep. *asti*. See *nibbɔn*.

saːʔlɛŋ$_a$ see *saːlaŋ*.

≡sɛ$_m$ see *≡se*^{1}.

sɛccap$_a$, **sɛccam**$_m$ *vt-2d* <sɛtt- ~ sɛn-> to kill, put to death, slaughter, murder, execute, slay. LSN I *sɛn-*, *sɛk-*; II *śɛ-t-*; III *set-*. Nep. *mārnu*, *vadh garnu*.

sɛkcap$_a$ *v(t)* to pluck (e.g. fruit). Nep. *phal ādi ṭipnu*.

sɛle$_m$, **sɛt**$_a$ *n* dance. Nep. *nāc*. **sɛle pacam**$_m$, **sɛt pacap**$_a$ *vt-2a* to dance. Nep. *nācnu*. **sɛt pottɔp** *v adj* dancer. Nep. *nācne*.

sɛra$_m$, **sɛru**$_a$ [term of reference] *n* father-in-law. Nep. *sasuro*.

sɛri$_{am}$ *n* body louse. Nep. *jumro*. **sɛri sɛccam**$_m$ *vt* to kill lice. Nep. *jumrā mārnu*.

sɛrme$_{am}$ [term of reference] *n* mother-in-law. Nep. *sāsū*.

sɛru$_a$ see *sɛra*.

sɛt$_a$ see *sɛle*.

≡se$^1_{am}$, **≡sɛ**$_m$, **-sa**$_a$, **≡s**$_{am}$ *suffix* similaritive marker. Nep. *jasto*. The suffixes *-sɛ* and *-sa* are found in adverbs of direction, e.g. *asɛl*$_m$ ~ *asal*$_a$ 'here'. LIT 1 *=se* in *krākromsem* 'the one like a gourd'.

=se$^2_{am}$, **=s**$_{am}$ *suffix* exactly, precisely, e.g. *ulu=s* 'exactly there'. LIT 1 *=se* in *uibyālāsse* 'at exactly that time', 5 *=s* in *uses* 'in just that way'; 6 *=se* in *jindagīse* 'exactly my life'; 7 *=se* in *ḍyālnase* 'exactly in the village', 7 *=s* in *pausāsbāṅmā* 'I am doing'. Nep. *nai*.

seicap$_a$, **sei-**$_m$ *v(t)* to know a person (by sight), make acquaintance with someone. LIT 6 *sei-* in *seisī* 'learn'. Nep. *cinnu*, *paricaya garnu*.

seri$_{am}$ *n* husked and polished grain, especially rice. Nep. *cāmal.* See *labji.*

Setalcu$_{a}$ *n* the name of a particular Jero clan. LIT 7 *Setālco.*

sĩ$_{a}$ *n* blowing one's nose. **sĩ pacap**$_{a}$ *vt-2a* to blow one's nose.

sĩgan$_{a}$ [<Nep. *sĩgān*] *n* snot, nasal mucus. See *nusum-khli.*

-si$^{1}_{am}$ *suffix* marker of fruit.

-si$^{2}_{am}$ *suffix* marker of a tree or wood.

-si$^{3}_{am}$ *suffix* marker of a small object.

-si$^{4}_{am}$ *suffix* middle marker, which is only used in third person singular middle verb forms.

-si$^{5}_{am}$ *suffix* marker of the infinitive. LIT 2 4 *-sī* in 2 *ḍumsī* 'become' / 4 *sāmsīparcha* 'we must lose'; 6 *-sī* in *seisī* 'learn'; 7 *-sī* in *bāksī-parcha* 'we must be', 7 *-si* in *tyārsis parcha* 'we must meet'.

sicap$_{a}$, **sicam**$_{m}$ *vi-1a-i* <si-> to die, be dead, be in heaven. LSN I *si-ŋ-*; II *śi-ś-*; III *si-*. LIT 1 4 *si-* in 1 *sĩma* 'I will die' / 4 *siṅm* 'I will die'. Nep. *marnu, svarge hunu.*

sikʌi$_{a}$ [<Nep. *sikāi*] *n* study, learning. **sikʌi lacap**$_{a}$ *vi-1a-i* to learn, study. Nep. *siknu.* See *cei-.* **sikʌi pacap**$_{a}$ *vt-2a* to teach, instruct. Nep. *sikāunu.*

sika$_{m}$ *n* resin, gum. Nep. *khoṭo.*

sikar$_{am}$ [<Nep. *sikār, śikār*] *n* hunting, prey, meat. **sikar pacap**$_{a}$, **sikar pacam**$_{m}$ *vt-2a* to hunt game. Nep. *sikār khelnu.*

sikri$_{m}$ [<Nep. *sikrī*] *n* chain.

silʌuŋta$_{m}$ [<Nep. *silauṭo*] *n* a slab of stone on which spices are ground up.

simbʌl$_{m}$ [<Nep. *simal*] *n* the kapok tree *Bombax malabaricum* (Turner 1931), the silk-cotton tree (Singh 1971).

siŋ$_{a}$ *n* wood, firewood. LIT 2 *sĩ*; 6 *siṅ.* Nep. *kāṭh, dāurā.*

sir$_{a}$ [<Nep. *siur*] *n* the comb of a cock.

siris$_{am}$ [<Nep. *siris*] *n* any kind of leguminous tree with pinnate leaves (Turner 1931).

sittɔp$_{a}$ *v adj* characterised by being dead. Nep. *marne.*

siʔlim$_{a}$ *n* greens, green leafy vegetable, especially spinach. Nep. *sāg.* See *sag.*

siːcap$_{a}$ *v(t)* to thread (bind flowers). Nep. *ghā̃snu.*

sɔblɛm$_{am}$ *n* bread, loaf. Nep. *roṭī.*

sɔcam$_{m}$ *v(t)* to say, talk, relate, tell. Nep. *bhannu, kahanu, batāunu, bolnu.*

sɔddɔndo$_{a}$, **sɔʔdɔndo**$_{m}$ *n* wasp. Nep. *bārulo.* See *sɔʔdɔndo.*

sɔkane$_{a}$ *n* cough. Nep. *khokī, khokne rog.* **sɔkane pacap**$_{a}$ *vt-2a* to cough. Nep. *khoknu.*

sɔlcap$_{a}$, **sɔl-**$_{m}$ *v(t)* to take out (e.g. from a hole), bring out, remove. Nep. *jhiknu, tānnu.*

sɔllɔm$_{m}$, **sɔlɔm**$_{a}$, **sɔʔlɔm**$_{a}$ *n* the tree *Shorea robusta* (Panday 1982; HMG 1984). Nep. *sāl.*

sɔm$_{m}$, **swam**$_{a}$ *n* hair. Nep. *keś, kapāl.*

sɔmdu$_{a}$ *n* chanted sacred text of the oral tradition. Nep. *mundhum.*

sɔmdu-khadu$_{a}$ *n cmp* chanted sacred text of the oral tradition.

sɔndɔm$_{a}$ *n* voice. Nep. *sor.* See *sor.*

sɔŋku$_{a}$ *postp* without. Nep. *vinā, bāhek.*

sɔrga$_{a}$ [<Nep. *sargā*] *n* sky, heaven. Nep. *ākāś.*

sɔrcap$_{a}$, **sɔr-**$_{m}$ *v(i)* to dry, dry up, decrease, become less. Nep. *suknu.*

sɔrewa$_{am}$ *n* bee. Nep. *māhurī.*

sɔrki$_{am}$ *n* urine, piss. Nep. *pisāb.* **sɔrki pacap**$_{a}$, **sɔrki pacam**$_{m}$ *vt-2a* to urinate, piss. Nep. *pisāb garnu.*

sɔyam$_{a}$, **sɔʔyɔm**$_{m}$ *n* fly, housefly. Nep. *jhĩgo.*

sɔʔdɔndo$_{m}$ see *sɔddɔndo.*

sɔʔlɔm$_{a}$ see *sɔllɔm.*

sɔʔyɔm$_{m}$ see *sɔyam.*

-so$^{1}_{am}$ *suffix* marker of day.

-so$^{2}_{am}$ *suffix* marker of the irrealis.

solu$_{m}$, **sol**$_{am}$ *n* hail, hailstone. Nep. *asinā.* **solu yacam**$_{m}$ *vi-1a-ii* hail.

sor$_{am}$ [<Nep. *sor, svar*] *n* voice, sound. See *sɔndɔm.*

-su$^{1}_{m}$ *suffix* marker of the gerund of manner. See *-sa*^{1}.

-su$^{2}_{am}$ *suffix* marker of flesh or meat.

su-$^{3}_{m}$ *v* A to be hot, be spicy. B to itch. Nep. *piro hunu, cilāunu.*

su$^{4}_{am}$ *n* flesh, meat. LSN I *su*; II *śu*; III *šu*. Nep. *māsu.*

Subba$_{a}$ [<Nep. *subbā*; a hypocoristic term] *n* Limbu.

suga$_{a}$ [<Nep. *sugā*] *n* parrot.

suk-$_{m}$ *v(t)* A to prick, pierce. B to stab, point, hit with pointed object, prick. Nep. *ghopnu, hānnu, ghocnu.*

sukmul$_{a}$, **sukul**$_{m}$ *adv* three days from now, day after the day after tomorrow. Nep. *niparsi, nikoparsi, nikorsi.* See *nunusso.*

sumcam$_{m}$ *v(t)* to cover, cover up (e.g. to put a lid on a pot). Nep. *chopnu, ḍhāknu.*

sumlo$_{a}$ *n* large mortar made of stone or wood, used to husk paddy or beat rice. Nep. *okhal.*

sumpuru$_{a}$, **sumpur**$_{m}$ *n* umbilicus. Nep. *nāiṭo.*

suntʌla$_a$ [<Nep. *suntalā*] *n* tangerine, mandarin orange.
supari$_m$ [<Nep. *supārī*] *n* areca nut, betel nut.
Suriya-Bwaŋsi$_a$ [$^?$<Nep. *surya* 'sun' + *buwā̃so* 'wild dog'] *n cmp* the name of a subdivision of the Jero *Rɔke* clan.
surta$_m$ [<Nep. *surtā*] *n* worry, care. **surta pacam**$_m$ *vt-2a* to worry, care. Nep. *surtā garnu.*
suru$_m$ [<Nep. *śuru*] *n* beginning, commencement, inception.
swam$_a$ see *sɔm.*
syal$_m$ [<Nep. *syāl*] *n* jackal.

— t —

-**t**$_a$ see *-ta*^{1}.
tʌrʌ$_m$ [<Nep. *tara*] *conj* but. LIT 4 *tara.*
tʌrʌi$_a$ [<Nep. *tarāi*] *n* crossing. **tʌrʌi lacap**$_a$ *vi-1a-i* to cross. Nep. *tarnu.*
tʌruni$_a$ [<Nep. *taruṇī*] *n* young woman, girl of marriageable age, young woman in the full bloom of youth. See *salme.*
tʌtʌi$_a$ [<Nep. *tatāi*] *n* heating. **tʌtʌi pacap**$_a$ *vt-2a* to heat. Nep. *tatāunu.*
tʌusɛl$_a$, **tosɛl**$_m$ *n* moon, moonshine. LSN I *ṭosyal*; III *toːsɛl.* Nep. *jūn.*
tʌya$_a$ *adv* yet, still. Nep. *ajhai.* See *tɛŋu.*
-ta^1_a, **-t**$_a$, **-to**^1_m *bound morph* marker which indicates a location at a higher elevation than the point of reference.
ta-^2_m *v* to kick (with the sole of foot), hit with stick. Nep. *godnu, lāttīle hānnu.*
taccap$_a$ *vt-2d* <tatt- ~tan-> A to stop, quit, give up. B [in Āmboṭe] terminative auxiliary, which is used with an infinitive. Nep. *choḍnu.* See *plɛcam.*
takcap$_a$ *v(t)* to place, set up, appoint. Nep. *thāpnu.*
talim$_m$ [<Nep. *tālim*] *n* training, instruction.
talu$_a$ [<Nep. *tālu*] *n* the top of the head.
ta[k]-$_m$ *v* to take. LSN II *tak-.* Nep. *linu.*
tara$_{am}$ [<Nep. *tārā*] *n* star.
tato$_a$ [<Nep. *tāto*] *adj* hot (of touch), hot-tempered, impetuous.
tɛccap$_a$ *v(t)* to cut, kill (time). Nep. *kāṭnu.*
tɛm$_a$, **tɔm**$_m$ *n* heart, mind. LIT 1 *ṭyām.* Nep. *man, dil, hr̥daya.*

tɛmbar$_{am}$ *adv* today. LSN I *tɛmbara*; II *tɛmbar*; III *tɛmbar*. LIT 5 *tyāmbār*. Nep. *āja*. **tɛmbar=me kam**$_{m}$ *n* today's work, today's chores. Nep. *ājako kām*.

tɛm-cinci$_{a}$, **tɔm-cinci**$_{m}$ [Jero *tɛm* ~ *tɔm* 'heart' + *cinci* 'seed, grain'] *n cmp* heart. LSN II *tyamcinci*; III *tɛmcinci*. LIT 6 *tyamcincī*. Nep. *hr̥daya, muṭu*.

tɛncap$_{a}$ *v(t)* to make somebody drink something. Nep. *pilāunu, pilāpila garnu*. See *teicap*.

tɛŋ$_{am}$ see *tɛŋu*.

tɛŋthoce$_{a}$ *adv* this year.

tɛŋu$_{a}$, **tɛŋ**$_{am}$ *adv* now, from now on. Nep. *aba*. LIT 2 *tyā̃pip* 'nowadays'.

tɛrcap$_{a}$, **tɛrcam**$_{m}$ I *vt-2g* <tɛrt- ~ tɛr-> A to get, receive. B to meet (by catching up). II *vm-1c* <tɛr-> A to be received. B to be met (by catching up). LIT 7 *tyār-* in *tyārsis parcha* 'we must meet'. Nep. *pāunu, prāpta garnu*.

teicam$_{a}$ *v(t)* to make somebody drink something. Nep. *pilāunu, pilāpila garnu*. See *tɛncap*.

tep$_{a}$, **teʔme**$_{am}$ *n* daughter, girl. Nep. *chorī*.

teʔu$_{am}$ *n* son, boy. LIT 5 *ṭeu*. Nep. *choro*.

-ti$_{am}$ *suffix* marker of the connective gerund. LIT 5 *-ti* in *pitigvākce* 'the one coming suddenly', 5 *-ṭi* in *plāṭigvākṭvāk*.

ticcam$_{m}$ *v(t)* to comb, shuffle (hair). Nep. *kornu, keś bāṭnu*.

ticu$_{am}$, **tit**$_{am}$ *number* nominal plural number marker. LIT 1 *ticu*; 7 *ticu* in *kāvāticu* 'friends and the like'.

tikhra$_{a}$ [<Nep. *tighro*] *n* thigh.

tilɛm$_{am}$ [$^{?}$<Nep. *tel*] *n* oil.

tin$_{am}$ [<Nep. *tīn*] *num* three.

tit$_{am}$ see *ticu*.

tɔ-$^{1}_{am}$ *bound morph* demonstrative which indicates a position at a higher elevation which is relatively far away from the point of reference or from the speaker and hearer.

-tɔ$^{2}_{a}$, **-ttɔ**$_{a}$, **-to**$_{m}$, **-tto**$_{m}$ *suffix* marker of the attributive verbal adjective. LIT 5 *-ṭvā* in *bākṭvāk* 'being'. Nep. *-ne*.

tɔi$_{am}$ *dem pron* that (up). LSN I *ṭoi̯*. Nep. *tyo māthi*.

tɔicu$_{am}$ *dem pron* that which is higher than *tɔi*$_{am}$, another thing that is relatively far away and higher than the point of reference. Nep. *tyo māthi*.

tɔk-$_{m}$ *v* to swallow, eat. Nep. *nilnu, khānu*.

tɔksi$_{am}$ *n* A mango. B cucumber. Nep. *ā̃p, kā̃kro.*

tɔm$_{m}$ see *tɛm.*

tɔm-cinci$_{m}$ see *tɛm-cinci.*

tɔmala$_{m}$, **tɔmal**$_{am}$ I *adv* above, up, towards the upper side. II *postp* towards the upper side of, above, e.g. *phutur tɔmal*$_{a}$ 'above the head'. Nep. *māthi, māstira, ũbho.*

tɔpcap$_{a}$, **tɔpcam**$_{m}$ *v(t)* A to strike. B to play an instrument. Nep. *bajāunu, vādan vā tāḍan garnu.*

tɔsal$_{a}$, **tɔsɛl**$_{m}$ *dem adv* up there (of direction). Nep. *tyatā-māthitira.*

tɔse=p$_{a}$ *dem adj & adv* (something) like that (at a higher elevation than the point of reference), thus, so. Nep. *tyasto māthi.* **tɔse=p =na=se=p**$_{a}$ *dem adj & adv* (something) like that (at a higher elevation than the point of reference).

tɔta$_{a}$, **tɔt**$_{a}$, **tɔto**$_{m}$ *dem adv* up there (of place). Nep. *tyahā̃ māthi.* **tɔta=ku**$_{a}$, **tɔta=k**$_{a}$, **tɔta=na=ku**$_{a}$, **tɔta=na=k**$_{a}$ [with the source marker or with the locative and source compound marker] *dem adv* from up there (of place). Nep. *tyahā̃ māthi dekhi.*

-to$^{1}_{m}$ see *-ta*^{1}.

-to$^{2}_{m}$ see *-tɔ*^{2}.

Tolupe$_{a}$ *n* the name of a particular Jero clan.

Topile$_{a}$ *n* the name of a particular Jero clan.

tosɛl$_{m}$ see *tʌusɛl.*

toʔla$_{a}$ I *adv* above, up. II *postp* on top of, above, e.g. *kul toʔla* 'on to of the house'. Nep. *māthi.*

-ttɔ$_{a}$, **-tto**$_{m}$ see *-tɔ*^{2}.

tublo$_{a}$ *n* request, question, interrogation. Nep. *praśna.* **tublo pacap**$_{a}$ *vt-2a* to ask, inquire, make a request. Nep. *sodhnu.* See *cel.*

tumcap$^{1}_{a}$, **tumcam**$_{m}$ *vm-1b* <tum-> A to beat oneself. B to be or get beaten. Nep. *kuṭinu.* **tum pocap**$_{a}$ *vm-1a* to beat each other. Nep. *kuṭākuṭ garnu.*

tumcap$^{2}_{a}$ *v(t)* to finish, complete. Nep. *siddhyāunu, saknu.*

tuŋ$_{a}$ *n* manner of squatting. Nep. *ṭukrukka.* **tuŋ niːcap**$_{a}$ *vm-1a* to squat. Nep. *ṭukrukka basnu*

tupcap$_{a}$, **tupcam**$_{a}$ *vt-2c* <tupt- ~ tum-> to beat, strike, hit, molest, thrash. Nep. *piṭnu, kuṭnu.*

tuːcap$_{a}$, **tuːcam**$_{m}$ *vt-2b* <tuːt- ~ tuː-> to drink, smoke. LSN I *ṭut, tutni, tupũ*; II *tu*^{w}*-*; III *tụ̂(?)-*. Nep. *piunu, curoṭ, tamākhu adi khānu.*

— th —

thʌkʌi$_{a}$ [<Nep. *thakāi*] *n* weariness, fatigue. **thʌkʌi lacap**$_{a}$ *vi-1a-i* to become tired, be exhausted. Nep. *thakinu*.

thʌr$_{m}$ [<Nep. *thar*] *n* caste, sub-caste, clan, tribe.

thaccum$_{m}$ *adv* two days ago, the day before yesterday. Nep. *asti*, *hijo-ko hijo*. See *saʔni*.

thalʌi$_{am}$ [<Nep. *thalāi*] *n* beginning, start. **thalʌi pacap**$_{a}$, **thalʌi pa-cam**$_{m}$ *vt-2a* A to begin, start. B [in Āmboṭe] ingressive auxiliary, which is used with an infinitive. Nep. *thālnu*. See *jɛkcam*.

thalu$_{am}$, **thal**$_{am}$ *ind* where, somewhere (of place). LSN I *t̪*^{h}*alo*; II *thalu*; III *t̪*^{h}*alu*. LIT 1 4 *thālu* in 4 *thālulvānne* 'where will you^{s} go to?'; 7 *thālu* in *thālu-thālu* 'where and where'. Nep. *kahā̃*. **thalu=na=ku**$_{a}$, **thalu=na=k**$_{a}$, **thalu=ŋ**$_{m}$ *ind* from where. Nep. *kahā̃dekhi*, *kahā̃bā-ṭa*.

thamalu$_{a}$, **thamal**$_{am}$ *ind* whereto, whither. Nep. *katā*, *katātira*.

thamcap$_{a}$ *v(t)* to sell, put up for sale, dispose. Nep. *bikrī garnu*.

thapu$_{a}$ *n* maternal uncle. Nep. *kākā*.

thaːcap$_{a}$, **thaːcam**$_{m}$ *vm-1a* <thaː-> A to warm oneself (near a fire), take the sunlight or the heat of the fire in the body. B to be or get warm-ed up (near a fire). Nep. *tāpnu*.

thaːthaccum$_{m}$ *adv* three days ago, the day before the day before yes-terday. Nep. *tīn din aghi*, *asti-asti*.

thɛkcap$_{a}$, **ṯhɛkcam**$_{m}$ *v(t)* to shut, lock, close, cover, shut off (e.g. a door). Nep. *thunnu*, *banda garnu*. See *thunʌi*.

thiyo$_{am}$ [<Nep. *thiyo*] *part* marker of past time.

thɔcap^{1}$_{a}$, **thɔ-**$_{m}$ *v(t)* to hear, smell, absorb a noise, sound or smell. LSN I *t̪*^{h}*ɔ-*; II *t*^{h}*o*^{w}*-*; III *t*^{h}*ɔ̞-*. Nep. *sunnu*, *dhvani grahaṇ garnu*.

thɔcap^{2}$_{a}$ *vt-1* <thɔ-> to ask for, beg, request, solicit. Nep. *māgnu*. See *phɔicam*.

thɔmbar-thoni$_{a}$ [Jero *thoni* 'one year ago'] *adv cmp* two years ago, the year before last. Nep. *parār*.

-thoce$_{am}$, **-thot**$_{a}$, **tho-**$_{a}$ *bound morph* year. Nep. *sāl*.

thoni$_{a}$ *adv* one year ago, last year. Nep. *pohar*, *pohor*.

thok$_{m}$ [<Nep. *thok*] *n* thing, affair, matter, commodity.

-thot$_{a}$ see *-thoce*.

thu$_{a}$ [<Nep. *thuk*] *n* spittle, spitting. **thu pacap**$_{a}$ *vt-2a* to spit. Nep. *thuknu*.

thukcap$_{a}$ *v(t)* to spit at someone. Nep. *thuknu*, *thukka garnu*.

-thum$_{a}$ *suffix* marker of the negative state gerund. LIT 4 *-thu* in *āhipthu* 'in order to not see'.

thunʌi$_{a}$ [<Nep. *thunāi*] *n* prevention, restraint. **thunʌi pacap**$_{a}$ *vt-2a* to prevent, restrain, hinder (e.g. water). Nep. *thunnu*. See *thɛkcap*.

thupro$_{a}$ [<Nep. *thupro*] *quant* a heap of, a pile of, a lot of. **thuprʌi**$_{a}$ [<Nep. *thuprai*] *quant emph* a large heap of, a large pile of.

— ʈ —

ʈaɖo$_{m}$ [<Nep. *ṭāḍho*] *adv* far. LIT 5 *ṭāḍhā*.

ʈaŋgai$_{m}$ [<Nep. *ṭā̃gāi*] *n* hanging. **ʈaŋgai pacam**$_{m}$ *vt-2a* to hang, hang up, suspend. Nep. *ṭā̃gnu*.

ʈãsʌi$_{am}$ [<Nep. *ṭā̃sāi*] *n* sticking. **ʈãsʌi lacam**$_{m}$ *vi-1a-i* to stick, attach, glue. Nep. *ṭā̃sinu*. **ʈãsʌi pacap**$_{a}$, **ʈãsʌi pacam**$_{m}$ *vt-2a* to stick, attach, glue. Nep. *ṭā̃snu*. See *kɛpcap*.

ʈupi$_{m}$ [<Nep. *ṭupī*] *n* tail, pigtail.

— ʈh —

ʈhaũ$_{am}$ [<Nep. *ṭhāũ*] *n* place.

ʈhɛkcam$_{m}$ see *thɛkcap*.

— u —

u-$^{1}_{am}$ *bound morph* demonstrative which indicates a position relatively far away from the point of reference or near the hearer.

-u$^{2}_{am}$ see *-ŋu*^{1}.

ubrʌi$_{a}$ [<Nep. *ubrāi*] *n* surplus. **ubrʌi lacap**$_{a}$ *vi-1a-i* to be left over (said of food). Nep. *ubranu*.

ubhinɖo$_{m}$ [<Nep. *ubhiṇḍo*] *adj* standing on one's head.

uɖʌi$_{am}$ [<Nep. *uḍāi*] *n* flight. **uɖʌi lacam**$_{a}$ *vi-1a-i*, **uɖʌi dumcam**$_{m}$ *vi-1c* to fly. Nep. *uḍnu*. **uɖʌi pacam**$_{m}$ *vt-2a* to lift up, sweep away. Nep. *uḍāunu*.

uɖus$_{m}$ [<Nep. *uḍus*] *n* bedbug, *Cimex lectularius*.

ui$_{a}$ see *uya*.

ulṭo$_{m}$ [<Nep. *ulṭo*] *adj* opposite, reversed, turned inside out, upside down, inside out.

ulu$_{am}$, **ul**$_{a}$ *dem adv* there (near the hearer). LIT 1 2 *ulu* in *uluṅ* 'from there'. Nep. *tyahā̃*. **ul=na=ku**$_{a}$, **ul=na=k**$_{a}$, **ulu=k**$_{a}$ I *dem adv* from there. II *conj* and, and than. LIT 1 2 *uluṅ* 'from there'. Nep. *tyahā̃-dekhi, ani.*

umlʌi$_{a}$ [Nep. *umlāi*] *n* boil, state of bubbling. **umlʌi pacap**$_{a}$ *vt-2a* to boil, simmer, bubble up. Nep. *umālnu*. See *lɔkcap.*

uniu$_{m}$ [<Nep. *uniũ*] *n* fern.

-uŋ$^{1}_{m}$ see *-ŋ*^{3}.

-uŋ$^{2}_{m}$ see *-ŋu*^{1}.

uŋgu$_{am}$, **uŋ**$_{am}$ *pers* I, we. LSN I *uŋgu*; II *uŋgu*; III *ungu*. LIT 1 *uṅgu*; 7 *uṅ*. Nep. *ma, hāmī*. **uŋ nimpha**$_{am}$ *pers* we^{d}. **uŋ ticu**$_{am}$ *pers* we^{p}. LIT 7 *uṅticu.*

uphrʌi$_{a}$ [<Nep. *uphrāi*] *n* jump, leap. **uphrʌi lacam**$_{a}$ *vi-1a-i* to jump up, jump over, leap. Nep. *uphranu.*

usal$_{a}$ *dem adv* there (of direction, towards the hearer). Nep. *tyatātira.*

use$_{m}$, **us**$_{am}$ *dem adv* in that way, like that, thus, so. LIT 1 *us*, 1 *use*, 5 *use* in *uses* 'in just that way'. Nep. *tyaso*. **use=p**$_{a}$, **use=m**$_{m}$ *dem adj & adv* (something) like that (near the hearer), thus, so. Nep. *tyasto.* **use=p=na=se=p**$_{a}$ *dem adj & adv* (something) like that (near the hearer).

usu$_{m}$, **yusu**$_{a}$ *n* blood. LSN I *usu*; II *yuśu*; III *yušu*. LIT 2 *usūṃ*, 5 *usu*. Nep. *ragat.*

uya$_{a}$, **ui**$_{a}$ *dem pron* that (near the hearer). LSN II *u̯i*. LIT 1 *ui* in *uibyā-lāsse* 'at exactly that time', 4 *uī*; 7 *uī*. **uya=ku**$_{a}$ [With the source marker] *dem pron* because of that.

— w —

wa$_{am}$ *n* clothes, cloth. LSN I *wa*; II *wa*; III *wa*. Nep. *lugā, kapaḍā.*

waccɛm$_{a}$ *n* needle. LSN I *watcɛm*. Nep. *siyo*. See *jyambale.*

wacu$_{m}$ *n* husband. LSN I *wa̤tcu*; II *wa̤ttɛp*; III *wa̭ttɛʔm*. Nep. *logne, poi, pati.*

wakcap$^{1}_{a}$ *v* to plough. Nep. *jotnu, halo calāunu*. See *khɔrcap.*

wakcap$^{2}_{a}$ *vi-2* <wak- ~ wa:-> to scream, shriek, screech, shout, yell, howl, call with a loud voice. Nep. *ciccyāunu, ṭhūlo svarle karāu-nu*. See *wa:cap.*

wakewa$_{m}$ *n* lizard. Nep. *chepāro.*

walcap$_{a}$, **walcam**$_{m}$ *vi-1d* <wal-> to walk, go, move, pace, travel on foot, make a journey. LSN I *wal-*; II *wal-* 'follow'; III *wal-*. LIT 3 4 5 *vālcām.* Nep. *hīḍnu, prasthān garnu.* **wal paccam**$_{m}$ *vt-2d* to make walk, make go, make move, conduct, steer. Nep. *hīḍālnu.*

wam$_{am}$ *n* bear. Nep. *bhālu.*

warlʌi$_{a}$ [<Nep. *orlāi*] *n* descend, climb down. LIT 3 *varlai.* **warlʌi lacap**$_{a}$ *vi-1a-i* to descend, climb down, get off. LIT 3 *varlaidumcām.* Nep. *orlanu.* **warlʌi pacap**$_{a}$ *vt-2a* to cause to descend, bring down. Nep. *orālnu.*

warsi$_{m}$ see *hwarsi.*

watɛwa$_{m}$, **wattɛp**$_{a}$ *n* boy. Nep. *choro.*

waʔlo$_{m}$ *n* scrotum.

waʔɔmjimo$_{m}$ *adj* yellow. Nep. *pahẽlpur, pahẽlāmme, pītmaya.* See *waʔɔmjɔkto, pʌhẽlo.*

waʔɔmjɔkto$_{m}$ *adj* yellow. Nep. *pahẽlpur, pahẽlāmme, pītmaya.* See *waʔɔmjimo, pʌhẽlo.*

waːcap$_{a}$ *v(i)* to scream, shriek, screech, shout, yell, howl, call with a loud voice. Nep. *ciccyāunu, ṭhūlo svarle karāunu.* See *wakcap*^{2}.

— y —

=ya^{1}$_{am}$, **=i**$_{am}$ *suffix* also, too, even. Nep. *pani.* LIT 1 *=e* in *āmmee* 'that of mine too', 5 *=ī.*

-ya^{2}$_{a}$, **-yo**$_{m}$, **-i**$_{am}$ *bound morph* marker which indicates a location at a lower elevation than the point of reference.

-ya^{3}$_{a}$, **-i**$_{am}$ *suffix* nominalising element in demonstrative pronouns. LIT 1 *-i*, 2 4 5 *-ī.*

yacap^{1}$_{a}$, **yacam**$_{m}$ *vi-1a-ii* <ya-> to come down. Nep. *māthibāṭa tala āunu.*

yacap^{2}$_{a}$ *v(i)* to be sharp. Nep. *lāgnu, tīkho dhār hunu.*

yak-$_{m}$ *v(t)* to cut down, fell, chop down, knock over, tip over. Nep. *kunai vastulāī laḍāunu vā ḍhalāunu.*

yaksi$_{am}$ *n* salt. LSN I *yɔksɛ*; II *yaksi*; III *yaksi.* Nep. *nūn, nimak, lavaṇ.* **yaksi lucap**$_{a}$, **yaksi lucam**$_{m}$ *vi* to be salty. Nep. *nunilo hunu.*

yamcap$_{a}$ *v(i)* to be rotten, be spoilt. Nep. *kuhinu.*

yɔ-$_{\text{am}}$ *bound morph* demonstrative which indicates a position which is relatively far away from the point of reference or from the speaker and hearer and at a lower elevation.

yɔi$^{1}_{\text{am}}$ see *yɔya*^{1}.

yɔi$^{2}_{\text{am}}$ see *yɔya*^{2}.

yɔicu$_{\text{m}}$ *dem pron* that which is lower than *yɔi*$_{\text{am}}$, another thing that is relatively far away and lower than the point of reference. Nep. *tyo tala.*

yɔkcu$_{\text{am}}$ *n* child, infant, any human from birth until eighteen years of age. LSN I *yokcuṯicu*; II *yɔkcuti*; III *yokticu* (plural forms). Nep. *nānī, bacco.*

yɔkko$_{\text{m}}$ *adj* small, little, inferior. Nep. *sānu.*

yɔm$_{\text{m}}$ *adv* completely, without a trace. Nep. *birsihālne vā harāihālne kisimsita.* **yɔm ma[p]-**$_{\text{m}}$ *v* to forget completely. Nep. *birsihālnu.*

yɔmala$_{\text{m}}$, **yɔmal**$_{\text{am}}$ I *adv* below, down, towards the lower side. II *postp* towards the lower side of, below, e.g. *phutur yɔmal*$_{\text{a}}$ 'below the head'. Nep. *māthi, māstira, ũbho.*

yɔmcap$_{\text{a}}$, **yɔmcam**$_{\text{m}}$ *vi-1c* <yɔm-> to stand, stand up. Nep. *ubhinu, khaḍā hunu.*

yɔsɛl$_{\text{m}}$ *dem adv* down there (of direction). Nep. *tyatā talatira.*

yɔse=p$_{\text{a}}$ *dem adj & adv* (something) like that (at a lower elevation than the point of reference), thus, so. Nep. *tyasto tala.* **yɔse=p=na=se=p**$_{\text{a}}$ *dem adj & adv* (something) like that (at a lower elevation than the point of reference). **yɔse=p=se kul**$_{\text{a}}$ *n* a house like that.

yɔya$^{1}_{\text{a}}$, **yɔyo**$_{\text{m}}$, **yɔi**$_{\text{am}}$ *dem adv* down there (of place). Nep. *tyahā̃ tala.* **yɔya=ku**$_{\text{a}}$, **yɔya=k**$_{\text{a}}$ [With the source marker] *dem adv* from down there (of place). Nep. *tyahā̃ tala dekhi.*

yɔya$^{2}_{\text{a}}$, **yɔi**$_{\text{am}}$ *dem pron* that (down). Nep. *u tala.*

yɔyo$_{\text{m}}$ see *yɔya*^{1}.

-yo$_{\text{m}}$ see *-ya*$^{2}_{\text{a}}$.

yocam$_{\text{m}}$ *v(t)* to swing, sway from side to side, shake, move, agitate. Nep. *jhalāunu, hallāunu.*

yoccam$_{\text{m}}$, **yuccap**$_{\text{a}}$ *v(t)* to throw overhand, toss overhand, throw away, cast, fling. Nep. *phyā̃knu, phālnu, milkāunu.*

yunti$_{\text{am}}$ *n* lip. Nep. *oṭh.*

yupcap$_{\text{a}}$ *v(t)* to suck, hold something in the mouth and make movements with the tongue and lips as if drawing liquid out of it. Nep. *cusnu.*

yusu$_{a}$ see *usu*.
yuːcap$_{a}$ *v(t)* to keep (animals or other dependants), support, maintain. Nep. *pālnu*.

— **ʔ** —

-ʔ$^{1}_{m}$ *suffix* third person dual agent simplex agreement morpheme.
-ʔ$^{2}_{a}$, **-ʔim**$_{m}$, **-ʔmi**$_{a}$ see *-mi*^{1}.
-ʔ$^{3}_{am}$, **-ʔu**$_{am}$ see *-ŋu*^{1}.
-ʔu$_{am}$ *suffix* masculine gender marker. LIT 5 *-u* in *ṭeu*. See *-pa*^{1}, *-pu*^{1}.

APPENDIX TWO

ENGLISH-JERO LEXICON

— a —

abandon *plɛcam*$_{m}$.
ablative marker *=ŋo*$^{2}_{m}$, *≡ŋ*$_{m}$.
able in **be able** *capcam*$_{m}$; *phaccap*$_{a}$.
above *gattu*$_{a}$, *gatthu*$_{m}$; *tɔmala*$_{m}$, *tɔmal*$_{am}$; *toʔla*$_{a}$.
absorb (a sound or smell) *thɔcap*$^{1}_{a}$, *thɔ-*$_{m}$.
abuse *burcap*$_{a}$.
abyss *gʌira*$_{m}$.
accord in **of one's own accord** *daŋma*$_{a}$.
according to *ʌnusar*$_{a}$.
acquaintance in **make acquaintance with someone** *seicap*$_{a}$, *sei-*$_{m}$.
acquire *placap*$_{a}$.
active in **marker of the general active verbal adjective** *-ce*$_{am}$. **marker of the particular active verbal adjective** *-cu*$^{3}_{am}$.
adolescent *salco*$_{m}$.
affair *thok*$_{m}$.
affirmative marker *-me*$^{2}_{am}$, *-ma*$_{am}$, *-m*$_{am}$, *-ne*$_{am}$.
afraid in **be afraid** *nim lucam*$_{m}$; *ni:cap*$^{2}_{a}$.
after *nʌuţhaŋ*$_{am}$.
afternoon *dɛre*$_{a}$.
afterwards *nʌuţhaŋ*$_{am}$.
again *pheri*$_{am}$.
aged A (male) *buḑa*$_{a}$. B (female) *buḑi*$_{a}$.
agitate *dukcam*$_{m}$; *yocam*$_{m}$.
agree *milʌi lacap*$_{a}$, *milʌi dumcam*$_{m}$.
agreeable *broto*$_{m}$, *brottɔp*$_{a}$. **be agreeable** *brocap*$_{a}$.
agreement *milʌi*$_{am}$.
air *hawa*$_{a}$.
alive in **be alive** *blecap*$_{a}$, *ble-*$_{m}$.

all A *sʌb*$_{a}$, *sʌp*$_{m}$. B (more emphatic) *sʌbʌi*$_{a}$, *sʌpʌi*$_{m}$. C (even more emphatic) *sʌppʌi*$_{m}$. **not be all right** *anucap*$_{a}$, *anucam*$_{m}$.
allot *bãḍʌi pacap*$_{a}$.
allotment *bãḍʌi*$_{a}$; *dɔyo*$_{m}$, *do*$_{a}$.
alone *khamma*$_{a}$, *kha:ma*$_{m}$.
already *na*$^{4}_{am}$.
also *=ya*$^{1}_{am}$, *=i*$_{am}$.
alter *pherʌi pacam*$_{m}$.
amount in **an amount of** *khɔlse*$_{a}$.
ancestor *pitrʌ*$_{a}$; *purkha*$_{a}$.
and (and than) *ul=na=ku*$_{a}$, *ul=na=k*$_{a}$, *ulu=k*$_{a}$.
anger *ris*$_{m}$.
angle *kuna*$_{a}$.
angry in **make angry** *ris phukcam*$_{m}$.
animal *nake*$_{a}$.
ant A (in general) *rapcimtep*$_{a}$. B (species of red ant) *bɛŋge*$_{a}$; *rwate*$_{a}$. C (a white or brown ant-like insect) *krɛktum*$_{m}$, *krɛktup*$_{a}$.
anus *plɔŋkhi*$_{m}$.
appear *himcap*$_{a}$; *jocam*$_{m}$.
application *binti*$_{m}$.
appoint *daccam*; *takcap*$_{a}$.
areca nut *supari*$_{m}$.
arise *bukcap*$_{a}$, *bukcam*$_{m}$.
arm A (in general, including the hand) *la*$^{2}_{am}$. B (upper arm, including the shoulder) *pakhra*$_{a}$.
armful *ʌŋgalo*$_{m}$.
armpit *kakhi*$_{am}$.
aroma *ŋaba*$_{m}$, *ŋab*$_{am}$.
arouse *rakcap*$_{a}$, *rakcam*$_{m}$; *ra:cap*$_{a}$.
arrange and give food *mɛccap*$_{a}$, *mɛccam*$_{m}$.
arrive A (from no fixed direction) *blakcap*$_{a}$, *blak-*$_{m}$; *blaccap*$_{a}$, *bla[k]-*$_{m}$. B (by going) *blandicap*$_{a}$. C (go up and arrive somewhere) *blaŋkha-*$_{m}$. **characterised by arriving** *blattɔp*$_{a}$.
arrow *baḍ*$_{a}$; *blu*$_{am}$. **arrow and bow** *blu-lekhe*$_{m}$.
article *gɔṭa*$_{a}$, *gɔṭ*$_{a}$.
as for *bhʌne*$_{a}$.
ascend *ca:cap*$_{a}$, *ca:-*$_{m}$.
ash *phucul*$_{m}$.
ashes A (black) *pusmi*$_{a}$. B (white) *pɔkhal*$_{a}$. C (wet) *phucul*$_{m}$.

aside *pʌrʌ*$_{a}$. **aside from** *bahek*$_{a}$.
ask *cel pacam*$_{m}$; *tublo pacap*$_{a}$. **ask for** *phɔicam*$_{m}$; *thɔcap*$^{2}_{a}$.
asleep in **be asleep** *mɛlcap*$_{a}$, *mɛlcam*$_{m}$. **fall asleep** *glecap*$_{a}$, *glecam*$_{m}$; *mɛlcap*$_{a}$, *mɛlcam*$_{m}$.
assertive marker *ni*$^{5}_{am}$.
assistant priest *ŋa:bu*$_{a}$.
attach *kɛpcap*$_{a}$, *kɛpcam*$_{m}$; *ţãsʌi lacam*$_{m}$; *ţãsʌi pacap*$_{a}$, *ţãsʌi pacam*$_{m}$.
attributive in **marker of the attributive verbal adjective** *-tɔ*$^{2}_{a}$, *-ttɔ*$_{a}$, *-to*$_{m}$, *-tto*$_{m}$.
aunt A (paternal) *ma:mu*$_{am}$. B (mother's brother's wife) *mʌiju*$_{a}$.
await *locam*$_{m}$.
awake *bukcap*$_{a}$, *bukcam*$_{m}$; *phukcam*$_{m}$.
aware in **become aware of** *cɛkcam*$_{m}$, *cikcam*$_{a}$.
awareness in **marker of recent awareness** *rʌi*$_{am}$, *rʌicha*$_{a}$.
axe *khu*$_{am}$.
Azedarachta indica (plant) *bʌkʌino*$_{m}$.

— b —

baby *nunu*$_{m}$.
back I n A (of the head) *lɛpsu*$_{a}$. B (of the neck) *ghuccuk*$_{a}$. II adv *nʌuthal*$_{a}$, *nʌuţhal*$_{m}$. **back tooth** *baŋra*$_{am}$.
bag *jhola*$_{am}$.
bamboo *pha:pu*$_{am}$. **bamboo bow** A (with a bent handle) *dhʌnu*$_{a}$. B (with a straight handle) *lekhe*$_{m}$.
banana *jɔmbal*$_{am}$.
bark^{1} *hu:cap*$_{a}$, *hu:-*$_{m}$. **barking deer** (*Muntiacus muntjak*) *gɛpsu*$_{m}$, *mirgʌ*$_{a}$.
bark^{2} *kɔkte*$_{am}$.
barley *jʌu*$_{am}$.
base *pum*$^{1}_{am}$.
Bassia butyracea (tree) *hipsu*$_{a}$, *hispu*$_{m}$.
bat (species) *pɔkti*$_{am}$.
bathe *mɛrcap*$_{a}$, *mɛrcam*$_{m}$.
Bauhinia vahilii (tree) *bhorla*$_{am}$.
Bauhinia variegata (tree) *jilli*$_{a}$, *jitli*$_{m}$.

be A (sit) *bakcap*$_{a}$, *bakcam*$_{m}$. B (become) *dumcap*$_{a}$, *dumcam*$_{m}$; *lacap*$_{a}$, *lacam*$_{m}$. C (be like) *jocam*$_{m}$. D (auxiliary of identification and categorisation) *nɔcap*$_{a}$, *nɔcam*$_{m}$.

bear *wam*$_{am}$.

beard *dari*$_{a}$.

beat A (somebody) *tupcap*$_{a}$, *tupcam*$_{a}$. B (each other) *tum pocap*$_{a}$. C (oneself) *tumcap*$^{1}_{a}$, *tumcam*$_{m}$. be **beaten** *tumcap*$^{1}_{a}$, *tumcam*$_{m}$.

beautiful *broto*$_{m}$, *brottɔp*$_{a}$. be **beautiful** *brocap*$_{a}$.

because A *haŋ-bhʌne*$_{a}$. B (because of that) *uya=ku*$_{a}$.

become *dumcap*$_{a}$, *dumcam*$_{m}$; *lacap*$_{a}$, *lacam*$_{m}$.

bed A (in general) *lɛtam*$_{am}$. B (made of wood) *kaṭh*$_{a}$. put to **bed** *khlɔmcap*$_{a}$, *khlɔm-*$_{m}$.

bedbug [*Cimex lectularius*] *uḍus*$_{m}$.

bedding *lɛtam*$_{am}$.

bee *sɔrewa*$_{am}$.

beer A (home-brewed beer made from fermented rice, maize or barley) *nasi*$_{m}$, *nassi*$_{a}$, *ŋasi*$_{m}$. B (made from finger millet, *Eleusine coracana*) *caksi*$_{a}$.

before A *lapphu*$_{am}$; *lapthɔl*$_{a}$. B (much before) *na ke*$_{a}$, *na=se*$_{am}$.

beg *phɔicam*$_{m}$; *thɔcap*$^{2}_{a}$.

beget *jʌnmʌi pacap*$_{a}$, *jʌnmʌi pacam*$_{m}$.

beggar *phɔice mucu*.

begin *jɛkcam*$_{m}$; *thalʌi pacap*$_{a}$, *thalʌi pacam*$_{m}$.

beginning *suru*$_{m}$; *thalʌi*$_{am}$.

behind *nʌuthal*$_{a}$, *nʌuṭhal*$_{m}$.

belly *bhũḍi*$_{a}$; *mɔl*$_{am}$.

below *hɛttu*$_{a}$, *hɛtthu*$_{m}$; *yɔmala*$_{m}$, *yɔmal*$_{am}$.

bend down *kum bɔm-*$_{m}$.

beneath *hɛttu*$_{a}$, *hɛtthu*$_{m}$.

bent arm *ʌŋgalo*$_{m}$.

beside *nɔmala*$_{m}$, *nɔmal*$_{a}$; *pum*$^{2}_{a}$.

betel nut *supari*$_{m}$.

beyond *nɔmala*$_{m}$, *nɔmal*$_{a}$; *pʌrʌ*$_{a}$.

big A *khɔltɔp*$_{a}$, *khɔlto*$_{m}$. B (little big) *asi khɔlto*$_{m}$.

billy-goat *boka*$_{a}$.

bind *pɔccam*$_{m}$.

bird A (in general) *cikmu*$_{m}$, *cipmu*$_{a}$. B (species of black river bird with a long neck) *jʌlewa*$_{a}$. **bird** marker *-mu*$^{2}_{am}$.

birth *jʌnmʌi*$_{am}$. give **birth** to *jʌnmʌi pacap*$_{a}$, *jʌnmʌi pacam*$_{m}$.

bite A (by a snake) *kɔkcap*$^{2}_{a}$. B (with molars or snout) *kraccap*$_{a}$, *kra[k]-*$_{m}$.
bitter *khatto*$_{m}$.
black *khucɛm*$_{m}$, *khucɛŋmo*$_{a}$, *khucɛp*$_{a}$.
blanket *kɔmcap*$_{a}$, *kɔmcam*$_{m}$.
blend *milʌi lacap*$_{a}$, *milʌi dumcam*$_{m}$; *misʌi pacam*$_{m}$.
blending *milʌi*$_{am}$; *misʌi*$_{m}$.
blind (of both eyes) *ʌndha*$_{m}$.
blister *mari*$_{am}$.
blood *usu*$_{m}$, *yusu*$_{a}$.
blow A (wind) *phuḍim pacam*$_{m}$. B (fire) *huccap*$_{a}$, *hu[k]-*$_{m}$. C (one's nose) *sĩ pacap*$_{a}$.
boar *pa*$^{3}_{am}$.
boat (small) *ḍuŋga*$_{a}$.
body *jiu*$_{a}$; *ram*$_{m}$. **body louse** *sɛri*$_{am}$.
boil^{1} (liquid) A (in water) *hum-*$_{m}$. B (rice) *khɔkcap*$_{a}$, *khɔkcam*$_{m}$. C (simmer) *lɔkcap*$^{1}_{a}$, *lɔkt-*$_{m}$; *umlʌi*$_{a}$ *pacap*$_{a}$.
boil^{2} (wound) *mari*$_{am}$.
Bombax malabaricum (kapok tree) *simbʌl*$_{m}$.
bone *rusu*$_{am}$.
book *kitap*$_{a}$.
boss *khɔltɔp mucu*$_{a}$.
bottom A (lower part) *pum*$^{1}_{am}$. B (buttocks) *jɛnje*$_{am}$.
bow^{1} (weapon) A (with a bent handle) *gurtha*$_{a}$. B (for shooting mud pellets) *guleli*$_{a}$.
bow^{2} (bend) *kum bɔm-*$_{m}$.
boy *keṭa*; *teʔu*$_{am}$; *watɛwa*$_{m}$, *wattɛp*$_{a}$.
brain *gidi*$_{a}$; *nɛm*$_{m}$.
branch (of a tree) *hãga*$_{a}$, *haŋga*$_{m}$.
bread *sɔblɛm*$_{am}$.
break *brakcap*$_{a}$; *cɛkcap*$^{1}_{a}$, *cɛkcam*$_{m}$.
break down *bhʌtkʌi pacap*$_{a}$, *bhʌtkʌi pacam*$_{m}$. characterised by **breaking** *braktɔp*$_{a}$. **break off** *peicam*$_{m}$. **break open** *phrakcap*$_{a}$.
breast *chati*$_{a}$.
breath *sas*$_{a}$.
breather in **take a breather** *naicam*$_{m}$.
bridge *pul*$_{m}$; *sãghu*$_{a}$.
bring A (from no fixed direction) *blaccap*$_{a}$, *bla[k]-*$_{m}$. B (across a horizontal plane) *phiccap*$_{a}$, *phiccam*$_{m}$. C (down) *hɛccap*$_{a}$. D (down)

warlʌi pacap$_{a}$; *rɔlcam*$_{m}$, *rwalcap*$_{a}$. E (up) *khaccap*$_{a}$, *khaccam*$_{m}$. **bring back** *phʌrkʌi pacam*$_{m}$. **bring out** *sɔlcap*$_{a}$, *sɔl-*$_{m}$.

brother A [younger than ego] *bhai*$_{a}$. B [older than ego] *daju*$_{a}$. **brothers** *daju-bhai*$_{a}$.

brow *nidhar*$_{a}$.

bruise *mari*$_{am}$.

brush I n *kuco*$_{am}$. II v *brɛkcap*$_{a}$, *brɛk-*$_{m}$.

bubble up *lɔkcap*$^{1}_{a}$, *lɔkt-*$_{m}$; *umlʌi pacap*$_{a}$.

bubbling in state of **bubbling** *umlʌi*$_{a}$.

buffalo *mesu*$_{am}$.

build *bʌnʌi pacam*$_{m}$.

bull A (wild) *sãḍe*$_{m}$. B (young buffalo bull) *paḍa*$_{a}$.

bullock *biya*$_{a}$; *goru*$_{m}$.

burglar *khus pɔce mucu*$_{m}$; *khus pottɔp*$_{a}$.

burn A (lamps) *mi lagʌi lacap*$_{a}$, *mi lagʌi dumcam*$_{m}$. B (wood) *hocame*$_{a}$, *ho-*$_{m}$. C (something) *cɛccap*$^{2}_{a}$.

burst *brakcap*$_{a}$.

bush (*Colebrookia oppositifolia*) *dhursiŋ*$_{m}$; *sa:limo*$_{a}$.

but *tʌrʌ*$_{m}$.

butterfly *julɛmo*$_{m}$; *putʌli*$_{a}$.

buttocks *jɛnje*$_{am}$.

buy *japcap*$_{a}$, *japcam*$_{m}$.

— c —

Cābahil [a division of Kathmandu] *Cabʌhil*$_{a}$.

calf (of the leg) *pɔpɔl*$_{a}$, *phɔphɔl*$_{m}$.

call I n *cɛm*$_{am}$. II v *cɛm paccap*$_{a}$, *cɛm paccam*$_{m}$; *khamcap*$_{a}$; *wakcap*$^{2}_{a}$; *wa:cap*$_{a}$.

can (be able) *capcam*$_{m}$; *phaccap*$_{a}$.

capture *cumcap*$_{a}$, *cumcam*$_{m}$; *makcam*$_{m}$.

care I n *surta*$_{m}$. II v *surta pacam*$_{m}$.

carrot *gajʌr*$_{a}$.

carry *kurcap*$_{a}$, *kurcam*$_{m}$.

carve *cɔk-*.

cast (throw) *hɔpcap*$^{2}_{a}$; *yuccap*$_{a}$, *yoccam*$_{m}$.

caste *thʌr*$_{m}$.

cat *biralo*$_{am}$.

catch A (in general) *cumcap*$_{a}$, *cumcam*$_{m}$; *makcam*$_{m}$. B (fire) *mi lagʌi lacap*$_{a}$, *mi lagʌi dumcam*$_{m}$.
causative auxiliary *paccap*$_{a}$, *paccam*$_{m}$.
cave *gupha*$_{a}$.
centipede *braphu*$_{a}$.
centre *kha:ci*$_{am}$.
ceremony A (performed as a funeral ceremony after the death of a relative) *khauma*$_{a}$; *nul*$_{a}$. B (life cycle ceremony of giving a child its first solid food) *pasmi*$_{a}$.
chaff *bhus*$_{m}$.
chain *sikri*$_{m}$.
change I n *pherʌi*$_{m}$. II v *pherʌi pacam*$_{m}$.
chase away *dalcap*$_{a}$, *dalcam*$_{m}$.
cheek *gala*$_{a}$; *mambu*$_{am}$. **cheek bone** *mambu-rusu*$_{m}$.
chest *chati*$_{a}$.
chew *makcam*[2]$_{m}$, *nakcap*$_{a}$.
chick *cɛ̃kmu*$_{a}$, *cɛũmu*$_{a}$, *cɛʔmu*$_{m}$.
chicken A (in general) *mɔkɔm*$_{am}$. B (which lays eggs) *kuryam*$_{a}$, *kuryaŋma*$_{a}$, *kuryaŋmo*$_{m}$.
chief *khɔltɔp mucu*$_{a}$.
chignon *pukulum*$_{m}$.
child *nani*$_{am}$; *nunu*$_{m}$; *yɔkcu*$_{am}$.
chill *khoku*$_{a}$, *khokhu*$_{m}$.
chilli pepper *khursani*$_{am}$, *khursan*$_{a}$.
Cimex lectularius [bedbug] *uḍus*$_{m}$.
chin *rɛpmu*$_{am}$.
chop down *yak-*$_{m}$.
clan A (in general) *pāchā*$_{a}$; *thʌr*$_{m}$. (names of some Jero clans) *Bhau-Cacu*$_{a}$; *Dʌŋkhʌmcu*$_{a}$; *Gʌurathoke*$_{a}$; *Laimcu*$_{a}$; *Rɔke*$_{a}$ (divided into *Suriya-Bwaŋsi*$_{a}$ and *Mʌha-Rɔke*$_{a}$); *Setalcu*$_{a}$; *Tolupe*$_{a}$; *Topile*$_{a}$
clap one's hands *la tɔpcam*$_{m}$.
classifier A (human) *jʌna*$_{am}$, *jʌn*$_{m}$. B (non-human) *gɔṭa*$_{a}$, *gɔṭ*$_{a}$.
claw *gwarji*$_{am}$.
clay *kaksi*$_{am}$.
climb *hedicap*$_{a}$. **climb down** I n *warlʌi*$_{a}$. II v *warlʌi lacap*$_{a}$.
close[1] (near) *nʌjik*$_{m}$.
close[2] (shut) *bʌndʌ pacam*$_{m}$; *thɛkcap*$_{a}$, *ṭhɛkcam*$_{m}$.
closed *bʌndʌ*$_{m}$.

cloth A (in general) *wa*$_{am}$. B (worn over the shoulder by women) *ghʌlɛk*$_{a}$.
clothes *wa*$_{am}$. put on **clothes** *paicap*$_{a}$.
cloud *badʌl*$_{a}$; *kɔksɛl*$_{a}$, *kuksɛl*$_{m}$.
cob (of maize) *bobo*$_{a}$.
cock (male animal) *bhale*$_{am}$.
cold A (wet) *ciso*$_{a}$, *cisʌi*$_{a}$. B (of temperature) *khoku*$_{a}$, *khokhu*$_{m}$. **be cold** *khokhu pacam*$_{m}$. **feel cold** *khokhu sicam*$_{m}$. **make cold** *me pacap*$_{a}$, *me pacam*$_{m}$.
comb I n A (of a cock) *sir*$_{a}$. B (hair) *kaŋgyu*$_{m}$. II v *ticcam*$_{m}$.
come A (from no fixed direction) *blakcap*$_{a}$, *blak-*$_{m}$; *blaccap*$_{a}$, *bla[k]-*$_{m}$. B (across a horizontal plane) *picap*$_{a}$, *picam*$_{m}$. C (down) *yacap*$^{1}_{a}$, *yacam*$_{m}$; *dɔkcam*$_{m}$; *docap*$_{a}$. D (up) *gacap*$_{a}$, *ga-*$_{m}$; *-kha-*$^{2}_{m}$. **come across, come together** *rɛmcam*$_{m}$. **come back** I n *phʌrkʌi*$_{m}$. II v *phʌrkʌi dumcam*$_{m}$, *phʌrkʌi lacam*$_{m}$. **cause to come out** *mɔrcap*$_{a}$.
comitative marker *=na*$^{2}_{a}$, *=no*$_{m}$, *=n*$_{am}$.
commencement *suru*$_{m}$.
commodity *thok*$_{m}$.
company in **in the company of** *kwa*$_{a}$. **in company with others** *kwa-ya*$_{a}$.
comparable to *=na=se*$_{a}$, *=na=s*$_{a}$; *=na=se=p*.
complete *tumcap*$^{2}_{a}$.
completely *yɔm*$_{m}$.
comrade *sathi*$_{a}$.
conceal *kliccap*$_{a}$, *kliccam*$_{m}$.
conditional in **marker of the conditional gerund** *-dɔŋo*$_{a}$, *-dɔŋ*$_{am}$.
conduct *wal paccam*$_{m}$.
confined *bʌndʌ*$_{m}$.
connective in **marker of the connective gerund** *-ti*$_{am}$.
consciousness *maʔla*$_{a}$.
consideration *bicar*$_{a}$.
considering in **not considering** *bahek*$_{a}$.
construct *bʌnʌi pacam*$_{m}$.
construction *bʌnʌi*$_{m}$.
contemporaneous time suffix *-bu*$^{1}_{am}$.
contrary in **marker of contrary expectation** *ke*$_{a}$.
contrastive topic marker *cai*$_{a}$.
conversation *samsa*$_{a}$.
converse *ma:la sɔcam*$_{m}$.

cook *hum-*$_{m}$; *khɔkcap*$_{a}$, *khɔkcam*$_{m}$.

cool *cisʌi pacap*$_{a}$. **let cool off** *me pacap*$_{a}$, *me pacam*$_{m}$.

corn *mʌkʌi*$_{am}$.

corner *kuna*$_{a}$.

cotton A (plant) *buisi*$_{am}$. B (wool) *buisi*$_{am}$; *ruwa*$_{a}$.

couch *glecap*$_{a}$, *glecam*$_{m}$.

cough I n *sɔkane*$_{a}$. II v *sɔkane pacap*$_{a}$.

count *khripcam*$_{m}$; *nɛrcap*$_{a}$.

cover I n *chopʌi*$_{a}$. II v *bʌndʌ pacam*$_{m}$; *chopʌi pacap*$_{a}$; *kɔmcap*$_{a}$, *kɔmcam*$_{m}$; *sumcam*$_{m}$; *thɛkcap*$_{a}$, *ʈhɛkcam*$_{m}$. be **covered** *bɔm-*$_{m}$; *chopʌi lacap*$_{a}$.

cow *gai*$_{am}$.

craziness *bʌulʌi*$_{am}$.

crazy in **go crazy** *bʌulʌi lacap*$_{a}$, *bʌulʌi lacam*$_{m}$.

cross *tʌrʌi lacap*$_{a}$.

crossing *tʌrʌi*$_{a}$.

cross-legging *phɛmto*$_{a}$.

crow *gagmu*$_{m}$, *gaːgab*$_{a}$; *kag*$_{a}$.

cry I n *khrɔm*. II v *huːcap*$_{a}$, *huː-*$_{m}$; *khrɔmcap*$_{a}$, *khrɔmcam*$_{m}$. **cause to cry** *khrɔm paccap*.

cucumber *tɔksi*$_{am}$.

cut I n *cirʌi*$_{m}$. II v *cirʌi pacam*$_{m}$; *tɛccap*$_{a}$. **cut down** *yak-*$_{m}$. **cut off** *rikcam*$_{m}$.

— d —

damage *bigrʌi pacap*$_{a}$. **become damaged** *bigrʌi lacap*$_{a}$. **becoming damaged** *bigrʌi*$_{a}$.

dance I n *sɛle*$_{m}$, *sɛt*$_{a}$. II v *sɛle pacam*$_{m}$, *sɛt pacap*$_{a}$.

dancer *sɛt pottɔp*.

daughter *tep*$_{a}$, *teʔme*$_{am}$.

day A (in general) *din*$_{am}$. B (three days ago, the day before the day before yesterday) *ninibbɔn*$_{a}$; *thaːthaccum*$_{m}$. C (two days ago) *nibbɔn*$_{a}$; *saʔni*$_{m}$; *saːsatni*$_{a}$; *thaccum*$_{m}$. D (yesterday) *saiso*$_{m}$; *satni*$_{a}$. E (today) *tɛmbar*$_{am}$. F (tomorrow) *phɔpma*$_{am}$. G (day after tomorrow, two days from now) *nuso*$_{m}$, *nusso*$_{a}$. H (three days from now, the day after the day after tomorrow) *nunusso*$_{a}$; *sukmul*$_{a}$, *sukul*$_{m}$. I (four days from now) *pyakmul*$_{a}$. **day marker** *-ni*$^{4}_{am}$; *-so*$^{1}_{am}$.

daybreak *bihan*$_{am}$.
dead in **be dead** *sicap*$_{a}$, *sicam*$_{m}$. characterised by being **dead** *sittɔp*$_{a}$.
deal out (a meal) *phɛccap*$_{a}$, *phɛccam*$_{m}$.
death in **put to death** *sɛccap*$_{a}$, *sɛccam*$_{m}$.
decrease *sɔrcap*$_{a}$, *sɔr-*$_{m}$.
deed *karjʌi*$_{a}$.
deep (place) *gʌira*$_{m}$.
deity A (in general) *sama*$_{m}$; B (who resides indoors in a Jero household) *kul-deuta*$_{a}$.
delay *ḍhilo*$_{am}$.
delicious *jiji*$_{m}$.
demolish *bhʌtkʌi pacap*$_{a}$, *bhʌtkʌi pacam*$_{m}$.
demonstrative morpheme A (near the speaker) *a-*$^{2}_{am}$. B (far, horizontally) *nɔ-*$_{am}$. C (far, up) *tɔ-*$^{1}_{am}$. D (far, down) *yɔ-*$_{am}$. E (near the hearer) *u-*$^{1}_{am}$. **marker of comparative demonstrative pronouns** *-cu*$^{4}_{am}$.
depress *cepʌi pacap*$_{a}$.
depression A (area) *khalṭa*$_{m}$. B (pressure) *cepʌi*$_{a}$.
descend I n *warlʌi*$_{a}$. II v *warlʌi lacap*$_{a}$; *dɔkcam*$_{m}$; *docap*$_{a}$. cause to **descend** *warlʌi pacap*$_{a}$; *rɔlcam*$_{m}$, *rwalcap*$_{a}$.
destroy *bhʌtkʌi pacap*$_{a}$, *bhʌtkʌi pacam*$_{m}$.
destruction *bhʌtkʌi*$_{am}$.
detransitivising marker *-s*$^{1}_{am}$.
devil *bhut*$_{a}$.
diarrhoea in **suffer from diarrhoea** *saŋkhi prit-*$_{m}$.
die *sicap*$_{a}$, *sicam*$_{m}$.
difficult *saro*$_{m}$.
dig *dɛcap*$_{a}$; *kɔkcap*$^{1}_{a}$; *phuicap*$_{a}$, *phuit-*$_{m}$.
directive marker *lam*$^{1}_{a}$; *-la*$_{am}$, *-l*$_{am}$.
dirtiness (on the body) *riku*$_{am}$.
dish in **cooked liquid vegetable or meat dish** *khamsi*$_{am}$.
dislocated in **be dislocated** *khuskʌi lacam*$_{m}$.
dislocation *khuskʌi*$_{m}$.
dispatch *pʌṭhʌi pacap*$_{a}$, *pʌṭhʌi pacam*$_{m}$.
dispose *thamcap*$_{a}$.
distort *curcap*$_{a}$, *curcam*$_{m}$.
distribute A (something) *bā̃ḍʌi pacap*$_{a}$; *dɔyo pacam*$_{m}$. B (to someone) *do paccap*$_{a}$.
distribution *bā̃ḍʌi*$_{a}$; *dɔyo*$_{m}$, *do*$_{a}$.

divide *bā̃ḍʌi pacap*$_{a}$.
divinity *deuta*$_{a}$; *sama*$_{m}$.
division *bā̃ḍʌi*$_{a}$.
dizzy in **be dizzy** *niwa ri-*$_{m}$.
do *pacap*$_{a}$, *pacam*$_{m}$. **make do** *paccap*$_{a}$, *paccam*$_{m}$. **characterised by doing** something *pottɔp*$_{a}$. **something done** *bʌnʌi*$_{m}$.
dog *saŋmu*$_{am}$.
door *ḍhoka*$_{am}$; *kimsul*$_{am}$.
dove *pʌrewa*$_{a}$.
down *hɛttu*$_{a}$, *hɛtthu*$_{m}$; *yɔmala*$_{m}$, *yɔmal*$_{am}$.
downwards *hɛttu*$_{a}$, *hɛtthu*$_{m}$.
draw A (pull) *jɛccap*$_{a}$. B (the liquid out of something with one's mouth) *bipcap*$_{a}$, *bipcam*$_{m}$. C (write) *rɛkcap*$_{a}$, *rɛk-*$_{m}$.
dream I n *ŋabu*$_{m}$. II v *ŋabu mɔ-*$_{m}$.
dress oneself *paicap*.
drink *tu:cap*$_{a}$, *tu:cam*$_{m}$. **make drink** *tɛncap*$_{a}$; *teicam*$_{a}$.
drive out *dalcap*$_{a}$, *dalcam*$_{m}$; *mɔrcap*$_{a}$.
drop *rɔlcam*$_{m}$, *rwalcap*$_{a}$. **drop off** *dɔkcam*$_{m}$; *docap*$_{a}$.
drown *ḍubʌi lacap*$_{a}$.
dry (up) *sɔrcap*$_{a}$, *sɔr-*$_{m}$. **make dry** *plɛccap*$_{a}$, *plɛccam*$_{m}$.
dual number marker *nim*$^{3}_{m}$, *nimpha*$_{am}$.
duck *hā̃s*$_{a}$.
Dūdhkosī river *Dudhkosi*$_{a}$, *Glɔku*$_{m}$.
dung *saŋki*$_{a}$, *saŋkhi*$_{m}$.
dust-pit *kurti*$_{a}$; *kʌreso*$_{a}$.

— e —

ear A (organ) *nɔbu*$_{am}$. B (of grain) *bobo*$_{a}$.
earring *jhumka*$_{m}$; *mundri*$_{m}$.
earth *bhuĩ*$_{am}$; *kaksi*$_{am}$.
earwax *kanaguju*$_{a}$.
easy *sʌjilo*$_{m}$.
eat A (swallow) *tɔk-*$_{m}$. B (soft food) *jacap*$_{a}$, *jacam*$_{m}$. C (by biting and tearing the food with the teeth) *macap*$_{a}$, *macam*$_{m}$.
eating *jocu*$_{a}$. **characterised by eating** *jottɔp*$_{a}$.
edge *cheu*$_{am}$.
education *pʌḍʌi*$_{a}$.

eel *phuŋmũ*$_{a}$.
egg A (in general) *magge*$_{a}$; *mayaŋga*$_{am}$. B (of a louse) *pɛkmar*$_{a}$.
Elaeagnus parvifolia (tree) *mɛsi*$_{m}$.
elbow *kuhina*$_{a}$, *kuina*$_{m}$; *nɛksi*$_{m}$.
elder *buḍa*$_{a}$; *buḍi*$_{a}$.
embrace *ʌŋgalo*$_{m}$.
emphatic marker *-ʌi*$^{2}_{am}$.
enclosure *khor*$_{a}$.
end *cheu*$_{am}$.
endow *gɔkcap*$_{a}$, *gɔkcam*$_{m}$.
enlarge *bʌḍʌi pacap*$_{a}$.
enlargement *bʌḍʌi*$_{a}$.
enough in **be enough** *dɔkcap*$_{a}$, *dɔkcam*$_{m}$.
enter *hedicap*$_{a}$.
entrance in **main entrance which gives way to the courtyard** *kimsu-l*$_{am}$.
erect *bukcap*$_{a}$, *bukcam*$_{m}$; *phukcam*$_{m}$.
escape *prakcam*$_{m}$.
escort *lɛccap*$_{a}$, *lɛccam*$_{m}$.
essential marker *-sano*$_{a}$.
ethnic group *jat*$_{a}$.
even A (used after a negative) *=ya*$^{1}_{am}$, *=i*$_{am}$. B (yes, used to say that something is true) *ʌ̃*$_{a}$.
ever *hus bulu*$_{a}$, *hus bul*$_{a}$; *husɛl*$_{m}$, *husulu*$_{a}$, *husul*$_{a}$.
evil spirit *bhut*$_{a}$.
exactly A (used to add emphasis when specifying something) *=se*$^{2}_{am}$, *=s*$_{am}$. B (used to indicate complete agreement with what has been said) *ʌ̃*$_{a}$.
except *bahek*$_{a}$.
excrement *saŋki*$_{a}$, *saŋkhi*$_{m}$.
execute *sɛccap*$_{a}$, *sɛccam*$_{m}$.
exhausted in **be exhausted** *thʌkʌi lacap*$_{a}$.
extract (with one's mouth) *bipcap*$_{a}$, *bipcam*$_{m}$.
eye *misi*$_{am}$.
eyebrow *pʌrela*$_{am}$.
eyelash *rɔmpu-sɔm*$_{m}$; *pʌrela*$_{am}$.

— f —

fable *kʌtha*$_{m}$.
face *ʌnuhar*$_{a}$; *kuli*$_{m}$.
factual in **marker of the factual verbal adjective** *-mei*$_{am}$, *-maya*$_{a}$, *-mai*$_{am}$, *-nei*$_{am}$, *-mʌi*$_{am}$.
faeces *saŋki*$_{a}$, *saŋkhi*$_{m}$.
falcon (kind) *besura*$_{am}$.
fall *dɔkcam*$_{m}$; *docap*$_{a}$. **let fall** *rɔlcam*$_{m}$, *rwalcap*$_{a}$.
family priest *naksu*$_{a}$.
far *ṭaḍo*$_{m}$. **as far as** *sʌmba*$_{m}$, *sʌmma*$_{a}$.
farm *khet*$_{m}$.
fast *dʌro*$_{a}$.
fat *jɔʔmu*$_{am}$.
father *papa*$_{am}$.
father-in-law A (in general) *sɛra*$_{m}$, *sɛru*$_{a}$. B (one's own child's father-in-law) *hilpu*$_{a}$; *sʌmdhi*$_{a}$.
fatigue *thʌkʌi*$_{a}$.
fear I n *nim*$^{1}_{m}$. II v *nim lucam*$_{m}$.
feather A (big) *masrɛmpu*$_{a}$. B (small) *bhutla*$_{a}$.
feed *mɛccap*$_{a}$, *mɛccam*$_{m}$.
feel *chamʌi pacap*$_{a}$, *chamʌi pacam*$_{m}$; *mɔ-*$_{m}$.
feeling *chamʌi*$_{am}$.
fell *yak-*$_{m}$.
female animal A (in general, especially a bird) *pothi*$_{a}$. B (sow) *khɔp-me*$_{m}$.
feminine gender marker *-ma*$^{3}_{am}$; *-me*$^{3}_{am}$; *-mu*$^{1}_{am}$.
fence *bar*$_{m}$.
fern *uniu*$_{m}$.
fetch *blaccap*$_{a}$, *bla[k]-*$_{m}$.
fever *ʌul*$_{a}$; *jʌro*$_{a}$.
few *asi*$_{am}$; *asi khɔlse*$_{a}$; *cicir*$_{a}$; *cimmaŋ*$_{m}$; *cimtɛp*$_{a}$.
Ficus bengalensis (tree) *bʌr*$_{m}$
Ficus cunia (tree) *kuksi*$_{am}$.
Ficus religiosa (tree) *pipʌl*$_{m}$.
field to grow vegetables *khirki*$_{a}$.
find (a trace of someone) *rɛmcam*$_{m}$. **find out** *cɛkcam*$_{m}$, *cikcam*$_{a}$.
fine *rance*$_{m}$; *rantɔp*$_{a}$, *ranto*$_{m}$.

finger A (in general, also toe) *brεmci*$_{am}$. B (index finger) *cor-brεmci*$_{am}$. C (little finger) *kanchi-brεmci*$_{am}$. D (middle finger) *maili-brεmci*$_{m}$. E (third finger) *saili-brεmci*$_{m}$. F (thumb) *bɔmti*$_{m}$; *buḍi-bɔmti*$_{m}$; *buḍi-brεmci*$_{a}$.
finish *tumcap*$^{2}{}_{a}$.
fire *mi*$^{2}{}_{am}$. be set on **fire** *sʌlkʌi lacap*$_{a}$. setting on **fire** *sʌlkʌi*$_{a}$.
firefly *dalcip*$_{a}$; *dalaciŋma*$_{m}$.
fireplace (for cooking) *culo*$_{a}$.
firewood *siŋ*$_{a}$.
firm *dʌro*$_{a}$.
first-born male *jeṭha*$_{am}$.
fish *mõ*, *mũ*$_{a}$, *mu*$_{m}$.
fist A (in general) *muṭhi*$_{am}$. B (clenched) *muḍki*$_{m}$.
five *pãc*$_{am}$.
flee *prakcam*$_{m}$.
flesh *su*$^{4}{}_{am}$. **flesh** marker *-su*$^{2}{}_{am}$.
flight *uḍʌi*$_{am}$.
fling *yoccam*$_{m}$, *yuccap*$_{a}$.
floor *bhuĩ*$_{am}$.
flour *phuli*$_{am}$.
flower *phuri*$_{am}$.
flute *murʌli*$_{m}$.
fly^{1} (insect) *sɔyam*$_{a}$, *sɔʔyɔm*$_{m}$.
fly^{2} (travel) *uḍʌi lacam*$_{a}$, *uḍʌi dumcam*$_{m}$.
fog *badʌl*$_{a}$; *kɔksεl*$_{a}$, *kuksεl*$_{m}$.
fold *khor*$_{a}$.
follow *khɔccap*$_{a}$; *manʌi pacam*$_{m}$.
fond in **be fond of** *dakcap*$_{a}$, *dakcam*$_{m}$.
food *jacam thok*$_{m}$; *jacap cis*$_{a}$.
for (duration of time) *sʌmba*$_{m}$, *sʌmma*$_{a}$.
forbid *rokʌi pacap*$_{a}$, *rokʌi pacam*$_{m}$.
forehead *nidhar*$_{a}$.
foreigner *bidesi*$_{a}$.
forget *ma[p]-*$_{m}$. **forget completely** *yɔm ma[p]-*$_{m}$.
forgive *maph gɔkcam*$_{m}$.
forgiveness *maph*$_{m}$.
former *num-*$_{m}$.
formerly *lapphu*$_{am}$; *lapthɔl*$_{a}$; *na*$^{4}{}_{am}$. **much formerly** *na-na*$_{m}$, *na ke*$_{a}$, *na= se*$_{am}$.

forsake *plεcam*$_{m}$.
foundation *pum*$^{1}_{am}$.
four *car*$_{am}$.
fowl *mɔkɔm*$_{am}$.
fracture *cεkcap*$^{1}_{a}$, *cεkcam*$_{m}$.
fragrance *ŋaba*$_{m}$, *ŋab*$_{am}$.
free in **set free** *peicam*$_{m}$.
friend *kaʔu*$_{am}$; *sathi*$_{a}$.
frog A (in general) *bhyaguta*$_{am}$. B (big) *paha*$_{a}$.
from *=na=ku*$_{a}$, *=na=k*$_{a}$.
front in **in front** *lapphu*$_{am}$; *lapthɔl*$_{a}$.
fruit *phʌl-phul*$_{am}$. **fruit marker** *-si*$^{1}_{am}$.
fry *kharcap*$_{a}$, *kharcam*$_{m}$.
full in **in full** *jʌmma*$_{a}$.
further *nɔmala*$_{m}$, *nɔmal*$_{a}$; *pʌrʌ*$_{a}$.

— g —

gallop in **make gallop** *kudʌi pacap*$_{a}$, *kuɖʌi pacam*$_{m}$.
galloping *kudʌi*$_{a}$, *kuɖʌi*$_{m}$.
game *camda*$_{a}$, *cam*$_{a}$, *camdo*$_{m}$; *khel*$_{a}$.
garland *mala*$_{a}$.
Garuga pinnata (tree) *krampu*$_{a}$, *krampa*$_{m}$.
gate *kimsul*$_{am}$.
genitive marker *=ŋaŋ*$^{2}_{m}$, *=ŋ*$_{am}$.
get *hipcam*$_{m}$; *tεrcap*$_{a}$, *tεrcam*$_{m}$; *rεmcam*$_{m}$. **get out** *mɔrcap*$_{a}$. **get up** *bukcap*$_{a}$, *bukcam*$_{m}$.
ghost *bhut*$_{a}$; *mʌsan*$_{a}$.
giddy in **be giddy** *niwa ri-*$_{m}$.
ginger *phipuwa*$_{a}$.
girl A (in general) *mεtεme*$_{m}$, *mεttεp*$_{a}$; *tep*$_{a}$, *teʔme*$_{am}$. B (of marriageable age) *salme*$_{m}$; *tʌruni*$_{a}$.
give *gɔkcap*$_{a}$, *gɔkcam*$_{m}$. **give up** *plεcam*$_{m}$; *taccap*$_{a}$.
glad *khusi*$_{m}$. **be glad** *khusi bakcam*$_{m}$.
glue *kεpcap*$_{a}$, *kεpcam*$_{m}$; *ʈãsʌi lacam*$_{m}$; *ʈãsʌi pacap*$_{a}$, *ʈãsʌi pacam*$_{m}$.
gnaw *kraccap*$_{a}$, *kra[k]-*$_{m}$.
go A (and come back, go working) *-di-*$_{a}$, *-du-*$_{a}$; *dicap*$_{a}$, *dicam*$_{m}$. B (away) *lɔcap*$_{a}$, *lɔcam*$_{m}$. C (up) *caːcap*$_{a}$, *caː-*$_{m}$. D (walk) *walcap*$_{a}$,

walcam$_{m}$. **keep on the go** *kudʌi pacap*$_{a}$, *kuḍʌi pacam*$_{m}$. **make go** *wal paccam*$_{m}$. **go about** *ghumʌi lacap*$_{a}$. **go after, go later** *khɔccap*$_{a}$. **go back** *phʌrkʌi dumcam*$_{m}$, *phʌrkʌi lacam*$_{m}$. **go out** *mɔrcap*$_{a}$.

god *deuta*$_{a}$; *sama*$_{m}$.

good *jati*$_{a}$; *rance*$_{m}$; *rantɔp*$_{a}$, *ranto*$_{m}$. **be good** *nucap*$_{a}$, *nucam*$_{m}$.

grain A (in general) *cicila*$_{a}$; *cinci*$_{am}$. B (cooked grain, especially rice) *hepa*$_{am}$, *hep*$_{a}$. C (husked and polished, especially rice) *labji*$_{a}$; *seri*$_{am}$. **grain marker** *-ji*$_{am}$.

granary (for storing maize) *kholma*$_{a}$.

granddaughter *cacume*$_{m}$, *cacuŋma*$_{a}$.

grandfather (especially paternal) *hupu*$_{am}$.

grandmother (especially paternal) *humu*$_{am}$.

grandson *cacu*$_{am}$.

grass *ghãs*$_{a}$.

grasshopper *kaŋkoṭ*$_{a}$, *kaŋkaŋ*$_{m}$.

graze *cʌrʌi lacap*$_{a}$, *cʌrʌi lacam*$_{m}$.

grazing *cʌrʌi*$_{am}$.

grease (of a living creature) *jɔʔmu*$_{am}$.

great *khɔltɔp*$_{a}$, *khɔlto*$_{m}$; *saro*$_{m}$.

great-grandfather *gupsu-hupu*$_{am}$.

great-grandmother *gupsu-humu*$_{a}$.

green *hʌriyo*$_{a}$. **becoming green** (of plants) *pʌlʌi*$_{m}$. **become green** *pʌlʌi dumcam*$_{m}$. **green leafy vegetable** (especially spinach) *siʔlim*$_{a}$; *sag*$_{m}$.

greeting *nʌmʌskar*$_{m}$.

grief *dukhʌ*$_{a}$.

grind *khricap*$_{a}$, *khricam*$_{m}$.

grope *chamʌi pacap*$_{a}$, *chamʌi pacam*$_{m}$.

groping *chamʌi*$_{am}$.

ground A (in general) *bhuĩ*$_{am}$; *kaksi*$_{am}$. B (immediately round a house) *kʌreso*$_{a}$; *kurti*$_{a}$.

grub *phuicap*$_{a}$, *phuit-*$_{m}$.

guard *locam*$_{m}$; *rim pacap*$_{a}$.

gum *sika*$_{m}$.

Gurkhali knife *bɛthɔŋ*$_{am}$.

— h —

hail I n *solu*$_{m}$, *sol*$_{am}$. II v *solu yacam*$_{m}$.
hair *sɔm*$_{m}$, *swam*$_{a}$.
handful *muṭhi*$_{am}$.
handle A (in general) *bĩḍ*$_{a}$. B (of an axe) *khusiŋ*$_{m}$.
hang up *cεccap*$^{1}_{a}$; *jhunḍʌi pacam*$_{m}$; *ṭaŋgai pacam*$_{m}$. **hang down** *kum bɔm-*$_{m}$.
hanging *jhunḍʌi*$_{m}$; *ṭaŋgai*$_{m}$.
happen *lagʌi dumcam*$_{m}$. **it will happen** *lagchʌ*$_{a}$.
happening *lagʌi*$_{m}$.
happy *khusi*$_{m}$. **be happy** *khusi bakcam*$_{m}$.
hard *saro*$_{m}$.
hatchet *khu*$_{am}$.
hate I n *gramji*$_{a}$, *gramsu*$_{m}$. II v *gramsu pacam*$_{m}$. feel **hate** *gramji lucap*$_{a}$.
he *aŋgu*$_{am}$, *aŋ*$_{am}$.
head *phutir*$_{m}$, *phutur*$_{a}$.
head strap *nobir*$_{m}$, *noʔmar*$_{a}$.
healthy in **be healthy** *nucap*$_{a}$, *nucam*$_{m}$.
heap in **a heap of** *thupro*$_{a}$. a large **heap** of *thuprʌi*$_{a}$.
hear *thɔcap*$^{1}_{a}$, *thɔ-*$_{m}$.
hearsay in **marker of hearsay** *nεʔe*$_{a}$.
heart A (in general) *tεm*$_{a}$, *tɔm*$_{m}$. B (the organ) *tεm-cinci*$_{a}$, *tɔm-cinci*$_{m}$.
heat *tʌtʌi pacap*$_{a}$.
heating *tʌtʌi*$_{a}$.
heaven *sɔrga*$_{a}$.
heel *kurkucca*$_{a}$.
heifer in **young buffalo heifer** *paḍi*$_{a}$.
hen *kuryam*$_{a}$, *kuryaŋma*$_{a}$, *kuryaŋmo*$_{m}$.
her *aŋ*$_{m}$, *aŋam*$_{a}$.
here *alu*$_{am}$, *al*$_{am}$. **until here** *al sʌmba*$_{m}$.
hide *chopʌi pacap*$_{a}$; *kliccap*$_{a}$, *kliccam*$_{m}$. **be hidden** *chopʌi lacap*$_{a}$.
high *roto*$_{m}$. **very high** *bʌḍe roto*$_{m}$.
hill *ḍãḍa*$_{a}$.
hinder I n *chekʌi*$_{a}$; *rokʌi*$_{am}$. II v *chekʌi pacap*$_{a}$; *rokʌi pacap*$_{a}$, *rokʌi pacam*$_{m}$.
his *aŋ*$_{m}$, *aŋam*$_{a}$.

hit A (strike) *hɔpcap*$^{2}_{a}$; *tupcap*$_{a}$, *tupcam*$_{a}$. B (with a pointed object) *suk-*$_{m}$. C (with a stick) *ta-*$^{2}_{m}$.
hog *pa*$^{3}_{am}$.
hold *cumcap*$_{a}$, *cumcam*$_{m}$; *makcam*$_{m}$.
hole *dulo*$_{a}$; *dhɔŋga*$_{m}$; *dhɔndro*$_{m}$, *dhɔndhro*$_{a}$; *khalʈa*$_{m}$; *khopʌi*$_{a}$. **make a hole in** *khopʌi pacap*$_{a}$.
hollow *khalʈa*$_{m}$.
honey *khudo*$_{a}$, *khuɖo*$_{m}$.
hop *kudʌi lacap*$_{a}$.
horizontally *pɛttu*$_{a}$, *pɛtthu*$_{m}$.
horn *rosu*$_{am}$, *ros*$_{a}$.
horse *ghoɖa*$_{am}$.
hot (of touch) *tato*$_{a}$. **be hot** (spicy) *su-*$^{3}_{m}$.
house *kulu*$_{a}$, *kul*$_{am}$.
housefly *sɔyam*$_{a}$, *sɔʔyɔm*$_{m}$.
how *hujɔktɔp*$_{a}$; *hus*$_{am}$; *hus pasaku*$_{m}$.
how many, how much *hukɔl*$_{am}$.
howl *wakcap*$^{2}_{a}$; *waːcap*$_{a}$.
human (race) *mucu*$_{am}$.
hundred *sʌi*$_{am}$. **one hundred** *kɔʔl sʌi*$_{a}$.
hunger *krɛmku*$_{a}$, *krɛmkhu*$_{m}$.
hungry in **feel hungry** *krɛmkhu pacam*$_{m}$.
hunt (game) *sikar pacap*$_{a}$, *sikar pacam*$_{m}$.
hunting *sikar*$_{am}$.
hurt *nɛccap*$_{a}$, *nɛt-*$_{m}$. **characterised by hurting** *nɛttɔp*$_{a}$.
husband A *buɖa*$_{a}$; *wacu*$_{m}$. B [husband of one's eldest sister] *jeʈha-bhena*$_{a}$.
husk I n *bhus*$_{m}$. II v *peicam*$_{m}$.

— i —

I *uŋgu*$_{am}$, *uŋ*$_{am}$.
idea *bicar*$_{a}$.
if *bhʌne*$_{a}$. **if it is** *nɔdɔŋ*$_{a}$.
ignite *mi lagʌi lacap*$_{a}$, *mi lagʌi dumcam*$_{m}$.
Ilam [district in Nepal] *Ilam*$_{a}$.
ill *birami*$_{am}$. be **ill** *anucap*$_{a}$, *anucam*$_{m}$.
imagination *mimti*$_{m}$.

imperative agreement suffix A (singular agent and subject) *-Ø*$^{2}_{am}$. B (second and third person dual) *-ci*$^{2}_{m}$. C (general marker) *-ka*$_{am}$, *-kha*$_{am}$, *-ha*$_{am}$, *-a*$_{am}$, *-pha*$_{am}$, *-pa*$_{m}$. D (which marks a transitive relationship between a singular agent and a third person non-singular patient) *-m*$^{1}_{am}$. E (plural subject) *-n*$^{1}_{am}$. F (second and third person plural) *-ni*$^{2}_{am}$, *-i*$_{a}$. G (dual subject) *-ŋ*$^{1}_{am}$. H (first person singular patient) *-ŋ*$^{2}_{am}$.
impetuous *tato*$_{a}$.
inception *suru*$_{m}$.
incessantly *lʌgatar*$_{a}$.
incision *cirʌi*$_{m}$.
increase I n *bʌɖʌi*$_{a}$. II v *bʌɖʌi pacap*$_{a}$.
index finger *cor-brɛmci*$_{am}$.
India *Bharʌt*$_{a}$; *India*$_{a}$.
infant *yɔkcu*$_{am}$.
infatuation *maya*$_{a}$.
inferior *cimtɛp*$_{a}$; *yɔkko*$_{m}$.
infinitive marker *-si*$^{5}_{am}$.
inflate *huccap*$_{a}$, *hu[k]-*$_{m}$.
influence *rakcap*$_{a}$, *rakcam*$_{m}$; *ra:cap*$_{a}$.
inform *necap*$_{a}$, *necam*$_{m}$.
injury *mari*$_{am}$.
inquire *cel pacam*$_{m}$; *tublo pacap*$_{a}$.
insane in **go insane** *bʌulʌi lacap*$_{a}$, *bʌulʌi lacam*$_{m}$.
insanity *bʌulʌi*$_{am}$.
insert *phikcap*$_{a}$.
inside *bhitra*$_{am}$. **inside out** *ulʈo*$_{m}$.
instruct *sikʌi pacap*$_{a}$.
instruction *talim*$_{m}$.
insufficient *kʌmti*$_{a}$.
interrogation *cel*$_{m}$; *tublo*$_{a}$.
ire *ris*$_{m}$.
irrealis marker *-so*$^{2}_{am}$.
irrigated field (used to grow grain crops) *khet*$_{m}$.
itch *su-*$^{3}_{m}$.

— j —

jack up *khricap*$_{a}$, *khricam*$_{m}$.
jackal *syal*$_{m}$.
jar A (small) *ghʌĩṭi*$_{am}$. B (small or medium sized copper water jar) *gag-ri*$_{a}$.
jaw in **lower jaw** *cyapu*$_{a}$.
Jero *Jero*$_{am}$. **Jero language** *Jero maːla*$_{m}$.
journey in **make a journey** *lɔcap*$_{a}$, *lɔcam*$_{m}$; *walcap*$_{a}$, *walcam*$_{m}$.
jump I n A (over) *nãghʌi*$_{a}$. B (up) *uphrʌi*$_{a}$. II v A (down) *ham phalʌi pacap*$_{a}$. B (over) *nãghʌi pacap*$_{a}$. C (up) *prɛkcam*$_{m}$; *uphrʌi lacam*$_{a}$.

— k —

kapok tree (*Bombax malabaricum*) *simbʌl*$_{m}$.
Kathmandu *Kaṭhmanḍu*$_{a}$.
keep A (in general) *cɔpcap*$_{a}$, *cɔpcam*$_{m}$. B (animals or other dependants) *yuːcap*$_{a}$.
kept for a long time *basi*$_{m}$.
kernel in **nut-like kernel of the tree *Bauhinia vahilii*** *bhorla=ŋ kokolo*$_{m}$.
kick with the sole of foot *ta-*$^{2}_{m}$.
kill A (in general) *sɛccap*$_{a}$, *sɛccam*$_{m}$. B (time) *tɛccap*$_{a}$.
Kiranti *Kirãt*$_{a}$.
kiss I n *cumma*$_{a}$; *cuʔ*$_{m}$; *moi*$_{a}$. II v *cuʔ pacam*$_{m}$.
knee *pumci*$_{am}$.
knock down *rɔlcam*$_{m}$, *rwalcap*$_{a}$. **knock over** *yak-*$_{m}$.
knot *gãṭho*$_{a}$.
knotty *ganʌ*$_{a}$.
know A (by learning) *jɔkcam*$_{m}$. B (a person, by sight) *seicap*$_{a}$, *sei-*$_{m}$. **characterised by knowing** *jɔktɔp*$_{a}$, *jɔkto*$_{m}$. **I don't know** *khʌi*$_{m}$.
knowledge *niwa*$_{am}$. **have knowledge** *cɛkcam*$_{m}$, *cikcam*$_{a}$. **marker of knowledge obtained through the senses** *-jimo*$_{m}$.

— l —

lacerate *cirʌi pacam*$_{m}$; *ciccap*$_{a}$.
landslide *pʌiro*$_{m}$.
language *maːla*$_{am}$.
large *khɔltɔp*$_{a}$, *khɔlto*$_{m}$.
larger *bʌḍe*$_{m}$, *bʌḍi*$_{a}$.
last *nʌuṭha=m*$_{m}$. **last year** *numthoce*$_{m}$; *thoni*$_{a}$.
late *mat*$_{a}$, *matto*$_{a}$, *mattol*$_{a}$, *mattɔlo*$_{m}$.
later A (in general) *nʌuṭhaŋ*$_{am}$. B (a little later) *mat*$_{a}$, *matto*$_{a}$, *mattol*$_{a}$, *mattɔlo*$_{m}$.
laugh I n *rɛnda*$_{am}$. II v *rɛnda recap*$_{a}$, *rɛnda recam*$_{m}$. **cause someone to laugh** *rɛnda re paccam*$_{m}$.
lead *lɛccap*$_{a}$, *lɛccam*$_{m}$.
leaf *moli*$_{m}$, *moʔli*$_{a}$.
leap I n *uphrʌi*$_{a}$. II v *kudʌi lacap*$_{a}$; *uphrʌi lacam*$_{a}$.
learn *cei-*$_{m}$; *sikʌi lacap*$_{a}$.
learning *pʌḍʌi*$_{a}$; *sikʌi*$_{a}$.
leave *plɛcam*$_{m}$. **cause to leave** (said of grains of corn) *peicam*$_{m}$.
left^{1} (as opposed to right) *debre*$_{a}$.
left^{2} in **be left over** *hecap*$^{1}_{a}$, *he-*$_{m}$; *ubrʌi lacap*$_{a}$. **characterised by being left over** *hettɔp*$_{a}$.
leg A (leg, including the foot) *lɔsu*$_{am}$, *lɔs*$_{a}$. B (the lower part of the leg) *kɔŋko*$_{a}$, *kɔŋku*$_{m}$. C (upper leg) *phila*$_{m}$.
lentils *dal*$_{a}$.
leopard *gupsu*$_{am}$.
less *asi*$_{am}$; *kʌmti*$_{a}$. **become less** *sɔrcap*$_{a}$, *sɔr-*$_{m}$.
let *gɔkcap*$_{a}$, *gɔkcam*$_{m}$.
letter *ciṭhi*$_{m}$.
liar *nim pottɔp*$_{a}$.
lick *lɔkcap*$^{2}_{a}$.
lie (untruth) I n *nim*$^{2}_{a}$, *nima*$_{m}$. II v *nima han-*$_{m}$, *nim pacap*$_{a}$.
lie down *glecap*$_{a}$, *glecam*$_{m}$.
lift *phukcam*$_{m}$. **lift up** *uḍʌi pacam*$_{m}$.
lightened in **be lightened** *sʌlkʌi lacap*$_{a}$.
lightening bug *dalcip*$_{a}$; *dalaciŋma*$_{m}$.
lightning *gʌrjʌi*$_{a}$; *gurum*$_{a}$.
like^{1} (similar to) *=na=se*$_{a}$, *=na=s*$_{a}$; *=na=se=p*. **be like** *jocam*$_{m}$.
like^{2} (be fond of) *dakcap*$_{a}$, *dakcam*$_{m}$; *daː-*$_{a}$.

Limbu (Kiranti group) *Subba*$_{a}$.
lime (big, species) *bɔmbar*$_{am}$.
line *rekha*$_{a}$.
lip *yunti*$_{am}$.
liquor *rʌksi*$_{a}$.
Litsea polyantha (tree) *kuṭmiro*$_{m}$.
little *cicir*$_{a}$; *cimtɛp*$_{a}$; *yɔkko*$_{m}$. **a little** *cimmaŋ*$_{m}$; *cimtɛp*$_{a}$.
liver *kʌlejo*$_{a}$; *ma*$^{5}_{a}$; *ni*$^{6}_{m}$.
living in **be living** *blecap*$_{a}$, *ble-*$_{m}$.
lizard *cheparo*$_{a}$; *wakewa*$_{m}$.
loaf *sɔblɛm*$_{am}$.
location in **marker of location** A (up) *-ta*$^{1}_{a}$, *-t*$_{a}$, *-to*$^{1}_{m}$. B (down) *-ya*$^{2}_{a}$, *-yo*$_{m}$, *-i*$_{am}$. C (horizontally) *-na*$^{3}_{a}$, *-n*$_{a}$, *-no*$_{m}$.
locative marker *=na*$^{1}_{a}$, *=no*$^{2}_{m}$, *=n*$_{am}$, *=ma*$_{a}$; *-lu*$_{am}$, *-l*$_{am}$.
lock *bʌndʌ pacam*$_{m}$; *thɛkcap*$_{a}$, *ṭhɛkcam*$_{m}$.
locust *kaŋkoṭ*$_{a}$, *kaŋkaŋ*$_{m}$.
long *hitto*$_{m}$, *hiṭṭɔp*$_{a}$. be **long** *hi:cap*$_{a}$.
look (after, at) *kicap*$_{a}$, *kicam*$_{m}$. **look for** *malcam*$_{m}$. **look like** *jocam*$_{m}$.
loose in **let loose** *klɔ[k]-*$_{m}$.
loosen *phukʌi pacap*$_{a}$; *phuklʌi pacap*$_{a}$, *phuklʌi pacam*$_{m}$. **be loosened** *khuskʌi lacam*$_{m}$.
loot *khus pacam*$_{m}$.
lose *damcap*$_{a}$. **be lost** *damcap*$_{a}$. **get lost** *harʌi dumcam*$_{m}$.
loss *harʌi*$_{m}$.
lot in **a lot of** *thupro*$_{a}$.
love I n *maya*$_{a}$. II v *dakcap*$_{a}$, *dakcam*$_{m}$. **be in love** *maya pacap*$_{a}$.
lower *rɔlcam*$_{m}$, *rwalcap*$_{a}$.
lungs *jɔpre*$_{m}$, *jɔpro*$_{a}$; *phɔkso*$_{a}$.
lying in **act of lying** (telling a lie) *nim*$^{2}_{a}$, *nima*$_{m}$.

— m —

maintain *yu:cap*$_{a}$
maize *mʌkʌi*$_{am}$.
make *bʌnʌi pacam*$_{m}$; *pacap*$_{a}$, *pacam*$_{m}$. **something made** *bʌnʌi*$_{m}$.
man A (person, in general) *mucu*$_{am}$. B (old) *buḍa*$_{a}$. C (young) *salco*$_{m}$.
mandarin orange *suntʌla*$_{a}$.
mango *tɔksi*$_{am}$.

mankind *mucu*$_{am}$.
manner in **in what manner?** *hus*$_{am}$*?*; *hus pasaku*$_{m}$*?*. **marker of the gerund of manner** *-sa*$^{1}_{am}$; *-su*$^{1}_{m}$.
many *as khɔlse*$_{a}$. **very many** *dherʌi*$_{m}$.
mark *rekha*$_{a}$.
marriage *biha*$_{a}$.
marrow *mʌsi*$_{a}$.
marten *kɔŋgale*$_{a}$, *kaŋgale*$_{m}$.
masculine gender marker *-pa*$^{1}_{am}$; *-pu*$^{1}_{am}$; *-ʔu*$_{am}$.
masticate *makcam*$^{2}_{m}$, *nakcap*$_{a}$.
mat in **woven straw mat** *gundri*$_{am}$.
maternal grandfather *kɔr-hupu*$_{a}$. **maternal grandmother** *kɔr-humu*$_{a}$. **maternal great-grandfather** *kɔr-gupsu-hupu*$_{a}$. **maternal great-grandmother** *kɔr-gupsu-humu*$_{a}$. **maternal uncle** *kɔro*$_{a}$, *kɔr*$_{a}$; *thapu*$_{a}$. **maternal uncle-in-law** *buḍi-mauli*$_{a}$.
matter *bat*$_{a}$; *dɔt*$_{a}$; *thok*$_{m}$.
mattress *lɛtam*$_{am}$.
meat B (in general) *sikar*$_{am}$; *su*$^{4}_{am}$. B (of a living creature) *jɔʔmu*$_{am}$. **meat** marker *-su*$^{2}_{am}$.
meet *rɛmcam*$_{m}$; *tɛrcap*$_{a}$, *tɛrcam*$_{m}$. **be met** *tɛrcap*$_{a}$, *tɛrcam*$_{m}$.
memory *daku*$_{a}$, *dak*$_{a}$, *dakhu*$_{m}$; *mimti*$_{m}$. **not have the memory** *ma[p]-*$_{m}$.
middle *kha:ci*$_{am}$. **middle marker** *-si*$^{4}_{am}$.
mild *nʌrʌm*$_{m}$.
milk *dudh*$_{am}$.
millet A (uncooked *Eleusine coracana*) *carji*$_{am}$. B (cooked *carji*) *khicul*$_{a}$.
mind *tɛm*$_{a}$, *tɔm*$_{m}$.
mist (in sky) *badʌl*$_{a}$; *kɔksɛl*$_{a}$, *kuksɛl*$_{m}$.
mix I n *misʌi*$_{m}$. II v *misʌi pacam*$_{m}$.
molar *baŋra*$_{am}$.
molest *tupcap*$_{a}$, *tupcam*$_{a}$.
money *pʌisa*$_{am}$; *rɔkso*$_{a}$.
monkey A (in general, especially the white langur) *buḍim*$_{m}$, *buḍum*$_{a}$. B (small red species) *pɛku*$_{a}$.
moon *tʌusɛl*$_{a}$, *tosɛl*$_{m}$.
more A (larger) *bʌḍe*$_{m}$, *bʌḍi*$_{a}$. B (other) *ʌru*$_{a}$
morning *bihan*$_{am}$.
mortar (large, made of stone or wood) *sumlo*$_{a}$.
mosquito *bhusna*$_{a}$; *gaŋayɔma*$_{m}$.

mother A (in general) *mama*$_{am}$. B (sow) *jyaŋli*$_{a}$. C (mother-hen) *kuryam*$_{a}$, *kuryaŋma*$_{a}$, *kuryaŋmo*$_{m}$.

mother-in-law A (term of address) *ma:mʌi*$_{m}$. B (term of reference) *sɛrme*$_{am}$. C (one's own child's mother-in-law) *hilmu*$_{a}$.

mount *hedicap*$_{a}$.

mountain *himal*$_{a}$.

mouse *cicimo*$_{m}$, *cicum*$_{m}$; *musa*$_{a}$.

moustache *juŋga*$_{a}$.

mouth *hur*$_{am}$.

move I n *hʌlʌi*$_{am}$. II v *cʌlʌi pacam*$_{m}$; *dukcam*$_{m}$; *hʌlʌi pacap*$_{a}$, *hʌlʌi pacam*$_{m}$; *sarʌi dumcam*$_{m}$; *sarʌi pacam*$_{m}$; *walcap*$_{a}$, *walcam*$_{m}$; *yocam*$_{m}$. **make move** *wal paccam*$_{m}$.

movement *cʌlʌi*$_{m}$; *sarʌi*$_{m}$.

mow *rikcam*$_{m}$.

much *as khɔlse*$_{a}$; *saro*$_{m}$. **this much** *ɛti*$_{a}$.

mud *hilo*$_{a}$, *kaksi*$_{am}$.

murder *sɛccap*$_{a}$, *sɛccam*$_{m}$.

muzzle *hur*$_{am}$.

my *am*$_{am}$.

myth *kʌtha*$_{m}$.

— n —

nail *gwarji*$_{am}$.

name *ni*$^{7}_{am}$.

nasal mucus *nusum-khli*$_{m}$; *sĩgan*$_{a}$.

near *cheu*$_{am}$; *nʌjik*$_{m}$.

necessary in it is generally necessary *pʌrchʌ*$_{am}$. **it is not generally necessary** *pʌrdʌinʌ*$_{a}$. **it is now necessary, it was then necessary** *pʌryo*$_{m}$.

neck *kligji*$_{a}$.

needle *jyambale*$_{a}$; *waccɛm*$_{a}$.

negative marker *a-*$^{1}_{am}$.

Nepal *Nepal*$_{a}$

nest *gũḍ*$_{a}$.

net *jala*$_{a}$.

netting *jal*$_{a}$, *jalu*$_{m}$.

new *ebo*$_{m}$; *nɛntha*$_{a}$.

next to *cheu*$_{am}$.
nice *rance*$_{m}$; *rantɔp*$_{a}$, *ranto*$_{m}$.
night *rat*$_{a}$.
nip *naccam*$_{m}$.
nominaliser A (of loan verbs) -*ʌi*$^{1}_{am}$. B (in demonstrative pronouns) -*ya*$^{3}_{a}$, -*i*$_{am}$.
nose *nusum*$_{am}$. **nose ring** *mundri*$_{m}$.
notice *daku*$_{a}$, *dak*$_{a}$, *dakhu*$_{m}$.
now *ɛti bɛla*$_{a}$; *maŋ*$_{am}$; *tɛŋu*$_{a}$, *tɛŋ*$_{am}$. **from now** *tɛŋu*$_{a}$, *tɛŋ*$_{am}$. **just now** *mɔkke*$_{m}$, *mɔkko*$_{a}$, *mɔko*$_{a}$.

— o —

oar *bɔna*$_{a}$.
obeisance *nʌmʌskar*$_{m}$.
object *cij*$_{m}$.
obliterate *bhʌtkʌi pacap*$_{a}$, *bhʌtkʌi pacam*$_{m}$.
obliteration *bhʌtkʌi*$_{am}$.
observe *manʌi pacam*$_{m}$.
observing *manʌi*$_{m}$.
obstruct *chekʌi pacap*$_{a}$.
obstruction *chekʌi*$_{a}$.
obtain *hipcam*$_{m}$.
occupation *karjʌi*$_{a}$.
oil *tilɛm*$_{am}$.
old *buḍa*$_{a}$; *buḍi*$_{a}$.
one *kɔʔlo*$_{a}$, *kɔʔl*$_{a}$, *kwal*$_{m}$.
oneself *daŋma*$_{a}$.
onion *pyãc*$_{a}$.
only *khamma*$_{a}$, *khaːma*$_{m}$; *naʔa*$_{am}$, *naʔ*$_{a}$.
open *hɔl*-$_{m}$. **make open** *kholʌi pacap*$_{a}$, *kholʌi pacam*$_{m}$.
opening *kholʌi*$_{am}$.
opinion *bicar*$_{a}$.
opposite *ulṭo*$_{m}$.
optative marker -*ano*$_{a}$, -*no*$_{am}$.
or *a*$_{a}$; *ki*$_{a}$.
other A [usually of two] *ʌrko*$_{a}$. B [of more than two] *ʌru*$_{a}$.

our A (dual exclusive) *ancum*$_{am}$. B (dual inclusive) *incim*$_{am}$. C (plural exclusive) *akkum*$_{am}$. D (plural inclusive) *ikkim*$_{am}$.
overthrow *ghopṭʌi lacam*$_{a}$.
owl *kope*$_{a}$.
ox *goru*$_{m}$.

— p —

pace *walcap*$_{a}$, *walcam*$_{m}$.
paddy *garji*$_{am}$.
pain *dukhʌ*$_{a}$.
paint I n *lipʌi*$_{a}$. II v *lipʌi pacap*$_{a}$; *khlɛkcap*$_{a}$, *khlɛk-*$_{m}$.
palm (of the hand) *jajale*$_{m}$.
panther *gupsu*$_{am}$.
papaya (*Carica papaya*) *mɛwa*$_{am}$, *mewa*$_{a}$.
pardon *maph*$_{m}$.
parents *papa-mama*$_{a}$.
parrot *suga*$_{a}$.
passive in **marker of the passive verbal adjective** *-mamcu*$_{a}$.
past in **marker of past time** *thiyo*$_{am}$. **past prior time marker in past perfect gerunds** *-ma*$^{1}{}_{am}$.
path *lam*$^{2}{}_{am}$.
patient in **grammatical patient marker** *lai*$_{am}$.
peacock *mʌjur*$_{a}$.
pebble *asi khɔlto phuluŋ*$_{m}$.
peel I n *bɔkra*$_{m}$. II v *peicam*$_{m}$.
pellet-bow *gɛtis*$_{a}$.
pen *kʌlʌm*$_{a}$.
penis *pli*$_{am}$.
penknife *cʌkku*$_{a}$.
pepper *khursani*$_{am}$, *khursan*$_{a}$.
perceive *mɔ-*$_{m}$.
perfect in **marker of the perfect gerund** *-ku*$^{2}{}_{am}$, *-k*$_{am}$
perforate *phɛrcap*$_{a}$, *phɛr-*$_{m}$.
person *jʌna*$_{am}$, *jʌn*$_{m}$; *mucu*$_{am}$. **person marker** *-cu*$^{1}{}_{am}$.
petition *binti*$_{m}$.
physic *jiu*$_{a}$; *ram*$_{m}$.
pick^{1} (bone) *kraccap*$_{a}$, *kra[k]-*$_{m}$.

pick^{2} (up) *gicap*$_{a}$, *gicam*$_{m}$.
piece *gɔʈa*$_{a}$, *gɔʈ*$_{a}$.
pierce *suk-*$_{m}$.
pig *pa*$^{3}_{am}$.
pigeon *pʌrewa*$_{a}$.
piglet *cuppa*$_{am}$.
pigtail *ʈupi*$_{m}$.
pile in **a pile of** *thupro*$_{a}$. **a large pile of** *thuprʌi*$_{a}$.
pinch *naccam*$_{m}$.
pinion *masrɛmpu*$_{a}$.
pipe *murʌli*$_{m}$.
piss I n *sɔrki*$_{am}$. II v *sɔrki pacap*$_{a}$, *sɔrki pacam*$_{m}$.
pit *khalʈa*$_{m}$.
place I n *ʈhaũ*$_{am}$. II v *cɔpcap*$_{a}$, *cɔpcam*$_{m}$; *daccam*$_{m}$; *takcap*$_{a}$. **place** upright *phukcam*$_{m}$.
plait *calcap*$_{a}$, *calcam*$_{m}$.
plaster (with mud and dung) *khlɛkcap*$_{a}$, *khlɛk-*$_{m}$; *lipʌi pacap*$_{a}$.
play A (a game) *khelʌi pacap*$_{a}$; *camda pacap*$_{a}$, *cam pacap*$_{a}$; *camdo pacam*$_{m}$. B (an instrument) *tɔpcap*$_{a}$, *tɔpcam*$_{m}$.
playing *khelʌi*$_{a}$.
pleased *khusi*$_{m}$. **be pleased** *daksi raːcap*$_{a}$; *khusi bakcam*$_{m}$.
plough *khɔrcap*$_{a}$, *khɔr-*$_{m}$; *wakcap*$^{1}_{a}$.
plural number marker *ticu*$_{am}$, *tit*$_{am}$.
pluck *pɛk-*$_{m}$; *sɛkcap*$_{a}$. **pluck out** *mɔrcap*$_{a}$.
plunder *khus pacam*$_{m}$.
point *suk-*$_{m}$.
poor *gʌrib*$_{am}$. **be poor** *gʌrib dumcap*$_{a}$, *gʌrib dumcam*$_{m}$.
pop (fry) *kharcap*$_{a}$, *kharcam*$_{m}$.
porcupine *dumsi*$_{m}$.
pork *pa-su*$_{a}$.
pot *bhãɖo*$_{am}$.
potato A (tuber) *rɛnjab*$_{a}$. B (sweet potato) *parkoti*$_{m}$, *parkot*$_{a}$.
pounce upon *cumcap*$_{a}$, *cumcam*$_{m}$.
practice I n *manʌi*$_{m}$. II v *manʌi pacam*$_{m}$.
pray *binti pacam*$_{m}$.
prayer *binti*$_{m}$.
precisely *=se*$^{2}_{am}$, *=s*$_{am}$.
prefer *dakcap*$_{a}$, *dakcam*$_{m}$.
presence (in mind) *maʔla*$_{a}$.

present in **marker of a specific fact in present time** *ho*$_{a}$. **marker of the present gerund** *-lu*$_{am}$, *-l*$_{am}$.
presently *mɔkke*$_{m}$, *mɔkko*$_{a}$, *mɔko*$_{a}$.
press A (squeeze) *cepʌi pacap*$_{a}$. B (sugar cane, oil) *curcap*$_{a}$, *curcam*$_{m}$. **press forward** *ghʌcca gɔkcam*$_{m}$; *nɛpcap*$_{a}$, *nɛpcam*$_{m}$.
pressure *cepʌi*$_{a}$.
prevent *rokʌi pacap*$_{a}$, *rokʌi pacam*$_{m}$; *thunʌi pacap*$_{a}$.
prevention *thunʌi*$_{a}$.
previous *lapphu*$_{am}$; *lapthɔl*$_{a}$; *na*$^{4}_{am}$; *num-*$_{m}$.
previously in **much previously** *na-na*$_{m}$, *na ke*$_{a}$, *na=se*$_{am}$.
prey *sikar*$_{am}$.
prick (pierce) *suk-*$_{m}$.
probability marker *hɔla*$_{m}$.
proceed *lagʌi dumcam*$_{m}$.
proceeding *lagʌi*$_{m}$.
produce *bʌnʌi pacam*$_{m}$.
profound *gʌira*$_{m}$.
provoke *rakcap*$_{a}$, *rakcam*$_{m}$; *ra:cap*$_{a}$.
publish *mɔrcap*$_{a}$.
pull *jɛccap*$_{a}$; *ki:t-*$_{m}$; *klɔ[k]-*$_{m}$. **pull out** *pɛk-*$_{m}$.
pulse *nari*$_{a}$.
punch *muḍki*$_{m}$.
puppy *kurtima*$_{a}$.
purpose in **marker of the verbal adjective of purpose** *-ca*$_{am}$.
pursue *dalcap*$_{a}$, *dalcam*$_{m}$.
pus *hupmi*$_{m}$, *hupni*$_{a}$.
push I n *ghʌcca*$_{m}$. II v *ghʌcca gɔkcam*$_{m}$; *nɛpcap*$_{a}$, *nɛpcam*$_{m}$.
put down *cɔpcap*$_{a}$, *cɔpcam*$_{m}$. **put in** *phikcap*$_{a}$. **manner of setting up or putting down** *ba*$_{a}$.
python *ʌjiŋgʌr*$_{a}$.

— q —

queen *rani*$_{a}$.
question *cel*$_{m}$; *tublo*$_{a}$.
quiet *cup*$_{a}$; *manto*$_{m}$, *manthu*$_{a}$. **be quiet** *cup pacap*$_{a}$.
quit *plɛcam*$_{m}$; *taccap*$_{a}$.
quote *necap*$_{a}$, *necam*$_{m}$.

— r —

Rai *Ra:du*$_{a}$, *Ra:ḍu*$_{m}$. **Rai person** *Ra:ḍu mucu*$_{m}$.
rain I n *hwarsi*$_{a}$, *warsi*$_{m}$. II v *warsi yacam*$_{m}$.
rainbow *indreni*$_{a}$.
raw cotton *buisi*$_{am}$.
read *pʌḍʌi lacap*$_{a}$.
reading *pʌḍʌi*$_{a}$.
reason in **for what reason?** *haiŋa*$_{m}$, *haiŋaŋ*$_{m}$, *haiŋo*$_{m}$, *hayaŋ*$_{m}$, *hayɔŋ*$_{m}$; *haŋ*$_{a}$.
rebuke *burcap*$_{a}$.
receive *tɛrcap*$_{a}$, *tɛrcam*$_{m}$. **be received** *tɛrcap*$_{a}$, *tɛrcam*$_{m}$.
reciprocal auxiliary *pocap*$_{a}$.
rectum *berne*$_{a}$.
red *laka*$_{a}$; *lakcip*$_{a}$. very **red** *laka-laka*$_{a}$.
reifying marker *≡me*[1]$_{am}$, *≡p*$_{a}$, *≡m*$_{am}$.
relate *necap*$_{a}$, *necam*$_{m}$; *sɔcam*$_{m}$.
relax *naicam*$_{m}$.
remain *bakcap*$_{a}$, *bakcam*$_{m}$.
remember *mimcap*$_{a}$; *mimti pacam*$_{m}$; *sʌmjhʌi lacap*$_{a}$; *samjhʌi pacap*$_{a}$, *sʌmjhʌi pacam*$_{m}$.
remembrance *daku*$_{a}$, *dak*$_{a}$, *dakhu*$_{m}$; *mimti*$_{m}$; *sʌmjhʌi*$_{am}$.
reminder *sʌmjhʌi*$_{am}$.
remove *klɔ[k]-*$_{m}$; *sɔlcap*$_{a}$, *sɔl-*$_{m}$.
rend *ciccap*$_{a}$.
repose *glecap*$_{a}$, *glecam*$_{m}$.
request I n *binti*$_{m}$; *cel*$_{m}$; *tublo*$_{a}$. II v *binti pacam*$_{m}$; *phɔicam*$_{m}$; *thɔcap*[2]$_{a}$. **make a request** *cel pacam*$_{m}$; *tublo pacap*$_{a}$.
reserve *krɔtni*$_{m}$; *laji*$_{a}$.
resin *sika*$_{m}$.
rest *glecap*$_{a}$, *glecam*$_{m}$; *naicam*$_{m}$.
restrain *thunʌi pacap*$_{a}$; *rokʌi pacap*$_{a}$, *rokʌi pacam*$_{m}$.
restraint *thunʌi*$_{a}$.
return I n *phʌrkʌi*$_{m}$. II v *phʌrkʌi dumcam*$_{m}$, *phʌrkʌi lacam*$_{m}$; *phʌrkʌi pacam*$_{m}$.
reverse *pherʌi pacam*$_{m}$.
reversed *ulṭo*$_{m}$.
revolution *ghumʌi*$_{a}$.
revolve *ghumʌi pacap*$_{a}$.

rib *kʌrʌŋ*$_{a}$.
rice A (plant, unhusked) *garji*$_{am}$. B (husked and polished) *garji-seri*$_{m}$.
ridge *ḍãḍa*$_{a}$.
right A (as opposed to left) *daine*$_{a}$. B (good) *jati*$_{a}$.
rind *bɔkra*$_{m}$.
ring (small) *mundri*$_{m}$.
rinse *murcap*$_{a}$.
rip *ciccap*$_{a}$; *phrakcap*$_{a}$; *cirʌi pacam*$_{m}$.
rise (of the sun) *nɔm mɔrcap*$_{a}$.
river *nʌdi*$_{a}$.
road *lam*$^{2}{}_{am}$.
rob *khus pacam*$_{m}$.
roll up *calcap*$_{a}$, *calcam*$_{m}$.
roof *chana*$_{a}$.
room *koṭha*$_{a}$.
rooster *bhale*$_{am}$.
root (in the soil) *phuicap*$_{a}$, *phuit-*$_{m}$.
root *jʌra*$_{a}$.
rope *ḍeri*$_{m}$, *ḍori*$_{a}$. **make a rope** *calcap*$_{a}$, *calcam*$_{m}$.
rotation *pala*$_{a}$.
rotten in **be rotten** *yamcap*$_{a}$.
round *golo*$_{a}$.
route *lam*$^{2}{}_{am}$.
rub *khlecap*$_{a}$.
ruin I n *bigrʌi*$_{a}$. II v *bigrʌi pacap*$_{a}$. **be ruined** *bigrʌi lacap*$_{a}$.
run *prakcam*$_{m}$. **make run** *kudʌi pacap*$_{a}$, *kuḍʌi pacam*$_{m}$.
running *kudʌi*$_{a}$, *kuḍʌi*$_{m}$.
rupee *rupiyã*$_{m}$.

— S —

sale in **put up for sale** *thamcap*$_{a}$.
saliva *nɛmki*$_{am}$.
salt *yaksi*$_{am}$.
salty in **be salty** *yaksi lucap*$_{a}$, *yaksi lucam*$_{m}$.
salutation *nʌmʌskar*$_{m}$.
Sampang (Rai group) *Sampaŋ*$_{a}$.
sand *baluwa*$_{a}$.

saved in **be saved** *blecap*$_{a}$, *ble-*$_{m}$.
saw *aro*$_{a}$.
say A (something) *necap*$_{a}$, *necam*$_{m}$; *sɔcam*$_{m}$. B (to someone) *nɛ[ŋ]-*$_{a}$, *nɛ[ʔ]-*$_{m}$. **having said** *nesaku*$_{a}$. **something said** *ma:la*$_{am}$.
scarce *asi*$_{am}$.
scatter *bracap*$_{a}$, *bracam*$_{m}$.
scent *ŋaba*$_{m}$, *ŋab*$_{am}$. **bad scent** *arance ŋab*$_{m}$.
scorpion *bicchi*$_{a}$.
scratch A (by cat) *mircap*$_{a}$, *mircam*$_{m}$. B (by chicken) *phuicap*$_{a}$, *phuit-*$_{m}$. **scratch** up *khɔsrʌi pacap*$_{a}$.
scratching *khɔsrʌi*$_{a}$.
scream *wakcap*[2]$_{a}$; *wa:cap*$_{a}$.
screw up *khricap*$_{a}$, *khricam*$_{m}$.
scrotum *waʔlo*$_{m}$.
sear *kharcap*$_{a}$, *kharcam*$_{m}$.
search *malcam*$_{m}$.
seated in **be seated** *ni:cap*[1]$_{a}$, *ni:-*$_{m}$.
see *hipcap*$_{a}$, *hipcam*$_{m}$. **see oneself** *himcap*$_{a}$. **be seen** *himcap*$_{a}$.
seed *biu*$_{a}$; *cicila*$_{a}$; *cinci*$_{am}$.
seek *malcam*$_{m}$.
seem *jocam*$_{m}$.
seize *cumcap*$_{a}$, *cumcam*$_{m}$; *makcam*$_{m}$.
self *daŋma*$_{a}$.
sell *thamcap*$_{a}$.
send *khamcap*$_{a}$; *pʌṭhʌi pacap*$_{a}$, *pʌṭhʌi pacam*$_{m}$.
sending in **act of sending** *pʌṭhʌi*$_{am}$.
sensation in **cause a mental or bodily sensation** *lucap*$_{a}$, *lucam*$_{m}$. **causing a mental or bodily sensation** *luttɔp*$_{a}$.
sense *mɔ-*$_{m}$.
set (moon, sun) *hɔmcap*$_{a}$, *hamcam*$_{m}$. **set up** *daccam*; *takcap*$_{a}$. **manner of setting up or putting down** *ba*$_{a}$.
sew *phɛrcap*$_{a}$, *phɛr-*$_{m}$.
shade (of a tree) *rimsa*$_{m}$; *riptɛwa*$_{a}$.
shake I n *hʌlʌi*$_{am}$. II v *hʌlʌi pacap*$_{a}$, *hʌlʌi pacam*$_{m}$; *yocam*$_{m}$.
shake *dukcam*$_{m}$. **shake down** *rɔlcam*$_{m}$, *rwalcap*$_{a}$.
shaman *jɔmcu*$_{am}$.
shame *krɔtni*$_{m}$; *laji*$_{a}$.
share I n *bãḍʌi*$_{a}$. II v *bãḍʌi pacap*$_{a}$.
sharp in **be sharp** *yacap*[2]$_{a}$.

she *aŋgu*$_{am}$, *aŋ*$_{am}$.
shed[1] (structure) *kʌṭerʌ*$_{a}$.
shed[2] (go down) *rɔlcam*$_{m}$, *rwalcap*$_{a}$.
she-goat *beli*$_{m}$, *beʔli*$_{a}$.
shell *peicam*$_{m}$.
shelter *chopʌi*$_{a}$.
shift I n *sarʌi*$_{m}$; *hʌlʌi*$_{am}$. II v *hʌlʌi pacap*$_{a}$, *hʌlʌi pacam*$_{m}$; *sarʌi dumcam*$_{m}$; *sarʌi pacam*$_{m}$.
shin *ḍuḍuna*$_{a}$; *kɔŋko*$_{a}$, *kɔŋku*$_{m}$.
shit *saŋki*$_{a}$, *saŋkhi*$_{m}$.
shoot *hɔpcap*[2]$_{a}$.
Shorea robusta (tree) *sɔllɔm*$_{m}$, *sɔlɔm*$_{a}$, *sɔʔlɔm*$_{a}$.
shoulder *masɛm*$_{m}$.
shout *burcap*$_{a}$; *hu:cap*$_{a}$, *hu:-*$_{m}$; *wakcap*[2]$_{a}$; *wa:cap*$_{a}$.
shove *ghʌcca gɔkcam*$_{m}$; *nɛpcap*$_{a}$, *nɛpcam*$_{m}$.
shower I n *hwarsi*$_{a}$, *warsi*$_{m}$. II v *warsi yacam*$_{m}$.
shriek *wakcap*[2]$_{a}$; *wa:cap*$_{a}$.
shuffle (hair) *ticcam*$_{m}$.
shut I adj *bʌndʌ*$_{m}$. II v *bʌndʌ pacam*$_{m}$; *thɛkcap*$_{a}$, *ṭhɛkcam*$_{m}$.
sick *birami*$_{am}$. **be sick** *anucap*$_{a}$, *anucam*$_{m}$.
side *cheu*$_{am}$.
silence *cup*$_{a}$; *manto*$_{m}$, *manthu*$_{a}$.
silent in **be silent** *cup pacap*$_{a}$.
similar *=na=se*$_{a}$, *=na=s*$_{a}$; *=na=se=p*.
similaritive marker *≡se*[1]$_{am}$, *≡sɛ*$_{m}$, *-sa*$_{a}$, *≡s*$_{am}$.
simmer *lɔkcap*[1]$_{a}$, *lɔkt-*$_{m}$; *umlʌi pacap*$_{a}$.
simplex agreement suffix A (second and third person singular) *-Ø*[1]$_{am}$. B (marks a transitive relationship between a third person singular agent and a first person singular patient) *-aŋti*$_{m}$, *-ŋti*$_{m}$. C (dual) *-ci*[1]$_{am}$. D (first person dual exclusive agent and subject) *-cuwa*$_{a}$, *-cu*$_{am}$. E (third person non-plural agent) *-i*[1]$_{am}$, *-Ø*$_{am}$. F (marks a transitive relationship between a second person agent and a first person singular patient) *-iŋ*[1]$_{m}$. G (first person plural inclusive agent and subject) *-ki*$_{am}$. H (first person plural exclusive agent and subject) *-kuwa*[1]$_{a}$, *-ku*$_{am}$. I (marks that minimally one of the actants involved in the verbal scenario is a second or third person and that minimally one actant) *-mi*[1]$_{am}$, *-im*$_{am}$, *-m*$_{am}$, *-ʔ*$_{a}$, *-ʔim*$_{m}$, *-ʔmi*$_{a}$, *-Ø*$_{a}$. J (marks a transitive relationship between a third person singular agent and a second person singular patient) *-nati*$_{m}$. K (second per-

son) *-ni*$^{3}{}_{am}$, *-n*$_{am}$. L (marks a transitive relationship between a first person singular agent and a second person patient) *-ni*$^{1}{}_{am}$. M (dual subject) *-ŋ*$^{3}{}_{am}$, *-ŋaŋ*$_{a}$, *-ŋu*$_{a}$, *-uŋ*$_{m}$, *-iŋ*$_{m}$. N (first person singular) *-ŋu*$^{1}{}_{am}$, *-ŋ*$_{am}$, *-uŋ*$_{m}$, *-u*$_{am}$, *-ʔ*$_{am}$, *-ʔu*$_{am}$, *-Ø*$_{a}$. O (third person dual agent) *-ʔ*$_{m}$.

simultaneous in **marker of the simultaneous gerund** *-sʌi*$_{am}$.

sing *sa:laŋ pacam*$_{m}$.

singer *sa:ʔlɛŋ pottɔp*$_{a}$.

sink *ḍubʌi lacap*$_{a}$; *hɔmcap*$_{a}$, *hamcam*$_{m}$.

sinking *ḍubʌi*$_{a}$.

sister A [younger than ego] *bʌini*$_{a}$. B [older than ego] *didi*$_{a}$. **sisters** *didi-bʌini*$_{a}$.

sit *bakcap*$_{a}$, *bakcam*$_{m}$. **sit cross-legged** *phɛmto pacap*$_{a}$. **sit down** *ni:-cap*$^{1}{}_{a}$, *ni:-*$_{m}$.

six *chʌ*$_{a}$

skin *bɔkra*$_{m}$; *chala*$_{m}$.

skull *khʌppʌr*$_{a}$.

sky *sɔrga*$_{a}$.

slackness *ḍhilo*$_{am}$.

slaughter *sɛccap*$_{a}$, *sɛccam*$_{m}$.

sleep *mɛlcap*$_{a}$, *mɛlcam*$_{m}$. **go to sleep** *glecap*$_{a}$, *glecam*$_{m}$. **put to sleep** *khlɔmcap*$_{a}$, *khlɔm-*$_{m}$.

slime *hilo*$_{a}$.

small *cimtɛp*$_{a}$, *yɔkko*$_{m}$. **small object marker** *-si*$^{3}{}_{am}$.

smear I n *lipʌi*$_{a}$. II v *khlɛkcap*$_{a}$, *khlɛk-*$_{m}$; *lipʌi pacap*$_{a}$.

smell I n *ŋaba*$_{m}$, *ŋab*$_{am}$. II v *ŋab dɔmcap*$_{a}$; *ŋaba ŋɔmcam*$_{m}$; *ŋɔmcap*$_{a}$, *ŋɔmcam*$_{m}$; *thɔcap*$^{1}{}_{a}$, *thɔ-*$_{m}$. **bad smell** *arance ŋab*$_{m}$.

smoke I n *khumci*$_{a}$, *kunci*$_{a}$. II v *tu:cap*$_{a}$, *tu:cam*$_{m}$.

snail *gyaŋgu*$_{a}$.

snake A (big) *ʌjiŋgʌr*$_{a}$. B (small) *phucu*$_{a}$.

snare *jala*$_{a}$.

snatch *makcam*$_{m}$.

sniff *ŋɔmcap*$_{a}$, *ŋɔmcam*$_{m}$.

snot *nusum-khli*$_{m}$; *sĩgan*$_{a}$.

snout *hur*$_{am}$.

so A (like this) *ase*$_{m}$, *as*$_{m}$; *ase=p*$_{a}$, *ase=m*$_{m}$. B (like that, horizontally) *nɔse*$_{m}$; *nɔse=p*$_{a}$, *nɔse=m*$_{m}$. C (like that, up) *tɔse=p*$_{a}$; *use*$_{m}$, *us*$_{am}$. D (like that, near hearer) *use=p*$_{a}$, *use=m*$_{m}$. E (like that, down) *yɔse=p*$_{a}$.

soft A (in general) *nʌrʌm*$_{m}$. B (especially pertaining to cartilage or gristle) *kurkure*$_{a}$.
soil *kaksi*$_{am}$.
sole (of a foot or shoe) *pʌital*$_{a}$.
solicit *phɔicam*$_{m}$; *thɔcap*$^{2}{}_{a}$.
some *asi khɔlse*$_{a}$; *cicir*$_{a}$; *cimmaŋ*$_{m}$; *cimtɛp*$_{a}$.
somebody *munu*$_{am}$, *mun*$_{a}$; *mundo*$_{m}$.
something *hai*$_{am}$. **something done** *bʌnʌi*$_{m}$. **something made** *bʌnʌi*$_{m}$. **something said** *ma:la*$_{am}$.
somewhere (of place) *thalu*$_{am}$, *thal*$_{am}$.
son *teʔu*$_{am}$.
song *sa:laŋ*$_{m}$, *sa:ʔlɛŋ*$_{a}$.
sorcerer *dhami*$_{a}$.
sound *sor*$_{am}$.
sour *jurtɔp*$_{a}$, *jurto*$_{m}$. **be sour** *jurcap*$_{a}$, *jur-*$_{m}$.
source marker *≡ku*$^{2}{}_{a}$, *≡khu*$_{m}$, *≡k*$_{am}$.
sow^{1} (pig) *jyaŋli*$_{a}$; *khɔpme*$_{m}$.
sow^{2} (scatter) *bracap*$_{a}$, *bracam*$_{m}$.
speak *ma:la sɔcam*$_{m}$.
speech *ma:la*$^{1}{}_{am}$.
spices *mʌsala*$_{a}$.
spicy in **be spicy** *su-*$^{3}{}_{m}$.
spider *bosrɛmpu*$_{a}$; *ma:jari*$_{m}$; *makura*$_{a}$.
spirit A (vital force) *maʔla*$_{a}$. B (of the dead) *pitrʌ*$_{a}$. C (alcoholic drink made from fermented barley) *rʌksi*$_{a}$.
spiritual leader *naksu*$_{a}$.
spit *thu pacap*$_{a}$; *thukcap*$_{a}$.
spitting *thu*$_{a}$.
spittle *nɛmki*$_{am}$; *thu*$_{a}$.
split *cirʌi pacam*$_{m}$; *phrakcap*$_{a}$.
spoil *bigrʌi lacap*$_{a}$. **be spoilt** *yamcap*$_{a}$.
spread I n *bichʌi*$_{a}$; *ochʌi*$_{a}$. II v *bichʌi pacap*$_{a}$; *ochʌi pacap*$_{a}$; *bracap*$_{a}$, *bracam*$_{m}$; *klecam*$_{m}$.
spring *kudʌi lacap*$_{a}$.
sprout in **begin to sprout** *pʌlʌi dumcam*$_{m}$.
sprouting *pʌlʌi*$_{m}$.
squat *tuŋ ni:cap*$_{a}$. **manner of squatting** *tuŋ*$_{a}$.
squeeze *cepʌi pacap*$_{a}$; *naccam*$_{m}$.
squirrel *lokhʌrke*$_{am}$.

stab *suk-*$_{m}$.
stable *dʌro*$_{a}$.
stale *basi*$_{m}$.
stall *kʌṭerʌ*$_{a}$.
stand *bukcap*$_{a}$, *bukcam*$_{m}$; *yɔmcap*$_{a}$, *yɔmcam*$_{m}$. **be standing** *bukcap*$_{a}$, *bukcam*$_{m}$. **standing on one's head** *ubhinḍo*$_{m}$.
star *tara*$_{am}$.
start I n *thalʌi*$_{am}$. II v *jɛkcam*$_{m}$; *thalʌi pacap*$_{a}$, *thalʌi pacam*$_{m}$.
state in **marker of the negative state gerund** *-thum*$_{a}$.
steal *khus pacam*$_{m}$.
steer[1] (cattle) *biya*$_{a}$; *goru*$_{m}$.
steer[2] (guide) *wal paccam*$_{m}$.
stench *ŋɔmcap*$_{a}$, *ŋɔmcam*$_{m}$.
stick[1] (bar) *lʌura*$_{am}$.
stick[2] (fasten) *ṭãsʌi lacam*$_{m}$; *ṭãsʌi pacap*$_{a}$, *ṭãsʌi pacam*$_{m}$; *kɛpcap*$_{a}$, *kɛp-cam*$_{m}$.
sticking *ṭãsʌi*$_{am}$.
still *tʌya*$_{a}$.
sting *kɔkcap*[2]$_{a}$; *naccam*$_{m}$.
stinging nettle *culle*$_{a}$, *cutle*$_{m}$.
stink *ŋɔmcap*$_{a}$, *ŋɔmcam*$_{m}$.
stir up *rakcap*$_{a}$, *rakcam*$_{m}$; *raːcap*$_{a}$.
stomach *mɔl*$_{am}$.
stone A (in general) *phuluŋ*$_{am}$. B (slab of stone on which spices are ground up) *silʌuŋta*$_{m}$.
stool (faeces) I n *saŋki*$_{a}$, *saŋkhi*$_{m}$. II v *saŋki pacap*$_{a}$.
stoop *kum bɔm-*$_{m}$.
stop I n *rokʌi*$_{am}$. II v *plɛcam*$_{m}$; *rokʌi pacap*$_{a}$, *rokʌi pacam*$_{m}$; *taccap*$_{a}$.
stopped *bʌndʌ*$_{m}$.
storm I n A *hundʌri*$_{a}$; *huri*$_{a}$; *phuḍim*$_{m}$. B (severe) *dikkur*$_{m}$. II v (blow strongly) *dikkur pacam*$_{m}$.
stormy in **be stormy** *phuḍim pacam*$_{m}$.
story *kʌtha*$_{m}$. **tell a story** *kʌtha sɔcam*$_{m}$.
stretch *kiːt-*$_{m}$.
strike *hɔpcap*[2]$_{a}$; *tɔpcap*$_{a}$, *tɔpcam*$_{m}$; *tupcap*$_{a}$, *tupcam*$_{a}$.
strong *bʌliyo*$_{a}$.
study I n *sikʌi*$_{a}$. II v *cei-*$_{m}$; *pʌḍʌi lacap*$_{a}$; *sikʌi lacap*$_{a}$.
stunt in **a kind of mischievous trick or silly stunt done for amusement** *pacewa*$_{a}$.

sub-caste *thʌr*$_{m}$.
subject *bisʌya*$_{a}$.
submerged in **be submerged** *ḍubʌi lacap*$_{a}$.
suck *bipcap*$_{a}$, *bipcam*$_{m}$; *yupcap*$_{a}$.
suckle *dudh teicam*$_{a}$.
suddenly *kwal coṭiku*$_{m}$.
sufficient in **be sufficient** *dɔkcap*$_{a}$, *dɔkcam*$_{m}$.
sugar *cini*$_{am}$. **sugar cane** *khudo*$_{a}$, *khuḍo*$_{m}$.
summon I n *cεm*$_{am}$. II v *khamcap*$_{a}$.
sun *nɔm*$_{am}$. **feel the sun** *nɔm pacam*$_{m}$.
Sunkosī river *Briŋmu*$_{a}$, *Briŋku*$_{m}$.
sunlight *nɔm*$_{am}$.
sunny in **be sunny** *nɔm pacam*$_{m}$.
supernatural being *sama*$_{m}$.
supine in **marker of the supine** *-phu*$_{am}$, *-pu*$_{a}$.
supplicate *binti pacam*$_{m}$.
supplication *binti*$_{m}$.
support *yu:cap*$_{a}$. **take support on one's feet** *dimcap*$_{a}$.
sure *dʌro*$_{a}$.
surplus *ubrʌi*$_{a}$.
surround *gerʌi pacap*$_{a}$, *gerʌi pacam*$_{m}$.
surrounding *gerʌi*$_{am}$.
survive *blecap*$_{a}$, *ble-*$_{m}$.
suspend *cεccap*$^{1}_{a}$; *jhunḍʌi pacam*$_{m}$; *ṭaŋgai pacam*$_{m}$.
suspension *jhunḍʌi*$_{m}$.
swallow *tɔk-*$_{m}$.
sway (from side to side) *yocam*$_{m}$.
swear *burcap*$_{a}$.
sweep *brεkcap*$_{a}$, *brεk-*$_{m}$. **sweep away** *uḍʌi pacam*$_{m}$.
sweet *jiji*$_{m}$. **be sweet** *jiji lucam*$_{m}$.
swim *jos pacap*$_{a}$, *jos pacam*$_{m}$.
swimming *josu*$_{a}$, *jos*$_{am}$.
swine *pa*$^{3}_{am}$.
swing *yocam*$_{m}$.
syrup *khudo*$_{a}$, *khuḍo*$_{m}$.

— t —

tail *mɛʔlum*$_{a}$, *muʔlum*$_{m}$; *pucchʌr*$_{a}$; *ṭupi*$_{m}$.

take *placap*$_{a}$; *ta[k]-*$_{m}$. **take away** *lɛccap*$_{a}$, *lɛccam*$_{m}$. **take down** *rɔl-cam*$_{m}$, *rwalcap*$_{a}$. **take in one's hand** *makcam*$_{m}$. **take off** *klɔ[k]-*$_{m}$; *phukʌi pacap*$_{a}$; *phuklʌi pacap*$_{a}$, *phuklʌi pacam*$_{m}$. **take out** *klɔ[k]-*$_{m}$; *mɔrcap*$_{a}$. **take out of the pot** *phɛccap*$_{a}$, *phɛccam*$_{m}$. **take** with *lɛccap*$_{a}$, *lɛccam*$_{m}$.

talk I n *samsa*$_{a}$. II v *bat pacap*$_{a}$; *maːla sɔcam*$_{m}$; *sɔcam*$_{m}$.

tall *roto*$_{m}$. **very tall** *bʌḍe roto*$_{m}$.

talon *gwarji*$_{am}$.

tangerine *suntʌla*$_{a}$.

tasted in **be tasted** *dɔmcap*$_{m}$.

tasty *broto*$_{m}$, *brottɔp*$_{a}$; *luttɔp*$_{a}$. **be tasty** *brocap*$_{a}$.

taunt *rakcap*$_{a}$, *rakcam*$_{m}$; *raːcap*$_{a}$.

tea *ciya*$_{m}$.

teach *sikʌi pacap*$_{a}$.

tear[1] (drop from) *pimis*$_{a}$; *pitaŋke*$_{m}$.

tear[2] **apart** *ciccap*$_{a}$. **tear down** *bhʌtkʌi pacap*$_{a}$, *bhʌtkʌi pacam*$_{m}$. **tear up** (soil with an implement) *dɛcap*$_{a}$; *phuicap*$_{a}$, *phuit-*$_{m}$.

tease *rakcap*$_{a}$, *rakcam*$_{m}$; *raːcap*$_{a}$.

tell *necap*$_{a}$, *necam*$_{m}$; *sɔcam*$_{m}$.

tempest *phuḍim*$_{m}$.

ten *dʌs*$_{m}$.

tender *nʌrʌm*$_{m}$.

termite *krɛktum*$_{m}$, *krɛktup*$_{a}$.

text in **chanted sacred text of the oral tradition** *sɔmdu*$_{a}$; *sɔmdu-khadu*$_{a}$.

than *bhʌnda*$_{am}$.

that A (horizontally) *nɔya*$_{a}$, *nɔi*$_{am}$. B (up) *tɔi*$_{am}$. C (near the hearer) *uya*$_{a}$, *ui*$_{a}$. D (down) *yɔya*[2]$_{a}$, *yɔi*$_{am}$. **like that** A (horizontally) *nɔse*$_{m}$; *nɔse=p*$_{a}$, *nɔse=m*$_{m}$, *nɔse=p=na=se=p*$_{a}$. B (up) *tɔse=p*$_{a}$, *tɔse=p=na =se=p*$_{a}$. C (near hearer) *use*$_{m}$, *us*$_{am}$; *use=p*$_{a}$, *use=m*$_{m}$; *use=p=na =se=p*$_{a}$. D (down) *yɔse=p*$_{a}$, *yɔse=p=na=se=p*$_{a}$.

thatch *chana*$_{a}$.

theft *khus*$_{am}$.

their[d] A (dual) *ancim*$_{am}$. B (plural) *anim*$_{am}$.

theme marker *da*$_{a}$, *ḍa*$_{m}$.

then *hus bulu*$_{a}$, *hus bul*$_{a}$.

there A (of place, near the hearer) *ulu*$_{am}$, *ul*$_{a}$. B (of direction, near the hearer) *usal*$_{a}$. C (of place, horizontally) *nɔna*$_{a}$, *nɔn*$_{a}$, *nɔno*$_{m}$. D (of direction, horizontally) *nɔsal*$_{a}$, *nɔsɛl*$_{m}$. E (of place, down) *yɔya*$^{1}_{a}$, *yɔyo*$_{m}$, *yɔi*$_{am}$. F (of direction, down) *yɔsɛl*$_{m}$. G (of place, up) *tɔta*$_{a}$, *tɔt*$_{a}$, *tɔto*$_{m}$. H (of direction, up) *tɔsal*$_{a}$, *tɔsɛl*$_{m}$.

they A (in general) *aŋgu*$_{am}$, *aŋ*$_{am}$. B (dual) *aŋ nimpha*$_{am}$. C (plural) *aŋ ticu*$_{am}$.

thief *cor*$_{a}$; *cor pottɔp*$_{a}$; *khus pɔce mucu*$_{m}$; *khus pottɔp*$_{a}$.

thigh *tikhra*$_{a}$; *phila*$_{m}$.

thing *bat*$_{a}$; *cij*$_{m}$; *dɔt*$_{a}$; *thok*$_{m}$; *ma:la*$_{am}$.

think *mimcap*$_{a}$; *mimti pacam*$_{m}$.

thirsty in **feel thirsty** *ka:k-daku sicap*$_{a}$, *ka:k-dakhu sicam*$_{m}$; *ka:k-daku pacap*$_{a}$.

this *ɛs*$_{a}$; *aya*$_{a}$, *ai*$_{am}$. **like this** *ase*$_{m}$, *as*$_{m}$; *ase=p*$_{a}$, *ase=m*$_{m}$, *ase=p=na=se=p*$_{a}$.

thought *bicar*$_{a}$.

thrash *tupcap*$_{a}$, *tupcam*$_{a}$.

thread I n *dhago*$_{am}$. II v *si:cap*$_{a}$.

three *tin*$_{am}$.

thresher (saw-shaped, for rice) *ḍhiki*$_{a}$.

throat *kligji*$_{a}$.

throw I n *phalʌi*$_{a}$. II v *hɔpcap*$^{2}_{a}$; *phalʌi pacap*$_{a}$; *yoccam*$_{m}$, *yuccap*$_{a}$.

thrust *ghʌcca*$_{m}$.

thumb *bɔmti*$_{m}$; *buḍi-bɔmti*$_{m}$; *buḍi-brɛmci*$_{a}$.

thunder I n *gʌrjʌi*$_{a}$; *gurum*$_{a}$. II v *gʌrjʌi lacap*$_{a}$, *gurum pacam*$_{a}$.

thus A (like this) *ase*$_{m}$, *as*$_{m}$; *ase=p*$_{a}$, *ase=m*$_{m}$. B (like this, near hearer) *use*$_{m}$, *us*$_{am}$; *use=p*$_{a}$, *use=m*$_{m}$. C (like that, horizontally) *nɔse*$_{m}$; *nɔse=p*$_{a}$, *nɔse=m*$_{m}$. D (like that, up) *tɔse=p*$_{a}$; E (like that, down) *yɔse=p*$_{a}$.

tie *pɔccam*$_{m}$.

tiger *gupsu*$_{am}$.

time *bɛla*$_{a}$, *bɛl*$_{a}$; *bu-*$^{2}_{a}$; *khera*$_{a}$; *coṭi*$_{m}$; *pala*$_{a}$. **at the time when or of which one is writing or speaking** *maŋ*$_{am}$. **one time** *kwal coṭiku*$_{m}$. **this time** *ɛs pala*$_{a}$.

tip over *yak-*$_{m}$.

tired in **become tired** *thʌkʌi lacap*$_{a}$.

today *tɛmbar*$_{am}$.

toe A (in general) *brɛmci*$_{am}$. B (big) *bɔmti*$_{m}$; *buḍi-bɔmti*$_{m}$; *buḍi-brɛmci*$_{a}$.

together *kwaya*$_{a}$. **make go together** *milʌi lacap*$_{a}$, *milʌi dumcam*$_{m}$.
tomato *rambhɛnda*$_{a}$.
tomorrow *phɔpma*$_{am}$.
tone ball used to grind spices with *gutulum*$_{a}$.
tongue *lɛm*$_{am}$.
too *=ya*$^{1}_{am}$, *=i*$_{am}$; *dherʌi*$_{m}$.
tooth *gumsu*$_{am}$.
top (of the head) *talu*$_{a}$. **on top of** *toʔla*$_{a}$.
topic *bisʌya*$_{a}$.
tortoise *kʌchuwa*$_{a}$.
toss *hɔpcap*$^{2}_{a}$; *yoccam*$_{m}$, *yuccap*$_{a}$.
touch I n *chamʌi*$_{am}$. II v *chamʌi pacap*$_{a}$, *chamʌi pacam*$_{m}$.
touch *khɛlcap*$_{a}$, *khɛlcam*$_{m}$.
towards A (the speaker) *asal*$_{a}$. B (the horizontal side) *nɔmala*$_{m}$, *nɔmal*$_{a}$. C (the upper side) *tɔmala*$_{m}$, *tɔmal*$_{am}$. D (the hearer) *usal*$_{a}$; E (the lower side) *yɔmala*$_{m}$, *yɔmal*$_{am}$.
trace in **without a trace** *yɔm*$_{m}$.
training *talim*$_{m}$.
trample *dimcap*$_{a}$.
transgress *nãghʌi pacap*$_{a}$.
transgression *nãghʌi*$_{a}$.
transport *sarʌi pacam*$_{m}$.
trap *paso*$_{a}$; *jala*$_{a}$.
travel (on foot) *walcap*$_{a}$, *walcam*$_{m}$.
tread *dimcap*$_{a}$.
tree A (in general) *rukh*$_{am}$. B (*Bassia butyracea*) *hipsu*$_{a}$, *hispu*$_{m}$. C (*Bauhinia vahilii*) *bhorla*$_{am}$. D (*Bauhinia variegata*) *jilli*$_{a}$, *jitli*$_{m}$. E (the cotton-tree *Bombax malabaricum*) *simbʌl*$_{m}$. F (*Elaeagnus parvifolia*) *mɛsi*$_{m}$. G (*Ficus bengalensis*) *bʌr*$_{m}$. H (*Ficus cunia*) *kuksi*$_{am}$. I (*Ficus religiosa*) *pipʌl*$_{m}$. J (*Garuga pinnata*) *krampu*$_{a}$, *krampa*$_{m}$. K (*Litsea polyantha*) *kuṭmiro*$_{m}$. L (*Shorea robusta*) *sɔllɔm*$_{m}$, *sɔlɔm*$_{a}$, *sɔʔlɔm*$_{a}$. M (any kind of leguminous tree with pinnate leaves) *siris*$_{am}$. N (an unidentified species) *nalmu*$_{a}$. **tree marker** *-si*$^{2}_{am}$.
tribe *thʌr*$_{m}$.
trick in **a kind of mischievous trick or silly stunt done for amusement** *pacewa*$_{a}$.
turn I n A (time) *coṭi*$_{m}$; *pala*$_{a}$. B (winding) *ghumʌi*$_{a}$. C (upset) *ghopṭʌi*$_{a}$. II v *ghumʌi pacap*$_{a}$.
turned inside out *ulṭo*$_{m}$.

turtle *kʌchuwa*$_{a}$.
turtledove (species) *ḍhukur*$_{m}$.
twist *calcap*$_{a}$, *calcam*$_{m}$; *curcap*$_{a}$, *curcam*$_{m}$.
two *dui*$_{am}$.

— **u** —

ulcer *mari*$_{am}$.
umbilicus *sumpuru*$_{a}$, *sumpur*$_{m}$.
uncle-in-law *hupu*$_{am}$.
understand *sʌmjhʌi lacap*$_{a}$; *samjhʌi pacap*$_{a}$, *sʌmjhʌi pacam*$_{m}$.
unfasten *klɔ[k]-*$_{m}$; *phukʌi pacap*$_{a}$; *phuklʌi pacap*$_{a}$, *phuklʌi pacam*$_{m}$.
unfastening A (used in connection with animate beings) *phukʌi*$_{a}$. B (used in connection with inanimate beings) *phuklʌi*$_{am}$.
unfold *phukʌi pacap*$_{a}$; *phuklʌi pacap*$_{a}$, *phuklʌi pacam*$_{m}$.
unhealthy in **be unhealthy** *anucap*$_{a}$, *anucam*$_{m}$.
unknot *klɔ[k]-*$_{m}$.
untie *klɔ[k]-*$_{m}$; *phukʌi pacap*$_{a}$; *phuklʌi pacap*$_{a}$, *phuklʌi pacam*$_{m}$.
until *sʌmba*$_{m}$, *sʌmma*$_{a}$.
untying *phukʌi*$_{a}$; *phuklʌi*$_{am}$.
up *gattu*$_{a}$, *gatthu*$_{m}$; *tɔmala*$_{m}$, *tɔmal*$_{am}$; *toʔla*$_{a}$.
upright *bukcap*$_{a}$, *bukcam*$_{m}$.
upset I n *ghopṭʌi*$_{a}$. II v *ghopṭʌi lacam*$_{a}$.
upside down *ulṭo*$_{m}$.
upwards *gattu*$_{a}$, *gatthu*$_{m}$.
urinate *sɔrki pacap*$_{a}$, *sɔrki pacam*$_{m}$.
urine *sɔrki*$_{am}$.
uvula *kilkile*$_{a}$.

— **v** —

vagina *laci*$_{m}$; *poʔle*$_{a}$.
valley *gʌira*$_{m}$.
vapour in **visible vapour given off by a burning substance** *kunci*$_{a}$, *khumci*$_{a}$.
vegetable (especially spinach) *siʔlim*$_{a}$.
vertebral column *kuma=na=p rusu*$_{a}$; *kuŋma-rusu*$_{m}$.

very *dherʌi*$_{\text{m}}$; *saro*$_{\text{m}}$.
vessel A (in general, especially one made from a large dried gourd) *kakhrɔm*$_{\text{a}}$. B (big-mouthed copper or brass vessel) *baṭa*$_{\text{m}}$. C (big earthenware vessel used to store alcoholic drinks) *dubɔlki*$_{\text{a}}$; *himpu*$_{\text{a}}$; *li:phu*$_{\text{m}}$. D (earthenware vessel in which rice-spirit is distilled) *pʌini*$_{\text{a}}$.
village *dɛl*$_{\text{am}}$; *gaũ*$_{\text{a}}$.
visible *himtɔp*$_{\text{a}}$. **be visible** *himcap*$_{\text{a}}$.
visit *rɛmcam*$_{\text{m}}$.
voice *sɔndɔm*$_{\text{a}}$; *sor*$_{\text{am}}$.
vomiting *banta*$_{\text{a}}$.
vulture *giddhʌ*$_{\text{a}}$.

— W —

wait I n *rim*$_{\text{a}}$. II v *locam*$_{\text{m}}$; *rim pacap*$_{\text{a}}$.
wake *bukcap*$_{\text{a}}$, *bukcam*$_{\text{m}}$; *phukcam*$_{\text{m}}$.
walk I n *ḍulʌi*$_{\text{am}}$. II v *walcap*$_{\text{a}}$, *walcam*$_{\text{m}}$. **make walk** *wal paccam*$_{\text{m}}$. **take for a walk** *ḍulʌi pacap*$_{\text{a}}$, *ḍulʌi pacam*$_{\text{m}}$. **walking stick** *lʌura*$_{\text{am}}$.
wall A (of a building) *garo*$_{\text{a}}$. B (inner wall) *bhitta*$_{\text{am}}$.
Wambule *Ɔmbule*$_{\text{a}}$.
wander *ghumʌi lacap*$_{\text{a}}$.
warm oneself (near a fire) *tha:cap*$_{\text{a}}$, *tha:cam*$_{\text{m}}$.
wash A (something) *murcap*$_{\text{a}}$. B (oneself) *mɛrcap*$_{\text{a}}$, *mɛrcam*$_{\text{m}}$.
wasp *sɔddɔndo*$_{\text{a}}$, *sɔʔdɔndo*$_{\text{m}}$.
watch *kicap*$_{\text{a}}$, *kicam*$_{\text{m}}$. **keep watch** *locam*$_{\text{m}}$; *rim pacap*$_{\text{a}}$.
water *ka:ku*$_{\text{am}}$, *kak*$_{\text{am}}$. **water marker** *-ku*[3]$_{\text{am}}$, *-k*$_{\text{am}}$.
water-hole *kuwa*[2]$_{\text{m}}$.
wave *dukcam*$_{\text{m}}$.
way *lam*[2]$_{\text{am}}$. **in that way** *use*$_{\text{m}}$, *us*$_{\text{am}}$. **in this way** *ase*$_{\text{m}}$, *as*$_{\text{m}}$.
we A (in general) *uŋgu*$_{\text{am}}$, *uŋ*$_{\text{am}}$. B (dual) *uŋ nimpha*$_{\text{am}}$. C (plural) *uŋ ticu*$_{\text{am}}$.
wear (around one's neck) *hecap*[2]$_{\text{a}}$.
weariness *thʌkʌi*$_{\text{a}}$.
web *jal*$_{\text{a}}$, *jalu*$_{\text{m}}$.
weep *khrɔm*; *khrɔmcap*$_{\text{a}}$, *khrɔmcam*$_{\text{m}}$. **make weep** *khrɔm paccap*.
well[1] in **be well** (good) *nucap*$_{\text{a}}$, *nucam*$_{\text{m}}$.

well^{2} (hole) *kuwa*$^{2}{}_{m}$.
wet *ciso*$_{a}$.
what *hai*$_{am}$; *hujɔktɔp*$_{a}$.
when *hus bulu*$_{a}$, *hus bul*$_{a}$; *husɛl*$_{m}$, *husulu*$_{a}$, *husul*$_{a}$; *hai bɛl?*$_{a}$.
where *thalu*$_{am}$, *thal*$_{am}$.
whereto *thamalu*$_{a}$, *thamal*$_{am}$.
white *bubjɛŋmo*$_{a}$; *bubu*$_{a}$; *bupcip*$_{a}$. **very or purely white** *bubuyaya*$_{a}$.
whither *thamalu*$_{a}$, *thamal*$_{am}$.
who *munu*$_{am}$, *mun*$_{a}$; *mundo*$_{m}$; *mun dɔt*$_{a}$.
whole *sʌb*$_{a}$, *sʌp*$_{m}$.
wholesome *jati*$_{a}$.
why *haiŋa*$_{m}$, *haiŋaŋ*$_{m}$, *haiŋo*$_{m}$, *hayaŋ*$_{m}$, *hayɔŋ*$_{m}$; *haŋ*$_{a}$.
wife *buɖi*$_{a}$.
wind (air) *hawa*$_{a}$; *phuɖim*$_{m}$.
winding *ghumʌi*$_{a}$.
windy in **be windy** *phuɖim pacam*$_{m}$.
wing *maphlɛm*$_{am}$.
winnow *hɔpcap*$^{1}{}_{a}$, *hɔpcam*$_{m}$.
wisdom *niwa*$_{am}$.
without *sɔŋku*$_{a}$.
wizard *dhami*$_{a}$.
woman A (old) *buɖi*$_{a}$. B (young) *salme*$_{m}$; *tʌruni*$_{a}$.
womb *nani=ŋ kul*$_{a}$; *nunu=ŋ kul*$_{m}$.
wood *siŋ*$_{a}$. **wood** marker *-si*$^{2}{}_{am}$.
word *ma:la*$_{am}$.
work I n *kam*$_{am}$; *karjʌi*$_{a}$; *khasi*$_{a}$. II v *kam pacam*$_{m}$.
world *prithibi*$_{a}$.
worry I n *surta*$_{m}$. II v *surta pacam*$_{m}$.
wound *mari*$_{am}$.
wrap around oneself *kɔmcap*$_{a}$, *kɔmcam*$_{m}$.
wring *curcap*$_{a}$, *curcam*$_{m}$.
wrist *nari*$_{a}$.
write *rɛkcap*$_{a}$, *rɛk-*$_{m}$.

— y —

year A (in general) *bʌrsa*$_{m}$; *sal*$_{a}$; *-thoce*$_{am}$, *-thot*$_{a}$, *tho-*$_{a}$. B (two years ago) *thɔmbar-thoni*$_{a}$. C (one year ago) *numthoce*$_{m}$; *thoni*$_{a}$. D (this year) *tɛŋthoce*$_{a}$. E (next year) *naːthot*$_{a}$.
yell *wakcap*$^{2}_{a}$; *waːcap*$_{a}$.
yellow *pʌhẽlo*$_{a}$; *waʔɔmjimo*$_{m}$; *waʔɔmjɔkto*$_{m}$.
yes *ʌ̃*$_{a}$; *ho*$_{a}$.
yesterday *saiso*$_{m}$; *satni*$_{a}$.
yet *tʌya*$_{a}$.
you A (in general) *inne*$_{am}$, *in*$_{am}$. B (dual) *in nimpha*$_{am}$. C (plural) *in ticu*$_{am}$.
youngest-born A (male) *kancha*$_{m}$. B (female) *kanchi*$_{am}$.
your^{s} A (singular) *im*$^{2}_{am}$. B (dual) *incim*$_{am}$. C (plural) *inim*$_{am}$.
youth *salco*$_{m}$.

APPENDIX THREE

AFFIRMATIVE AND IMPERATIVE PARADIGMS

Below are given the affirmative and imperative paradigms of several Jero verbs. Āmboṭe forms are given in the left-hand columns, and Mohanṭāre verbs are given in the right-hand columns. The form *sim(e)* reads as '*sime* alternates with *sim*'.

3.1 *Class (vi-1a-i)*

· <si-> vi-1a-i ‘to die’
· <di-> vi-1a-i ‘to go (and come back)

S	*sicap*	*sicam*
1s	*siŋma*	*siŋma*
2s	*sinne*	*sinne*
3s	*sim(e)*	*sime*
1di/2d/3d	*siŋcim*	*siŋcim*
1de	*siŋcuma*	*siŋcum*
1pi	*sikime*	*sikim*
1pe	*sikuma*	*sikum*
2p	*sinimme*	*sinimme*
3p	*simme*	*simme*
2s IMP	*sisa*	*disa*
2d IMP	*siŋaci*	*diŋaci*
2p IMP	*sinani*	*dinani*

3.2 *Class (vi-1a-ii)*

· <ya-> vi-1a-ii 'to come up'

S	*yacap*
1s	*yaŋma*
2s	*yanne*
3s	*yam(e)*
1di/2d/3d	*yaŋcim*
1de	*yaŋcuma*
1pi	*yakime*
1pe	*yakuma*
2p	*yanimme*
3p	*yamme*
2s IMP	*yaka*
2d IMP	*yaŋaci*
2p IMP	*yanani*

3.3 *Class (vi-1c)*

· <dum-> vi-1c 'to become'
· <khrɔm-> vi-1c 'to cry'

S	*dumcap*	*khrɔmcam*
1s	*duŋŋuma*	*khrɔŋma*
2s	*dumnim*	*khrɔmnim*
3s	*dumme*	*khrɔmme*
1di/2d/3d	*duŋŋaŋcim*	*khrɔmiŋcim*
1de	*duŋŋaŋcum*	*khrɔmuŋcum*
1pi	*dumkim*	*khrɔmkim*
1pe	*dumkum*	*khrɔmkum*
2p	*dumnimme*	*khrɔmnimme*
3p	*duimme*	*khrɔmimme*
2s IMP	*dumsa*	*khrɔmsa*
2d IMP	*dumŋaci*	*khrɔmaŋci*
2p IMP	*dumnani*	*khrɔmnani*

3.4 *Class (vi-2)*

· <blak- ~ bla:-> vi-2 'to come'
· <bak- ~ ba:-> vi-2 'to be'

S	*blakcap*	*bakcam*
1s	*blaŋma*	*baŋma*
2s	*blanne*	*banne*
3s	*bla:m(e)*	*ba:me*
1di/2d/3d	*blaŋcim*	*baŋcim*
1de	*blaŋcum*	*baŋcum*
1pi	*bla:kim*	*ba:kim*
1pe	*bla:kum*	*ba:kum*
2p	*bla:nimme*	*ba:nimme*
3p	*blamme*	*bamme*
2s IMP	*baksa*	*baksa*
2d IMP	*ba:ŋaci*	*ba:ŋaci*
2p IMP	*ba:nani*	*ba:nani*

3.5 *Class (vm-1a)*

· <ca:-> vm-1a 'to go up'
· <ne-> vm-1a 'to say'

S	*ca:cap*	*necam*
1s	*caŋma*	*neŋma*
2s	*canne*	*nenne*
3s	*ca:sim*	*nesim*
1di/2d/3d	*caŋcim*	*neŋcim*
1de	*caŋcum*	*neŋcum*
1pi	*ca:kim*	*nekim*
1pe	*ca:kum*	*nekum*
2p	*ca:nimme*	*nenimme*
3p	*camme*	*nemme*
2s IMP		*nesa*
2d IMP		*neŋaci*
2p IMP		*nenani*

3.6 *Classes (vm-1b) and (vm-1c)*

· <tum-> vm-1b ‘to hit oneself’
· <mεr-> vm-1c ‘to wash oneself’

S	*tumcap*	*tumcam*
1s	*tuŋŋum(a)*	*tuŋma*
2s	*tumnim*	*tumnim*
3s	*tumsim*	*tumsime*
1di/2d/3d	*tuŋumcim*	*tumiŋcim*
1de	*tuŋumcum*	*tumuŋcum*
1pi	*tumkim*	*tumkim*
1pe	*tumkum*	*tumkum*
2p	*tumnimme*	*tumnimme*
3p	*tuimme*	*tumimme*
2s IMP		*mεrsa*
2d IMP		*mεrŋaci*
2p IMP		*mεrnani*

3.7 *Class (vt-2a)*

· <pa- ~ po-> vt-2a 'to do, make'
· <ja- ~ jo-> vt-2a 'to eat'

A→P	*pacap*	*jacam*
1s→3s	*pauma*	*jaum*
2s→3s	*panne*	*janne*
3s→3s	*paime*	*jaim*
1di/2d→3s	*pocim*	*jocim*
1de→3s	*pocum*	*jocum*
3d→3s	*paicim*	*jaicikm*
1pi→3s	*pokim*	*jokim*
1pe→3s	*pokum*	*jokum*
2p→3s	*ponimme*	*jonimme*
3p→3s	*pamme*	*jamme*
2s→3s IMP	*paha*	*paha*
2d→3s IMP	*pahaci*	*pahaci*
3p→3s IMP	*pahani*	*pahani*

3.8 *Class (vt-2b)*

· <tu:t- ~ tu:-> vt-2b 'to drink'

A→P	*tu:cap*	*tu:cam*
1s→3s	*tu:ʔma*	*tu:ʔma*
2s→3s	*tu:ʔnim*	*tu:ʔnim ~ tu:nim*
3s→3s	*tu:tim*	*tu:ʔtim ~ tu:tim*
1di/2d→3s	*tu:cim*	*tu:cim*
1de→3s	*tu:cum*	*tu:cum*
3d→3s	*tu:cim*	*tu:ʔcikm*
1pi→3s	*tu:kim*	*tu:kim*
1pe→3s	*tu:kum*	*tu:kum*
2p→3s	*tu:nimme*	*tu:nimme*
3p→3s	*tu:ʔme*	NEG *atu:ʔim*
2s→3s IMP		*tu:ha*
2d→3s IMP		*tu:haci*
2p→3s IMP		*tu:hani*

3.9 *Class (vt-2c)*

· <hipt- ~ him-> vt-2c ‘to see’
· <japt- ~ jam-> vt-2c ‘to buy’ (also negative forms)

A→P	*hipcap*	*japcam*
1s→3s	*hipma*	*jaʔma*
2s→3s	*hipnim*	*japnim*
3s→3s	*hiptim*	*japtim*
1di/2d→3s	*himcim*	NEG *ajamci*
1de→3s	*himcum*	NEG *ajamcu*
3d→3s	*hipcim*	NEG *ajapciʔ*
1pi→3s	*himkim*	NEG *ajamki*
1pe→3s	*himkum*	NEG *ajamku*
2p→3s	*himnimme*	NEG *ajamnim*
3p→3s	*hipme*	*jaʔimme*
2s→3s IMP		*jappha*
2d→3s IMP		*japphaci*
2p→3s IMP		*japphani*

3.10 *Class (vt-2d)*

· <phatt- ~ phan-> vt-2d 'can'
· <kratt- ~ kran-> vt-2d 'to bite'
· <plɛtt- ~ plɛn-> vt-2d 'to dry'

A→P	*phaccap*	*plɛccam*
1s→3s	*phapma*	*plɛʔma*
2s→3s	*phatnim*	*plenim*
3s→3s	*phattim*	*plɛttim*
1di/2d→3s	*phancim*	*plɛncim*
1de→3s	*phancum*	*plɛncum*
3d→3s	*phaccim*	*plecikm*
1pi→3s	*phaŋkim*	*plɛŋkim*
1pe→3s	*phaŋkum*	*plɛŋkum*
2p→3s	*phannimme*	*plenimme*
3p→3s	*phaːʔme*	*pleʔimme*
2s→3s IMP	*krakka*	*plɛkkha*
2d→3s IMP	*krakkaci*	*plɛkkhaci*
2p→3s IMP	*krakkani*	*plɛkkhani*

3.11 *Class (vt-2e)*

· <gɔkt- ~ go-> vt-2e 'to give'
· <makt- ~ maː-> vt-2e 'to catch'

A→P	*gɔkcap*	*makcam*
1s→3s	*gɔkma*	*maʔma*
2s→3s	*gɔknim*	*maknim*
3s→3s	*gɔktim*	*maktim*
1di/2d→3s	*gocim*	*maːcim*
1de→3s	*gocum*	*maːcum*
3d→3s	*gɔkcim*	*makcikm*
1pi→3s	*gokim*	*maːkim*
1pe→3s	*gokum*	*maːkum*
2p→3s	*gonimme*	*maːnimme*
3p→3s	*gɔkme*	*maːʔimme*
2s→3s IMP	*gɔkka*	*makkha*
2d→3s IMP	*gɔkkaci*	*makkhaci*
2p→3s IMP	*gɔkkani*	*makkhani*

3.12 *Class (vt-2g)*

· <kurt- ~ kur-> vt-2g 'to carry'
· <tɛrt- ~ tɛr-> vt-2g 'to receive'

A→P	*tɛrcap*	*kurcam*
1s→3s	*tɛrʔma*	*kurʔma*
2s→3s	*tɛrnim*	*kurnim*
3s→3s	*tɛrtim*	*kurtim*
1di/2d→3s	*tɛrcim*	*kurcim*
1de→3s	*tɛrcum*	*kurcum*
3d→3s	*tɛrcim*	*kurcikm*
1pi→3s	*tɛrkim*	*kurkim*
1pe→3s	*tɛrkum*	*kurkum*
2p→3s	*tɛrnimme*	*kurnimme*
3p→3s	*tɛrʔme*	*kurʔimme*
2s→3s IMP		*kura*
2d→3s IMP		*kuraci*
2p→3s IMP		*kurani*

APPENDIX FOUR

COMPARATIVE KIRANTI WORD LIST

Morphosemantically non-identical roots are not claimed to be reflexes of the same etymon. Semantic leaps are kept to a minimum.

BE ABLE:

- /*c-/: Jero *capcam*$_{m}$; Wambule *capcam*; Bahing *chápo*; Sunwar *tsap-tsa*; Thulung *caps-*; Khaling *'cäm-nä*; Dumi *tsa:pnɨ*; Chamling *camma*; Bantawa *cap-(a)*; Limbu *cuptama* 'be convenient, appropriate, favourable, opportune'.
- /*ph-/ or $^{?}$/*ʔp-/: Jero *phaccapa*$_{a}$; Hayu *phat-*.
- /*h-/: Yamphu *he'ma*; Limbu *heʔma*.

BE ALIVE, SURVIVE:

Proto-Tibeto-Burman **s-riŋ* × **s-ryaŋ*.

- /*bl-/: Jero *blecap*$_{a}$, *ble-*$_{m}$; Wambule *blecam*, *blyancam*; Bahing *bleno* 'live'; Sunwar *broyn-tsa* 'be spare, live'; Dumi *letnɨ* 'survive'; Chamling *let-*; Kulung *leima*.
- /*h-/: Bantawa *hüŋ-(a)*; Yamphu *hiŋma*; Limbu *hiŋma*.

ALSO:

- /*y-/: Jero *=ya*$_{am}$, *=i*$_{am}$; Wambule *=ya*, *=i*; Bahing *yó*, *yo*; Sunwar *yo*; Thulung *o*, *wo* (LTH *bo*); Khaling *yo*; Dumi *ye*, *ya*, *yə*.
- /*s-/: Kulung *so*; Yamphu *so*.

ARM, HAND:

Proto-Tibeto-Burman **g-l(y)ak*.

- /*ʔl-/: Jero la_{am} (*ʔlā*); Wambule *ʔla*$_{\mathrm{w}}$, *la*; Thulung *loa*.
- /*g-/: Bahing *gú* 'arm', *gúblem* 'hand'; Sunwar *guy*; Hayu *got*.
  ≈ /*h-/: Bantawa *chuk* (initial unexplained; /h-/ expected); Kulung *hu*; Yamphu *huk*; Limbu *huk*.
- /*kh-/: Khaling *khar*; Dumi *khɨr*.

ARROW:

Proto-Tibeto-Burman **g/b/m-la-y*.

- /*bl-/: Jero blu_{am}; Wambule *blo*; Bahing *blá*; Sunwar *-bra* in *libra*; Hayu *blo*, *bo*, *liwo*; Thulung *blə* 'metal arrow head'; Bantawa *bhe* (/b-/ expected); Kulung *bei* (loss of /*l-/); Yamphu *-la* in *thula*; Limbu *-la* in *to:ŋ-la* 'arrow-stick'.

ASHES:

Proto-Tibeto-Burman **pla* (Benedict 1972).

- /ʔp-/: Sunwar *'pulu* Khaling *püyü*; Kulung *-bui* in *c^hubui*.
  /*ph-/: Jero $phucul_{\mathrm{m}}$; Wambule *phucul*.
- /*m-/: compounds with 'fire': Chamling *mi-dhima*, *musep-pa*; Bantawa *mi+rak* 'fire+heat'.

ASK FOR, BEG:

- /*ʔp-/: Bahing *puno* 'beg'; Sunwar *puyn-tsa*; Thulung *bi-*.
  /*ph-/: Jero $phɔicam_{\mathrm{m}}$; Wambule *phwaicam*; Khaling *phi-nä*; Dumi *phi:tnɨ*.
- /*ŋ-/: Chamling *ngoma*; Kulung *ŋo:ma*; Yamphu *na·kma* Limbu *na:kma*.

AXE:

Proto-Tibeto-Burman **r-p^w a*.

- /*kh-/: Jero *khu*$_{am}$; Wambule *khu*; Bahing *khá*; Sunwar *khraa* (initial unexplained; /kh-/ expected); Hayu *khoʔ-joŋ*; Thulung *kho*.
- /*ʔp-/: Khaling *pwaandu*; Dumi *pəndhi*; Bantawa *ban+tük* 'knife-strike'; Kulung *bati*; Yamphu *ændhi*.
- Limbu *tɔti*, *tɔːndi*.

BACK, BEHIND, AFTER:

Proto-Tibeto-Burman **s-nuŋ* × **s-nuk*.

- /*n-/: Jero *nʌuthal*$_{a}$, *nʌuṯhal*$_{m}$, *nʌuṯhaŋ*$_{am}$; Wambule *nʌuṯha*, *nʌuthaŋ*; Bahing *nótha*; Sunwar *'noole*; Hayu *noŋ-*.
- /*y-/: Khaling *yaathaa*; Dumi *yoː*; Limbu *yaŋsi*.
- /*ʔt-/ or /d-/: Chamling *dõsi*; Bantawa *deŋ*; Kulung *dos*.

BAMBOO:

Proto-Tibeto-Burman **g-p^w a* × **r-p^w a*.

- /*ʔp-/: Jero *phaːpu*$_{am}$; Wambule *phaphu*; Bahing *pálám*; Sunwar *'palaa*; Thulung *bephum*; Bantawa *ba+hu;* Kulung *bap^h u*; Yamphu *a'bhu*; Limbu *pha*.

BANANA:

Proto-Tibeto-Burman **s-ŋak* 'plantain, banana'.

- /*b-/: Jero *-bal* in *jɔmbal*$_{am}$; Wambule *bal-* in *balci*.
- /*m-/ or /*ʔm-/: Bahing *-mo-* in *grámochi*; Sunwar *mu-* in *mugi*.
- /*ŋ-/: The element *-ŋak* in Thulung *leə̃si* (LTH *leŋaksi*); Khaling *lengaasi*; Dumi *ŋye'ləksi*; Bantawa *ŋak+si*; Kulung *liŋoːsi*.
  ≈ Limbu *tɛllaseʔ* (*teːʔlaːseːʔ*, van Driem 1987).
- Yamphu *cemmeʔla*.

BARK (V):

Proto-Tibeto-Burman *u = (m-)u* (Benedict 1972).

- /*h-/: Jero *hu:capa*$_{a}$, *hu:-*$_{m}$; Wambule *hukcam*; Sunwar *hook-tsa*; Thulung *huk-*; Khaling *'hu-nä*; Chamling *hukma*; Bantawa *hukt-(a)*; Kulung *hu:ma*; Limbu *hɔ:ma*.

BARK, SKIN:

Proto-Tibeto-Burman **kok × kwa(:)k*.

- /*k-/: Jero *kɔkte*$_{am}$; Wambule *kwakte*; Bahing *kokte* 'skin'; Sunwar *krusul* 'bark', *'kusul* 'skin'; Hayu *kuktsho*; Thulung *kokte*; Khaling *'kaa*.
  - ≈ /*k-/: Dumi *-kə* in *səkkə*; Kulung *-ko-* in *sokowar*; Yamphu *-k* in *sauk*.

BARK, PEEL:

- /*h-/: Thulung *hokte* 'chaff', *hok(s)-* 'peel, strip'; Bantawa *hok-wa*; Bantawa *hou* 'bark of a tree'; Yamphu *u'kma* 'peel'; Limbu *ho:rik*.

BAT:

Proto-Tibeto-Burman **ba:k*.

- /*p-/: Jero *pɔkti*$_{am}$; Wambule *pwakti*; Bahing *pákati*; Sunwar *'pakatiyti*; Thulung *pakti*; Khaling *'paakti*; Kulung *papi-wa*.

BE (IDENTITY):

- /*n-/ or /*ʔn-/: Jero *nɔcapa*$_{a}$, *nɔcam*$_{m}$; Sunwar *na-* (identity); Hayu *not-*.
- /*g-/: Bahing *ká, khe, gno* (initials unexplained; /g-/ expected); Khaling *gö-nä* 'be (inanimate)'; Dumi *gɨni* 'existential to be'.

BE, SIT:

Proto-Tibeto-Burman **m-duŋ/k* × **m-tuŋ/k* (Matisoff 2003), **bam ~ pam* (Benedict 1972).

- /*b-/: Jero *bakcap*$_a$, *bakcam*$_m$; Wambule *bakcam*; Bahing *bwakko*; Sunwar *'baak-tsa* 'sit, stay, live'; Thulung *b(a)-*; Yamphu *pemma* 'sit, live'; Limbu *po:ŋma* 'be, become'.
- /*m-/ or /*ʔm-/: Hayu *mut-*; Khaling *mu-nä* 'be, stay, remain'; Dumi *mɨnɨ* 'sit, be, stay'.

BEAR (N):

Proto-Tibeto-Burman **d-wam*.

- /*w-/: Jero *wam*$_{am}$; Wambule *wam*; Bahing *wam*; Sunwar *waan*; Thulung *hōmu* (LTH *wə̄mu*).
- /*m-/ or /*ʔm-/: Khaling *mos*; Dumi *mo:ksɨ*; Bantawa *mak+sa*; Kulung *moksi*; Yamphu *ma'ksa*; Limbu *ma:kyu*.

BEAT, PLAY (INSTRUMENT):

- /*ʔt-/: Jero *tɔpcap*$_a$, *tɔpcam*$_m$; Wambule *twapcam*; Khaling *'tam-nä*; Thulung *Diup-*; Dumi *tipnɨ*; Kulung *dumma*.
- /*m-/ or /*ʔm-/: Bantawa *mutt-(u)*; Limbu *mukma*.

BEAT, STRIKE:

Proto-Tibeto-Burman **dip* × **tip*, **dup* × **tup*.

- /*ʔt-/: Jero *tupcap*$_a$, *tupcam*$_a$; Wambule *tupcam*; Bahing *teuppo*; Sunwar *'tup-tsa*; Hayu *top-*; Thulung *Dep-*; Khaling *'thu-nä* 'beat (heart)' (initial unexplained; /t-/ expected); Dumi *da:pnɨ* (initial unexplained; /t-/ expected); Chamling *dip-*; Bantawa *dup-(u)* 'work metal' (*dhup-(u)* 'hit'; /d-/ as expected); Kulung *dəima*; Yamphu *upma* 'batter'; Limbu *thamma* 'beat (cloth in washing), smash, thrash, knock down'.

BECOME:

- /*d-/: Jero *dumcap*$_{a}$, *dumcam*$_{m}$; Wambule *dumcam*; Bahing *dyúmo*; Sunwar *dum-tsa* 'be made, become'; Hayu *dum-*.
  ≈ Thulung *diums-* 'be, be finished'.
- /*l-/: Jero *lacap*$_{a}$, *lacam*$_{m}$; Khaling *lü-nä*; Chamling *lama*; Bantawa *lis-(a)*; Yamphu *li'ma* 'start to be, become'; Limbu *lɔʔma* 'be, look like'.
- /*ʔc-/ or /*ch-/: Dumi *tsɨknɨ*; Kulung *cʰuma* 'be, has to'.

BEE:

Proto-Tibeto-Burman **was* 'bee, honey', **s-braŋ* 'fly, bee', **bya* 'bee, bird'.

- /*s-/: Jero *sɔrewa*$_{am}$; Wambule *swarewa*; Bahing *syúra*; Hayu *siŋwo*; Sunwar *surbu*; Thulung *'seor*; Khaling *sür*; Bantawa *sun-ya(p)*; Kulung *suwer*; Yamphu *suama*; Limbu *-sɔ-* in *khɛsɔʔma*, *sɔk-wa*.

BEFORE, FRONT:

Proto-Tibeto-Burman **s-ŋa* (Benedict 1972).

- /*l-/: Jero *lapphu*$_{am}$, *lapthɔl*$_{a}$; Khaling *läl*; Dumi *lal* 'in front'; Kulung *lais*.
- Wambule *ɗambi*.
- /*ŋ-/: Bahing *gnallá*; Sunwar *ngoynti*; Hayu *nõ'ku*; Thulung *ŋaddo* (LTH *ŋaDDo*); Bantawa *ŋa+lüŋ* 'face'; Yamphu *najik* 'face'; Limbu *na* 'countenance, face'.

BEND:

Proto-Tibeto-Burman **gu(:)k* × **m-ku(:)k* 'crooked, bent, knee, angle'.

- /*g-/: Wambule *gupcam*; Bahing *guk-* (Michailovsky 1994); Sunwar *'guk-* (Michailovsky 1994); Hayu *guk-*; Thulung *gum-*; Khaling *'ghu-nä*; Dumi *kɨm'sini*; Bantawa *kuŋt-(u)*; Kulung *kumma*; Yamphu *kuŋliŋ* 'curly, twisted'; Limbu /-kɔk/ in *pɛgɔk* 'manner of being twisted'.

BIG, LARGE, GREAT:

Proto-Tibeto-Burman **ta-y*, **tay* 'big'.

- /*k-/ or /*ʔk-/: Bahing *gnólo* (initial unexplained; /k-/ expected); Sunwar *kol-tsa* 'grow up'; Thulung *kol-*, *kəl-* 'be large'; Dumi *golpɨ* (initial unexplained).

  /*kh-/: Jero *khɔltɔp*$_{a}$, *khɔlto*$_{m}$; Wambule *khwalbo*; Khaling *ghwaalpä* (initial unexplained; /kh-/ expected).

- /*d-/: Sunwar *threebe* (initial unexplained; /d-/ expected); Bantawa *dhi+waŋ* (/d-/) expected; Kulung *dema* 'be big'; Yamphu *tu-* in *tuba* 'grandfather' and *tuma* 'grandmother', *thappa* 'big, old' (initial unexplained; /t-/ expected); Limbu *tumba* 'elder, eldest'.

BIND, TIE:

Proto-Tibeto-Burman **s-dar* 'bind, fasten, tether', **g(y)it/k* × **k(y)it/k* 'tie, bind', **grak*, **ki:l* × *hi:l* 'bind, twist, roll, angle'.

- /*ʔp-/: Jero *pɔccam*$_{m}$; Wambule *pwaccam*; Sunwar *'payk-tsa* 'tether (an animal)'; Hayu *pot-*; Thulung *bət-* 'tie up'; Khaling *'pwaan-nä*; Dumi *pa:tnɨ* 'wrap, spool, bandage'; Bantawa *bokt-(u)* 'hold tight, mend, patch up'; Kulung *bəmma* 'tie in a bundle'.

  ≈ Yamphu *pukma* (initial unexplained).

BIRD:

Proto-Tibeto-Burman **bya* 'bee, bird', **wa* 'bird, feather', **s-ŋak* 'bird'.

- /*ʔc-/: Jero *cikmu*$_{m}$, *cipmu*$_{a}$; Wambule *cwagbo*; Bahing *chikba*; Sunwar *'tsiikbi*; Thulung *cəkpu*; Bantawa *choŋ-ga*, *choŋ-wa*. Kulung *c*^{h}*owa*; Yamphu *soŋ(w)a*.

- /*s-/: Khaling *salpu*; Dumi *silpu*.

  ≈ Limbu *pu*.

BITE, PECK:

Proto-Tibeto-Burman **hap* 'bite, snap at, mouthful', **g-wa-t* 'bite, chew'.

- /*ʔk-/: Jero *kɔkcap*$_a$; Wambule *kwakcam*; Sunwar *kook-tsa*; Thulung *kək-* 'dig, peg'; Khaling *'kaa-nä*; Dumi *kokni*; Bantawa *khokt-(u)* 'cut into pieces', Kulung *k*^{h}*oma*.
  ≈ /*o-/: Yamphu *o'kma* 'peck, bite suddenly'; Limbu *ɔkma* 'peck, bite'.

BITE; GNAW:

Proto-Tibeto-Burman **hap* 'bite, snap at, mouthful', **g-wa-t* 'bite, chew'.

- /*kr-/: Jero *kraccap*$_a$, *kra[k]-*$_m$; Wambule *kraccam*; Bahing *kráto*; Khaling *'kän-nä*; Dumi *ka:tni*.
  /*khr-/: Sunwar *'khrayk-tsa* 'bite'; Thulung *khret-* 'bite, rend, nibble', *ghrək-* 'gnaw'; Bantawa *khett-(u)*; Yamphu *hæ'ʔma* 'bite, nibble'; Limbu *haʔma* 'bite'.

BITTER:

Proto-Tibeto-Burman **b-ka-n* 'bitter, liver'.

- /*k-/ or /*ʔk-/: Bahing *kaba*; Sunwar *'ka-sho*.
  /*kh-/: Jero *khatto*$_m$; Wambule *khaco*; Thulung *khes-* 'taste bitter'; Khaling *khäpä*; Dumi *kha:kpi*; Bantawa *khük*; Kulung *khikpa*; Yamphu *khiʔiye*; Limbu *khi:k*.

BLACK:

Proto-Tibeto-Burman **s-maŋ* × **s-mak* 'black, ink, deep'.

- /*k-/ or /*ʔk-/: Bahing *kekem*; Sunwar *kyer*; Thulung *kekem*; Khaling *kekem*; Dumi *kulim*; Kulung *gugurpa* (initial unexplained; /k-/ expected).
  /*kh-/: Jero *khucɛm*$_m$, *khucɛŋmo*$_a$, *khucɛp*$_a$; Wambule *khucyam*; Hayu *khaktshiŋmi*.
- /*m-/ or /*ʔm-/: Chamling *mõ-* (<**mak-*) in *mõwa*; Bantawa *mak-ko*; Yamphu *maik*; Limbu *mak-la*.

BLOOD:

Proto-Tibeto-Burman **s-hywəy*.

- /h-/: Jero *usu*$_m$, *yusu*$_a$ (<**husu*); Wambule *usu* (<**husu*); Bahing *hési*; Sunwar *hush*; Khaling *hi*; Dumi *hiː*; Hayu *ji* (<**hi*); Bantawa *hü*; Kulung *hi*; Yamphu *hari*; Limbu *-khiʔ* in *makkhiʔ* (<**mak-hiʔ*).

BLOW (BY MOUTH):

Proto-Tibeto-Burman **s-mut*.

- /*h-/: Jero *huccap*$_a$, *hu[k]-*$_m$; Wambule *huccam*; Hayu *hot-*.
- /*m-/ or /*ʔm-/: Bahing *múto*; Sunwar *muyk-tsa*; Bantawa *mutt-(u)*; Kulung *muima* 'blow out'; Yamphu *mi'ʔma*; Limbu *mupma*.
- /*d-/: Khaling *dham-nä* (/d-/ expected); Dumi *dɨmni*.

BODY:

Proto-Tibeto-Burman **guŋ*.

- /*ry-/ > /y-/: Bantawa *yam*; Lohorung *yam* (H); Yamphu *yami* 'body hair'; Limbu *yam*.

  /*ry-/ > /r-/: Jero *ram*$_m$; Wambule *ram*; Bahing *ram*; Sunwar *raan*; Thulung *reom*, *reop*; Khaling *rwaam*; Dumi *ram*.

  /*ry-/ > /g-/: Kulung *gam*.

BOIL, SIMMER:

Proto-Tibeto-Burman **klak* × **glak* 'cook, boil'.

- /*bl-/: Jero *lɔkcap*$_a$, *lɔkt-*$_m$; Wambule *lwakcam*; Sunwar *'bruyk-tsa*; Hayu *lek-* 'boil over'; Thulung *lok/t-* 'boil', *bliut-*; Khaling *'blan-nä*; Dumi *lɨmni* 'boil something in water'; Chamling *lhoma*; Bantawa *lokt-(u)*; Limbu *laŋ-ma*.

BONE:

Proto-Tibeto-Burman **s/m/g-rus*.

- /*r-/: Jero *rusu*$_{am}$; Wambule *rusu*; Bahing *reusye*; Sunwar *rush*; Hayu *ru*.

  ≈ /s-/: compounds with 'flesh, meat': Thulung *'ser*, *sasar*, *seser*; Khaling *solu*; Dumi *saːlu*; Chamling *saruwa*; Bantawa *sa+yü-wa*, *yüwa*; Kulung *-ri* in *tupri*.

BOW:

Proto-Tibeto-Burman **d/s-ləy* 'bow, slingshot'.

- /*l-/: Jero *lekhe*$_{m}$; Wambule *likhi*; Bahing *li*; Thulung *lin*; Khaling *laaphu*; Bantawa *li(t)* in *ta+li* or *ta+lit* 'bow (made of bamboo)'; Kulung *lip^{h}u*; Limbu *liʔ*.

BRAIN:

Proto-Tibeto-Burman **s-niŋ* × *g*s-nik* 'heart, mind, brain', **s-nuk* 'brain'.

- /*n-/: Jero *nεm*$_{m}$; Wambule *nyam*; Sunwar *'nipsi*; Thulung *nepci*, *neopci*; Khaling *nes*; Yamphu *-nasi* in *taŋnasi*; Limbu *nisiːk*.

BREAK:

Proto-Tibeto-Burman **tsyat* 'break, cut'.

- /*j-/: Wambule *jikcam*; Bahing *dzik-* (Michailovsky 1994); Sunwar *dzik-* (Michailovsky 1994); Hayu *dzik-*; Thulung *jəks-*; Yamphu *ciˑma*; Limbu *cεkma*.

BREAK, BURST:

- /*br-/: Jero *brakcap*$_{a}$; Wambule *brikcam*; Bahing *bukko, pwákko* (initial unexplained; /br-/ expected); Sunwar *broy-tsa* 'break (as a rope)'; Thulung *breos-* (*bhreos-*; /br-/ as expected) 'break off'; Khaling *'bhro-nä* (/br-/ expected); Dumi *boknɨ*.
- /*ph-/: Bantawa *phek-(u)* 'break (nut, ginger)'; Kulung *p^{h}omcima* (root *p^{h}ok-*); Yamphu *phœkma* 'divide, break off a little'.

BRING (ACROSS A HORIZONTAL PLANE):

- /*ʔp-/: Bahing *pito*; Sunwar *'pit-tsa*; Hayu *pit-*; Khaling *'pan-nä*; Dumi *pitnɨ*; Chamling *baid-*; Bantawa *bitt-(u)*; Kulung *baima*.
  /*ph-/: Jero *phiccap*$_{\mathrm{a}}$, *phiccam*$_{\mathrm{m}}$; Wambule *phiccam*; Thulung *phit-*; Limbu *phɛpma*.

BUFFALO:

Proto-Tibeto-Burman **broŋ* 'wild yak, buffalo'.

- /*ʔm-/: Jero *mesu*$_{\mathrm{am}}$; Wambule *ɓeiso*; Bahing *mésyeú*; Sunwar *meshe*; Thulung *meosiu*, *miusiu*, *mesi*; Khaling *mes*; Dumi *meːsi*; Kulung *meːsi*.
- /*s-/: Bantawa *saŋ-wa*; Yamphu *saŋa*; Limbu *sɔŋwɛtla* (van Driem 1987).

BUY:

Proto-Tibeto-Burman **g/m/s-lay* × **r-ley* 'change, exchange, buy, barter', **par* 'trade, buy, sell', **rey* 'buy, barter', **ywar* 'sell, buy'.

- /*j-/: Jero *japcap*$_{\mathrm{a}}$, *japcam*$_{\mathrm{m}}$; Wambule *japcam*; Bahing *jyappo*; Sunwar *'gyap-tsa*.
- /*ʔk-/: Dumi *kiːtnɨ*; Bantawa *khit-(u)*; Kulung *k^{h}eima*.
- /*i-/: Khaling *u-nä*; Yamphu *imma*; Limbu *iŋma*.

CALF OF LEG:

Proto-Tibeto-Burman **bop*, **bwap* × **bwam*.

- /*ʔp-/: Jero *pɔpɔl*$_{\mathrm{a}}$; Sunwar *polpol*; Thulung *palseo*; Khaling *pälsö*.
  /*ph-/: Jero *phɔphɔl*$_{\mathrm{m}}$; Wambule *phwapwal*; Bahing *phó-phól*.

CALL (V):

Proto-Tibeto-Burman **gaw*.

- /*kh-/: Jero *khamcap*$_a$; Wambule *khamcam*; Yamphu *kha* 'speech, words, talk'.
- /*br-/: Bahing *bréto*; Sunwar *bret-tsa* 'invite, call to come'; Khaling *bhrwaan-nä* (/br-/ expected); Dumi *photnɨ* (initial unexplained; /b-/ expected); Chamling *buima*; Bantawa *butt-(u)*; Limbu *pa:pma* 'speak'.

CARRY:

Proto-Tibeto-Burman **ba* 'carry on back', **tam* 'carry on shoulder'.

- /*ʔk-/: Jero *kurcap*$_a$, *kurcam*$_m$; Wambule *kurcam*; Bahing *kúro*; Sunwar *kur-b mur* 'porter'; Thulung *kur-*; Khaling *kar-nä*; Dumi *kɨrnɨ*; Chamling *khur-*; Bantawa *khuy-(u)*; Kulung *khurma*; Yamphu *khi'ma*; Limbu *ku:ma* (initial unexplained; /kh-/ expected).

CATCH:

Proto-Tibeto-Burman **s-grim* 'catch, hold fast'.

- /*c-/ or /*ʔc-/: Jero *cumcap*$_a$, *cumcam*$_m$; Wambule *cumcam*; Khaling *'cam-nä* 'catch up'.
- /*m-/: Jero *makcam*$_m$; Wambule *mwakcam*; Thulung *mok-* 'use, take, borrow'.
- /*l-/ or /*ʔl-/: Hayu *la-* 'snatch'; Khaling *'lwaam-nä* 'catch a ball'; Dumi *lopnɨ*; Chamling *lhap-* (initial unexplained; /l-/ expected); Bantawa *lap-(u)*; Kulung *lamma*; Yamphu *ra'pma*.

CAUSATIVISER:

Proto-Tibeto-Burman **s-ter* ‘give, causative’.

- /*ʔp-/: Jero *paccap*$_{a}$, *paccam*$_{m}$; Wambule *paccam*; Bahing *páto*; Sunwar *'payk-tsa*; Hayu *piŋ*; Thulung *bet-* ‘act on, inflict, affect’.
- /*m-/ or /*ʔm-/: Khaling *man-nä*; Dumi *mɨtnɨ*; Chamling *maid-*; Bantawa *mett-(u)*; Kulung *mima*; Yamphu *meʔ-ma*; Limbu *mɛpma*.

CHASE AWAY:

- /*d-/: Jero *dalcap*$_{a}$, *dalcam*$_{m}$; Wambule *dalcam*.
- /*k-/: Sunwar *'kher-tsa* ‘drive away’ (initial unexplained; /k-/ expected); Thulung *kol-* ‘drive off’; Khaling *kwaal-nä*; Kulung *kəlma*.

CHEEK:

- $^{?}$/*kw-/: Jero *mambu*$_{am}$; Wambule *ɓambu*; Thulung *phosiu*, *phosip*; Khaling *phosu*; Dumi *busu*; Kulung *p*^{h}*ousi*.
- /*c-/ or /*ʔc-/: Bahing *chocho*; Sunwar *tsootso*.
- /*ŋ-/: compounds with ‘face’: Bantawa *ŋam+yaŋ*; Yamphu *namdaŋ*; Limbu *nɛdɛŋba*.

CHEW, MASTICATE:

Proto-Tibeto-Burman **g-wa-t* ‘bite, chew’.

- /*ʔd-/: Jero *nakcap*$_{a}$; Wambule *ɗakcam*, *ɗaŋcam*; Sunwar *'nak-tsa* ‘chew’.
- /*ʔk-/: Hayu *hwap-* (initial unexplained; /k-/ expected); Thulung *kam-*; Khaling *käm-nä*; Chamling *kemdhyu* ‘chewed’ (initial unexplained; /kh-/ expected); Bantawa *khup-(u)*, *khupt-(u)*; Kulung *k*^{h}*amma*; Yamphu *khemma* ‘bite, set your teeth into something’; Limbu *khaːmma*.
- Yamphu *yœˑkma*; Limbu *yeːŋma*.

CHICKEN:

Proto-Tibeto-Burman **ʔa:r*, **ha:r* 'fowl, chicken, quail'.

- $^{?}$/*kw-/: Jero *mɔkɔm*$_{am}$ 'chicken', *ma-* in *maphlɛm*$_{am}$ 'wing'; Wambule *ɓo* 'chicken', *ɓa-* in *ɓaphlyam* 'wing'; Bahing *ʔbá* (Michailovsky 1994); Sunwar *bwa* (Michailovsky 1994); Hayu *xo'co*; Thulung *po*, *pa-* in *pasiurium* 'feather', *ba-* in *baphlem* 'wing'; Khaling *phö*; Dumi *pa-wœm*; Chamling *wasa*; Bantawa *wa*; Kulung *wa:*; Yamphu *wa*; Limbu *waʔ*.

CLOTH, WEAR:

Proto-Tibeto-Burman **gwa-n* × **kwan* 'wear, put on, clothe', **s-g-w(y)a-n/t* 'wear, clothe', **w(y)a-t* × **wit* 'wear, clothe'.

- /*w-/: Jero *wa*$_{am}$; Wambule *wa*; Bahing *wá'*; Sunwar *waa*; Khaling *gö* (initial unexplained; /w-/ expected); Dumi *gu* (initial unexplained; /w-/ expected); Hayu *-wa* in *cuʔwa*; Chamling *wa-kha*; Bantawa *war-a* 'is worn'; Kulung *waima* 'wear (cloths and jewellery)'; Yamphu *wæ'ʔma* 'wear ornaments or a watch'; Limbu *wa:pma* 'adorn, decorate'.
- /*t-/ or /*d-/: Bantawa *tit*; Kulung *tei* 'cloth'; Limbu *te:t*.

CLOUD:

Proto-Tibeto-Burman **r-məw* 'sky, heavens, clouds'.

- /*ʔk-/: Jero *kɔksɛl*$_{a}$, *kuksɛl*$_{m}$; Wambule *kuksyal*; Bahing *kuksyal*; Sunwar *'gossu* (initial unexplained; /k-/ expected); Thulung *khase* (initial unexplained; /k-/ expected); Khaling *köm*; Dumi *ki'hɨm*; Yamphu *khimmiʔ-ma*; Limbu *kha:pmedhɔ:mba*, *khamdɔmba*.
- /*m-/ or /*ʔm-/: Bantawa *muk+sa*; Kulung *mom*.

COME (ACROSS A HORIZONTAL PLANE):

Proto-Tibeto-Burman **byon* 'come, go', **pay* 'come, go'.

- /*ʔp-/: Jero *picap*$_a$, *picam*$_m$; Wambule *picam*; Bahing *piwo*; Sunwar *'pi-tsa*; Hayu *phi-* (initial unexplained; /p-/ expected); Thulung *bik-*; Khaling *pi-nä*; Dumi *pi:nɨ*; Bantawa *ban-(a)*; Kulung *baima*; Limbu *phɛmma*.
  ≈ Yamphu *apma*.

COME DOWN:

- /*y-/: Jero *yacap*$_a$, *yacam*$_m$; Wambule *ywacam*; Bahing *yúwo*; Sunwar *'yi-tsa* 'descend'; Hayu *ju(t)-*; Thulung *yok-*; Khaling *ye-nä*; Dumi *yi:nɨ*; Chamling *i-* (<**yi-*); Bantawa *yi-(a)*; Kulung *yuma*; Yamphu *yu'ma*; Limbu *yu:ma*.

COME OUT, GO OUT:

Proto-Tibeto-Burman **s-pro-k* 'come out, emerge, bring out', **s-twak* 'come out, go out, emerge'.

- ?/*kw-/: Jero *mɔrcap*$_a$; Wambule *ɓwarcam* 'come out', *ɓarcam* 'throw out, throw away'; Bahing *ward-* (Michailovsky 1994); Sunwar *bwar-tsa* 'shoot up'; Thulung *par-* 'throw, discard'; Dumi *wərnɨ* 'toss, throw';
- /*l-/ or /*ʔl-/: Hayu *lɪ-* 'sprout, shout'; Khaling *läy-nä* 'come out', *'län-nä* 'go out'; Dumi *lənnɨ* 'come out'; Chamling *laida-*, *lond-*, *lud-*; Bantawa *lont-(a)*; Kulung *ləima*; Limbu *lɔmma*.

COME UP:

- /*g-/: Jero *gacap*$_a$, *ga-*$_m$; Wambule *gacam*; Bahing *kúwo* (initial unexplained; /g-/ expected); Sunwar *'ngoyk-tsa* 'ascend' (initial unexplained; /g-/ expected); Thulung *ge(t)-*; Khaling *kho-nä* (derived from *kho-nä* 'bring up') Dumi *khoŋnɨ* (derived from *khotnɨ* 'bring up'); Yamphu *kæʔma*.
- /*th-/: Bantawa *thaŋ-(a)*; Kulung *tho:ma*; Limbu *tha:ŋma*.

COOK, BOIL:

Proto-Tibeto-Burman **klak* × **glak* 'cook, boil'.

- /*k-/: Bahing *kúko*; Sunwar *'ke-tsa* 'cook'; Bantawa *kok-mu-(a)* 'cook (rice)'; Limbu *koːma* 'be hot'.
  /*kh-/: Jero *khɔkcap*$_a$, *khɔkcam*$_m$; Wambule *khwakcam*; Hayu *khot-*; Thulung *khok-*; Khaling *kham-nä*; Dumi *khipni*.
- /*ŋ-/: Bantawa *ŋü-(u)* 'cook (curry)'; Kulung *ŋima*; Yamphu *ni'ma*.

COOKED LIQUID VEGETABLE OR MEAT DISH:

- /*k-/ or /*ʔk-/: Thulung *ke*; Dumi *kœ*.
  /*kh-/: Jero *khamsi*$_{am}$; Wambule *khamsi*; Bantawa *khan* 'curry'; Kulung *k*^{h}*ai*; Yamphu *khœŋ*.

COOL (V):

Proto-Tibeto-Burman **glaŋ* 'cold freeze', **graŋ* 'cold, freeze', **m/ʔ-glak* 'cold, freeze', **kyam* 'snow, ice, cold'.

- /*kw-/: Jero *me pacap*$_a$, *me pacam*$_m$; Wambule *ɓecam*; Bahing *ʔbet-* (Michailovsky 1994); Thulung *pəs-*; Khaling *ke-nä*; Kulung *keːma*.
- /*r-/: Dumi *remni*; Bantawa *ʔems-(u)* (<**yems-*); Yamphu *yemma*.

COUGH (N):

Proto-Tibeto-Burman **səw-t* 'cough'.

- /*s-/: Jero *sɔkane*$_a$; Wambule *swakwane*; Bahing *sheúkhé*, *syókhé*; Thulung *seoki*, *seokhe*; Khaling *söki*.
  /*ʔc-/ or /*ch-/: Kulung *c*^{h}*uːma*; Limbu *suŋ*.
- /*th-/: Sunwar *'thuuksu*; Chamling *thungma*; Bantawa *thuŋs-(a)* (v).

COUNT:

Proto-Tibeto-Burman **graŋ* × **kraŋ* 'measure, count', **b-rəy* × **b-ris* × **rit* × **ri:n* 'draw, write, count', **r-tśrəy* 'count, number', **r-tryəy* 'count, number'.

- /*khr-/: Jero *khripcam*$_{m}$; Wambule *khripcam*; Bahing *hikko*; Sunwar *hiik-tsa*; Hayu *hi-*; Khaling *'khran-nä*; Dumi *khi:tnɨ*; Chamling *khimma*, *khipma*; Bantawa *khipt-(u)*.
- /*ŋ-/: Jero *nɛrcap*$_{a}$; Thulung *ŋar-*; Kulung *ŋirma*; Yamphu *neʔma*; Limbu *ni:pma*.

COVER:

Proto-Tibeto-Burman **ʔup* × **gup* 'hatch, cover', **klup* 'cover, wrap'.

- /*ʔk-/: Jero *kɔmcap*$_{a}$, *kɔmcam*$_{m}$; Wambule *kwamcam*; Thulung *kəp-* 'thatch'; Dumi *kam'sinɨ*; Kulung *k^{h}amma*; Yamphu *khamma*; Limbu *khapma*.

  ≈ /*ŋ-/: Sunwar *ngeek-so-tsa*; Khaling *'ne-nä* 'cover'.
- /*ʔc-/: Thulung *ciup-*; Chamling *chupda*.

  /*s-/: Jero *sumcam*$_{m}$; Wambule *sumcam*; Bahing *sheumo*; Sunwar *sum-tsa*; Hayu *sɷp-* 'thatch'; Khaling *säm-nä* 'cover (head)'; Bantawa *sept-(u)*; Limbu *su:pma*.
- /*d-/: Dumi *depnɨ*; Bantawa *dipt-(u)*; Kulung *demma*; Limbu *tɛpma*.

COW:

- /*b-/: Jero *biya*$_{a}$ 'bullock'; Wambule *biya*; Bahing *bing* 'bull'; Sunwar *bii*; Thulung *beno* (LTH *beoneo*); Khaling *bay*; Dumi *bhiʔi* (/b-/ expected); Chamling *pyupa*; Bantawa *pit-ma*; Kulung *pi*; Yamphu *bik* (initial unexplained; /p-/ expected); Limbu *pit*.

CROW:

Proto-Tibeto-Burman **ka-n*.

- /*g-/: Jero *gagmu*$_{m}$, *ga:gab*$_{a}$; Wambule *gagbo*; Bahing *gagágpa*; Sunwar *khada* (initial unexplained; /g-/ expected); Thulung *gāpu*, *goāpu* (LTH *gagakpu*); Khaling *'gaakphö*; Dumi *gogo*; Bantawa *ka-gak*, *gagak*; Kulung *gagappa*; Limbu *ka:k-wa*, *a:k-wa*.

  ≈ Yamphu: *araʔwa*.

CUT OFF, MOW:

  ≈ ?/*kr-/: Jero *rikcam*$_{m}$; Wambule *rikcam*; Bahing *riko* 'reap'; Sunwar *'riik-tsa* 'saw'; Thulung *krip-* 'cut (rope, nail, hair, etc.)'; Khaling *'kramnä* 'cut, saw'; Dumi *ropnɨ* 'fell', *ripnɨ*; Kulung *rumma* 'cut wood'.

  ≈ /*h-/: Bantawa *hekt-(u)*; Yamphu *hœkma*; Limbu *hɛkma*.

DAMAGE, DESTROY:

Proto-Tibeto-Burman **ri-* 'decay, rotten' (Benedict 1972).

- /*ry-/ > /y-/: Yamphu *yokma* 'break down, cause to collapse'; Limbu *yɔ:ma* 'collapse, fall down'.

  /*ry-/ > /r-/: Jero *ri-*$_{m}$ in *niwa ri-*$_{m}$ 'become dizzy'; Wambule *ricam*; Bahing *ruko* 'eradicate'; Thulung *ri-*.

  /*ry-/ > /g-/: Kulung *gəma*.

DANCE (N):

Proto-Tibeto-Burman **gan* 'run, dance, kick', **ga:r* × **s-ga* 'dance, sing, leap, stride'.

- /*s-/: Jero *sɛle*$_{m}$, *sɛt*$_{a}$; Wambule *sili*; Bahing *sili*; Sunwar *'sil*; Kulung *sili*.
- /*ch-/: Thulung *cheoms-*; Khaling *chwaam-nä* (V); Dumi *tsəm*; Chamling *themma* (initial unexplained; /ch-/ expected); Yamphu *simmama* (V).
- /*l-/ or /*ʔl-/: Kulung *lak+lu-(a)*; Limbu *la:ŋ*.

DAY AFTER TOMORROW:

- /*n-/: Jero *nuso*$_{m}$, *nusso*$_{a}$; Wambule *nusso*, *nusswam*; Bahing *niti*; Sunwar *'nit-naakti*; Hayu *niha*; Khaling *'näm*; Dumi *na:mnɨ*.
- /*ch-/: Bantawa *chin+to+len*; Kulung *c^hindi*; Yamphu *siŋ-ʔa*; Limbu *-chinda:n* in *achinda:n*.

DIE:

Proto-Tibeto-Burman **səy*.

- /*s-/: Jero *sicap*$_{a}$, *sicam*$_{m}$; Wambule *sicam*; Thulung *si-*; Chamling *si-*; Bantawa *sü-(a)*; Kulung *sima*; Yamphu *si'ma*; Limbu *sima*, *si:ma*.
- /*b-/: Bahing *byákko*; Sunwar *'beek-tsa*.
- /*m-/: Khaling *man-nä*; Dumi *mitnɨ*. See 'forget'.

DIG:

Proto-Tibeto-Burman **tu* × **s/m-du*.

- /*d-/: Jero *dɛcap*$_{a}$; Wambule *dwacam*; Sunwar *'do-tsa*; Thulung *da-* (or *dha-*; /d-/ as expected); Khaling *dhö-nä* (/d-/ expected); Dumi *dhunɨ* (/d-/ expected); Bantawa *dhokt-(u)* /d-/ expected); Kulung *doma*; Yamphu *to'ma*; Limbu *tɔ:ma*.

DIRTINESS ON THE BODY:

Proto-Tibeto-Burman **d-ri(y)* 'dirt, filth, ordure, stench'.

- /*r-/: Jero *riku*$_{am}$; Wambule *riku*; Bahing *ríku*; Sunwar *'riku* in *'riku 'baak-maakt* 'dirty'.
- /*n-/ or /*ʔn-/: Yamphu *-nuak* in *muknuak*, *miknuak*; Limbu *na:mma* 'get dirty (on a human body)'.

DO, MAKE:

Proto-Tibeto-Burman **mow* (Benedict 1972).

- /*ʔp-/: Jero *pacap*$_{a}$, *pacam*$_{m}$; Wambule *pacam*; Bahing *páwo*; Sunwar *'pa-tsa*; Hayu *pa-*; Thulung *b(e)-*.
- /*m-/ or /*ʔm-/: Thulung *mun-* 'be created'; Khaling *mü-nä*; Dumi *minnɨ*; Chamling *maima*; Bantawa *mü-(a)*; Kulung *məma*.
- Yamphu *lœ'ʔma*.
- Limbu *co:kma*.

DOG:

Proto-Tibeto-Burman **d-k*^{w}*əy-n*.

- /*khl-/: Bahing *khlicha*; Thulung *khlewa*, *kheya* (LTH *khleba*); Khaling *khlep*; Dumi *khi:bɨ*, *khi:bu*; Chamling *khlipa* (northwestern dialect), *khipa* (southeastern dialect); Kulung *kheba*; Limbu *khya*, *khyaba*.

  ≈ Sunwar *kutsum*.

DOOR:

Proto-Tibeto-Burman **m-ka* 'open, opening, mouth, door'.

- /*k-/ or /*ʔk-/: Jero *kimsul*$_{am}$; Wambule *kimsul*; Hayu *ka'mu*.
- /*l-/ or /*ʔl-/: Bahing *lapcho*; Sunwar *'laptso*; Khaling *'laaskaa*; Dumi *lamtsɨkœ*; Bantawa *lam*; Kulung *lamsko*; Limbu *lamdhe:ppa*.

DREAM:

Proto-Tibeto-Burman **r/s-maŋ* × **mak*.

- /*ŋ-/: Jero *ŋabu*$_{m}$; Wambule *ŋabu*; Bahing *gnámung*; Thulung *ŋīma*.
- /*s-/: Thulung *sema*; Khaling *semö*; Dumi *syemma*; Bantawa *sen+mi*, *sen+mit*; Kulung *se:mo:*; Yamphu *semmaŋ*; Limbu *sɛpmaŋ*.

DRESS:

- /*ʔp-/: Jero *paicap*$_{a}$; Wambule *paicam*; Thulung *ban-*.
  /*ph-/: Bahing *phiso*; Sunwar *'pheek-tsa*; Thulung *phəmsi-*; Khaling *gö bhäy-nä* (initial unexplained; /ph-/ expected).
- /*c-/ or /*j-/: Yamphu *caŋma*; Limbu *caŋma*.

DRINK:

Proto-Tibeto-Burman **ʔam* 'eat, drink'.

- /*ʔt-/: Jero *tu:cap*$_{a}$, *tu:cam*$_{m}$; Wambule *tu:cam*; Bahing *túg-no*; Sunwar *tuu-tsa*; Hayu *tũ'ta* 'drunk'; Thulung *Du(ŋ)-*; Khaling *tu-nä*; Dumi *tiŋnɨ*; Chamling *dungma*; Bantawa *duŋ-ma*; Kulung *du:ma*; Yamphu *uŋma*; Limbu *thuŋma*.

DRY, DRY UP:

Proto-Tibeto-Burman **kan*.

- /*s-/: Jero *sɔrcap*$_{a}$, *sɔr-*$_{m}$; Wambule *swarcam*; Bahing *syeu-wo*; Sunwar *soo-tsa*; Thulung *sa(t)-* 'become dry', *seor-* 'become dry'; Khaling *sär-nä* 'boil'.
- /*ch-/: Chamling *sipd-* (initial unexplained; /ch-/ expected); Bantawa *choms-*; Limbu *sɔmma* 'dry up (water)'.
- /*h-/: Khaling *hey-nä*; Bantawa *haŋs-(u)*; Kulung *harma* 'be dry'; Yamphu *he'ma*; Limbu *he:ma* 'dry up (especially in the sun).

EAR:

Proto-Tibeto-Burman **r/g-na* 'ear, hear, listen'.

- /*ʔn-/: Jero *nɔbu*$_{am}$; Wambule *ɗwabu*; Bahing *-neu* in *sámaneu*; Sunwar *'nopha*; Thulung *nəphla*, *nophla*; Khaling *ngeco* (initial unexplained; /n-/ expected); Dumi *ŋi-tso* (initial unexplained; /n-/ expected); Bantawa *na+bak*; Kulung *nobo*; Yamphu *næʔæk*; Limbu *nɛkkhoʔ*. See 'hear'.

EARTH, SOIL:

Proto-Tibeto-Burman **ha* × **r-ka* 'earth, ground, soil'.

- /*k/ or /*ʔk-/: Jero *kaksi*$_{am}$; Wambule *kaksi*; Hayu *ko*; Thulung *koa*.
  /*kh-/: Bahing *khápi* 'the earth'; Sunwar *khapi*; Yamphu *kham*; Limbu *kham*.
- /*ʔp-/: Khaling *'pök*; Dumi *pɨkhɨ*; Chamling *bokha*; Bantawa *bak-kha*; Kulung *boho* 'mud, earth'.

EAT:

Proto-Tibeto-Burman **dzya* 'eat, food, feed', **dzya-s* 'eat, food, feed', **dzya-t* 'eat, food, feed'.

- /*j-/: Jero *jacap*$_{a}$, *jacam*$_{m}$; Wambule *jacam*; Bahing *jáwo*; Sunwar *'dza-tsa*; Hayu *dza-*; Thulung *jam* 'cooked rice, food'; Khaling *jö-nä*; Dumi *dzunɨ*; Chamling *ca-ma*; Bantawa *ca-(a)*, *ca-(u)*; Kulung *cama*; Yamphu *ca·ma*; Limbu *cama*.

EAT, BITE:

Proto-Tibeto-Burman *g-wa-t* 'bite, chew'.

- ?/*kw-/: Jero *macap*$_{a}$, *macam*$_{m}$; Wambule *ɓacam*; Bahing *ʔba-*, *ʔba-* (Michailovsky 1994); Sunwar *'ba-tsa* 'gnaw'; Thulung *p(e)-*; Khaling *bət-* (Michailovsky 1994).
  ≈ Bantawa *ŋek-(u)*; Kulung *ŋe:ma*.

ELBOW:

- /*n-/: Jero *nɛksi*$_{m}$; Wambule *nyaksi*; Bahing *nyaksi*; Limbu *nɔksu:mba*.
- /*kh-/: Thulung *khiciuli*; Khaling *khecülü*; Dumi *kɨtna* (initial unexplained; /kh-/ expected); Kulung *k^{h}acalu*; Yamphu *khænsrukma*.

ERECT, ARISE, WAKE UP:

Proto-Tibeto-Burman **m-sow* 'arise, awake(n)'.

- /*p-/: Bahing *pok-* (Michailovsky 1975); Sunwar *pook-tsa* 'pick up'; Hayu *pɶk-*; Kulung *po:ma*; Yamphu *pu'kma*.

  /*ph-/: Jero $phukcam_{m}$; Wambule *phukcam*; Thulung *phək-* 'raise, waken'; Khaling *'phu-nä* 'raise'; Dumi *bhoknɨ* 'put' (initial unexplained; /ph-/ expected); Limbu *pho:ŋ-ma*.

EYE:

Proto-Tibeto-Burman **s-mik* × **s-myak*.

- /*ʔm-/: Jero $misi_{am}$; Wambule *ɓisi*; Bahing *michi*; Sunwar *miiktsi*; Thulung *miksi*; Khaling *mas*; Dumi *miksi*; Chamling *micu*; Bantawa *mük*; Kulung *muksi*; Yamphu *mik*; Limbu *mik*.

FAECES, STOOL:

Proto-Tibeto-Burman * *kləy* 'excrement'.

- /*khl-/: Jero *-ki* in $saŋki_{a}$ and *-khi* in $saŋkhi_{m}$ (loss of /l-/); Wambule *khli*; Sunwar *'khrii* 'faeces'; Thulung *khli*; Khaling *khli*; Dumi *khil*; Chamling *-khle* in *nakhle* 'snot' (lit. 'nose-shit'); Bantawa *khü*; Kulung $k^{h}il$; Yamphu *hi*; Limbu *hi*.

FALL DOWN, FALL OFF:

- /*d-/: Jero $dɔkcam_{m}$, $docap_{a}$; Wambule *dwakcam*, *docam*; Bahing *doko*; Sunwar *'dook-tsa*; Hayu *dɶk-*; Thulung *Dəks-*, *dəks-*.
- /*t-/: Thulung *ta(n)-* 'fall down as when walking'.

  /*ʔt-/ or /d-/: Chamling *dha-* (/d-/ expected); Bantawa *dha-(a)* (/d-/ expected); Kulung *dima*.

  /*th-/: Khaling *thi-nä*; Dumi *thi:ni*; Limbu *tha:ma* 'come down, fall down'.

FATHER:

Proto-Tibeto-Burman **pu* 'male, father, grandfather', **p^{w}a* 'man, father, husband, person', **wa* 'man, father, husband, person'.

- /*p-/: Jero *papa*$_{am}$; Wambule *papa, pap, po*; Bahing *-po* in *ápo*; Hayu *-pɯ* in *uxpɯ*; Thulung *pap*; Khaling *'päp*; Chamling *-pa* in *kok-pa* 'grandfather'; Dumi *papa, pu*; Bantawa *(-)pa, pa=pa*; Kulung *pa*; Yamphu *-pa*; Limbu *pa*.

FEAR (N):

Proto-Tibeto-Burman **kri(y)* 'fear', **k/grok* × **k/grak* 'fear, frighten'.

- /*ŋ-/: Jero *nim*$_m$; Wambule *ŋi:ma, ŋim*; Bahing *níma* (n), *gnito* (v); Sunwar *'hiin-tsa* 'fear, worry' (initial unexplained; /ŋ-/ expected); Thulung *ŋim/(t)/s-*; Khaling *ngay-nä* (v); Dumi *niŋ*.
- /*k-/ or /*g-/: Chamling *kurma* (v); Bantawa *kin+ca, kü-ma, kü-wa*; Kulung *kima* (v); Yamphu *kiʔma* (v); Limbu *ki:ma* (v).

FINGER, TOE:

Proto-Tibeto-Burman **m-yuŋ* 'finger'.

- /*br-/: Jero *brɛmci*$_{am}$; Wambule *bryamci*; Bahing *brepcho*; Sunwar *breptso*; Thulung *brepco*; Khaling *'brepco*.
- /*ʔc-/: Dumi *tsopmsi*; Bantawa *chuk+ku+si*; Kulung *c^{h}ok-c^{h}o:me*.
- /*h-/: Yamphu *hukkhœtciʔwa*; Limbu *hukco*.

FINGERNAIL:

Proto-Tibeto-Burman **m-(t)syen* 'nail, claw'.

- /*g-/: Jero *gwarji*$_{am}$; Wambule *gwarji*; Bahing *gyáng*; Sunwar *gee*.
- /*s-/: Khaling *sendü*; Dumi *sali*; Kulung *sen*; Yamphu *semdumma*; Limbu *sɛndiba*.

FINISH, COMPLETE:

Proto-Tibeto-Burman **s-dut* 'tie, knot, conclude, finish'.

- /*t-/ or /*ʔt-/: Jero *tumcap*$_{a}$ Wambule *tumcam.*
  /*th-/: Bahing *theumo*; Sunwar *'thum-tsa.*
  ≈ Thulung *diums-* 'be finished'.
- /*ŋ-/: Khaling *ner-nä*; Dumi *ŋyi:rnɨ.*
- /*m-/ or /*ʔm-/: Kulung *məima*; Limbu *mɛŋma.*
- /*c-/ or /*j-/: Bantawa *ciy-(u)*; Yamphu *cæʔma.*

FIRE:

Proto-Tibeto-Burman **mey.*

- /*m-/: Jero *mi*$_{am}$; Wambule *mi*; Bahing *mí*; Sunwar *mii*; Thulung *mu*; Khaling *mi*; Dumi *mi*; Chamling *mi-* in *midhima* 'ashes'; Bantawa *mi*; Kulung *mi*; Yamphu *mi*; Limbu *mi.*

FIREFLY:

Proto-Tibeto-Burman **kraŋ* mosquito, firefly'.

- ?/*d-/: Jero *dalaciŋma*$_{m}$, *dalcip*$_{a}$; Wambule *ɗalacimo* (initial unexplained; /d-/ expected); Sunwar *dzamkeri*; Thulung *dodikham*; Khaling *dodikhäm*; Bantawa *dok=dok+ʔi*; Kulung *didik*^{h}*am*; Limbu *odiŋga* (loss of /*d-/).

FISH:

Proto-Tibeto-Burman **s-ŋya.*

- /*ŋ-/: Jero *mõ*$_{a}$, *mũ*$_{a}$, *mu*$_{m}$ (initial unexplained; /ŋ-/ expected); Wambule *ŋwaso*; Bahing *gná*; Thulung *ŋō*; Khaling *ngö*; Dumi *ŋi*; Chamling *ngasa*; Bantawa *ŋa*, *ŋa+sa*; Kulung *ŋa*; Yamphu *na*; Limbu *na*, *ŋa.*

FLESH, MEAT:

Proto-Tibeto-Burman **sya-n* 'animal, body, flesh, meat'.

- /*s-/: Jero *su*$_{am}$; Wambule *so*; Bahing *syé*; Sunwar *she*; Thulung *seo*; Khaling *sö*; Dumi *su*; Chamling *-sa* 'animal noun class marker'; Bantawa *sa*; Kulung *sa*; Yamphu *sa*; Limbu *sa.*

FLOUR:

- /*ph-/: Jero *phuli*$_{am}$; Wambule *phuli*; Thulung *phul*; Kulung *p^{h}ul*; Limbu *phe:rum*.
- /*ʔk-/ or /kh-/: Yamphu *khaʔmi*; Limbu *khyup*.

FLOWER:

Proto-Tibeto-Burman **ba:r* 'bloom flower', **b^{w}at* 'flower', **b/s-wat* 'flower'.

- /*ʔp-/: Jero *phuri*$_{am}$; Wambule *phuri*; Bahing *phúng*; Sunwar *phuu*; Thulung *buŋma*; Khaling *pungme*; Dumi *puma*; Chamling *bungwa*; Bantawa *buŋ+ga*; Kulung *buŋ*; Yamphu *œʔwa*.

FLY (N):

Proto-Tibeto-Burman **s-braŋ* 'fly, bee', **m-tow* 'fly'.

- /*c-/ or /*ʔc-/: Sunwar *'tsurmu*.
  /*j-/: Hayu *dzama*; Kulung *cəiəmma*.
  /*s-/: Jero *sɔyam*$_{a}$, *sɔʔyɔm*$_{m}$; Wambule *swaywamo*; Bahing *sheúmo*; Thulung *seōmu*; Khaling *saayaame*; Limbu *sija*.

FOLLOW, GO AFTER:

Proto-Tibeto-Burman **s-naŋ* 'follow, repeat', **m/s-yuy* 'follow', **ywi* 'follow'.

- /*kh-/: Jero *khɔccap*$_{a}$; Wambule *khwaicam*; Sunwar *'khoyk-tsa*; Thulung *khlək-*.
- /*t-/: Thulung *tium-* 'follow, track, trace'; Khaling *'tam-nä* 'track'.
  /*ʔt-/ or /*d-/: Bantawa *dhumt-(u)* (/d-/ expected); Kulung *dumma* 'track'.
  ≈ /*t-/ or /*d-/: Yamphu *tiŋma*; Limbu *ti:kma*.
- /*t-/ or /*ʔt-/: Hayu *tot-*.
  /*d-/: Dumi *dhitni* (initial unexplained; /d-/ expected).
- Chamling *nhai-*.

FORGET:

Proto-Tibeto-Burman **ma-t* 'lose, disappear' (Benedict 1972).

- /*m-/: Jero *ma[p]*-$_{\mathrm{m}}$; Wambule *maccam*; Thulung *man/t-* 'kill'; Khaling *'mannä* 'die'; Dumi *mitnɨ* 'die'; Chamling *məima*; Bantawa *mant-(u)*; Kulung *maima* 'forget'; Yamphu *mindeʔma*; Limbu *mu:mma*. See 'die'.
- /*pl-/: Bahing *plendo*; Sunwar *'preen-tsa*; Thulung *ploas-*.

FRY:

Proto-Tibeto-Burman **r-ŋaw* 'roast, fry'.

- /*kh-/: Jero *kharcap*$_{\mathrm{a}}$, *kharcam*$_{\mathrm{m}}$; Wambule *kharcam*; Sunwar *kar-tsa* (initial unexplained; /kh-/ expected); Thulung *khər-* 'parch, cook (dry or in oil)'; Khaling *khwaar-nä*; Dumi *kharnɨ* 'pop, sear'.
- /*ŋ-/: Bantawa *ŋü-(u)*; Kulung *ŋəma*; Yamphu *nu'ma*; Limbu *ŋɔ:ma*, *nɔ:ma*.

GAME:

Proto-Tibeto-Burman **r-tsya:y* 'play'.

- /*c-/: Jero *camda*$_{\mathrm{a}}$, *cam*$_{\mathrm{a}}$, *camdo*$_{\mathrm{m}}$; Wambule *camdo*; Bahing *chamso*; Dumi *tsemnɨ* 'play'; Thulung *camdo*; Limbu *ca:pma* 'play'.

GET UP, STAND UP, ARISE:

Proto-Tibeto-Burman **m-sow* 'arise, awake(n)'.

- /*b-/: Jero *bukcap*$_{\mathrm{a}}$, *bukcam*$_{\mathrm{m}}$; Wambule *bukcam*, *bu:cam*; Bahing *bwóko*; Sunwar *'book-tsa*; Hayu *bɶk-*; Thulung *bək-*; Bantawa *puk-(a)*; Kulung *po:ma*; Yamphu *pu'kma*; Limbu *po:kma*.
  - ≈ 'Transitive' initial /*ph-/: Khaling *'phu-nä*; Dumi *phɨknɨ*.

GINGER:

Proto-Tibeto-Burman **kyaŋ*.

- /*ʔp-/: Bahing *peúrim*; Kulung *bic^{h}u*.
  /*ph-/: Jero *phipuwa*$_{\mathrm{a}}$; Wambule *phipiwa*; Thulung *phiurium*; Dumi *phiri:*.

GIVE:

Proto-Tibeto-Burman **bəy-k*, **s-bəy-n*.

- /*g-/: Jero *gɔkcap*$_a$, *gɔkcam*$_m$; Wambule *gwakcam*; Bahing *giwo*; Sunwar *ge-tsa*; Thulung *goak-*.
- /*b-/: Khaling *bi-nä*; Dumi *bi:ni*; Chamling *pid-*; Bantawa *pü-(a)*; Kulung *pima*; Yamphu *pi'ma*; Limbu *pima*.
- Hayu *ha-*.

GO:

Proto-Tibeto-Burman **m/s-ka-y* 'go, stride', **pay* 'come, go', **s-wa* 'go'.

- /*l-/: Jero *lɔcap*$_a$, *lɔcam*$_m$; Wambule *lɔcam*$_w$, *lwacam*; Bahing *lawo*; Sunwar *'la-tsa*; Hayu *lat-*; Thulung *ləks-*.
- /*kh-/: Khaling *'khwaan-nä*; Dumi *khotni*; Chamling *khai-ma*; Bantawa *khat-(a)*; Kulung *k^{h}aima*; Yamphu *khœʔma*.
- Limbu *pe:kma*.

GOOD, NICE, FINE:

Proto-Tibeto-Burman **l(y)ak* × **l(y)aŋ* 'good, beautiful'.

- /*r-/: Jero *rantɔp*$_a$, *ranto*$_m$; Wambule *ranco*; Bahing *rimmo* 'be handsome'; Sunwar *rim-sho*.

BE GOOD, BE HEALTHY:

Proto-Tibeto-Burman **s-nam* 'good'.

- /*ʔn-/: Jero *nucap*$_a$, *nucam*$_m$; Wambule *ɗucam*; Bahing *neu-ba*, *nyúba* 'good'; Thulung *niu-* 'be well, be right'; Khaling *nappä* 'good'; Dumi *nini* 'be good'; Chamling *nu-*, *nyo-*; Bantawa *nu*; Kulung *nəma*; Yamphu *numa*; Limbu *nu:ma* 'be good'.

GRANDCHILD:

Proto-Tibeto-Burman **syu(w)-n* (Matisoff 2003), **tsa* (Benedict 1972).

- /*c-/: Jero *cacu*$_{am}$ 'grandson'; Wambule *caco* 'grandson'; Bahing *chácha* 'grandson'; Hayu *tha'tso* (initial unexplained; /c-/ expected); Thulung *ciusiu*; Khaling *'cäs*; Dumi *tsatsu* 'grandson'; Kulung *casi*.
  - ≈ Bantawa *chok+cha*; Limbu *-chaʔ* in *mɛnchaʔ*.

GRIND:

Proto-Tibeto-Burman **kri:t*.

- /*khr-/: Jero *khricap*$_{a}$, *khricam*$_{m}$; Wambule *khricam*; Bahing *khrina* 'grinded'; Sunwar *'khraak-tsa* 'grind, press through'; Thulung *khuruk* 'hand mill'; Khaling *khürü* 'grinding stone'.
- /*y-/: Thulung *hik-*, *yik-*; Dumi *yɨknɨ* 'turn around; grind'; Chamling *ik-*, *yu-ma*; Kulung *yi:ma*; Yamphu *yi'ʔma* 'grind by means of a mill stone'; Limbu *yu:mma*.

HAIL:

Proto-Tibeto-Burman **s-p^{w}al* 'snow, ice, frost, hail', **ryal* 'hail', **ser* 'hail, sleet'.

- /*s-/: Jero *solu*$_{m}$, *sol*$_{am}$; Wambule *solu*.
  - ≈ /*l-/ or /*ʔl-/: Thulung *lōsiu*; Khaling *laas*.
- /*m-/ or /*ʔm-/: Bahing *músi*; Sunwar *'mupsi*; Dumi *mulu*; Bantawa *mut+luŋ*; Kulung *mulu*.

HAIR:

Proto-Tibeto-Burman **tsam* × **sam* 'hair (head)'.

- /*s-/: Jero *sɔm*$_{m}$, *swam*$_{a}$; Wambule *swam*; Bahing *swóng*; Sunwar *tsaan* 'hair' (initial unexplained; /s-/ expected); Thulung *sem*; Khaling *-swaam* in *rwaamswaam* 'hair of body'; Dumi *səm* 'body hair'; Kulung *-səm* in *to:səm*; Limbu *-saŋ* in *miksaŋ* 'eyelash'.

HANG UP, SUSPEND:

Proto-Tibeto-Burman **k(w)a:y.*

- /*c-/ or /*ʔc-/: Jero *cɛccap*$_{a}$; Wambule *cyaccam*; Hayu *jet-* (initial unexplained; /c-/ expected); Thulung *cet-*.
- /*k-/: Sunwar *kyayk-tsa*; Khaling *'ku-nä*; Bantawa *küŋs-(u)*; Kulung *ka:ma*.

  /*kh-/: Thulung *kheak-*; Khaling *'khe-nä*; Dumi *khyokni*; Chamling *khyo*.
- /*p-/ or /*b-/: Yamphu *paŋma*.

  /*ʔp-/ or /*ph-/: Limbu *pho:mma*.

HATE (N):

- /*gr-/: Jero *gramji*$_{a}$, *gramsu*$_{m}$; Wambule *gramji*; Bahing *gramdo* (v); Thulung *ghram-* 'despise, regard as dirty and disgusting' (/gr-/ expected; /ghr-/ under influence of Nep. *ghin*, *ghr̥ṇā*); Khaling *ghräm-nä* (/gr-/ expected; /ghr-/ under influence of Nep. *ghin*, *ghr̥ṇā*).
- /*ʔc-/: Dumi *tsi:ŋni*; Chamling *chə̃ima* 'disgust'; Bantawa *cip-ma+katt-(u)* 'hate someone' (initial unexplained; /ch-/ expected); Yamphu *si·tca·ma* (v); Limbu *ci:tchiŋ* (initial unexplained; /s-/ expected).

HEAD:

Proto-Tibeto-Burman **d-bu-s* 'head, centre'.

- /*ʔp-/: Jero *phutir*$_{m}$, *phutur*$_{a}$; Wambule *phutir*; Bahing *píya*; Sunwar *'piya*; Thulung *buy*.
- /*d-/: Khaling *dhong* (/d-/ expected); Dumi *dəkhlœ* 'head'; Chamling *ta-khlo*, *tõ*; Bantawa *taŋ*; Kulung *toŋ*; Yamphu /-taŋa/ in *nindaŋa*; Limbu *thage:k* (initial unexplained; /t-/ expected).

HEAD STRAP:

- /*ʔn-/: Jero *nobir*$_{m}$, *noʔmar*$_{a}$; Wambule *ɗobir*; Sunwar *nook-bu* 'headband'; Hayu *noʔro*.

  ≈ /nVm/: Bantawa *nem+laŋ*; Kulung *bə:nam*; Yamphu *wa-nam*; Limbu *khɛʔnam*.

HEAR:

Proto-Tibeto-Burman **r/g-na* ‘ear, hear, listen’, **s-ta-s* ‘hear’.

- /*th-/: Jero *thɔcap*$_a$, *thɔ-*$_m$; Wambule *thwacam*; Hayu *tha(t)-*; Thulung *theos-*; Khaling *thö-nä* ‘see, get’.
- /*ŋ-/: Bahing *ninno*; Sunwar *nee-tsa* ‘hear’, *neen-tsa* ‘listen’; Khaling *ngi-nä*; Dumi *ŋyi:nɨ*. See ’ear’.
- /*y-/: Chamling *yen-*; Bantawa *ʔen-(u)* (<**yen-*); Kulung *ye:ma*.
- /*ʔk-/ or /kh-/: Yamphu *khemma*; Limbu *khɛmma*.

HEART:

Proto-Tibeto-Burman **s-niŋ* × **s-nik*.

- /*t-/ or /*ʔt-/: Jero *tɛm*$_a$, *tɔm*$_m$; Wambule *twam*.
  /*th-/: Bahing *thim*, *theum*; Sunwar *thun*.
- /*c-/: Dumi *tsuba*; Kulung *cowa*.

HIDE, CONCEAL:

Proto-Tibeto-Burman **hway* × **kwa(:)y* ‘hide, conceal, shun’, **s=yip* × **s-yup* ‘sleep, put to sleep, conceal, hide’.

- Jero *kliccap*$_a$, *kliccam*$_m$; Wambule *kliccam*; Bahing *khleúto*; Sunwar *’khruyk-tsa*; Hayu *khi-* (loss of /*l-/).
- /*g-/: Khaling *’gam-nä*; Bantawa *kums-(u)*.
- /*s-/: Khaling *salsi-nä* ‘disappear’; Dumi *sɨlnɨ*; Kulung *sulma*.
- /*c-/ or /*j-/: Yamphu *cumma* ‘hide something’; Limbu *ciŋma*.

HORN:

Proto-Tibeto-Burman **gruŋ* ‘horn’, **g-ruŋ* ‘horn, corner’.

- /*gr-/: Jero *rosu*$_{am}$, *ros*$_a$; Wambule *roso*; Bahing *grong*; Sunwar *groo*; Thulung *rəŋ* (initial unexplained; /gr-/ expected); Khaling *grang*; Dumi *go*.

HOUSE:

Proto-Tibeto-Burman **k-yim* × **k-yum*.

- /k-/ or /ʔk-/: Jero *kulu*$_{a}$, *kul*$_{am}$; Wambule *kuḍu*; Hayu *kem*; Khaling *kam*; Dumi *ki:m*.

  /kh-/: Bahing *khyim*; Sunwar *khiin*; Chamling *khim*; Bantawa *khim*; Kulung *k*^{h}*im*; Yamphu *khim*; Limbu *khim, him*.

HURT, ACHE:

Proto-Tibeto-Burman **na-n* × **na-t* 'ill, suffer, hurt, evil spirit', **s-nyen* 'hurt, oppress'.

- /*ŋ-/: Jero *nɛccap*$_{a}$, *nɛt-*$_{m}$; Wambule *nyaccam*; Thulung *neo-*; Khaling *ngen-nä*; Dumi *ŋyetnɨ*.

  ≈ Limbu *ŋɛmakpa* 'worried, sad'.

- /*t-/ or /*d-/: Bantawa *tuk-ma* 'pain'; Kulung *tu:ma*; Yamphu *tukma*; Limbu *tukkhe*.

HUSBAND:

Proto-Tibeto-Burman **p*^{w}*a* 'man, father, husband, person', **wa* 'man, father, husband, person'.

- /*w-/: Jero *wacu*$_{m}$; Wambule *waco*; Bahing *wancha*; Sunwar *'woyshmur* 'man'; Thulung *wociu* (LTH *bociu*).

  ≈ Hayu *xwaptso*.

  ≈ /*b-/ or /*w-/: Khaling *-bu* in *dumbu*; Dumi *-bu dumbo*; Limbu *-baʔ* in *yɛmbaʔ*.

HUSKED AND POLISHED GRAIN, ESPECIALLY RICE:

Proto-Tibeto-Burman **b-ras* 'bear fruit, rice'.

- /*s-/: Jero *seri*$_{am}$; Wambule *sera*; Bahing *shéri*; Sunwar *sheri* 'uncooked rice'; Thulung *sor*; Khaling *-sör* in *rösör* 'husked rice'; Dumi *sura* 'uncooked rice'; Kulung *se:ri*; Yamphu *siya*; Limbu *syaʔ*.

  ≈ Chamling *rõ*.

ITCH:

Proto-Tibeto-Burman **m-sak*, **g-ya*.

- /*s-/: Jero *su-*$_{m}$; Wambule *sucam*; Sunwar *-su-* in *raksu-tsa*; Hayu *sot* 'be spicy'; Thulung *sius-*; Khaling *sü-nä*; Chamling *syus-*; Bantawa *sus-(a)*; Kulung *səma*; Yamphu *su'ma* 'be spicy'; Limbu *so:ma*.

JUMP:

Proto-Tibeto-Burman **p(r)ok*.

- /*pr-/: Jero *prɛkcam*$_{m}$; Wambule *pryakcam*, *precam*; Bahing *próko*; Sunwar *preek-tsa*; Thulung *prok-*; Khaling *'pro-nä*; Chamling *phũima* (initial unexplained); Bantawa *phint-(a)* (initial unexplained); Yamphu /-pruk-/ in *ambrukma* 'jump up and down'; Limbu *pimma*.

KICK:

Proto-Tibeto-Burman **r/g-dek* 'kick', **k(y)at* 'run, dance, kick'.

- /*t-/ or /*ʔt-/: Jero *ta-*$_{m}$; Wambule *taccam*; Bahing *táto*; Sunwar *tayk-tsa*.
  ≈ Thulung *theak-*.

KILL:

Proto-Tibeto-Burman **g/b-sat*.

- /*s-/: Jero *sɛccap*$_{a}$, *sɛccam*$_{m}$; Wambule *syaccam*; Bahing *sáto*; Sunwar *'sayk-tsa*; Hayu *sɪt-*; Thulung *set-*; Khaling *'sen-nä*; Dumi *setnɨ*; Chamling *seima*; Bantawa *set-(u)*; Kulung *seima*; Yamphu *seʔma*; Limbu *sɛpma*.

KISS:

Proto-Tibeto-Burman **dzyup* × **dzyip* 'suck, kiss, breast, milk'.

- /*c-/: Jero *cuʔ*$_{m}$; Wambule *cup*; Bahing *chup*; Khaling *cüp*; Bantawa *cup-ma*. See 'suck'.

KNEE:

Proto-Tibeto-Burman **put-s*.

- /*p-/ or /*ʔp-/: Jero *pumci*$_{am}$; Wambule *pumci*; Bahing *pok-chi*; Sunwar *pooktsi*.
- Hayu *khokali*; Thulung *kokci*, *kōciuka*, *kōciuwa*.
- /*t-/: Khaling *tamcu*; Kulung *tumc^{h}i*; Yamphu *tumruk*; Limbu *thumboʔ*, *thuŋboʔ* (initial unexplained; /t-/ expected).

KNOW (BY LEARNING):

- /j-/: Jero *jɔkcam*$_{m}$; Wambule *jwakcam*; Sunwar *'dzook-tsa*, *'dzoo-tsa*; Hayu *dzœk-*.

  ≈ Khaling *'cu-nä* (initial unexplained; /j-/ expected).
- /*l-/ or /*ʔl-/: Bantawa *les-(u)*; Kulung *lema*; Yamphu *le'-ma*; Limbu *lɛːma*.

LANGUAGE, WORD, SPEECH:

Proto-Tibeto-Burman **glaŋ* × **klaŋ* 'word, language, speech, sound', **ka* 'word, speech, language', **rey* 'language, speech'.

- /*l-/: Jero *-la* in *maːla*$_{am}$; Bahing *ló*; Sunwar *loo*; Thulung *loa*; Chamling *la*.
- ?/*kw-/: Bahing *ʔbak-* 'speak' (Michailovsky 1994); Sunwar *bwaːk-* 'speak' (Michailovsky 1994); Khaling *'braa*; Dumi *boʔo*; Limbu *paːn*.
- /*r-/: Bantawa *yüŋ*; Kulung *riŋ*.

LAUGH:

Proto-Tibeto-Burman **r(y)ay* × **r(y)a-t(s)*.

- /*ry-/ > /y-/: Hayu *jɪt-*; Lohorung *yichae* (H); Yamphu *yi't-cama*; Mewahang *yúcha'* (H); Limbu *eːpma* (<**yeːpma*).

  /*ry-/ > /r-/: Jero *rɛnda recap*$_{a}$, *rɛnda recam*$_{m}$; Wambule *ryanda ryacam*; Bahing *riso*; Sunwar *'rit-tsa* 'laugh, smile'; Thulung *ris-*; Khaling *ren-nä*; Dumi *riːni*; Chamling *ri-* ~ *rya-*; Bantawa *réta* (H); Dungmali *ríge* (H); Nachiring *rhésa* (H); Yakkha *rísa* (H).

  /*ry-/ > /g-/: Kulung *gema* (Tolsma 1999), *gésa* (H); Sampang *ghísá* (H).

LEARN, STUDY:

Proto-Tibeto-Burman **s-lwap* 'practice, learn'.

- /*c-/: Jero *cei-*$_{m}$; Wambule *ceicam*; Bahing *cháyin̲so*; Sunwar *'sheen-si-tsa* (initial unexplained; /c-/ expected); Thulung *cen-* 'teach'; Khaling *'ceysi-nä*; Dumi *tsen'sini*; Chamling *cuima*; Bantawa *cint-(a)ncin-*; Yamphu *cimma*.

LEAVE, QUIT, ABANDON:

Proto-Tibeto-Burman **gar* 'leave, abandon'.

- /*pl-/: Jero *plɛcam*$_{m}$; Wambule *plyacam*; Bahing *pleno* 'set at liberty'; Sunwar *'preentsa*; Khaling *'len-nä*.
  - ≈ /*l-/ or /*ʔl-/: Kulung *ramma*; Yamphu *leʔma*; Limbu *lɛpma*.

LEG, FOOT:

Proto-Tibeto-Burman **kan* × **keŋ* 'leg, foot, stem, stalk' (Matisoff 2003), **g-la* 'foot' (Benedict 1972).

- /*ʔl-/: Jero *lɔsu*$_{am}$, *lɔs*$_{a}$; Wambule *ʔlɔsu*$_{w}$, *lwasu*; Bahing *-li* in *kho'li*; Sunwar *-li* in *khoyli* 'foot, leg', *-laa* in *dimlaa* 'foot, sole'; Thulung *khel*; Hayu *le*; Dumi *-lɨ* in *phoʔlɨ* 'leg, foot'; Bantawa *laŋ*; Kulung *lɔŋ*; Yamphu *laŋ*; Limbu *laŋ*.
- /*s-/: Thulung *siul* 'track, trace, footprint'; Khaling *säl*.

LICK:

Proto-Tibeto-Burman **m/s-lyak* 'lick, tongue, eat (of animals), feed (animals)'.

- /*l-/: Jero *lɔkcap*$_{a}$; Wambule *lɔkcam*$_{w}$, *lwakcam*; Khaling *'laa-nä*; Dumi *lyəknɨ*; Bantawa *lek-(u)*; Kulung *loːma*; Yamphu *rœˑkma*; Limbu *lakma*. Thulung *lep-* can perhaps also be added. See 'tongue'.
- /*t-/ or /*ʔt-/: Bahing *tukko*; Sunwar *'tuuk-tsa*.

LIE DOWN, GO TO SLEEP:

Proto-Tibeto-Burman **s-yip* × *s-yup* 'sleep, put to sleep, conceal, hide'.

- /*gl-/: Jero *glecap*$_a$, *glecam*$_m$; Wambule *glwamcam*; Bahing *gléso*; Sunwar *'gol-tsa*; Thulung *ghleom-* 'hatch, keep something warm (inside one's clothes)'; Khaling *'lansi-nä*; Bantawa *lims-(a)* 'lie down'.
- /*i-/: Sunwar *'ip-tsa*; Hayu *ɪm-*; Thulung *əms-*, *ums-*; Dumi *iːbdẓinɨ*; Chamling *imma*; Bantawa *ʔims-(a)*; Kulung *im-ma*; Yamphu *imma*; Limbu *imma*.

LIE, ACT OF LYING:

Proto-Tibeto-Burman **haːy* 'lie, deceive, dissemble'.

- /*ʔl-/: Jero *nim*$_a$, *nima*$_m$ (<**ʔlima*); Wambule *ʔlima*$_w$, *lima*; Bahing *limo*; Thulung *lima*; Khaling *'lemaa*; Yamphu *remdeʔma*.
- ≈ /*w-/: Dumi *waːlə*; Kulung *walili*; Limbu *illɛk* 'false'.

LIKE, BE FOND OF:

- /*d-/: Jero *daː-*$_a$, *dakcap*$_a$, *dakcam*$_m$; Wambule *dakcam*; Bahing *dwakto* 'desire, like'; Sunwar *'daak-tsa*; Thulung *doak-*.
- /*y-/: Khaling *yän-nä*; Dumi *yaːtnɨ*.
- /*n-/ or /*ʔn-/: Bantawa *nü-ʔa nu-ma*; Kulung *nəima*; Yamphu *nenjama*; Limbu *nanuʔma*.

LIVER:

Proto-Tibeto-Burman *m-luŋ* 'mind, heart, liver'.

- ?/*ʔl-/: Jero *ni*$_m$ (<**ʔli*); Wambule *ḍi* (<**di*); Bahing *ding*; Sunwar *-di* in *aydi*; Thulung *duŋ* (LTH *diuŋa*); Khaling *lum*; Dumi *lum*; Chamling *lui*; Bantawa *luŋ+ma*; Kulung *luma*; *ruŋmajuwa*; Limbu *luŋmaʔ*.

LIZARD:

Proto-Tibeto-Burman **r-saŋ.*

- /*k-/: Jero *wakewa*$_{m}$ (loss of /*k-/); Wambule *kwakyawa*; Sunwar *khote* (initial unexplained; /k-/ expected); Khaling *kokcaalaap*; Dumi *kokte:*; Bantawa *khok+ca* (initial unexplained; /k-/ expected); Kulung *kokcilipa*; Yamphu *koŋgriŋ* 'a species of coloured lizard'.

LOOK:

Proto-Tibeto-Burman **hyen* 'hear, listen, look, see'.

- /*ʔk-/: Jero *kicap*$_{a}$, *kicam*$_{m}$; Wambule *kwacam*; Bahing *kwógno* 'see'; Sunwar *koo-tsa* 'see, look at'; Khaling *'ko-nä* 'know how to do something'; Chamling *khanga-*, *khõ-*; Bantawa *kha-(u)*, *khaŋ-(u)*; Kulung *kho:ma* 'see'; Yamphu *khaŋma*.

  ≈ Limbu *ni:ma*.
- /*s-/: Khaling *sey-nä* 'look'; Dumi *syennɨ*.

LOUSE:

Proto-Tibeto-Burman **s-r(y)ik*, **s(y)ar*.

- Jero *sɛri*$_{am}$; Wambule *syari*; Bahing *-syar* in *túsyar*; Sunwar *rii* ($^{?}$<**serii*); Thulung *ser*; Khaling *ser*; Dumi *se:r*; Bantawa *sit*; Kulung *si*; Yamphu *sik*; Limbu *siʔ*.

LUNGS:

Proto-Tibeto-Burman **tsi-wap*, **tsywap*.

- /*j-/: Jero *jɔpre*$_{m}$, *jɔpro*$_{a}$; Wambule *jwapro*; Thulung *jan, ja*.
  /*s-/: Bahing *syeúporeú*; Khaling *swaapraap*.

  ≈ /*s-/ in 'breath': Bantawa *som*; Kulung *səm*; Yamphu *som*; Limbu *so:m*.

MAKE DRINK:

- /*ʔt-/: Jero *tɛncap*$_{a}$, *teicam*$_{a}$; Wambule *teicam*; Bahing *tundo*; Sunwar *'tuyn-tsa* in *duud 'tuyn-tsa* 'wean'; Chamling *dungd-*.
  /*th-/: Hayu *thun-*; Thulung *theo(n)-*.

MANKIND, PERSON:

Proto-Tibeto-Burman **r-mi(y)-n* 'man, person'.

- /*m-/: Jero *mucu*$_{am}$; Wambule *muyo*; Bahing *múryeu*; Sunwar *mur*; Thulung *miuciu*; Khaling *min*; Dumi *mi:n*; Chamling *mina*; Bantawa *mü+na* 'man'; Kulung *misi*; Yamphu *-mi* in *yaʔmi*; Limbu *mɔna*.

MATERNAL UNCLE:

Proto-Tibeto-Burman **kuw* = **kəw* (Benedict 1972).

- /*k-/: Jero *kɔro*$_a$, *kɔr*$_a$; Wambule *kwaro*; Bahing *kuku*; Thulung *kuk*; Dumi *kiki*, *kira*; Chamling *kurungpa*; Bantawa *kü+yaŋ+pa*; Limbu *kuvaʔ*, *kukkvaʔ*.

MEET, VISIT:

Proto-Tibeto-Burman **grim* × **krim*, **grum* × **krum*.

- /*gr-/: Jero *rɛmcam*$_m$; Wambule *rwamcam*; Sunwar *grumtsa* 'meet'; Thulung *ghreom-*, *kreom-* (/gr-/ expected).
- /*d-/: Hayu *do(t)-*; Khaling *dam-nä*; Dumi *dɨmnɨ*; Chamling *tip-*; Bantawa *tup-(u)*; Kulung *tumma*; Limbu *tumma*.

MILLET:

- /*c-/ or /*ʔc-/: Jero *carji*$_{am}$; Wambule *carja*; Bahing *chárjá*; Sunwar *'tsirsi*.
- /*l-/ or /*ʔl-/: Hayu *le'i*; Khaling *lujaa*; Dumi *lidzəm*, *lidzə*; Kulung *lisi*.
- /*b-/: Bantawa *büŋ+ku* 'species of large millet'; Yamphu *paŋgiya*; Limbu *pɛna*.

MOON:

Proto-Tibeto-Burman **s/g-la* 'moon, month'.

- /*t-/ or /*ʔt-/: Jero *tʌusɛl*$_a$, *tosɛl*$_m$; Wambule *tosyal*; Bahing *taúsaba*; Sunwar *'tasla*.
- /*khl-/ or /*l-/: Thulung *khleomu*; Khaling *'lö*; Bantawa *la+dip*; Kulung *la*; Yamphu *la*; Limbu *la:*, *la:ba*.

MORTAR:

Proto-Tibeto-Burman **t(s)um* × *(t)sum*, **tśrum*.

- /*ʔc-/: Sunwar *'tsumlo*; Chamling *chippu*, *chippukhung*; Bantawa *chum+puk*; Kulung *c*^{h}*umbo*.

  /*s-/: Jero *sumlo*$_{\mathrm{a}}$; Wambule *sumlo*; Thulung *'siuŋkhra*; Khaling *samkhraa*; Dumi *siŋkho*; Yamphu *summak*; Limbu *sumdaŋ*.

MOTHER:

Proto-Tibeto-Burman **ma-n* 'mother, feminine suffix', **m-na* 'mother'.

- /*m-/: Jero *mama*$_{\mathrm{am}}$; Wambule *mama*, *mam*; Bahing *-mó* in *ámó* 'my mother'; Hayu *u'mu*; Thulung *mam*; Khaling *'mäm*; Dumi *mama*, *mu*; Chamling *-ma* in *kok-ma* 'grandmother'; Bantawa *ma*, *ma=ma*; Kulung *ma*; Yamphu *ma'ma*; Limbu *mɔmma*.

MOUSE:

Proto-Tibeto-Burman **syow* 'rat', **b-yəw-n* 'rat, rabbit, hare', **sya-yəw* 'rat'.

- /*ʔc-/: Jero *cicimo*$_{\mathrm{m}}$, *cicum*$_{\mathrm{m}}$; Wambule *cicimo*; Bantawa *cü-ʔyü*, *cük-yü* (initial unexplained; /ch-/ expected); Kulung *c*^{h}*uwi*; Yamphu *siʔnuma*; Limbu *suba*.
- /*y-/: Bahing *yeu*; Sunwar *'yitsu*.

  ≈ Thulung *'jal*.

NAME:

Proto-Tibeto-Burman **mi:n* 'name (v), order, command', **r/s-miŋ*.

- /*ʔn-/ ($^{?}$< /*s-m-/): Jero *ni*$_{\mathrm{am}}$; Wambule *dî*; Bahing *ning*; Sunwar *ne*; Hayu *miŋ* ($^{?}$/*s-m-/ > /m-/); Thulung *nəŋ*; Khaling *nang*; Dumi *ni*; Chamling *nung*; Bantawa *nüŋ*; Kulung *niŋ*; Yamphu *niŋ*; Limbu *miŋ* ($^{?}$/*s-m-/ > /m-/).

NET:

Proto-Tibeto-Burman *gwa-n × *kwa-n 'net (casting)'.

- ?/*kw-/: Wambule *ɓallu* 'fishing net'; Bahing *ʔba:luŋ* (Michailovsky 1994); Sunwar *'gyayli*; Thulung *paluŋ*.
- /*y-/: Chamling *-yu* in *cãyu*; Limbu *yo:ŋ*.

NEW:

Proto-Tibeto-Burman **g-sar* 'new, fresh', **sar* 'new', **g-sik* 'new'.

- /*n-/ or /*ʔn-/: Jero *nɛntha*$_{a}$; Bahing *-ninta* in *aninta*; Sunwar *'nak*; Hayu *nesi*; Khaling *'nin* 'freshness, newness'; Thulung *niuDa* (LTH *neoDa*); Kulung *nus* 'soon, early'.
  ≈ Limbu *nakusɔŋ*.
- Wambule *ebo*.
- /*c-/ or /*j-/: Bantawa *coŋ-wa*; Yamphu *coŋ*.
  /*ʔc-/, /*ch-/, /*s-/: Limbu *sɔŋ*.

NOSE:

Proto-Tibeto-Burman **s-na* × **s-na:r*.

- /*ʔn-/: Jero *nusum*$_{am}$; Wambule *ɗusum*; Bahing *néu*; Sunwar *neen*; Hayu *-no* in *tsoʔno*; Thulung *neo*, or *na-* in *nakhli* 'nasal mucus'; Khaling *nö*; Dumi *nu*; Chamling *nabro*; Bantawa *na+bu*; Kulung *nap*; Yamphu *naʔu*; Limbu *nɛboʔ*.

OBEY:

- /*r-/: Wambule *ryapcam* 'obey someone'; Khaling *'rem-nä*; Dumi *repnɨ*; Bantawa *yüŋ+ca+ka-ba*; Kulung *remma*; Yamphu *khemma* (initial unexplained, perhaps < /*γ/); /y-/ expected).

ONE:

Proto-Tibeto-Burman **ʔit* 'one', **tyak* × **g-t(y)ik* 'one, only'.

- /*k-/ or /*ʔk-/: Jero *kɔʔlo*$_a$, *kɔʔl*$_a$, *kwal*$_m$; Wambule *kwalo*, *kwal*; Bahing *kwong*; Sunwar *kaa*; Hayu *kolu*; Thulung *ko*, *koŋ*.
- /*ʔt-/: Khaling *'tu*, *'tubaa*; Dumi *tɨk*, *tɨkbo*; Limbu *thik*.
- /*i-/: Chamling *i-*; Bantawa *ʔük*; Kulung *i:bum*; Yamphu *ik-ko*.

ONE'S OWN CHILD'S FATHER-IN-LAW:

- /*h-/: Jero *hilpu*$_a$; Wambule *ilpo* (<**hilpo*); Thulung *həlbo* 'child's parent-in-law'; Khaling *helpö*; Kulung *helpa*.

ONE'S OWN CHILD'S MOTHER-IN-LAW:

- /*h-/: Jero *hilmu*$_a$; Wambule *ilmo* (<**hilmo*); Thulung *həlbo* 'child's parent-in-law'; Khaling *helmö*; Kulung *helma*.

OPEN:

Proto-Tibeto-Burman **m-ka* 'open, opening, mouth, door'.

- /*h-/: Jero *hɔl-*$_m$; Wambule *hwalcam*; Bahing *hókko*; Thulung *hoak-*, *hol-* 'open'; Khaling *'haa-nä* 'open', *hwaal-nä* 'break open'; Hayu *ho-*; Dumi *ha:knɨ*; Bantawa *hok-(u)*; Kulung *həlma*; Yamphu *hemma*; Limbu *hɔmma*.

OWL:

Proto-Tibeto-Burman **gu* × **ku*.

- /*ʔp-/: Wambule *phwapwaci*; Sunwar *'buuksu* (initial unexplained; /p-/ expected); Thulung *bobok*; Khaling *po-pwaap* 'forest eagle-owl'; Dumi *-popo* in *dilipopo* '*Bubo nipalensis*'; Bantawa *bu-wa*; Limbu *phɔkti:mba*; *khɔk-ti:mba*.

PICK UP:

Proto-Tibeto-Burman **s-g-ruk.*

- /*g-/: Jero *gicap*$_{a}$, *gicam*$_{m}$; Wambule *gucam*; Bahing *gup-* (Michailovsky 1994); Sunwar *gup-tsa*; Chamling *kup-* (Michailovsky 1994); Bantawa *kup-(u)*; Kulung *kəmma*; Yamphu *ku·pma*; Limbu *khɔmma* (initial unexplained; /k-/ expected).
- /*s-/: Khaling *su-nä*; Dumi *siŋni*.

PIG, HOG:

Proto-Tibeto-Burman **p^{w}ak, *wak.*

- /*ʔp-/: Jero *pa*$_{am}$ 'pig', *cuppa*$_{am}$ 'piglet'; Wambule *pa* 'pig', *cuppa* 'piglet'; Bahing *po*; Sunwar *poo*; Thulung *boa*; Khaling *'po*; Dumi *poʔo* 'pig', *poksœ* 'piglet'; Chamling *bose*; Bantawa *bak*; Kulung *bo:* 'pig', *bokc^{h}a* 'piglet'; Yamphu *akma* 'pig', *akpasa* 'piglet'; Limbu *phak*.

PINCH, NIP; STING (BY INSECT):

Proto-Tibeto-Burman **s-ni(:)p* × **r/s-nyap* × **s-nu(:)p.*

- /*n-/: Jero *naccam*$_{m}$; Wambule *naccam*; Sunwar *'nayk-tsa* 'sting', *nayk-tsa* 'pinch'; Thulung *nat(s)-* 'crush'.
- /*k-/ or /*ʔk-/: Khaling *'kem-nä*; Dumi *kepni*.
- /*ʔc-/: Chamling *chik-ma*; Bantawa *chük-(u)*; Kulung *c^{h}e:-ma*; Yamphu *ci·kma* (initial unexplained; /s-/ expected); Limbu *se:kma*.

PLASTER:

- /*kl-/: Thulung *klək-* 'smear, anoint, rub on'; Khaling *'kle-nä*;

  /*khl-/: Jero *khlɛkcap*$_{a}$, *khlɛk-*$_{m}$; Wambule *khlyakcam*; Bahing *khlyakko*; Sunwar *'tel 'khreek-tsa* 'rub in (oil)'; Dumi *leŋni* 'smear on (mud or clay)'; Bantawa *leŋs-(u)*; Kulung *kilma*; Limbu *lɛŋma*.

PLOUGH:

- /*j-/: Bahing *jóto*; Thulung *jo(t)-* (*jho(t)-*; /j-/ as expected); Khaling *jho-nä*; Kulung *jo:ma*.

POTATO, YAM:

Proto-Tibeto-Burman **grwa* 'taro, potato', **s-r(y)a* 'yam, potato'.

- /*r-/: Jero *rεnjab*$_{a}$; Wambule *rwanjabi* 'k.o. jam'; Sunwar *reekbe*; Yamphu *yaksi* 'a species of edible root'.
- /*kw-/: Bahing *ʔbe* (Michailovsky 1994); Sunwar *-be* in *reekbe*; Hayu *xi* (Michailovsky 1994); Thulung *pə* 'cultivated yam', *bələkpu* 'yam, potato'; Khaling *ki*; Dumi *ki:*; Chamling *-ki* in *soki* (Michailovsky 1994); Bantawa *-ki* in *sak+ki*; Kulung *k*^{h}*e* (archaic); Limbu *khe* 'yam, potato'.

PRIEST:

- /*n-/: Jero *naksu*$_{a}$; Wambule *nakso*; Thulung *nokcho* 'ritual officiant'; Khaling *'nokco*; Dumi *naksœ*; Bantawa *nak+choŋ* 'male shaman'; Kulung *nokc*^{h}*o*.

PUS:

Proto-Tibeto-Burman **s-na:y*.

- /*h-/: Jero *hupmi*$_{m}$, *hupni*$_{a}$; Wambule *hwabdi*.
- /*n-/ or /*ʔn-/: Sunwar *nene*; Khaling *'ni* 'sap'; Limbu *ni:kwa*.
- /*kh-/: Khaling *khünüwä*; Dumi *khɨ'ni*; Thulung *kən* (initial unexplained; /kh-/ expected); Bantawa *kho-wa+wa*; Kulung *k*^{h}*unwa*.

PUSH:

- /*n-/: Jero *nεpcap*$_{a}$, *nεpcam*$_{m}$; Wambule *nyapcam*; Bahing *nyapto*; Sunwar *'nep-tsa*.
- /*t-/ or /*d-/: Bantawa *tol-(u)*; Kulung *təlma*.

  /*th-/: Khaling *thwaal-nä*; Yamphu *the·ma*.

QUESTION:

- /*c-/ or /*ʔc-/: Jero *cel*$_{m}$; Wambule *cela*.
- /*h-/: Bahing *hilo*; Sunwar *hillo*; Thulung *hila*.
- /*s-/: Khaling *su-nä* 'ask'; Dumi *siŋnɨ* 'ask'; *sen-pa* 'asking'; Yamphu *simma*; Limbu *se:ndo*, *se:nlap*, *se:llap* 'question'.

RAIN, SHOWER:

Proto-Tibeto-Burman **rwa-s*, **r-wa* ×**s-wa* ×**g-wa*.

- /*w-/: Jero *hwarsi*$_a$ (initial unexplained; /w-/ expected), *warsi*$_m$; Wambule *warsi*; Thulung *wō*; Khaling *wö*; Dumi *hu* (initial unexplained; /w-/ expected); Bantawa *wa-ta-(a)* (v); Kulung *wa*; Yamphu *wari*; Limbu *wage:k*.
  ≈ /*r-/: Bahing *ryá-wá*; Sunwar *rew*.

RED:

Proto-Tibeto-Burman *t(s)a:y*, **t(y)a*.

- /*ʔl-/: Jero *laka*$_a$; Wambule *ʔlaka*$_w$, *laka, lak*; Bahing *lalam*; Sunwar *lal*; Thulung *lalam*.
  ≈ /*h-/: Khaling *haalaalaam*; Bantawa *ha+la, ha+la=la*; Kulung *halala:pa*; Yamphu *harra*; Limbu *hɛ:t*.

REMEMBER, THINK:

- /*ʔm-/: Jero *mimcap*$_a$; Wambule *ɓimcam*; Bahing *mimto*; Sunwar *mim-tsa*; Thulung *mim-*; Khaling *mam-nä*; Dumi *minni*; Bantawa *mitt-(a)*; Kulung *mi:ma*; Yamphu *miʔma*; Limbu *niŋ-waʔ*.

REST, RELAX:

Proto-Tibeto-Burman **g-na-s* 'be, live, stay, rest, alight, perch'.

- /*n-/: Jero *naicam*$_m$; Wambule *naicam*; Bahing *náso* 'take rest'; Sunwar *'nayk-tsa*; Thulung *ŋemsi-* (initial unexplained; /n-/ expected); Khaling *nöl mü-nä*; Bantawa *nant-(a)*; Kulung *nomcima*; Yamphu *næ'ʔma* 'rest a burden'; Limbu *naʔsiŋma*.

ROAD, PATH:

Proto-Tibeto-Burman **lam*.

- /*ʔl-/: Jero *lam*$_{am}$; Wambule *ʔlam*$_w$, *lam*; Bahing *lam*; Sunwar *'laan*; Hayu *lom*; Thulung *lam*; Khaling *läm*; Dumi *lam*; Chamling *lam*; Bantawa *lam*; Kulung *lam*; Yamphu *ram*; Limbu *lam*.

RUB:

Proto-Tibeto-Burman **nu:l* 'rub, wear down'.

- /*ry-/ > /y-/: Wambule *yalcam*; Bahing *yállo*.
  /*ry-/ > /r-/: Khaling *ral-nä* 'roll out (dough)'.
  /*ry-/ > /g-/: Kulung *galma*.
- /*n-/ or /*ʔn-/: Khaling *'nu-nä*; Bantawa *nul-(u)*; Yamphu *nukma*; Limbu *nukma*.

RUN (AWAY):

Proto-Tibeto-Burman **gyar* × **hyar* 'run, ride, go by vehicle', **ploŋ* 'run, flee'.

- /*pr-/: Jero *prakcam*$_{\mathrm{m}}$; Wambule *prwakcam*, *procam*; Sunwar *prook-tsa*.
- Khaling *ghar-nä* 'run'.
- /*b-/: Dumi *bɨlnɨ*; Kulung *bulma*.
- /*o-/: Thulung *on-*; Yamphu *oŋma*.
- /*l-/ or /*ʔl-/: Hayu *lɷn-*; Bantawa *lot-(a)*; Limbu *lo:kma*.

SALT:

Proto-Tibeto-Burman **gryum*, **g-ryum*.

- /*ry-/ > /y-/: Bantawa *yum*; Dungmali *yúm* (H); Lohorung *yúm* (H); Yamphu *yum*; Mewahang *yúm* (H); Yakkha *yúm* (H); Limbu *yum*.
  /*ry-/ > /r-/: Khaling *ram*; Dumi *rɨm*; Chamling *rúm* (H); Nachiring *ram* (H); Sampang *rúm* (H).
  /*ry-/ > /g-/: Kulung *rum* (Tolsma 1999), *gúm* (H).
- /*y-/: Jero *yaksi*$_{\mathrm{am}}$; Wambule *yaksi*, *ywaksi*; Bahing *yuksi*; Sunwar *hiikshi*; Thulung *yo*.

SAY:

Proto-Tibeto-Burman **s-br(w)aŋ* × **br(w)ak* 'speak', **g-tam* × **g-dam* 'speak'.

- ?/d-/: Jero *necap*$_a$, *necam*$_m$; Wambule *decam*, *dyancam*; Sunwar *deen-tsa* 'say, talk'.
- /*bl-/: Khaling *blän-nä*; Dumi *ba:tnɨ*; Kulung *pi:ma*; Limbu *pa:pma*.
- /*r-/: Chamling *rungma*, *ringma*; Bantawa *yüŋ-(a)*.
- /*i-/: Hayu *ɪt-*; Yamphu *i'ma*.

SCREAM, CROW:

Proto-Tibeto-Burman *ʔa:w* 'shout'.

- /*o-/: Jero *wakcap*$_a$, *wa:cap*$_a$; Wambule *wakcam*; Hayu *ok-* ; Thulung *ok-*, *hok-*; Khaling *'o-nä*; Dumi *u:knɨ*; Bantawa *ʔokt-(a)*; Kulung *o:ma*; Yamphu *wo'ma*; Limbu *u:ma*.

SEARCH, LOOK FOR:

Proto-Tibeto-Burman **pa* 'search, for, seek', **m-pup* 'turn over, search for, seek'.

- /*m-/: Jero *malcam*$_m$; Wambule *malcam*; Sunwar *mal-tsa* 'search for, want, long for'; Hayu *mot*; Thulung *mal-*.
- /*l-/ or /*ʔl-/: Bahing *lamo*; Khaling *lwaam-nä*; Dumi *ləm-nɨ*; Chamling *lam-*; Bantawa *lam-(u)*; Kulung *lamma*.
- Yamphu *yokma*.
- Limbu *ko:pma*.

SELF:

Proto-Tibeto-Burman **ŋay* 'first person pronoun, self', **tay* 'self'.

- ?/*t-/ or /*d-/: Jero *daŋma*$_a$; Wambule *ɗaŋma*; Bahing *dau-bo*, *dwabo*; Sunwar *aanmaa*; Thulung *tap*; Khaling *taam*, *taap* 'own'; Yamphu *taŋba*; Limbu *abaŋe* (initial unexplained).
- /*h-/: Dumi *ho:p*; Bantawa *ʔan+haŋ+paŋ*; Kulung *-ho:p*.

SELL, EXCHANGE:

Proto-Tibeto-Burman **g/m/s-lay* × **r-ley* 'change, exchange, buy, barter', **par* 'trade, buy, sell', **rey* 'buy, barter', **ywar* 'sell, buy'.

- /*ʔl-/: Wambule *ʔliːcam*$_w$, *liːcam*; Bahing *légno*; Sunwar *'lee-tsa*; Dumi *leŋ'sinɨ* 'change (esp. clothes)'; Chamling *lo-ma*; Bantawa *lent-(u)*; Yamphu *lemma* 'exchange, swap'; Limbu *lɛkma* 'change, exchange, interchange'.
- /*th-/: Jero *thamcap*$_a$; Hayu *tham-*.
- /*i-/: Dumi *innɨ*; Bantawa *ʔint-(u)*; Yamphu *injama*.

SET (SUN), SINK:

Proto-Tibeto-Burman **g(l)im* ×**g(l)um* 'set (of the sun)'.

- /*h-/: Jero *hamcam*$_m$, *hɔmcap*$_a$; Wambule *hamcam*; Bahing *nam wamtana* 'at sun-set' (<**hwamtana*); Khaling *hem-nä*; Dumi *hɨmnɨ*; Bantawa *khopt-(u)* 'sink (vt)' (initial unexplained; /h-/ expected); Kulung *kamma* (initial un-explained; /h-/ expected); Limbu *humma* 'sink in'.

SEW:

Proto-Tibeto-Burman **byar* × **pyar* 'affix, sew', plait, braid'.

- /*ʔp-/: Hayu *pi-*; Kulung *burma*.
  /*ph-/: Jero *phɛrcap*$_a$, *phɛr-*$_m$; Wambule *phyarcam*; Bahing *phyéro*; Sunwar *pher-tsa*; Thulung *phir-*; Khaling *pher-nä*.
- /*th-/: Dumi *thɨpnɨ*; Bantawa *thup-(u)*; Yamphu *thi'ʔma*.

SHADE:

Proto-Tibeto-Burman **g/s-rip* 'shade, shadow', **rum* × **rim* 'dark, shade, dusk'.

- /*ry-/ > /y-/: Hayu *ji'li*; Yamphu *yi'pma* 'disappear from sight'.
  /*ry-/ > /r-/: Jero *rimsa*$_m$, *riptɛwa*$_a$; Wambule *rimsa*; Thu-lung *ribjuŋ*, *rimjuŋ*'; Khaling *ramjhung*; Dumi *ri(m)* in *kiri*, *kɨrim*; Bantawa *rim=rim+da* 'at down'.
  /*ry-/ > /g-/: Kulung *gimju*.

SHADOW, SPIRIT:

Proto-Tibeto-Burman **m-hla* 'god, soul, beautiful'.

- ?/*kw-/: Jero *maʔla*$_a$; Wambule *ɓala*; Bahing *ʔbala* 'spirit'; Sunwar *wala* 'ghost, spirit'; Thulung *pel.*
- /*l-/ or /*ʔl-/: Thulung *leo* 'spirit'; Khaling *lö* 'senses, feeling'; Dumi *luː* 'mind, soul'; Bantawa *la-wa*; Kulung *loŋ-ma* 'shadow'; Yamphu *lawa.*

SHAKE, MOVE, AGITATE:

Proto-Tibeto-Burman **tur* 'tremble, shake, pulse'.

- /*d-/: Jero *dukcam*$_m$; Wambule *dukcam*; Bahing *dukba* 'drunken, moving'; Sunwar *duuk-tsa* 'move, stir'; Hayu *duk-*; Thulung *dos-*; Khaling *'thu-nä* 'move' ('transitive' initial; /d-/ expected); Bantawa *tuŋ-(a)* 'move (vi)'; Kulung *toːma*; Yamphu *ta·ma* 'move'.

  ≈ Limbu *thɔŋma* 'shake up and down in a winnowing disc'.

BE SHARP:

Proto-Tibeto-Burman **s-ryam* 'sharp'.

- /*ry-/ > /y-/: Jero *yacap*$_a$; Wambule *yacam*; Yamphu *yem-ma*; Limbu *yarapma* 'whet, sharpen, make sharp'; Thulung *ya* 'blade'.

  /*ry-/ > /r-/: Khaling *'ren-nä* 'sharpen, whet'.

  /*ry-/ > /h-/: Bahing *héba* 'sharp'; Sunwar *hesh-sho* 'sharp (edged)'; Thulung *hən-*; Khaling *henpä.*

  /*ry-/ > /g-/: Kulung *geːpa.*

SHAVE:

- /*kh-/: Jero *khɔrcap*$_a$, *khɔr-*$_m$ 'plough'; Wambule *khwarcam* 'plough; shave'; Thulung *khur-*; Bantawa *khos-(u)*; Kulung *k*^{h}*oːma*; Yamphu *kho·kma.*

SHOULDER:

- ?/*kw-/: Jero *masεm*$_{m}$; Wambule *ɓasyam*; Bahing *balam*; Sunwar *balaa*; Thulung *'balam* 'shoulder blade'; Khaling *'bhaataa* (/b-/ expected); Dumi *bokto*; Bantawa *bak+taŋ*; Kulung *bouto* (?<**bokto*); Yamphu *akkɓaŋ* (<**paktaŋ*); Limbu *phɔkthaŋ*.

SHUT, CLOSE:

Proto-Tibeto-Burman **dzyi:p* 'shut, close, close together'.

- /*t-/ or /*ʔt-/: Wambule *tyakcam*, *ṭyakcam*; Bahing *tyakko* 'retain, shut'.

  /*th-/: Jero *thεkcap*$_{a}$, *ṭhεkcam*$_{m}$; Wambule *thyakcam*, *ṭhyakcam*; Bantawa *dhekt-(u)* (initial unexplained; /th-/ expected).

  ≈ Chamling *doma*.
- /*ʔc-/: Bahing *tsok-* (Michailovsky 1994); Sunwar *'tsookshо* 'shut, lock'; Thulung *cəks-* 'shut up'; Khaling *'cenä*; Bantawa *chekt-(u)*; Kulung *cʰima*; Yamphu *sækma*; Limbu *sakma*, *supma*.

SILENCE, QUIETNESS:

Proto-Tibeto-Burman **ŋoy* 'gentle, silent'.

- /*ʔl-/: Wambule *ʔliba*$_{w}$, *liba*, *lib*; Bahing *líba*, *liba*; Sunwar *bwaale*; Thulung *liwa* (LTH *leba*); Kulung *lebaleba*.
- /*m-/ or /*ʔm-/: Jero *manto*$_{m}$, *manthu*$_{a}$ (see Thulung *manthi* 'without'); Khaling *majepä* 'silent'; Bantawa *man-cep*.

SIT DOWN:

- /*ŋ-/: Jero *ni:cap*$_{a}$, *ni:-*$_{m}$; Wambule *ni:cam*; Bahing *niso* 'sit'; Sunwar *nit-tsa* 'sit', *'nit-tsa* 'sit cross legged'; Khaling *ngäy-nä*; Dumi *ŋa:nsinɨ* 'sit down'.
- ?/*h-/: Chamling *hing-*; Bantawa *yuŋ-(a)*; Limbu *yuŋma*, *yuŋsiŋma*.

SMALL, LITTLE:

Proto-Tibeto-Burman **z(y)əy* 'little, small, tiny'.

- /*y-/: Jero *yɔkko*$_m$; Wambule *ywakka*; Bahing *yáke*; Thulung *yakke*; Hayu *jaŋ-* 'be small'; Khaling *yaahki*.
- /*c-/ or /*j-/: Bantawa *cup*, *cup-pa*; Kulung *ci:ma*; Limbu *cuk*.

SMELL:

Proto-Tibeto-Burman **m/s-nam*.

- /*n-/: Jero *ŋɔmcap*$_a$, *ŋɔmcam*$_m$ (initial unexplained; /n-/ expected); Wambule *ŋwamcam* (initial unexplained; /n-/ expected); Bahing *námo*; Sunwar *nam-tsa* 'smell, sense odour'; Hayu *nam-*; Thulung *nem-*; Khaling *nwaam-nä*; Dumi *nəmnɨ*; Chamling *namma*; Bantawa *nam*; Kulung *namma*; Yamphu *namma*; Limbu *namma*.

SMOKE (N):

Proto-Tibeto-Burman **kəw-n/t*.

- /*k-/ or /*ʔk-/: Jero *kunci*$_a$; Bahing *kúni*; Sunwar *kun*; Thulung *kuyku*.

  /kh-/: Jero *khumci*$_a$; Wambule *khunimo*.
- /*m-/: The root 'fire' is reflected in Khaling *'mikmö*; Dumi *mo:sisom*; Bantawa *mi+khü*; Kulung *mikma*; Yamphu *mækkhu*; Limbu *mighu:ma*.

SONG:

Proto-Tibeto-Burman **ga:r* × **s-ga* 'dance, sing, leap, stride'.

- /*ch-/: Jero *sa:laŋ*$_m$, *sa:ʔlɛŋ*$_a$; Wambule *sa:laŋ*; Bahing *swálong*; Bantawa *cham*; Kulung *c^{h}am*; Yamphu *semluma* 'song', *semla* 'voice'; Limbu *sam*, *sam-lo*.
- /*k-/ or /*ʔk-/: Sunwar *kumso*; Thulung *kamso*.
- /*l-/ or /*ʔl-/: Thulung *leolam* 'voice'; Khaling *lel*; Dumi *le:*.

SOUR:

Proto-Tibeto-Burman **su:r* × **swa:r* 'sour, be acid', **s-kyu:r* × **s-kywa:r* 'sour, be acid'.

- /*j-/: Jero *jurtɔp*$_a$, *jurto*$_m$; Wambule *jurco*; Bahing *jeujeum*; Sunwar *gyur-sho*; Thulung *jhiur-* 'be sour', *jiujiur* 'variety of bitter fruit'; Khaling *jujur*; Dumi *tsirpɨ* (initial unexplained; /j-/ expected); Kulung *jujurpa*.

  ≈ /*s-/: Chamling *syiraha* 'sour (things)'; Bantawa *sun-ko*; Yamphu *si'ye*; Limbu *su:pma*.

SPIDER:

Proto-Tibeto-Burman **m-kaŋ* 'spider'.

- ?/*kw-/: Jero *majari*$_m$; Wambule *ɓajirimo*, *ɓajirim*; Bahing *bájeringmo*; Thulung *proŋjiu* (<**paroŋjiu*); Khaling *'proci* (<**paroci*); Kulung *punc^{h}iri*.

  ≈ Dumi *gotsu*; Bantawa *ghaŋ=ghaŋ-ma*; Yamphu *yaŋ-ghakpa*; Limbu *khamda:kpa*, *khirippa*.

SPIT:

Proto-Tibeto-Burman **m/s-tu:k* 'spit, spew', **ts(y)il* × **til* 'spit, spittle, saliva'.

- /*t-/ or /*ʔt-/: Bahing *téwo*; Sunwar *'took-si-tsa*.

  /*th-/: Jero *thukcap*$_a$; Wambule *thukcam*; Thulung *thaŋki*, *thəŋki*; Khaling *khi 'thu-nä*; Kulung *t^{h}uwa*; Limbu *tho:ŋ-ma*.

- /*c-/ or /*j-/: Bantawa *cent-(u)*; Yamphu *ce'ʔma*.

SPITTLE, SALIVA:

Proto-Tibeto-Burman **ts(y)il* × **til* 'spit, spittle, saliva'.

- /*ʔn-/: Jero *nɛmki*$_{am}$; Wambule *ɗyamki*; Sunwar *'naaktsuka*.
- /*k-/ or /*ʔk-/: Bahing *-kú* in *ríchukú*; Thulung *-ki* in *thaŋki*.

  /*kh-/: Khaling *khi*; Dumi *khi:m*.
- /*th-/: Bantawa *thet-ma*; Kulung *thuwa*; Limbu *thɛt*.

SPREAD:

Proto-Tibeto-Burman *bra 'scattered' (Benedict 1972).

- /*br-/: Jero *bracap*$_a$, *bracam*$_m$; Wambule *bracam*; Bahing *bráwo*; Sunwar *'phra-tsa* 'scatter, spread (e.g. mats)' (initial unexplained; /br-/ expected).
- /*ph-/: Khaling *'phen-nä*; Dumi *phiŋni* 'spread out, grow wider'; Bantawa *phes-(u)*; Yamphu *phe'ma* 'spread out'.

STAND:

Proto-Tibeto-Burman **g-r(y)ap*.

- /*r-/ > /y-/: Jero *yɔmcap*$_a$, *yɔmcam*$_a$; Wambule *yamcam*; Thulung *yem-*, *yep-*; Bantawa *ʔep(a)* (Winter 2003), *yéba* (H); Lohorung *yébe* (H); Yamphu *ye'pma*; Mewahang *yépok* (H); Yakkha *yé-bá-chi-ni*; Limbu *yɛpma*.

  /*r-/ > /r-/: Bahing *rápo* (H); Sunwar *'rap-tsa*; Khaling *'rem-nä* 'erect'; Dumi *repni*; Chamling *repa-*; Dungmali *rebe* (H); Kulung *t^{h}o remma* (Tolsma 1999), *thórépa* (H); Nachiring *répa* (H); Sampang *ripá* (H).

STICK, ATTACH:

Proto-Tibeto-Burman **g(y)it/k* × **k(y)it/k* 'tie, bind'.

- /*k-/: Jero *kɛpcap*$_a$, *kɛpcam*$_m$; Wambule *kyapcam*; Bahing *kyapcho* 'glue'; Sunwar *keptsok* 'greasy'; Hayu *kik-*; Thulung *kep-;* Khaling *kay-nä* 'stick into', *'kem-nä* 'stick'; Dumi *kepni*; Bantawa *khep* in *cük+khep=cük+khep* 'sticky' (initial unexplained; /k-/ expected); Kulung *kemma*; Yamphu *ki'pma* 'stick onto'; Limbu *kapma*.

STONE:

Proto-Tibeto-Burman **r-luŋ* × **k-luk*.

- /*ʔl-/: Jero *-luŋ* in *phuluŋ*$_{am}$; Wambule *ʔluŋ*$_w$, *luŋ*; Bahing *lung*; Sunwar *-lu* in *phullu*; Hayu *lœphœ*; Thulung *luŋ*; Khaling *lung*; Dumi *lu*; Chamling *longto*; Bantawa *luŋ*; Kulung *luŋ*; Yamphu *ruŋguʔwa*; Limbu *luŋ*.

STRETCH:

- /*ʔk-/: Jero *ki:t-*$_{m}$; Wambule *ki:cam*; Sunwar *kii-tsa*; Thulung *ki-*; Bantawa *khünt-(u)*, *künt-(u)*; Kulung *ki:ma* (initial unexplained; /kh-/ expected); Yamphu *khiŋma*; Limbu *khiŋma*.
- /*th-/: Khaling *'than-nä*; Dumi *thɨtnɨ*; Limbu *thiŋma*.

SUCK:

Proto-Tibeto-Burman **dzyup* × **dzyip* 'suck, kiss, breast, milk'.

- /*y-/: Jero *yupcap*$_{a}$; Wambule *yupcam*; Sunwar *yup-tsa*.
- /*p-/ or /*ʔp-/: Hayu *pip-*.

  /*ph-/: Thulung *phip/m-*; Khaling *'pham-nä*; Dumi *phipnɨ*; Bantawa *phüpt-(u)*; Kulung *p^{h}imma*, *p^{h}ɔima*; Yamphu *phi'pma*.

  /*b-/: Jero *bipcap*$_{a}$, *bipcam*$_{m;}$ Wambule *ɓipcam*, *bipcam*; Bahing *bippo*; Limbu *pi:pma*.
- /*ch-/: Thulung *chip-*; Khaling *'cham-nä*; Yamphu *so'pma* 'suck, inhale',

SUFFICE:

Proto-Tibeto-Burman **luk* 'enough'.

- /*d-/: Jero *dɔkcap*$_{a}$, *dɔkcam*$_{m}$; Wambule *dwakcam*; Thulung *Doāsə(t)-*; Khaling *'do-nä*; Limbu *tɛkma* 'be sufficient for everyone'.
- /*l-/ or /*ʔl-/: Dumi *la:tnɨ* 'be enough for someone'; Bantawa *latt-(u)*; Kulung *laima*.

SUN:

Proto-Tibeto-Burman **nəy* 'sun, day' (Matisoff 2003), **nam* 'sun' (Benedict 1972).

- /*ʔn-/: Jero *nɔm*$_{am}$; Wambule *ɗwam*; Bahing *nam*; Sunwar *naa*; Thulung *nepsuŋ*; Khaling *nwaam*; Dumi *na:m*; Chamling *nam*; Bantawa *nam*; Kulung *nam*; Yamphu *nam*; Limbu *nam*.

SWALLOW:

Proto-Tibeto-Burman *mlyəw-k.*

- /*ʔt-/: Jero *tɔk-*$_{m}$; Wambule *twakcam, twaŋcam*; Bahing *dwakko, dwangso* ('intransitive' initial; /t-/ expected); Sunwar *daak-tsa* ('intransitive' initial; /t-/ expected); Hayu *tœk-* 'let fall'; Thulung *Dok-*.
- /*l-/ or /*ʔl-/: Khaling *ley-nä*; Dumi *lenni*; Bantawa *lunt-(u)* 'make sink'; Kulung *luima*; Yamphu *rimma*; Limbu *lɔpma*.

SWEEP:

Proto-Tibeto-Burman **py(w)ak* 'sweep, broom'.

- /*br-/: Jero *brɛkcap*$_{a}$, *brɛk-*$_{m}$; Wambule *bryakcam*; Sunwar *braaksu* 'broom'; Chamling *byu-ma*; Bantawa *bük-ka-ba* 'sweeper'.

  ≈ Hayu *pek-*; Dumi *phi:kni*; Yamphu *phi'kma*.
- /*ch-/: Thulung *chi-*; Khaling *chi-nä*; Kulung *c^{h}ima*; Limbu *sɛ:ma*.

SWEET POTATO:

- /*p-/: Jero *parkoti*$_{m}$, *parkot*$_{a}$; Wambule *parkoti, parkot*[17]; Thulung *palkoti*; Dumi *pa:lkokti*; Kulung *palkokti*.

SWEET:

Proto-Tibeto-Burman **dz(y)im* 'sweet, delicious', **s-klum* 'sweet'.

- /*j-/: Jero *jiji*$_{m}$; Wambule *jiji*; Bahing *jijim*; Sunwar *dzidzi*; Thulung *jijiwa*.
- /*l-/ or /*ʔl-/: Thulung *lem-* 'be sweet', *lempa* 'sugar'; Khaling *lempä*; Dumi *lempi*; Bantawa *lem+chok*; Kulung *lemlempa*; Yamphu *rimʔiye*; Limbu *lipma* 'be sweet'.

---

[17] Note that the loss of syllable-final /-k/ yields a long vowel in Wambule, viz. /*parkokti/ > /parkoti/ [parko:ti].

TAIL:

Proto-Tibeto-Burman **r-may*, **r-mey*, **r-mi*.

- /*ʔm-/: Jero *mɛʔlum*$_a$, *muʔlum*$_m$; Wambule *ɓulum*; Bahing *méri*; Sunwar *'miilu*; Thulung *'mer*; Khaling *mer*; Dumi *miri*; Bantawa *mi+rip*; Kulung *meri*; Yamphu *mira*; Limbu *me*.

TASTE (EAT AN EXAMPLE):

- /d-/: Jero *dɔmcap*$_m$ 'be tasted', Wambule *dwapcam*; Bahing *damso*; Sunwar *tham-tsa* 'taste' (initial unexplained; /d-/ expected); Thulung *deop-*; Khaling *'däm-nä*; Dumi *da:p-ni*; Bantawa *dutt-(u)* (also *dhutt-(u)*; /d-/ as expected); Kulung *damma*.

TASTY:

- /*br-/: Jero *broto*$_m$, *brottɔp*$_a$; Wambule *broco*; Bahing *broba* 'fresh, sweet'; Sunwar *broo-sho* 'savoury'; Thulung *brəs-* 'taste nice'.
- /*c-/: Khaling *cänüpä*; Dumi *tsa:nikpa*; Bantawa *ca+nu-(a)*; Kulung *ca nəma* 'taste good'; Yamphu *canuma*; Limbu *ca:noʔba*.

TEAR (N):

- /*p-/ or /*ʔp-/: Jero *pimis*$_a$, *pitaŋke*$_m$; Wambule *pitaŋke*.
- /*pl-/: Sunwar *prekku*; Thulung *plə*.
- /*ʔm-/: compounds with 'eye': Khaling *'mikmö*; Dumi *mik-khi:m* 'eye-spit'; Chamling *mik-wa* 'eye-water'; Bantawa *mük+wa*; Kulung *mikwa*; Yamphu *miʔwa*; Limbu *mik-wa*.

TEAR, REND:

Proto-Tibeto-Burman **dzyit* × **dzyut*.

- /*c-/: Jero *ciccap*$_a$; Wambule *ciccam*; Bahing *chiso*; Dumi *tse:tni*; Chamling *cetma*.
- [?]/*y-/: Thulung *eak-*; Khaling *'e-nä*; Bantawa *rek-(u)* 'tear open'; Kulung *e:ma*; Yamphu *yiŋma*.

THEFT, THIEF:

Proto-Tibeto-Burman **r-kəw* × **r-kun* × **r-kut* 'steal, thief'.

- /*kh-/: Jero *khus*$_{am}$ 'theft'; Wambule *khus* 'theft', *khujiwa* 'male thief'; Bahing *kunchaniwa* 'theft', *kuncha* 'thief' (initial unexplained; /kh-/ expected); Sunwar *khuy 'patsa* 'steal'; Thulung *khu-* 'steal', *khuciubo* 'thief'; Khaling *'khepä* 'thief'; Dumi *khi:ni* 'steal'; Chamling *khuma* 'steal'; Bantawa *khü+ka+ba*; Kulung *k^{h}uma* 'be a thief'; Yamphu *khusubaŋ* 'thief'; Limbu *khu:pma* 'steal'.

THIGH:

- /*s-/: Yamphu *se·bræk*; Limbu *-sɛmbo* in *laŋsɛmbo.*

THUMB:

- /*b-/: Jero *bɔmti*$_{m}$; Wambule *bwamti*; Bahing *bombo*; Thulung *bomla.*

TIGER, LEOPARD:

Proto-Tibeto-Burman **d-key* × **dkəy* 'tiger'.

- /*g-/: Jero *gupsu*$_{am}$; Wambule *gupso*; Bahing *gupsa*; Sunwar *gupsu* 'tiger'; Thulung *gupsiu*; Bantawa *ki-wa*; Yamphu *ki·ba*; Limbu *keba.*
- /*s-/: Thulung *'saw*; Khaling *saa*; Bantawa *sak+suŋ+ma.*
- /*n-/ or /*ʔn-/: Khaling *nör*; Dumi *nuri*; Kulung *nari.* See Thulung *ŋor-* 'roar (of tiger)'.

TOMORROW:

- /*d-/: Wambule *diskana, diskan, disna*; Bahing *dilla*; Sunwar *'diisa*; Thulung *dīka, dika*; Khaling *disä*; Kulung *desa*; Limbu /-tik/ in *ta:ndik.*
- /*s-/: Dumi *-selma* in *a'selma*; Chamling *selama.*

TONGUE:

Proto-Tibeto-Burman **s-lyam* 'tongue, flame'.

- /*l-/: Jero *lɛm*$_{am}$; Wambule *lɛm*$_{w}$, *lyam*; Bahing *lyam*; Sunwar *leen*; Thulung *lem*; Khaling *lem*; Dumi *le:m*; Chamling *lem*; Bantawa *lem*; Kulung *lem*; Yamphu *lem*; Limbu *lɛso:t*, *lɛso:ppa*.

TOOTH:

Proto-Tibeto-Burman **d-ŋa*, **swa*, **s-wa*.

- /*g-/: Jero *gumsu*$_{am}$; Wambule *gumso*; Bantawa *küŋ*; Kulung *kaŋ*.
- /*l-/ or /*ʔl-/: the elements /-lV/ or /-rV/ in Bahing *khleu*; Sunwar *khruy*; Hayu *lu*; Thulung *liu*, *li*; Khaling *ngalu*; Dumi *ŋilo:*.

TOSS, THROW, SHOOT:

Proto-Tibeto-Burman **ga:p* × **ʔap* 'shoot'.

- /*o-/: Jero *hɔpcap*$_{a}$ (<**ɔp-*); Wambule *wapcam*; Bahing *appo*; Sunwar *'ap-tsa*; Hayu *op-*; Thulung *op-*; Dumi *opni*; Chamling *am-ma*, *ap-ma*; Bantawa *ʔapt-(u)*; Kulung *amma*; Yamphu *apma*; Limbu *apma*.

TOUCH:

- /*kh-/: Jero *khɛlcap*$_{a}$, *khɛlcam*$_{a}$; Wambule *khyalcam*; Bahing *khúto*.
- Sunwar *'thi-tsa* 'touch'.
- /*b-/: Khaling *bhwaay-nä* (/b-/ expected); Dumi *bənni* 'feel, touch'; Kulung *pəima*.
- /*s-/: Bantawa *sopt-(u)*; Limbu *su:ma*.

TWIST:

- /*c-/ or /*ʔc-/: Jero *calcap*$_{a}$, *calcam*$_{m}$; Wambule *calcam*; Thulung *cal-* 'twist (as rope)'.
  ≈ Bahing *chéwo* 'twist'.
- /*r-/: Sunwar *rop-tsa*; Thulung *rim-* 'twist'; Khaling *'ram-nä* 'twist, wring'; Dumi *ri:pni*; Bantawa *ript-(u)*; Kulung *rəmma*; Limbu *lipma* (initial unexplained; /*y-/ expected).

URINE:

Proto-Tibeto-Burman **g-ts(y)i-t/n*, **zəy.*

- /*ʔc-/: Bahing *charníku*; Sunwar *'tsarnaku*; Hayu *tsɪ-*; Khaling *'cekmö*; Dumi *tsirkhim*; Chamling *chʌrs-* 'urinate'; Bantawa *cheys-(a)*; Kulung *c*^{h}*ema* 'urinate'; Yamphu *se'ma* 'urinate'; Limbu *seʔma:t* 'urinate'.
  /*s-/: Jero *sɔrki*$_{am}$; Wambule *swarki*; Thulung *sar(s)-* 'urinate'.

VILLAGE:

Proto-Tibeto-Burman **dyal* × **tyal.*

- /d-/: Jero *dɛl*$_{am}$; Wambule *dyal*; Bahing *dyal*; Thulung *del*, *Del*; Khaling *del*; Dumi *de:l*; Bantawa *ten*; Kulung *tel*; Limbu *tɛn* 'place'.

WAIT (FOR):

Proto-Tibeto-Burman **dzoŋ* 'wait, watch for', **lyaŋ* 'wait'.

- /*r-/: Jero *rim pacap*$_{a}$; Bahing *rimdo*; Sunwar *'rim-tsa*; Hayu *rim-*.
- /*l-/: Wambule *locam*$_{w}$, *locam*; Thulung *lə(t)-*.
- /*h-/: Khaling *hu-nä*; Dumi *hiŋni*; Chamling *hung-ma*; Bantawa *huŋ-(u)*; Kulung *hu:ma*; Yamphu *huŋma*; Limbu *haŋma*.

WASH (UP, ONESELF), BATHE:

Proto-Tibeto-Burman **hur* × **hir* 'wash', **m/b-s(y)il* × **m/b-syal* 'wash, bathe'.

- /*m-/: Jero *mεrcapa*$_a$, *mεrcam*$_m$; Wambule *mwarcam* 'wash somebody or something'.
- /*c-/ or /*ʔc-/: Bahing *chikso* 'cause to bathe'; Sunwar *'tsiik-si-tsa*.
- /*s-/: Thulung *seol-* 'wash (body)'; Khaling *sarnä*; Dumi *sirni*; Bantawa *seŋs-(a)ncin-*; Kulung *səmma*.
- compounds with *wa* 'water': Yamphu *wasokma* 'wash, wash oneself, wash somebody'.
- Limbu *ɔrumma*, *ɔrumsiŋma*.

WASH, RINSE:

Proto-Tibeto-Burman **hur* × **hir* 'wash', **m/b-s(y)il* × **m/b-syal* 'wash, bathe'.

- /*m-/: Jero *murcap*$_a$; Wambule *murcam*; Sunwar *mur-tsa*.
- /*s-/: Bahing *syappo* 'wash'; Hayu *tshup-* (initial unexplained; /s-/ expected); Thulung *seop-* 'wash (clothes)'; Khaling *'swaam-nä* 'wash'.
- /*h-/: Chamling *hupd-*; Yamphu *-hapma* in *wahapma*; Limbu *-hɔpma* in *wahɔpma* 'wash, rinse' (with *wa* 'water').

WATER:

Proto-Tibeto-Burman **m-ti-s* 'wet, soak', **ti(y)* 'water'.

- /*kw-/: Jero *ka:ku*$_{am}$, *ka:k*$_{am}$; Wambule *ka:ku*, *kak*; Bahing *pwáku*; Sunwar *baakku*; Thulung *ku*; Khaling *ku*; Dumi *kɨ*; Kulung *kawa*.
  - ≈ /*kw-/: Chamling *wa*; Bantawa *caʔ+wa*; Yamphu *wa-* in *wajokma* 'water'; Limbu *wa*.

WEEP, CRY:

Proto-Tibeto-Burman **krap*.

- /*khr-/: Jero *khrɔmcap*$_{a}$, *khrɔmcam*$_{m}$; Wambule *khramcam*; Thulung *khrap-*; Chamling *kham-*; Bantawa *khap-(a)*; Kulung *k^h amma*; Yamphu *ha'pma*; Limbu *ha:pma*.
- /*ŋ-/: Bahing *gnwákko*; Sunwar *ngaak-tsa*; Khaling *'ngo-nä*; Dumi *ŋokni*.

WHAT:

Proto-Tibeto-Burman **ma-y*.

- /*m-/: Wambule *ama*, *am* (<**a-mar*); Bahing *mára*; Sunwar *'mar* 'what'; Khaling *maang*; Dumi *mwo:*.
- /*h-/: Jero *hai*$_{am}$; Thulung *ham*.
- /*ʔt-/ or /d-/: Chamling *de*, *do*, *dyo*; Bantawa *di*.

WHITE:

Proto-Tibeto-Burman **bok*.

- /*b-/: Jero *bubu*$_{a}$; Wambule *bubu*, *bub*; Bahing *bubum*; Sunwar *bush*; Thulung *bubum*; Khaling *bubum*; Chamling *bat-* 'get white'; Limbu *phɔ:* (initial unexplained; /p-/ expected).

WIND (N):

Proto-Tibeto-Burman **buŋ*, **g-ləy*.

- /*ph-/ or ?/*ʔp-/: Jero *phuḍim*$_{m}$; Wambule *phuḍim*; Sunwar *phash*.
- /*j-/: Bahing *júnam* 'windy'; Thulung *ju* 'wind, breeze, cold'; Khaling *jung*.
- /*h-/: Dumi *hiʔi*; Bantawa *hük*; Kulung *hik*; Yamphu *hiʔwa-ba*.

WINNOW:

- [?]/*khr-/: Jero *hɔpcap*$_{a}$, *hɔpcam*$_{m}$; Wambule *hwapcam*; Sunwar *'krap-tsa* 'winnow', *khrap-tsa* 'winnow (small quantities)'; Hayu *hop-* 'jump down'; Dumi *khopnɨ*; Yamphu *yepma*; Limbu *aːmma*.
- /*c-/ or /*ʔc-/: Thulung *ce(t)-* 'sift'.
  /*ch-/: Khaling *'che-nä*.
  /*s-/: Khaling *'se-nä*; Kulung *saːma*.

WOMAN:

Proto-Tibeto-Burman **mow* 'woman, female relative'.

- /*ʔm-/: Jero *mɛtɛme*$_{m}$, *mɛttɛp*$_{a}$ 'girl'; Wambule *ɓiːco* 'female'; Sunwar *'miishmur* 'woman'; Hayu *mixtso*; Thulung *mēsem*, *mociu*; Khaling *melsem*; Dumi *meːʔe* 'wife'; Chamling *maricha* 'girl'; Bantawa *mec+cha+cha*; Yamphu *meʔnamiʔ*; Limbu *meːt*.

WOOD, FIREWOOD:

Proto-Tibeto-Burman **siŋ* × **sik* 'tree, wood'.

- /*s-/: Jero *siŋ*$_{a}$; Wambule *siŋ*; Bahing *sing* 'tree'; Sunwar *shii*; Hayu *siŋ*; Thulung *səŋ* 'wood, tree'; Khaling *sang*; Dumi *sɨ*; Chamling *suŋ*; Bantawa *süŋ*; Kulung *siŋ*; Yamphu *siŋ*; Limbu *siŋ*.

WOUND:

Proto-Tibeto-Burman **r-ma-t* 'wound, injured'.

- /*kw-/: Jero *mari*$_{am}$; Wambule *ɓari*; Bahing *ʔbar* (Michailovsky 1994); Sunwar *gaar*; Hayu *buʔma* (Michailovsky 1994); Thulung *par* 'sore, skin lesion of any kind'; Khaling *'kwaar*; Dumi *kar*; Bantawa *khen*; Kulung *k*^{h}*er*; Yamphu *huwa*; Limbu *kaːn*.

WRING, SQUEEZE:

Proto-Tibeto-Burman **tsyir* × **tsyu:r*.

- /*c-/ or /*ʔc-/: Jero *curcap*$_a$, *curcam*$_m$ Wambule *curcam*; Bahing *chyúrdo*.
  ≈ /*s-/: Thulung *siur-* 'press (as wood into basket)'.
- /*p-/: Thulung *pum-*; Dumi *pipni*; Kulung *pumma* 'twist, entwine'; Yamphu *pupma* 'squeeze out'.
- /*r-/: Bantawa *rükt-(u)*; Yamphu *yiŋma* 'wring, wrench'; Limbu *ikma*.

WRITE:

Proto-Tibeto-Burman **b-rəy* × **b-ris* × **rit* × **ri:n* 'draw, write, count'.

- /*r-/: Jero *rɛkcap*$_a$, *rɛk-*$_m$; Wambule *ryakcam*; Bahing *ryangso*; Sunwar *breek-tso* (initial unexplained; /r-/ expected); Thulung *reak-*; Khaling *'re-nä*.
- /*ʔc-/: Hayu *sat-* (Michailovsky 1994; initial unexplained; /c-/ expected); Dumi *tsəpni*; Chamling *chappa*; Bantawa *chapt-(u)*; Kulung *c^{h}amma*; Yamphu *sapma*; Limbu *sapma*.

YEAR:

Proto-Tibeto-Burman **s-ni(:)ŋ* × **s-nik*.

- /*th-/: Jero *-thoce*$_{am}$, *-thot*$_a$, *tho-*$_a$; Wambule *-thoce*, *-thoḓ*; Bahing *thó*; Sunwar *-thotse*; Thulung *thə*; Khaling *tho*.
  ≈ /*d-/: Bantawa *doŋ*; Kulung *-doŋ*; Limbu *tɔŋ*.
- /*n-/ or /*ʔn-/: Yamphu *niŋ*; Limbu *-niŋ* in *ɛnniŋ* 'this year'.

YELLOW:

Proto-Tibeto-Burman **b-wa* 'white, yellow'.

- /*o-/: Jero *waʔɔmjimo*$_m$; Wambule *waʔwamjwam*, *waʔwamjim*; Bahing *womwome*; Sunwar *haw* (initial unexplained); Thulung *om-om*; Khaling *ööm*; Bantawa *ʔom+pi*; Kulung *omlo:pa* 'white'; Limbu *ɔm*.

YESTERDAY:

- /*s-/: Jero *saiso*$_m$, *satni*$_a$; Wambule *saiso*; Bahing *sanamti*; Sunwar *'sinaakti*; Dumi *-sina* in *asina*; Chamling *-se* in *ase*; Yamphu *-seʔŋa* in *aseʔŋa*.

BIBLIOGRAPHY

Allen, Nicholas K. 1975. *Sketch of Thulung Grammar with Three texts and a Glossary* (East Asian Papers No. 6). Ithaca: Cornell University.

Benedict, Paul K. 1972. *Sino-Tibetan: A Conspectus.* Cambridge: Cambridge University Press.

Bieri, Dora, and Marlene Schulze. 1971. *A Vocabulary of the Sunwar Language.* Kathmandu: Summer Institute of Linguistics [38-page typescript].

Clark, T.W. 1989. *Introduction to Nepali.* Kathmandu: Ratna Pustak Bhandar [Revised edition by John Burton-Page].

Driem, George van. 1987. *A Grammar of Limbu.* Berlin: Mouton de Gruyter.

Driem, George van. 1990, 'The fall and rise of the phoneme /r/ in Eastern Kiranti: sound change in Tibeto-Burman. *Bulletin of the School of Oriental and African Studies* LIII (1): 83-86.

Driem, George van. 1993. *A Grammar of Dumi.* Berlin/New York: Mouton de Gruyter.

Driem, George van. 2001. *Languages of the Himalayas.* Volumes 1 and 2. Handbook of Oriental Studies. Section Two: India. Leiden/Boston/Köln: Brill.

Ebert, Karen. 1997a. *Athpare.* München: Lincom Europa.

Ebert, Karen. 1997b. *Camling (Chamling).* München: Lincom Europa.

Glover, Warren William. 1971. *Swadesh List Calculations on Thirty Tibeto-Burman Languages.* Kathmandu: Summer Institute of Linguistics [16-page mimeograph].

Grierson, George A. 1909. *Linguistic Survey of India. Vol. III. Tibeto-Burman Family. Part I. General Introduction, Specimens of the Tibetan Dialects, The Himalayan Dialects, and the North Assam Group.* Calcutta: Government of India [Reprinted: Delhi, Varanasi, Patna. Motilal Banarsidass 1967. XXIII. 641 pp].

Hanßon, Gerd. 1991. *The Rai of Eastern Nepal: Ethnic and Linguistic Grouping.* Findings of the Linguistic Survey of Nepal. Kirtipur/Kathmandu: Linguistic Survey of Nepal and Centre for Nepal and Asian Studies, Tribhuvan University [Edited and provided with an introduction by Werner Winter].

His Majesty's Government of Nepal. 1982. *Medicinal Plants of Nepal.* Bulletin of the Department of Medicinal Plants No. 3. Kathmandu: His Majesty's Government Press [Third edition].

His Majesty's Government of Nepal. 1984. *Medicinal Plants of Nepal.* Supplement volume of the Bulletin of the Department of Medicinal Plants No. 10. Kathmandu: His Majesty's Government Press.

His Majesty's Government of Nepal. 1995. *Statistical Year Book of Nepal 1995.* National Planning Commission Secretariat. Central Bureau of Statistics. Kathmandu: His Majesty's Government Press.

His Majesty's Government of Nepal. 2002. *Nepal Population Report 2002*. Ministry of Population and Environment. Electronic publication at the internet site <http://www.mope.gov.np/population/chapter5.php>.

Hodgson, Brian Houghton. 1857. 'Comparative Vocabulary of the languages of the broken Tribes of Népál', in *Journal of the Asiatic Society of Bengal* XXVI: 333-371.

Hodgson, Brian Houghton. 1858. 'Comparative Vocabulary of the languages of the broken Tribes of Nepál', in *Journal of the Asiatic Society of Bengal* XXVII: 393-456.

Kā̃lā, Vairāgī *et al.* (VS 2059). *Limbū-Nepālī-Aṅgrejī Śabdakoś* [Limbu-Nepali-English Dictionary]. Kathmandu: Royal Nepal Academy.

Matisoff, James A. 2003. *Handbook of Proto-Tibeto-Burman. System and Philosophy of Sino-Tibetan Reconstruction*. UC Publications in Linguistics, 135.

Matthews, David. 1990. *A Course in Nepali*. Kathmandu: Tiwari's Pilgrim Book House, in arrangement with Heritage Publishers, New Delhi, and School of Oriental & African Studies, London.

Michailovsky, Boyd. 1975. 'Notes on the Kiranti verb (East Nepal). 1. The Bahing verb. 2. The origin of tone in Khaling', *Linguistics of the Tibeto-Burman Area* 2/2: 183-218.

Michailovsky, Boyd. 1981. *Grammaire de la langue hayu*. Ph.D. thesis. University of California at Berkeley (University Microfilms International).

Michailovsky, Boyd. 1988a. *La langue hayu* (Collection sciences du langage). Paris: Éditions du Centre National de la Recherche Scientifique.

Michailovsky, Boyd. 1988b. 'Phonological typology of Nepal languages', *Linguistics of the Tibeto-Burman Area* Volume 11.2: 25-50.

Michailovsky, Boyd. 1994. 'Manner vs. place of articulation in the Kiranti initial stops', pp. 59-78 in Current Issues in Sino-Tibetan Linguistics. Hajime Kitamura, Tatsuo Nishida and Yasuhiko Nagono, eds. Osaka: Organizing Committee of the 26th International Conference on Sino-Tibetan Languages and Linguistics.

Michailovsky, Boyd. 1995. 'Internal reconstruction and the Dumi verb', Paper presented at the 1st Himalayan Languages Symposium, Leiden 16–17 June 1995.

Michailovsky, Boyd. 2003. 'Suffix-runs and counters in Kiranti time-ordinals', in David Bradley, Randy LaPolla, Boyd Michailovsky and Graham Thurgood, eds, *Language Variation: Papers on variation and change in the Sinosphere and in the Indosphere in honour of James A. Matisoff*. Pacific Linguistics. Canberra: ANU.

Opgenort, Jean Robert. 2002. *The Wāmbule Language*. Amsterdam: Jean Robert Opgenort [doctoral dissertation, 6 June 2002].

Opgenort, Jean Robert. 2004a. 'Implosive and preglottalized stops in Kiranti', *Linguistics of the Tibeto-Burman Area* Volume 27.1: 1-27.

Opgenort, Jean Robert. 2004b. *A Grammar of Wambule. Grammar, Lexicon, Texts and Cultural Survey of a Kiranti Tribe of Eastern Nepal*. Brill's Tibetan Studies Library, Languages of the Greater Himalayan Region, 5/2. Leiden: Koninklijke Brill.

Panday, Krishnakumar. 1982. *Fodder Trees and Tree Fodder in Nepal*. Bern/Birmensdorf: Swiss Development Cooperation and Swiss Federal Institute of Forestry Research.

Pokhrel, Bālkṛṣṇa *et al*. VS 2040. *Nepālī Bṛhat Śabdakoś*. Kāṭhmāḍaũ: Nepāl Rājkīya Prajñā-Pratiṣṭhān.

Rāī, Aṅgadhan. VS 2051. 'Dyāl piṅmāī bāṅmā', in *Libju-Bhumju* 2: 69-70.

Rāī, Aṅgadhan. VS 2052. 'Ām jīvan', in *Libju-Bhumju* 3: 21.

Rāī, Aṃga Dhan (= Aṅgadhan). VS 2053. 'Jero Rāī bhāṣā', in *Libju-Bhumju* 5: 36.

Rāī, Aṃgadhan (= Aṅgadhan). VS 2054. 'Gāmuncvam mandir rim rai', in *Libju-Bhumju* 7: 18.

Rāī, Aṅgadhan. VS 2056. 'Sālāṅ', in *Libju-Bhumju* 11: 49.

Rāī, Ramilā. VS 2051. 'Āmme jindagī', in *Libju-Bhumju* 2: 69.

Rutgers, Roland. 1998. *Yamphu. Grammar, Texts & Lexicon*. Leiden: Research School CNWS.

Setālco, Nain Bahādur. VS 2057. 'Kavāticu', in *Libju-Bhumju* 15: 38.

Shafer, Robert. 1966. *Introduction to Sino-Tibetan, Part I*. Wiesbaden: Otto Harrassowitz.

Shrestha, Keshab. 1979. *Nepali Name for Plants*. Kathmandu: Natural History Museum.

Singh, Chandra Lal. 1971. *Nepali to English Dictionary*. Kathmandu: Singh Brothers [Fourth revised edition 1991].

Starostin, Sergei. 1994-2000. Electronic publication at the internet site <http://www.iiasnt.leidenuniv.nl/starling.html>. Also presented at the Sino-Tibetan conference in Paris, 1994.

Toba Sueyoshi, and Ingrid Toba. 1975. *A Khaling-English English-Khaling Glossary*. Kirtipur: Summer Institute of Linguistics and the Institute of Nepal and Asian Studies of Tribhuvan University.

Toba, Sueyoshi. 1979. *Khaling*. Asian & African Grammatical Manual 13d. Tokyo: Asia Africa Gengo Bunka Kenkyūzyo.

Toba, Sueyoshi. 2004. 'Tilung: an endangered Kiranti language. Preliminary observations', in *Nepalese Linguistics. Journal of the Linguistic Society of Nepal* 20 (November 2004). Kirtipur, Kathmandu, Nepal: Linguistic Society of Nepal, Tribhuvan University.

Tolsma, Gerard Jacobus. 1999. *A Grammar of Kulung*. Rijksuniversiteit te Leiden: unpublished doctoral dissertation [2 June 1999].

Turner, Ralph Lilley. 1931. *A Comparative and Etymological Dictionary of the Nepali Language*. New Delhi: Allied Publishers Limited [Reprinted in 1997].

Winter, Werner. 1986. 'Aus der Arbeit des Linguistic Survey of Nepal', in B. Kölver & Siegfried Lienhard, eds, *Formen Kulturellen Wandels und Andere Beiträge zur Erforschung des Himalaya*. Nepalica 2. Sankt Augustin: VGH Wissenschaftsverlag.

Winter, Werner. 1987. 'Differentiation within Rai', *A World of Language: papers presented to Prof. S.A. Wurm on his 65th birthday*. Pacific Linguistics C 100: 729-734.

Winter, Werner. 2003. *A Bantawa Dictionary*. Trends in Linguistics. Documentation 20. Berlin/New York: Mouton de Gruyter.

Wolfenden, Stuart. 1929. *Outlines of Tibeto-Burman Linguistic Morphology, with special reference to the prefixes, infixes, and suffixes of Classical Tibetan, and the languages of the Kachin, Bodo, Naga, Kuki-Chin, and Burma groups*. Prize Publications 12. London: Royal Asiatic Society.

BRILL'S TIBETAN STUDIES LIBRARY

ISSN 1568-6183

1. Martin, D. Life and Contested Legacy of a Tibetan Scripture Revealer, with a General Bibliography of Bon. 2001. ISBN 90 04 12123 4
2.1 Blezer, H. (ed.). Tibetan Studies I. 2002. ISBN 90 04 12775 5
2.2 Blezer, H. (ed.). Tibetan Studies II. 2002. ISBN 90 04 12776 3
2.3 Ardussi, J., & H. Blezer (eds.). Tibetan Studies III.2002. ISBN 90 04 12545 0
2.4 Epstein, L. (ed.). Visions of People, Place and Authority. 2002 ISBN 90 04 12423 3
2.5 Huber, T. (ed.). Society and Culture in the Post-Mao Era 2002. ISBN 90 04 12596 5
2.6 Beckwith, C.I. (ed.). 2002. ISBN 90 04 12424 1
2.7 Klimburg-Salter, D. & E. Allinger (eds.). 2002. ISBN 90 04 12600 7
2.8 Klieger, P.C. (ed.). Voices of Difference. 2002. ISBN 90 04 12555 8
2.9 Buffetrille, K. & H. Diemberger (eds.). 2002. ISBN 90 04 125973
2.10 Eimer, H. & D. Germano. (eds.). 2002. ISBN 90 04 12595 7
3. Pommaret, F. (ed.). Lhasa in the Seventeenth Century. The Capital of the Dalai Lamas. 2003. ISBN 90 04 12866 2
4. Andreyev, A. Soviet Russia and Tibet. The Debacle of Secret Diplomacy, 1918-1930s. 2003. ISBN 90 04 12952 9
5.2 Opgenort, J.R. A Grammar of Wambule. Grammar, Lexicon, Texts and Cultural Survey of a Kiranti Tribe of Eastern Nepal. 2004. ISBN 90 04 13831 5
5.3 Opgenort, J.R. A Grammar of Jero. With a Historical Comparative Study of the Kiranti Languages. 2005. ISBN 90 04 14505 2
6. Achard, J.-L. Bon Po Hidden Treasures. A Catalogue of gTer ston bDe chen gling pa's *Collected Revelations*. 2004. ISBN 90 04 13835 8
7. Sujata, V. Tibetan Songs of Realization. Echoes from a Seventeenth-Century Scholar and Siddha in Amdo. 2005. ISBN 90 04 14095 6
8. Bellezza, J.V. Spirit-mediums, Sacred Mountains and Related Bon Textual Traditions in Upper Tibet. 2005. ISBN 90 04 14388 2